The Dawn of Modern Warfare

Other Volumes of Delbrück's *History of the Art of War*
Available in Bison Book Editions

Warfare in Antiquity, Volume I

The Barbarian Invasions, Volume II

Medieval Warfare, Volume III

The Dawn of Modern Warfare

HISTORY OF THE ART OF WAR

VOLUME IV

By Hans Delbrück

Translated from the German by Walter J. Renfroe, Jr.

University of Nebraska Press
Lincoln and London

First Bison Book printing: 1990
Most recent printing indicated by the last digit below:
10   9   8   7   6   5   4   3

Library of Congress Cataloging-in-Publication Data
(Revised for volumes 3–4)
Delbrück, Hans, 1848–1929.
History of the art of war.
Translation of: Geschichte der Kriegskunst im Rahmen der politischen Geschichte.
Reprint • Originally published: History of the art of war within the framework of political history.
Westport, Conn.: Greenwood Press, c1975–c1985.
Contents: v. 1. Warfare in antiquity—[etc.]—v. 3. Medieval warfare—v. 4. The dawn of modern warfare.
1. Military art and science—History. 2. Naval art and science—History. 3. War—History. I. Title.
U27.D34213 1990   355′.009   89-24980
ISBN 0-8032-6584-0 (set) ISBN 0-8032-6586-7 (Vol. IV)

Reprinted by arrangement with Greenwood Press, Inc.

Originally titled *HISTORY OF THE ART OF WAR WITHIN THE FRAMEWORK OF POLITICAL HISTORY,* by Hans Delbrück, Volume IV, THE MODERN ERA. Translated from the German by Walter J. Renfroe, Jr., and published as part of the Greenwood Press Series, Contributions in Military History, in Westport, CT, 1985. Copyright © 1985 by Walter J. Renfroe, Jr. Maps drawn by Edward J. Krasnoborski. Originally published in German under the title GESCHICHTE DER KRIEGS-KUNST IM RAHMEN DER POLITISCEN GESCHICHTE. All rights reserved.

Table of Contents

Translator's Foreword   viii
Preface   ix

Volume IV
The Dawn of Modern Warfare

BOOK I
The Nature of the Military in the Renaissance

    I.   The Establishment of a European Infantry   3
    II.   Firearms   23
    III.   Tactics of the Spear Units   53
    IV.   Internal Organization of the Mercenary Armies   59
    V.   Individual Battles   73
    VI.   Machiavelli   101

BOOK II
The Period of the Wars of Religion

    I.   The Transformation of Knights into Cavalry   117
    II.   Increase in Numbers of Marksmen.
         Refinement of Infantry Tactics   147
    III.   Maurice of Orange   155
    IV.   Gustavus Adolphus   173
    V.   Cromwell   185
    VI.   Individual Battles   193

BOOK III
The Period of Standing Armies

        General Remarks   223
    I.   France   227
    II.   Brandenburg-Prussia   241

III.   Drills. Changes in Tactics in the Eighteenth Century   269
IV.   Strategy   293
V.   Strategic Sketches and Individual Battles   319
VI.   Frederick as a Strategist   369

BOOK IV
The Period of National Armies

I.   Revolution and Invasion   387
II.   The Revolutionary Armies   395
        Generals of the Republic and Napoleon's Marshals   417
III.   Napoleonic Strategy   421
IV.   Scharnhorst, Gneisenau, Clausewitz   449

Index   457

Translator's Foreword

This translation of the fourth and last volume of Hans Delbrück's *Geschichte der Kriegskunst im Rahmen der politischen Geschichte* completes my task of translating the four volumes written by Delbrück personally. This volume was originally published in Berlin in 1920.

I have followed the same guidelines here as in my translations of the first three volumes. It should be noted that, in the many references to strategy, I have translated *Ermattungs-Strategie* as "strategy of attrition," and *Niederwerfungs-Strategie* as "strategy of annihilation," the same terms I used in the preceding volumes. While some readers may prefer other terminology, I believe the meaning is clear in each case.

In the occasional references to the varying minimum requirements for the height of soldiers, it should be remembered that the foot and inch were not standard measurements throughout Europe, and a height measurement of 5 feet, 7 inches, for example, is not the equivalent of those figures in British or American usage.

Once again I am indebted to Dr. Everett L. Wheeler for his translations of the Latin passages appearing in the text.

Finally, I take heartfelt pleasure in expressing my gratitude to my wife Ruth, who not only wrote out the translation of each of the last three volumes as I dictated but also bore the long ordeal with great patience.

Preface

This fourth and last volume of the *History of the Art of War* is appearing in the year in which the greatest of all wars has just ended. The research for this volume was practically complete in 1914, and the work was in large part already composed at that time. But the storm into which we were plunged, instead of spurring me on to complete this task and finish this subject, as one might have imagined, drew my attention away from it. I interrupted my work, only to bring it finally to completion without constructing a bridge between it and the present. Whenever it is a question in this book of the conditions of our time, this means the period before the World War, in which I was actually writing, and occasionally also the period in which I myself gained practical knowledge of warfare. (In 1867 I became a soldier and was discharged in 1885 as a first lieutenant of reserves.)

Originally, I planned to have my work finish with the German wars of unification and to add a presentation of the development of the Napoleonic strategy into that of Moltke. But I dropped this idea, since it would have led directly into the problems of the World War, which are not yet sufficiently well defined for a scholarly treatment in the spirit of this work. That does not mean that I would not risk devoting any consideration at all to the latest period but only that it cannot yet be done in the systematic, detached manner which a work of this kind requires. Consequently, this work ends with Napoleon and his contemporaries. The continuation up to the present time, however, is already at hand, even though in another form. What I have to say and have been able to say concerning the phenomena of military history of the later nineteenth century, especially about Moltke's strategy and the events of the World War, has been written in individual articles and in the three volumes of the collection *War and Politics, 1914 to 1918* (*Krieg und Politik, 1914 bis 1918*), which are being published at the same time as this book. The Moltke articles appear in the collection *Recollections, Articles, and Speeches* (*Erinnerungen, Aufsätze und Reden*), supplemented by an article concerning Caemmerer's "Development of the Science of Strategy in the Nineteenth Century" ("Entwickelung der strategischen Wissenschaft im 19. Jahrhundert"), in the *Preussische Jahrbücher*, 115 (1904): 347. Here, in association with Schlichting's viewpoint, the new thinking of Moltke, the strategic approach march on two fronts, which Schlieffen then developed into the idea of the double envelopment in association with my analysis of the battle of Cannae, is explained in more detail and clarified both technically and psychologically. This, in turn, leads over into the strategic observations which I made concerning the events of the World War.

It was only natural that I was able to let the technical aspects of warfare, weapons as well as tactics, fade into the background in my treatment of the modern period. This was not because these points were less important than previously; on the contrary, the technical side of warfare has indeed grown stronger and stronger at an ever-increasing pace. Rather, it is because these technical aspects appear so clearly in their form and their importance that they require no further investigations. Abundant literature on this subject is available, and I could therefore limit myself to establishing the practical results. I have been able to confine myself to the most essential points with all the more justification in that Max Jähns's invaluable *History of the Military Sciences* (*Geschichte der Kriegswissenschaften*) presents the material in systematic fashion for the reader seeking further enlightenment. This limitation of the technical aspects has made it all the more possible for me, I hope, to bring out clearly the basic theme of this work, the relationship between the organization of the nation, tactics, and strategy—"The History of the Art of War Within the Framework of Political History," as the title indicates. Recognition of the mutual interaction between tactics, strategy, national organization, and politics throws light on the relationship of these subjects to universal history, and this has clarified many points which were previously obscured or misunderstood. This work has been written not for the sake of the art of war but in the interest of world history. If military men read this and derive stimulation from it, I can only find that satisfying, and I am honored; but this work is written by a historian for friends of history. I would even have no objection if this work, which treats of warfare and specifically within the framework of political history, were to be classified in the category of works of cultural history. For the art of war is an art like painting, architecture, or pedagogy, and the entire cultural existence of peoples is determined to a high degree by their military organizations, which in turn are closely related to the technique of warfare, tactics, and strategy. All these things have mutual influences on one another. The spirit of each age reveals itself in its multifaceted individual phenomena, and the knowledge of each individual, as in my case of the art of war, furthers the knowledge of mankind's overall development. There is no epoch in world history which would not be affected in its foundations by the results of this work. But it has required great effort and even struggle to have the idea accepted that there was something to be gained in this way. Even Leopold Ranke directly rejected my plan when I explained it to him. The faculty to which I now have the honor of belonging raised obstacles at the time of my nomination, objecting that study of the military did not belong in the university. When I handed the first volume, which, after all, reaches quite deeply into ancient history and especially Roman history, to Theodor Mommsen, he thanked me but stated that he would hardly have time to read this book. And since, on other hand, I also had the General Staff against me, one will have to admit that my struggle was not easy. Nobody who was recognized as one of my students was allowed to become an instructor at the *Kriegsakademie*, and historians who had become convinced of the logic of the conclusions from my research were nevertheless careful enough to let that fact be known as little as possible. In the cases of other scholars, as will be seen, I have not been able to succeed up to the most recent time in having them even correctly repeat my concept. New ideas have to fight against not only the obstinate opposition of the traditional concepts but also against misunderstanding, which is almost even more unshakable.

Just as I felt obliged, at the time of publication of my first volume, to point out in the preface the book by Julius Beloch, *The Population of the Greco-Roman World (Die Bevölkerung der griechisch-römischen Welt)*, as a work which was an essential precursor to mine, this time I must not neglect to name here and now a work that forms both an indispensable prelude and the most valuable supplement to this volume. It is *Machiavelli's Renaissance of the Art of War (Machiavellis Renaissance der Kriegskunst)* by Martin Hobohm. I have been able to accept completely the conclusions of this work that is just as scholarly as it is brilliantly written, and Dr. Hobohm has also given me very important further assistance by assembling material for the continuation of the research. In addition to Dr. Hobohm, I am also indebted to Dr. Siegfried Mette for his assistance in proofreading this work and drawing up the index.

Berlin—Grunewald, 7 August 1919.

Hans Delbrück

BOOK I

The Nature of the Military in the Renaissance

Chapter I

The Establishment of a European Infantry

The surprising power of the Swiss military system was based on the mass effect of the large, closed squares in which each individual was filled with the self-confidence nurtured by 200 years of uninterrupted victories. The warlike spirit that was spread throughout the entire population made it possible for all the men to be led en masse into battle, and their massive formation in turn overwhelmed all the personal courage, no matter how great, of the older professional warriorhood. With the battle of Nancy, this Swiss warfare by masses had come down out of the mountains, which had been such important allies for its previous victories. As had already been the case in the war that was finally decided at Grandson and Murten, where the Confederates had fought more for the king of France than for their own political interest, now their military power began to make itself felt far from their homeland, in the service of foreigners. In doing so, this small fraction of a German people had a significant historical effect. Much more important, however, from the viewpoint of world history, was the change brought about everywhere as the other nations, recognizing the superiority of the Swiss method of warfare, began to imitate it.

Of course, it had long been true that, in addition to the heavy, armored mounted warriors, there had existed not only marksmen but also foot troops with close-combat weapons who supported the knights in battle. The progress that was to be made and the changes that were to be carried out consisted of grouping these foot troops, who had previously formed only a supporting arm, together in much larger numbers in tightly formed units.

At first this progress was fully realized only among two peoples, the Germans and the Spanish. While we find trends in this direction among the French and the Italians, these beginnings were not carried through to completion, or they were not completed until considerably later. There exists here a very remarkable difference, which deserves special attention.

First of all, however, let us turn to the clarification of the first positive example of this development of the modern period, which took place on German soil.

THE DUTCH AND THE BATTLE OF GUINEGATE[1]
7 AUGUST 1479

The first battle in which the Swiss combat methods appear in use by other than Swiss warriors is the battle of Guinegate, two and a half years after the battle of Nancy. Here Archduke Maximilian, the son-in-law of Charles the Bold, defeated a French army. Thus it was precisely the Burgundians, who had so sorely suffered from the Swiss superiority, who now successfully made the first attempt to practice this tactical art themselves.

Maximilian was besieging the small border stronghold of Thérouanne, and he moved out to engage and throw back a French relief army that was moving up from the south under des Cordes. The French army was composed in the usual way of knights and marksmen. In addition to the marksmen of the *compagnies d'ordonnance* who were assigned to the individual knights, there were also many *francs-archers*. In these two arms Maximilian was considerably weaker, but, on the other hand, he had no fewer than 11,000 foot troops with close-combat weapons, spears and halberds, who had been led up to join him by Jean Dadizeele, bailiff of Ghent and captain general of Flanders. Maximilian was only twenty years old, and he had himself neither the experience nor the authority, here in the territories of his wife, to create the new military system. But in his army was the count of Romont, whose possessions were situated in the immediate neighboring area of Bern and Fribourg, on Neuenburg Lake. In the service of the duke of Burgundy he had fought the battles against the Swiss. He had become their enemy very much against his wishes and his desires; no one was better acquainted with them in peace and in war than he. According to the sources, it was this Swiss count who now formed up the Flemish foot troops in the Swiss manner. We may assume that it was also he who advised his present commander to provide himself with masses of such foot troops, and nowhere in the world could he find better material for this new formation than precisely in the Burgundian Low Countries. Indeed, a combat method quite similar to that of the Swiss had already been seen once in this area, when the rebellious Flemish cities defeated the French knights in the battle of Courtrai in 1302. In 1382 at Rosebeke this method of warfare had failed, because in the Flemish plain, against the knights, it lacked the terrain strong points that the Swiss had in their mountains. Nevertheless, a large warrior group and a strong warlike spirit had been maintained in these lowlands. Even the armies of Charles the Bold were composed in large part of Netherlanders, and the Swiss example now provided the form in which this warlike spirit could once again be made effective.

All together, the Burgundian army was probably stronger by a few thousand men than the French army, even if we include in the latter force the garrison of Thérouanne, 4,000 men, who threatened the rear of the Burgundians during the battle.

Both armies had their horsemen on the flanks and their foot troops in the center—on the one side marksmen and on the other principally pikemen. The Burgundian pikemen were divided into two large, deep squares, one of which was commanded by Count Engelbert of Nassau, who had fought at Nancy under Charles the Bold, while the other square was commanded by the count of Romont. Maximilian himself, instead of fighting with the knights in keeping with the traditional knightly custom, joined these squares on foot with spear in hand, accompanied by a number of nobles.[2] In his memoirs Maximilian tells us that, after he had come to the Low Countries as a young prince, he had had long spears fabricated and had carried out drills with these weapons. And so it might be said that the foot troops were trained systematically with long spears, accompanying nobles, and drills. The addition of nobles, who naturally stood in the first rank, as an effort to strengthen the square of foot troops, is a procedure that we have already observed quite often in the late Middle Ages. The significant difference, however, is that they now took up the long spear, the arm of the foot troops, and did not simply fight in front of these troops but joined with them in a unified tactical body. "There stood," the "most excellent chronicle" reports to us, "the count of Romont right in the formation, and over there stood the duke (Maximilian) among the common soldiers on foot and among the pikes."

On his right flank des Cordes succeeded in throwing back the Burgundian knights accompanying the infantry square and also in capturing the Burgundian cannon drawn up on that flank. Although the Burgundian marksmen were quite numerous, they are not mentioned at all in the battle account. They had no doubt immediately given way in the face of the French superior forces and had either fled or pushed into the squares of pikemen.

The victory of his knights gave des Cordes the possibility of attacking from the flank the left square of Burgundian pikemen, the unit commanded by Nassau. This attack brought the Burgundians to a standstill. They received heavy fire, both from front and flank, from the French marksmen, who were also supported by the captured Burgundian cannon. The Burgundians were thus sorely pressed, even though most of the victorious French knights, instead of participating in this fight, rode off in pursuit of the fleeing Burgundian knights and thus left the battlefield.

If the action on the other flank had been similar, the Burgundians could not have avoided defeat. But there the larger part of the knights held fast against the French and did not allow them to move into the flank of the pikemen. Consequently, Romont's unit continued to move forward, drove the French marksmen to flight, thus relieving the other unit, and decided the outcome of the battle.

We do not have any contemporary report telling us in so many words that in the infantry squares at Guinegate we have the adopted Swiss tactics. It is particularly noteworthy that there is no such mention in the reports on the battle, no fewer than four of which come from Maximilian himself or can be traced back to him. But as remarkable as that might seem at first glance, it is, after all, not so rare that contemporaries are not conscious of the significance of a theoretical change, and it is only in following generations that the importance of this factor is recognized. In the military history of antiquity we have found, for example, that a change as fundamental as the formation of echelons during the Second Punic War was not directly mentioned at all in the sources. Nevertheless, both here and in the Punic War the fact is completely certain. Dadizeele, Molinet, de But, and Basin all agree that the Flemish foot troops were responsible for the victory. De But says: "Dux Maximilianus cum picariis fortiter instabat, ut equitatus Francorum, qui ab utraque parte cum aliis suis obpugnare quaerebat eundem, non posset in eum praevalere." ("Duke Maximilian bravely stood firm with his pikemen, so that the French cavalry, which sought to attack him from both sides with their other men, could not prevail against him.") And Basin states even more definitely that the Flemish foot soldiers with their long spears repulsed the penetration of the enemy horsemen. ("Nam ipsi Flamingi pedites, cum suis longis contis praeacutis ferramentis communitis, quos vulgo piken appellant, hostium equites, ne intra se se immitterent, viriliter arcebant": "For the Flemish infantry with their long spears strengthened by sharp iron heads, which they commonly call pikes, courageously prevented the enemy horsemen from charging among them.")

We should not, however, overlook the fact that the victory was due in part to the flank protection the knights provided for at least one of the Burgundian squares of pikemen. If that had not happened, the Flemish foot troops might well have lost the battle, as had happened at Rosebeke.

Up to the present there is no explanation of why the victory did not result in the fall of Thérouanne. Instead, Maximilian gave up the campaign and disbanded his army. If the events and the outcome of the battle were not so definitely proven in many reports, we would probably find this victory incredible, judging from the final result. It is said that the Flemish were not willing to serve any longer. It was presumably a question of the old hostility between the prince and the provincial estates; the Netherlanders feared their own master, Maximilian, no less than they feared the French, and they did not wish that he should become too powerful as a result of his victory. Perhaps Maximilian's treasury was also so empty that he could not even assemble the pay for the small army force which would then have been needed to continue the siege.

It is obvious, then, that the battle of Guinegate attained no importance from the political point of view. Militarily, however, it was a critical turning point. The band of Netherland foot troops that played a role throughout the next generation no doubt had its start in the victors of Guinegate, and the French derived from their defeat there the momentum for the reform of their military organization, which may have carried over to Spain. Primarily, however, these Netherland foot troops were the precursors of the lansquenets.

THE LANSQUENETS[3]

The victory at Guinegate was fruitless for the victor because after the battle he no longer had his army intact. Soon Maximilian, who of course initially administered the country only as the prince consort and then, after the death of his wife, as regent for their son Philip, found himself in open conflict with the Estates. In order to hold his own in this conflict, he was obliged to obtain an army other than the citizen levies.

He recruited serving men from the countries of every lord, from the Low Countries themselves, from the Rhine, from Upper Germany, and from Switzerland. In the years 1482 to 1486 the name "lansquenets" (*Landsknechte*) came into use for these common soldiers.

Why were they called *Landsknechte*? (provinciae servi: servants of the province; patriae ministri: attendants of the country; compagnons du pays: companions of the country). Why were they not called *Fussknechte* (foot soldiers), *Soldknechte* (mercenary soldiers), *Kriegsknechte* (military serving men), or some such other combination? The designation *Landsknecht* (lansquenet) was used for about a century, into the period of the Thirty Years' War. Then it disappeared, because the free mercenary, who frequently changed his affiliation, entered a more permanent and definite relationship to a country or a general and was named accordingly.

The word has been explained in numerous ways, but they are all to be rejected. It does not mean "soldiers of their own country" in contrast with the Swiss, for the lansquenets served together with them under the same colors and in the same unit. The word also does not mean "soldiers of the flat country" in contrast with the Swiss mountains. It does not mean "soldiers for the defense of the country," or "soldiers who serve the country." It also does not mean "soldiers who are not provided by the Estates but are recruited from the country." It does not mean "soldiers

of the same country," that is, "compatriots." The word also has nothing
to do with the lance, for the weapon that these soldiers carried was called
a "spear" or a "pike."[4]

The word *Landknecht* (as distinguished from *Landsknecht*) was to be
found in the fifteenth century in both High German and Low German,
and it meant a bailiff, a court messenger, a mounted or dismounted
gendarme who also assumed combat functions. Thus Johann von Posilge,
in his 1417 chronicle, recounts that a Prussian stronghold, Bassinhayen,
was traitorously surrendered to the Polish king "by a few *Lantknechte*."
The period 1482–1486, in which the name "lansquenet" took on its specific meaning in the Low Countries, was the period in which Maximilian
was at peace with France but was waging war against his Estates, who
deprived him of the regency for his son Philip. It was precisely the
mercenaries whom Maximilian took into his service in increasing numbers
and who wished to be paid and who also oppressed the country that the
Estates wanted to get rid of. What was the purpose of these mercenaries?
After all, the country was at peace. It was specifically for this reason that
Maximilian supposedly gave them the harmless name "*Landknechte*,"
which up to that time meant not primarily warriors, but simply policemen.

The development occurred through the fact that Maximilian trained
the colorful mixture of his mercenaries in the tactical formations that the
Swiss had created and that had already won the battle of Guinegate for
the Netherland citizen levy. The most important factor in this training
was not simply that a number of Swiss were in the mercenary units but
that the duke himself took spear in hand and obliged his nobles to join
the unit of foot soldiers in order by this camaraderie to heighten the
soldiers' self-confidence and to inspire them with a touch of the warrior
spirit carried over from knighthood. The chroniclers later recounted that
Emperor Maximilian created the Order of the Lansquenets. That means
that these soldiers in the new combat formations with their formal training
were no longer regarded as a simple supporting arm but developed a
warlike esprit de corps which caused them to appear as something new
and created a significant distinction from the earlier mercenary soldiers.

Among the oldest and more famous lansquenet leaders was Martin
Schwarz, who was initially a shoemaker from Nuremberg, was raised to
knighthood for his bravery, and united Swabians and Swiss under his
command. His lieutenant was a Swiss, Hans Kuttler of Bern, who was
also known by other names.

The first definite mention of the new phenomenon in which the name
appears with this meaning is found in the minutes of a session of the
Confederation in Zurich on 1 October 1486, where there were complaints
concerning the recruiting by a Swabian knight in Maximilian's service,
Konrad Gäschuff. The knight had reportedly spoken abusively and had
boasted that he would equip and train the Swabians and other lansquenets

in such a way that one of them would be worth more than two soldiers of the Confederation.

From this document we see that in the autumn of 1486 the word "lansquenet" was already a definite concept, that he was trained in his profession, and that there was a difference and a contrast between the Swiss and lansquenets.

Just ten years earlier the German common soldiers were held in low regard. When René of Lorraine in 1476 attempted to reconquer his duchy with Upper Rhenish mercenaries, they did not prove themselves but took flight before the Burgundians at Pont-à-Mousson. The Swiss had to be called in, and the squares at Nancy on 5 June 1477 consisted of a mixture of Swiss and Swabians. But the Swiss were so conscious of their superiority that they treated the Germans scornfully, and claimed for themselves alone almost all the booty taken in these campaigns.

When the lansquenets were brought through systematic training to a degree of competence that gave them self-confidence, the Swiss separated themselves from their company, and from that moment on teachers and pupils stood jealously opposing each other. The Swiss with their proud tradition of victory wanted to uphold their position of an incomparable warriorhood, superior to all others. The lansquenets were told by their leaders that they could do just as much, and they began to be filled with this belief. Organized units moved from the Low Countries to England and to Savoy. Under Duke Sigismund of Tyrol and the direct command of Friedrich Kappeler, they defeated Venetian condottieri in the battle of Calliano on 10 August 1487. Initially, Sigismund still had Swiss mercenaries, but instead of their looking down scornfully on their fellow warriors, as was previously the case, now the Swiss captains reported back home that they were threatened by the lansquenets and were hardly sure of their lives.

In 1488 an imperial army moved into the Netherlands to the aid of Maximilian against the Estates, which had temporarily taken him prisoner. Before the gates of Cologne there appeared Swiss also, but the commanders were not willing to accept them, "because of the lansquenets," in order to avoid dissension, and so the Swiss returned home.

Two years later, in 1490, we again find Swiss and lansquenets together, when Maximilian moved against the Hungarians. Watt, a chronicler of St. Gall in a somewhat later period, reports: "In this campaign there were many men from the Confederation with the lansquenets and also a few men from our region of St. Gall." Thus, they were thrown together again quite often.

This campaign of 1490, in which Stuhlweissenburg was taken by storm, seems to have directed general attention for the first time to this new phenomenon, so that the chroniclers felt obliged to add a few words of clarification or explanation concerning the word "lansquenets."

The word "lansquenet" appears for the first time in 1495, in a folk song that can be specifically dated: "There is many a lansquenet in the country."[5]

These were recruited private soldiers such as we have known since the eleventh century. In the fifteenth century we find a number of names for them, such as "*Böcke*" ("goats") and "*Trabanten*" ("guardsmen"). The difference is that they are no longer simple individual warriors, but they form definite tactical bodies and have been accustomed to finding their strength precisely in this closed formation, this mutual relationship, and this physical relationship is paralleled by their inner relationship, their new esprit de corps. What the Swiss, who set the example, had in the way of community spirit and its warlike tradition was represented in these free mercenary bands, once they were formed, by the continuing military training.

For the first time in world military history we encountered a tactical body in the phalanx of the Spartans, whom, in conscious contrast to the individual warrior, Demarat reportedly praised before King Xerxes, saying that the individual Spartans were as brave as other men but that their real strength was based on the law that bade them hold fast in their ranks and win or die.

Although Low German units were also continuously to be found, the name "lansquenets" was applied principally to the Upper Germans, the Swabians and Bavarians, no doubt because on the one hand in those regions the closeness to the Swiss attracted men to follow the drum, and on the other hand Maximilian's possessions were situated there and consequently serving men in large numbers from these areas were particularly anxious to join him. At the beginning it was natural that regional groupings and special units were formed, and the strongest group, the Swabian, finally set the tone for the whole army. In his autobiography Maximilian uses the expression "lansquenets and Hollanders," and in another passage he equates the "lansquenets" to the Upper Germans. The "Hollanders" also continued in existence, appeared as mercenaries along with the Swiss in the campaigns of Charles VIII to Italy in 1494, and probably were destroyed as the "Black Band" in the battle of Pavia in 1525.

From the complaint of the Swiss against Konrad Gäschuff we have seen that there was a systematic training of the lansquenets. This point is confirmed in the account of a military exercise that Count Friedrich of Zollern ordered to be carried out on 30 January 1488 in the marketplace of Bruges. We have various reports on this event that are not completely in agreement, especially as to who actually carried out the exercise. One report states it was German nobles from Maximilian's retinue, while another says it was German foot soldiers. Still others report that it was Netherlanders who were being instructed by the Germans. In any case, the weapon carried by the unit was the long spear. Then came the com-

mand for the formation of a "snail" ("limaçon à la mode d'Allemagne"),
then the command to lower spears. This was accompanied by a battle
call, "Sta, sta." The watching burghers thought they heard "Sla, sla"
and, fearing a sudden attack, they dispersed, terror-stricken.

By the word "snail" we are to understand an orderly movement in
which the unit shifted from a march column into an attack column and
vice versa. That cannot possibly be done automatically but has to be
practiced, and this practice can be done in various ways.[6] This movement
has nothing to do with a later maneuver of the marksmen, which was
also called "snail" ("limaçon," "caracole").

The use of the long spear was not as simple as it might appear.[7] The
Swiss writer Müller-Hickler, who attempted it, reports as follows:

> The most unfavorable aspect was the vibrating of the long shaft. I
> have personally learned from fighting with the long spear that it is
> almost impossible to hit the target, because with a strong thrust the
> point quivers so much. This is particularly true when one makes
> energetic jabs and most apparent when the full length of the lance
> is used and it is thrust out far by stretching the right arm.
>
> There was also a more certain, relatively slower thrust to be used
> when the opportunity offered itself if the person fighting with the
> armored "double-pay mercenary" wanted to aim the desired thrust
> at the neck and the lower body in such a way as to strike the joint
> of the harness.[8]

Instead of the long spear, quite a number of lansquenets were armed
with heavy swords which were manipulated with both hands, but they
did not play a significant role. Böheim has stated, certainly correctly, on
this point that there were only a few unusually strong men armed with
these swords, specifically for the protection of the colors, and later for
the protection of the colonel.[9] He goes on to say that they were systematically trained in the use of this sword, but in reality the bragging sons
of Anak who were armed with it had precisely the same worth as the
giant drum-majors in Napoleon's army.

The sources also repeatedly praise the orderly marching of the soldiers.
Ranks of four, five, and eight men are mentioned. No such statement
ever appears in medieval sources.

In the autumn of 1495, 10,000 Germans moved to the aid of Duke
Ludovico Moro of Milan, who was besieging the duke of Orleans in
Novara. The physician Alessandro Benedetti thoroughly described a pa-
rade in which the duke, with his wife, reviewed his troops in front of
Novara:

All eyes were attracted to a phalanx of Germans which formed a square and was composed of 6,000 foot soldiers commanded by Georg von Eberstein (Wolkenstein) on a splendid horse. In keeping with the German custom, a large number of drums was heard in this battle formation, almost strong enough to burst one's ears. Wearing only breast armor, they strode along with but little interval between their ranks. The leading men carried long lances with a sharp point, while the following ranks held their lances high. They were followed by halberds and men with two-handed swords. They were accompanied by color bearers whose signals caused the entire unit to move to the right, to the left, and to the rear, as if it were moving along on a float. These units were followed by men armed with the harquebus, with crossbowmen on their right and left. When opposite Duchess Beatrix, on a signal, they suddenly shifted the square into a wedge (that is, the broad formation into a narrow one, or the square with sides of equal length into a square with equal numbers of men on each side). Then they divided into two wings, and finally the entire mass swung about as one part moved very slowly and the other very quickly so that one part revolved about the other, which stood still, so that they appeared to form a single body.[10]

In addition to their drills, the participation of the nobles was of special significance in the training of the lansquenets. It is reported again and again that they stood in the ranks of the foot troops, with spear in hand. In a battle at Bethune in 1486 the Germans suffered a defeat at the hands of the French. Duke Adolf of Geldern and Count Engelbert of Nassau placed themselves among the foot troops, saying that they intended to live and die with them, and, as the chronicler says, they shed their blood "for the protection of the foot soldiers."

An account in the opposite sense shows us what that meant. When Emperor Maximilian was besieging Padua in 1509 and the lansquenets were supposed to storm the place, they demanded that the noblemen participate in the attack. But Bayard said: "Are we supposed to risk our lives at the side of tailors and shoemakers?" And the German knights said they were there to fight on horseback and not to storm the fortifications. Thereupon the emperor gave up the siege.

The first large clash between the lansquenets and the Swiss took place in the Swabian War in 1499. The older warriorhood of the Swiss, strengthened by success and experience, was still victorious. At Hard, the Bruderholz, Schwaderlow, Frastenz, the Calven Pass, and at Dornach the Swabians were beaten. Nevertheless, when negotiations were taken up, Maximilian made the most demanding conditions, and in the following peace treaty the Swiss eventually gained hardly anything of a positive nature; indeed, they even gave something back. Of course, the fact that Louis XII had captured Milan in the meantime provided the motive for the peace.

THE FRENCH, SPANISH, AND ITALIANS

The military organization of France in the fifteenth century was based on the *compagnies d'ordonnance* and the *francs-archers*. After the latter had conducted themselves so poorly at Guinegate, Louis XI wanted to convert them into foot troops like the Swiss. He replaced their bows with long spears and halberds, and for their training he assembled them, more than 10,000 men strong, in a camp near Hedin in Picardy. The following year their training was conducted at Pont de l'Arche, near Rouen.

The Swiss ambassador, Melchior Russ, reported back home that the king was having a large number of long spears and halberds fabricated in the German style.[11] If he were also able to fabricate men who could manipulate them, he would no longer need the services of anybody else. Later historians have believed themselves justified in considering the camp of Pont de l'Arche as the cradle of the French infantry, claiming that the troops were systematically trained there after 6,000 Swiss were brought there as demonstration troops. The training camp supposedly existed for three years; the Swiss instructors reportedly remained there for one year. But closer study of the evidence has destroyed this imaginary picture.[12] In reality, no source has reported anything of drills or a Swiss instructional unit. The intention of the king was undoubtedly directed toward the same thing that was created at that time under Maximilian in the Netherlands. We also hear expressly that 1,500 knights of the *compagnies d'ordonnance* were brought to the camp in order to fight on foot if necessary. That must therefore mean that they were to form up with the foot soldiers. But such changes are not effected with a simple command.

The infantry that came from that camp was never considered the equal of the Swiss or the lansquenets. A similar type of unit to that on the Belgian border was also formed on the Italian border. In addition to these units, which were later designated as the "old units" of Picardy and Piedmont, there were other, more or less loose-knit mercenary bands named "adventurers," the members of which were partially equipped with close-combat weapons but for the most part served as marksmen. Before Genoa in 1507 they distinguished themselves when Bayard and other knights took position at their head for the attack, so that Susane, the historian of the French army, believes he can establish this as the origin of the French infantry. He says that since that occasion it became customary for young noblemen who did not have the wherewithal for mounted equipment to serve with the infantry in return for higher pay. An Italian expression, *"lanze spezzate,"* was applied to these nobles. The expression *"lanspessades"* is said to have existed in the French army until the middle of the eighteenth century as the title for privates first class, between the corporals and the privates.

In the so-called *Mémoires de Vieilleville* it is recounted that there were twelve *lanspessades* in each company. They carried neither a halberd nor a harquebus but a spear.

But despite this social reinforcement, the French infantry units continued to play only a secondary role in comparison with the Swiss and lansquenets who entered the service of their king. They appeared in the large battles from Ravenna to Pavia; Gascons and Burgundians are also mentioned, but the sources never mention them as entirely competent. The French kings from Charles VIII on always preferred to fight their important battles with German foot soldiers. In 1523 their general, Bonnivet, sent the French home from Italy when he was able to obtain Swiss to replace them. It was not until 1544, in the battle of Ceresole, that a Gascon unit of spearmen fought not only in the Swiss manner but also with success.

In 1533 Francis I made another attempt to create a national French infantry, more of a militia-type character, to which he gave the proud name "legions." He even intended to create new tactical formations with them, units that were to be a mixture of the phalanx, the Roman legion, and the formations of modern warfare. The unit described for us is the large square, which is divided up into small sections with little intervals in a highly contrived manner. It is impossible to recognize any purpose or function of these small units. This was apparently a question simply of theoretical musing. In 1543, when 10,000 French legionaries were supposed to defend Luxembourg, they deserted in masses and surrendered the stronghold to the imperial troops. The same thing happened in 1545 at Boulogne. In Marshal Vieilleville's memoirs for 1557 it is stated that these legionaries were no warriors. On the basis of evidence inscribed in the documents of their district, it appears that they left their farming in order to avoid taxes by serving from four to five months.

The French leaders no doubt realized how intolerable it was to conduct the French wars with foreigners, but they found that the French character simply was not suited for infantry service and by taking into their pay Germans, Swiss, and Italians, they not only obtained good soldiers but they also took these good soldiers away from the enemy.

Around 1500 the cavalry in France was called "l'ordinaire de la guerre" and the infantry "l'extraordinaire de la guerre," because in peacetime there was only cavalry on hand.[13] The word "infantry" (*infanterie*), however, supposedly did not appear until the reign of Henry III. Around 1550 the term *"fanterie"* was still in use, based on the Italian word "*fante*," meaning the same as "fellow" ("*Bursche*") or "serving man" ("*Knecht*").[14]

The development in Spain was different from that in France. As early as 1483—that is, just after Louis XI is supposed to have established the camp in Picardy and while the struggle for Granada was still taking place—King Ferdinand of Aragon reportedly called a Swiss unit that was to serve as a model for the formation of a similar infantry. On the Swiss side, however, nothing is known of this unit beyond the Pyrenees, and research to date has discovered nothing concerning this formation of a new infantry in the following twenty years.

Since, aside from the Germans, it was initially only the Spanish who formed useful foot troops in the Swiss manner, their military system in this period holds a special interest for us, and at my request and with the backing of the Ministry of Culture, Doctor Karl Hadank undertook a voyage to Spain in order to conduct research in the archives and references there. The results, however, were only meager and did not lead significantly beyond what Hobohm had already said. While the source references concerning the Spanish-French campaigns in Lower Italy are quite comprehensive—prominent among them is the life of the "Gran Capitan," Gonzalo of Cordova, by Jovius—they offer very little toward the solution of our problem, the development of the tactical body of infantry. A militia organization that was authorized at a junta in 1495 and was provided for several other times gives no indication of the spirit of the new art of war. When the Spaniards took up the fight with the French for the possession of Naples and brought over their troops under Gonzalo of Cordova in 1495, these troops could not hold their own against the Swiss who were fighting for the French. They were not up to the Swiss "either in the quality of their weapons or in the steadfastness of their formation," and, despite their numerical superiority, they took to their heels. But this did not cause Gonzalo to give up. During the war and by means of the fighting itself he trained his troops and with the support of lansquenets won his first victory in the battle of Cerignola in 1503. The human material he had to deal with was supposedly initially very poor. Not only adventurers and vagabonds who were accustomed to follow the beat of the drum but also men impressed into service were among his troops. But he was aided by the fact that they were in a foreign country far from their homeland. For their own good the men had no choice but to stand by their colors, and a few years later there was no doubt that the Spanish infantry compared favorably in their competence with the Swiss and the lansquenets. This fact was to be demonstrated in the battle of Ravenna in 1512, even though they were defeated there by the lansquenets fighting with the French knights. For the next century and a half the Spanish enjoyed the reputation of being an outstanding body of infantry.

With the Spaniards we also learn on one occasion something of the theoretical opposition which the new organization ran against. A certain Gonzalo of Ayora, who intended to form and train square units at home at the same time Gonzalo of Cordova was doing this, was ridiculed for his efforts. We hear that on one occasion he drilled his foot soldiers the whole day long. He requested that the king provide the additional wine and rations necessitated by this long drill, and he wanted a reinforcement of his authority through the title of colonel. He also asked for express instructions to his captains to obey him to the letter. In a great council of war it was debated as to whether Ayora's ideas should be approved. It is reported that the courtiers joked about this for a long time. But in 1506 Philip the Handsome, the son of Maximilian and prince consort of the crown princess, brought 3,000 lansquenets to Spain, and their example presumably overcame the last opposition.

In Italy things went differently than in Spain. In the fourteenth and fifteenth centuries Italy was a very warlike country. It produced the great condottieri who formed an exemplary tradition in the art of war. Distinctions were made between certain differences in the strategic principles of the school of the Sforzas and the school of the Braccios, even though these differences were not very significant. The great historians of the Renaissance, Machiavelli, Guicciardini, and Jovius, were agreed in stating that the condottieri waged war simply as a game and not in bloody earnest. It was their judgment that these men, guided by self-interest, in order to extend the war as long as possible so that they might obtain the most possible pay, did not seek a decision in battle. On the contrary, they avoided that, and when it did finally come down to a battle, the men on both sides, who regarded themselves mutually as comrades, spared one another and shed no blood. In the battle of Anghiari in 1440, for example, it is reported that one man died, to be sure, but he was not struck down but drowned in a swamp. Later scholars have no doubt characterized this kind of warfare as having raised war to a work of art, that is, the skill of maneuver, through the efforts of these condottieri.

Close examination of the contemporary reports has shown that there is not a true word in this entire description, despite the opinions of the three great authorities. The only correct aspect in this judgment is the fact that the condottieri did not wage war in the cruel manner that Machiavelli and his contemporaries saw as characteristic of the Swiss, who were forbidden to take prisoners and even killed all the men in the cities they captured. The combat of the condottieri was similar to that of the knights, who likewise showed mercy whenever their military mission permitted and also, for the sake of ransom money, not only allowed but even strove for the taking of prisoners. But the condottieri did not go any further than this in their mercy, and their battles were often quite bloody.[15]

Through the entire fourteenth and fifteenth centuries the Italian marksmen, Genoese and Lombards, enjoyed a special reputation. These troops also played an important role in the army of Charles the Bold.

The armies of the condottieri, like the medieval armies in general, were composed principally of horsemen. That, too, was a reason why Machiavelli hated and scorned them, since he considered infantry in the Roman style to be the decisive arm.

When the reports of the deeds of the Swiss and the lansquenets spread through Italy also, there were soon perspicacious warriors who wished to bring this new practice into their land as well. The population offered much more and better material than did the French, for example, at that time. The Spaniard Gonzalo of Ayora had learned the new art in Milan, and a respected family of condottieri, the three Vitelli brothers, who possessed the small domain of Città di Castello in the Romagna district, took it upon themselves in 1496 to create an Italian infantry that was nonexistent up to that time. They recruited among their own subjects, mixed them in with experienced warriors, armed them with spears that were an ell longer than those of the Germans, and taught them, as Jovius very clearly reports, "to follow the colors, to keep step by the drumbeat, to move forward in column and to turn, to form the snail, and finally to strike the enemy with great skill and maintain the formation exactly." ("Signa sequi, tympanorum certis pulsibus scienter obtemperare, convertere dirigereque aciem, in cocleam decurrere, et denique multa arte hostem ferire, exacteque ordines servare.") Vitellozzo actually succeeded with a unit of 1,000 men in defeating at the battle of Soriano (26 January 1497) 800 German lansquenets in the service of Pope Alexander VI. But the creators of this new order survived their accomplishment only briefly. Camillo Vitello died in the French service in Naples as early as 1496, Paolo was beheaded by the Florentines in 1499, and Vitellozzo was throttled in 1503 at the command of Caesar Borgia.

Caesar Borgia himself took up and continued the work of the Vitellis. After his downfall, men of Romagna entered the service of Venice as mercenaries, and they proved to be very skillful. But in the long run these attempts were too small and did not have the support of a dominant political power that could have maintained them even after crises. Machiavelli's attempt to organize a native, skillful militia for the Republic of Florence was erroneous in its concept, and it failed. The conditions in the Republic of Venice, which had a large and dependent peasant population under its control, would have been the most favorable ones for the new organization. But the government was not willing to militarize its own subjects and preferred to recruit men elsewhere, especially in the Romagna. These men of Romagna, who could have become the nucleus for a national Italian infantry, were beaten and destroyed in the battle of Vaila (1509) by the Swiss and the battle of La Motta (1513) by the Spanish and lansquenets. After that time, wherever Italian foot troops appeared, they were regarded as of just as little value as the French, or even of less value, even though the individual Italian had such a good military reputation that the captains of the French adventurers were in no small measure Italians.

From all these points we can expressly establish that, if the French and Italians remained behind the Germans and Spanish in the new art of war, there was no question of racial tendencies in this phenomenon, since of course in later times the French showed outstanding warrior characteristics and the Italians were regarded as very competent fighters up into the period of the Renaissance. It was rather a question of the product of circumstances and the result of events. The Germans benefited from the fact that they were the first to serve with the Swiss under Maximilian's colors. As a result, the Swiss themselves became the nucleus of the lansquenets, whom they later regarded, after they had split up, not only as their rivals but also as their deadly enemies. A few important men under the leadership of Maximilian himself, recognizing the principles of their task, carried it out by holding drills. When a certain nucleus of lansquenets, filled with the new spirit and their own self-confidence, was created and when a number of captains and colonels who enjoyed the general respect and trust had worked their way to the top, the institution of the lansquenets continued to expand uninterruptedly as a result of its own strength.

Contemporaries often asked why nothing similar happened among the French. It was believed that this resulted from an intention to keep the people from becoming warlike so that they could easily be kept under control. That was supposedly the concept of the nobility, and the king allowed himself to be influenced by this attitude.[16] This viewpoint is contradicted by the fact that repeated attempts were made to create a national French infantry. But these attempts did not succeed; that is, they did not attain the competence and the self-confidence of the Swiss and the lansquenets, and we may have no doubt that the French kings preferred to have fully competent troops instead of those of little value. The basis for the failure of the French, therefore, is that, first of all, they did not have the proper point of departure, the dependence on the Swiss. It is true, of course, that the French kings also had Swiss soldiers themselves, but it was impossible to unite French units in a larger organization with the Swiss, as was done with the Swabians and Tyroleans. The Swiss were able to serve as examples for the French only in a theoretical way. The French infantry had to be drawn from new seed. But the French did not feel obliged to expend the necessary work and energy on this task because they had the convenient means of drawing the best warriors from Switzerland through recruitment. It was to the benefit of the French kings that the Swiss and lansquenets became enemies. In 1509, when Louis XII was at odds with the Swiss and they provided him no soldiers, he recruited lansquenets.

at odds with the Swiss and they provided him no soldiers, he recruited lansquenets.

In Spain the opposite situation prevailed. As soon as the new art of war was understood, hard necessity forced them to train their own men in the new methods. Where would the kings of Aragon and Castile supposedly have gotten the money to fill the demands of the German soldiers, even if that would have been easier from a geographical view-point? The source of precious metals across the ocean was just starting to be tapped. Finally, it is also very important to remember that for Italy the formation of a more or less standing army of foot troops would have brought the republics and other areas of only mediocre strength into a very dangerous dependence on the leaders. The great kings, as military leaders, did not have to fear that possibility very much.

NOTES FOR CHAPTER I

1. The standard monograph is "The Battle of Guinegate" ("Die Schlacht bei Guinegate") by Ernst Richert. Berlin dissertation, 1907.

2. Dadizeele, *Mémoires*, ed. Kerwyn de Lettenhove, p. 19. According to Comines, there were 200 noblemen.

3. All the earlier works and studies on the lansquenets have been superseded by the book by Martin Nell, *The Lansquenets, Origin of the First German Infantry (Die Landsknechte, Entstehung der ersten deutschen Infanterie)*, Berlin, 1914. This work is exemplary in its penetrating study and perspicacious critique. The first part was published as a Berlin dissertation. The author, who was justified in having the finest hopes for the future and looked on life with youthful trust, fell on the field of honor in France in 1914.

Erben, *Historische Zeitschrift*, 116:48, had a few reservations concerning Nell's conclusions, which we can agree with, but they do not eliminate anything of importance.

4. In the first seven documents in which the name appears, Nell found that it was written twice as "*Lanzknechte*," twice in the Swiss minutes in 1486 as "*landtsknechte*," and three times as "*lantknechte*."

5. Lilienkron, 2:362, 20.

6. Hobohm treats this more thoroughly in *Machiavellis Renaissance der Kriegskunst*, 2:394, with the references at 2:405. I cannot agree with Nell's interpretation.

7. Hobohm, 2:426 ff., basing his opinion on Jovius, has expressed the belief that the Swiss spear was initially only 10 feet long and was gradually lengthened to 17 or 18 feet as the squares of spearmen fought against one another. Nell, p. 158, observed that the lengthening of the

spear must therefore have started in 1483. Presumably the spears never had a "normal" length but had always been of greatly varying lengths.

8. "Studies on the Long Spear" ("Studien über den Langen Spiess"), *Zeitschrift für historische Waffenkunde*, 4 (1908): 301.

9. Böheim, in the *Zeitschrift für historische Waffenkunde*, 1:62.

10. The work appeared in Venice as early as 1496. I am using the version reprinted in Eccard, *Corpus Historicum*, II, 1612. I do not wish to present the above translation as completely confirmed. The expressions used by the author are not absolutely clear, even though he was an eyewitness. An Italian translation (Venice, 1549) does not shed any more light on the matter. Jähns, 1:727, has interpreted this not as a wheeling movement but a caracole. Because of these uncertainties, I quote the original text here:

> Ab his phalanx una peditum Germanorum erat, quae omnium oculos in se convertebat, quadratae figurae, quae VI M. peditum continebat, Georgio Petroplanensi Duce integerrimo, in equo eminente. In ea acie tympanorum multitudo audiebatur germanico more, quibus aures rumpebantur; hi pectore tantum armato incedebant per ordines primo a posteriore parvo intervallo. Primi longiores lanceas in humeris ferebant, infesto mucrone sequentes lanceas erectiores portabant post hos bipennibus et securibus armati; ab his signiferi erant, ad quorum inclinationem agmen totum ac si una rate veherentur, in dextrum, laevum, retro regrediuntur; a tergo pilularii dicti parvorum tormentorum; hos a laeva et sinistra scorpionum Magistri sive manubalistarii sequuntur. Hi in conspectu Beatricis Ducis quadratum agmen uno signo in cuneum subito commutavere, paulo post in alas sese divisere: demum in rotundum altera tantum parte levi motu, altera cursim movebant, prima parte circumacta, postrema immota, ita ut unum corpus esse videretur.

11. *Jahrbücher für Schweizer Geschichte*, 6:263. Basin: "Surrogavit enim in eorum locum alios pedites, quos appellabant halbardurios, qui similibus armis induti ut franci sagittarii, loco arcuum contos longos ferratos, quos Flamingi piken appellant, aut latas quasdam secures, secundum Alemannorum peditum ritum, deferebant" ("For he put other infantry in their place, whom they call halberdiers. These, similarly equipped to French archers, carried instead of bows long iron-tipped poles, which the Flemish call pikes, or broad axes following the custom of German infantry.")

12. Hobohm, 2:329, 345.

13. According to Spont, *Revue des Questions Historiques*, 1899, p. 60.

14. According to Susane, *Histoire de l'infanterie française*, 1:14.

15. Proof based on the sources is to be found in Willibald Block, "The Condottieri: Studies on the so-called 'Unbloody Battles' " ("Die Condottieri. Studien über die sogenannten 'unblutigen Schlachten' "), Berlin dissertation, 1913.

16. Hobohm, 2:336.

Chapter II

Firearms

I have waited until this point to insert a chapter on firearms, for, although they had already been in use for 150 years and I have often mentioned them, they did not take on a real and significant importance before the period we are now discussing.[1]

Even in the most recent period, opinions on the discovery of gunpowder have varied greatly, and even now research on this subject has not reached definitive conclusions either with respect to the country of origin or the period. A few years ago it was considered as certain that "Greek fire," of which we first hear in the seventh century (at the siege of Cyzicus in 678 A.D.), had nothing to do with gunpowder, the explosive material made of saltpeter, charcoal, and sulfur. Instead, it was thought to be a combustible composition principally of unslaked lime or something similar. Now, however, a sketch has been found in Byzantine manuscripts going back to the tenth century that can hardly be explained in any other way than by an explosion of gunpowder. The studies of the descriptions of Greek fire which were resumed after this discovery have also led to the conclusion that the best and most natural interpretation points to a use of gunpowder after all.[2] If that is correct, we have here the oldest historically confirmed appearance of gunpowder. Nevertheless, there are some indications that this discovery was not made here, but in China. Explosive gunpowder results from a mixing of some six parts of saltpeter, one part of charcoal, and one part of sulfur. This produces a flourlike substance which burns away very quickly and which in burning results in products, principally gaseous, that require about a thousand times as much space as the original gunpowder. The principal ingredient of gunpowder, then, is saltpeter. But this substance is seldom found in its natural condition in our ancient civilized world, whereas in Mongolia and China it is very common. It must have been noticed there in an early period how much the energy of any burning process was increased if saltpeter was mixed in with older combustible materials, and this realization could easily have led to the discovery of gunpowder. Furthermore, the Arabs call saltpeter "snow from China," and this point also seems to indicate that the correct mixture of the three ingredients was first discovered in China and then made its way to the Arabs and the East Romans.

The Chinese also arrived at the use of gunpowder for military purposes, but not before the thirteenth century. This was a long time after the Greeks had arrived at such a use of gunpowder and only a short time before we find references to formulas for powder and to firearms in the Occident.

During the defense of a besieged city, Pien-King, in 1232, rockets were fired, iron hand grenades were thrown, and ground mines were laid. In 1259 gunpowder was used to project burning wads from bamboo canes. The Chinese called this instrument the "lance of the raging fire." In present-day pyrotechnics this is known as the "Roman candle." This procedure can already be designated as a shooting, for we have a tube from which, through explosive power, missiles are projected to a distance of some 100 feet. But since the purpose of this is limited to setting fire to combustible objects, the "lance of the raging fire" cannot yet be called a firearm, and the Chinese did not push their discovery any further.

The earliest correct recipe for gunpowder that has been preserved, that indicating the three ingredients in the ratio 6:1:1, is found in a Latin document attributed to a certain Marcus Graecus and can be dated around the middle of the thirteenth century. It is undoubtedly a Latin translation of a Greek document dealing with all kinds of pyrotechnics. The powder recipes to be found in the writings of Albertus Magnus (died 1280) and Roger Bacon (died 1294) were taken either directly or indirectly from this source. But what we find in all these documents concerning the use of gunpowder shows that it was not yet used for shooting at that time. This point is made clear by the very title of Marcus Graecus's book, "liber ignium ad comburendos hostes" ("Book of Fires for Burning up the Enemy"). Contemporary Arabic writings and those of a somewhat later period from Spain are not different from those mentioned above. Written by Hassan Alrammah (around 1290), Jussuf, and Schemaeddin-Mohammed, these works contain recipes for gunpowder and instructions for its use in which the energy of the powder is to be used as fire to burn the enemy but not to shoot him. This applied particularly to an instrument called *madfaa*, which, as had been the case with the Chinese, used the power of the gunpowder to project a burning substance (not a projectile and not a ball) against the enemy.[3]

Consequently, the secret of the formula for gunpowder came to the Occident from the East Roman Empire via translation from a Greek document. The name "Roman candle" for the instrument that the Chinese called the "lance of the raging fire" leads to the supposition that with the formula this use, too, of the new substance was brought to us from the Eastern Empire.

The mighty effect of gunpowder was explained by the alchemists as resulting from the heat of the sulfur and the cold of the saltpeter, which could not tolerate one another.

It is of interest that Hassan Alrammah describes an instrument that we can consider as a primitive but, in its way, completely developed, self-propelled torpedo.[4] The torpedo, therefore, was invented earlier than the cannon or the musket, and this may serve as an illustration of the fact that, even when gunpowder was already available, it was not so easy to arrive at the invention of the firearm.[5]

The first historically confirmed use of firearms in warfare in Europe took place in 1331 at the time of Louis the Bavarian, in the Italo-German border area in Friuli, when the two knights de Cruspergo and de Spilimbergo attacked the town of Cividale. The expressions in the chronicle read "ponentes vasa versus civitatem" and "extrinseci balistabant cum sclopo versus Terram, et nihil nocuit" ("setting vessels against the city ... those from a distance shot with a sclopus against the ground and did no damage"). *Sclopus* or *sclopetum*, in Italian *schioppo* (thunderer), later meant a hand firearm in contrast to cannon.

In 1334, three years after the battle of Cividale, the chronicle of Este reports that the margrave had a large number of cannon of various types fabricated ("praeparari fecit maximam quantitatem balistarum, sclopetorum, spingardarum": "He had made ready a very great number of *balistae*, *sclopeti*, and *spingae*"). At that time the *spingardarum* ("*Springarden*") did not necessarily mean firearms, but no doubt *vasa* and *sclopeta* did refer to firearms.

The third oldest reliable testimony of firearms has only recently been discovered in the papal accounts.[6] It is stated there that in 1340 at the siege of Terni by the papal army thunder jars that shot bolts ("edificium de ferro, quod vocatur tromba marina," "tubarum marinarum seu bombardarum de ferro": "a construction of iron, which is called a naval tube," "naval tubes or stone-throwers of iron") were used on a trial basis. And the account also states that at the siege of the stronghold of Saluerolo in 1350 bombards that shot iron balls weighing some 300 grams were employed.

In the first references to the new weapons in the chronicles, then, we find various designations, and that may be taken as meaning that even at that early date various types were in use and that the invention therefore occurred somewhat earlier. Since these weapons were not yet known by Albertus Magnus, Roger Bacon, and Hassan Alrammah, the discovery was probably made around the year 1300 or shortly thereafter.

We have no descriptions or illustrations of these oldest firearms. To be sure, an English illuminated manuscript from around the years 1325–1327 contains an illustration that is undoubtedly supposed to portray a powder-fired cannon.[7] It is therefore somewhat earlier than the events at Cividale. A vessel in the form of a large, pot-bellied bottle is lying on a wooden bench. A block is inserted in the neck of the bottle, and a heavy arrow is fastened to the block. A man who remains cautiously at a certain distance is extending a match to a touchhole that can be distinguished in the vessel. The instrument is aimed at the closed gate of a stronghold. As interesting as this picture is, it is impossible that we have here the reproduction of a firearm actually in use at that time. If this vessel were filled with powder in a quantity compatible with the heavy weight of the inserted block and its attached arrow or with the strength of the target gate, and if the vessel were of sufficiently strong metal, not only would the recoil have shattered the light wooden bench on which the vessel lay loosely, but also the cannoneer, even if he maintained a cautious distance, would hardly have escaped with his life. It is therefore conceivable in no other way than that the illustrator himself had never seen a cannon but had only heard of the wonderful new invention and had drawn his picture after hearing vague descriptions. Nevertheless, this picture remains interesting as a proof of the fact that the use of this force, newly introduced in the Occident, was discussed in learned circles, and it shows the nature of their ideas. But we must reconstruct the actual form of the oldest cannon, not after the pattern of this picture, but from the realistic pictures that appeared later and the artifacts we have available.[8] These bits of evidence leave no doubt that the earliest firearms were rather small and quite short. At an early point in this development two diverse basic forms appeared. On one of these the tube was provided with a rather long handle that the marksman either held under his arm or braced against the ground. The other was of a somewhat larger caliber and had its tube fastened to a beam that was either laid on the ground or had its rear part dug into the earth. It is impossible to decide which of these two oldest known forms was actually the original one. It does not seem impossible, however, to trace back the line of development from this stage to the earlier uses of gunpowder as fire for combat purposes. The handle used in extension of the tube is similar to the handle that is also found on the *madfaa*. As for the larger caliber, we could imagine as its precursor that Byzantine instrument already mentioned, the illustration of which we can trace back to the tenth century. This instrument has about the same size and form of a large beer tankard, with a handle underneath and a touchhole above. The intention was to shoot a stream of fire into the enemy's face at the moment one was closing in the assault. Of course, here we may doubt once again if we are dealing with a weapon that ever had a practical use or with a figment of somebody's imagination. For, since the stream of fire did not even extend for 1 meter, the man carrying this instrument was too exposed to the danger that the enemy, with his close-combat weapon, sword or spear, would reach him faster than he could blow his fire at the enemy, a fire, furthermore, that at best could create fear but do little damage.[9]

A particular difficulty in the use of gunpowder was caused by the fact that saltpeter was often mixed with other salts or was polluted with dust. This pollution attracted moisture, so that within a short time after its manufacture the powder became useless. Consequently, an effective method of purifying or crystalizing saltpeter was a necessity in the fabrication of a useful gunpowder. This purifying process was already being sought in the thirteenth century, but it was attained only very gradually.

As we can see from the facts mentioned above, the discovery of gunpowder did not yet mean the discovery of firearms, that is to say, expressed specifically, transformation of the explosive power of gunpowder into the power of penetration. Gunpowder was known and used in warfare many centuries before firearms came into use. How were they finally invented? In Byzantium the fire vessel with the touchhole was known, and the Arabs in Spain had the *madfaa*. In order to progress from these instruments to the firearm, it was not sufficient, for example, that a metal or stone ball be placed on top of the powder load. The oldest gunpowder, in flourlike form, did not ignite simultaneously throughout its mass but required several moments until the fire had reached the entire mass. Consequently, a ball simply placed on top of a load of powder would not be projected with the full force of the explosion. Instead, it would roll out slowly, and only afterward would the full force of the explosion push out of the tube. *Therefore, the real invention that led from gunpowder to shooting was the invention of the loading process.* The ball had to be pressed so firmly into the tube—or better, between the gunpowder and the ball there had to be placed a cramming substance that closed the tube so tightly that it and the ball would not be projected until the entire load of powder had ignited and developed its full explosive power. That was best accomplished when an open space was left between the load of powder and the cramming substance. The concentration of power due to the cramming of the tube also caused the sharp crack. Since the Byzantines speak of the thunder they created with their Greek fire, we may assume that at an early stage they had already discovered the method of placing a cramming substance on the powder.[10] But from that point to a weapon with penetrating power is still a considerable leap. The explosive power worked not only forward against the projectile but in all directions. Consequently, the tube had to be very firm and heavy. And so it could not be held in the bare hand, but, as we have seen, it had to be attached to a handle that allowed the marksman to take up the recoil with all the strength of his body, or, if the caliber and, consequently, the load were too strong for that, it had to be based in some way on the ground.

Therefore, neither the Byzantine fire vessel nor the Arab *madfaa* could have been the direct precursor of the firearm—if indeed there existed any link at all between the two. As a result of the lack of sources, there exists here a wide-open area for fantasy. For example, it would be imaginable that the Byzantine fire vessel developed into the firearm as men based it on the ground, ramming in the powder load with a cramming substance, instead of holding it in the hand. And we can further imagine that it was then developed into a hand firearm by imitating the external shape of the *madfaa* with the handle. The fact that we find the first firearms in Italy, which had relationships with both Byzantium and Spain, could be a factor in such an hypothesis.

We do not know where and by whom the first firearm was constructed. We can only determine approximately the time this occurred, around 1300. We may regard Upper Italy as the area of this invention, and we may also be sure that not only gunpowder was at the base of the invention of the firearm but also the purification of saltpeter, the strong tube with the touchhole, the loading with a cramming substance, and the addition of a shaft.

A few years after the appearance of this discovery in Italy, the first reports of thunder jars appeared in France in 1339, in England in 1338,[11] and in Spain in 1342. A few years later they were also mentioned in Germany. First mention appears in the city accounts of Aachen in 1346, then in Deventer in 1348, Arnheim in 1354, Holland in 1355, Nuremberg in 1356, Wesel in 1361, Erfurt in 1362, Cologne in 1370, Meissen around 1370,[12] and Trier in 1373. The earliest report of the presence of a harquebus in Switzerland is from Basel in 1371. It is stated there that the use of firearms came "from the other side of the Rhine."[13]

The generals whom the surviving sources indicate as the first ones to use firearms in warfare were, as we have seen, the knights von Kreuzberg and Spangenberg (1331). Although both of them were Germans, the relatively later appearance of these new weapons in Germany contradicts the legend that their invention took place in our fatherland. Not even any kind of important improvement which might have been made in Germany, for example, and thus have formed the basis for the legend has been proven.[14]

We see from instructions concerning the use of the oldest firearms what a short range they had. In 1347 the stronghold of Bioule of the knight Hugues de Candilhac was armed with twenty-two cannon. One man served as crew for every two pieces; consequently, it was not contemplated that they could be reloaded during the battle. The marksman simply had to fire one and then the other. First of all, however, the large crossbows were to fire, and then the slings, and finally the cannon, which therefore had the least distant effect.[15]

The alleged first use of cannon in the battle of Crécy in 1346 is a fable. According to Froissart, the men of Ghent supposedly used in a battle against the forces of Bruges 200 *ribaudequins*, which are vaguely described as carts bearing small cannon and with a spear extending out in front.[16] We do not know how great their effect was.

In order to have useful gunpowder, it was necessary, as we have seen, to pay particular attention to purifying the saltpeter. Gradual progress was made in this purification process, and eventually good saltpeter could be distinguished from the bad. It was of decisive importance, however, that they learned how to granulate the gunpowder. The powder was dampened and made into small lumps, which were then dried again. This process offered the advantage of making the combustion proceed much faster, because of the small intervals between the lumps. Furthermore, with fine powder it happened easily that while it was being transported the various ingredients were partially separated from one another as a result of the shaking, whereas powder in lumps remained intact. From these lumps one went on to the granulation process by pressing the moistened mush through a sieve. As a result of the improvement of the powder by granulation, the empty space between the cramming substance and the ball disappeared, and after the middle of the fifteenth century the ball was placed directly on the powder, with or without a cramming block.[17]

There also occurred the search for the best proportion of the mixture. In Germany in the nineteenth century a mixture of 74 parts of saltpeter, 10 parts of sulfur, and 16 parts of charcoal was considered the best (also 74:12:13). In the fifteenth century we find similar prescriptions. But along with these there were others with a much smaller proportion of saltpeter, which indicates that it was undesirable to have powder that was too strong, in view of the weak cannon that might possibly explode and seriously endanger their crews.

With insufficient purification of the saltpeter, however, judgment of the effectiveness of the various compositions was uncertain, and the efficiency of the powder was not uniform.

The first literary reference to the new weapon is found in one of Petrarch's writings entitled "de remediis utriusque fortunae" ("On the Remedies of Good and Bad Fortune"), which he dedicated to his friend Azzo da Coreggio but which he did not complete until after Azzo's death. After Azzo sold his city of Parma to the Estes in 1344, he had many sad experiences—sickness, exile, the death of relatives, the unfaithful defection of friends. Petrarch's composition seeks bases for consolation in the misery of this world. In the dialogue somebody who boasts of his possessions in engines and catapults is jokingly asked whether he does not also possess those instruments that project brass acorns with thunder and flames. Until recently, it is said, this plague was so rare that it was looked on with the greatest amazement. But, continues the dialogue, it has now become as widely used as all the other weapons.

Köhler, Jähns, Feldhaus, and others place Petrarch's composition in

or around the year 1340 or 1347. If that were correct, we would have to
assume that Italy was still further ahead of the other countries in the use
of the new weapon than is otherwise believed. In fact, this document was
not finished until 1366,[18] when firearms were already quite widespread
throughout Europe. Therefore, Petrarch's observation is eliminated as
evidence for the earlier date of this weapon, but several expressions in
his work are worthy of note, and it is worth our trouble to become
completely acquainted with this passage. It reads:[19]

Mirum, nisi et glandes aeneas, quae flammis injectis horrisono tonitru iaciuntur. Non erat satis de coelo tonantis ira Dei immortalis, nisi homuncio (O crudelitas iuncta superbiae) de terra etiam tonuisset: non imitabile fulmen (ut Maro ait) humana rabies imitata est, quod e nubibus mitti solet, ligneo quidem, sed tartareo mittitur instrumento, quod ab Archimede inventum quidam putant ... Erat haec pestis nuper rara, ut cum ingenti miraculo cerneretur; nunc ut rerum pessimarum dociles sunt animi; ita communis est, ut unum quodlibet genus armorum.	A marvel except for the bronze bullets, which are shot with spewing flames and awful-sounding thunder. The anger of immortal God thundering from the sky was not enough, unless poor mortal man (O cruelty joined to pride) had also thundered from the ground: human madness copied the inimitable thunderbolt (as Maro [Vergil] says), which is accustomed to be sent from the clouds. Certainly it is shot with a wooden but hellish instrument, which some think was invented by Archimedes. ... This plague was recently rare, so that it was seen with tremendous amazement; now, as minds are easily trained by the worst affairs, so it is common as any one type of weapons.

The invention of firearms must have taken place around the time of
Petrarch's birth (1304) or as he was growing up. Consequently, he knew
nothing about the inventor and actually gave the credit to Archimedes.
We may therefore conclude that even at that time the inventor was not
known. Furthermore, Petrarch called the weapon an "instrument that
was, to be sure, of wood, but still hellish." It is difficult to say just what
he meant. Only the shaft was of wood. With its long and very massive
handle the shaft no doubt was much larger than the quite short iron tube
but could not possibly be considered the important part. We have a choice
between assuming that Petrarch had hardly seen the weapon itself and
had no true idea of what it was like or had only allowed himself to be
misled into the unsatisfactory description by his antithesis of "wooden"
and "hellish."[20]

The third point of interest in Petrarch's discussion lies in the word
"hellish." This strikes a note that persisted throughout the centuries, a
note taken up by Ariosto and Luther in their condemnations of the cruel
instruments of war and still heard today whenever the pacifists complain
of the invention of newer machines of death.

Today we see in the invention of gunpowder one of the most important steps in the technological progress of mankind. Even those who have recognized as false and have rejected the idea that the firearm overcame knighthood and feudalism and thereby created the modern concept of national citizenship, with its social equality, will not hesitate to ascribe to the technique of the firearm, and especially its later development, an important share in the development of mankind. In the force of gunpowder and the related explosives of the most recent period we have gained a power over nature and barbarism that renders impossible a repetition of an overthrow such as that suffered by ancient civilization in the *Völkerwanderung*. The contemporaries, however, had different ideas on that subject.

In 1467 the Florentine exiles under Colleoni fought against Florence, led by Federigo of Urbino, near Imola. Because Colleoni was using field pieces in unusual numbers, Urbino forbade his men to give quarter.

In 1498 Paolo Vitelli, who himself used heavy cannon, ordered that captured harquebusiers have their hands cut off and their eyes pierced out because it seemed unworthy, according to Jovius, for noble knights to be killed by common foot soldiers without revenge.[21]

Frönsberger writes in a similar vein: "And so hardly any man or courage is needed any more in matters of warfare, because all kinds of ruse, deception, and treachery, together with the cruel cannon, have spread so extensively that neither individual fighting, scuffling, striking, harquebus, weapons, strength, skill, or courage can any longer help or have some importance, for it happens often that a manly, brave hero is killed by a dissolute, outlawed youngster by means of the cannon, a person who otherwise would not even be allowed to look at one or address one in a gross manner."

Luther, too, denounced harquebuses and cannon as the very work of the devil and hell, as did Sebastian Münster. On the other hand, Fugger compared them with water and fire, saying they could be just as useful as they were harmful.

Quite often it is reported that captured cannoneers were stuck into their own large cannon and shot out.

LARGE CANNON

Even if it is certain that the oldest firearms were only small,[22] there soon arose a distinction between smaller hand pieces, precursors of the musket, and larger ones, precursors of cannon. Both were manufactured, and the larger ones then grew very quickly. From about 1370 the giant bombards, which were supposed to smash breaches in walls with their mighty stone cannonballs, were under construction, and this first took place once again in the Romanic region.[23]

A simple enlargement was not sufficient, since with a tube having a diameter of one-half meter it was not possible to obtain the definite blocking of the powder load which, as we have seen, was so necessary. Consequently, the cannon was divided into the chamber, which had only a moderate diameter, was filled with powder, and was firmly crammed and blocked with a plug of soft wood, and the forward housing, or the barrel, in which the huge stone cannonball was placed and which was also blocked off as tightly as possible with tow or clay. The gigantic size of the stone balls was required by the nature of the material. They took effect as a result of their weight, even if they were projected with only a moderate velocity. Smaller balls would have had to be shot with all the greater velocity, but then they easily disintegrated on striking the walls they were supposed to destroy.

By separating the forward housing and the chamber from each other and bringing them together only at the time of firing, either by means of their platform or by some kind of lock, the chamber could be loaded more easily, it was easier to transport the cannon, and it was even possible to have several chambers for each forward housing, thereby attaining a faster rate of fire. But these cannon cannot be described as breechloaders.

The forward housing of the earlier stone-firing cannon of this type was so short that the ball barely fit inside or possibly even protruded. It was only gradually that men realized the advantages of a long tube, and they lengthened it accordingly.

In order to protect such a cannon and its crew from the shots of the besieged garrison whenever the cannon was set up before an enemy city or stronghold, a wooden screen was erected in front of it, with a firing slit that could be closed with a cover.

In 1388 the city of Nuremberg sent out its large cannon, "Chriemhilde," to destroy a stronghold. It weighed almost 6,200 pounds, fired a ball of about 600 pounds, and was drawn by twelve horses. The base for the cannon, the "cradle," was drawn by sixteen horses. The screen was transported on three carts drawn by two horses each. Four 4-horse wagons were loaded with eleven stone balls. Other tools—hoists, shovels and ropes, the baggage of the cannon-master—required two wagons, each drawn by four horses. The crew consisted of eight men with breastplates and iron hats, and they rode on one wagon. The cannon-master, Grunwald, was mounted on horseback. The powder supply that was carried for the huge cannon seems remarkably small, not more than about 165 pounds. But since they contemplated, of course, firing not more than eleven shots, that supply was sufficient, allowing about 15 pounds for each shot. In order to accomplish the eleven shots, certainly several days were required.

The great bombard that is still preserved in Vienna is more than 2 1/2 meters long. Its stone balls had a diameter of 80 centimeters and weighed about 1,300 pounds. The bombard itself is considerably heavier than 22,000 pounds. It was probably fabricated between 1430 and 1440.

A Frankfurt cannon that was used in the siege of the stronghold of

Tannenberg in Hesse in 1399 was even somewhat larger.

The earlier tubes were no doubt made of iron and forged over a mandrel. But as early as the fourteenth century the technique of casting in bronze became predominant. Every effort was made to attain the necessary strength without too much weight by tapering the tube toward the muzzle. The interior of the barrel was made as smooth and even as possible by boring and filing, but by the end of the fifteenth century this process had still not led to exactly cylindrical tubes.[24]

The larger the cannon became, the more important was the task of basing them firmly, absorbing the recoil, and being able to move them easily, in order to change their positions and aim them. One attempt followed another, and one invention came on the heels of another until a carriage that was useful in every respect was achieved. The gun mounts in the army of Charles the Bold were already being praised, but the balancing trunnions did not appear until the campaign of Charles VIII in Italy in 1494, and the trunnion discs, which eliminated the play in the trunnion bearing, were first seen in the cannon of Maximilian. It was not until the eighteenth century that the trunnions everywhere attained the form necessary for a reliable cradling of the barrel in the carriage.[25] As late as 1540 the engineer Biringuccio complained that the carriages were generally built so heavy that the cannon could hardly be moved and their slowness also held up the movements of the troops.

The large cannon fired not only full-sized balls but also groups of small balls or flint pebbles, precursors of the canister, and at the end of the fifteenth century bombs also appeared.[26]

The most important improvement that was still to be made, however, was the construction of a useful ball. The stone balls were not sufficiently solid and firm, and the crossed iron rings that were placed around them naturally helped but little. But now, in the fifteenth century, through the utilization of water power, the process of casting iron was developed. The water power made it possible to produce a strong enough blast to heat the iron to a liquid state. It has been said that the use of water power, which only then began serving mankind, did as much for technical progress as did steam power 300 years later. The casting of iron produced the iron cannon ball. It is not clear when iron balls were first used, but it is certain that the French used them in their first move into Italy in 1494 and with them quickly blasted the walls of the enemy cities into dust.[27] Since iron cannon balls did not have to be so very large, the French were able to move their siege guns with them without difficulty and quickly overcame one city after the other. Not until now, that is, more than five generations after the first appearance of firearms, do we have, as a result of the incidental invention of the casting of iron balls, really useful cannon.[28]

The cannon-masters formed a kind of guild that treated its skill as a secret and passed it down in their families, or through their students. Even when, around 1420, and therefore about a century after the new discovery, an unknown master wrote the *Book of Pyrotechnics* (*Feuer-werksbuch*), which treated the entire technique of powder fabrication, casting of cannon, loading, aiming, and firing, and this book was distributed in numerous copies and was even translated into French, it was nevertheless guarded as such a secret that it was not printed until 1529. For more than a century and a half this book, as its copies were revised in keeping with the progress of the art, remained the standard instructional manual for artillerymen. It is perhaps because of the fame of this book that the legend concerning the invention of powder in Germany found acceptance.

In about the period we are discussing, the protection of the artillery became an assignment of special honor, but the artillerymen themselves were not yet considered as soldiers, but rather as technicians.[29]

In 1568, de la Noue named St. Anthony as the patron saint of this guild,[30] but in the end St. Barbara, whose aid was invoked in cases of danger from lightning, took over that position.

It is difficult to say how effective the earliest siege cannon, that is, those of the last decades of the fourteenth century and beginning of the fifteenth, projecting stone balls, really were. In 1388 Archbishop Friedrich of Cologne besieged the city of Dortmund and managed to fire 33 balls in a single day and a total of 283 balls in fourteen days. In 1390 Blaubeuren was reportedly captured as a result of such bombardment, and in 1395 the stronghold of Elkershausen presumably fell in the same way. When the Appenzellers in 1401 besieged the castle of Klanx in their rebellion against their lord, the abbot of St. Gall, they reportedly captured it finally with the help of the burghers of St. Gall, who brought up cannon.

In February 1414, when Friedrich of Brandenburg with his allies moved out against the Quitzows, his enemies, too, already had cannon. According to a statement in his will, Friedrich had cannon cast from the bells of the church of the Virgin Mary in Berlin. But there remains the question of whether that was done for this campaign or perhaps later for the war with the Hussites.[31] From the landgrave of Thuringia he had borrowed the gigantic cannon that was called the "lazy Greta" in the legend. This cannon was used first at Friesack near Rathenow and then at Plaue near Brandenburg. Friesack was defended by Dietrich von Quitzow, while Hans von Quitzow defended Plaue, but both of them fled before the critical moment arrived, and the strongholds then surrendered. We probably cannot assume that the cannon played a decisive role at those places, since the numerical superiority of the burgrave, who was allied with the archbishop of Magdeburg and the duke of Saxony, would have sufficed in any case to overcome those strongholds. In 1437 the prince elector still had *bliden* [a type of catapult] as well as cannon in his siege equipment.[32]

In 1422 the Hussites in five months fired almost 11,000 projectiles against the Bohemian fort of Karlstein, and yet they still had to withdraw without attaining their goal.

In 1428 the English fired stone balls weighing from 130 to 180 pounds against Orléans without damaging the wall. Only individual buildings in the city were beaten into ruins and a few persons were killed or wounded, but their total did not reach 50.

In 1453 the Turks took Constantinople by storm, using the same means that were already in use before the employment of firearms. The artillery had contributed nothing to their success, even though a giant cannon shot stone balls weighing 1,300 pounds against the city.[33]

Rudolf Schneider has established the fact that the engine with which the ancients had obtained the greatest effect was lost in the *Völkerwanderung*.[34] This weapon was based on the power of torsion, that is, the tension created by the twisting of animal sinews or hairs. This power is unusually great, but the construction of an engine of this kind is quite complicated, and when the conduct of war became more barbaric, the armies were unable to continue using this technique. The Middle Ages were familiar only with enlarged crossbows and engines based on the principle of leverage (the *blide*). Schneider believes that if the torsion engines had survived, cannon using gunpowder would perhaps never have appeared, since, in their earlier forms—indeed, until 1600—they would not have been able to compete in effectiveness with the torsion engines.

As conclusive as this idea may seem, it has nevertheless recently been contradicted by the discovery that at about the same time the cannon appeared, the ancient torsion engine was again invented and put in use. Such an engine was used in 1324 in the defense of Metz, and in 1346 and later Johann Gui of Metz built such instruments in Avignon for the pope, in return for an extremely high price.[35]

How remarkably the spirit of invention can go astray! Johann Gui or his mentor in Metz, who studied the ancients and, borrowing from them, again built the torsion engine, was certainly a man of genius, and he created anew a weapon that was surely far superior to the contemporary cannon. But the cannon lent itself to further development, while the torsion engine did not, and Johann Gui would have accomplished something much more important from a practical viewpoint if he had been able to teach his contemporaries how to cast iron cannon balls.

Nevertheless, as late as 1740, Dulacq, in his *Théorie nouvelle sur le méchanisme de l'artillerie*, proposed reintroducing the projectile engines of the ancients instead of the high-angle guns, since the performance of these firearms was too irregular.

However small we may estimate the effectiveness of the large stone balls, their performance cannot have been so very insignificant, since new versions of these huge engines would not otherwise have been cast and used again and again. If we consider as the true test of their effectiveness a corresponding change in the defense, in the design and construction of strongholds, then we must note that these changes are to be observed from the second half of the fifteenth century on.[36]

The names of the various types of cannon were very numerous, but we cannot establish specific limits for the meaning of each. The term "culverin," which was an individual firearm at the time of Charles the Bold, meant a cannon in the sixteenth century. Furthermore, we can also list: bombards, cannon firing stone balls (*Steinbüchse*), block cannon (*Klotzbüchse*), main cannon (*Hauptbüchse*), "Metze," mortar, breaker (*Tummler*), mortar (*Böller*), howitzer, cannon-royal (*Karthaune*: that is, actually *Quartane*: quarter-cannon), "snake," "emergency snake," "serpentine," "falcon," "falconette," "sparrow-hawk," "Tarras cannon," "singer," "nightingale," "fowler," "pelican," "basilisk," "dragon," "*Saker*," "*Kanone*."[37]

Initially, the Italians and Spanish used oxen to draw cannon. When the French appeared in Italy in 1494, it was noticed that their numerous cannon were drawn by unusually strong horses.[38] The mobility this permitted them was a great advantage, but the cost of such teams was also very high. When Emperor Maximilian took the field in 1507, it is recounted in the *Life of Bayard* that he had teams for only half of his artillery, so that when the first half had completed its march, the teams had to return and bring up the second half.

Despite this disadvantage, Maximilian, the Swiss,[39] and the French were praised in various passages because of their artillery.[40]

As late as the beginning of the sixteenth century, the effectiveness of artillery in battle was relatively small. The technique and art of aiming was still too undeveloped. The cannon balls flew too high. The tight units of infantry lay down whenever they had to remain under cannon fire, or they sought to run up under it, so that the cannon could not fire more than one shot.[41]

For this reason, in 1494, when the French cannon were praised, the famous mercenary leader Trivulzio declared that they were of hardly any use in battle.[42] Machiavelli, in his *Discorsi*,[43] written between 1513 and 1521, said that it was mainly the unaccustomed noise of the cannon that created fear. In the 1580s Montaigne was of the same opinion, and he hoped, therefore, that these "useless things" would be abandoned.[44] Nevertheless, Jovius says in his *Life of Pescara* that no wise general would go into battle under any circumstances without artillery.[45] Avila praises the excellent manner in which Landgrave Philip and his officers had understood how to use cannon in the Schmalkaldic War.[46] On one occasion, before Ingolstadt, they fired 750 cannon balls in nine hours, and that was considered a fearful cannonade.

HAND FIREARMS

As we have seen, a distinction must have been made very early between hand firearms, which in Germany were called "*Lotbüchsen*" ("perpendicular muskets"), and cannon. But with all their differences, there were analogies between the development of the two types. With small arms also the barrel was lengthened and sometimes divided into two pieces, or a ringlike bulge was placed inside, separating the chamber from the barrel, so that when the wooden cramming block was inserted, it did not move all the way to the powder but left some empty space for the complete development of the gases.

The large cannon were ignited by placing an iron hook, heated to the glowing point, into the touchhole. In the case of hand arms, a slow match was pressed onto the touchhole, which was filled with powder. As long as the touchhole was on top of the barrel, this prevented any aiming, especially because a flame shot up from the touchhole. For this reason, two men were sometimes assigned to one piece; one aimed and gave the sign to the other, who fired. Later the touchhole was placed on the side of the barrel, and a pan was provided there for the ignition powder. The cock was then invented, in the mouth of which the match was held, which the marksman could push down with his hand while aiming, without looking at the pan.

The match hammer, which the marksman pressed down with his hand, was followed by the matchlock, which by means of a spring enabled the hammer to be snapped down with a simple pressure of the finger, a procedure already used on the crossbow.

Loading was simplified by having the marksman carry small wooden powder measures, each of which contained the proper amount of powder for a shot, measured out in advance. In order to have these cartridges, as they can be called, available as quickly as possible, the marksman carried eleven of them on a bandoleer over his shoulder. In addition, he had a bag of bullets and a powder horn from which he shook powder onto the pan. For this igniting powder or priming, a different, finer kind of powder was used than for the shot itself. A cover was placed on the pan.

The earlier hand arms were manipulated in widely varying ways. The extension rod was placed against the ground, or it was held in the armpit or on the shoulder, or it was braced against the chest. In some cases the firearm was even held freely with both hands away from the body.

But none of these stances was able to produce either a distant or an accurate shot. When, in order to improve these aspects of firing, the barrel was lengthened, the resulting increased recoil caused new difficulties. To take up the recoil, an iron hook was placed under the barrel near the muzzle, starting in 1419.[47] Weapons with such hooks were very common, but since they required a firm support, a wall or a piece of timber, they were hardly usable in the open field. And even when individual stocks were constructed as supports, very little was gained for use in the open field, since the transportation of such supports and every change of position were too difficult.[48]

A more accurate aiming was facilitated through the invention of front and rear sights. From 1430 on competitive shoots were held by the burghers. But accuracy in battle, where the marksman was more or less affected by the excitement of the situation, was not a particular consideration. Later, in the eighteenth century, accuracy of firing was intentionally ignored in favor of mass fire and rapid fire.

The advantage of the new weapon over the bow and crossbow was its great penetrating power and its long range. At the shooting tournaments toward the end of the fifteenth century shots were made with firearms to distances of 230 to 250 paces, whereas the range for a crossbow amounted to only 110 to 135 paces.[49] Rifled barrels, which had already been invented at that time, were normally expressly prohibited. Other provisions can hardly be understood in any other way than applying to freehand shooting (and not, for example, to supported hook weapons).

The balls of the harquebus, however, often proved to be too weak to penetrate the heavy knightly armor. Consequently, the musket was built, an infantry weapon that shot a ball weighing 2 ounces (that is about twice the weight of our old needle-gun bullet); and since the marksman could not control it simply with his hands, it was supported on a fork. Du Bellay writes of this invention in 1523, that is, after Bicocca and before Pavia.

The fork was so light that the marksman could carry it along with his musket, and when in position it could be turned in all directions. During loading the marksman held it on a leather sling around his left arm.

The stock was only very gradually shaped in such a way that the musket could be placed against the shoulder.

Both the lighter harquebus and the heavier musket remained in use throughout the sixteenth century. (See the excursus below.)

When the barrel was forged over a spindle, the finished product was still so rough that it detracted from the effectiveness of the powder gases and the accuracy of aiming. Attempts to arrive at completely smooth interior surfaces were made by means of careful boring.

Other inventions already included double-barrel pieces, revolving and organ firearms, which are somewhat similar to the modern *mitrailleuse* and machine gun. The firing of bolts was also attempted.

The uncertain success of the firearm led to the idea of making it in such a form as to be used also as a striking weapon. Battle clubs were fabricated from which one could also fire. Some of these even had several barrels.[50]

These inventions and fabrications are valuable only as experiments and curiosities. The real development followed the process of continually perfecting the instrument of the hand firearm in its basic form.

As early as the meeting of the diet in Nuremberg in 1431 it was decreed for the campaign against the Hussites that half of the marksmen were to be armed with harquebuses and half with crossbows. Similar prescriptions were quite frequent. In the armies of Charles the Bold there were archers, crossbowmen, and marksmen with firearms all serving together. In 1507, however, Emperor Maximilian eliminated the crossbow.

At that time some 200 years had passed since the invention of the first firearm. The barrel had been lengthened, the stock with the butt had been invented, as well as the powder pan with its cover, the matchlock, the fork, the powder cartridges, and the boring of the barrel. But let us listen to how a modern expert describes the manipulation of this greatly improved harquebus:[51]

> The manipulation of harquebuses equipped with matchlocks was slow, complicated, and highly dangerous. First of all was the lighting of the match with stone, steel, sparker, and sulfur (if there did not happen to be another burning match or a campfire at hand). Then there was the caution that was necessary to protect the match from being extinguished by humidity and to protect oneself, one's clothing, and the munitions from the flame of the match. This was followed by the awkward loading from the little powder cartridge and the bullet bag, and finally the shaking out of powder on the pan, which required a good breath to blow away the superfluous powder, after the pan was closed, from all the edges of the lock to avoid the danger of accidental ignition. And if the firing did not take place immediately or shortly after loading, it was usually necessary to seal shut the cover of the pan with tallow to protect the priming powder—a somewhat dirty operation. Then came the insertion of the match into the mouth of the hammer—not protruding too much, where it would not have struck the pan; not too far back, where it might easily have been smothered; not too firmly, because, of course, with the short burning time it was often necessary to push it out further; not too loose, because it could then easily slip through and be extinguished. And with all of this the constant anxious attentiveness to avoid bringing one of the two burning matchpoints or the sparks emitted by them too close to the open powder container or one's clothing. And to cap it all, the poor matchlock marksman who was called a dragoon was placed on a horse, where he was supposed to accomplish all these complicated manipulations and still control his mount!

No wonder that Machiavelli speaks in quite a number of passages of his *Art of War* of the dangerous nature of the harquebus and the field cannon, whereas in other places he treats them as of little value and claims that the harquebus was useful to terrify peasants when they had occupied a pass, for example.

A French work of 1559 recommended again adopting the crossbow, because it had advantages against cavalry, in rain, and in sudden attacks.[52]

The bow, especially, retained its advocates and defenders for a long time. As late as 1590 a literary controversy took place in England over the advantages of the bow and the harquebus. Sir John Smythe favored the bow, claiming it shot faster and more accurately and the marksman was not troubled by poor or wet powder or by unreliable matches. Furthermore, it could be shot from several ranks, and the arrows frightened the horses. Barwick replied that dampness was just as harmful for bowstrings as for powder. He claimed that good archers were rare, since it was easier to aim with the harquebus than with the bow, and that fatigue made the archer downright incapable. The shots were often fired too quickly and with only half-force. While horses might be more frightened by arrows, men feared bullets more. Smythe replied that if a musketeer fired more than ten times in an hour, he was no longer capable of hitting a target.[53]

In 1547 the English bow defeated the Scots at Pinkin Cleugh. In 1616 archers were mentioned in the battles between Venice and Austria. In 1627 the English appeared before La Rochelle with bows and arrows. In 1730 in the camp of Mühlberg Saxon hussars were armed with bows and arrows. In the Seven Years' War the Russians had in their ranks Kalmucks of whom a diary reported: "They are armed with bows and arrows with which they shoot incredibly far and accurately, but in wet and windy weather these shots are not so much to be feared." General Fermor is said to have sent "most of the Kalmucks" home in the end because they would not submit to military discipline and also, like the Cossacks, they feared the firing.[54] Indeed, even in 1807 and 1813 the Russian army had Kalmucks, Bashkirs, and Tungus who were armed with bows and arrows. The French general Marbot recounts in his *Mémoires* that he himself was wounded by an arrow in the battle of Leipzig. He says that, although the number of these mounted archers was huge and they constantly swarmed around the French like wasps, filling the air with their arrows, only a single Frenchman was killed by an arrow, to the best of his knowledge, and the wounds caused by the arrows were mostly only light ones. This ineffectiveness would be incompatible with the medieval reports if we were not to take into account the fact that Marbot greatly exaggerates the number of these primitive warriors and that, faced with firearms, they naturally maintained a respectful distance.[55]

If the French in 1495,[56] the Swiss in 1499,[57] and Frundsberg's lansquenets in 1526 defended themselves on the march against pursuing enemies by means of marksmen in the rear guard,[58] no doubt archers and crossbowmen also did that in similar situations in earlier times.

Whereas the cannon was a completely new factor in open battle, the cannon in siege warfare and the hand firearm were instruments that were initially used only to complement other weapons having similar effects, and only very gradually did they succeed in completely supplanting the older weapons. Consequently, the tactical employment of the new hand firearms was not initially different from the use of the earlier missile weapons.

In the battles that marked the end of the medieval system of warfare and introduced the new epoch in the area of weapons, at Grandson, Murten, and Nancy—to emphasize this point once again—this new force was on the side of the knights. It was not as a result of the firearm that they were overcome; on the contrary, they were overcome despite the fact that they had understood how to make use of the new techniques and to adapt themselves to such use.

The first rather large battle in which we see a significant influence of hand firearms appears to have taken place at the beginning of 1503 in Lower Italy between the French and the Spanish. It is recounted by Jovius, who apparently had good sources, in his *Life of Gonzalo of Cordova*.[59] The French general, the duke of Nemours, attempted to lure Gonzalo from his fortified strongpoint, Barletta. Gonzalo held back, but when the French withdrew, he followed them with his light horsemen and attached to these mounted men two groups of men armed with the harquebus. They moved along on both flanks of the horsemen. The French men-at-arms turned about and charged the Spanish horsemen, who pretended to take flight and thus drew the French between the two groups of harquebusiers, which now poured heavy fire on them. The men-at-arms could now have turned against the marksmen to ride them down, but they did not manage to do so, since the Spanish horsemen, reinforced, returned to the attack, forcing the French to flee with heavy losses.

Soon thereafter (28 August 1503) the battle of Cerignola took place. On that field, the hand firearm, in conjunction with a field fortification, determined the nature of the battle, and this influence then increased steadily from one battle to another.

PISTOLS

As early as the second half of the fourteenth century firearms were also made for mounted men,[60] and at the end of the fifteenth century Camillo Vitelli formed a corps of mounted marksmen.[61] But they did not last long, and in 1535, when Emperor Charles V explained to Jovius his campaign in Tunisia, he added that he intended to incorporate again into his troops mounted crossbowmen. Consequently, it appears that at that time the emperor had not yet found a sufficiently useful firearm for his horsemen. A few years later we learn from Jovius that the horsemen of the imperial army were armed with wheel lock pistols. When Stuhlweissenburg was forced to capitulate to Sultan Suleiman in September 1543, the garrison was allowed to withdraw freely with its property. The terms of the capitulation were observed by the Turks with the one exception that they took from the withdrawing troops their wheel lock pistols, which aroused their curiosity and their greed because of their wonderful construction. In the following year, 1544, the dismounted lansquenets used this type of pistol in the battle of Ceresole.[62] Charles V himself recounts in his memoirs how the *"pistolets"* or *"petites arquebuses"* of the German horsemen had dealt damage to the French in a battle at Châlons.[63] Again in the Schmalkaldic War they are mentioned by the Spanish historian Avila, who uses the circumlocution "harquebuses two spans long" or "small harquebuses." We see, then, that the name "pistol" had not yet come into use.[64]

In 1547 we hear from France that the mounted marksmen were now armed, not with the bow, which they had carried before "this devilish pistol was invented," but with the pistol.[65]

The wheel lock, which made use of the pistol possible for a mounted man, was based on the principle that a sharp-toothed wheel, rotated by a wound spring, struck a spark from a sulfuric stone, igniting the powder on the pan. Nevertheless, this type of lock had such great shortcomings in actual practice that the matchlock continued to be preferable for the foot soldier.[66]

Finally, let us add the following passage (p. 65) from the *War Booklet* (*Kriegs-Büchlein*), 1644, by the Zurich captain, Lavater: "But when a soldier fires an iron or tin ball dipped in fat and chewed, shaved, or quartered, you should grant him no mercy. All those who are armed with a rifled barrel and a French musket have forfeited any mercy. Therefore, you should strike dead all those who shoot shot of iron, or of rectangular shape, or of steel or who have swords with undulating blades."

EXCURSUS

MUSKETS

It is not easy to say what we should understand as the significant difference between the harquebus and the musket. Consequently, what we have said in the foregoing text may be open to some doubt. See Hobohm in the *Guide to the Berlin Ordnance Museum* (*Führer durch das Berliner Zeughaus*), p. 83. As early as 1321 crossbow bolts were called *muschettae* by Marino Sanuto (Jähns, *Kriegswesen*, p. 637; Schneider, *Artillerie des Mittelalters*, p. 48). In Germany the name *"Muskete"* did not appear until 1587.[67] Fork harquebuses were supposedly cast in Bordeaux in the spring of 1504; they had not yet been mentioned in 1499.

Martin du Bellay, *Mémoires*, Book II (Ed. Paris, 1586), p. 43, says in 1521, speaking of the siege of Parma by the imperial army: Splendid skirmishes took place—"from that hour on, the harquebuses that were fired on a fork were invented." Jovius, in his *Life of Pescara*, reports that, when the imperial cuirassiers were sorely pressed by the French in the battle of Pavia:[68]

Piscarius . . . hispanos sclopettarios circiter octingentos subsidio mittit, qui repente circumfusi a tergo et a lateribus edita terribili pilarum procella, ingentem equorum atque hominum numerum prosternunt. . . . Hispani natura agiles, et levibus protectis armis, retro sese celeriter explicant, equorumque impetum tortuosis discursibus eludunt: auctique numero, uti erant cum longo usu, tum novis Piscarit praeceptis edocti, manipulatim toto campo sine ordine diffunduntur. Erat id pugnae genus per se novum et inusitatum, sed in primis saevum et miserabile, quod magna rerum iniquitate praeoccupantibus sclopettariis, praeclarae virtutis usus in equite penitus interiret: nec ullae vel fortissimae dextrae diu proficerent, quin conferti a raris et paucis, plures et clarissimi saepe duces et equites inulta caede passim ab ignobili et gregario pedite sternerentur. . . . Erat pugna omnium maxime funesta, et magnopere iniqua Gallis equitibus: nam a circumfusis et expeditis Hispanis in omnem partem ad lethales ictus pilae plumbeae spargebantur: quae non jam tenuioribus (uti paulo ante erat solitum) sed gravioribus sclopettis quos vocant arcabusios, emissae, non cataphractorum modo, sed duos saepe milites et binos equos transverberabant: sic ut miserabili nobilium equitum strage, et morientium equorum cumulis constrati campi, et alarum virtuti simul officerent, si densato ordine irrumpere conarentur, et passim veluti objectis aggeribus, si cui decore vita potior foret, minime expeditum ad fugam iter praeberent.

Pescara sent about 800 Spanish *sclopettarii* as a reinforcement, who were suddenly surrounded on their flanks and rear and leveled a huge number of horses and men, when they shot an awful hail of balls. . . . The Spanish, naturally mobile and lightly armored, quickly retreated and avoided the attack of the cavalry by serpentine rushes. Reinforced, the Spanish were scattered by units all over the field without a definite battle line, as they had been instructed not only by long experience but also by the new orders of Pescara. This type of battle was in itself strange and unusual, but especially savage and pitiable, because while the *sclopettarii* were taking advantage from the inequity of affairs, the practice of valorous courage among the cavalry utterly perished: nor for a long time did any or even the strongest sword arms gain an advantage; rather, more, and often the most famous commanders and knights, gathered in small scattered groups, were prostrated here and there in unavenged slaughter by the ignoble and common infantry. . . . Of all the soldiers, the battle was especially deadly and very unequal for the French cavalry, for lead balls were sprayed by the Spanish surrounding them and ready on every side for their deadly volleys. These were shot no longer with the lighter *sclopetti* (as had been customary a little before) but with the heavier ones, which they call arquebuses, and they penetrated not only an armored horseman, but also often two soldiers and two horses. Thus the fields were covered with the pitiful slaughter of noble horsemen and by heaps of dying horses. Both of these would at the same time obstruct the capability of the mounted units if they tried to break out in a close formation, and here and there, as if embankments had been thrown up, would offer the least expedient route for flight, if someone had a stronger desire for life than for glory.

When the Spanish had suffered a defeat at the hands of the French in 1544 at Ceresole, their general, del Guasto, still remembered the earlier success of their marksmen at Pavia. Jovius (*Hist. B.* 44) recounts that del Guasto himself had spoken with him about that, saying he had believed that the French knights were now no longer to be feared.

When Italian mounted troops and infantry fought unsuccessfully against janissaries before Budapest in 1542, Jovius says (*Hist. lib.* 42, opera tom. I, p. 517): "Janizeri summa agilitate suspensa ad utrunque latus anteriore tunica, peritissime longioribus sclopettis utebantur" ("The janissaries, of the greatest nimbleness with their tunics pinned up on both sides, used most skillfully the longer *sclopetti*").

NOTES FOR CHAPTER II

1. From the abundant literature on the invention of gunpowder and the oldest firearms, I mention the following works: Napoleon III, *Du Passé et de l'Avenir de l'Artillerie*. This work, which was written during the imprisonment of Louis Napoleon in Ham, is still worthy of note today. With a certain amount of abridgment and the omission of notes and tables, it was copied in the *Oeuvres de Napoléon III*, Vol. IV, 1856, and was translated by Lieutenant (later Lieutenant General) H. Müller, Berlin, 1856. A. Essenwein, *Sources on the History of Firearms. Facsimile Illustrations of Old Original Drawings, Miniatures, Wood Cuts, and Etchings, together with Photographs of Authentic Old Weapons and Models (Quellen zur Geschichte der Feuerwaffen. Faksimilierte Nachbildung alter Originalzeichnungen, Miniaturen, Holzschnitte und Kupferstiche nebst Aufnahmen alter Originalwaffen und Modelle)*. Published by the Germanic National Museum. Text by A. Essenwein. With 213 facsimile illustrations. Leipzig, 1872–1877. Thierbach, M., *The Historical Development of Hand Firearms (Die geschichtliche Entwicklung der Handfeuerwaffen)*, Dresden, 1886. Supplement, 1899. Köhler, G., *The Development of the Military System and Warfare in the Knightly Period (Die Entwicklung des Kriegswesens und der Kriegführung in der Ritterzeit)*, Vol. III, Breslau, 1887 (probably the most valuable part of this broadly conceived work). Romocki, S. J. von, *History of Explosives (Geschichte der Explosivstoffe)*, Vol. I, Berlin, Hanover, 1898. Very valuable, especially because of its corrected reprint of Marcus Graecus. Jähns, M., *History of the Development of Old Offensive Weapons (Supplement on Firearms) (Entwicklungsgeschichte der alten Trutzwaffen [Anhang Feuerwaffen])*, Berlin, 1899. Sixl, P., "Development and Use of Hand Firearms" ("Entwicklung und Gebrauch der Handfeuerwaffen"), *Zeitschrift für historische Waffenkunde*, I ff., 1899 ff. Reimer, P., "Gunpowder and Ballistic Concepts in the Fourteenth and Fifteenth Centuries" ("Das Pulver und die ballistischen Anschauungen im XIV. und XV. Jahrhundert"), *Zeitschrift für historische Waffenkunde*, 1:164 ff. Also 4:367. Oskar Guttmann, *Records of Gunpowder (Monumenta pulveris pyrii)*,

London, 1906. Karl Jacobs, *The Development of Firearms on the Lower Rhine up to the Year 1400* (*Das Aufkommen der Feuerwaffen am Niederrheine bis zum Jahre 1400*), Bonn, Peter Hanstein, publisher, 1910. An excellent document that presents much more than the title indicates. Rudolf Schneider, in the *Zeitschrift für historische Waffenkunde*, Vol. 6, Book 3, "A Byzantine Firearm" ("Eine byzantinische Feuerwaffe"). See also in this connection the article by R. Forrer, "Archeological and Technical Aspects of the Byzantine Firearm of the cod. Vat 1605 c. Eleventh Century" ("Archäologisches und Technisches zu der byzantinischen Feuerwaffe des cod. Vat 1605 c. 11. Jahrhundert") in the fourth book of the same periodical (1909). These two articles overtake Romocki's work with completely new material. M. Feldhaus, in his *Great Pages of Technology* (*Ruhmesblätter der Technik*), Leipzig, 191–[*sic*], gives a valuable survey based on his own research. Recently, a new contribution in this field with very valuable new conclusions has been added by Rathgen (Lieutenant General) and Schäfer, "Firearms and Long-range Weapons in the Papal Army in the Fourteenth Century" ("Feuer- und Fernwaffen beim päpstlichen Heer im 14. Jahrhundert"), *Zeitschrift für historische Waffenkunde*, Vol. VII, Book 1, 1915.

2. Schneider and Forrer, op. cit.

3. See Romocki, *Geschichte der Explosivstoffe*, for the best and most thorough treatment of this subject.

4. Romocki, p. 31.

5. Under these circumstances, I may be permitted to pass over the question as to whether and to what extent gunpowder and firearms were known in ancient India. On this point see Oppert, Gustav, "On the Question of Gunpowder in Ancient India" ("Zur Schiesspulverfrage im alten Indien"), *Mitteilungen zur Geschichte der Medizin und Naturwissenschaften*, 4:421–437.

6. Rathgen and Schäfer, "Feuer- und Fernwaffen beim päpstlichen Heer im 14. Jahrhundert."

7. This work by Walter de Millemete is entitled *De officiis regum* (*On the Duties of Kings*) and was presumably written in 1325 or at the beginning of the reign of Edward III, that is, shortly after 1327. The manuscript is in Oxford. The illustration is to be found in Guttmann, figure 69, reproduced in the *Zeitschrift für historische Waffenkunde* and also, very unclearly, in Feldhaus, p. 100. I handed my colleague, Tangl, the sample given in Guttmann, and he told me that no conclusion could be drawn from the passage. While he was certain it belonged in the fourteenth century, it was of the type of elegant writing which contains so little of an individual character that it is impossible to establish a closer date. But he went on to say that if the manuscript can be proved to stem from the years to which it has been attributed (1325–1327), then we may also assume that the illustration is from the same period. The fact that the

projectile with the arrow point is aimed at the gate of a stronghold could perhaps be interpreted as indicating that we are dealing with a purely decorative composition that does not necessarily show firing against the strong gate. Shooting with bolts instead of balls was actually done.

8. The most important are two frescoes in the church of the former monastery of St. Leonardo in Leccetto near Siena, on which a siege with a cannon and a hand firearm are shown (Guttmann, p. 28). According to an account book, the master Paul was paid 16 L., 12 R. for these works in June 1343. Professor Tangl told me, however, that the writing in the account book is of a much later period.

9. On this point see the articles by Schneider and Forrer named in note 1 above.

10. Of course, Rathgen and Schäfer point out that in the papal accounts, as detailed as they are in other respects, there is no entry for wood for the blocks. They say, however, that these blocks may have been made on the spot.

11. According to Clephan, "A Sketch of the History and Evolution of the Handgun," *Festschrift für Thierbach*, pp. 35, 40, gunpowder and various types of cannon are mentioned for the first time in England in 1338, in a procurement contract.

12. With respect to Meissen, see Baarmann in the *Festschrift für Thierbach*, p. 67, where it is said that the defender of Salzderhelden successfully used a lead firearm several years earlier.

13. "On the Oldest Cannon in Switzerland, with a Document from the Year 1391" ("Ueber älteste Geschütze in der Schweiz, mit einer Urkunde vom Jahre 1391"), by Dr. J. Häne in Zurich. *Anzeiger für schweizerische Altertumskunde*, new series, 2(1900): 215–222.

14. Jacobs, p. 136.

15. Favé, 3:80 ff., according to Köhler.

16. The *ribaudequins* were originally large crossbows that were installed on the walls. In the fifteenth century they were often named as cannon. The most important passages are cited in Köhler, *Kriegswesen der Ritterzeit*, 3:178, 279, 315.

17. In an extract from the *Book of Pyrotechnics (Feuerwerksbuch)* of 1429 it is already stated how "lump powder" was made and the fact that this powder was more effective than fine powder. Köster (p. 336) and Jähns (p. 401) believe that this lump powder was not yet a true granulation but only a preliminary step. Romocki, p. 182, and Clephan, p. 36, call it simply granulation. Clephan adds that, nevertheless, fine powder continued to be used for a long time and granulated powder was again used at the beginning of the sixteenth century. As the reason for this, he assumes, as does Köhler, 3:255, that the explosion of the granulated powder was so strong that the weak cannon could not withstand it. This explanation is not very enlightening, since one could have used less powder.

18. G. Körting, *Petrarch's Life and Works* (*Petrarcas Leben und Werke*), p. 542, says that the poet devoted many years to this work but did not finish it until he was old—on 4 October 1366, according to a reliable source. Azzo died in 1362. This date is also accepted by Karl Förster, *Petrarch's Collected Canzonas* (*Petrarcas sämtliche Canzone*, usw.), translation, 2d ed., 1833, p. XI. This report is based on Baldelli, *Del Petrarca e delle sue opere*, Florence, 1797. 2d ed., Fiesole, 1837. Blanc, in Ersch and Gruber, III, 19, p. 237, reports that Petrarch started the work in 1358 and finished it in 1360. In 1360 or early 1361 he supposedly presented it to the Dauphin, later Charles V of France, on the occasion of a diplomatic mission, and Charles had it translated into French. Blanc also bases his statements on Baldelli, but Baldelli, in his second edition at any rate, names 1366 as the year of completion.

19. Published in Geneva by Jacob Stoer in 1645, p. 302.

20. In the word "wooden" Jähns saw indirect proof of its derivation from the *madfaa*. That does not seem clear to me.

21. Jovius, *Elogia virorum bellica virtute illustrium* (*Aphorisms of Men Distinguished by Military Virtue*), Basel, 1575, p. 184. Also Guicciardini, *Historia d'Italia*, Venice, 1562, 4:100.

22. Jacobs, p. 53.

23. Jacobs, p. 51 ff., p. 136.

24. Napoléon, *Etudes*, p. 66.

25. Baarmann, "The Development of the Gun Carriage up to the Beginning of the Sixteenth Century and Its Relationship to that of the Rifle Stock" ("Die Entwicklung der Geschützlafette bis zum Beginn des 16. Jahrhunderts und ihrer Beziehungen zu der des Gewehrschaftes"), *Festschrift für Thierbach*, p. 54. A very valuable study. I cannot agree with the differing opinions in Essenwein and Gohlke (*Geschichte der Feuerwaffen*). According to von Graevenitz, *Gattamelata and Colleoni and Their Relationships to the Art* (*Gattamelata und Colleoni und ihre Beziehungen zur Kunst*), Leipzig, 1906, p. 96, Colleoni placed cannon on mobile carriages and thereby became the creator of the field artillery in Italy.

26. Robertus Valturius, *de re militari* (*On Military Affairs*), Verona, 1482, has a series of illustrations of cannon in Book X. Among them are also bombs with burning tinder, but in other respects the pictures are fantasies.

27. On his rapid march from Rome to Naples in 1495, Charles VIII bombarded the city of Monte Fortino so that it could be taken by storm (Pilorgerie, *Campagne de 1494–1495*, p. 174). The same procedure was repeated at Monte di San Giovanni (p. 174). Charles VIII himself gives testimony in a letter written on the day of the victory (9 February 1495) of "a bombardment of four hours." During that time an extensive breach had been made (p. 176). In a letter dated 11 February, Charles refers to

Monte Fortino as "one of the fortified places of this country famous for its strength." He did not move out against this city until after the midday meal, and less than an hour after the first shot the attack had already succeeded (pp. 177–178). A letter from a high-ranking French officer from Naples, written in February 1495, states: "Our artillery is not large, but we have found more in this city and large stocks of powder. But we have a shortage of iron bolts because here they have only stones" (p. 197). —In the presence of the king the shooting was better—"Today the king went to dine with the artillery, and in short order the cannoneers fired so well that they knocked down a tower" (13 March 1495). (Pilorgerie, *Campagne de 1494–1495*, p. 211).

28. Beck, *History of Iron (Geschichte des Eisens)*, 1:906, says that iron balls were among the earliest proof for the invention of iron casting and existed long before 1470, when Louis XI supposedly bought the secret from a German Jew (p. 910). On p. 915 he even claims they go back to the beginning of the fifteenth century. But that certainly seems false. In those cases where iron balls are mentioned earlier, they may have been, as Beck himself says, forged balls, and the cast-iron balls that appeared toward the end of the fifteenth century were regarded as something entirely new. Jähns, 1:427, cites the statement from an anonymous military book dated 1450 to the effect that stone balls were to be preferred because they were much less expensive than those of iron or lead. The high price, however, can hardly have been a decisive factor when we realize that, although the individual stone ball was much cheaper, the manufacture, transportation, and manipulation of the cannon that it required were all the more costly. The manuscript of a book on pyrotechnics that Jähns, 2:405, places in the year 1454 recommends covering iron balls with cast lead. This can no doubt refer only to forged iron balls which were rounded off with the lead casting, something that could not be done easily by forging. This would therefore seem to be indirect proof that the casting of iron itself was not yet understood. A Nuremberg inventory of 1462 that is mentioned in Jähns, 1:427, does not show iron cannon balls.

29. Liebe, "The Social Rank of Artillery" ("Die soziale Wertung der Artillerie"), *Zeitschrift für historische Waffenkunde*, 2:146.

30. De la Noue, 26. *Discours, Observations militaires*, ed. of 1587, p. 755.

31. Sello, "The Campaign of Burgrave Frederick in February 1414" ("Der Feldzug Burggraf Friedrichs im Februar 1414"), *Zeitschrift für Preussische Geschichte*, 19 (1882): 101.

32. Sello, p. 101.

33. The last three examples are taken from the collected passages in R. Schneider, *Neue Jahrbücher für das klassische Altertum*, 1909, p. 139. The effectiveness of the giant Turkish cannon before Constantinople is

pictured on the other side, however, as very strong. See Essenwein, p. 34, and Jacobs, p. 128 ff.

34. Rudolf Schneider, *Anonymi de rebus bellicis liber*, 1908. Schneider, "Beginning and End of the Torsion Engines" ("Anfang und Ende der Torsionsgeschütze"), *Neue Jahrbücher für das klassische Altertum*, 1909. Schneider, *The Artillery of the Middle Ages* (*Die Artillerie des Mittelalters*), 1910. In these otherwise excellent writings I consider as erroneous what is said about the Carolingian period. The capitularies are not "laws," but simple prescriptions for individual cases, and there is no proof that leverage engines did not exist at the time of Charlemagne. Consequently, nothing prevents us from considering that the passages from Paulus Diaconus and from the *vita Hludowici* (*Life of Hludowicus*) cited by Schneider, p. 24 f., refer to such leverage engines. There is no basis (p. 61) for ascribing their invention to the Normans. Erroneous, too, is the rationale on p. 22 for the inability of the *scara* to manufacture and use projectile weapons.

35. Rathgen and Schäfer, "Feuer- und Fernwaffen beim päpstlichen Heer."

36. Jähns, p. 429. Burckhardt, *Geschichte der Renaissance in Italien*, Sect. 108, p. 224, says that Federigo of Urbino (1444–1482) introduced low forts instead of high ones, since the cannon was less effective against the lower ones. Von Stetten, *Geschichte von Augsburg*, 1:195 ff., reports that, whereas in that city in the second half of the fifteenth century the very energetic work on the city fortifications still consisted of raising the height of the walls, with the turn of the century a clearly recognizable turnabout took place. Walls and towers were lowered to a certain height, strong mounds of earth were erected, the moats were deepened and "lined," bastions and ravelins were installed, and so on. The law governing the radius became stricter and stricter; in 1542, despite the protests of the clergy, even a church was razed. For further information, see the considerations of Guicciardini in *Historia d'Italia*, Venice, 1562, pp. 388, 425. According to this source, the conquest of Otranto by the Turks in 1480 and the reconquest by Duke Alfonso of Calabria in the following year were landmarks in siege warfare. De la Noue, *18. discours, 2. Paradox.* Ed. 1587, p. 387. I shall go no further into the techniques either of fortification or of the attack; instead, I refer the reader to the corresponding sections in Jähns, *Geschichte der Kriegswissenschaften*. From a methodological viewpoint, it is interesting to see what kinds of exaggerations gain credence in something that is new and surprising. In his *History of the Artillery*, Napoleon III establishes the fact that Charles VIII in his campaign into Italy in 1494 transported 100 cannon of medium caliber and 40 heavy cannon. A whole series of authors, however, give him as many as 240 cannon and 2,040 field pieces, indeed as many as

6,000 light cannon. These exaggerations are due in part to copying errors and in part to the fact that the 6,000 "*vastardeurs*" (pioneers, workers) who accompanied the army were misunderstood as cannon.

37. According to *Sources for the History of Firearms* (*Quellen zur Geschichte der Feuerwaffen*), p. 100, the word "cannon" appears for the first time in a Spanish ordnance book of Charles V.

38. Guicciardini, *Historia d'Italia*, 1:24. Jovius for the year 1515. *Hist. Lib.* XV, 1:298.

39. von Ellgger, *Military System and Military Art of the Swiss Confederation* (*Kriegswesen und Kriegskunst der schweizerischen Eidgenossen*), Lucerne, 1873, p. 139.

40. Jovius *lib.* I for the year 1494 and *lib.* XV before Marignano.

41. *The Swiss at Frastenz* (*Die Schweizer bei Frastenz*): Stettler, 342, cited in Ranke, *Werke*, 34:115. Valerius Anshelm, *Bern Chronicle*, Bern, 1826, 2:396. Jovius, *Leben Gonsalvos*, Venice, 1581, p. 292, at Cerignola in 1503. Likewise at Suriano in 1497: Jovius, *Hist. lib.* IV. At Marignano: Jovius, *Lib.* XV. At Ravenna in 1512: Jovius, *Leben Leos*, X, *lib.* II; Guicciardini, *Historia d'Italia*, lib. XI; Reissner, *Leben Frundsbergs*, Frankfurt, 1620, fol. 41–42. At Novara the Swiss supposedly fired with conquered French cannon they had turned around: Fleuranges, *Mémoires*, p. 151.

The Venetian ambassador Quirini wrote the following description of the German battle square at the end of 1507:

> . . . as soon as they see the fire of the cannon, the infantrymen automatically have to lift the halberds and long lances all together over their heads and to cross one lance over the other, and likewise the halberds, and at the same time to drop to the ground so low that the cannon, which do not fire downward, pass over them or hit in the halberds and long lances, not doing much harm to the infantrymen of the formation. For this reason, the Germans customarily now make the wheels of the gun carriages so small and low that the enemies can be harmed, even if they drop down as indicated; and when the formation is about to assault, the halberdiers and likewise those with the long lances all lower their halberds and also their long lances, with the points forward and not above their shoulders. (*Relazioni degli Ambasc. Veneti* [*Reports of the Venetian Ambassadors*], Ed. Albèri, Series I, 6:21–22).

In 1537 de Langey taught that the best defense against the artillery was to take it by storm so that it would not have time for a second shot, or to approach it in a wide formation so that it would hit fewer men. *Trewer Rath*, fol. III, recommends having 300 "runners" (including a few good musketeers) close quickly on the cannon.

42. "Nullo prope usui fore" ("It would be nearly useless"), Jovius, *Hist. Lib.* I, Venice, 1553, 1:30.

43. Book II, Chap. 17. See also the account in Comines, 2:258. Ed. Mandrot.

44. *Essais*, Book I.

45. *Le vite de dicenove huomini illustri* (*The Lives of Nineteen Famous Men*), Venice, 1581, lib. III.

46. Avila, *Schmalkaldic War* (*Schmalkaldischer Krieg*), Venice, 1548, p. 40.

47. Sixl, 2:167.

48. The name "hook firearm" was derived from this hook and survived for a long time, taking the form "haquebutte" in French. This word may also have been influenced by its similarity to *"arkebuse"* (harquebus). Jähns, however, has surmised that the name "hook firearm" was derived from the hook into which the match was clamped, and this interpretation is actually supported by common sense. The invention of this "hook" represented a much more important step forward than the invention of the recoil hook. The latter, of course, could only be used in a prepared defensive position and in target shooting. The fork did not provide any resistance for the recoil; even a three-legged stand would have been too weak for that.

49. Sixl, *Zeitschrift für historische Waffenkunde*, 2:334, 407, 409, on the basis of firing reports from Zurich in 1472, Würzburg in 1474, Eichstädt in 1487, and others. In noteworthy contradiction to these is Guicciardini's comment that before Pavia in 1525 the entrenched lines of the two sides were only 40 paces apart and the bastions were so close that the harquebus marksmen could have fired on each other. The greater distances in competitive shooting are so extensively confirmed that we cannot doubt them, but even if the paces were taken to be of the smallest possible length, it is still difficult to understand why they wanted to shoot at targets at such distances with the firearms of that period.

50. Forrer, *Zeitschrift für historische Waffenkunde*, 4:55.

51. *Zeitschrift für historische Waffenkunde*, 1:316.

52. *Institution de la discipline militaire au Royaume de France*, Lyon, 1559, Vol. I, Chap. 10, p. 46. According to Jovius, Charles V suffered heavy losses in Algiers in 1541 because a rainfall extinguished the matches. A similar report appears in Vieilleville, *Mémoires*, Vol. III, Chap. 22.

53. According to the *Badminton Archery Book*, by Charles Longman. London, 1894.

54. Tielcke, *Contributions to the Art of War and History of the War of 1756 to 1763* (*Beyträge zur Kriegskunst und Geschichte des Krieges von 1756 bis 1763*), 2:22.

55. The astonishing accuracy of the present-day Mongolians with the bow and arrow is reported by von Binder in the *Militär-Wochenblatt*,

8(1905):173. For the accomplishments with the bow and arrow in the Middle Ages, see Giraldus Cambrensis, cited in Oman, *History of the Art of War*, p. 559. On the occasion of a siege, Welsh archers reportedly shot their arrows through an oak door 4 inches thick. Giraldus himself claimed to have seen in 1188 the arrows, which had been left in the door as a matter of curiosity. The iron points could just be seen on the interior of the door. An arrow was also reported to have penetrated a knight's coat of mail, his mail breeches, his thigh, through the wood of his saddle, and deep into the flank of his horse.

56. Comines, Ed. Mandrot, 2:296.

57. Escher, *Neujahrsblatt der Züricher Feuerwerker*, 1906, p. 23.

58. Ranke, *Werke*, 2:269.

59. *De vita magni Consalvi* (*On the Life of Gonsalvo the Great*), *Opere*, 1578, 2:243.

60. According to the very careful and enlightening study by R. Forrer, *Zeitschrift für historische Waffenkunde*, 4:57.

61. Jovius, *Elogia vir. ill.* (*Aphorisms of Distinguished Men*), Book III.

62. Martin du Bellay as an eyewitness. *Mémoires*, Ed. 1753, 5:296.

63. See also Martin du Bellay, *Mémoires*, Ed. 1753, Book X, 6:35.

64. "Pistol" ("*Pistole*") comes from the Slavic (Bohemian) "*pistala*" (tube, firing tube). In a Breslau inventory of 1483 are listed 235 "*Pisdeallen*." This number indicates that these were hand weapons, but we cannot tell what kind of weapon. *Sources for the History of Firearms* (*Quellen zur Geschichte der Feuerwaffen*), published by the Germanic Museum, Leipzig, 1877, pp. 46, 112. The name of the weapon has nothing to do with the word "*Pistoja*."

65. Susane, *Histoire de la cavallerie française*, 1:48.

66. According to the *Quellen zur Geschichte der Feuerwaffen*, p. 118, a pistol appears in an illustration dated as early as 1531; another pistol, with a wheel lock, "judging from its component parts and form," is dated "approximately" in the second decade of the sixteenth century.

67. *Quellen zur Geschichte der Feuerwaffen*, p. 123.

68. Paulus Jovius, *vitae illustrium virorum* (*Lives of Famous Men*), Tome I, in *opera* Tome II, pp. 403, 405.

Chapter III

Tactics of the Spear Units

The large infantry square armed with the close-combat weapon had been formed by the Swiss in order to withstand defensively attacking knights and, on the offensive, to run down knights and marksmen. The spread of this infantry among other peoples resulted in the new mission in the combat of such infantry units not only against mounted men and marksmen but also against one another. Indeed, this kind of combat now became not only a new type but also the principal kind. For the superiority of infantry in close formation over the old arms had become so obvious that it had to be regarded as the main arm, forming the mass and the power of the army, and the other arms faded in importance. The decision in battle depended on the victory or defeat of the infantry. Machiavelli recognized from his studies that also in antiquity the infantry with its close-combat weapon formed the nucleus of the army, and he therefore promoted and prophesied a renewal of the art of war based on the ancient pattern.

The formations of the new infantry, however, were quite different from those of the ancient units. The ancients had had the phalanx, a broad formation armed either with the spear or with the *pilum* and sword. The newer infantry had several deep squares, normally three, armed with long spears; it was more similar to the later Macedonian phalanx, armed with the *sarissa*, but the difference between the single broad formation and the three squares is basic. We shall return to this point later.

The new mission of the infantry in combat against infantry perhaps also brought on a certain change in the formation of the squares and their armament. In the preceding volume, in my description of the Swiss military system, I held fast to the traditional concept that the long spear, that is, the spear about 5 meters long, even if it was perhaps not yet used at Morgarten and Sempach, nevertheless was generally adopted in the course of the fifteenth century, because it was so well fitted to ward off knights. Now we find in two passages in Jovius, with a certain emphasis, the report that the Swiss, when they appeared in Italy in 1494 in the service of Charles VIII of France, had spears 10 feet long. Rüstow interpreted that as indicating that the Confederates, in their heightened self-confidence and because the long spear was so very uncomfortable to carry, had shortened it to 10 feet. Hobohm, on the other hand, expressed the opinion that the Swiss had never previously carried longer spears and that the true long spear, that is, the spear lengthened from 3 to 5 meters, only came into being as the result of the combat of infantry units against one another. Even with spears 3 meters long, the early Confederates were able in closed formation to ward off the knights satisfactorily, and later in individual combat this spear was immeasurably more useful than the very long one. If now this weapon was nevertheless lengthened, this change was first of all the technique of the lansquenets, to whom it gave the inestimable advantage in combat with the Swiss of being able to strike the first blow. Consequently, the Swiss were obliged to follow suit. The illustrated manuscripts give a certain indication that the manipulation of the spear was somewhat different among the Swiss and the lansquenets.

If this was the development—of course, I am not ready to accept it as completely certain—it would be similar to the history of the Macedonian *sarissa*, which of course did not attain the reported length of 21 feet from the very start but only in its last phase.

The question as to the length of the spear is not of such very great importance, because the advantage on the one side of being able to strike the first blow with the longer spear is offset by the much greater ease of manipulation of the shorter spear. The Spanish, who from the start placed more emphasis on the agility of the individual warrior as they developed their infantry, therefore retained a length of only about 14 feet for their spear, and the French and Italians followed their example.

Hobohm now sees the development of the long spear in the following way: First of all, the knights lengthened their lances in order to be able to reach the dismounted spearmen. The first opportunity to do this was provided in the fifteenth century by the plate armor, because it had the hook for couching the lance, which could not be held long without the hook.

Then experiments were held with the lengthening of the lansquenets' spears.

The experimental stage was not yet complete when the Swiss moved into Italy in 1494 with Charles VIII, that is, still armed with spears 10 feet long.

It was only from that time on that the real lengthening of the spears began.

If two such units with long spears clashed with one another, there resulted a powerful pressure. The sources speak again and again of "pressure" or of "pressure from the rear," with which the deep units sought to surge over the enemy and press him down. At Bicocca, where the Swiss were defeated, it was pointed out that the "pressure from the rear was not for the best" (since the men were held up by the ditch). At Ceresole the captain of the Swiss held his unit back so that the opposing lansquenet unit would spread apart in its approach and would strike the Swiss with a formation not tightly closed. And it occurred in that way. Monluc recounts that in the same battle the Gascons struck the lansquenets with such a mighty shock that the first rank on each side fell to the ground ("Tous ceux des premiers rangs, soit du choc ou des coups, furent portés par terre"). This should not be taken entirely literally, but when it goes on to say that the second and third ranks decided the victory, since they were pushed forward by the following ranks (". . . car les derniers rangs les poussaient en avant"), that is compatible with everything that is reported elsewhere.

One might think that, with such pressure from the rear and with the men tightly pressed against one another, the foremost ranks would necessarily have speared one another. This did occur to a certain extent, but since the leading ranks were well armored, the spears no doubt also splintered or were pushed up into the air, or they slid backward through the soldiers' hands despite the notches that they carved to enable them to hold fast. Finally, therefore, the fighters pressed against one another, hardly able to use their weapons.

We have no report of such a picture from antiquity, since of course the late Macedonian phalanx never had occasion to fight with a similar opponent.[1]

Even in the lansquenet period, however, the normal situation portrayed above underwent some changes. To the first rank were assigned a few strong and trusted warriors with particularly good armor who wielded two-handed swords or halberds. It is reported of Frundsberg himself "that in the battle of La Motta (1513) he stood in the first rank, swung his sword and fought like a woodsman who was felling an oak in the forest." Marksmen, too, were placed in the first or second rank, for example at Ceresole. In the battle of Ravenna the Spanish had selected foot soldiers, experienced fighters, crawl along the ground under the long spears and strike the lansquenets with their short Spanish swords.

Nevertheless, all these expedients can only have had a secondary significance. For as soon as one attempted to mix with the spearmen either swordsmen or men armed with the halberd, or marksmen, or men with short arms in rather large numbers, one would have broken up one's own formation more than that of the enemy, for the formation was based on the gigantic weight of the tightly pressed spearmen.

We have a document, *True Advice and Reflections of an Old Well-tested and Experienced Warrior (Trewer Rath und Bedencken eines Alten wol versuchten und Erfahrenen Kriegsmans)*, which was probably written toward the end of 1522 and perhaps was the work of no less a person than Georg Frundsberg. This document rejects the opinion that "the formation should be tight" and should give the decision as a result of pressure from the rear, "for the foremost men, who are supposed to do the work, do not wish to be too closely pressed; they must be left room for freely jabbing," otherwise they would be pushed in "as one pushes people into a ditch."

Trewer Rath therefore recommends another method. The old Swiss unit, in the form taken over by the lansquenets, was a square of men—the same number of ranks as of files—which means that it was considerably deeper than wide, at least in the approach march, since more interval was required between men in file than those in line. *Trewer Rath* requires that the front be three times as wide as the depth, for, it says, to the extent that a formation is wider than that of the enemy, to the same extent one can break into the flanks "and grip the narrow formation between one's arms. That means certain death and the winning of the battle," even if the enemy is stronger, "for if he is attacked in the flanks, he is lost." It is supposedly the first five or six ranks that win or lose the battle, and the more men "who can go to work" as a result of the broad formation, the easier it is.

In support of its envelopment concept, *Trewer Rath* attaches to the main body several small units, which are to skirmish and strike the enemy's flank.

Nothing seems to be more plausible than this observation. Nevertheless, not only is the main body of the *Trewer Rath* still extremely deep and powerful (with 6,000 men, some 45 men deep and 135 wide), but also up to the end of the century and beyond, the principle of the square formation actually remained dominant. One theoretician after another recommended a shallower formation, but in practice the deep formation was maintained, except when the space square was used instead of the square with equal numbers of men, and that, of course, would have meant more width and less depth.[2] We shall have further occasion to speak of this when we reach the point at which the change starts. Let us only suggest here the reason for continuing retention of the old formations: broad formations are much more difficult to move and to lead than narrow ones. Let us determine here and now that the actual development of a broad front did not result from the idea of gaining an advantage from the broader formation, as we might express it in military history terms, shifting from the square or wedge formation to the phalanx.[3]

The change that the heavy infantry developed of itself is only that one gradually gave up the triple units of the Swiss. When the Schmalkaldic army stood facing Charles V on the Danube, it was regarded as a double army, and Charles drew up two groups of three squares each, with the mounted men side by side between them. The Spanish had in fact already freed themselves from the traditional scheme in the battle of Ravenna (1512), and in the second half of the century they went over to a larger number of units, according to the circumstances, with each unit retaining the square shape. This freer formation is also found in the Huguenot wars. But this temporary increase in the number of squares did not yet mean a basic theoretical change in infantry tactics.

NOTES FOR CHAPTER III

1. We might be reminded of the battle of Sellasia, but the sources for that battle are much too uncertain. See Vol. I, p. 241.

2. The Spanish theoreticians of the school of Alba—Valdes, Eguiluz, and Lechuga—favored a shallower formation for the infantry (Jähns, 1:729 ff.). At any rate, they preferred the square by space to the square of men, but they also favored an even shallower formation, going as far as a ratio of 1:7. Valdes gives as an example that Alba once formed his 1,200 spearmen, three *terzios*, 60 men wide and 20 men deep.

Mendoza gives no positive prescription but simply mentions that they had both wider formations and deeper formations. In the *Institution de la discipline militaire au Royaume de France*, Lyon, 1559, p. 73, the space square, which has twice as many files as ranks, is prescribed.

3. The Italian Giovacchino da Coniano, who was a sergeant major in the English service against France in the 1540s, sketched and described a series of thirty-two battle formations. There were supposed to have been even more. (Comment by the editor at the end of the document: "It was entitled *Dell' Ordinanze overo battaglie del capitan Giovacchino da Conjano*, printed in Book III of the work *Della Fortificatione delle città di Girolamo Maggi e Jacomo Castriotto*. Venice, 1583, 115 ff.) The whole work was already assembled in 1564. (See Maurice I. D. Cockle, *A Bibliography of English Military Books Up to 1642 and of Contemporary Foreign Works*. London, 1900, pp. 141, 200.) Although the somewhat boastful soldier refers again and again to practical testing of his formations in the face of the enemy, we can probably not lend him too much credence. The accomplishments on the English side before Boulogne at that time did not evoke much respect elsewhere in the world. Nevertheless, it is interesting that the sergeant major was already sketching very shallow formations, with the justification that he had experienced how much better it was to have more weapons in the front line in action simultaneously (Fol. 119–720).

Chapter IV

Internal Organization of the Mercenary Armies[1]

In the Middle Ages the military leader was always at the same time the organizer of his troops. That held true for the feudal levies as well as for the mercenary bands, and it now continued in the mercenary armies of the sixteenth century up to those of the Thirty Years' War. In larger situations the national leader gave to a few colonels, and in smaller ones to one or a few captains, a lump sum of money and the mission of recruiting and maintaining the lansquenets or mounted men. Often, however, these colonels and captains were also entrepreneurs in the sense that they advanced the necessary money or a part of it at the start or in the course of the procedure. In very large situations, a general entrepreneur, like Wallenstein, also undertook the assembling of the army of which he was at the same time the commanding general.

The colonel appointed his captains, and they in turn named their lieutenant (*locotenente*), their ensign, their first sergeant,[2] their quartermaster sergeant, and their file leaders (corporals), the last of which were probably also elected by the men themselves.

A varying number of detachments, some ten to eighteen, together formed a regiment, an expression that originally meant that a colonel had established his regimen, that is, his authority, over the individual units. Each such unit numbered around 400 men and even more. Consequently, the strength of the regiments differed greatly. The subordinate unit, like the regiment, was only an administrative organization and not a tactical one. The tactical body, as we have seen, was the group, the square, which was also called a battalion.

We do not know much about the internal structure of the mercenary bands of the Middle Ages. They appear to have been based entirely on the arbitrary disciplinary power of the commander and the strength of his personality. Then the practice was started of establishing written field regulations, the oldest surviving example of which is the camp regulation of Barbarossa (Vol. III, p. 246). In order to assure obedience to such regulations, the Confederation started the practice of obligating the troops by means of the oath of obedience. This example was followed in Germany around the turn of the fifteenth century, just as the lansquenets had appeared. It called for the wild fellows to swear on entering the service to a field regulation, a "letter of articles," that became more and more detailed, in order to keep them under control. The author of the *Trewer Rath* (Frundsberg) recommended administering the oath one after the other in small units, for "if they are all assembled unsworn in one unit, you will not succeed in having them swear to this letter of articles, for they will establish a regimen for you as they wish it, according to their pleasure, and then you will have to abide by it and thereafter you will never be sure of your life, for when one cannot obligate soldiers by force, one must remind them of the law that they have sworn to maintain." The content and form of this combination of the oath of loyalty and the field regulations naturally vary considerably among the different commanders, in the different regions, and in the course of different times. The basic idea is a two-sided contract between the mercenaries on the one side and the commander or condottiere on the other. The men swear to their obligations in return for the promises of the mercenary leader. Gradually, with the shift from mercenary bands recruited for a limited time into a standing army, the mutuality of the contract disappeared and the democratic element was eliminated and replaced by the one-sided disciplinary power of the commander. The letters of articles, which led to the articles of war that are still in use today, are documents of great importance from the viewpoints of both cultural and military history.

From the plethora of details, completed and clarified from other sources, I point out a few particularly characteristic traits.

A basic provision is that the soldiers obligate themselves not to form any "community," that is, expressed in modern terms, they do not have the right to establish a labor union. They may, however, bring their complaints on any kind of grievance to the attention of their senior captain through their double-pay mercenary, whom they have the right to choose.

In order to give emphasis to their commands, the leaders under certain circumstances undoubtedly used great force.[3] In addition, a legal procedure was integrated into the disciplinary power. From the Middle Ages came the practice of having the field marshal originally stand at the head of the court, because the warriors were horsemen and the marshal had the horses and everything pertaining to them under his control. He was replaced by the *Schultheiss* (royal inspector) and the *Profoss* (provost), both of whom were experienced old soldiers. For a long time, however, the field marshal retained the supervision of the division of booty.[4]

The procedure in the military court followed the organization and procedure of German jury courts. The hearings were public.

The jury members or the officers sitting with them had to be comrades or superiors of the accused.

In addition to this true military court, there was the "law before the common man," with its variation of the "law of the long spears." It could function only by order of the colonel, but it was a democratic people's court and amounted in practice to a raw form of lynch justice. It disappeared with the establishment of stricter order in the armies.

The rights of the mounted men were for a long time quite different from those of the foot soldiers, because the mounted man was a successor to the feudal knights. Consequently, there existed for a long time the custom for the mounted troops of recruiting not the individual man but a nobleman with a larger or smaller following of serving men, a practice that naturally affected the everyday life of the mounted troops. The artillery, too, had its special privileges.

As a result of the esprit de corps that dominated this military system, in the seventeenth century the soldiers were completely removed from the civilian juridical system and even for civilian transgressions were tried only by their own legal system.

The administration was relatively simple, in that the man was generally responsible for taking care of his equipment, his weapons, his clothing, and his horse. The rations, too, were left principally to the purveyors, and they were controlled by fees established by the provost.

Philip of Hesse himself sold the necessities to his mercenaries and thus hoped to get back half of the soldiers' pay, that is, as it is called in modern industry, an exchange system.[5] If Philip himself had nothing to sell, he exacted a toll from the purveyors in order to be indemnified. For larger units this system of rations was, of course, insufficient, and the soldiers took whatever they needed from the land. This practice not only oppressed the countryside in the most fearful manner, but it also led to the greatest inconveniences from the military viewpoint. In friendly and neutral country, Philip and Johann Friedrich of Saxony required that their soldiers might take only fodder and oats for the horses, bread, vegetables, bacon, dried meat, and other foodstuffs. But they were to spare cattle and household equipment and were not to break into cupboards, crates, and chests. De la Noue reports that Coligny was careful to have clever commissars and to maintain a sufficient pool of vehicles.[6] Whenever it was a question of raising an army, he used to say "Let us start to build this monster with the stomach." There was a baker for each squadron, and as soon as the unit arrived in billets, he immediately started baking. Through the threat of burning everything to the ground, the villages within a certain radius of the billets were forced to provide foodstuffs.

The monthly pay was established in the articles of war (4 guilders for the foot soldier in the sixteenth century). But there was often controversy as to how the month should be reckoned. The soldiers demanded that the month should end and a new one start after each battle or the storming of a city. King Francis I once had to obligate himself to retain the soldiers in his service for ten months and to pay them for an extra month the day before a battle. Philip of Hesse finally recommended to his sons in his will that they wage only defensive wars, since the demands of the mercenaries could no longer be satisfied.[7]

In the obligation for obedience it was expressly added that the commands were to be carried out by the soldiers "whether they be nobles or commoners, small fellows or important ones."[8] Not only the individual soldier but also each detachment and each file had to obey its captain or his substitute.

When 6,000 mercenaries were dispatched in 1480 in the service of the king of France, the Swiss diet decreed that there should be peace in the army "and whoever disturbs the peace or breaks it by his speech, whether it be by swearing or disputing, the captains are authorized in accordance with their oath to punish them through dishonor, or by corporal punishment, or by taking their life. And whoever breaks the peace while on duty shall have his head cut off, but if somebody kills another in peacetime, he shall be brought before a council as a murderer."

In 1499 the diet of the Confederation issued an order that every soldier was to obey *all* captains.[9]

If a city was conquered, the soldiers were expressly obligated under the articles of war to obey the orders of their colonel, even if they had not yet been paid. Garrison troops were obligated to carry out entrenching and construction tasks. When the Bohemian troops were supposed to prepare entrenchments in 1619, they refused, saying it was against their honor, since they had received no pay.

In altercations it was expressly forbidden to shout "the nation." It happened only too often that when their compatriots came to the aid of two men who were fighting, the soldiers then fought veritable battles among themselves. There were only too many occasions for controversies—rations, booty, women, and especially gambling, where the loser was ready to charge cheating.

The "tussle" (*Balgen*), that is, the duel, was not punished as such on an absolute basis but was only limited in one way or another. For example, no deadly weapons were to be used, or it was to take place only at a specified place or only in the morning.

Various provisions applied to booty, but the basis was: "What an individual wins remains his own in keeping with the nature of war and good order." Captured cannon and powder belonged to the field captain.

As we have seen, the warrior of the Middle Ages was a quality fighter. Not only the knight but also the common mercenary soldier always had to be a man of pronounced physical courage and ability in order to be useful in war. These qualities were also required of the lansquenets, but their principal effectiveness was based on their mass and their steadfastness. This cohesiveness also carried along the individual who was initially less capable, trained him, and through the spirit of the group made of him a useful soldier. With the awkward tactical formation of the square unit in which they fought, difficult drills and a rather long period of training were not necessary in order to make a strong man into a soldier. A few ways of manipulating one's weapons and simple indoctrination in the formation in rank and column were sufficient. Consequently, once the framework was created, it was not difficult to assemble large masses of these mercenaries. The masses determined the outcome; whichever side led the largest units into the attack was necessarily victorious. The Middle Ages had been too weak economically to be able to send such units into the field, and without the tactical body they would also not have been correspondingly more effective. Consequently, the political-economic prerequisite for this new aspect of warfare was the formation of large nations—the French national state, the unification of Castile and Aragon, the unifying of the Hapsburg and Burgundian possessions resulting from Maximilian's marriage to the daughter and heiress of Charles the Bold. As strong and capable as these new national entities were, nevertheless, by seeking in their struggles to outdo one another, they went not only to the limits of their capabilities but beyond, for we have seen that it was not difficult to increase the number of soldiers, and only a large number of soldiers gave the prospect of victory. The natural limit for the size of an army should have been the financial capability of the ruler. But what if the enemy exceeded this limit, estimating that such an increase would bring him victory and that victory would also fill his needs for mercenary payments? From the start this hope drove both sides beyond their capabilities. The size of the armies grew far beyond those of the Middle Ages, not only to the extent that there were now national leaders who could pay for that, but they also became much larger than the rulers were able to pay for. With an initial bonus and further promises of pay, there were enough soldiers available. It was known from the start that these promises would hardly be kept. Even in the articles of war there appeared the clause that if the pay was not promptly dispensed, the soldiers were not to become immediately impatient and refuse to serve. In fact, pay was very often unavailable, even for long periods. We shall have more to say about the strategic effects of this shortcoming. Now, however, it is a question of the effect on the interior nature of the lansquenet system. Despite the oath of obedience, the courts-martial, the royal inspector (*Schultheiss*), and the provost, it was impossible to bring these mercenaries to a true state of discipline. How were they supposed to feel themselves bound by their oath when the ruler, for his part, did not keep the promises he had made to them? Practically inseparable from the system of the lansquenets was the idea of mutiny. As early as 1490, when they had captured Stuhlweissenburg, they refused to continue Maximilian's campaign because they were not paid. This kind of occurrence was repeated again and again.

In 1516 before Milan, lansquenets mutinied because they received less pay than the Swiss. Maximilian addressed them as "his dear, honorable, German lansquenets," but "no matter how much His Imperial Majesty spoke to the soldiers in this manner and even more flatteringly, they were still not pleased," says the chronicler.

The lansquenet demanded that his missing pay be replaced with booty, and how could the ruler oppose him in that respect, since he was unable to give him his pay? The result was cruel mistreatment of the population and the countryside through which a campaign was conducted. Nothing is further from the truth than the idea that such excesses were shown only by a later, degenerate soldiery.[10] It is also untrue that only riff-raff and criminals followed the call of the recruiter's drum. Certainly many unprincipled men did join up, but the great mass consisted of the sons of burghers and peasants, often from good families. Patricians and knights also served with them as mercenaries with double pay. Force, however, where it is not restrained by another force—that is, in this case, discipline—only too quickly believes itself justified in wild excesses. Even among the knights, who to some extent were held in bounds by their education and class customs, we hear only too often of robbery and cruelty. The soldiers were individually even worse and more frightful because of their numbers. In a city taken by storm everything was permitted, and all the women were sacrificed to them. The most extreme case occurred when the captured burghers and peasants were systematically tortured, either to force them to produce supposedly hidden treasures or to oblige relatives to pay a ransom. Even when the field commander had agreed with the city on a capitulation and had solemnly promised to spare life and property, often enough the soldiers were unwilling to let the booty escape them, and they plundered and created havoc just as in a place taken by storm. The leaders did not have the power to prevent that, and from the start they gave up any idea of opposing the savage band.

It is true that the soldiers, through their oath to the articles of war, had obligated themselves particularly to give no resistance to the provost when he led soldiers off. The colonels and captains had a number of special mercenaries (*Trabanten*) as personal bodyguards, but we read accounts that even field commanders like Gonzalo of Cordova or Pescara did not dare to take a strong position in the face of the raging mob. Instead, they had a miscreant seized and hanged during the night or otherwise took later revenge on the leaders of an insubordination.

The colonels and captains were all the less capable of exercising a moral authority in that the lansquenets knew only too well to what extent their officers were inclined not only to take booty themselves but also to deceive the ruler by not having the agreed number of soldiers under their banner and pocketing the extra pay themselves. Similar things no doubt had already occurred in the *Völkerwanderung* and among the Arabs (Vol. II, p. 285; Vol. III, p. 206). In the Middle Ages, where we hear so little about numbers and it was the quality of the warriors that was decisive, this abuse cannot have played such an important role. In the mercenary armies of the sixteenth and seventeenth centuries, however, it was a normal and incredibly extensive occurrence. Lazarus Schwendi calls deception over the muster the "ruin of the Germans." In the musters, train servants and even women were equipped as lansquenets and placed in the ranks to fill up the numbers. At times it was prescribed that the impostors were to have their noses cut off in order to punish them and at the same time make it impossible for them to participate in such deception in the future.

All the evils of the lack of discipline were multiplied as a result of the train that was attached to each unit of lansquenets. The lansquenet, demanding as he was, wanted to have his woman near him or at least a youth to serve him. With the existing lack of field hospitals, such support was also indispensable in cases of sickness and wounds. In these closely grouped masses, with their dissolute lives, varying between excesses and privations, often with insufficient shelter in camp, without any concern and care for health, sicknesses played a large role. The armies were helpless whenever an epidemic broke out. In the winter of 1618–1619, the Bohemian army in front of Budweis lost through sickness two-thirds of its effective strength, more than 8,000 men. Among the Spaniards, fraternal groups were formed for mutual help.[11] But the main support was provided by the women, both wives and prostitutes.

When the duke of Alba moved from Italy to Flanders in 1567, his army was followed by 400 courtesans on horseback, "as pretty and worthy as princesses," said Brantôme. Others described them as shrews, meaner than the men. In any case, this train formed a great obstacle for the movement and feeding of every army and an increase of suffering for the countryside that was traversed. A handwritten war diary describes the soldier women as follows:[12]

> It is to be noticed that the Romans allowed no women in their campaigns, neither for persons of high or low rank, a practice much to be desired in our times in our nation and among the Walloons. Because this is so greatly abused and misused, however, not only the common soldiers but also many of the higher officers and the commander himself are guilty.... How very helpful the German women in Hungary were to the soldiers in carrying necessities and

in their care in sickness. Seldom is one found who does not carry
at least 50 or 60 pounds. Since the soldier carries provisions or other
materials, he loads straw and wood on her, to say nothing of the
fact that many of them carry one, two, or more children on their
back. Normally, however, aside from the clothing they are wearing,
they carry for the man one pair of breeches, one pair of stockings,
one pair of shoes. And for themselves the same number of shoes
and stockings, one jacket, two *Hemmeter*, one pan, one pot, one
or two spoons, one sheet, one overcoat, one tent, and three poles.
They receive no wood for cooking in their billets, and so they pick
it up on the way. And to add to their fatigue, they normally lead
a small dog on a rope or even carry him in bad weather.

Count Johann of Nassau proposed replacing the women with food
purveyors, doctors, and nurses. The unmarried common soldiers were
to form fraternal groups among themselves like the Spaniards, and they
were to help each other in cases of sickness and other emergencies.

In the contract of the horsemen with the Huguenots in 1568 it was
specified that they were to have one wagon for every four or six horses.
The lansquenets had one wagon for every ten men.[13]

Discipline is a matter not only of the power to punish and of punishments but also of training and habit. If the irregularity of distribution of
pay formed an obstacle to the development of discipline, an almost greater
obstacle was the fact that the lansquenet was always taken into service
only for a limited time, for specified months, or the duration of a campaign. Wallhausen reports how the soldiers, after their discharge, "as
soon as the banners were ripped from their staff and the regiments were
dismissed," took revenge on strict superiors and thereby intimidated
them:[14]

Then the lowliest, most dissolute, most irresponsible scoundrel can
challenge his captain, his lieutenant, his ensign, his first sergeant,
his corporal, his wagon master, his quartermaster, the provost with
his assistants—who may not let themselves be seen—and say to
them: "Ha, rascal, you were my commander, but now you are not.
Now you are not one hair better than I am. Now a pound of hair
(and that taken right out of one spot where it doesn't smell good)
is worth as much as a pound of cotton. Come on out, fight with
me. Are you better than a knave or a thief? Do you remember how
now and then you slapped me on guard duty and how you now
and then tormented me?"

The German soldiers served first this prince, then that one—first the emperor, then the king of France, now the pope, then the Republic of Venice or the Netherlands or in England, and later the king of Denmark and especially the king of Sweden. On the other hand, we find quite often Poles in the service of German princes and, of course, Hungarians and Croats in the service of the emperor.[15] The mercenary went wherever there was pay, without asking for what cause he was fighting. Of course, the question of religion did have an influence at times. Frundsberg's lansquenets were Lutherans, but the important thing with them was less this positive aspect than the negative one, that is, their hate for the priests. In the Huguenot wars, the Catholic Swiss helped Charles IX, and German Protestants sent aid to their fellow believers. In the Thirty Years' War one would be inclined to believe that the armies facing each other were divided along strictly religious lines. In principle, this was the case, and the German Catholics were supported by Spaniards and Italians, while the Protestants received aid from Hungarians, English, and Scots. But this difference was not felt deeply enough in the masses to prevent defection from one side to the other. The prisoners, in particular, were quickly ready to enter the service of the winner. When Groningen capitulated in 1594, Count Eberhard Solms reported to his cousin, Johann of Nassau,[16] Maurice guaranteed a free withdrawal and "graciously honored and permitted the retention of the nine colors" of the garrison. When they came out, many ran away from their captains and enlisted in the service of the victor. If the colors had been torn down in the city, it is reported, a good half of the soldiers would have gone over. When the Netherlanders conquered the fortress of Saint Andreas in 1600, almost the entire garrison, 1,100 men, entered the service of the States.[17] After the battle of Breitenfeld, Gustavus Adolphus wrote home that he had taken so many prisoners as to make up for his losses. In the battle of Leipzig in 1642, toward the end of the battle, imperial infantry was surrounded in the open field and partly cut down,

> but a part of the unit asked for quarter, offering to serve the victor, and thus they saved their lives. In complete squares or companies, some with their banners, they marched along in such good order against the electoral city and then to the Swedish train as if they had sworn allegiance to the queen and crown of Sweden. Then Colonel Daniel, who was taken prisoner with them, with a large number adhering to him, went over to the field marshal (Torstensson). With the permission of the latter, he formed almost a whole new regiment of his own, because his former unit was very depleted. And this regiment continued for a long time thereafter and did good service in the Swedish army.[18]

In 1647 the emperor and Wrangel stood facing one another in fortified camps near Eger. The imperial troops were in needy circumstances. "Many old soldiers fled to the Swedes, so that the infantry had to be guarded by the mounted troops."[19]

When the Swiss earlier opposed the knightly system of battle with their own, the cruelty of warfare increased to an extreme degree. The knights had often gone into battle more for the purpose of capturing their enemies than of killing them, but the Swiss not only granted no mercy in battle but even struck down all the men in conquered cities. The Swiss and the lansquenets, too, were for a long time such mortal enemies that they showed no mercy. Gradually, however, a certain moderation began to take hold. A distinction between "good" and "bad" wars was recognized, and agreements were signed providing for the exchange of prisoners; for example, one month's pay was established as a ransom. Limitations were also placed on murdering, robbing, and burning in the countryside. In time, this mutual granting of mercy even became dangerous from the military viewpoint. On one occasion, Wallenstein considered it necessary to forbid taking men into captivity unless a real fight had previously taken place.[20]

But we also find quite often that the storming of a place resulted in the killing of the entire enemy garrison, and at the next opportunity the other side took revenge in the same way.

A particular phenomenon of this system of warfare was the lansquenet after his discharge. He was rarely inclined to return to a civilian trade, or in a position to do so. He waited until he was called again, or he went in search of another commander. In the meantime, he supported himself by begging, stealing, and robbing. According to an expression that has not been clarified with certainty and perhaps meant simply "to wait," this was called "auf die Gart gehn" ("to go on the wait"?). The expressions "gardende Knechte" ("waiting serving men"?) or "Gardebrüder" ("waiting brothers"?) were also used. These men were, of course, a plague for the countryside. As early as the twelfth century, Barbarossa and Louis VII of France had signed a treaty providing for their suppression (Vol. III, p. 317). In the fifteenth century they left a particularly bad memory behind them under the names of "Armagnacs" and "extortioners" ("*Schinder*") (Vol. III, p. 507).

In January 1546 the following states and cities assembled to establish agreed measures against these "*gardende*" lansquenets: Denmark, Cologne, Electorate of Saxony, Münster, Lüneburg, Hesse, Mansfeld, Teklenburg, Augsburg, Hamburg, Goslar, Magdeburg, Braunschweig, Hildesheim, Hanover. Wallhausen explains very well that it would have been much less expensive for the population to have kept the soldiers continuously under the colors and consequently in good order than to allow them to scrape up their means of livelihood for themselves.[21] But that would have required an orderly system of taxation, and, as we shall see, tax systems are not easily created. And thus it came to a grotesque intermediate position between the "waiting" of the lansquenets and a systematic collection of taxes. On 5 May 1620 Elector Georg Wilhelm of Brandenburg issued an edict that I want to reproduce verbatim here as a cultural document of the highest significance and descriptiveness. It reads:

Let it hereafter be known that we...are having sundry foot soldiers recruited and accepted, but that in doing so we can easily consider that these men, particularly up to the time specified for their muster, move about and would be a burden for the poor inhabitant of the countryside to the extent that the latter is not given a certain protection and order. And we hereby earnestly command these same men, our soldiers, not to roam about in groups of more than ten and not without the knowledge of their captains and commanders. They are also to be satisfied whenever in a troop of ten they are given in each village three imperial guilders or 36 pennies in return for presentation of their papers. But if they roam about individually and each peasant or farmer gives them two pennies and the cottager or gardener gives them one penny, they are to be satisfied with that and are not to injure anybody, nor are they to remove chickens or other possessions, or if one or several are treated irregularly, that is, so that he or they are driven off with blows, or otherwise have to suffer in various ways, they will have nobody to blame but themselves.

We also do not wish that they customarily go too often or in too great numbers to a place, consequently draining off completely the poor possessions of that locality. Instead, as soon as they arrive in a village, they are, as it is reported, to show their papers, and because there is seldom or never a village where there is not someone who can write, in each place the names of those who are received at that time as well as the day on which they are received are to be recorded and retained.

We also leave it up to the inhabitant of the countryside whether he himself wishes to give each wandering soldier the aforementioned two pennies or one penny or whether the inhabitants together wish to gather a few guilders and leave it up to their squire to distribute them to the arriving soldiers. In that case, the arriving soldiers will be directed each time to the squire. In those places where there is no squire in residence, this could be done in the same way by the village mayors.

Consequently, the edict assumes that the wandering soldier might sometimes receive a beating instead of the modest gift. Actually, it may be that whenever one or more wild rascals with their sword at their side or their halberd over their shoulder came into the farmyard, perhaps while the man was in the field, the peasant's wife was glad enough to see them march on, satisfied with a few groschen or a chicken. But let us not joke about the ineptitude and thoughtlessness of our ancestors; the "unemployed person" who is sent tramping to look for work and in the meantime to live from begging is also not unknown in our time.

EXCURSUS

In the *Zeitschrift für deutsche Wortforschung*, 1912, Helbling has assembled in a very interesting way those foreign military words that had already penetrated into the German language by the start of the Thirty Years' War.

Tross (train), French, in the Middle Ages. *Proviant* (*Profandt*, provisions) and *Bastei* (bastion) as early as the fifteenth century. *Leutnant, Quartier, Furier, Munition, Marschie-, Profoss* (*propositus*, provost), *Säbel* (saber), Slavic, since the beginning of the sixteenth century. *Soldat*, Italian, since about 1550 and in more common use since 1600. *General* (initially in the combination *General-Hauptmann* [captain general] and similar expressions), *Commiss* (for the feeding of the soldier), *Marketender* (purveyor), Italian, middle of the sixteenth century. *Offizier* (initially a court official; also used for military ranks at the end of the sixteenth century). *Disziplin*, end of the sixteenth century. *Infanterie, Front*, first used in Wallhausen's writings. *Armee, Kompagnie, Kavallerie, Kanone, Garnison, Bagage* (*Paggagie*), *Exerzieren* around 1600 or early in the seventeenth century.

NOTES FOR CHAPTER IV

1. The standard document for this subject is the careful and worthwhile study by Wilhelm Erben, "Origin and Development of the German Articles of War" ("Ursprung und Entwicklung der deutschen Kriegsartikel"), in the *Festgabe für Theodor Sickel, Mitteilungen des Instituts für östreichische Geschichtsforschung*, supplementary Vol. VI, 1900, with a few later additions by the same author. Closely linked with this work is the equally excellent book by Burkhard von Bonin, *Bases of the Legal System in the German Army at the Beginning of the Modern Era (to 1600) (Grundzüge der Rechtsverfassung in dem deutschen Heere zu Beginn der Neuzeit [bis 1600]).* Weimar, 1904. Also very important and providing good orientation by its comprehensiveness is the work by Wilhelm Beck, *The Oldest Letters of Articles for the German Infantry (Die ältesten Artikelbriefe für das deutsche Fussvolk)*, 1908. See Erben's review in the *Historische Zeitschrift*, 102:368.

2. *"Weibel"* (*Feldwebel*: first sergeant) is related to the word *"weben"* ("to weave") and means the servant who moves quickly here and there, running back and forth. The *Feldwebel* was initially assigned by the colonel as responsible for lining up the whole regiment and only later gradually became a functionary for the company. The *"Gemeinweibel,"* who are supposed by some scholars to have been elected by the troops in order to present their possible complaints to the captain, seem to me somewhat questionable. On this point, see Bonin, p. 50, and Erben, p. 14.

3. Bonin, p. 170, cites a few passages that indicate that the first sergeant was not to strike with his fist or with staffs, but with the shaft of his halberd. The captain and the lieutenant were supposed "to strike in their command duties with short sticks," but "not without great reason therefor."

4. Bonin, p. 21.

5. Georg Paetel, *The Organization of the Hessian Army under Philip the Magnanimous* (*Die Organisation des hessischen Heeres unter Philipp dem Grossmütigen*), 1897.

6. *26. Discours. Observations militaires*, Ed. 1587, p. 750.

7. Paetel, p. 231.

8. *Saxon Articles of War of 1546* (*Sächsische Kriegsartikel von 1546*). Published in the *Militär-Wochenblatt*, No. 157, 1909, by G. Berbig.

9. *Eidgenössische Abschiede*, 3.1.599.

10. When the wars of religion started in 1562, the soldiers on both sides initially conducted themselves very properly. Among the Huguenots no swearing was heard, and no gambling or prostitutes were to be seen. The population was not bothered. But Coligny said at that time to de la Noue: "That will not last two months." He was completely right. Furthermore, on occasion he took stringent steps and had robbers hanged. De la Noue, *Discours 26, Observations militaires*, Ed. 1587, pp. 681–686.

11. De la Noue treats these fraternal groups thoroughly. *Discours 16*, Ed. 1587, p. 352 ff.

12. Jähns, 2:924.

13. S. C. Gigon, *La troisième guerre de religion*. Jarnac-Moncontour (1568–1569), p. 376.

14. *The Art of Dismounted War* (*Kriegskunst zu Fuss*), pp. 20–21.

15. For example, Georg von Lüneburg had no fewer than 1,200 Poles in his service in 1636.

16. *Archives Oranien-Nassau*, 2d Series, 2:275.

17. *Archives*, p. 10.

18. Chemnitz, *Swedish War* (*Schwedischer Krieg*), Part IV, Book 2, p. 141.

19. Pufendorf, B. 19, Ed. 1688, 2:320. Apparently from Chemnitz.

20. Such a convention "de bonne guerre" ("of good war") was signed by Gonzago and Brissac in 1553. Hardy, *Histoire de la tactique française*, p. 463. Men-at-arms and private soldiers "will suddenly be released," without having to pay, after they have been *"dévalisés"*—that is, disarmed and relieved of their possessions.

21. *Kriegskunst zu Fuss*, pp. 16, 22. Jähns, 2:1018.

Chapter V

Individual Battles

BATTLE OF CERIGNOLA
28 APRIL 1503

This encounter between Spaniards and French in Lower Italy may well be considered the first full-fledged example of the new art of war since the creation of a European infantry. I shall not attempt a detailed analysis at this point but simply note that Fabricio Colonna, who participated, told Jovius that it was not the courage of the troops and not the *"valore"* of the commander (Gonzalo) that brought victory, but the small earthen wall and trench that the Spanish occupied with marksmen in advance of their front. The infantry then moved out into the offensive from this position.

Frontal obstacles; effectiveness of the marksmen; attack or lack of attack against the obstacles or originating from the obstacles—from now on these are the dominant factors in the battle accounts. Gonzalo of Cordova was the creator of the basic form. The commanders who used it later came from his school.[1]

BATTLE OF RAVENNA[2]
11 APRIL 1512

On the one side stood Pope Julius II, who was allied with Venice and the Spanish, and on the other side was Louis XII of France, who held Milan. The Spanish under the viceroy Cardona moved up from Naples, while from the north the Swiss, who had made themselves available to the pope, moved out of their mountains (autumn, 1511). But since it was not so easy to arrive at a cooperative procedure, especially in the bad winter weather, perhaps also because of the role played by French money, the Swiss turned back again. Now the French had the numerical superiority. They relieved Bologna, which was being besieged by the allies, recaptured Brescia, which had been taken by the Venetians, and when further reinforcements now arrived for the French infantry, Gaston de Foix, the overall commander, decided, in response to an order from his king, to drive forward in a large-scale offensive perhaps as far as Rome itself.

On the other hand, the Spanish commander sought to delay the decisive action, since the emperor, the king of England, and the Swiss all seemed to be on the verge of intervening in behalf of Spain. When the French army, complete with a column of provisions (Guicciardini), approached at the end of March, Cardona took position on the eastern slope of the Apennines, and the enemy, despite his superior numbers, did not dare attack. While the Spanish easily obtained rations from the towns of Aemilia, the French ran short of provisions. Then Gaston turned toward Ravenna. At the very last moment the Spaniards succeeded in sending reinforcements for the garrison into the city, and an attack the French risked making was repulsed. But the city would not have been able to hold out for long against the French artillery. The field army had to do something to save the place. It moved up closer and found a position southeast of Ravenna that, in the opinion of Fabricius Colonna, commander of the mounted troops, fulfilled every requirement. It could be attacked only with difficulty, its garrison could easily be fed, and it could seriously threaten any continuation of the siege of Ravenna and prevent provisions from reaching the siege army. Navarro, the leader of the infantry, believed he had discovered an equally favorable position one Italian mile closer to the enemy. Cardona ordered that this position be occupied, although Colonna protested, claiming that would bring on a battle.[3]

The left flank rested on the deep gorge of the Ronco River, the opposite side of which was held by the French. Consequently, before they could move up, there was time to strengthen the front with artificial measures. Navarro was already famous for such fortifications. A number of carts were emplaced behind a ditch, and a spear extended toward the enemy from each of them.[4] Marksmen and culverins were placed between the carts. Behind this fortified line stood the infantry, the Spaniards in line in the first echelon and the Italians in two squares in the second. On the left of the infantry, on the high bank of the Ronco, stood the heavy cavalry, which had no continuous obstacle in front of it, presumably because there had not been enough time to extend the ditch up to the river. The distance between the end of the ditch and the river was said to be about 20 fathoms. Posted on the right flank were the light horsemen under the command of the young Pescara, husband of Vittoria Colonna.

The sources report nothing of any terrain feature on which this flank might have rested. But the Italian survey map shows that, something over 1 kilometer from the Ronco, wet meadows start. They are crisscrossed by ditches and are therefore hardly passable for troops. It was no doubt precisely for this reason that the light horsemen had been separated from the heavy cavalry and placed on this flank. Since the front line, moreover, starting perpendicular to the Ronco, ran along somewhat inclined to the rear, an envelopment there was all the less feasible.

The French numbered some 23,000 men, including a strong corps of German lansquenets, 5,000 to 6,000 men under Jacob von Ems.[5] The Spanish had about 16,000 men and were therefore weaker almost by half. Furthermore, the French had a double superiority in artillery, about 50 cannon against 24. Given the Spanish position that was rendered so extremely advantageous by nature and artifice, the French council of war hesitated as to whether to risk an attack. But since, on the other hand, there was no alternative but to give up the siege and withdraw ignominiously, the youthfully bold Prince Gaston finally decided to attack, and he also found the means of depriving the enemy of the advantage of his position.

At first light the French army crossed the Ronco, partly on the bridge and partly by fording, and formed up facing the enemy.

Colonna had also proposed to the viceroy that, since they were now so close to the enemy, they should move out before daylight and attack him as he crossed the river. The bridge was only half a kilometer from the Spanish position. The commander, however, had adhered to Navarro's plan to await the enemy in the unexcelled defensive position.

The French, therefore, deployed on a front facing the Spanish, with their heavy horsemen on the right, their light horse on the left, and their foot troops in the middle. The center was reportedly held back somewhat, giving the formation the shape of a half-moon. It is not clear what that was supposed to accomplish, however, and it had no effect on the course of the battle.

On neither side do we find anything similar to the three squares of the Swiss tactics. These three-unit tactics were based on a strong assault by at least one or two of the squares, if not all three. But the Spanish were standing in a purely defensive position, and the French did not move directly from their deployment into the attack. Something completely new took place. The attacking army came up to within a certain distance of the enemy, but then it first had its artillery go into action, so that the other troops carried out their mission under the protection of this arm.

The Spanish artillery successfully replied to the French fire, since, even if it was numerically weaker, it had the advantage of its position. But on the side of the French was Duke Alfons of Este (Ferrara), who had taken a special interest in the development of the new artillery arm. His arsenals were filled with cannon, and it was thanks to his contingent that the French were so strong in this arm and their crews so excellently trained. The duke recognized the disadvantage of the position that had been taken up and led a number of his cannon from behind the infantry to a spot, presumably a slight rise in the ground, from which they could fire on the Spaniards' flank.[6] Navarro ordered his foot troops to lie down in order to escape the effect of the fire, but the Spanish knights on the left flank were now caught critically in the crossfire from front and flank. In a similar situation modern cavalry would certainly withdraw from the deadly effect of the enemy fire by changing its position, taking advantage of any available rise in the terrain. The Spanish knights were not sufficiently under the control of their leaders to carry out correctly movements of this kind. Quite to the contrary, as the enemy cannon balls were striking among them, they demanded that their leader, Colonna, allow them to ride out to the attack. The numerical losses that they suffered were probably not so very great, since even the best trained artillery crew of that period could fire only slowly and inaccurately. But it required only a few of the heavy cannon balls that flew through the mass or hit the target and blew apart horses and riders to make the situation appear intolerable. Colonna sent a demand to Navarro and Pescara that the whole line move forward simultaneously into the attack. Naturally, Navarro rejected such an unreasonable request, since the Spaniards would then have sacrificed the entire advantage of their carefully chosen defensive position. That point is so clear that even Colonna cannot possibly have failed to recognize it. But it is not so easy to fight a defensive battle. In order to do so, the troops must be under the control of the commander. Colonna, however, was not the master of his knights. In order to escape the cannon balls, they stormed forward against the French knights who were facing them. In the fight that then developed, they were beaten all the more badly when the French brought up a reserve of 400 lances that had remained behind at the Ronco bridge and sent them into the flank of the Spaniards.

On the other flank, among the light horse, a very similar action took place. The Italian-Spanish horsemen under Pescara moved forward against the enemy cannon and were overcome by the superior force of the enemy.

In the center, Navarro had held his foot soldiers in place. With completely rational leadership, the French foot troops should have held back in the same way until their mounted troops had been victorious on the flanks, and then they should have moved forward to the attack together with them. But it appears that the Spanish cannon reached the enemy foot troops sooner than they had expected, and then they could no longer be held in place. Instead, they stormed forward. Navarro had his men get up, the units in the rear closed up on the forward line, and the consolidated group charged on the enemy just as he, already shaken by the preceding salvo of the hook muskets, was seeking to cross the ditch. The Picards and Gascons gave way before the onslaught of the Spaniards, but the lansquenets held fast, even though the Spanish, who were better armed with short weapons, caused them heavy losses wherever they were able to push in between the long spears.

The decision was brought on by the fact that in the meantime the French horsemen on both flanks had been victorious and now fell on the flanks of the Spanish-Italian infantry. The retreating Picards and Gascons also moved forward again, and Navarro's troops, attacked on all sides by strongly superior forces, finally had to give way. But despite all the losses they suffered, their formation was not broken up. Instead, still 3,000 men strong, they moved in close formation along the Ronco dike and escaped. Their leader, Navarro, was captured, as were Fabricius Colonna and Pescara, the two leaders of the mounted troops. Gaston de Foix, the French commander, however, had been killed when he attempted with a number of knights to break up the withdrawing square of the Spanish pikemen.

The remarkable aspect of the battle of Ravenna is the role the artillery played on the side of the attacker. Gaston intentionally had it go to work alone at first, not only to tire the enemy for the following attack by the knights and foot soldiers, but also, by the effect of the fire, to lure the enemy himself to attack from his fine defensive position. The fact that this was not an incidental development but was a conscious intention is not only proven by Guicciardini, who shows Gaston telling of this in his talk to the troops, but particularly by the Florentine ambassador, Pandolfini, who was present at the battle on the French side. Machiavelli, too, says in the *Discorsi*, 1:206: "The Spanish were driven from their fortified positions by the enemy cannon and were forced to fight." This force was exercised exclusively on the Spanish knights on the left flank. We may therefore raise the question as to why these horsemen were not withdrawn and the protection of the cannon emplaced in front of them taken over by an infantry unit that could have protected itself to a certain degree by lying down, just as the main body of the infantry did. The answer to this question is that the knights could not easily be led back from the position where they stood.

As a result of the forward movement of the Spanish knights, which was contrary to the plan, first they themselves were lost and then also the infantry, which was indeed on the point of being victorious but was defeated as a result of the flank attack of the French knights. If the Spanish knights had awaited the French attack in their position, they would presumably have been capable of holding their own, for the distance between the front ditch and the Ronco, through which the attack had to go, was, of course, only 20 fathoms (*braccia*), according to Pandolfini, and Navarro had a detachment of 500 pikemen ready to bring assistance wherever it might be needed, that is, to bring aid to the knights as soon as they were attacked and involved in hand-to-hand combat.

As brilliant as the victory of Ravenna was, the French derived no benefit from it. The German lansquenets, who had had such an important share in the victory, were recalled from the French camp by imperial order, and they followed this command, with the exception of about 800, who did not submit to the imperial authority. The Swiss, however, who had given the French a free hand against the Spaniards by their withdrawal in the winter, now came again into the picture. As allies of the pope and of the Republic of Venice and with the approval of Emperor Maximilian, they moved through the Tyrol, 18,000 men strong, to join the Venetians and thus assembled such a powerful army that the French left Italy without even risking a new battle. It was only two months after the battle of Ravenna that they had withdrawn to France on the route over Mount Cenis, continuing to hold in the region of Milan only a few fortified castles. One might read that the death of their commander, Gaston de Foix, had robbed the French of all the fruits of their victory. It is undoubtedly more correct, however, to turn this sentence around: that the knightly battle death of the youthful French prince guaranteed him against seeing his name associated with the strategic defeat that followed immediately. I do not see that he could have acted in an essentially different and better way than his successor, La Palice, did. In the face of an absolute numerical superiority, even the strategic genius must give way.

BATTLE OF NOVARA[7]
6 JUNE 1513

As quickly as the political alliance had forced the French out of Italy, despite their victory at Ravenna, just as quickly did the situation change again, once more opening the door to them. The Venetians changed over to the side of the French, and the politics of the Confederation became uncertain. A French army appeared once again with a strong contingent of German lansquenets, captured Milan, and besieged Duke Maximilian Sforza with his Swiss auxiliaries in Novara. When the situation in this city had become a matter of great emergency through the effects of the excellent French cannon, a Swiss relief army appeared from the north, and the French decided to fall back eastward before it on their Venetian allies.

Since only half of the Swiss army, after extremely long marches, arrived in Novara in the evening and since the lifting of the siege and the withdrawal of the cannon and of the very large train were very troublesome and required time, the French army on that day did not move any farther than 4 kilometers from Novara and pitched camp opposite the small town of Trecate in a rather swampy area, crisscrossed with ditches.

This lack of caution did not escape the leaders of the Confederates. Nothing was better suited to their tactics than a sudden attack. Since Morgarten they knew what strength resided in a strategy that understood how to surprise the enemy. They had just arrived in Novara in the evening, and that same night the leaders held a council of war and decided to move out to the attack at once without even awaiting the second half of the army. Until almost midnight the French heard the Swiss making noise in the city, and they assumed that the lifting of the siege was being celebrated with drinking bouts. Trivulzio, who, along with Trémouille, was in command of the army, reportedly said: "Now the drunkards are sleeping it off, so we can go to bed without concern." The French were hauling along with them a kind of wooden fortress composed of posts and planks that were fit together, invented by Count de la Marck. This burden must have made the movements of their train quite difficult. Furthermore, this fortress could not have been very effective, because it was so small that it could enclose only a part of the army. But that night the French felt so secure that they had not even erected this fortress.

Suddenly there rang out through the camp the cry that the Swiss were there and were attacking. These tough mountaineers had rested only a few hours after their forced march and their carousing, and then, even before daybreak, they were assembled again and, like "irascible bees" had streamed out through the gates and over the fallen walls into the countryside "in order to seek out their enemies and risk their luck with them."

Again we find the old formation in three units, but suited to the situation in a well-considered manner. The unit which, coming from the north, was to envelop the right flank of the French and which was weak in infantry was accompanied by Duke Maximilian with his Italian knights. The middle unit, which attacked the front of the camp, where the French cannon were emplaced, was also weak. Its mission was not to attack directly but at first, supported by a few cannon, to occupy the enemy and make feints. The main body, however, concealed by a small woods, enveloped the French camp from the south, thus avoiding the dangerous cannon fire, and it fell with all its weight on the true strength of the French army, the unit of German lansquenets.[8]

The two armies were of approximately equal strength in infantry, 10,000 men. But the French also had their strong artillery and no fewer than 1,100 heavy horsemen and 500 light horse. We may also attribute to the Swiss, who had never yet lost a battle—and such self-confidence gives great strength—a certain qualitative superiority over the lansquenets and the French infantry. But these latter units, too, especially the lansquenets, had their experience in battle, their self-confidence and their ability, and one might hardly consider it possible that in a pitched battle the Swiss derring-do would have been equal to the opposing superiority in horse-men and cannon. But the suddenness of the attack equalized everything. It is true, of course, that the surprise was not as great as at Murten, for example, and there was no panic. The lansquenets formed up their main body, the knights put on their armor and mounted their horses, and the other troop units also formed up, but there was no rational cooperation. The French commander, La Trémouille, had sprung on his horse only half-armored in order to direct the battle, but we cannot discern anything in the way of actual leadership. The two small Swiss units occupied the attention of a relatively large part of the enemy army, but the French did not move out offensively on that side, where, after winning a success, they could have turned toward the left flank, where the main battle was raging around the lansquenets. It is particularly curious that the otherwise so brave knights did but little. At the end no more than forty men-at-arms had been killed, and Guicciardini accused them of outright cow-ardice. Since that appears incredible, scholars have sought the reason for this in the unfavorable soft terrain, and this might also have contributed somewhat. But the French cannot possibly have chosen for their camp a place so unfavorable that their heavy horsemen could not be used at all. Military history gives us another explanation. From the Persian horsemen at Marathon and through numerous battles of the Middle Ages we en-counter again and again the phenomenon that knights are almost unlead-able. If they are directed in a pitched battle against a specific, visible target, they accomplish what only they can be required to do. But as soon as distractions of any type occur, they lose their effectiveness, be-cause the individual, who is not accustomed to form a tight group with the others and obey commands or signals but is inclined to act only according to his own ideas, cannot possibly manage to act jointly with his comrades in the correct place, for the proper purpose, and at the right moment. A few, driven by their courage, attack in one place, others in another place, and still others want to wait until more come to join them or the situation becomes clearer. And there are still others who already see their cause as lost and are not willing to sacrifice themselves in vain. The lansquenets succeeded in turning some of the cannon around and moving them over so that they formed a new front against the enveloping Swiss. Their hook muskets, too, were effective against the enemy mass. If a few hundred French men-at-arms had been directed at that moment into the flank of the Swiss main body, when it was just about to enter the melee with the lansquenets, the lansquenets would surely have held their own, but, although a few knights boldly charged the enemy unit, they delayed it just as little as did the cannon and muskets. In their wild attack, and at the end supported by the other units, after the French detachments in the center and on the right flank, panic-stricken, had left the field, the Swiss overcame the lansquenets and, since they had driven them back from their natural line of retreat as a result of the envelopment, they destroyed the lansquenets almost completely, showing no mercy.[9] The French infantry, like the knights, had fled without very great losses. One group had retreated eastward toward Trecate, and another group had withdrawn toward the north and then around the north side of Novara toward Vercelli, which was situated southwest of Novara. In Vercelli, the unit that had marched toward Trecate with the rescued war treasury joined them, after marching around on the south of the Swiss.

The Swiss took as booty the enemy camp with all its cannon. Although, according to Duke Maximilian's letters, the battle had lasted only between one and two hours, the victory had been more costly for them than earlier ones. They may well have had up to 1,500 killed. In the fire of the cannon and the muskets, and finally in the desperate opposition of the surrounded unit of the lansquenets, such forces came into play as had never yet been felt in the old Swiss battles.

BATTLE OF LA MOTTA (CREAZZO)
7 OCTOBER 1513

Alviano, the Venetian general, attacked with considerable numerical superiority a Spanish-German-papal army north of Vicenza. He was defeated because a flanking movement by heavy horsemen that he had ordered became mired in a swamp and because his Italian infantry did not withstand the feared Spanish and German soldiers, who were led by Pescara and Frundsberg, respectively.[10]

BATTLE OF MARIGNANO
13–14 SEPTEMBER 1515

The Swiss followed up their victory of Novara by making an incursion into France itself in the autumn of that same year. They had formed a close alliance with Emperor Maximilian, who reinforced their campaign with horsemen and cannon and accompanied them. At the same time, the English invaded France from the north, and the French lost the battle of Guinegate, so that, with extravagant fantasy, they were already envisaging Paris itself as the common target and meeting place of the allied armies.

When the imperial-Swiss army, moving into Burgundy, appeared before Dijon and the city was on the point of being subjected by the fire of the cannon, the French saw no other salvation than to submit to the Swiss demands. La Trémouille, who was in command in the city, made a treaty with the Swiss in order to save the city from the attack. This treaty provided that the king of France renounce his claim to Milan and promise to pay 400,000 crowns as war indemnity.

But the treaty was not carried out. The Swiss, whose army had become less disciplined and more greedy with each campaign, were unable to hold their troops together before Dijon until the ratification by the French king was received. As soon as the immediate danger had disappeared, the king took a deep breath and declared he was ready to pay the stipulated amount but intended to retain his claim to Milan.

The Swiss had taken Milan from the French in 1513 as mercenaries in the service of Duke Maximilian Sforza. But this youthful ruler had himself thereby come into a position of full dependence on his allies. Not only had he been obliged to turn over directly to them a series of border areas and to pay them 200,000 ducats, but he had also had to place himself and his entire duchy under the lasting protection of the Confederation. He wrote to them that they could consider his person, his land, his people, and his possessions as their own and, as his legal fathers, hold him and his city of Milan under their protection, in return for which he would regard them as a son regards his father. The Swiss took that literally. They occupied the fortified castles, demanded 40,000 ducats annually, and through their resident ambassadors told the duke how he was to govern. This relationship can be compared with that of the French to the present-day Tunisia (1906) and its bey, of the English to Egypt, or of the Germanic federated tribes to the Roman Empire at the beginning of the *Völkerwanderung*. The Swiss, by demanding so energetically that the French king renounce his claim to Milan, were therefore fighting not for Sforza, but for themselves. If this relationship had lasted, the duchy of Milan, to which, in a broader sense, Genoa also belonged, would have become a subject country of the Confederation, a Swiss province. Switzerland would have formed a nation extending from the Lake of Constance to the Mediterranean. If we could imagine that a princely dynasty stood at the head of the union of cantons, following a constant policy, as had the Merovingians at the head of the Frankish tribes, or some other kind of firm government, the military forces of the Alpine inhabitants would have created a nation with far-flung borders. The loose union of the cantons, however, was not capable of following great political goals. The very same conditions that had produced their great military strength prevented its political exploitation. The warrior strength of the ancient Franks was based on their barbarian nature, which willingly subjected itself to Clovis's leadership en route to booty and dominance. The military strength of the Swiss had as a prerequisite the participation of each individual in the political life. The defiant self-confidence that animated every single soldier gave the irresistible force to the undertakings of the Confederation. From the political viewpoint, this self-confidence could exist only in small cantons, each of which was sovereign, which united for a political purpose from case to case.[11] The mutual jealousy between the cantons, however, and the will of the masses, who always wanted an immediate gain, did not allow the establishment of large-scale objectives. Half-way in the pay of France and half-way because the Bernese aristocrats were eager for conquest, the Confederates had attacked and defeated Charles the Bold. Finally, after the most brilliant victories, Bern had been permitted to keep only a few small places and areas. Vaud and Franche-Comté, however, were given back in return for repeated payments of money. The same game now started over Milan. If formerly the eastern cantons had not been willing to make conquests for Bern, it was now Bern and its neighbors, Fribourg and Solothurn, that showed no inclination to support the mastery over Milan, which was principally to the benefit of the original cantons.

When Francis I, the successor to Louis XII, crossed the Alps again in the summer of 1515 with a large army, including a body of lansquenets reportedly no less than 23,000 strong, in order to recapture Milan, he was enough of a statesman not simply to threaten the Swiss with the sword. Instead, he knew how to lure them at the same time with his gold. In addition to the 400,000 crowns already promised in Dijon, he offered a further 300,000 and annual payments, if the Confederates would turn Milan over to him. At the same time he was willing to indemnify Duke Maximilian by offering him the Duchy of Nemours in France and an annual payment.

The Swiss had already been long divided among themselves over their relationship with France. After all, they had always been allied with Louis XI and with Charles VIII. Then, as a result of errors that were made half-way by chance, especially because of extravagant claims by the Swiss, they had fallen into dispute with Louis XII. The pope, who wanted to drive the French out of Italy, had cleverly encouraged this dissension and, through the bishop of Sitten, Cardinal Schinner, a very energetic church diplomat and passionate enemy of the French, he had drawn the Confederation completely into the enemy camp. But the partisans of France among the Swiss continued to be active. By means of generously distributed presents, they kept alive the memory of the old alliance. Even the campaign to Dijon was carried out only with the help of a popular movement against the Francophiles, the "crown-eaters," who were accused of bribery and treason. The combination of offers and threats with which Francis now appeared finally gained for him an attentive ear in the council of captains. For a total of a million crowns the Confederation turned over to the king in the peace treaty of Gallerate (8 September 1515) the Duchy of Milan with all its dependencies. At the same time the Confed-

eration formed an alliance with him for his lifetime plus ten years in return
for an annual payment of 2,000 francs for each of the places.

The Bernese with their friends, including the men of Valais, returned
home. In the contingents of the other cantons, however, a great rage
broke out, and in the Swiss camp there was a man who was rash and
scheming enough to attempt, despite the completed treaty and the departure of a large part of the army, to bring the enemies against each
other in order to force the Swiss by their ensuing victory to adopt a
different policy from that decided in the council. It was the ambassador
of the pope, Cardinal Schinner, who inspired this furious desire for battle.

The French army may well have numbered 30,000 men; the reports
indicate much higher numbers. The infantry was composed of the main
corps, the lansquenets, and also of French. In addition, there were 2,500
lances and sixty pieces of heavy artillery. The Swiss, after the departure
of such a large part of their army, hardly numbered 20,000 foot soldiers,
supported by a very small number of horsemen, some 200, and a few
pieces of artillery.

The army of the Confederation was in the city of Milan; the French
had approached from the south to less than 9 miles' distance from the
city. Suddenly the cry rang through the billets that fighting was taking
place before the city, that the Confederates were being attacked by the
French. Schinner had persuaded the captain of the duke's life guard,
Arnold Winkelried of Unterwalden, to start a little skirmish with the
advanced troops of the French. Immediately the men of Uri, Lucerne,
and the other forest cantons, who wanted to maintain their mastery of
Milan and have nothing to do with the peace treaty with the French,
rushed out the gate in order to help. Although the French had immediately
withdrawn, the report was sent into the city that the fight was continuing.
Now the other cantons, even though the withdrawal was already decided,
especially at the insistence of Zurich and Zug, believed they could not
fail their comrades, and so they followed.

The sun was already sinking when they came to the camp of the French
advance guard, attacked, and drove it back, capturing a few cannon. But
the king, who had encamped with the main body somewhat farther to
the rear, was already hastening forward with his knights, and the fall of
darkness brought an end to the battle. Both armies camped so close to
one another that individual fights took place throughout the night. By
morning, however, Francis had overcome all the disorder that the sudden
attack of the Swiss had created in the advance guard and had drawn up
his army very advantageously behind several ditches in alternating units
of knights and spearmen, with cannon and marksmen in front or between
them, ready to receive the attack of the Swiss.

The Swiss formed their usual three squares, but those on the left and
in the center did not actually attack. Despite the numerous sources, we

have very little information on the left unit, and it is quite clear that the involvement of the center unit, which was directly opposed by Francis himself, did not extend beyond the cannonade, firing by marksmen, and individual sorties. The Swiss leaders who were in command in the center apparently intended to wait, as had been done at Novara, until one of the two enveloping columns had been successful before starting the actual attack in the center. King Francis, however, had no reason for moving out of his advantageous defensive position, behind the flooded ditches and supported by his superior cannon.

The real attack of the Swiss was carried out by the right flanking column, and at the start it had a certain degree of success. But the French had a very large overall numerical superiority, and the German lansquenets withstood the Swiss attack. It appears that Francis, on noticing the critical situation of his left flank, which his brother Alençon commanded, sent help from the center, and eventually the advance guard of the Venetian army also arrived and went to the aid of the French on that flank.

Thus all the boldness and courage of the Swiss was in vain. The cardinal, who on the preceding day had mounted on horseback in his purple robes and had ridden along with the army, encouraging them on all sides, supposedly realized during the night, when the sudden attack in the evening had had no decisive success, that the battle could no longer be won, and he advised a withdrawal. When the right flank now gave way, it was generally recognized that any hope of success for the center was also lost, and the entire Swiss army took up the withdrawal.

If the French king had now had his army with its strong mounted units take up the pursuit, things would probably not have gone much better for the Swiss than they had two years earlier for the lansquenets at Novara. But, of course, Francis had not wanted the battle. In the defeated attackers he saw his future friends rather than his momentary enemies. If he had now had the largest possible number of the retreating men cut down and shot, he would have been killing his own future mercenaries and would perhaps have awakened in the Swiss a desire for revenge that would have destroyed again the incipient friendship. Consequently, the king rejected the idea of pursuing, out of consideration for the courage that the Swiss had shown, as his contemporaries interpreted the situation. Nevertheless, the Swiss losses were considerable, since the French cannon had had a strong effect among the tight units of the Swiss, even in those places where there was no mass attack. Finally, a few units were cut off during their retreat, and one detachment was completely destroyed in a burning house.

The battle of Marignano belongs among those battles which have been completely distorted in the traditional accounts. The expression of Guicciardini, repeated again and again, to the effect that Marshal Trivulzio had said that it was a battle, not of human beings but of giants, whether or not this was actually said, is in any case better not applied to this battle as a whole. It evokes the impression of a warrior action of especially great, unprecedented dimensions, whereas in reality the battle, on the contrary, belongs among those that were not completely fought through to a decision. The political factor played a much greater role than the military. In this "History of the Art of War," we could, in fact, have omitted the entire battle, if it were not desirable to reject the false accounts by a more correct presentation and at the same time useful to give an example of a battle distorted in this way by politics.[12]

This battle, which, of course, was only the work of a popular passion cleverly exploited by schemers, had no results at all. King Francis granted the Swiss exactly the same peace agreement after his victory that he had already signed with them before, with the single difference that they chose, since it was left up to them, to retain a part of the Milan border region (as the border runs today), and in return they received 300,000 crowns less. There is no indication, however, that the Swiss felt this to be a military defeat or that, with their bold aggressiveness, they had lost any of their absolute self-confidence. The next battle, Bicocca, will demonstrate this point.

The beginnings of the Confederation toward developing into a great power were cut off in 1515. It is true that in 1536 Bern still took advantage of a favorable opportunity to win over Vaud. But that was, so to speak, only a delayed fruit of the Burgundian War, and after 1515 there was never again a large-scale, consistently followed Swiss policy. The military strength of the Confederation entered more or less continuously into the pay of France, and in doing so it gradually sank from its dominant position to one of equality with the troops of other nations. If the Swiss had wanted to develop into an independent great power militarily, they would not only have had to give themselves another, centralized form of government but would also have had to develop their mounted troops and their artillery up to the contemporary standard. Their strength, of course, lay exclusively in their infantry; even for the siege of Dijon, Emperor Maximilian had had to provide the cannon. That requirement exceeded the powers of the small mountain regions and cities.[13] Only the creation of the infantry, which became the model for all countries, was the contribution of the Swiss to world history. Up to Marignano they had been invincible, and even their failure in that battle was determined too greatly by special circumstances to lessen their reputation.

BATTLE OF BICOCCA[14]
27 APRIL 1522

For six years the French remained in possession of the Duchy of Milan, undisturbed. Then Emperor Charles V, in whose person as great-grandson of Charles the Bold and grandson of Emperor Maximilian and the Spanish monarchs Ferdinand and Isabella was united all the inherited enmity against the French kingdom, again took up the fight for the mastery of Upper Italy. Francis recruited Swiss mercenaries, but the imperial commander, Prosper Colonna, maneuvered so long around the French army without letting affairs come to the point of battle that there was no more money in the French war chest, and the Swiss returned home. Then Colonna moved into Milan without opposition, since the French had so antagonized the citizens that they opened the gates to the imperial army.

The following year the French appeared again with such a large army as to enable them to besiege Milan. An imperial relief corps of 6,000 lansquenets and 300 horsemen caused the French to withdraw from Milan and concentrate on a smaller objective, Pavia. When this siege, too, remained unsuccessful and flood conditions in the Ticino interrupted the supply of rations, and an attempt by means of an envelopment to force the imperial army to fight failed, the French army was again on the point of breaking up, because the Swiss were no longer willing to continue. Their mode of operation was to seek out the enemy as soon as they had taken to the field, attack and defeat him, and return home again with their booty and their pay. Besieging cities and spending time maneuvering and taking up defensive positions were actions at odds with their nature and their concepts of warfare, especially when their pay was not even forthcoming on a regular basis. The last move of the French army was supposedly determined by the fact that the army was to march out to Monza to meet the war chest, which was being brought from France via the Simplon Pass. When the money still did not appear, the Swiss refused to be consoled further with promises. They intended either to fight or go home.[15]

The French-Venetian army was probably about half again larger than the imperial army, or even more so—around 32,000 against 20,000. Prosper Colonna, the commander of the imperial troops, however, held a position that was almost unassailable. He stood about 4 miles north of Milan near the little hunting castle of Bicocca. A sunken road ran parallel to his front; his left flank was protected by a swamp and his right flank by a deep ditch filled with water, which was crossed only by a narrow bridge. His front, which faced north and was of a very appropriate length for his army, some 600 meters, was occupied by cannon and a line of marksmen four men deep, whose weapons had recently been improved and who were trained to fire by ranks. After the first and second ranks had fired, they threw themselves to the ground so that the third and fourth ranks could fire over them. Behind the marksmen stood the deep units of German lansquenets under Georg Frundsberg and the Spanish soldiers under Pescara. The mounted men were posted farther to the rear in order to counter a possible envelopment against the right flank across the bridge.

The position was even much stronger than the one the Spanish had occupied at Ravenna. The artifice of luring the defender out of his position by the action of the artillery, forcing him either to withdraw or move forward, which had succeeded so brilliantly at Ravenna, could not be repeated here, since the French hardly had any significant superiority in artillery and the Spanish horsemen, against whom the artillery had been so effective at Ravenna, were not posted on the front this time but in the second echelon. Furthermore, it was very difficult to envelop the imperial position completely and attack it in the rear with a corps, since the city of Milan lay so close behind the imperial battle formation. Moreover, when the approach of the French attack was observed, Colonna had had Duke Franz Sforza ring the alarm and lead out the armed citizenry, 6,000 men, to cover the rear of the imperial army.

Despite his numerical superiority, Lautrec, the French commander, would naturally have preferred under such circumstances to avoid the battle and to continue to operate in the manner in which he had been proceeding, that is, besieging and capturing the individual towns of the duchy in the hope that the enemy's counteroperations would perhaps give him an opportunity to use his superiority in a battle in the open field. Even though, as a result of the alertness and cleverness of his enemy, he had had little success in the two months the campaign had been under way, such success was certainly not ruled out for the future. But the impatience of the Swiss did not permit lengthy maneuvering. No matter how much Lautrec pointed out to them the strength of the enemy position, their boldness and their confidence were still in no way broken by their experience at Marignano. They recalled to the French how, with their smaller numbers, they had beaten the French themselves at Novara, and now they intended to do the same thing to the Spaniards, who may have exceeded them in ruses and deception but not in courage.

Consequently, Lautrec had no alternative but to send them in to attack the imperial front. For this purpose, they formed two squares with their 15,000 men, each square 100 men wide and 75 men deep. Each unit was accompanied by marksmen, and a third unit, principally the horsemen, was assigned the mission of enveloping the right flank of the enemy and attacking over the bridge. All together, they were about 18,000 men strong. The Venetians, however, and the other Italian troops, a total of about 14,000 men, remained in reserve. It is not reported why Lautrec adopted this disposition. It appears that, since the blustery Swiss, boasting of their invincibility, had demanded the battle, it was decided to leave it up to them to overrun the enemy. It is also possible that there was hardly enough room in the front line for a third and fourth assault unit. Finally,

Lautrec may also have had a positive idea for the use of the reserve. He could be thinking that, if the Swiss did not succeed in their furious attack but were thrown back, the enemy would storm out after them, giving Lautrec the opportunity to fall on them, in their disorder and without the protection of their defensive position, with his fresh troops. If the Swiss then turned about, Lautrec's great numerical superiority could defeat the enemy.

While the Swiss were already moving forward, Lautrec still attempted to hold them up so that at least his flanking corps could move into position and enter the action. But the Swiss, mistrustful because they had only been able to force him into the battle through their obstinacy, saw in this order to stop only a last attempt to avoid the fight, and with enraged shouts they demanded the attack. The mass of soldiers even showed mistrust of their own leaders, saying the captains, the young nobles, the pensioners, and the triple-pay mercenaries should move to the front of the column and not shout from the rear. And so the mass stormed forward through the hail of balls from cannon and harquebuses, which could hardly miss their mark in the thickly pressed squares. The attackers reached the sunken road, and the marksmen moved back. The Swiss climbed the slope beside the sunken road, about 3 feet high, to come to grips with the enemy spearmen.

As was dictated by their tactics, the lansquenets and Spaniards were not in position directly beside the sunken road but a short distance behind it, so that their marksmen, as the Swiss closed with them, could easily fade back through and around the front line. Then came the clash, not while the defenders stood awaiting the assault of the Swiss but as a result of their moving forward against the attackers just as the latter came over the edge of the sunken road, intending to continue their push forward. With a halberd in his hand, Frundsberg himself had taken position in the first rank of his lansquenets, who were on their knees to pray. "Everybody up, in a good hour, in the name of God!" cried the leader and stormed forward with his men. On the other side, at the point of the Swiss square, came Arnold Winkelried of Unterwalden, who seven years earlier had opened the battle at Marignano and once had also fought in the imperial service at Frundsberg's side. "You old rascal, now that I find you there, you must die by my hand," he shouted. "That will happen to you, God willing," replied Frundsberg. Frundsberg was wounded by a stab in the thigh; Winkelried was killed by the spears of the lansquenets.

The Swiss were forced to withdraw. They were tired from the long approach, many had fallen under the fire of the imperial cannon and marksmen, and their formation had been broken up as they crossed the sunken road, so that their "pressure from the rear was not the best," as the Appenzellers reported back home. The rearmost ranks, separated from the leading ranks by the sunken road, could not exert the pressure on them on which, of course, the tactical system of this deep square was based.

At the same time, the attempt by the French knights to cross the bridge and attack the right flank of the emperor's troops was also thrown back.

Pescara, who with his Spaniards had repulsed the troops of the cities under Albrecht von Stein in the same way in which Frundsberg had beaten back the other Swiss square with his lansquenets, now proposed following up the victory and pursuing the Swiss. Frundsberg, however, declined, saying: "We have won enough honor today," and Colonna, the overall commander, agreed with him. Despite the heavy losses they had suffered, the Swiss had withdrawn in good order, and, as we know, behind them stood 14,000 men, who presumably were only waiting for the imperial troops to come toward them in the open field.

Since that did not occur, the French finally had to acknowledge defeat, and, since the Swiss marched back home, the campaign was also a failure.

The lansquenets had defeated the Swiss for the first time, and they were very proud of that. They sang songs mocking the defeated troops, who replied with other songs. In the continuation of this battle of songs, the various battles became confused with one another, and finally the battle of Bicocca, with the squares of tightly aligned lansquenets and the brave Arnold Winkelried, who was their victim, was transposed into the knightly battle of Sempach, 136 years earlier.

According to the smallest number reported, the Swiss had 3,000 men killed at Bicocca, perhaps no fewer than in all their great victories together. Guicciardini writes that they lost more in boldness, however, than in numbers, for it was certain, according to him, that the damage they suffered at Bicocca so weakened them that for many years afterward they did not show their old spirit. Indeed, their boldness had been based on their unconditional confidence in being invincible, nurtured for two centuries, and this confidence, it was thought, was now broken. In reality, however, later military history does not confirm this judgment. If the importance of the Swiss gradually diminished, that was not because their own ability had decreased, as we shall see, but in the overall developments, which limited more and more the area of action for the power of the Confederation.

Ranke characterizes the Swiss at Bicocca as follows:

> They had a savage warrior courage without any higher inspiration, and it took pride only in itself and believed it needed no leadership. They knew they were hirelings, but each one was bound to do his duty and wanted to do so. Their only thought was to fight things out, body to body, to earn their pay for the attack, and to overcome their old opponents, the Swabians, the lansquenets.

BATTLE OF PAVIA[16]
24 FEBRUARY 1525

Despite their defeat at Bicocca, the French continued their fight for the mastery of Italy. Two campaigns followed, which, although full of maneuvering, did not result in any battles and ended with the imperial army, which had pushed forward to Marseilles, almost breaking up, while King Francis crossed the Alps again, captured Milan (with the exception of the citadel), and besieged Pavia.

The city was defended by Spaniards and lansquenets, who repelled the French attacks, so that the king finally limited himself to surrounding the city for the purpose of starving the inhabitants into submission. Meanwhile, newly recruited lansquenet units under Frundsberg and Marx Sittich of Embs crossed the Alps, joined forces with the Spaniards under Pescara, and moved up from the east to relieve the city. The French, however, who had already been besieging the city more than two months, since 24 November, had used the time to fortify their camp on the outer side, so that it appeared unassailable. Pescara pushed his fortifications so close to the enemy camp that the marksmen stood facing one another in a number of places only 40 fathoms apart. But the king considered his position so strong that he felt it unnecessary to take any positive measures against the relief army. He drew the majority of his troops to the east side, where the relief army was threatening him, and he believed he could win by simply waiting. He was all the more confident that this plan would succeed because there was a complete lack of money in the imperial army, and the lansquenets were threatening to return home if they were not finally paid. Individual units were already actually beginning to march off. The soldiers finally obligated themselves to wait a few more days in return for the promise of forcing the enemy to do battle. "May God give me one hundred years of war and not one day of battle," said Pescara, "but now there is no other solution."

Along its front the siege army was entrenched in an impregnable position toward both the interior and the exterior, but the north flank extended into a deer park surrounded by a brick wall. The flank seemed to be completely covered by this wall, and that was indeed the case when it was kept under careful observation. Before the wall could be torn down and a considerable part of the relief army could penetrate, superior forces of the French army would always be at hand to drive out the attackers.

For the imperial army, everything depended on their succeeding in weakening the alertness of the French and penetrating into the park with large numbers before the French could be assembled for the counterattack.

On the night of 23-24 February, a number of Spanish labor troops (*vastadores*) with battering rams and similar instruments were sent to the most northerly part of the wall, which was quite distant from the French camp. They were careful not to use any cannon to knock down the wall, so that the French would not be alerted by their thunder. The night was dark and stormy, so that the work was done without attracting the enemy's attention. Contributing, no doubt, to this lack of caution was the fact that the armies had now stood facing each other for three weeks, small attacks had taken place almost every night, and so they did not suspect something of a larger nature behind various small movements.[17]

While the *vastadores*, working through the night, opened three large breaches in the city wall, the entire army moved out. It started in deep darkness and arrived before the breaches at daylight. If the French noticed this move, they may have interpreted it as the beginning of a withdrawal.

Now the imperial troops streamed into the park in three columns and deployed. First came 3,000 marksmen, Spaniards and lansquenets. Then came the horsemen and then the lansquenets. The latter were last perhaps because they formed the largest mass and therefore needed the most time to pass through the narrow breach.

The terrain in the park formed a rolling meadowland, through which a small stream ran. Here and there stood individual trees and small sections of woods, and about in the middle there was a dairy house or a small hunting lodge, Mirabello. The imperial troops had already reached that point when they found themselves facing the French. King Francis himself came galloping up with the men-at-arms, and the French artillery began to fire. The imperial troops, who were in any case very weak in cannon, did not succeed in firing them at all. The French, who had a total of not fewer than fifty-three pieces, were firing with success. But the brave French men-at-arms were especially successful in beating back the emperor's horsemen, so that King Francis already said to a companion that that day would make him master of Milan.

But this success was short-lived. The Spanish and German marksmen, part of whom were no doubt already armed with the new firearms, the muskets, which had greater accuracy at long range and powerful penetrating force, came to the aid of their horsemen. The trees, woods, and even the stream offered them cover against the French men-at-arms, and their shots felled so many that the imperial horsemen were able to come back into the fight. In the meantime, however, the large infantry squares were marching up. The French artillery could not stop them, and they charged into the foremost square of the French army, the "Black Band," 5,000 Low German soldiers, who were just coming on the field.

The two armies were of approximately equal strength in infantry, about 20,000 men, but the French had greater numbers of mounted men and cannon. As a result, however, of the sudden appearance of the imperial army at dawn in an unexpected place, this army now stood completely deployed in the middle of the park, whereas the 8,000 Swiss, that part of the French army that occupied the southern portion of the camp, were not yet in position. Consequently, Frundsberg and Embs, with their two units, 12,000 men strong, were able "to seize the 'Black Band' as if with tongs" from both sides and completely cut them up. The Swiss did not appear until the remnants of the "Black Band," together with the French horsemen, were streaming to the rear. But the Swiss were all the less able to change the fate of the day in that the garrison of Pavia, making a sortie, now appeared in their rear. In their desperate situation, the Swiss were not even able to make an attack in closed formation, and they were attacked from all sides and cut to pieces by the superior force of the enemy, just as the "Black Band" had been destroyed, or they sought their salvation in flight.

The rear guard of the French army, under the command of the duke of Alençon, which was posted principally on the other side of Pavia, had not yet been engaged. The duke, however, saw that there was no prospect of success, and he destroyed the bridge that the French had erected on the south side across the Ticino. In doing so he saved himself and his command but caused all the greater losses in the other parts of the army, where many men died in the waters of the river or were captured, like King Francis himself and many of his men-at-arms. This victory, which destroyed the enemy army, reportedly cost the imperial troops no more than some 500 killed, and that is no doubt possible, since, owing to the surprise attack and the assault from the flank, they had been able to fight in every single phase of the battle with great numerical superiority. And with this point, the charge of lack of energy that Guicciardini made against the Swiss also collapses. In reality, there was nothing they could do.

THE MUSTER AT VIENNA IN 1532

In addition to the battle analyses, a troop muster that Charles V caused to be conducted at Vienna in 1532 also deserves our attention. Jovius, who was personally present in the retinue of the papal legate, has provided a thorough description of this event, using, it appears, an official report with a sketch. A letter from King Ferdinand to his sister, dated 2 October, stated that the army numbered 80,000 foot troops and 6,000 mounted men. Schärtlin von Burtenbach gives 65,000 on foot and 11,000 horsemen, whereas Sepulveda and Jovius state the numbers as 120,000 men all together, including 30,000 horsemen and 20,000 marksmen. This total, however, presumably also included garrison troops.

These great differences in the numbers given by witnesses who would normally deserve full credence are worthy of note. Of course, the number 30,000 horsemen is completely incredible.

The formation for the muster had the huge mass of pikemen forming three squares with equal numbers of men on each side, that is, between 140 and 150 men wide and deep. All the mounted troops were formed in the intervals between these squares and with the same depth, and the entire formation was surrounded by a band of marksmen five ranks deep. The artillery was drawn up in front, and the light Hungarian horsemen were outside the formation.

Jovius says the reason for this formation was that the horsemen might not be exposed to the superior forces of the Turks, which he places at 300,000.

Rüstow understood this as meaning that it was a question of a defensive position that then stood as "Hungarian Order" for more than 100 years in the wars against the Turks.

I see in this muster only a parade formation without any tactical significance. I do not know of any battle where the troops were drawn up in this manner.

The entire mighty levy of 1532 had no positive results, since Sultan Suleiman, not willing to risk letting a battle develop, withdrew, and the Protestants were unwilling to make any conquests for the emperor. Because of poor rations and a lack of pay, mutiny broke out among the troops, and the army was disbanded.

BATTLE OF CERESOLE[18]
14 APRIL 1544

The French were besieging Carignano, south of Turin. An imperial army under del Guasto sought a position that would force the French either to give up the siege or to attack the relief army under unfavorable conditions. But the maneuver, although it was very carefully planned, failed, partly because rainy weather softened the roads and the army with its large columns of provisions was unable to reach the march objective in the assumed time.

The youthful and bold commander of the French, the prince of Enghien, foreseeing del Guasto's relief attempt, had sought and gained his king's permission to risk a battle. Now, as the imperial army approached, the French, who had become alert at the proper time, moved out from their camp at Carignano at three o'clock in the morning and appeared on the right flank of the enemy march columns, so that del Guasto had to decide either to withdraw and sacrifice Carignano or accept battle.

The opposing forces were approximately even. Del Guasto had numerical superiority in foot troops, while Enghien had more men-at-arms. At the last moment, more than 100 French nobles moved to join him, rushing forward to fight in the ancient knightly manner as soon as they heard the cry that a battle was imminent. Del Guasto believed, however, as he later told Jovius, that the experience of Pavia showed that the musketeers were superior to the knights and his lansquenets would then bring him victory. He therefore accepted the battle, and both armies deployed at the place where they had happened to make contact.

Both armies, however, sought to gain for themselves the tactical advantage of the defensive and to force the other army to attack. Consequently, the battle, reminiscent of quite modern events, opened with a duel between marksmen and artillery lasting several hours. The marksmen moved back and forth, and whenever they were sorely pressed, they called for help from the horsemen. As soon as the horsemen arrived, the marksmen in the open terrain naturally had to fall back.

It was finally del Guasto who decided to attack, perhaps because he could no longer tolerate the effects of the French artillery, and perhaps in the belief that he was countering an enemy push that was already under way.

Both sides had deployed their pikemen in three large squares in the old Swiss manner. On the evenly rolling terrain, these squares simply stood side by side. When the Swiss in earlier days had deployed their three squares in echelons, that was done in order to gain complete freedom of movement in their stormy attack. Here, where each side awaited the attack and each square was accompanied and flanked by horsemen, the linear deployment resulted automatically.

As the troops made contact, the best square of pikemen of the imperial army, the advance guard on the right flank, consisting of lansquenets and Spaniards, clashed with a unit of newly recruited Swiss (from Gruyères) and Italians that was numerically superior but rather loosely organized. The latter troops were thrown back and pursued, and even the French men-at-arms, who attacked the advancing lansquenets and Spaniards, were unable to hold them up.

In the center, however, a unit of newly recruited lansquenets encountered a corresponding unit of especially experienced Swiss in the French service. This unit, initially held back carefully by its captain, Fröhlich, did not attack the lansquenets until they had come close to them and, because of a lack of experience and the difficult terrain before the front, were somewhat disorganized. These Swiss, even though significantly weaker in numbers, were superior to their enemies in military ability. And it also happened that the French men-at-arms overcame the light Spanish horsemen who were accompanying the lansquenets, and finally the third French square of pikemen, composed of Gascons, struck the lansquenets in the flank. This was made possible by the fact that the third square of imperial infantry, which was supposed to attack the Gascons, did not do so but held back. This unit was composed of Italians who had not yet accomplished anything with the new infantry tactics, and the unit was only a small one. Del Guasto probably depended on the fact that these Italians were very strong in marksmen, but the marksmen had been obliged to withdraw before the enemy horsemen. The Florentine horsemen, too, who were accompanying the Italian infantry, were defeated by the French, and thus the unit of Gascon spearmen had been free to turn its attention, under skillful leadership, to the decisive point. The sources do not agree as to the moment at which the Gascons fell upon the lansquenets. It is not clear whether they simply completed the defeat after the Swiss had already thrown the enemy back, or whether both units worked together, or the Gascons accomplished the principal work. Since the Swiss themselves reported only forty killed, some of whom must have been lost in the preceding firefight, their clash with the lansquenets cannot have been so very hard. The intervention of the Gascons was also no doubt already effective when they were seen approaching, before their weapons could be used. Monluc's account to the effect that the clash was so strong that the first rank on each side was thrown to the ground can probably not be repeated as an actual fact.

The initially victorious right flank of the imperial army, which had committed the fundamental error of following up its victory immediately instead of first helping to overcome the enemy main body, the Swiss, was now attacked from all sides and destroyed when it attempted to return to the battlefield.

The unique features of this battle all seem to have been determined by the firearms, both as a result of what they accomplished and of what was expected from them but not actually accomplished. Whereas in the preceding large battles we have had a clearly defined defender and also a clearly defined attacker, we have here the phenomenon that both sides wished to gain tactically until the last moment the advantage of the defense. It is obviously not simply the terrain advantage that they hoped for—for in earlier battles the Swiss, of course, never considered this— but the advantage of long-range weapons. Furthermore, it is reported of both the lansquenets and the Gascons that marksmen with harquebuses or pistols had been placed in the second rank with the mission of firing into the enemy mass immediately before the clash. The weight and tightly closed formation of the square of spearmen were thereby reduced to a certain extent. It was like the beginning of a disintegration, and the Swiss gave no evidence of this new style of artifice, and yet they continued to be victorious. Since even the musket had to give way before the French knights, Ceresole shows that the success of the musketeers at Pavia was significantly determined by the cover that the terrain in the park offered the marksmen. The artillery, even though not numerous, had a greater effect on the course of the battle than did the hand firearms. But it was still the large squares of pikemen that produced the real decision.

The losses of the imperial army in killed and captured were tremendous, approximately half of the army, of which there were 5,000 killed. Nevertheless, the positive results of the victory for the French were only small. After some time, they captured Carignano, but they were unable to do anything more, since Emperor Charles was just preparing for an invasion of France from Germany and King Francis recalled troops from Italy to protect against that invasion. Of course, if del Guasto had been victorious at Ceresole and had then crossed the Alps and invaded France, the pressure on the French would have become very intense. But even then it would certainly not have been sufficient for a complete defeat.

NOTES FOR CHAPTER V

1. Hobohm, 2:518.

2. This battle is thoroughly treated by Rüstow in *History of the Infantry (Geschichte der Infanterie)*, by Jähns in *Manual of a History of Warfare (Handbuch einer Geschichte des Kriegswesens)*, and by Ranke, *History of the Romanic and Germanic Peoples (Geschichte der romanischen und germanischen Völker)*, Werke, 33:25. All these accounts, which differ significantly from one another, need serious correcting. Rüstow based his work too exclusively on Guicciardini, while Ranke and Jähns used as their principal source Coccinius, who can hardly be compared to the better sources. The standard study, based on the sources, is the Berlin dissertation by Erich Siedersleben (1907). Published by Georg Nauck. His principal sources are a letter written by Fabricius Colonna, who commanded the knights on the Spanish side (printed in Marino Sanuto, *Diarii*, 14:176. Venice, 1886), and a report from the Florentine ambassador, Pandolfini, who was present at the battle in the French headquarters (printed in Desjardins, *Négociations diplomatiques de la France avec la Toscane*, 2:581. Paris, 1861).

3. According to Colonna's letter.

4. The Italian survey map indicates that the ditch still exists today but does not extend as close to the Ronco as it did, according to our sources, at the time of the battle in 1512.

5. I include the 400 lances that were in position at the Ronco bridge under Alègre and intervened in the battle.

6. The artillery maneuver is not completely clear, since we cannot assume, as Guicciardini recounts, that Este drove completely into the right flank of the enemy, and the cannon certainly did not have enough range to shoot along the entire enemy front. Perhaps another inspection of the battlefield would clarify this point.

7. This battle is treated in two valuable monographs that appeared in

quick succession: *Novara and Dijon. Apogee and Decline of the Swiss Great Power in the Sixteenth Century (Novara und Dijon. Höhepunkt und Verfall der schweizerischen Grossmacht im 16. Jahrhundert)*, by Doctor of Philosophy E. Gagliardi. Zurich, 1907. Published by Leemann Brothers and Co. "The Battle of Novara" ("Die Schlacht bei Novara"), by Georg Fischer. Berlin dissertation, 1908. Published by Georg Nauck.

8. Gagliardi and Fischer arrange the individual elements of the battle very differently, indeed even contradicting one another, since Fischer places on the right flank what Gagliardi seems to report for the left flank. I agree with Fischer. Nevertheless, when Fischer assigns only 1,000 men to the north square of the Swiss, 2,000 to the center square, and 7,000 to the south square, I do not say that that is impossible, but I do not consider it as certain. If the Swiss had good information on the enemy and knew that the lansquenets were in the southern part of the camp but that there was no favorable terrain there for horsemen, they may well have made the northerly and central columns of infantry very weak, assigning in return the horsemen to the former and the cannon to the latter. But they may have given these two units only missions calling for demonstrations, while assigning the actual attack exclusively to the third square and giving it seven-tenths of the entire infantry. But we may believe such fine points only if we have direct and reliable sources concerning them. Consequently, although I agree essentially with Fischer, I have expressed myself more carefully and with more restraint and have avoided giving specific numbers for the various troop units.

9. The sources speak of 400 Swiss halberdiers who reportedly first drove off the harquebusiers of the lansquenets and then attacked the main body in the flank. Gagliardi (p. 162) considers them to be a unit that arrived by chance, while Fischer (p. 138) considers this a detachment that was sent out intentionally. I suspect that these were men who welled out on one side when the main bodies clashed.

10. This battle is studied in an exemplary way by Otto Haintz in the dissertation "From Novara to La Motta" ("Von Novara bis La Motta"). Berlin, 1912.

11. This polarity is developed excellently by Gagliardi, *Novara und Dijon*, p. 327.

12. The monograph by Heinrich Harkensee (Göttingen dissertation, 1909), while also contributing to the research in detail, did not arrive at tactically correct concepts of the overall battle. The corrections that need to be made are apparent when this work is compared with the account above. In particular, Harkensee attributes too much credibility to the exaggerations in the figures for the French strength. Hadank's review in the *Deutsche Literaturzeitung*, No. 26, 1910, concentrates too much on details and unjustly raises the accusation that the author did not understand the strategic situation. He may, however, be correct in his reckoning

of the French strength as 30,000. He also justifiably defends the report that the Gascons had large shields that could be placed on the ground as a base. Such shields (*pavesen*) were used by the marksmen. He refers to a miniature showing crossbowmen with large shields of this kind in front of them. Hewett, *Ancient Armour and Weapons*, 3:543 (Supplement).

13. On page 36 above there is a quote that praises the Swiss artillery. The facts do not justify this.

14. "The Battle of Bicocca" ("Die Schlacht bei Bicocca"), by Paul Kopitsch. Berlin dissertation, 1909. Published by E. Ebering.

15. In Guicciardini the account reads: "They wanted to return home, but in order to show the whole world that it was not because of fear, they first wanted to defeat the enemy." It is possible that this statement was made, but if they had been victorious, the Swiss would no doubt still have remained, and so they no doubt intended in the bottom of their hearts to do so from the start.

16. The standard monograph is the Berlin dissertation by Reinhard Thom (1907), which, as a result of precise source analysis, corrects many individual errors in earlier accounts. A few additional sources mentioned in the review of this monograph in the *Deutsche Literaturzeitung*, No. 8, 1909, are not of concern to us.

17. The report by the ambassador from Siena specifically gives this as the reason for the carelessness of the French.

18. Berlin dissertation by Karl Stallwitz, 1911. Review by Hadank in the *Deutsche Literaturzeitung*, No. 16, 1912.

Chapter VI

Machiavelli

The new art of war also produced at once its great theoretician. Even in the Middle Ages men had not stopped reading Vegetius. Charles the Bold had translations of Vegetius and Xenophon made for himself, and they are still preserved. His translation of the *Cyropaedia* by Vasque de Lucenne was lost on the flight from Nancy.[1]

Charles V studied Caesar's writings in great detail and wrote many annotations in the margin of his copy. On his orders, a commission of scholars was sent to France to determine the locations of Caesar's camps, and they made forty plans of them.

The classical military author of the period, however, was Niccolo Machiavelli, on whose *Renaissance der Kriegskunst* (*Renaissance of the Art of War*) Martin Hobohm has recently favored us with a work that is at the same time basic and definitive.[2]

Machiavelli was strongly impressed by the fact that, whereas in his youth (born 1469) mounted troops had still been almost exclusively the dominant arm, now it was the infantry that decided the outcome of battles. He combined this belief with the results of his classical studies, namely, that the Romans had ruled the world thanks to their legions, and he now set for himself the task of showing the world and particularly his compatriots that a competent citizen infantry represented the ideal of an army organization and was capable of freeing Italy and especially Florence from the fearful mercenary bands with which war was now being waged. His patriotism and his constructively inclined intellect, his literary studies, and his realistic outlook on the surrounding world joined to drive him forward both to the construction of a theoretically conceived system and to the practical creation of a Florentine national militia in which he intended to renew the system of the ancient Romans.

The position of chancellor that Machiavelli held in the Republic of Florence was not the leading office but, as we would express it today, one of the higher subaltern posts. From this lower position, Machiavelli was able, through the power of his word and his personality, to persuade the republic in 1506 to organize a militia, which eventually grew to a strength of nearly 20,000 men.

The country was divided into districts. Governmental commissars traveled through these districts, designated the men who seemed suitable, and drew up lists of them. Each district provided a company, at the head of which was assigned an experienced captain. The men were issued weapons—a spear and a body harness—and uniform, a white jerkin and breeches with one red leg and one white leg. Each company carried a banner of distinctive cloth, but they were all decorated with the same figure of the Florentine lion. The captain was aided by a chancellor for the administration, keeping of rosters, and all correspondence, an ensign, a number of corporals, and one or several drummers, who drummed "in the fashion of those beyond the mountains." From time to time, on a holiday, the captain assembled his men in their district, reviewed them either by himself or together with a governmental commissar from the capital, and drilled them in military movements "in the manner of the Swiss." Sometimes large parades were held in Florence itself.

In peacetime the militiamen had the right to bear arms and also had certain juridical privileges. In wartime they received (or were supposed to receive) the same pay as recruited men, 3 ducats per month. The captains received a regular salary up to 12 ducats a month, or, instead, partial provision of foodstuffs, free lodging, and fodder for a horse.

The companies were gradually built up to great strength, 800 men, and were consequently much too large for a single officer, but it was reckoned that in case of war only about a third of that number would really take the field, and in fact these numbers were even much smaller, some 150 men per company.

At least 70 percent of the men in the companies were armed with long spears, some 10 percent were marksmen, and the remainder were divided between light halberds (the "ronca"), hog-spears, and other close-combat weapons. They formed the large square, learned to march to a certain extent in time with the drumbeat, to maintain position in file and in rank, and to face to the right and the left. These movements, like the manipulation of the weapons, were so simple that they could probably be learned in the few holiday drills. The Swiss and the lansquenets, too, were probably not drilled any more thoroughly. The only weapon that required special skill, the missile weapon, was borne by those men who practiced on their own and who themselves owned such weapons. Whether the weapon was a crossbow or a harquebus was left up to the individual.

Up to this point, the organization of the Florentine militia seems to be in line with all reasonable requirements. But there were other conditions. In the very first memorandum in which Machiavelli recommended this militia to the Florentines, he raised the question as to whether the creation of a force armed in this way might not possibly become dangerous for the republic itself: The organization was based, first of all, on the dominant position of the city over the countryside, a considerable area with many farms and smaller towns. Only a part of this area, which was called the "*contado*," was considered to be absolutely reliable. The larger part, the "*distritto*," had been gradually subjected by force and could possibly decide once again to refuse obedience to the city. In the city itself there reigned a very artificially organized middle class with an aristocratic stamp. At the head of the republic stood a gonfalonier, Soderini, who was elected for life, but his jurisdiction was limited. The real governmental power was in the hands of a number of councils, the Council of 80, the Council of 10, the Council of 9, and the Council of 8, the composition of which always changed after a few months and the jurisdiction of which overlapped in many respects. Above all these groups was a citizen assembly composed of men whose father, grandfather, or great-grandfather had once belonged to one of the councils or had been eligible for such membership.

The basic distinction from the constitution of ancient Rome is immediately obvious. In Rome the peasant had the same rights as the city dweller, and there was no opposition between city and countryside. The officials of the republic had complete authority. The rich aristocratic families enjoyed an inherited respect, which was supported by religion, and they exercised their influence in wavering balance with the democratic masses. These masses formed the army.

On the other hand, as loose, indeed diffuse, as was the Florentine governmental machinery, it was, in addition, constantly threatened from without and within by the pretensions of the exiled Medici family. Everything was therefore built on a basis of mutual suspicion and mutual limitations. In peacetime the militia was under the Council of 9, but if war broke out, the command shifted to the Council of 10. Machiavelli believed that this was precisely an advantage, the fact that the militiamen did not know who their master really was. But how could a government that was so loose itself create a firm army organization? Everything that was done actually depended on Machiavelli, who, as the official secretary in various councils, created and represented in his person the unity which enabled the various groups to function consistently.

Even Machiavelli, however, was not able to do other than seek a middle course between the desire of the republic to have an army and the fear of the republic of being swallowed up by its own army.

The first requirement for a useful militia would have been the closest possible mutual growth of the captain with his company. The men had to have confidence in their captain, and the captain had to know his men. What could not have been accomplished by captains who had accustomed their men to their command in this manner! To avoid such dangers, it was prescribed that the captains were to be transferred each year to another district, so that "their authority would not take root."

The captain, however, was to have no true power over his company. The militiaman who did not want to attend drill did not need any leave but only had to excuse himself in any kind of manner. The captain had no direct power of punishment but could only arrest men, on a temporary basis, in case of open mutiny. The power of punishment was in the hands of the governmental commissar and the authorities in Florence. A few captains once received the following written instructions:

> In consideration of the small compensation that our enlisted men receive for their trouble and discomfort in their training as members of the militia, we desire that they be treated humanely and corrected in a kind manner whenever in drill they make mistakes as a result of their inexperience. We desire this so that they will carry through with this work all the more gladly and with joyous hearts. For from the foregoing consideration, we consider this means to be the most effective to maintain their obedience and positive attitude toward this training. It appears to us that to bully and irritate them ("el bistractarli et exasperarli") would serve to produce the exact opposite. For this reason we have wished to exhort you to deal with them in a kindly manner ("*amorevolente*") and to take the trouble to maintain a good attitude in them. You must be careful to avoid everything that you know or believe could cause any kind of incident ("*disordine*").

Whereas the captain was a stranger who was assigned to the district by the authorities, the ensign and the corporals were respected local inhabitants. We find, however, that they were not assigned any military function, so that the actual management of the service rested on the captain alone.

Just as the captains had no effective agencies under them for the execution of their mission, so too was the militia as a whole lacking in a unified military higher command. The captains themselves told Machiavelli he should see to it that a colonel be appointed. And in fact Machiavelli did accomplish that one week before the final collapse. On 25 August 1512 Jacopo Savelli, a veteran Florentine condottiere of mounted units, was appointed as supreme commander, but he was no longer capable of saving the situation. If he had been able to do so and had succeeded in establishing discipline among the 20,000 militiamen, it would soon have been a simple matter for him to lead his units against the treasury of the tyrannical city and to place his boot on the paper on which the people's constitution was written, provided that he had not previously been assassinated (Hobohm).

After the foot militia was organized on an impressive scale, Machiavelli also put through the creation of a mounted militia at the end of 1510.

Machiavelli's militia existed for some seven years. It was used to subject the city of Pisa once again to Florence. Supplies to Pisa were cut off, and its harvest was destroyed twice annually right up to the city walls. This enforced starvation finally forced the city to surrender. But the militia did not have to stand a true test until a great league had formed in 1512 to restore the Medici family in Florence. At the head of this league were the Spaniards. It was the same Spanish infantry that had been defeated at Ravenna but despite this defeat avoided destruction because of its unbreakable cohesiveness. When these Spaniards crossed the Florentine border, the militia was called up. It would have been easy to send 12,000 men against the 8,000 Spaniards. But from the start it seemed to be an impossible risk to move against this experienced army in the open field. Consequently, the militia occupied Florence and the small town of Prato, some 9 miles north of the capital, which was initially threatened by the Spaniards. Prato still had the medieval defenses, a high, thin wall. An attempt by the besiegers to scale the wall with ladders was repelled. The Spaniards had only two siege cannon, and one of them exploded. With the one remaining cannon they shot a breach in the wall, or, as one source expresses it, more a window than a breach, a hole 4 meters wide and 2 meters high. The besiegers were already in extreme need because of a lack of provisions. If Prato had held out for two more days, the Spanish army would have had to withdraw and might perhaps have disbanded during its retreat. It was precisely this extreme need that drove the army to attempt the attack on the breach. The breach was not only small and so high that ladders had to be used, but it could also be taken under fire from a second wall behind it. But the Spanish harquebusiers moved up close to the city wall and covered it with such heavy fire that the defenders no longer dared to expose themselves in the crenelations. When the Spaniards, led by a few ensigns, were about to attack, the Tuscan militiamen took flight, and within a half-hour the town was conquered.

A frightful butchery followed, and not only murder but also rape and plundering. Those prisoners still alive, after they had given up everything, were tortured by the Spaniards for three weeks in order to force ransoms from their relatives living at some distance. The Florentines complained to the Spanish commander, Cardona, about the unprecedented size of the ransoms being demanded. He himself admitted that the demands were too high but said that he was powerless against his troops.

The fall of Prato was also the end of the Republic of Florence. It announced it was ready to receive the Medici again, and within a short time that family again had the reins of control in its hands. The militia, too, came to an end along with the republic.

The garrison of Prato was no smaller than 3,000 militiamen and 1,000 armed citizens. They all knew what was facing them if the Spaniards took the town. How was it possible, even if their warlike spirit and patriotism were not sufficient, that they did not gather enough combat strength to defend the breach in order to save themselves from the most horrible fate? After all, they were something more than a simple civilian levy. They had captains experienced in battle and were trained to a certain extent in the use of their weapons and maintaining their formation. But this is again a situation like that in the *Völkerwanderung*, where the richest provinces with millions of inhabitants fell victim to a few thousand Germans almost without opposition, and town after town went up in flames simply because that gave pleasure to the savage barbarians.

Machiavelli had studied the Roman military system, but, remarkably enough, he had not discovered the decisive concept, the Roman discipline. Discipline was, indeed, positively excluded as a result of his regulations that the captains had no direct power of punishment and it was not to be allowed that their authority should become rooted among the troops. Nothing is more interesting than to note from this point why Rome was able to become the greatest center of power and, on the other hand, Florence's attempt to do so failed so miserably. The city of Rome did not dominate its peasant population but formed a single unit with it. The peasants, together with the burghers, elected the authorities in the committees. In Rome, too, as in Florence, there was a certain suspicion of the city council, and for that reason there was no unified army commander; instead, the command was divided between two consuls. But from that point down, the authority of the empire ruled with iron might, supported by the religion and the system of auguries. The drilling of the centurion with his grapevine staff gave the Roman troops the steadfastness to withstand the Gauls and the Cimbri, a steadfastness that Machiavelli's militiamen were sadly missing in the breach of Prato.

The Swiss, the lansquenets, and the Spaniards were also lacking in the Roman discipline. What still made them irresistible in the heat of battle was their long-standing habit of maintaining their formation and, finally, the mutual trust that had developed as a result of their victories. Machiavelli was able to give his militiamen neither discipline nor the warlike spirit developed in battle itself, and he did not even recognize theoretically the value and the importance of either the one factor or the other. But let us not reproach him on that account. In his concept of the national army lay the vision of a prophet. It was impossible for the Florentine nation at the beginning of the sixteenth century actually to form such a popular army, because the basic organization was lacking, and the passage of centuries was necessary for the creation of that concept of discipline, at once brutal and ideal, which also forms a people's levy into a militarily useful body. But Machiavelli, by wishing to relate the infantry of the future to the Roman system, had a correct presentiment of this subject.

Basically, two precursors, from whom he also derived inspiration, came closer to the true target than Machiavelli himself. They were the condottiere Vitelli and Caesar Borgia, each of whom created in his territory a combination of a mercenary system and a militia, and the result was undoubtedly better than the pure militia of the Florentine. We may attribute that to the fact that Vitelli and Borgia were no idealists but practical soldiers. Primarily, they were at the same time general and lord in their territory. They did not have to fear, as did the Florentine citizens of the Council of 9 and the Council of 10, that, if their creation really succeeded, it could someday become dangerous to them, and so they did not weaken the military authority artificially but developed it according to the requirements of military necessity. Of course, their work, too, had no permanence, because the basis of their own ruling position did not withstand the storms of the times.

Just as Machiavelli's organization of the Tuscan militia was anything but irreproachable, so too did he have but little success in formulating an incontrovertible, consistent theory of strategy. Here too, we may say, he saw the problem of his period and in his pronouncements there was something that was prophetic but did not yet create a well-rounded theory.

The transition from the Middle Ages to the modern period was marked by the great increase in the means of waging war. The mighty combat squares replaced the small numbers of foot soldiers with close-combat weapons of the medieval armies. And the technology of the new firearms can be said to have increased from moment to moment. We might suspect that these increased military means in strategy led all the more quickly toward the final, powerful resort to battle, and we have actually presented as a matter of fact a series of the most excellent battle descriptions from a very short period of time. In the Middle Ages, even if the concepts of tactics and strategy were not to be eliminated in theory, one could speak of them only to a limited degree, in detail, under special circumstances, in particularly intensified moments. The knight was too much of an individual personality to have leadership, and his armament was too limited, so that first of all the concept of tactics becomes almost inapplicable, and without tactics there can be no strategy. The new infantry, combined with the new firearms of both large and small caliber and with the old form of mounted troops, both light and heavy, made possible an abundance of combinations with the changing terrain, possibilities for attack and for defense that were unknown in the Middle Ages. Can we perhaps be entering a period in which the general, like Alexander or Caesar, drives directly at his goal, breaks all opposition, and does not rest until he has imposed his will on the enemy?

Such is not the case. In the large battles that we have already examined more closely we have repeatedly had to point out in the end that the victory evaporated without lasting effects. There is something remarkably fortuitous, inorganic, in all these battles. How brilliantly the French had been victorious at Ravenna in 1512 with the help of their lansquenets, and yet it was not a full year until they had to evacuate Italy without being defeated in a battle. The victory that had the largest and most lasting effects, the victory of the imperial troops at Pavia, was, after all, not the reasonable result of a long-term, thoroughly developed strategic plan but the final and most extreme expedient in a desperate situation. Pescara expresses it as follows: "Would that God give me 100 years of war and not a single day of battle, but here there is no alternative." The new means of waging war, just as they had increased the power of the attack, had not only given the defense new means as well, but also had certain inherent weaknesses that could make it appear possible and advisable to overcome an enemy without the risk of a battle. Firearms could make a terrain obstacle impregnable. The new massed infantry units were often a very transient military tool precisely because of their massiveness. Superiority of numbers had always been one of the most important means of success. In the Middle Ages, however, numbers did not play such a decisive role, because everything depended on the quality of the individual warrior, and quality warriors were to be found only in certain limited numbers. But Swiss and lansquenets, once they were organized, could easily be increased with volunteers by assigning them to the mass, and it was, of course, the mass pressure that now gave the decision in battle. Consequently, the national war leaders strove for masses, not only up to the extreme limit of their finances, but even beyond. If they were not in a position to disburse the promised pay to the soldiers, they could hope to nourish the war itself on the war. The troops were reminded of the booty, and entire regions and cities were sacrificed to them to be plundered. This procedure had the most serious repercussions on the conduct of war itself, as well as on strategy. Sometimes the soldiers became impatient because they were not paid, and they demanded battle, whereas at other times, on the contrary, they refused to attack until they were paid. Principally, however, we find again and again that a general estimated that if he only waited, the enemy army would automatically break up because its commander would not be able to pay it any longer. That was such a tempting idea that it could no doubt seduce the general to the extent of not exploiting otherwise favorable opportunities for a battle but letting the campaign stretch out into a simple war of maneuver. In this manner, King Francis was close to victory at Pavia, but it was despair over that fact that drove the enemy to attempt the most extreme means. They attacked him in his secure position and conquered him.

For this kind of strategy, I have previously coined the name "strategy of attrition," or "bipolar strategy," that is, that strategy in which the general decides from moment to moment whether he is to achieve his goal by battle or by maneuver, so that his decisions vary constantly, so to speak, between the two poles of maneuver and battle, now swinging toward one pole and then to the other.

This strategy stands in opposition to the other one, which sets out directly to attack the enemy armed forces and destroy them and to impose the will of the conqueror on the conquered—the strategy of annihilation. We shall have further occasion to deal thoroughly with these two basic forms of all strategic action. But let us remain first of all with Machiavelli.

Often enough he makes statements proclaiming as the highest aim of military action the principle of defeat of the enemy armed forces in open battle. "The weight of warfare rests on open battles; they are the purpose for which armies are created." "Whoever understands well how to offer battle to the enemy can be pardoned other errors that he makes in the conduct of war." "The strategic style of the Romans consisted primarily in the fact that they conducted their wars, as the French say, briefly and stoutly." "Marching, fighting, and camping are the three principal activities of war." "Not gold, as the common opinion cries out, but good soldiers form the nerve of war; for gold does not suffice to find good soldiers, but good soldiers are capable of finding gold." "When one wins the battle, one must follow up the victory with all haste."

Machiavelli's logic borrowed these and similar statements from the concept of war, which he analyzed. But the practical aspects of the warfare of his period in no way reflected this picture, and in the theoretician of antiquity, Vegetius, he found completely different basic principles. He could not tear himself away completely from these impressions, and thus we find him writing, in contradiction to the foregoing tenets, also the statement: "Good generals fight battles only if necessity forces them to do so or the occasion is favorable." Or we find him explaining that one must not drive an enemy army into despair but must build golden bridges for it. Or we find an observation that the Romans after a victory did not pursue with the legions but only with light troops and horsemen, because the pursuer, in his disorder, can easily lose his victory. In one passage he says it is better to conquer the enemy by hunger than by iron, for victory depends much more on luck than on courage. Despite the huge battles that took place precisely during Machiavelli's lifetime (Agnadello, Ravenna, Novara, Creazzo, Marignano, Bicocca, Pavia [Machiavelli died in 1527]), the period was still completely imbued with the idea of the strategy of attrition.

In an instructional military poem that was supposedly given to Emperor Maximilian in his youth,[3] it is said of battle that one should not be ashamed to move back into a fortified position whenever the enemy is stronger. "Do not risk yourself and your men because of fame or anger. First consider carefully: if it may not be today, it can happen tomorrow."

Guicciardini praises Prosper Colonna, the victor of Bicocca, as being by nature very cautious and worthy of being called "*cunctator*" ("delayer").[4] He deserved praise, according to Guicciardini, for waging war more with his mind than with the sword and for showing how one defends nations without exposing oneself, except in dire necessity, to the chance of decision in battle and the fortune of arms.

Jovius writes in the same spirit:[5]

> When Duke Francesco Maria of Urbino had become supreme Venetian commander (1523), he moderated his earlier fiery eagerness for battle, as was unavoidably required by the conditions of the time and the habits of the wise senate, and turned to a healthier, carefully analytical deliberation. He intended preferably to hold off the mighty and unconquerable legions of foreign peoples than to challenge them to battle. For the fathers, aware of this through Alviano's double foolhardiness and defeat (1509 and 1513), preferred a general like Quintus Fabius rather than one like Marcus Marcellus. Such a man would best the enemy, and would keep him continuously worn down by the art of careful fortification of the camp, by unexpected attacks ("*extraordinariis proeliis*"), by cutting off his supplies and his money. At the same time, it would confidently be expected that he would accept a general battle ("*universum proelium*") in the open field as soon as that might become necessary.

The most noteworthy example of a campaign of maneuver in this period is perhaps the invasion by the imperial army in Southern France in 1524.

The animating spirit of the expedition was the constable of Bourbon, who, by his title, commanded the imperial army. He intended to march directly to Lyons, which he wanted to make the capital of his future kingdom. He had definitely in mind risking a battle against Francis I, who was concentrating his troops at Avignon. But when he was in Aix, Pescara, the real delegate of the emperor and the man with the most influence in the army, pointed out to him that Charles wanted to capture a French port such as England possessed at Calais, and this port was to serve as a support base for undertakings against France. There was not enough money for the quick fortification of Toulon, which was already being held. Bourbon had to go along with this, and they proceeded to besiege Marseilles. But when, after five weeks, a large breach had been shot in the wall and the constable was calling for an attack, Pescara again considered it too dangerous. The garrison, under the Roman Renzo da Ceri, showed that it was determined to defend the port to the utmost. A sufficient emergency fortification was erected behind the breach. "Whoever wants to eat supper in hell," said Pescara, "may attack!" Meanwhile, King Francis assembled a large relief army, but he did not attack the besiegers of Marseilles. Instead, he crossed the Alps and pushed into Italy. Now Bourbon also turned about, and the two armies made a forced parallel march over the mountains. The imperial troops arrived in Milan two days before the French, but they had suffered such great losses that they no longer dared to remain in the field and they were divided up among the strongholds. Ranke wrote:

> This mighty military force, which only a few months earlier appeared to intend to make the emperor the master of the world, had suddenly disappeared from the field. Master Pasquin in Rome expressed his opinion as follows, not without good humor: "An imperial army has been lost in the Alps. The honest finder is requested to turn it over in return for a good reward."

The French now had the task of conquering the strongholds. While they were besieging Pavia, a new imperial army came from Germany, and the knot was untied when Pescara and Frundsberg resolved to attack the besiegers in their fortified position. This decision, however, had in no way been a part of their plan. Instead, it was a last resort to save themselves from an otherwise hopeless situation. The campaign, which ended with the complete destruction of the French army and the capture of King Francis, therefore belongs, insofar as its plan and the ideas of the generals are concerned, in the strategy of attrition.

In Machiavelli's writings we find the principles of the strategy of annihilation and the strategy of attrition side by side but unbalanced. The logician and empiricist in him both have their say but have not yet found one another. For centuries the problem remained in this fluid condition. We shall not consider it again until we come to Frederick the Great.

It is extremely questionable that Machiavelli can be considered as a witness for the military system of his time. One might believe that a man of such sharp perceptiveness, a man who, as a result of his inclination and his position, was constantly pushed to concentrate his attention on warfare, who had traveled extensively in Germany, Italy, and France, and who also concerned himself with warfare in a practical way—that the statements of such a man on the actual conditions surrounding him would have a claim to unconditional reliability. But this is not the case. It can very often be proved that the strength figures he gives are false. He reports erroneously of the Swiss that they always placed one rank of halberds behind three ranks of spears.[6] While Machiavelli is also an observer, he is primarily a theoretician and a doctrinaire. Everything he saw and heard was immediately fit into the schematics of his theory, and whenever it would not fit, the facts had to give way before the theories. In places he also shows a remarkable lack of critical analysis, as, for example, when he blithely repeats some Frenchman or other to the effect that France had 1,000,700 parishes, and each parish provided one armed *franc tireur* for the king. But these are isolated examples of inattentiveness; much more serious are the distortions that result from his revulsion to the mercenary system and from a noteworthy division into armed and unarmed nations that he constructed for himself.

In antiquity we have a great author who, it seems to me, offers a certain analogy to Machiavelli. I am thinking of Polybius. He, too, combines the qualities of a high intellect, outstandingly placed powers of observation, and a strong inclination to theory. Whoever has been convinced by Hobohm as to how often and how extensively Machiavelli missed the mark in his statements on the warfare of his period will perhaps become even more careful with respect to Polybius than scholars have already become with the passage of time.

NOTES FOR CHAPTER VI

1. Guillaume, p. 165.

2. E. Fueter, in a review of Hobohm's work in the *Historische Zeitschrift*, 113:578, while recognizing the high value of the work, nevertheless takes exception in detail to many points, charges the author with a lack of methodological schooling and even insufficient knowledge of warfare and of the Italian language. I have checked on these accusations and have compared them with a handwritten countercritique by Hobohm. The result is that the reproach falls back on the critic. Even if all the details that he criticizes were real errors, in comparison with the stupendous scholarship and the critical perceptiveness with which Hobohm sweeps aside mountains of misjudgments appearing in the sources and constructs positive new knowledge, those errors would have very little significance. But my study shows that of all the objections and corrections made by Fueter, not even a single one—really not a single one—is justified. It is not that Hobohm's understanding of Italian is insufficient, but rather that Fueter did not know the differences between modern Italian and the Italian of the sixteenth century. It is not Hobohm who introduces erroneous material concerning the warfare of that time but Fueter. Let us give but three examples: Machiavelli recommends that in the selection of corporals for the militia it should be taken into consideration that they are acceptable to the other conscripts ("*scripti*"). Fueter is not familiar with this principle and this language. He claims he is bringing sense into this prescription by translating conscripts ("*scripti*") with the word "instructions" and says that Hobohm, because of what is actually his correct translation of the passage, is unknowledgeable. Furthermore, Machiavelli recruited his militia exclusively from the peasants of the subjected countryside, and not from the burghers. Fueter read

Hobohm's book so hastily that he attributed to these peasants the attitudes of the "Florentine merchant nation."

A third feature of Machiavelli's militia system was the fact that Florence did its best, even though not always with success, to prevent its subjects from going off as mercenaries, whereas in Switzerland and Germany that was officially permitted and often even more or less organized. Fueter had such little understanding of these opposite attitudes, which are explained by Hobohm in a very interesting and thorough manner, that he believes Machiavelli borrowed the official regulations for sending men off for mercenary service from the Swiss military system, and he attempts to correct Hobohm in this matter with strong emphasis. And thus it continues point by point, and I can only regret that the *Historische Zeitschrift* has misled its readers on such a basic work.

3. Jähns, 1:336.

4. *Historia d'Italia*, L. IX. Venice, 1562, p. 425.

5. Jovius, *Elogia virorum bellica virtute illustrium* (*Aphorisms of Men Distinguished by Military Virtues*), Basel, 1575, p. 323.

6. Hobohm, 2:457, 464. False army strengths for Novara and Marignano: *Discorsi*, 2:18. Also Escher, "The Swiss Foot Troops in the Fifteenth Century and at the Beginning of the Sixteenth Century" ("Das schweizerische Fussvolk im 15. und im Anfang des 16. Jahrhunderts"), *Neujahrsblätter der Züricher Feuerwerker*, 1904–1907, explains thoroughly that Machiavelli does not portray correctly either the armament or the formation of the Swiss.

BOOK II

The Period of the Wars of Religion

Chapter I

The Transformation of
Knights Into Cavalry[1]

We have found the change of warfare from the Middle Ages to the modern period based on the creation of an infantry—foot troops in tactical units.

In the course of the sixteenth century a similar procedure takes place among the mounted troops, the transformation of knights into cavalry.

The conceptual difference, as it has been repeatedly expressed, is that knighthood was based on qualified individual warriors, whereas cavalry consists of tactical bodies composed of horsemen. As certain as this difference exists in mounted troops as it does in foot troops, nevertheless there is less of an extreme in the polar opposites of the individual and the organization in the mounted troops. The external cohesiveness is more difficult to create and to hold in a mounted unit than among foot troops, and the combat of man to man was always carried out on a much larger scale by mounted troops than by foot troops. For the dismounted troops, this kind of combat often plays a minor role in comparison with the movements and the pressure of the masses. Consequently, we have, for example, left open the question as to whether the mounted troops of Alexander the Great are to be regarded as knights or as cavalry.

The change that we first observe in the transitional period is a sharper distinction of the armed branches already known to us among the horsemen. Whereas the primary medieval arrangement is that the knight, as principal warrior, was supported by light horsemen and marksmen and only seldom did the branches operate individually, we now find much more often that the three arms are organized independently and fight independently. In the battle of Ravenna in 1512, for example, the heavy horse on each side fought on one flank, while the light horse fought on the other flank.

Competent and useful light horsemen could not be found so easily in large numbers among the civilized peoples. First of all, the Venetians recruited for this purpose Albanians, the *stradioti*, who then also entered the service of one lord or another. We encounter them everywhere until the second half of the sixteenth century.

Similar to the *stradioti* were the hussars, Hungarians, who appeared in the fifteenth century and were more frequently named and praised in the sixteenth century, even in German wars.[2] They carried lance and shield.

Consequently, whereas the ability of the heavy horsemen was guaranteed by their knightly status, the light horsemen were recruited among half-barbarians, who in their savage condition showed a natural warlike spirit.

The marksmen gradually replaced their bows and crossbows with firearms, a harquebus between 2 1/2 and 3 feet long. Camillo Vitelli is thought to be the first person who organized mounted harquebusiers as a special fighting branch, in 1496. In Wallhausen and other sources we later find pictures of horsemen who are shooting with the harquebus at a full gallop; we can hardly imagine that they were supposed to have hit the mark.

Du Bellay's instructions (*Discipline militaire*) of 1548 distinguish four types of mounted men: the knights (men-at-arms), light horsemen (*chevaux légers*), *stradioti* (*estradiots* or *ginetères*), and harquebusiers.[3] The author adds that the young man could not become a horseman until he was seventeen years old, and then he could gradually move up in the sequence listed above from one armed branch to another, serving two or three years in each branch. He also stated that better and better horses were required in the same sequence. The knights were required to remain in service between three and four additional years. Then they were permitted to withdraw to the fief but had to be constantly ready to answer the levy.

In addition to these rather sharp distinctions between the mounted branches, however, we also still find in the second half of the century the combining of knights, marksmen, and lightly armored soldiers in units just as was the case in the old *compagnies d'ordonnance*. In du Bellay's instructions of 1548, 100 men-at-arms, 100 light horsemen, 50 mounted harquebusiers, and 50 *stradioti* were combined in one unit under a captain. When Henry II of France had overpowered the city of Metz, he held a large parade in 1552 before the city gates. An eyewitness, Rabutin, described it in his journal as follows:

The men-at-arms, 1,000 to 1,100 men strong, on large French, Spanish, or Turkish horses which were armored in the colors of the captains, and the knights were armored from head to foot and carried lance, sword, dagger, or hammer. Behind them came their support group of marksmen and soldiers, the leaders embellished in the richest manner in gilded and chased armor, with gold and silver embroidery, and the marksmen with the light lance, their pistol on their saddle, on light horses, and all of them as brilliantly arrayed as possible.

In the following year, 1553, the same Rabutin expressly reports (p. 594) that no special mounted companies of marksmen had been formed, but the king had ordered that each leader of a company of men-at-arms was also to recruit a corresponding number of mounted harquebusiers. They were said to be very useful whenever the knights came upon unfavorable terrain. But for a battle they were detached and combined in a special corps (p. 600).

If we replaced the harquebuses and pistols with crossbows, these descriptions could just as well be from the thirteenth century as from the sixteenth. We cannot trace directly any further development from this.

The sharper distinction between the mounted branches is only the result of a stronger need for light horsemen, who were capable of causing more damage to the strong infantry and artillery branches on the march by sudden attacks and pursuit than could the cumbersome knights. And in keeping with their larger number, they could now also act more independently in the battle.

Contrary to the sharper separation of the various mounted branches that we observe here, another process developed, namely a leveling movement, a closer approach of the knight and his support group toward a more similar type of armament, as knights, knightlike soldiers, and common soldiers were brought together in the same measure with a certain cohesiveness. We observe this development in the armies of Charles V during his last war against Francis I of France (1543–1544).

Jovius reports that, while the imperial forces were attacking Düren in 1543, two German infantry battle squares and two "quadrata equitum agmina" ("square columns of cavalry") had been formed to ward off a relief army.[4] In another passage he emphasizes the slow riding of the Germans (no doubt due to their closed formation).[5] A Venetian ambassador, Navagero, reported to his lord that the French were frightened by the steady approach ride of the German mounted troops (*cavalleria*).[6]

In the Schmalkaldic War, three years later, this phenomenon was even more definite.

A Venetian ambassador, Mocenigo, who was present during this war, distinguished two types of imperial horsemen, the men-at-arms and the marksmen (*archibusetti*). He reports that the latter wore armor, carried light lances and wheel lock pistols, stood close together, and maintained excellent order.[7]

The Spanish historian of these events, Avila, reports that the emperor's horsemen were drawn up in squares (squadrons) that were only seventeen ranks deep. He wrote:

This made their front very wide and showed more men, and that gave a very fine appearance. In my judgment, this is the better formation, offering more security, whenever the terrain permits it. For a squadron drawn up in breadth cannot easily be enveloped, something that happens without difficulty in the case of a narrow front. On the other hand, seventeen ranks in depth are sufficient for the shock, and such a squadron can stand up to another one. A clear example of this was seen in the battle that the heavy horsemen of the Netherlands fought against those of Cleves in 1543 at Sittard.

The order that the depth was to be *only* seventeen horses indicates that up to that point the horsemen had been drawn up in an even deeper formation. We have seen in the battle of Pillenreuth (1450) that the knights with their soldiers were drawn up with a breadth of about fourteen men and a depth of some twenty men,[8] and in a theoretical work from the year 1532 it is recommended that a formation of 6,000 horsemen be formed with a depth of eighty-three horses.[9]

Among the medieval horsemen we have found two basic formations: either the knights formed in a single rank and had the foot soldiers and marksmen follow (except when they moved out in front as skirmishers), or they were drawn up in a deep square. As fundamental as the difference between these two formations seems, it was not so in practice, since it is a question here not of battle formations but only of approach formations. In battle the deep square automatically spread out, and in the larger armies the formation of knights in a single rank was from the start not practicable.

In the document we have already cited, *True Advice and Reflections of an Old Well-tested and Experienced Warrior (Trewer Rath und Bedencken eines Alten wol versuchten und Erfahrenen Kriegsmanns)*, which was written in about 1522 and perhaps has as its author no less a person than Frundsberg,[10] "many squares and broad formations" are recommended, "so that many men can come into the encounter and the fighting, and the enemy will be attacked in the rear, in the front, and on the sides." In the same way Duke Albrecht of Prussia, who wrote an extensive work on warfare, a "war book" (finished in 1555), required in similar words "broad fronts and many small squares."[11]

One might think that these indications are actually to be conceived as truer precursors of the development of cavalry than those seventeen-deep squares of Charles V that always seem so astonishing. But such is not the case. The many small units of Frundsberg and Albrecht still belong in the sphere of knightly formations, simple approach formations, whereas the squadron that was seventeen horses deep contained a nucleus for further development.

The depth of seventeen horses was based on the computation, which was attributed to the duke of Alba,[12] that a horseman occupied about three times as much space in depth as in breadth, and that a front of 100 horsemen in seventeen ranks was therefore twice as wide as it was deep. Consequently, the *"agmen quadratum"* ("square column") of horsemen which Jovius reports had already been changed to a much shallower formation, which, as all reports unanimously emphasized, was maintained with great care. In order to accomplish that, they must have carried out drills, as the infantry had already done for a long time, and when a certain firmness and confidence had been attained in these drills, the depth was decreased further. In Tavannes we hear of a depth of ten horses,[13] and de la Noue seems to regard a depth of six to seven horses as normal for a squadron.[14] As the sixteenth century ends, therefore, we are approaching the formations of modern cavalry.[15] If that was satisfactory, why had this shallow formation not been adopted from the start? Presumably for the same reason that the infantry, too, began with the very deep square and progressed only gradually to shallower formations—that is, because the deeper masses could more easily be held together. Not until the drills and the related discipline had reached a higher degree was it possible to broaden the formations without sacrificing good order, and it was precisely for this reason that the squadrons of the Schmalkaldic War with their depth of seventeen ranks, and not the "many small units" of Frundsberg, are to be placed historically in the forefront of the development.

In the armies of the German princes who opposed the emperor in the Schmalkaldic War there still appeared the levied vassal or the recruited nobleman with a following of men armed in various ways.[16] Philip of Hesse considered it important to have as many nobles as possible as cuirassiers among his knights, but the simple mercenary horsemen that corresponded to those of the emperor were still larger in number. The feudal base that was still present did not prevent the horsemen of the Schmalkaldic army from also being noted for their ability and good order, especially in the excellent manner they obeyed the trumpet signals.[17]

All of this still appears to be very little, and we would conclude nothing further from it if we found similar reports about horsemen in the Middle Ages. The further developments, however, show us that we are in fact dealing here with the germ of something organically new.

The "Black Horsemen," as they were already called in the Schmalkaldic War, continued to exist just as the lansquenet bands did. Known for their plundering and mutiny, they appeared in both the external and internal wars of Germany under Albrecht Alcibiades,[18] now under Emanuel Philibert of Savoy, and now under Günther of Schwarzburg. The successors to these "Black Horsemen," in turn, were the "German Horsemen," who appeared on both sides in the Huguenot wars and who were called *"reîtres"* by the French, and *"raitri"* by the Italians. They are to be regarded as the fathers of European cavalry in the same sense that the

German Swiss are considered the fathers of European infantry. It was Germans who formed this new arm, but not on German soil. At that time Germany was enjoying the longest period of peace, more than sixty years, that it has ever been granted by world history, but France was filled with the thirty-year disorders of the Huguenot wars. Just as the wars of the French in the first half of the century had been fought mainly with the infantry of the Swiss and lansquenets, now principally German horsemen fought on the sides both of the Protestants and the Catholics. It was here on French soil that they developed the new method of mounted combat.

Following the example of these horsemen, the Spanish, too, created a national mounted force, which consisted of *herreruelos* or *ferraruoli*, designations taken from the short coat they wore, and they replaced the *stradioti*, who had still been used up to that point.[19]

The Spanish general Mendoza, who was present, reports that in the battle of the Mooker Heide (1574) the mounted squadrons of the squares rode up in such close formation that it was impossible to see through their ranks.[20]

Since, of course, the Middle Ages had also seen the approach ride to battle in close, deep units, the importance of the squadron formation depended on how firmly these tactical units were able to maintain their cohesiveness. This was now made significantly more possible, even though only indirectly, by the introduction of the new weapon, the pistol. In the 1550s the "Black Horsemen" still appeared with lances, but then this weapon disappeared and the German horsemen carried only pistol and sword, while the French knights, the men-at-arms, were still armed in the old manner with lances.

The wheel lock pistol that they used, also called a "little fist," was very long and heavy and had very uncertain ignition. The lock became clogged very quickly and was difficult to clean, and the flints wore out. But the pistol had the great advantage of being able to be manipulated with one hand, and the unreliability of its firing was compensated for by arming the individual with several pistols. The horsemen carried pistols not only in slings but also in their boots.[21]

Even if firing from horseback was not such a simple matter,[22] it still required much less practice than did the manipulation of the knightly lance. Furthermore, the man armed with pistols did not need as strong a horse as the knight did.

Wallhausen called the lance an offensive weapon and the pistol only a defensive one. This characterization becomes clear when we remember that the lance was 18 to 21 feet long,[23] and the pistol was effective at only a very short range. The instructions recommend firing only when one can almost touch his opponent. Since the armor could not be penetrated very easily, one should try to hit the horseman in the hip or to hit the horse in the shoulder or in the head. De la Noue says the pistol was effective only at three paces.

In the battle of Sievershausen in 1553, between Maurice of Saxony and Albrecht Alcibiades of Brandenburg, the elector himself reported in a letter to the bishop of Würzburg, written on the day of the battle,[24] that the horsemen of the two sides approached each other so closely that they could see the white of the enemy's eye. Then they fired their pistols (*sclopetos*) and dashed into the fight, and Schärtelin of Burtenbach says in his autobiography (p. 103): "In this battle the mounted marksmen caused great damage."

In order to make the most effective possible use of their pistols, the horsemen developed a maneuver of their own that we have already seen among the dismounted marksmen under the name of the "snail" ("*Schnecke*"; "*limaçon*") and that was most often called "*caracole*" among the horsemen. It was apparently not yet used in the battle of Sievershausen. I find the earliest mention of it ten years later in the account of the battle of Dreux (1562) in the memoirs of Marshal Tavannes.[25] He recounts that, since the time of Charles V, the pistol had been invented and the German nobles who served previously with the lansquenets had become mounted men and formed squadrons of fifteen and sixteen ranks. They had attacked with these units, but without penetrating. "The first rank turns toward the left, thus uncovering the second rank, which also fires" and immediately forms the snail in order to reload. The author adds, however, that at Dreux the horsemen did not need their flanking movements at all, since, with their deep squadrons, they had to deal only with French knights in the shallow hedge formation. When the French had also learned to form in squadrons, they easily defeated the horsemen, since they did not execute the caracole and turn about but penetrated into the enemy, and the rearmost ranks of the horsemen were composed only of common soldiers.

We also hear that these horsemen were trained by Maurice of Saxony and Albrecht of Brandenburg.[26] Their leader, the landgrave of Hesse, said that for his pay the warrior would attack once, for his country he would attack twice, and for his religion he would attack three times. At Dreux, however, the horsemen reportedly attacked four times for the French Huguenots.

I find the next mention of the caracole in the account of the battle of Moncontour, 1569, in the history of the civil war, from the pen of the Huguenot, de la Popelinière, which was published in Cologne in 1571.[27] There is a slight difference from the account by Tavannes in that de la Popelinière pictures the caracole as being made to the right or the left, depending on the available space, whereas Tavannes mentions only the wheel to the left, because the horseman was firing with the right hand. In a later passage he even says that only the left wheel was possible.[28]

De la Popelinière also points out that the best horsemen were carefully selected for the leading ranks and each casualty was immediately replaced by the next man in his file.

The caracole played a role well into the Thirty Years' War. In the drill instructions, which in this period grew to a literature in its own right, it is not treated as thoroughly as one might expect, since it might be presumed that the caracole appeared very impressive on the drill field but, like so many artificial movements, hardly practicable in actual combat.[29] In his *Discours* XVIII, de la Noue observes that the ranks farther to the rear also normally fired at the same time as the foremost ranks, that is, into the air, "just for the noise." I would therefore like to express the presumption that the significance of the often mentioned caracole is to be sought less in its direct, practical use than in the drill itself, that is, in the development of discipline that results willy-nilly from any regular drill. But it is precisely this development of discipline with which we are concerned at this moment of transition from knighthood to cavalry. It is clear that a captain of horse who has brought his unit to the point of executing an exact caracole has his men under control and has a truly disciplined troop. For this goal cannot be reached without much effort and work on the part of both men and horses, careful attention and will power, handling of weapons and habit. If the unit can execute the caracole with precise horsemanship and accurate firing, then it is a tactical body into which the individual horseman is integrated as a simple cog and whose head and soul is its leader, the captain.

The narrow limits of the practical use of the caracole are evident from the following considerations.

If a squadron executing the caracole clashed with horsemen who, for their part, were seeking a hand-to-hand fight and drove into the unit making the caracole, that meant the end of the complicated peeling off of the successive ranks, and the battle turned into a general fight, a melee. This is reported by Popelinière, and de la Noue even makes fun of this kind of combat, which he considers to be more reminiscent of the game of prisoner's base rather than suitable for war (*Discours* XVIII).

If the squadron encountered a closed body of foot troops while executing the caracole, it could cause great harm to the dismounted unit. This happened, for example, to the Swiss square in the battle of Dreux in 1562. But the infantry square was, of course, accompanied by marksmen, who, with their musket balls of much greater range and more reliable fire, were very superior to the short-range pistols and usually held the horsemen at a certain respectful distance. That is proven by Duke Henry of Guise, who was assassinated in 1588, when he said to Brantôme: "In order to defeat the *reîtres*, one must have a well-ordered troop of good musketeers and harquebusiers . . . ; this is the sauce with which one spoils their taste." He explains that it was in this manner that he was victorious over them in 1575 at Dormans (not far from Château-Thierry), even though he had only a few dismounted marksmen.[30]

Consequently, the caracole was best used in situations where the horsemen applied it on both sides, and then, of course, the outcome depended on which side carried out the maneuver the more smoothly and exactly—that is, which side was best trained and had the more reliable and better maintained pistols.

Since the horsemen fired with the right hand, they naturally executed the caracole better to the left. Therefore, Tavannes says (p. 118) it is wrong to place horsemen on the right flank because they would then cause disorder, as they made their caracole, among the troops on their left, whereas nobody would be affected by their caracole from the left flank.

The horsemen armed with pistols were called "cuirassiers," and that brought about a change in the meaning of this word.[31] Previously, it denoted the knight or the man wearing armor like the knight's. Now the "cuirassier" was a light horseman—that is, the opposite of the very heavily armored knight on a heavily armored horse. The latter were called men-at-arms (*gendarmes*), and we now find an army divided into men-at-arms, cavalry, and infantry.[32]

Although the cuirassiers were in no small part also nobles, they were preponderantly common mercenary soldiers and partially the men who formerly accompanied the knights, who, equipped with armor, attack helmet, and pistols, were part of the squadron in which the noblemen and the most trusted warriors formed the foremost ranks and the exterior files. Gradually, however, as a result of the cohesiveness in the squadron, the various elements blended into a homogeneous mass.[33]

But for a long time thereafter the commission that a general gave a colonel or a captain, authorizing the raising of troops, still remained different for the infantry and the cavalry. In the infantry each man was considered as an individual, whereas in the cavalry the feudal character, the knight with a number of followers, remained.[34]

Like the cuirassiers, the mounted harquebusiers were also assigned in squadrons, as we already found to be the case in the Schmalkaldic War, and they also executed the caracole.

In the middle of the sixteenth century the dragoons also became a special armed branch. In order to combine the advantages of the firearm, which, after all, could only be completely attained on the solid ground, with the advantage of the speed of the horse, infantrymen were given nags of little worth that were not satisfactory for an attack and could be abandoned without any great loss.[35] Dragoons, by their very concept, were therefore mounted infantry and they still wear the infantry helmet today, even though they were gradually transformed into cavalry.

Of course, the various mounted branches were not sharply distinguished, and, as we have just seen in the case of the cuirassiers, at various times the same names did not always have the same meanings.[36]

Wallhausen, in his *Art of Mounted Warfare (Kriegskunst zu Pferd)*, p. 2, says that the lancers and cuirassiers were heavy cavalry and the harquebusiers and dragoons were light cavalry. But the lancers could be both light and heavy.

To the best of my knowledge, the first rather large battle in which the victory of men armed with the pistol is positively reported took place at Saint-Vincent, not far from Nancy, on 28 October 1552. The German horsemen under Albrecht Alcibiades encountered French horsemen under Aumale. Both the light horsemen and the mounted harquebusiers, and finally even the men-at-arms, were forced to yield before the pistol balls of the German horsemen. Many horses were killed, and in the hand-to-hand melee a large number of prominent lords were also killed or captured. Aumale himself also received several pistol shots and was finally taken prisoner.[37]

In 1572 a Venetian ambassador, Contarini, reported back home that the French men-at-arms had declined in effectiveness. He reported that in battle with mounted pistol men they had first sought to strengthen their armor, carrying that to such an extreme that man and horse could no longer carry the weight. After that, however, a large part of the men-at-arms had adopted the combat methods of their enemies. Contarini added that the German lansquenets, who were previously so famous, had greatly declined in their performance, whereas the "cavalry of horsemen" gained new fame each day.[38]

The pistol, as a further development and new application of the firearm, aroused the aversion of the contemporaries, just as the cannon and the harquebuses had previously done. De la Noue called it devilish, and Tavannes complains how murderous battles had become because of it.[39] Formerly, he wrote, battles had lasted from three to four hours, and not 10 men out of 500 were killed; now everything was finished in an hour.

Nevertheless, the mounted squadrons of pistol men did not simply take the place of the knights with their supporting warriors, but instead the two combat methods confronted one another in a long struggle, both practical and theoretical. It was a double confrontation, intertwined within itself: on the one side the battle of the deep square of the squadron against the single line formation, the "hedge," and on the other side the struggle of the pistol against the lance. The authors often referred to them simply as the French and the German combat methods.[40]

At the end of the eighteenth century there arose once again a mounted branch with lances, the uhlans. Since they bore the principal weapon of the knights, one might be inclined to consider them as successors to the knights. But that was not the case; they were of Polish origin. The nature of events brought about the phenomenon that for several generations horsemen completely put aside the lance and then eventually took it up again, but only under completely changed circumstances.

Let us review the most important statements concerning the transition from the knightly combat methods to those of the cavalry, statements that are to be found partly in the authors of the Huguenot wars and partly in writings on military theory. Their diversity and their contradictions give a lively impression of the uncertain probings of the professionals.

The first important man who wrote about the problem of mounted combat in this period was Gaspard de Saulx-Tavannes (born 1505), who, as a page, was already fighting with King Francis at Pavia and fought in the Huguenot wars as a marshal on the side of the Catholics. He died in 1573. A work entitled *Teachings of a True Military Leader* (*Instruction d'un vrai chef de guerre*), which, on the basis of reports and perhaps also notes from the marshal, was published by his nephew, gives us hardly anything of value. But of importance and value are the memoirs that were written by his son Jean from his father's descriptions but that unfortunately, in view of the scattered military observations, cannot be identified as stemming from the father or the son. Since the father died in 1573, when the change was still in full development, that is a serious lack.

In Tavannes, p. 203, it is reported that the knights had their armor made heavier and heavier in order to protect themselves from the pistol balls. Against the heavy armor, however, the lance, too, was not effective. A light lance splintered without any effect, and a heavy one was so dangerous for its own bearer that he often preferred to let it fall rather than break.

The lance could only be effective at a full gallop on good terrain and when horse and rider were both fresh. The excessively heavy armor made its wearer incapable of fighting. For this reason Tavannes was opposed to lances and in favor of arming horsemen with pistols.

The *Memoirs* state that he first changed the tactical formation in the Catholic army in 1568, forming squadrons of pistol men like those of the *reîtres* and requiring that the men-at-arms form larger companies than previously, between 80 and 100 men instead of 30, and that they adopt the formation in squadrons instead of the "hedge" formation. He believed the squadron of 400 horsemen was the best. He wrote that the regulations of the *reîtres* called for squares of 1,500 to 2,000 horses but that these units would be defeated by three squadrons of 400 each. He believed that the excessively large square caused confusion and too few horsemen were able to use their weapons. He explained that the very large squares were formed by the *reîtres* because three-fourths of them were simple soldiers. For this reason, once their two leading ranks were penetrated, the rest of the formation offered little danger.[41]

On p. 291 he recounts that the *reîtres*, as a result of their formation in squadrons, had initially defeated the French men-at-arms. But as soon as the men-at-arms also adopted the squadron formation, they were victorious over the *reîtres* by attacking them strongly as they were executing the caracole.[42]

Tavannes therefore favors both the formation by squadrons and the pistol, but not the caracole. Instead, he requires that the attack lead up to the hand-to-hand melee and the penetration of the enemy formation.

Nevertheless, he considered the lance to be superfluous, and only his ebullient spirit and fame ("sa vogue"), as his nephew added, caused him to equip one rank in front and one on the right flank of the squadron with that weapon.

Tavannes raised the question (p. 116) as to whether it was better to go into combat at the trot or to await the enemy in place. Attacking would give horses and men more verve, but it would also give more opportunity for holding back to those who did not want to be involved in the melee. Consequently, he felt, at least in the case of new recruits or questionably reliable soldiers, it was better to await the enemy in good order or at any rate to go into the trot or gallop at a distance of only twenty paces, because the cowards would then hardly be able to abandon their posts and the captains would be able to force them to be brave, even against their wills.[43]

In several other passages (pp. 122, 123, 203–205), Tavannes comes back to the warning, discussed in detail and mixed with other observations, against attacking at a fast pace, because then the less courageous soldiers held back. A captain who covered fifteen paces at the gallop without paying attention to his soldiers ran the risk of attacking alone and being buried in the enemy formation. The cowards would stop their horses six paces in front of the enemy. But if they moved at a walk or a slow trot, the opportunity to exercise that dodge would be removed and the rearmost ranks would push them forward. He who attacked at a gallop would enter the fight with but few men, and they would be in disorder. Consequently, a squadron should march slowly, halt frequently, and the captains in front of the formation and at the corners should call to their men by name, and the first sergeants in the rear should drive the cowards forward. A leader who could depend on his men could take up the gallop at a distance of fifteen paces. And he who moved forward slowly and took up a brisk trot or a slow gallop at a distance of only ten paces from the enemy would not go into the clash alone.

As a counterpart to the advantage of attacking in tightly formed squadrons so graphically portrayed by Tavannes, let us repeat here an episode from the battle of Bicocca recounted by Reisner in his *Life of Frundsberg*. It proves that Tavannes was in no way exaggerating.

A French cuirassier, after the battle was engaged, dashed into Frundsberg's squadron, penetrating into the third rank, and as the soldiers were thrusting at him, intending to kill him, Frundsberg cried out: "Let him live." And when he questioned him through an interpreter as to how and why he had ridden into their midst so boldly, he answered that he was a nobleman and seventy of them had sworn that they would attack with him and strike the enemy. He had no other idea than that they were following close behind him.

In numerous passages Tavannes also recommends that the cavalry take position behind a terrain obstacle, such as a ditch, and await the enemy attack in place.

In many respects very similar to the observations of the Catholic commander, Tavannes, are those of a captain from the Huguenot ranks, de la Noue.

De la Noue (born 1531) had lost his left arm in a battle and replaced it with an iron one, so that the soldiers called him "iron arm" ("bras de fer"). While he was a prisoner of the Spaniards for five years (1580–1585), he wrote his famous twenty-eight political and military discourses, which were published in Basel in 1587.

He says that professional warriors agreed that a troop of lancers would necessarily defeat a troop of pistol men. He claims that Spaniards, Italians, and French all agreed on this point, but that the Germans thought otherwise. In a squadron of men-at-arms, even if it was composed of nobles, there were always some men of little courage, and if an attack was made in the "hedge" formation, holes opened up very quickly in the line. Even if the courageous men, who were normally in the minority, attacked energetically, the others, who had no desire to fight, remained behind. One would have a bloody nose, another one a broken stirrup, or another a horse that had lost a shoe. In brief, after moving 200 paces, one could see the long line thinning out and wide holes developing in it. That greatly encouraged the enemy. Of 100 horsemen, often not 25 actually clashed with the enemy, and when they saw that they had no support from the others, they would break their lances and make a few thrusts with their swords. Then, if they had not already been overpowered, they would turn back.

Consequently, the advantage of the reîtres lay in their tight cohesion. It was, according to de la Noue, as if they were glued together. Experience had taught them that the strong unit always defeated the weak one. Even if they were thrown back, they did not break their formation. But when they executed the caracole and offered their flank to the enemy at twenty paces in order to fire their pistol salvo, riding back then to the rear to reload or take up their other pistol, they were often defeated. For, after all, the pistol was effective only at three paces, and in order to throw back a whole unit, one had to attack it decisively.

De la Noue goes on to say that good order had to be maintained not only in combat but on the march as well. The French were lacking in this respect, whereas the Germans also insisted even on the march that each man remain in his place.[44]

If one objected that the formation in the "hedge" offered the possibility of enveloping the flanks of the enemy squadrons, still not much would be gained by this, since it was not possible to penetrate deeply into the thick square.

If the mounted lancers were again formed in greater depth, still only the leading ranks were capable of using their lances. The following ranks could do nothing with them in the melee, and there was nothing else for them to do but throw away their lances and draw their swords. In the hand-to-hand fight, however, the pistol man was the most dangerous combatant; while the lancer could actually execute only *one* thrust with his lance, the pistol man had six or seven shots, and the squadron was a mass of fire.

The preceding statements might lead us to believe that de la Noue was recommending that the lance be simply abandoned, that a tightly closed approach be guaranteed by a relatively deep formation, and that the decision in the melee be achieved by the pistol and without the caracole. But the conclusion of his repeated and detailed observations is not so clear. However strongly he emphasizes how much more fearful the power of the pistols was than that of the lance, he nevertheless values the lance and expressly protests that he does not want to abandon it. He does not recommend the pistol for the French nobleman in particular, for the latter would turn over its care and loading to his servant and then it would fail him at the decisive moment.

I shall now report what de la Noue says about the contemporary armor in his fifteenth discourse, as translated by Jacob Rathgeben in 1592. French nobles, he says, easily tend to exaggerate:

> The example that I wish to introduce is of the manner in which they now customarily protect themselves with armor. Now, if they perhaps have had good reasons, because of the danger and force of the pistol and musket, to have their armor made stronger and of better material than previously, they have nevertheless so greatly exceeded a reasonable measure in this that most of them have loaded on themselves, instead of armor, an entire anvil, so to speak. And with this the handsome aspect of an armored man on horseback has been changed into an ugly monster. For his helmet now resembles an iron pot. On his left arm he wears a large iron glove that covers his arm up to the elbow. On his right arm he wears such a poor arm guard that only his shoulder is protected by it. And ordinarily he wears no cuisses. Instead of a blouse, he wears a small round

bell jacket, and he carries no spear or lance. Our cuirassiers and light horsemen under King Henry in other times were much more handsome and pleasant to see. They wore their helmets, arm cuisses and greaves, and their blouses, and they carried spear and lance with a banner streaming from the top. This entire armor was so flexible and light that a man might easily wear it for twenty-four hours. But the armor that is commonly worn today is so uncomfortable and heavy that a nobleman thirty-five years old becomes paralyzed in the shoulders under such a heavy burden. In earlier days I have seen the Sire Eguilli and the knight Puigreffier, two honored and famous old men, ride along in front of their companies for a whole day, armored from head to foot, whereas now a much younger captain is either unwilling or unable to remain in such a situation for only two hours.

In *Discours* 15, p. 345, de la Noue says that some people raise the objection that in the "hedge" formation every man enters the fight, whereas in the squadron only one-sixth at most—that is, those in the front ranks—are in contact with the enemy. But, says de la Noue, it is not a question of the success of the individual, but rather a matter of breaking up the enemy formation, and that is done by the squadron. It throws back the enemy line at the point where the standard or the captains and best men are posted, and with these the whole formation is broken up. In a squadron the bravest men are placed in the first rank, and brave men will also be available for the second rank. The rest of the men then feel protected and follow along, for the leading men accept the danger when their side is victorious but all the men participate in the fame. A hundred well-armed and well-led soldiers in squadron formation would defeat 100 nobles drawn up in the "hedge."

But even de la Noue favors retaining the "hedge" formation in two special cases, namely, when a small detachment is fighting separately and when one is attacking infantry and detaches units that are to attack simultaneously from different directions.

Blaise Monluc (died 1577), who rose from a private soldier to marshal of France, in his *Memoirs* of the year 1569 praises the military efficiency of the *reîtres*, who did not let themselves be taken by surprise, maintained their horses and weapons in good condition, and were awesome in combat. In battle one saw among them nothing but iron and fire, and every stable boy was equipped and developed into a warrior.

The most important Spanish military theorist of the period was Bernardino Mendoza, who wrote in 1592 a history of the war in the Netherlands and whose *Theory and Practice of War (Theorie und Praxis des Krieges)* appeared in 1595 and was also translated into German a number of times.

Mendoza gives no definite prescription for the depth of the squadron formation, but he assumes that a commander will choose a broader or deeper formation, depending on the circumstances. In any case, however, he holds that the ratio of one to three should not be exceeded (*Theorie*, I, Chap. 42).

With respect to the question as to whether the lance or the pistol is preferable, Mendoza favors the lance (I, Chap. 44, Chap. 49). A company of lancers of 100 or 120 men could, according to him, overcome 400 to 500 *ferraruoli* if they attacked furiously and from several directions simultaneously. He adds, however, that one would do well to have the lancers supported by mounted harquebusiers or pistol men on their left flank (Chap. 43). If so many were favoring the pistol men, the reason was that this armed branch required much less practice than the lancers and was consequently much easier to establish, from the viewpoint of both men and horses.[45]

In his account of the battle on the Mooker Heide in 1574, which is not completely clear in other respects, Mendoza explains that the squadrons of lancers should not be stronger than 100 to 120 men, and they had to attack vigorously; then the pistols of the *reîtres* would be of little use in the melee.[46]

Georg Basta, born in Italy in 1550 as the son of an Epirote nobleman, commanded at a young age a regiment of Arnauts under Alexander Farnase, became a Spanish general, commanded an imperial army against the Turks, and, in addition to a work on the general-field colonel (*il maestro di campo generale*), he wrote a work of his own on light cavalry (1612), which also appeared in German translation in several versions.

Like Tavannes, Basta believes that a unit in combat is to be held together not only in its courage but also through strictness. In his Book 4, Chap. 5, he prescribes that, when going into an encounter, the captain should ride two or three horse-lengths in front of his company, whereas the lieutenant, with his drawn sword in hand, should ride behind the squadron in order to kill on the spot, if necessary, "anyone who did anything improper."

In a special chapter at the end of his work, Basta compared the advantages of the cuirassiers and the lancers and decided in favor of the cuirassiers. He wrote that lancers needed very good horses, much drill, and firm ground. Only the two leading ranks could bring their weapons into play, and consequently it was necessary to divide them into many small squadrons that attacked separately. But now it is not clear from this why the cuirassiers should actually be the superior arm. The author contradicts himself repeatedly and finally is even unclear as to whether he is actually talking about the heavy knightly lancers or the unarmored, light mounted lancers.

This ineptitude in Basta's discussion provoked the most famous theorist of the period, the colonel of the guard of the city of Danzig, Johann Jacobi von Wallhausen, to oppose him with sharp polemics in his work *The Art of Mounted Warfare (Kriegskunst zu Pferd)*, 1616. He scornfully derides the theories of Basta, the excellent cavalryman (who spent forty years in the cavalry and made it his profession), and he emphatically takes the side of the lance. Both authors agree that lancers should attack in small units and no deeper than in two ranks, indeed with an interval between these two. Wallhausen says (p. 21):

> The lancer gains his effectiveness in small squadrons and at most in two ranks, and a good interval should be left between these two ranks, which should not be in close formation. If a horse stumbles or falls in the attack, it cannot cause trouble or delay the following soldier but can get up again and rejoin its squadron's formation.
>
> But the cuirassier, who must keep in position in large squadrons in tight formation, close beside and behind his neighbors, cannot recover alone if a horse in the two leading ranks stumbles or is wounded by the enemy. Even if the rider is not yet wounded, he cannot get up, but all the men following him in his file crash into him and fall with their horses on him. Consequently, many a cuirassier runs greater danger to his life from being trampled by the horses of his following comrades than he does from the enemy. For if only one man in a forward rank or in the middle falls, the following man can move neither to the right nor the left nor to the rear nor forward, but he is pushed ahead by the man behind him, who does not see or know of the fall. Consequently, many a healthy, unwounded man and horse falls over another, is crushed and is killed. That is, more damage is done to them by this crushing, as this misfortune also tends to break up the squadron and throw it into confusion more effectively than is accomplished by the enemy. This situation has undoubtedly been experienced and witnessed more than one thousand times by Mr. Basta, just as I have seen this confusing example with my own eyes and could thus describe it. I believe, therefore, that the lancer has a greater advantage than the cuirassier in this situation as well.

Wallhausen goes on to say (p. 31) that if the lancer's good horse and lance are taken from him and he is given a smaller horse, he then becomes a cuirassier. Therefore, the latter is nothing more than half a lancer, so to speak.

In a later passage (p. 32), Wallhausen even claims that the second rank of horsemen is even harmful for the first rank, because it prevents the leading rank from being able to withdraw to the right or left in case its attack fails. Consequently, if the space is not sufficient for the whole unit to be drawn up in a single rank, the following ones should maintain a distance of twenty to thirty paces.

In this dispute an important point is missing on both sides—that is, the caracole. In order to judge the comparative advantages and disadvantages of the pistol and the lance, one would have to consider that the lancers made a real attack, while the pistol men in fact only skirmished. The latter, therefore, would necessarily be overcome. But not only Basta says nothing about this, but also Wallhausen fails to mention it, and it is precisely on this point that he could have found the strongest argument for his concept. But both of them are weak in their logic and did not understand the true sequence of the development.

When Wallhausen wrote these observations in 1616—indeed, even when Mendoza championed the lance in 1595—this arm was already essentially discarded.

Even if Wallhausen is undoubtedly objectively correct with his reasons, we ask all the more why the lances were discarded and the cuirassiers were historically victorious. Wallhausen himself has to admit that the great military leader of his time, Maurice of Orange, had done away with the lances, which he had inherited from his father, William I, and Wallhausen does not know why this was done.

Once again, then, we have here the not so infrequent case of eminent practitioners who attempt to grasp theoretically the problems of their period and do not succeed. They are still not able to explain clearly and logically the things that they see and understand. Basta comes closer to the matter when he remarks that there is much less to a cuirassier than to a lancer, since the cuirassier needed nothing more than to be able to wear his armor and ride along in the mass formation. Wallhausen replies: "There are more yokels who can ride than there are well-drilled mounted gentlemen and knights. Therefore the yokels have the advantage over the knights." Actually, Basta, according to his wording, was reasoning illogically. But he would have stated the correct and accurate point logically and historically if he had concluded that the lancer, especially if he were also equipped with pistols in addition to the lance, formed in his two ranks and small squadrons, was superior to the deep unit of cuirassiers, assuming equal numbers on both sides. But for lancers one depended on noblemen or other outstandingly skillful warriors, and there were always only a few of them available. On the other hand, the demands made on the cuirassiers, both man and horse, were so much smaller that it was possible to assemble a much larger number. As a result of this numerical superiority they would defeat the lancers, despite the lancers' higher quality and better formation.

The struggle between the "hedge" and the squadron, between lance and pistol, was therefore not simply a technical confrontation, but two periods were struggling with one another. At this point there is actually once again a small grain of truth in the legend that the Middle Ages were conquered by the firearm. But the ways of historical development are often not direct but very devious and tortuous. The direct development from knighthood to cavalry would have required a lightening of the knightly armor, faster horses, and discipline. Instead, however, we find that the truly knightlike combat method, the attack with the couched lance, disappeared completely and was replaced by a type of combat that seemed to be the direct opposite of everything associated with cavalry: thick, deep masses moving slowly, or even awaiting the enemy in place, and armed with the pistol instead of cold steel.[47] But as uncavalrylike as all that was, it was still the only way to attain what was lacking in knighthood and what could not possibly develop directly from the knightly system—the disciplined tactical body. From this viewpoint let us glance back once again into the Middle Ages in order to be convinced how wrong those men are who claim to see cavalry in the groups of knights.

From this comparison we can now see clearly why the history of cavalry had its beginnings in the very deep squadrons. The thicker the masses were, the more awkwardly they moved, but also the less skill was needed to form them. The more skill and discipline progressed, the more shallow the formation gradually became. Cavalry was no progressive development of the knightly method but a new system that replaced the knightly one.

Since we, of course, have already encountered the deep formations in the Middle Ages and they automatically occurred wherever a number of knights, each with his following of armored mounted soldiers, moved together into combat, one may trace, if one wishes, transitional forms much farther back than I have done above. But it was not until the middle and the third quarter of the sixteenth century that the actual transition took place and something new replaced the old method.

The change of the times is reflected very well in an observation concerning the mounted art in Tavannes' *Memoirs*, p. 204, which apparently stems from the younger Tavannes. The "six volts," he says, were necessary as previously, for combat in the "hedge" formation with lance and sword, but these skills were not necessary for the modern soldier. Men and horses could now be trained for battle in three months. The art of horsemanship, according to him, only lured men into a trap and was superfluous except on those occasions when cavaliers wished to fight a duel on horseback. Even the Jesuits were now learning in three years what had previously required ten years, and eventually one would arrive at a still shorter period.

For a time the two methods confronted each other harshly. In the Huguenot wars the French still fought as knights, but both the Catholics and the Protestants brought in German horsemen as support troops, and these mounted Germans on French soil developed the system of the new cavalry. The French knights formed a material that was too stubborn to accomplish this. As our sources agree in pointing out, they were too proud to let themselves be drawn up in squadrons, for each man wanted to stand in the first rank. Nobody wanted to allow another to be in front of him, and they all hated the pistol. Both discipline and weapon contradicted the knightly system. But the common mercenaries were willing to be formed in ranks, and with their mass they now overpowered the knights.

With the formation of the closed squadrons, there naturally also disappeared the mixed combat, the support of horsemen by accompanying foot troops. The last examples of which I am aware are recounted by Jovius for the year 1543 before Landrecy.[48]

In the last battles of the Huguenot wars, Coutras in 1587 and Ivry in 1590, the new arm, as we may express it, the cavalry, was so broadly developed that the infantry, which had played the primary role since the appearance of the Swiss, now had to fall back again. It is Henry IV of France who as a general may lay claim to the fame of correctly understanding and fully exploiting the new force. Although at Coutras his horsemen were less numerous, he was still victorious by having his mounted men supported by marksmen, holding together his closely formed units, and leading them effectively, whereas on the Catholic side the nobles still fought in the knightly manner without leadership. At Ivry Henry showed the same tactical superiority, further enhanced by a pursuit that stretched out for miles.

More than 200 years later it happened that once again knights and cavalry took the measure of each other. When the French under General Bonaparte planned to conquer Egypt in 1798, the Nile region was governed by a warrior caste, the Mamelukes. They fought on horseback, wore shirts of mail and helmets, were armed with a carbine and two pairs of pistols, and each of them had several servants and horses to support him. Despite their firearms, we can therefore call them knights, and Napoleon said that two of them could cope with three Frenchmen, but 100 French had nothing to fear from 100 Mamelukes, 300 French were superior to an equal number of Mamelukes, and 1,000 French would defeat 1,500 Mamelukes without fail. While no real test of this theory was carried out, since the French had not transported any true cavalry overseas, the description from this source gives us a very vivid outlook on the difference between the knight, the qualified individual fighter, and the tactical body of cavalry.

EXCURSUS

CONCERNING HERMANN HUGO

The work of the Jesuit Hermann Hugo, *De militia equestri antiqua et nova libri quinque* (*On Ancient and Modern Cavalry, 5 Books*), Antwerp, 1630, is a scholarly, well-organized compilation. I am adding a little to what Jähns, 2:1057 (para. 79), has to say about it, partially to show how little even contemporary authors understand about giving us a correct description.

Book III, Chap. 4, p. 184: the "cuirassiers"—*Quirassarii* or *Corassarii*—took the place of the lancers—*lancearii*; "hoc solo ab his differunt, quod sclopo utantur pro lancea, et gradario succussarioque equo pro expedito" ("They differ from these in this respect alone, that they use a pistol instead of a lance and a trotter instead of a charger"). (*gradarius*: [horse] moving step by step; *succussarius*: [horse] hitting hard; we are reminded of the "German trot").

Book IV, Chap. 5, p. 257: although Hugo said earlier (Book III, Chap. 4) that the cuirassiers (pistol men) had replaced the *lancearii*, he still assigns a significant role to the *lancearii* in his theory. He characterizes *lancearii* and *arcabusarii* as eminently suitable for the attack, whereas he believes the cuirassiers were effective defensively.

For the *lancearii* it is required that always only one rank is to *incurrere* (charge); otherwise, they would interfere with one another. Nevertheless, he says that they can be drawn up in as many as eight ranks, one behind the other, and can be sent in turn into the attack (p. 258; not up to *four* ranks, as Jähns says on p. 1058).

When he goes on to recommend forming two ranks for the attack "quasi in quincuncem" (as if in checkerboard formation), that is, with the second rank covering the intervals of the first, that is a slight improvement over the attack in a single line.

For the harquebusiers, he claims the caracole as the proper combat form against infantry. He pictures the horsemen handling their ramrods as they sprung back. Furthermore, he draws a distinction between the caracole against the front of the enemy infantry unit and the caracole against its flank. In the illustrations he shows the caracole being executed only to the left and only the right flank of the enemy being attacked. He does not have mounted harquebusiers carrying out the caracole against similarly armed opponents but has them only fire from the front (p. 268).

In accordance with the descriptions of other authors, he has the various mounted arms combined for all kinds of intricate battle formations.

In the following chapter (Book IV, Chap. 6) Hugo also speaks of combining cavalry and infantry. But almost all of his sources are only ancient authors. The only difference he points out between antiquity and his epoch is the fact that the mixed combat has disappeared, and he regrets that very much. He says that the loss of this art is obviously due to the fact that much drill was required for mixed combat; the ancients had carried that out, but not the men of more modern times.

CONCERNING THE EFFECTIVENESS OF THE LANCE

Interesting points have been made on this subject by Dr. Major Friedrich Schäfer in a document entitled *The Lance. An Historical and Military Medical Study*. Special reprint from the *Archives for Clinical Surgery* (*Archiv für klinische Chirurgie*), Vol. 62, Book 3. The German lance weighs 1.85 kilograms and is 3.20 meters long; it has an iron point 13 centimeters long.

General Sparre and General de Brack stated in a French commission study that the lance was much less deadly in combat than the straight saber. The wounds it caused were almost always light ones. The mounted lancer, they said, could not thrust with his whole strength, since he would fall from his saddle. The thrusts were inaccurate because of the movement of the horse and because they were easy to parry and to avoid.

As the result of a statistical medical study, Schäfer comes to the same conclusion. The tissues give way before the penetrating lance, and it is deflected by the bones. Consequently, these wounds heal easily and quickly. Schäfer says that the preconceived notion to the opposite effect, that is, that thrust wounds are particularly dangerous, is false. Nevertheless, it depends on the shape of the lance; if it also cuts at the same time with its edges, the wound is much more dangerous.

NOTES FOR CHAPTER 1

1. George T. Denison's *History of the Cavalry from the Earliest Times, with Observations Concerning Its Future (Geschichte der Kavallerie seit den frühesten Zeiten mit Betrachtungen über ihre Zukunft),* (German version by Brix, Berlin, 1879) has no scientific-historical value.

2. Concerning the dispute over the explanation of the name, see Mangold in the *Jahresbericht der Geschichtswissenschaften,* 3(1892): 247. The hussars are mentioned quite often in the Küstrin Battle Report on Mühlberg in Ranke, *Werke,* 6:244–246, and in the report of the Nuremberg participant in the war, Joachim Imhof, in Knaake, *Contributions to the History of Charles V (Beiträge zur Geschichte Karls V.),* Stendal, 1864, p. 46. Of particular interest is Avila, *History of the Schmalkaldic War (Geschichte des Schmalkaldischen Krieges),* German edition, p. 123. According to Susane, 1:150, there had been Hungarian cavalry in France since 1635; in 1693 a regiment of hussars was formed.

3. See Jähns, 1:498, concerning this book. Hauser, in *Les Sources de l'histoire de France,* 2:25, rejects du Bellay as the author and says, probably correctly, that the edition of 1548 was the oldest (Jähns assumes 1535). A very large part of the contents, but not the passage above copied from Vol. I, Chap. 8, is taken from Machiavelli. See Gebelin, *Quid rei militaris doctrina renascentibus litteris antiquitatis debuerit (What Military Doctrine Owed to the Renaissance),* Bordeaux, 1881, p. 44.

4. Jovius, Book 44, Ed. 1578, p. 555.

5. Book 45, p. 610.

6. *Report of the Venetian Ambassador Navagero of July 1546 (Bericht des venezianischen Gesandten Navagero vom Juli 1546),* in Albèri, Series I, Vol. I, pp. 314, 328. He also describes the arms of these horsemen (p. 314). The pistol, which another report shows them as having (Ranke, *Werke,* 4:223), is not yet mentioned in this report.

7. Alois Mocenigo, *Relazione di Germania,* 1548. Ed. Fiedler, *Fontes rer. austriacarum (Sources of Austrian History),* 30:120, Vienna, 1870.

8. Vol. III, Book 3, Chap. 2, p. 289.

9. Jähns, 1:740.

10. See the detailed extract in Jähns' *Geschichte der Kriegswissenschaften,* 1:474.

11. Jähns, 1:521.

12. Napoleon III writes in his article entitled "On the Past and Future of Artillery" ("Du passé et de l'avenir de l'artillerie"), *Oeuvres,* 4:200:

Saint-Luc says in his *Observations militaires* that the duke of Alba, having found the squadrons of the *reîtres* too deep, wanted to form his own men with their front twice as wide as their depth. In this way, supposing that each horse would occupy a space of 6 paces by 2, he estimated that a squadron of 1,700 horses in seventeen ranks would occupy a rectangle of 102 paces by 204.

The passage by Saint-Luc does not yet seem to have been printed.

13. Edited by Buchon, p. 122.

14. That may be concluded from *Discourse XV* (Ed. 1587, p. 345), where it is assumed that a victorious squadron would still only directly throw back fifteen or sixteen of the enemy drawn up in line, that is, with a normal strength of 100, one-sixth or one-seventh of the total. See *Discourse XVIII.*

15. Napoleon III, in the work cited in Note 12 above, says that Henry IV had squadrons of 300 to 500 horses, which were drawn up in five ranks. He states that Montgomery required that the men-at-arms were to form in ten ranks and the light horse in seven. Billon, in *Les principes de l'art militaire*, German edition, p. 254 (1613), would have the squadron formed with a depth of five ranks, "for the horses do not press one another strongly."

16. Georg Paetel, *The Organization of the Hessian Army under Philip the Magnanimous (Die Organisation des hessischen Heeres unter Philipp dem Grossmütigen)*, 1897. See especially pp. 38, 40. See also Jovius, Book 34, p. 278, concerning Spanish armor.

17. According to the reports of the Venetian ambassador Alois Mocenigo, who accompanied the emperor. Fiedler, *Fontes rer. Austriacarum*, 30:120. *Venetian Dispatches from the Imperial Court (Venetianische Depeschen vom Kaiserhof)*, published by the Historische Kommission der Akademie der Wissenschaften, Vienna, 1889, 1:668, 670–671.

18. They are first mentioned in Avila, *Schmalkaldic War*, German edition, 1853, p. 58. First edition, Venice, 1548, p. 34. In a letter dated 6 November 1552, Lazarus Schwendi refers to the horsemen of Albrecht Alcibiades as "black horsemen." Voigt, *Albrecht Alcibiades*, 2:8. In 1554, 1,500 "black horsemen" appear in the imperial camp before Namur, all with pennons on their lances. *Anonymous Journal* (1554–1557), edited by Louis Torfs, *Campagnes de Charles-Quint et de Philippe II*, Antwerp, 1868, pp. 23–24. There are numerous references in this journal to their mutinies. In 1554 there appears on the emperor's side "un ost de reistres" ("a host of *reîtres*") of 1,800 to 2,000 horses under Count Wolfram von Schwarzenburg. Rabutin, *Commentaires* L. VI, Ed. Buchon, 1836, p. 620: "In order to intimidate us, they had all made themselves black like handsome devils." For the campaign of 1558, Henry II, looking back to

the experiences of the previous year at St. Quentin, ordered the recruiting of as many *reîtres* as possible.

> . . . because, the previous year, the largest strength that his enemy (Philip II) had and which was estimated as giving him the advantage, was by means of these *reîtres*, who have since been called "black armor," all of whom being armed with pistols, furious and frightening firearms, seemed to have been invented for the amazement and the breaking up of the French men-at-arms. And yet, in order to take as many of them as possible away from his enemy and to accustom and teach the French how to use such arms with confidence, he wished to draw them into his service.

Rabutin, L. XI, Ed. Buchon, 1836, p. 738. The first German pistol men in French service appeared, as best I have found, in 1554 (Rabutin, p. 605). Susane believes they appeared still earlier. Rabutin, p. 701, makes a distinction in 1557 in the French army between men-at-arms, cavalry, and *reîtres*. The expression "horsemen" (*"Reiter"*) for cavalry, apparently with the intention of indicating something specific, appears in Marino Cavallis, *Relazione da Ferdinando Re de Romani*, 1543. Ed. Albèri, Series I, Vol. III, p. 122.

19. They are mentioned for the first time in an account of 1559, where they are given very little praise. *Relation de Michel Suriano*, made on the return from his ambassadorship to Philip II, in 1559. Gachard, *Relations des ambassadeurs vénitiens sur Charles-Quint et Philippe II*, Brussels, 1856, p. 116.

Clonard, 4:155, places their first mention in the *Ordinanza* of 1560.

20. *History of the Netherlands War (Geschichte des niederländischen Krieges)*, Book II, Chaps. 11, 12.

21. Mocenigo reports to the doge on 4 September 1546: "The imperial mounted troops fear their enemies very much, both because of their numbers and their excellent horses and because many of them have three small wheel lock harquebuses, one on the saddle, another behind the saddle, and the third in a boot, so that it is said of these light horsemen that in skirmishes they always consider themselves secure, because having dealt with their enemies with one harquebus, they seize another, and many times, even when fleeing, they put it on their shoulder and fire to the rear." *Venetianische Depeschen vom Kaiserhof*, Vienna, 1889, 1:670–671.

A similar report is made by Federigo Badoero (*Relazione di Carlo V e di Filippo II*, 1557. Ed. Albèri, Series I, 3:189–190) about *ferraruoli* who were equipped with four or five pistols.

22. In the "Recollections of an Old Officer" (Feuilleton of the *Post* of 21 May 1890) we read:

At that time (1847), it was still the practice to target-shoot from horseback, a frightful maneuver during which very few horses stood still. A noncommissioned officer would hand the loaded pistol, provided with a fuse, with the greatest care to the mounted horseman. Now the horseman was to ride a volt, halt in front of the target, and fire. But as soon as the horse noticed that the rider had a pistol in his hand, he usually started to buck and jump, and the horseman, his mount, and the bystanders were all most seriously endangered. And it then sometimes happened that the horse was shot in the ear. But now it happened that our good first lieutenant, von B., had an old sorrel mare named Commode, and whenever he was in charge of the practice firing, the whole platoon, one after the other, climbed aboard Commode, who stood quietly, and each man fired his shot accurately. Now this foolishness has been abandoned and the firing is done only in a dismounted position, although, of course, signal shots by mounted scouts are not excluded.

23. Wallhausen, *Kriegskunst zu Pferde*, p. 6.

24. Mencken, 2:1427.

25. Ed. Buchon, p. 291. On Tavannes, see p. 127, above.

26. I have just received a study by R. Friedrichsdorf on Albrecht as a leader of mounted troops (Berlin dissertation, 1919). It contains new and very valuable material.

27. In the second edition of this work, Basel, 1572, the description is somewhat expanded (Book IX, Fol. 309), but without adding anything of significance for us. Lancelot Voisin, Sire de la Popelinière, came from Poitou and was a student in Toulouse when the news of the blood bath of Vassy became public. He immediately took command of a Huguenot company of students, was eventually incapacitated as the result of a wound, and thenceforth he took up the pen.

28. In the account of the battle of Ivry, p. 386. Since this battle did not take place until 1590, it is the younger Tavannes who is speaking here.

29. In the fourth chapter of Book 2 of his *Kriegskunst zu Pferde*, p. 65, Wallhausen describes the execution of the caracole but without using that name. It is also described by Grimmelshausen in *Simplizissimus*, Ed. Gödecke, 1897, Vols. 10, 11, p. 36.

30. Brantôme, *Oeuvres*, Edit. Lalanne, 1864 ff., 4:201. See also 3:376. In Vol. I, pp. 339–340, he mentions this example in the same sense and speaks of the battle of Aulneau (1 November 1587) as a parallel.

31. At the base of this is the Italian "*corazza*," which is derived from "*corium*," "leather."

32. For example, Villar's *Mémoires*, L.X., Ed. 1610, p. 901; this appears to be for the year 1559, according to a contemporary document.

33. In the sixteenth century a certain Count Solms (Würdinger, 2:371) wrote correctly—but in the final analysis nevertheless falsely:

> When one has as horsemen only wagon servants and peasants who steal their horses from wagons and plows, there will be in the field bad conduct and desertion in battle and campaigns. And even if they do not flee but remain, they are still not sufficiently well mounted and armored, and they have not learned how to fight but they remain peasants on plowhorses and draft horses. Such men should not be brought by a noble to the lord who provides the pay, for the lord relies on their numbers without knowing that he has only a loosely formed, worthless unit. Every knightly man who intends to lead horsemen to a lord should ponder this, for it is a matter of his honor and his welfare. For if he has peasant yokels in his squadron or banneret and finds himself faced by a good, well-equipped unit, what can he expect to accomplish and what poor service he has provided his commander in return for his money.

34. Erben, *Bulletin of the Imperial and Royal Army Museum* (*Mitteilungen des kaiserlichen und königlichen Heeresmuseums*), 1902, *Articles of War*, etc.

35. Susane, *Histoire de la cavallerie française*, 1:73, gives a somewhat different origin of this armed branch. He does not relate it to firearms but regards as the significant factor only the speed that the infantry in general, both lancers and musketeers, could develop in this way during individual expeditions. Because of the terror that they inspired, these warriors had called themselves dragoons. They were created by the Marquis de Brissac in the Piedmont theater of operations between 1550 and 1560. According to Jovius, Book 44, Pietro Strozzi had already placed 500 selected marksmen (*sclopettarii*) on horseback in 1543 in order to occupy Guise as quickly as possible. Ludwico Melzo, *Regule militari . . . della cavalleria* (Antwerp, 1611) understands the dragoons to be mounted marksmen. Jähns, 2:1050. Wallhausen has them armed in part with pikes.

Basta, Book I, Chap. 8, believes the mounted marksman or carabinier was invented in Piedmont. He identifies this type, therefore, with the dragoons. Hugo includes among the dragoons also men armed with spears, who move on horseback but fight on foot. *Militia equestri*, 1630, S. 184, Book III, p. 4. See Book IV, Chap. 5, pp. 271–272, concerning their formation in battle, with the pikemen in the middle, marksmen on the right and left, and horses in the rear.

36. When, for example, the Venetian Soriano, *Relazione di Francia*, 1562, Ed. Albèri, Series I, 4:117, says that the king of France had, in addition to his knights, foreign *ferraiuoli e cavalli leggieri*, the latter principally Albanians and Italians, the difference is that here the *cavalli*

leggieri are the older arm, which does not fight in such close formation, whereas the *ferraiuoli* were grouped in tight squadron formation and at this time, 1562, were probably also armed only with the pistol.

37. Rabutin, *Commentaires*, Ed. Buchon, p. 573, as an eyewitness.

38. Aloise Contarini, *Relazione di Francia*, February 1572, Ed. Albèri, Series I, Vol. IV, pp. 232–233.

39. Ed. Buchon, pp. 202–203.

40. "The formation of the French is with a broad front and weak rear, because everybody wants to take position in the front rank; but the Flemish, increasing the files and enlarging the body, make it stronger and more secure." *Report of Michel Suriano, made on his return from his ambassadorship to Philip II in 1559 (Relation de Michel Suriano, faite au retour de son Ambassade auprès de Philippe II en 1559)* (In Gachard, *Relations des ambassadeurs vénétiens sur Charles-Quint et Philippe II*, Brussels, 1856, p. 116). Popelinière, *Histoire des troubles*, Livre 9 (edition of 1572, p. 309): "The *reître*, because he fights in a completely different way than the French . . . "

41. And the worst is that, in the past, they fought in a single line (*en haye*). These regiments marching in battle formation are separated from one another by the foot troops, the artillery, or other units, and they cannot conveniently be drawn together to form a large unit when the occasion calls for it. And while they might still be in open country, if they should close together, if by chance the king's lieutenant should not be there to command them, each of them wanting to show his worth, without considering that body of troops—or, so to speak, the mountain of enemies—that is coming to attack them, neither the fear the soldiers can have, who seeing themselves weak and outnumbered, run off, seeking not only to win, but to survive if they face up to these troops where they have a four to one superiority, united, pressed together, and in quantity, as it is said.

They were to make the companies 80 to 100 men strong, composed of compatriots who were all known to one another, in order to foster cohesiveness. The companies were to be formed in regiments of about 500 men ("hommes d'armes").

Cavalry in single line (*en haye*) is useless; squadrons composed of 400 riders are the best; squadrons of 1,500 and 2,000, as is prescribed for the *reîtres*, would defeat them if they were dealing only with these 400; and if there were 1,200 in three units, charging one after the other, I would consider them to have the advantage. So many men in close formation only create confusion, and only a fourth of them fight. This large number of soldiers in a squadron is useful for the *reîtres*, because three-fourths of their men are nothing but villeins. The first troops that charge against these large bodies throw them into disorder, principally striking them on the flank. And even if the body can hold off the first attackers, the second and third squadrons sweep them away and break them up, charging from one end to the other and passing through; after the first two ranks are penetrated, there is little danger from the rest. He who has the larger number of squadrons of 300 and 400 must win the victory. Gaspard de Saulx-Tavannes, *Mémoires*, Ed. Buchon, 1836, p. 328 ff.

42. I find a similar argument in a Venetian account of 1596:

The *reîtres* were easily broken up by the lances of the light cavalry. Formerly, when each rank had made its wheel, the *reîtres* customarily tightened their whole formation and awaited the assault, facing the lances that were coming toward them, and then, widening their formation, they would let them enter among them and would handle them roughly with their pistols and their arms. But now the lances no longer come all together in squadrons but, divided into diverse and small detachments, they assault the squadrons of *reîtres* from all sides and harass them and throw them back and run through them from one side to the other and break them up with great facility. Tommaseco Contarini, *Relazione di Germania*, 1596. In *Relazione degli Ambasc. Veneti.*, Ed. Albèri, Series I, 6:235.

43. It was a question in ancient times and among those of the present time whether it was better to go into combat at a trot or to await the enemy in place; it seems that the momentum and the gallop increase the power of the men and horses to mow down the squadrons but it also gives much more opportunity to those who have no desire to be involved in this charge to halt, hold their mounts in place, and separate themselves from the charge, such as new soldiers and those the captain does not trust. It seems that it would be better to have them wait in formation and firmly fixed in place or at least not to take up the trot or gallop before a distance of twenty paces from the enemy, because then those who would fall out would be recognized, and the cowards would be too ashamed to leave their position at the moment of encountering the enemy, being the more easily seen and recognized by their captains, who would force them to be courageous in spite of themselves. Jean Gaspard de Saulx-Tavannes, *Mémoires*, Ed. Buchon, 1836, p. 116.

44. French ordinance of 16 October 1568. "It is likewise ordered that the companies of each regiment of cavalry will march together and in the

formation that they are to maintain while fighting, in order that each man will be accustomed to holding his position." Nothing further was prescribed. H. Choppin, *Les Origines de la Cavalerie française*, Paris and Nancy, 1905, p. 22.

45. Quite similar descriptions and observations are found in the *History of the Civil Wars in France (Storia delle guerre civili di Francia)*, by the Italian Davila, and in the *Art of War*, "The Difference between Launtiers and Pistolers," 1590, by the Englishman Roger Williams. They are quoted by C. H. Firth in *Cromwell's Army*, p. 129.

46. In the *Commentaires*, Vol. XI, Chaps. 11, 12, Ed. Lonmier-Guillaume, 2:214–222.

47. In his *History of the Netherlands War (Geschichte des Niederländischen Krieges)*, Mendoza reports expressly in his account of the battle on the Mooker Heide that the "horsemen" on the Spanish side had awaited the attack of the enemy squadrons in place—as a result of which, to be sure, they were defeated. It was only a counterattack by another Spanish cavalry unit that threw back the Gueux.

48. *Historia*, Book 44. Ed. 1578, p. 560.

Chapter II

Increase in Numbers of Marksmen. Refinement of Infantry Tactics

After its spread throughout Europe, Swiss tactics came to a halt, so to speak. Under the method that called for attacking the enemy with three large squares wherever he was found, the prerequisite had obtained that whenever one or another encountered an obstacle that was initially insuperable, the broad formation would nevertheless break open the enemy line at some point, where one of the units would penetrate and thereby clear the way for the others. But if the enemy took up a position that could neither be attacked from the front nor enveloped on one of its two flanks, then even the most valiant assault was powerless. This had been proved at Bicocca, and at Pavia the Swiss, as a part of the French army, had themselves sought protection in a position that was thought to be unassailable. In time, the spread of firearms and improvements to them made it easier and easier to find similar positions that were impregnable or difficult to attack. We shall become acquainted later with the strategic factors that led to the situation that caused great battles to occur only rarely. But it was only in battle that the large square famous for its long spears realized its full significance. If it was not possible to bring on a decisive battle, or if the commander considered that to be inadvisable, and the war was limited to mutual attempts to outlast the enemy through small undertakings, surprise attacks, the capture of castles, and sieges, the missile weapon was more useful and more necessary than the long spear, and in addition to the increased employment of marksmen, the possibilities for action by light horsemen also increased.

The progress of events, therefore, brought about a constant increase in the number of marksmen, while at the same time their weapon was continuously being improved.

During the same period, knighthood was gradually being transformed into cavalry.

At the beginning of the sixteenth century the marksmen constituted perhaps one-tenth of the total of foot soldiers with close-combat weapons.

In 1526, under Frundsberg, they were one-eighth. In 1524 it is reported that the Spaniards were stronger than the Swiss in marksmen and were also better trained. In the Schmalkaldic War the marksmen with the lansquenets increased to one-third, and Philip of Hesse in his levy required that they be one-half of the total. Domenico Moro in 1570 and Landono in 1578 assumed one-half to be normal. Adr. Duyk in 1588 estimated sixty marksmen to forty lancers, and so it continued.[1]

The theorists opposed this much too strong increase of marksmen. De la Noue (*Discourse* XIV) claimed they should be limited to one-fourth and the pikemen (*corcelets*) should receive higher pay. Monluc believed that soldiers preferred to shoot rather than engage in hand-to-hand combat. In any case, the movement was irreversible. Domenico Moro, who dedicated a book to Ottavio Farnese in 1570, anticipated the future, so to speak, by decreasing the pikemen to one-third and forming the two arms abreast in independent units of six ranks each.[2]

The marksman of antiquity, like that of the Middle Ages, was by his nature a skirmisher. The disciplined English archers and the janissaries had already raised their art to mass firing, which was superior to skirmishing, but there did not take place an organic development of these accomplishments. The effectiveness of the bow was not great enough for this. Even the new firearms, initially and for a long time, allowed only a heightened skirmishing effectiveness. As effective as the shot from the harquebus and even more so from the musket was, when it hit the target— it was nevertheless too inaccurate and required too much time for the individual marksman to have become able to cope with the horseman, the halberdier, or the pikeman unless he had some kind of cover. How was this cover to be provided?

The first expedient was the mutual support of the marksmen by one another. As early as 1477 Albrecht Achilles prescribed in his instructions for the campaign against Hans von Sagan that the units of harquebusiers should fire alternately, so that one group would always be ready to fire. In 1507 a Venetian ambassador sent home the report that the same method was customary for the Germans,[3] and in 1516, when Cardinal Ximenez established a militia in Spain, it was prescribed that training "in forming up and in the caracole" was to take place on Sundays,[4] that is, a firing sequence in which the marksman who had fired always stepped back behind the others in order to reload, and so forth in a cycle.

In the battle of Marignano in 1515, Jovius tells us the king's marksmen maintained with great success such a "snail fire" from a covered position against the Swiss.[5] In 1532, in the parade in Vienna,[6] and in 1551 in a parade for the duke of Nevers, governor of Champagne, according to the account of an eyewitness, Rabutin, the "snail" (*le limaçon*) was carried out a number of times.[7]

But even firing regulated in this way was not sufficient to allow marksmen in the open field to face up to enemy horsemen or even only foot troops armed with close-combat weapons. In a battle situation it was difficult to maintain the orderly sequence of fire in the caracole, and we hear as popular opinion that the marksmen believed the enemy would already be frightened off even by the simple noise of firing, and the rearmost ranks, instead of awaiting their turn to come forward and aim accurately, fired into the air.[8]

De la Noue says infantry in close formation can withstand attacking horsemen only with the pike, "for the unit of harquebusiers without cover is easily overcome."[9] There were no doubt cases where marksmen moved forward very boldly against horsemen, for example in the pursuit of the French army by Pescara in 1524, in which Bayard was struck down by a musket ball.[10] There were also cases where they defended themselves independently against enemy horsemen, as Avila relates on one occasion in the Schmalkaldic War.[11] But these are still only exceptions. Normally, marksmen had to have support by one of the other arms. Either the horsemen moved forward and repelled the enemy,[12] or the marksmen pushed in among the spearmen of the main body by being posted all around it either from the start or by having the small units that were to form the snail attached to the main body as a "wing" or "sleeve,"[13] and, in case they could not hold off the enemy with their fire, having them flee to the spears.[14]

In a certain contradiction to this one-sided concept of practice and theory in the sixteenth century and the first half of the seventeenth century, that is, that the firearm could not hold its own independently but needed support and protection, stands the fact that the Turks had no pikemen, only horsemen and marksmen, the janissaries, who had gone over from the bow to the musket. Nevertheless, the Turks were so superior that they conquered Hungary and in 1529 appeared before Vienna. But, after they had won an easy victory over the Hungarians at Mohacz in 1526, there was never a great decisive battle in this period.[15] The Turks avoided such a battle, and the armies of the emperor and the various kingdoms were not formed long enough to force such a battle. The wars were spent in sieges, the storming of castles, and wasting campaigns. For a hundred years, from 1568 to 1664, the emperor and the sultan were at peace with one another, except for one war from 1593 to 1606. From 1578 to 1639—that is, during the principal period of the Thirty Years' War—the Turks were engaged in serious conflicts with the Persians. When the new period of warfare between the Turks and Germans began in 1664, the battalions of pikemen had almost disappeared.

But let us turn back now to the sixteenth century and the problem of the relationship between marksmen and pikemen. The number of marksmen who can withdraw among the spears of a large square of pikemen was naturally very limited. A square with an equal number of men on each side for a total of 10,000 men has, of course, a front of only 100 men. Even if on all four sides two ranks of marksmen move in among the spears of each side, that is still only 800 who are covered. Spanish theorists have up to five ranks crawling in under the spears, but even that would account for only 2,000 and would no doubt have created great difficulties. We hear of a battle in which the musketeers pushed in under the spears after firing, thus pushing the spears upward and allowing the enemy horsemen to penetrate, so that the entire square was broken up and massacred.[16]

A certain relief was brought about by making the units of spearmen smaller and more numerous. The reduced size of the units of spearmen was accomplished, naturally, on the one hand in order to be able to give protection to more marksmen, but also in order to offer smaller targets to the constantly expanding and improving artillery.[17] But since the number remained small and could still provide cover for only a moderate number of men, this method could prove less and less satisfactory as time went on.

The theorists invented cross-formations, hollow squares, octagons, and the like, all for the purpose of protecting the marksmen, but all of which were of course impracticable.[18] The combat formation of the infantry continued to be a small number of rectangular units, and that brings up the question as to how these squares, which were called "*terzios*" by the Spaniards, were drawn up with respect to each other.[19] Machiavelli had already praised the three Swiss squares as a special refinement in that they were formed neither beside nor behind one another but obliquely echeloned. That was a doctrinaire description without inherent value; the number, formation, and advance of the Swiss squares depended completely on existing circumstances and terrain conditions. At Bicocca, since there was no possibility for a flanking movement, the second Swiss square took position at once beside the first, "for no square wanted to be the last one" (Anshelm).

With a larger number of squares, however, if they were formed on a plain, for example, in order to move into battle against the enemy or to await his attack, we would have to ask whether they were to be drawn up simply side by side or in another way. The simple formation side by side would have guaranteed an equal cooperation of all the forces and would have been close to the method of an ancient legion phalanx. But, as we know, a completely even advance of such a front line is very difficult, and it must also be considered that the squares had not simply the task of attacking but also the very important function of providing cover for the marksmen, who were so numerous and so effective from a distance. The Spanish, who were the leaders in the art of tactics in this period, found it was right to form the squares in checkerboard formation in two or three lines and at a rather great distance from one another. I do not think it correct to regard these lines as echelons. Rüstow used the name "Spanish brigade" for this formation, a name that was not derived from the sources but coined by him. The foremost units, in their square form and considerable strength, were capable of starting any battle but were naturally too weak to carry it through. For that purpose the rear units also had to move up, and they were better able to do that from the rear than if they had stood in the forward line from the beginning. For they could then be directed to the point where their help was most needed and where their attack promised to be most effective in accordance with the terrain and the enemy action. And then the various squares would very soon come up on the same front. Consequently, the deployment in the "Spanish brigade" was not a formation that was to be maintained during the battle. It was, in fact, nothing of importance but only meant that each of the squares moved as independently as possible, accommodating itself to the terrain and the circumstances, and all of them supported each other mutually.

The dividing of the original huge squares of infantry raised once again the question as to how foot troops and horsemen were to be evaluated with respect to one another. The old main bodies had repulsed the knights on the defensive and had overrun them in the attack. Could units like the *terzios* also do that? Lipsius makes it clear that among the Romans it seldom happened that infantry was broken up by horsemen, whereas in his time that happened often. De la Noue also states that as the predominant opinion, but he bases his statement on the Romans and cites two examples from Spaniards of his time in order to prove that infantry in close formation was capable of standing up to a more numerous unit of horsemen. But of course, he goes on to say, with the contemporary French infantry one would not risk letting things get to that point, for that infantry had neither spears nor discipline.[20]

Inasmuch as horsemen were going over more and more to firearms and, on the other hand, spearmen were being joined in increasing numbers with marksmen, the question loses its practical significance, as Lipsius already realized—or rather, the question remains but takes on another form.

The knights, by becoming cavalry, became tactically controllable. In addition to the mission of breaking up infantry and riding down its individuals came the other task of rendering infantry immobile by attacking it from two sides. We shall hear more about this. Davila, in his *History of the Huguenot Wars (Geschichte der Hugenottenkriege)*, Book XI, Chap. 3, recounts with respect to the battle of Ivry (1590) that Henry IV divided his cavalry into smaller squadrons so that they could attack the lansquenets from all sides.

NOTES FOR CHAPTER II

1. Rüstow, *Geschichte der Infanterie*, 1:242 f., 349. Jähns, 1:724, 726, 731. Hobohm, 2:472. Pätel, *The Organization of the Hessian Army under Philip the Magnanimous (Die Organisation des hessischen Heeres unter Philipp dem Grossmütigen)*. Philip gave the marksmen one guilder more per month than the spearmen; nevertheless, they did not reach half the strength.

2. Jähns, 1:726.

3. *Relazione di Vincenzo Quirini*, December 1507 (*Relazione degli ambassadore Veneti* [Eugen Albèri, Series I, 6:21]).

4. Clonard-Brix, p. 57.

5. Book XV, Basel, 1578, 1:315.

6. *Truthful Description of the Other Campaign in Austria against the Turks . . . in the Past Year 1532. Described in Detail. And now Prepared in Print for the First Time in this Year of 1539.* Reprinted in J.U.D. Goebel, *Contributions to the National History of Europe under Emperor Charles V (Beiträge zur Staatsgeschichte von Europa unter Kaiser Karl V.)*, Lemgo, 1767, p. 326. Further information on the caracole is to be found in Hobohm, 2:394, 405–407, 468, 483, 508.

7. Rabutin, *Commentaires*, Ed. Buchon, p. 530.

8. Quoted in Rüstow, 1:264.

9. *Discourse XVIII*, Paradoxe 2, p. 384.

10. Jovius, *Life of Pescara (Le vite . . .)*, Venice, 1581, p. 213.

11. 1 September 1546. Avila, German edition, p. 39.

12. There are also reports of mixed combat of marksmen and horsemen (Rüstow, 1:314, from Monluc), but these can only have been exceptional cases that had no further development.

13. Jovius in 1535 before Goleta: "duas sclopetariorum manus, quas manicas vocabant, quod cornuum instar . . . " ("two bands of *sclopetarii*, which they call sleeves because they are like wings"). Book 34, Edition of 1578, p. 392. In 1542 before Ofen, the Italian infantry of Alessandro Vitelli "promoto hastatorum agmine et utrinque sclopettariis in cornua expansis Barbaros invadunt" ("After the column of the pikemen had been moved forward and on both sides the *sclopetarii* had been extended on the wings, they attacked the barbarians"). Jovius, *Histories*, Book 42, p. 518.

14. As we have already seen on p. 94 above, Rüstow called this formation the "Hungarian order," which he based on the Vienna parade of 1532. But that was only a schematic representation without practical significance. The expression is not derived from the sources any more than is the "Spanish brigade." Wallhausen speaks not of a "Hungarian order," but only of a "Hungarian installation," that is, an administrative

arrangement rather than a tactical one. In his *Art of Dismounted Warfare (Kriegskunst zu Fuss)*, Book I, Chap. 6, p. 110, he says that in Hungary no formation other than the square was used. Jähns, 1:711, calls it fatal that there had been acceptance of the procedure advocated by the Italian Tartaglia calling for placing the marksmen in the outer ranks of the square rather than as wings resting on the squares of spearmen, as had already been recommended by Seldeneck in 1480. This criticism seems to me to fail to recognize the principal point. While it is true that the formation of marksmen in wings offered the advantage of better sequence of fire and also a reasonably sure protection, nevertheless, when the attacking horsemen approached, the marksmen always had to find protection either among or inside of the spearmen.

15. As an example of how little we can depend on isolated reports, even when they appear to be well founded, let us note that Jorga, *History of the Ottoman Empire (Geschichte des osmanischen Reiches)*, 3:295, tells of a defeat of the Turks in 1593 in which "the janissaries were destroyed by the new cavalry of the West, the heavy horsemen clad in iron on armored horses, and by the harquebusiers." A Turkish source and a Polish one are cited as a basis. Consequently, the writers had heard of the "new cavalry of the West," but they had not understood in what respect it was new, and so they describe it as the ancient knights. If we were not informed from other sources, it would be absolutely impossible to recognize what is correct in this exaggerated description. This is a counterpart to the transposition of Winkelried into a knightly battle. A similar situation is to be found in the same work on p. 314.

16. 1608. *Archives of Oranien-Nassau*, 2d Series, 2:389.

17. *Institution de la discipline militaire au Royaume de France*, Lyons, 1559, p. 96 ff. The author himself is opposed to the reduced units and believes that, since there are marksmen and horsemen in the intervals, the cannon would find their target in any case. In his opinion, one should seek to prevent the second shot by skirmishing marksmen and horsemen.

18. Rüstow treated these formations very thoroughly in his *Geschichte der Infanterie*. I do not consider it necessary to go into that in detail, since we find nothing of this kind in the real battles.

19. The extent to which the *"terzio"* was an administrative or a tactical unit and designation requires further research.

20. Lipsius, *de militia Romana (On Roman Military Service)*, 5:20, *Opera*, 1613, 2:460. De la Noue, *Discourse* XVIII, 2d Paradoxe. Ed. 1587, p. 377 ff.

Chapter III

Maurice of Orange

In the first twenty years of the open struggle, the Spanish were militarily superior to the Netherlanders. Even though William of Orange and his brothers assembled a mercenary army, it was undisciplined and was defeated in the open field or had to be disbanded again because the soldiers' pay could not be assembled. The Netherlanders were able to continue the fight only because the fortified cities closed their gates to the Spaniards, and even though the invaders succeeded in capturing no small number of them and punishing them cruelly, they still did not take all of them. When Alba finally had to withdraw before the small city of Alkmar, he was relieved, and in a complicated mixture of fighting and negotiating, together with intervention by France and England, there developed from the rebelling provinces a union of cities and rural areas that was capable of maintaining a regular army in the field. In 1585, after the assassination of William the Silent, the siege of Antwerp had required all the strength of the Spaniards. Then came the time when they turned all their resources to the great armada and the struggle against England, in 1588. Immediately thereafter the crisis in France following the assassination of Henry III and the ascension to the throne of the apostate Henry IV brought about the intervention of the Spanish-Netherlands troops in the internal French struggle. The southern part of the Low Countries finally remained in the hands of the Spanish, but the northern provinces adhered more and more firmly to their freedom and now found in the young Maurice, son of William the Silent, the leader who understood how to mold the existing military resources into new forms and thus attain greater accomplishments.

We remember how Machiavelli promised himself to renew the military system of his time by taking up again the great heritage of antiquity. He had failed in that effort from both a practical and a theoretical viewpoint. It becomes clear, however, that we must recognize his genius when we now see that two generations after his death the military reforms were related not only to antiquity but directly to him, his ideas, and his studies.

In 1575 William of Orange had granted the city of Leyden, as a reward for its extremely heroic defense against the siege, a university that attracted the great philologists of the period. Among them was Justus Lipsius, who in 1589 published his work *Civilis doctrina (Political Instruction)*, the fifth book of which is titled "De militari prudentia" ("On Military Wisdom"). In 1595 Lipsius, who had moved to Louvain, followed with his book *De militia Romana (On Roman Military Service)*. These writings were of a purely philologic nature, but the author, as a disciple of Machiavelli, could not avoid casting glances at the present as well, of which one could not say, according to Lipsius, that the period had a poor discipline; instead, one could not avoid saying that it had no discipline at all. But he said that whoever understood how to link the troops of his day with the Roman art of war would be able to dominate the earth. "We cannot give prescriptions, only the motivation" ("gustum dare potuimus, praecepta non potuimus"), and he adds, "and so it happened."[1]

The year 1590, when Maurice, who until that time had been only the governor of Holland and Seeland and now became governor of Geldern, Utrecht, and Upper-Yssel as well, is to be regarded as the critical year in the history of the infantry.

Beside Maurice, at the head of the united Netherlands, as governor of Friesland, stood his cousin, William Louis of Nassau. It appears that William became imbued almost even more than Maurice with the idea of reforming the military system of the period after the pattern of the ancients, and the two related and friendly princes mutually influenced one another in the work of reform. Their correspondence and the writings of loyal co-workers that have been preserved give us an insight into their work.[2]

The classical work on which the princes of Orange depended particularly was the *Tactics* of Emperor Leo, which had appeared in a Latin translation in 1554 and had then been published in an Italian translation as well and was also published in Greek by Meursius in Leyden in 1612.[3] In the eighteenth century a French translation appeared, followed by a German version. The Prince of Ligne called the work "immortal" and claimed that Emperor Leo was the equal of Frederick the Great and superior to Caesar. For the most part, this work consisted of somewhat systematized extracts from older authors, particularly Aelian, whose work was also studied directly by the Netherlanders and used by them.

Let us now remember how poorly informed the philosophic theorists of antiquity were with respect to practical military matters and how, in particular, the principal passage on Roman manipular tactics in Livy (8:8) was based on a serious misunderstanding by this completely unmilitary historian and has confused concepts up to the present day. The question,

then, arises as to whether it was at all possible that the warriors at the
turn of the sixteenth and seventeenth centuries derived practical and useful
instruction from such a confused and erroneous source. But that was in
fact possible. Of course, they would not have been able simply to carry
out in a practical way information transmitted in this manner. But despite
all its shortcomings, the source nevertheless contained great general elements of truth. It was a question of detecting them and making them
useful, and Maurice and William Louis were the men to do it. Indeed,
as compared with Machiavelli, they had the advantage of neither being
required nor wishing to create a new military system but simply of developing further a system they inherited. With admirable perceptiveness
they discovered in the ancient source those elements that their period
could use.

The decisive point, from an external viewpoint, was drill, and from an
internal viewpoint it was discipline. Machiavelli had sought the system
of ancient warfare in the general armed levy, and he believed he could
make such a general levy militarily useful through the manipulation of
weapons learned through occasional drills. The men from Orange drew
from the ancient authors the realization of the value for a unit of a
cohesiveness attained through continuous practice, and on the base of
the ancient source they created the new drill techniques. If one can ever
do so, it is precisely here that we can speak of the renaissance of a lost
art. It is true, of course, that the Swiss, with the creation of their square
units, had had to accustom themselves to a certain order, and Jovius tells
us how they marched to the beat of the drum when they entered Rome
in 1494—that is, they sought to keep in step to a certain degree. The
Spanish presumably thought it still more important to maintain their
squares in order,[4] and the execution of the "snail" by the infantry, as
with the cavalry, presupposes a certain amount of drill. But that was still
only the most necessary step in order to maintain a certain degree of
orderliness in the mass. When the recruit had understood the basic movements, it was believed that was all that was necessary and no further
work was needed. They knew, of course, no other formation than the
square, and it was very simple, until the men of Orange began to form
shallow units and to maneuver them in the most varied manner. The
depths of these units were generally reported as ten ranks, but we also
hear of formations with five and six ranks.[5] Strangely enough, it is never
reported directly that the movements were carried out in step, unless it
be that the command "crane dance" ("*Kranendans*"), which is not to be
found anywhere else, refers to the stiff walk of the crane and is to be
interpreted as "to keep in step."[6]

The shallow formation of the unit was now a change of far-reaching
significance. Already, by increasing the number of the old square units
beyond three, it had automatically resulted that not all of them moved

out from the start on the same front, but a few were held back. The new shallow formation led to the practice of having the first line followed systematically by a second and perhaps even a third—that is, a true echelon formation. If all the units had been formed on one front, that front would have been broken up or penetrated much too easily, and with the lack of depth a unit penetrating into such a break would have been able to roll up the battle line easily. This tendency was further reinforced by the arrangement of the marksmen, whom Maurice increased to arrive at a ratio of some two marksmen to each spearman.[7] Nowhere do I find it directly reported that it was consideration for the marksmen, whose increased number was so difficult to work into the square, that now had brought about the need for the new formation. But when we consider the entire picture, we must assume that this was at least a strong factor in the creation of the new formation. In any case, a result of the new formation was the fact that even a large number of marksmen could now be given the desired support by the pikes. The marksmen, among whom a distinction was made between musketeers and harquebusiers, were formed on the right and left of the units of pikes. Rüstow called this formation the "Netherlands Brigade." The marksmen fired, executing the caracole from these positions beside the pikemen, or, under certain circumstances, they spread out in front of the pikemen.[8] But if they were attacked directly by enemy horsemen or pikemen, they withdrew behind the units of pikemen, while the pikemen of the second or third echelon sprang forward to close the intervals and fend off the enemy.[9] Consequently, from this viewpoint as well, the shallow formation required an arrangement of echelons in the rear.

Included in the drills was also one in which the unit broke ranks and was then able on a drum signal to reform at great speed, because every man knew his position. The Netherlanders were famous for being able to form 2,000 men in twenty-two to twenty-three minutes, whereas elsewhere it took one hour to form 1,000 men.[10]

In addition to the pikemen, halberdiers and *Rondhartschiere* (shield bearers) were also used. But it is not necessary to dwell on this, since they soon disappeared.

The decisive factor in the new formation was, even more than the arrangement itself, the extraordinary mobility of each one of the newly formed small tactical bodies and the certain control their leaders had, even in the excitement of combat. This factor enabled them to lead their units in good order to the spot required at any given moment; as John of Nassau expressed it, "in order to relieve one another, to turn and wheel quickly, and also be able to attack the enemy simultaneously and unexpectedly in two or three places."[11]

The more familiar we become with these factors, the more we realize that much more was needed to bring this new art into being than a simple knowledge of the situation and a simple decision or command. The biographer of William Louis reports that he studied everything in the way of military skills practiced by the ancient Greeks and Romans, and he spared neither trouble, nor work, nor expense. His secretary, Reyd, and Colonel Cornput assisted him in his study of the ancients and in transferring the tenets found there into practice. They first set up the formation on a table with lead soldiers before training their men. In order to be sure whether it was better to arm their men with the long spear without a shield or to use the Roman armament with sword and shield, Maurice set up a test in 1595.[12] The commands were translated from the Greek and Latin, and the soldiers were ordered to remain silent during the drill so that they would not fail to hear the commands. From the ancients they learned and adopted the prescription that in giving a command the specialized aspect (preparatory command) had to precede the general one (not "face right," but "right . . . face"), because otherwise one could not expect accurate execution. Drills were held not only in garrison but also in camp, in contact with the enemy, and also in bad weather.[13] There were desertions, because this was too much for some of the soldiers.

The old veterans, even including Count Hohenlohe, Prince Maurice's military mentor, laughed and joked about such skills, which they believed would break down in real battle, but the two princes of Orange did not let themselves be distracted. In winter officers traveled through the garrisons to inspect the service. They had started the new system in 1590, and we have a long letter dated 1594 from William Louis to Maurice, in which he makes a report and gives information. He recommends not making the units of pikemen too shallow, since they always had to be able to withstand a cavalry attack. He says that Emperor Leo had given the correct prescription on that point (a depth of sixteen men). He further points out the chapters in Leo's *Tactics* whose prescriptions should be followed,[14] and finally he gives a listing of the commands that he had composed in accordance with Aelian and that he had put into practice. There were about fifty of them, including a few that he said were not yet definite, and a number of them are still used in present-day commands. He added that one should not introduce more commands than necessary, so that the men could be thoroughly imbued with those in use. He said it was particularly important for the men to learn the difference between rank and file, to maintain the intervals, and to form and march closely pressed together. For this purpose they had to learn to move in closely, doubling up both in ranks and in files, and to face right and left and wheel to the right and left.[15] There are still a number of similar points, which I have already partially discussed above, and finally the author of the letter protests that, if Maurice should laugh at his letter, let it be "inter parietem ende amicos" ("within the walls, between friends").[16]

According to an expression of Wallhausen, Maurice was a "seeker of drills," but not only did he create the new art in collaboration with his cousin, but he also insisted on compliance with an absolute prerequisite: punctual payment of the soldiers. From the start of the lansquenet system, the darkest point in the new institution had always been that concerning the payment of the soldiers.

In his tract on mounted troops, General Basta says: "Let one give me an army with all these features (pay, rations, participation in booty), even though it be as spoiled as possible, I would venture to reform it and restore its effectiveness. On the other hand, I could not promise, indeed, would not be able, to keep a good army well disciplined if it were deprived of these most necessary features."

We have learned to what a great extent even strategic decisions are dependent on the possibility or impossibility of giving the men the promised pay. One would never have been able to demand the efforts of the difficult drills that the older men among themselves considered as not only unnecessary, but laughable games, if one were still somewhat indebted to the soldiers. The merchant spirit in the States-General was prudent and professional enough to realize the importance of punctual payment, and the commerce that was developing amidst all the confusion of war, like the thriftiness of the strict Calvinists, who saw sin in every kind of luxury, provided the means for payment. The king of Spain, with all the gold and silver from America, was still not capable of keeping up with the immeasurable series of political tasks that he established for himself. After the battle on the Mooker Heide in 1574, the Spanish army, which had received no pay for three years, refused further obedience, selected a commander, and on its own initiative took up quarters in Antwerp until the burghers found it convenient to pay 400,000 gold crowns. Now, finally, the soldiers were reimbursed their back pay, partly in cash and partly in goods. This happened several other times and led to the most frightful disorders and atrocities. It was often a matter of months before the troops were brought back to a condition of obedience. In 1576, in the "fury" of Antwerp, the city was completely plundered and partially burned to the ground, and the population was slain in masses. Of course, that also interfered with the conduct of the war.

The Netherlandish troops did not behave in this way. The States-General created an orderly economy, and that was all the more significant in that this army was very expensive. The old units of lansquenets were normally 300 to 400 men strong and often numbered even as high as 500. Maurice lowered their strength to somewhat over 100, but without decreasing the number of officer positions. The significance of this change is excellently described by Wallhausen in his *Art of Dismounted Warfare (Kriegskunst zu Fuss)*, p. 97:

The most outstanding war hero, Prince Maurice, uses for each company, which is often smaller than 100 men,[17] the following officers:

the captain, the lieutenant, the ensign, two or three sergeants, three corporals, three runners, a captain of arms, a corporal of noble youths or privates first class, a scribe, a provost, ten privates first class, and two drummers. Now each month almost as much has to be paid to so many leaders as to the soldiers and the entire company. Consequently, half of the expenses could be saved if the company were given a strength of 200 or 300 men, and it therefore appears unreasonable to make the companies so small. But let it be known that the highborn prince is not particularly concerned with having such strong companies and regiments as are normal elsewhere, but he has his resolution that with a regiment of his soldiers no stronger than 1,000 men he can stand up to a regiment of his enemy of 3,000, and as often as he has attacked his enemy with this formation, he has always been victorious, something which appears impossible, that is, that three could do no more than one, and great expenses could thereby be avoided. For the fewer soldiers and the more leaders one has, the better they are led.

The old lansquenet captains at the head of their units had been leaders and front-line fighters. The Netherlandish captains, with the other higher ranking soldiers supporting them, became officers in the modern concept. They did not simply lead, but they created; they first formed the soldiery that they later led. Maurice of Orange, by becoming the renovator of the art of drill and the father of true military discipline, also became the creator of the officer status, even if it was not until later that this took on its specifically exclusive character.

The new discipline, based on drill, which was intended to give to the small, shallow tactical bodies of pikemen and marksmen the ability to meet the old square unit on equal terms (and which actually did so) also immediately gave the Netherlandish soldiers a second capability, one which first showed even more significant success from a practical viewpoint than did the increased tactical skill. That was the possibility of requiring the soldiers to dig fortifications, something which no doubt had occurred earlier on a sporadic basis but was now elevated to a system. Here, too, the classical model had its effect. In his writings Lipsius particularly emphasized *castrametatio* (fortified camp), and of course the Romans themselves knew and stated that it was not only *virtus* and *arma*, but also their *opus* (work) that gave them the victory over their enemies. The old lansquenets had been too proud and conscious of their importance to stoop to the work of digging. The Netherlandish princes realized and saw to it, with their ample pay and their discipline, that the soldiers should also be ready to do this kind of work. When William Louis presented his program to the States-General in 1589 and demanded as first priority regular payment of the soldiers, he added at the same time that with the generous pay one also had to disabuse the soldiers of the false shame they had in not being willing to dig. He said that if they succeeded in this, they would be securing themselves from the dangers that otherwise accompanied war. In a fortified camp, he said, one could not be forced to do battle, and if such camps were situated on streams, their supplies could not be cut off. In this way they should invest the fortresses—he named Nijmegen, The Hague, Venlo, Roermond, Deventer, and Zutphen—and could take them without fighting, without the risk of a bad turn of fortune. For, he said, they could protect themselves by fortifications in such a way that Parma could not think of relieving them. And if one first had the cities along the streams, the others would not be able to hold out long, because of lack of provisions.[18]

We can cite an antithesis to this from the Thirty Years' War. When the Bohemian troops were to fortify their position in the summer of 1620, they found this effort to be debasing, refused to work, and demanded their outstanding pay.[19]

Maurice took the offensive, captured Nijmegen and a number of smaller places by assault or bombardment, and Steenwyk, Coeworden, Gertruidenborg, and finally Groningen (1594) by formal sieges with trenches and mines. It is reported that William Louis himself was present at the works day and night in front of Steenwyk.[20] The besieged garrison taunted the "workers" with scornful words, saying that they were lowering themselves from soldiers to peasants and ditch-diggers and were using shovels instead of spears. But neither these words nor the bombardment or sorties held up the progress of the work.

It is also reported that Maurice carried along palisades on the streams, and with their help, by having each soldier carry up two or three of them, he quickly secured his position in the direct proximity of the enemy.[21]

In front of Gertruidenborg in 1593, Maurice secured his position by circumvallation and countervallation, even though the work was made particularly difficult by the swampy terrain. Mansfeld came to the relief of the garrison with 9,000 men, but he was unable to do anything and had to stand by and watch the surrender. When the outcome had been decided, William Louis wrote to the victor:

This siege can definitely be called the second Alesia, and it means the restoration of a great part of the ancient art and science of war, which until now has been prized very little and laughed at by ignorant men and which has not been understood by even the greatest modern generals or at least has not been practiced by them.[22]

On the occasion of the capture of Delfzyl, Maurice had two soldiers hanged, one because he had stolen a hat and the other because he had stolen a dagger. At the siege of Hulst he had a man shot to death in front of the assembled troops because he had robbed a woman.

A generation later, in 1620, the Venetian ambassador Girolamo Trevisano reported back home from the Netherlands that the States-General then maintained even in peacetime an effective strength of 30,000 foot troops and about 3,600 mounted men.[23] He said that the distribution of pay had never been delayed by even one hour, no matter what the situation was, and that had the greatest influence on the discipline. He went on to say that it was amazing to see how the cities contended with one another for garrisons and the burghers for the billeting of soldiers, for they hoped to earn a great deal from them. If a person had a spare room with two beds, he could take in six soldiers, for two of them would always be on duty. He said that the burgher had no hesitation in leaving his wife and daughters alone with the soldiers, something that did not occur anywhere else.

The only open battle that Maurice fought, at Nieuport on 2 July 1600, has been thoroughly discussed by Rüstow, but still not completely satisfactorily or exhaustively. A member of my seminar, Kurt Göbel, had undertaken a special study on this subject. At the end of October 1914 he fell fighting for his country at Dixmuyden, very close to the Nieuport battlefield.

EXCURSUS

INTERVALS BETWEEN RANKS AND FILES IN A UNIT OF PIKEMEN

The first testimony on this question is to be found in a report by the Venetian ambassador Quirini in 1507. It states the interval between ranks as some 1 1/2 paces and says of the intervals within each rank that the men stood at such a distance from one another that they could march without bumping against each other.[24]

In his *Geschichte der Kriegskunst* (1519–1520), Machiavelli gives figures that are not completely consistent. He does not give any direct measure for the individual man, but in the third book he makes a reckoning for his battle formation which, when we break it down, amounts to 25 *bracci* (yards) for a battalion 20 men wide, which amounts to some 74 centimeters or 2 1/2 feet per man. In the second book, however, he says the men stood arm to arm, and in his discussion concerning Germany he says of the Swiss that their formation was such that they believed nobody could penetrate it[25]—from which statements we could conclude that he assumed a space of only about 1 1/2 feet for each man.

For the interval between men in the file, Machiavelli consistently gives in several places two *bracci* (apparently from Vegetius, 3:14), which amounts to some six feet and which in the combat of pikemen was reduced to three feet.[26]

In a work by an unknown author, perhaps du Bellay-Langey, that first appeared in Paris in 1535 and is normally cited under the title "Instruction sur le fait de guerre," it is stated that there was an interval of three paces between men in each rank while marching, two paces in battle formation, and one pace in battle. The distance between ranks was given as four paces, two paces, and one pace, respectively.[27] On the basis of this passage, Rüstow (1:253) assumes that the man in a rank required only 1 1/2 geometric feet.

The space that each soldier occupies in width while marching in simple formation is three paces and when in battle two, and when he is fighting, one. The distance from one rank to another when in simple march formation is four paces, in battle formation two, and when fighting, one. Thus the twenty-one men of each unit, when in battle formation, occupy forty-two paces in width and the twenty ranks occupy forty paces in depth, including the space that each soldier occupies, which is one pace.

Shortly after the work named above, there appeared in France (1559) a similar work, also anonymous, *Institution de la discipline militaire au Royaume de France*,[28] which gave the space within ranks as one ell, and the interval between ranks as about 3 feet.[29] In another passage (p. 100) it is said that the "closing in of the battalion should be done frequently, when one is approaching the enemy." This passage can hardly be interpreted other than that, in order to counter the loosening of the formation that always occurs while marching, halts should be made quite frequently in order to have the men close tightly together again.

The Italian Tartaglia (1546) and Duke Albrecht of Prussia in his *Kriegsordnung* (1552) state the intervals within a rank as 3 feet and between ranks as 7 feet, undoubtedly taking these figures from Vegetius.[30]

Tavannes (it is uncertain whether father or son) gives three paces within the rank, seven in the file:[31]

> The geometric square and the square of men are different in that there must be seven paces in each file between the ranks, and three paces between each soldier is sufficient in the rank, so that to form the battalion in the geometric square with sixty men in line, only thirty men are necessary in depth. The broad front is necessary so as not to be enveloped and the extraordinary depth of the battalions which would occur if one wished to form the square by men would be useless.

William Louis of Nassau, in a letter to his cousin Maurice (printed in Duyk's *Journal*, 1:717), states that in the "stretched formation" the interval between infantrymen to the side and to the rear is 6 feet. But he says that they could also form and march in accordance with Aelian's prescription in "close formation" ("*densatie*," "*constipatie*").

It is also said that in battle formation facing the enemy the interval between men is 3 feet and between ranks 7. But one can also have the men close in much tighter, both in the ranks and between files. They would then stand close to one another but in such a way as still to be able to use their weapons. The command for this is "tight," or if it is desired that they be even more closely formed, in order to be able to withstand enemy cavalry like a wall, the command is "tight, tight," or "*Heel dicht*"—that is, as is said in ungerman, "*Serre, serre*" ("Squeeze, squeeze"). When the danger has passed and one wishes to march more comfortably, the ranks and files are again allowed to take up larger intervals.

In the "Instructions" and the "Memoirs" of Landgrave Maurice of Hesse of the year 1600, the interval between files is given as 3 feet;[32] in close formation one should come no closer to the next man than to touch his sidearms, and in the most closed formation to touch elbows.

In Dilich's *Kriegsbuch*, 1607, pp. 246, 277, the foot soldier in each rank is given 3 feet and in the file 5 feet. In the second revision, that of 1647, the author repeats in one passage the same numbers (Part I, p. 156), but in another passage (Part II, p. 71) he says 4 feet and 6 feet, respectively.

In the edition of 1607, p. 290, he prescribes that in battle against lansquenets one should not stand still, as in combat against mounted men, but should move forward, closing tightly together and holding the spears in the rear somewhat higher.

Montgommery, *La milice française*, 1610, p. 80, writes that the sergeant-major has a staff 3 feet long and measures off the front with it, that is, an interval of 3 feet for each soldier

soldier and in the file 7 feet—that is, 3 feet in front of the man, 1 foot for him, and 3 feet behind him. A square of 2,500 men, 50 men wide and 50 men deep, would therefore be 150 feet wide and 200 feet deep. Actually, therefore, the author is reckoning only 4 feet per man in depth, because he is counting the interval of 3 feet twice when he says 7 feet. Wallhausen, in his translation of this work under the title *Militia Gallica*, did not notice this contradiction but accepted it without comment.

Billon, *Les Principes de l'art de guerre*, 1613, II, Chap. 11 (p. 65 of the original version, p. 184 of the translation) forms a battalion of 200 men 20 men wide and 10 men deep and reckons that, if there were an interval of 6 feet "between the files," the unit would have a width of 114 feet (that is, 120 minus 6). Despite the expression "between the files," the man is also included in the 6 feet. But the 114 feet are falsely reckoned in that not 6 feet but only 4 1/2 should be subtracted from 120.

The same figures appear in the second work of the same author, *Instructions militaires*, 1617, p. 63 f.

According to Billon, the distance of 6 feet can be decreased to 3 feet and to a single foot, so that the breadth and depth take only one-sixth of the original space. The last formation is taken up "pour choquer les ennemis," which the German translation renders as "to attack the enemy" (p. 185).

In another passage (Book II, Chap. 45) Billon seems to intend to say the same thing, but he is so unclear that, if we had only this one reference to depend on, we would remain uncertain.

In his *Kriegskunst zu Fuss*, 1615, p. 79 (see also p. 71), Wallhausen states that in battle against foot troops men stood with a distance of one and a half paces in both ranks and files, but in combat against horsemen very tightly closed together. When marching and drilling they had larger intervals, which could be varied.

In the *corpus militare*, 1617, p. 55, distinctions are made, although rather unclearly, in like manner between several kinds of intervals, so that Rüstow interpreted it as meaning only two different intervals, whereas it should obviously be three: the close interval, the ordinary interval, and the extended one. The normal interval is two paces between ranks and files, and the close one is "when ranks and files stand the most closely pressed together as is proper." The extended interval is four paces or even more.

In the *Little War Book (Kriegsbüchlein)* by the Zurich captain Lavater, 1644, it is stated on p. 88 that, when forming up, each man takes a full pace from the next man, both in his rank and his file. When assuming close formation (doubling), either the rear ranks deploy abreast of the foremost ranks or the men of the rear ranks step forward into the intervals of the foremost ranks, "according to whether you intend to fight with the enemy and have enough interval to do so" (p. 87). It goes on to say (p. 90): "When the entire formation is closed (thus principally to prevent the penetration by horsemen) . . ."

Gerhard Melder (1658) (Jähns, 2:1149) states: "A musketeer needs 3 feet of space in his rank and 3 in his file; in like manner, a horseman needs 3 in his rank and 10 in file."

The Hessian captain lieutenant Backhausen, in *Description of Practical Drills (Beschreibung der gebräuchlichen Exercitien)*, 1664, p. 2, gives the infantrymen an interval of 6 feet for drilling, and for skirmishing, that is, for combat, has them double up, so that six ranks become three (p. 26). He says: "Others would give each man in the front ranks 2 feet, which each man can take up according to his own wishes and the circumstances."

He goes on to say that when the infantry is attacking enemy artillery, he recommends taking double intervals between the files so that broad lanes are formed between them and the cannon balls can pass through without causing harm. The files are then twelve men deep. "But if the horsemen intend to drive into the formation, one must close the door in the meantime and have the files form again."

Johann Boxel, Netherlandish captain lieutenant, *Netherlandish Military Drills (Niederländische Kriegs-Exercitien)*, 1668. German translation of 1675, Book 3, p. 6: "The soldiers stand 6 feet apart between ranks and 3 feet apart between files."

According to the pictures, there is no doubt that the given interval does not include the man, for after execution of the command "double your ranks" the soldiers still have considerable room.

Montecuccoli, *Works (Werke)*, 2:224, gives the foot soldier in closed formation three paces of interval in his rank and three in his file. But immediately after that he says that in "closed formation" the soldiers are to stand as close to one another as possible.

Whoever reads these references, to which we could easily add others, is undoubtedly initially astonished that the authors, who may all qualify as professionals, can possibly make such varied statements on such a simple matter that could easily be determined on any drill field. To a certain degree it is possible and logical to assume that in the various periods and countries or training schools various figures were taught, but the very nature of things nevertheless establishes for such variations more narrow limits than appear here. Why then are there such differences? The question is more important than the subject itself, but this question must still be studied, both because of the lansquenets themselves and also because of the corresponding question in the military system of antiquity. On the basis of a somewhat incorrectly understood passage in Polybius, a whole system of ancient tactics has been fantastically associated with a false concept of the intervals in ranks and files, and the question arises as to what conclusion might be reached on this subject from the lansquenet period. It is a question of the similarity of the Swiss and lansquenet squares to the late Macedonian phalanx, which did, to be sure, use the very same weapon, the long spear.

First of all we should note that in two of the cited bits of evidence there are obvious errors. When Tavannes gives the intervals as three and seven "paces" ("*pas*"), there can be no doubt that he means not paces but feet. When Montecuccoli says first that the soldier in closed ranks needs three paces of interval in his rank and three in his file but then immediately says that in closed ranks the soldiers are to stand as close together as possible, it is clear that in the first sentence he mistakenly wrote "closed" for "open." This point is confirmed on p. 226, where a front of eighty-three men is reckoned as 124 1/2 paces in width, and similarly on pp. 350, 579, and 586, where an interval of 1 1/2 paces is assigned each infantryman.

We further notice that the authors are quite often unclear and on occasion even contradict themselves. Instead of specific figures, sometimes only simple descriptions are given. It amounts to the fact that the "pace," which is often given as the unit of measure, is a quite indefinite concept, and the "foot" and "shoe" are in no way to be accepted as uniform measures. As the actual normal spacing in battle formation we seem to have 3 feet between men in each rank, but also closer and even much closer formations, to as little as one ell and indeed even one foot per man, are mentioned. It is also required that the closeness of the formation be changed in the middle of combat, especially to close together as tightly as possible against horsemen. The fixed scheme of the ancient authors—6 feet, 3 feet, 1/2 feet—we do not find repeated here. Even when William Louis indicates this directly by referring to Aelian, he still does not actually repeat it. This is all the more remarkable in that we could say that it automatically results from a drill that William Louis himself mentions and that plays an important role in the drill regulations throughout the seventeenth century—that is, the doubling formation as we have mentioned it above in the citation from the Zurich author, Lavater. In the drill regulations of Frederick III of Brandenburg of the year 1689, just before the abandonment of the pikemen, the regulations on the doubling and tripling of the ranks and files were still discussed in detail.[33] Intervals were not specifically stated, but if one accepts the basic interval of 6 feet, which is stated so frequently, then we come to intervals of 3 feet and 1/2 feet, respectively, with doubling and tripling, just as the Greeks did.

If, nevertheless, we do not find again the fixed Greek scheme among the units of pikemen of the modern age, that certainly does not result from the idea that in the sixteenth and seventeenth centuries drills were performed less exactly than among the Greeks.

While the analogy exists between the late Macedonian phalanx and our square, it has its limitations. The *sarissa* and the long spear were no doubt as good as identical, but the tactics used were different. I remind the reader of the fact that I in no way consider the Macedonian phalanx, as described by Polybius, to be identical with the phalanx of Alexander the Great. The very long *sarissa* and the very tight formation were only the final result of a rather long development in this direction. This late Macedonian phalanx, with its broad front and tightly closed formation, moved very slowly. Its principle was to press down the enemy through its mass bristling with spears. Alexander's phalanxes had been much more mobile, but the main squares of the Swiss and lansquenets were still more mobile than his. The older Swiss tactics were based specifically on the sudden assault, by surprise if possible. While the late Macedonian phalanx could in fact normally function only on a flat plain, the Swiss and lansquenet squares were hardly impeded by any kind of terrain obstacles, especially in their enveloping movements. Consequently, their normal formation could not be too tight, but under certain circumstances, and especially whenever they had to withstand an attack by knights or mounted men, they pressed together as closely as possible.

In a combat situation this closing together took place very simply and naturally from rear to front as the rearmost ranks closed in on the forward ones. This was not so simple from the right toward the left. Whereas there was often automatically a certain pressing together toward the middle, as is reported of the Romans at Cannae and confirmed in general by Machiavelli, to plan to close in in this way in the face of an imminent attack could easily disrupt the entire formation. Consequently, the tightening of the front no doubt took place by having the ranks move up from the rear and at the same time having an individual from the rear move up anywhere where a space opened up between two soldiers in a rank. Later, this action of having men move forward from the rear into the looser leading rank was practiced systematically on the drill field. This was the doubling formation that has already been mentioned.

In the authors of antiquity, Vegetius and Aelian, we also find this drill mentioned and developed with Greek logic into the scheme of the 6-foot interval, the 3-foot interval, and the 1 1/2-foot interval. In actual combat conditions this could not possibly have been carried out so correctly. In their advance the men did not maintain the intervals so precisely. The more recent authors whose ideas we have sampled all had practical experience and took their figures directly from this experience, unless they simply repeated the figures of the ancient authors. They were less philosophically inclined than the Greeks. They did not give a logical scheme; instead, they judged what they themselves had experienced and seen, and in doing so they arrived at quite different analyses—or they let themselves be influenced by a tendency toward theorizing. How greatly practical men can differ from one another in such analyses I have recently experienced myself when I asked three cavalry sergeants how much space in width a horse required today (1909). The three estimates were: "one pace," "one good pace," "one-and-one-half paces." When we consider that these replies came from three men of completely similar training and experience, we see that they differed considerably.

I wish to add immediately that the French military author, Billon, lieutenant colonel of Monsieur de Chappes, whom I have already cited above, assumes on p. 259 that with ten ranks the spears of the last rank still just barely protrude, whereas Montecuccoli, 2:579, claims that pikemen should not be formed more deeply than in six ranks, since the pike would not reach beyond the fifth rank.

If we now make an overall review of our testimony after all these considerations, we come to the conclusion that the pikemen basically moved up in a rather loose formation, with 3 feet of interval per man in each rank, but that in combat they very frequently shifted to a much tighter formation. That happened especially on the defense, in order to repel mounted attacks. But that happened also in combat between infantry squares, when the attacking unit clashed with an opponent, came to a standstill, and then everybody pushed forward, even into the first rank. Then the loose 3-foot interval disappeared, as we learn not only from some of the theoretical writings cited above but also from the accounts of many battles, and the attackers sought, in tightly pressed masses similar to the Macedonian phalanx, to overpower the opponent. We have such descriptions at Cerignola (1503), Vaila (1509), Ravenna (1512), Novara (1513), where the Swiss, as they were attacking the lansquenets, were threatened on their flank by the French men-at-arms and because of this had to press closely together, at La Motta (1513), and at Bicocca (1522), Pavia (1525), where the square of Low German soldiers, the "Black Ones," was "seized as if with tongs" by the two squares of Embs and Frundsberg, and finally at Ceresole (1544). If the unit did not press closely together until the last moment, and perhaps not even all at the same time, it also easily assumed a looser formation during the fight itself and especially whenever the enemy yielded and the attackers gradually shifted into the pursuit. We may not be specific in this respect and go too far in establishing definite measures, an error into which the theoretical needs so easily lead us. But a mighty closing together, at least at specific moments, is certainly proved, if by nothing else, then by that legend of Ravenna to the effect that the agile Spaniards had jumped on the heads of the lansquenets and had fought them from above. In order for such a legend to be formed, there must have been in the tale-tellers and their hearers the concept of a mass closed together as tightly as possible.

NOTES FOR CHAPTER III

1. On the military library of Maurice of Orange, see Carl Neumann, *Rembrandt*, 1:95.

2. *Journal of Anthony Duyck (Journaal van Anthonis Duyck)*, fiscal advocate of the Council of State (1591–1602). Published under commission of the War Department, with introduction and notes by Ludwig Mulder, captain of infantry, 3 volumes, 1862–1866, s'Gravenhage and Arnhem. Duyck's office was that of a chief of the war chancellery of the Council of State and of the highest juridical official for the army (Mulder, preface, p. LXXXVI). He was normally present with the army and kept a daily account of events. To judge from an examination of his journal, he was so excellently informed on the thoughts of Maurice as to be possible only through direct verbal contact. In many passages we may consider the journal to be Maurice's legacy to posterity. Gustav Roloff, "Maurice of Orange and the Founding of the Modern Army" ("Moritz von Oranien und die Begründung des modernen Heeres"), *Preussische Jahrbücher*, Vol. 111, 1903.

3. Jähns, 1:869 f.

4. Jähns, 1:472, 705, says that in 1521 Della Valle recommended the parade march in step; Lodrono did likewise (Jähns, 1:724). See also Hobohm, 2:407. In a report on the battle of Ceresole by Bernardo Spina, published by Stallwitz as a supplement to his document on that battle (Berlin dissertation, 1911, p. 54), it is stated that the Spanish general del Guasto had the recruits drilled immediately before the battle. It is also reported that the French guards had conducted drills.

5. Jähns, 1:735.

6. Dilich, *Kriegsbuch*, 1607, p. 254, discusses the steps taken to maintain the formation on the march. Among them he says "that in marching, an even and steady step is to be maintained" and "that the drummers maintain a correct beat as if the soldier had to *dance* by it."

7. In March 1591 this proportion was 1:0.47. Mulder, preface to Duyck's *Journal*, 1:51 ff., 1862. He arrives at this number by taking the average of a large number of individual figures in the documents, figures that cannot be confirmed.

8. According to the sketches by John of Nassau, two ranks of musketeers were drawn up forward of the front of the "double-pay men," that is, the pikemen. Plathner, "Graf Johann von Nassau," Berlin dissertation, 1913, p. 57.

9. Dilich, *Kriegsbuch*, 1607, p. 290, is not very clear as to what is supposed to happen when a formation of pikemen and marksmen is attacked by mounted men or pikemen. They should either retire behind the pikemen or into the mass of them.

10. Stuttgart Manuscript of 1612. Jähns, 2:924. John of Nassau states that Maurice never allowed his system of march and battle formation to be changed, once it had been established, so that merely by drum and trumpet signals each man could take his place. Plathner, p. 58.

11. Plathner, p. 57.

12. A letter from Sandolin to Lipsius, dated 16 July 1595. Cited in Jähns, 2:880. Duke Henri Rohan reported later in his document (cited in Jähns, 2:951) that Maurice had found that the armament with shields was better but had not been able to have his opinion accepted, since, of course, he was not the sovereign. See Hobohm, 2:452.

13. Mulder, *Van Duyck's Journal*, 1:636 ff. From 9 August to 26 October 1595. Similarly in 1598. Reyd, *Niederländische Geschichte*, Vol. XV, Ed. 1626, p. 569. In the same year the brother of William Louis, John of Nassau, reported from Groningen to their father on drills in the garrisons. *Archives of Oranien-Nassau*, 2d Series, 2:403. Wallhausen, *Kriegskunst zu Fuss*, p. 23, reproaches those who say: "What is drilling? When one is fighting for the enemy, one does not drill long."

14. Chapters IV and VII and a particular paragraph, 144, of Chapter XVIII are erroneously identified in the letter as Folio 144. The three echelons are prescribed in it: "Has tres acies ad usum separatas, propinquitate conjunctas, ad se mutuo adjuvandas idoneas esse perspeximus" ("We observed that these three battle lines, separated for use and joined by their proximity, are suitable to aid each other mutually"). The depth of the echelons is given as ten men in Leo. It is interesting to note, incidentally, how understanding and misunderstanding are often confused. In a rather careless way, Leo transferred the tradition concerning the Roman infantry (which eventually goes back to Livy, 8.8) to the

cavalry. But this attracted so little attention that William Louis, apparently without noticing Leo's error, was able to transfer it back again to the infantry.

15. A set of instructions for the training of the individual man was *Handling of the Guns, Muskets, and Spears (Waffenhandlung von den Rören, Musqueten und Spiessen)* by Jacob de Geyn. The Hague, 1608. Dedicated to Joachim Ernst, Margrave of Brandenburg. The book is illustrated with large, handsome copper plates. Republished in 1640. The copper plates in Wallhausen's *Kriegskunst zu Fuss* are different ones, also quite often different in their arrangement. Geyn distinguishes between marksmen and musketeers; he has forty-two commands for the former and forty-three for the latter. The musketeers have wooden powder containers on bandoliers, while the marksmen do not. For the spearmen there are twenty-one commands, many of them to be carried out in three speeds.

16. Rüstow, 1:345, characterizes Maurice's reforms as having simplified to the maximum the tactical formations. This seems to be the direct opposite of my description, to the extent that I see in the new formations something that had to be worked out and was not at all simple but possible only through hard work. But the difference is apparent rather than real. Rüstow is thinking of those artificial theoretical formations which he thoroughly discusses, like the cross battalion and the eight-cornered unit; they were nothing more than ingenious contrivances and never played a role in actual practice. And in comparison with this, the Netherlandish formation was, of course, a simplification. In comparison with the square of men or the geometric square, which up to that point were the only ones under practical consideration, the Netherlandish method was not a simplification but a far-reaching refinement, and it is only with this explanation that the historical progress is placed in the right light.

17. John of Nassau gives 135 as the normal number, of which 45 have the long spear and 74 are musketeers and marksmen. Plathner, p. 40.

18. Everardus Reidanus, *Belgarum aliarumque gentium annales (Annals of the Belgians and other Nations)*, Leyden, 1633, 8:192. Emmius, *Guilelmus Ludovicus (William Louis)*, 1621, p. 67. See also Mulder's preface to Duyck's *Journal*, 1:16.

19. Krebs, *Battle on the White Mountain (Schlacht an dem Weissen Berge)*, p. 25 ff.

20. Reyd, p. 281.

21. Billon, p. 191.

22. Maurice (19 June 1593), *Archives-Oranien-Nassau*, 2d Series, 1:24.

23. Printed in the *Works* of the *Historical Society (Historisch Genootschap)* in Utrecht. New series, No. 37. Utrecht, 1883, p. 448 ff.

24. Ed. Albèri, Series I, 6:19.

25. Cited in Hobohm, 2:420.

26. Hobohm, 2:420.

27. I have used the edition of 1553, which is found in the University Library in Erlangen. Page 77.

28. I am using the copy of the Munich *Hof- und Staatsbibliothek*, p. 103.

29. I have not been able to find the earlier passage, to which the anonymous author refers. To him, "Reng" means "rank" (*Glied*), and "*file*" means "file" (*Rotte*). This is shown on pp. 73–74, Vol. II, Chap. 6. Kromayer, *Hermes*, 35:228, cited this passage as proof of the 3-foot file interval, because he translated "*file*" as "rank" and "*Reng*" as "file." That is incorrect. In Billon, too, *Instructions militaires*, 1617, the German "*Rotte*" (file) is shown as "file"; for example, on p. 25:

> Ils ne seraient alors que dix hommes de hauteur, qui est la file entière selon l'ordre du Prince Maurice, et de cinquante hommes en front, qui est cinq fois autant en front comme en file.

30. Jähns, 1:712.
31. Ed. Buchon, p. 75.
32. Jähns, 2:889, 902.
33. Published by Eickstedt, 1837.

Chapter IV

Gustavus Adolphus

The man who perfected Maurice's art of war was Gustavus Adolphus, who not only took over and expanded the new tactics but also established the new system as the base of a large-scale strategy.

At the end of the Middle Ages Sweden was close to being merged with Denmark and Norway into a unified nation, as occurred with Castile and Aragon at the same time. But the Swedes resisted this unification and, in the struggle for their national independence, developed a military nation of a strength unknown before that time. The country, including Finland and Esthonia, had hardly a million inhabitants (approximately no more than the Electorate of Saxony and Brandenburg together), but the common people, the estates, and the king had drawn together into a firm unity. In the German areas, on the other hand, under both the Hapsburgs and the Hohenzollerns, all power was paralyzed as a result of the animosity between the princes and the estates, and the common people merely existed in a condition of dull aimlessness. The kingdom of the Vasa dynasty, which had not sprung from feudal hereditary right but was created by the people's choice, was completely different from the German princely concept. And the Swedish estates, too, like their monarchy, differed very significantly from the representation in the estates typical of the rest of Germanic-Romanic Europe. The Swedish parliament is a kind of professional representative organization that is not representative of its own rights but is summoned by the king at his discretion and for his support. For this purpose the king summoned not only nobles, clerics, and burghers, but also peasants; in addition, there were representatives of officers, judges, officials, miners, and other professions and trades.[1] The latter groups finally were dropped, and the officers' representation was melded with that of the nobility, forming a definite representative group of four classes which was unified in a close relationship with the monarchy and presented a single will toward other countries. Gustavus Adolphus, grandson of Gustavus Vasa, ascended the throne in 1611 at the age of seventeen. In the wars with the Russians and Poles he won Karelia, Ingermanland, and Livonia, and increased his army to more than 70,000 men, a strength relative to the population greater than that raised by Prussia in 1813.[2] The financial resources of the poor Swedish nation must have been strained to the utmost to maintain such an army. That would have been impossible in the long term, but war nourished war. The army, once in existence, maintained itself and even grew in the countries it conquered.

The national manning of the army did not result simply from voluntary recruitment; with the help of the clergy a roster of all men in the country over fifteen years of age was drawn up, and men were levied at the discretion of the local officials. Consequently, the Swedes were the first people to form a national army. The Swiss had been a military people's levy but not an army. The lansquenets had a specifically German character but no relationship to the German nation. The French "bands" were not significant enough to be designated as a national army. The Spaniards did come closer to this concept, while the Netherlanders again represented a purely international mercenary type. The Swedish army, however, was a trained military organization serving the defense, the greatness, and the fame of the fatherland. The people provided its sons as rank and file, and the officer corps was formed from the native nobility. In wartime, to be sure, this national character was not maintained, but many foreign soldiers were also recruited. Even prisoners of war were enlisted in large numbers, and officers of foreign birth were accepted. When Gustavus Adolphus went into Germany, he had many Scots in his army, and the longer the war in Germany lasted, the more German the Swedish army gradually became in officers and men.

The army was disciplined and trained after the Netherlandish pattern. Whereas "in Germany the soldiers often trotted along like a herd of cattle or pigs," Traupitz taught in his *Art of War According to the Royal Swedish Manner (Kriegskunst nach königlich schwedischer Manier)*, 1633, that it was necessary to maintain the dress in ranks, to cover down in files, and to keep exact intervals. He, as well as other authors, described the formations that were taken up and were often so artificial that they could not possibly be executed in battle. Nevertheless, even the idea that such movements could be made shows the energy of a very active concept of drill.

The Scot Monro describes as follows a Scottish regiment that fought under Gustavus Adolphus at Breitenfeld and Lützen: "An entire regiment disciplined like this one is like a single body and a single movement; all ears listen in the same manner to the command, all eyes turn with the same movement, and all hands work like a single hand."

In his *History of the Infantry*, Rüstow has drawn a very graphic picture of the "Swedish Formation." Each regiment consists of pikemen and musketeers; the tactical unit is called a brigade. It is based on a shallow linear formation, six ranks deep, in which the pikemen and musketeer sections alternate with one another. The problem of having the pikemen protect the marksmen is solved in this manner: in case of a threatened cavalry attack, the musketeers withdraw behind the line of pikemen, and the spaces thus opened in the front are filled by units of pikemen that formed a second echelon behind the first line up to that point.

If we make accurate comparisons, however, we see that this picture is not supported by the passages on which Rüstow bases it, and other reports read quite differently. From an objective viewpoint, too, it is very questionable as to whether it is possible in the face of an approaching enemy attack to pull the musketeers back so quickly behind their neighboring pikemen and to close the front by moving forward the pikemen of the second echelon. Furthermore, in the original formation the musketeers of the second echelon are masked by the first echelon in such a way that they can make no use of their weapons, and we do not see how and where they are supposed to be used at all.

Nevertheless, I decline to delve into the questions raised by these points (see the excursus below), since they are, after all, of a technical nature, and there is no doubt concerning the significant aspect with respect to military and world history: that is, the large number of musketeers, as we have already found them in Maurice's system, combined with the improvement of their weapon. The muskets had become so much lighter that the fork could be abandoned, and that meant a faster rate of fire. Some still believe that musketeers alone could not withstand a mounted attack, but this concept is contradicted by the fact that there were already regiments consisting entirely of musketeers, and as early as 1630 Neumair von Ramssla wrote in his *Recollections and Rules of the Military System (Erinneurngen und Regeln vom Kriegswesen)*[3]: "The long spears are more like a weakening influence in war than its nerve. The firearms give strength to the long spears."[4]

One of the Scots who participated in the battle of Breitenfeld, Lieutenant Colonel Muschamp, commander of a musketeer battalion, gives the following account of the infantry combat:[5]

First I had three of the smaller cannon that I had in front of me fire, and I did not allow my musketeers to fire a salvo until we were within pistol range of the enemy. Then I had the first three ranks fire a salvo, followed by the other three ranks; then we drove in on them and struck away at them with our muskets or sabers.

Although we were already in hand-to-hand contact with the enemy, he fired two or three salvos at us with his muskets. At the start of our attack, four spirited cuirassier squadrons which were advancing in front of the enemy infantry attacked our pikemen.

They moved up close to them and fired their pistol salvos once or twice, killing all the Scottish color bearers, so that suddenly many colors fell simultaneously to the ground. Our men retaliated appropriately. A brave leader, dressed in scarlet and gold embroidery, was directly in front of us. We saw how he was beating his own men on their heads and shoulders with his saber to drive them on, because they were unwilling to advance. This gentleman maintained the fight longer than an hour, but when he was killed, we saw their pikemen and units stumble and fall over one another, and all his men began to flee. We pursued them until darkness separated us.

A similar clear description of an infantry battle is found in another English source, the biography of King James II. The account reads as follows:[6]

When the royal army at Edgehill in 1642 was within musket range of the enemy, the infantry on both sides began firing. The royal army moved forward, while the rebels held their position, so that they came so close to one another that several battalions were able to thrust with their pikes, especially the Guard Regiment under Lord Willoughby and a few others. Lord Willoughby himself killed an officer of the Lord Essex Regiment with his pike and wounded a second one. When the foot troops were engaged in such a close and heavy combat, one would have expected that one side would give way and break formation, but this did not happen, for both sides, as if in agreed alternation, withdrew a few paces, had their units take a firm position on the ground, and continued to fire at one another into the night, an action so unusual that it could hardly be believed if there had not been so many witnesses present.

After the introduction of the linear formation of the infantry, the fire fight still developed first of all in the form of the caracole. The line of musketeers was divided into several groups, with an alley between them. When the first rank had fired, it withdrew to the rear through the alley in order to reload, while the second rank moved up into its place to fire, and so forth. When the unit was moving forward, the caracole was turned about, so to speak; the rank that had fired stood fast and the following one moved out in front. This procedure was also developed to the point where two ranks fired simultaneously and moved back. In order to execute this action without interruption, it was necessary, of course, to load very quickly. The Scots at Breitenfeld had reduced their six-rank formation to three ranks by doubling up and then, by having the first rank kneel, they fired salvos from all three ranks. Since we cannot assume that the original formation was broad enough to allow the doubling up

without any further measures, there must have been available enough
time and space to extend the intervals at the start.[7]

The pike units had become too small to be able to execute the former
heavy overwhelming impact. But that was not all. The development of
cavalry tactics reacted on them. It was now easy to strike the advancing
pikemen in the flank with the maneuverable cavalry squadrons and to
bring the offensive movement to a standstill by striking from two sides.
Then the unit of pikemen was exposed almost without protection to the
pistol fire of the mounted men. And so the pikemen had sunk to the role
of a simple supporting arm for the marksmen.

Gustavus Adolphus now increased not only the firearms in the infantry
but also just as much in the artillery. It was a question of the introduction
of a type of very light cannon that were bound with leather and therefore
called leather cannon. We have no sure account as to when they were
built and how long they were used. At any rate, the Swedish king had
at his disposal a large number of light artillery pieces in the battle of
Breitenfeld.[8]

In the third place, however, Gustavus Adolphus also reorganized the
cavalry. We have seen how cavalry was formed in the sixteenth century
as the former knightly elements with their mounted soldiers were grouped
in definite units and used the pistol as their principal weapon in the
caracole movement. This caused the abandonment of the system of true
mounted attacks. The Netherlanders, too, who reduced the depth of the
squadron to five or six ranks, still retained firing by caracole as their
combat method. Gustavus Adolphus now prescribed that the cavalry be
drawn up in only three ranks and attack the enemy at a gallop with cold
steel, after the first two ranks, at the most, had fired a shot from very
close range. After the battle of Lützen, Wallenstein, too, forbade the
caracole.[9]

Further research is still needed on the discipline in the army of Gustavus
Adolphus and the armies of the Thirty Years' War in general. On the
one hand it is certain that the troops mistreated the land and people in
the most extreme manner, while on the other hand, from a strictly military
viewpoint, discipline was better and more severe than in the armies of
lansquenets. This was, of course, the natural result of the fact that the
men remained constantly under the colors and the commanders did their
best to rein them in sharply. It is reported of Gustavus Adolphus that
he invented the punishment of running the gauntlet between spears in
order to be able to mete out severe punishments without losing the services
of the punished soldiers. For corporal punishment administered by the
executioner made the soldier "dishonorable," and he was no longer tolerated in the ranks of his comrades. Running the gauntlet, however, was
a punishment administered by one's comrades themselves, and it was
therefore not considered as dishonoring the man.[10]

Just as in the Roman army the service of the Capitoline gods had gone hand in hand with a rigorous administration of punishment, so too did Gustavus Adolphus base the morale of his army not simply on the official power of the superior, but also on the nurture of the religious concept. As we have seen, the army had a Swedish national foundation, but even more importantly it had a specifically Protestant-Lutheran attitude. After the victory at Wittstock, we are told in detail by an English eyewitness how General Baner had a three-day period of thanksgiving to God observed, during which there was substituted for organ music the playing of drums, pipes, trumpets, the firing of salvos, and the thunder of cannon.[11]

What Cannae was for Hannibal, the battle of Breitenfeld was for Gustavus Adolphus: the victory of art over a military skill that was no doubt present to a high degree but was too unwieldy. We find similarities between Cannae and Breitenfeld even in a number of individual details. There follows below, in the series of battle descriptions, the detailed account of this decisive encounter, so important in world history, which will bring complete clarity to the new Swedish military system as well as the older Spanish one in their clash. Not until later will we take up Gustavus Adolphus also as a strategist, in the general context of the development of strategy.

Let us here add the remarkable characteristics of the Swedish king which have been reported by Philip Bogislav Chemnitz (Vol. I, Book 4, Chap. 60):

Since he felt proper concern not only for his royal dignity and authority but also especially for the welfare of his kingdom and his subjects, he removed every basis for internal uprising and lack of unity and joined and bound together in a special way two differing, indeed almost opposite, things, namely, the freedom of his subjects and the dignity of his majesty.

Furthermore, in his military system, as greatly as he outshone other high commanders of previous periods in his splendid deeds, just as greatly did he exceed them in knowledge of the art of war and establishment of good order. Let all his deeds be ascribed not to simple, blind luck but, in addition to the grace of God, to his outstanding virtue, high intelligence, and good conduct. He was able in masterful fashion to lead his army advantageously against the enemy, withdraw it again from the enemy without losses, encamp it comfortably in the field and hastily secure it with a fortified camp. Nobody could easily fortify a place or attack it better than he. Nobody could better appraise the enemy, judge accurately the chance circumstances of war, and quickly reach an advantageous solution on the spur of the moment. Especially in the matter of forming up for battle he had no equal. With respect to the cavalry, his maxim was not to give much heed to wheeling and the caracole; instead it was drawn up in three ranks, was to move forward directly against the enemy and drive into him. Only the first rank, or, at the very most, the first two ranks, when they were close enough to be able to see the whites of the enemies' eyes, were to fire. Then they were to draw their sidearms and the last rank was to go at the enemy with drawn swords, without firing a shot, and the men were to keep both their pistols in reserve for the melee (just as the first two ranks were to do with one of their pistols). The foot troops were divided into their regiments and companies and the companies into their definite squads and files, each of which had its leader and assistant leader. This was done in such an orderly manner that any common soldier, even without orders from the officers, already knew in advance in which position he was to stand and fight. And because the king found that in a battalion in deep formation, in accordance with the old system, the men in front hindered those behind in their fighting, and also the cannon, when fired through the troops, caused great damage to them, he had his infantry form in only six ranks. And when they went into an engagement, they had to double up their ranks so that there were only three. In this manner the enemy cannon were less effective, and furthermore the rearmost men could use their muskets as effectively against the enemy as did those in the first rank. This was accomplished by having the first rank kneel, the second bend over, and the third stand erect, so that each fired over the shoulder of the preceding one. He had invented an unusual manner of forming the infantry, with the musketeers covered by the pikemen and the latter, in turn, supported by the musketeers. In the same way, each squadron supported another, and each brigade, like a small mobile fort, had its forward cover and flanks, each of which was defended and covered by another. Thus the brigades also stood in well-defined echelons with sufficient distance, beside and behind one another. On the flanks and in the rear they were similarly protected by horsemen. In like manner the horsemen were mixed with selected musketeers so that either one could withdraw toward the other and one could relieve the other. The invention of the boar-spears, although the royal Swedish army did not have them in the German war, had given the king a good advantage over the large and wild cavalry of the Poles. He also used the leather pieces advantageously against the Poles in Prussia. And again, in the German war, he used the short, light regimental pieces with wide muzzles from which he peppered the enemy more with canister and hail shot than with balls. Their effect was particularly noticeable in the losses they caused Tilly's army in its defeat at Leipzig.

In other respects he was a hero in battle, not only because of his decisions but also in his acts. He was careful in his deliberations, prompt in his decisions, undaunted in heart and spirit, strong of arm, and ready both to command and to fight. And such a figure was a proper exemplar not only of a highly intelligent commander but also of a brave and fearless soldier. Consequently, these things were interpreted of him in an almost bad manner by many people, and specifically those who either did not know or did not reflect sufficiently that his scorn of every danger and of death itself sprang from his love of the fatherland, which exceeded the common measure and was therefore capable of passing judgment on human failings and crimes, for the quality of great heroes is such as can never be matched by a common, ill-bred soul.

EXCURSUS

THE SWEDISH FORMATION

We seem to be very well informed on the Swedish infantry tactics. In addition to the information in the *Theatrum Europäum* and in Chemnitz, we have the two special documents, *Arma Suecica (Swedish Arms)*, by Arlanibaeus (1631), and *The Art of War in the Manner of the Swedish King (Kriegskunst nach Königlicher Schwedischer Manier)*, by Traupitz (1633),[12] and twenty illustrations of his battle formations between 1630 and 1632, drawn by the king himself and published in the *Archives for Swedish Military History (Archiv für schwedische Kriegsgeschichte)*, Vol. I, 1854. But there is no agreement between these sources.

According to Rüstow's estimate, a brigade was composed of 576 pikemen and 432 musketeers. But Traupitz says that the Swedes' strength was two-thirds marksmen and one-third pikemen. He argues strongly and in detail against an effort to give those two arms equal strengths, and this despite the fact that he also gives his prescriptions for this latter case.

We could reconcile this contradiction between Rüstow's description and the testimony by Traupitz by assuming that in the brigade formation some of the musketeers are not employed. Even Rüstow himself assumes that. Nevertheless, this difference is no doubt too great to be accounted for in this way.

Furthermore, even the illustrations are not in agreement. On the king's sketches two units, one behind the other, are pushed forward in front of the brigade's front. The same configuration appears in Horn's brigades in their initial position on the battle plan of Breitenfeld in the *Theatrum Europäum*. I have still not arrived at any sure conclusion as to what these units mean, whether they are supposed to be pikemen or musketeers.

Traupitz divides the company (156 individuals, including officers) into three squadrons, each numbering forty-eight men formed in six ranks of eight men each. In the center is the squadron of pikemen, and on the right and left a squadron of musketeers. Between the squadrons are intervals into each of which, although they are given as only "three or four long ells," two cannon are supposed to be placed in line with the last rank, and there hardly seems to be enough room for them. These cannon, however, are very important.

Against cavalry, the squadron of pikemen moves forward, but the musketeers do not take cover behind it but instead stand only a small distance to the rear.

All the units, both individual ones and those divided into three, are always indicated in the text of the *Theatrum Europäum* as "four units (*Fahnen*) on foot." The difference between the sketch of Gustavus Adolphus and the one in the *Theatrum Europäum* is that the advanced units in the latter text are much shorter in width.

In the first echelon it is clearly seen that the units along the line are all uniformly composed of pikemen with marksmen on both flanks. Since the units are shown as very deep, the marksmen appear as outer clothing for them.

On the king's illustrations the intervals between the individual units are for the most part only small, but occasionally there are also large ones.

The first formation for a battle at Stettin bears a certain similarity to the formation of the Bohemians on White Mountain. It is obvious that a common pattern forms the base for both. In Gustavus Adolphus's situation, however, the cavalry is not divided up between the infantry units but is stationed on the flanks.

Traupitz (pp. 28–45) describes and sketches five—actually six—battle formations that the company can supposedly assume from the basic formation. Each one is intended for a particular tactical situation. The captain supposedly needs only to command: "Form up. The enemy is forming with his infantry, cavalry, his entire force, etc." Then the subordinate leaders are supposed to give immediately the proper commands for assuming the familiar formation appropriate to the indicated situation.

The individual movements are prescribed in detail. Not only individual squads but even half-squads are given specific indications as to their movements.

From the description of the Swedish tactics in Arlanibaeus's *Arma Suecica* of 1631 we learn nothing more than that all arms support each other mutually, that the marksmen stand in a shallow formation, and that the marksmen are covered by both pikemen and cavalry.

The advantage of such a battle formation was emphasized as being its unassailability rather than its offensive power.

NOTES FOR CHAPTER IV

1. Fahlbeck, *Preussische Jahrbücher*, 133:535.

2. According to G. Droysen, *Gustav Adolf*, 2:85, the king landed in Pomerania in 1630

with	13,000 men
He already had in Stralsund	6,000
Follow-up forces	ca. 7,000
Withdrawn from Prussia	13,600
Total: approximately	40,000

Some 36,000 men remained behind in Sweden, Finland, Prussia, and so forth. Consequently, the entire military strength amounted to 76,000 men, 43,000 of whom were levied nationals.

3. Jähns, 2:952.

4. In his writings of the year 1673 (*Schriften*, 2:672), Montecuccoli actually considers the usual ratio of two-thirds musketeers and one-third pikemen to be wrong. He believes more pikemen are needed to cover the musketeers in battle, for the latter, alone, would be overpowered by

the cavalry. He points out that this was what happened at Lens, for example, where Condé defeated the Lotharingians. At Breitenfeld, he says, the Holstein regiment held fast because of its pikemen until it was overcome by the artillery. He reports the same thing in 2:223. He claims that the ratio of two-thirds to one-third was acceptable only because on so many occasions outside of battle the musketeers were more useful than the pikemen.

5. "The Swedish Discipline," cited in Firth, *Cromwell's Army*, p. 105.

6. According to Firth, p. 104.

7. Firth, *Cromwell's Army*, p. 98, from the *Swedish Intelligencer*, 1:124.

8. On the leather cannon, see Gohlke in the *Zeitschrift für historische Waffenkunde*, 4:392, and Feldhaus, p. 121. "Leather pieces" are also mentioned in the introductory poem to the *Little War Book (Kriegsbüchlein)* of Lavater of Zurich, 1644. He says they did not come first from Sweden to Zurich, "but rather from us to them."

9. Letter to Aldringer, 2 January 1633, reproduced in Förster, *Wallenstein's Letters (Wallensteins Briefe)*. Daniel's statement in *History of the Military (Geschichte des Kriegswesens)*, 5:12, that Henry IV of France had already required that his squadrons fire a single salvo with their pistols and then attack with cold steel, must be based on a misunderstanding. I have found nothing on this in the sources, and the objective prerequisite for such action is missing, that is, a stricter discipline. Davila states expressly that at Ivry, the last large battle of Henry IV, his squadrons used the caracole.

10. This explanation has been preserved for us in the work of an English military author, Turner, and it goes back to English officers who had served under Gustavus Adolphus. I draw the quotation from Firth, *Cromwell's Army*, p. 289. The passages cited in Marcks, *Coligny*, p. 56, and Hobohm, *Machiavelli*, 2:373, 385, which seem to prove an earlier occurrence of the running of the spear gauntlet—especially Bouchet, *Preuves de l'histoire de l'illustre maison de Coligny (Evidence on the History of the Illustrious House of Coligny)*, 1642, p. 457—are based on erroneous translations. "Passer par les piques" ("to pass before the pikes") is the "law of the long spears," mentioned on p. 61 above. Of course, La Curne de St. Palaye, *Dictionnaire de l'ancien langage françois*, Vol. 8, understands this expression as meaning striking with the spear shafts. I consider that impossible; the spears are too long to be used that way.

11. Cited in Firth, *Cromwell's Army*, p. 321.

12. *The Art of War according to the Royal Swedish Manner of forming a Company in a Regiment and by Platoons: and to arrange it in battle formation, to lead into combat, to employ, and to feed effectively.* By

Laurentium Traupitz. Frankfurt am Main, 1633. University Library, Göttingen. In both the preface and the conclusion, reference is made to continuations of the work, which are supposed to deal with the battle formation of the army rather than the company.

Chapter V

Cromwell

One may doubt whether Cromwell should have a place in a history of the art of war, since it cannot be said that a link in the chain of continuing development bears his name. Nevertheless, he was such a mighty warrior and his army such an unusual and significant phenomenon that we may not pass them by.[1]

As we have seen, England, as a result of its strongly centralized monarchy, produced a very effective military organization in the Middle Ages. In the wars of the red and white roses this military system had consumed itself, so to speak. The great condottieri families had destroyed one another. The Tudor monarchy, which brought an end to the civil war and established an almost unlimited despotism, was not based on a strong military system but on a refined police organization.

There was the beginning of a recruited standing army, particularly for the suppression of the Irish, but it could not develop, since the Parliament, concerned lest this strengthen further the royal despotism, approved no money for the army.

The great mission would have been to go to the aid of the German Protestants in the Thirty Years' War. But just as Elizabeth, in order to spare her subjects from excessive taxes, had given only weak support to the Netherlanders against the Spaniards, so now her successors did not intervene in Germany, even though the Bohemians, specifically in the expectation of this support, had selected as their king the elector of the Palatinate, the son-in-law of King James of England. But a few reinforcements, equipped through voluntary contributions, formed the only aid that England provided.

For the defense of the country and the maintenance of good order in the interior there existed the militia, which is already known to us from the Middle Ages (Vol. III, Book 2, Chap. 5). Each county formed a body of troops corresponding to its size, with military organization and officers. The weapons were stored in special arsenals, and some military exercises were also held. They assembled for an exercise for one day each month in the summer. But as has been said, these militia units were called "trained bands" more because they were supposed to drill than because they actually had drilled. Their military value, just as we have also learned of the local armed units in many German territories, was small.

Legally, they were not supposed to be employed outside of the kingdom and, where possible, not even outside the boundaries of their own county. About 150 years passed during which England no doubt waged war occasionally but could point to only very minor military accomplishments. Although the warrior traditions of the fathers lived on in the English nobility, as in Germany and France, wars could no longer be won with levies of knights, and if mercenaries were recruited, they were lacking in the tradition that made the German lansquenets valuable. By far the strongest of all the Protestant countries, England was nevertheless incapable of playing any significant role in European politics, because of her lack of a military organization—neither in the Huguenot wars, nor in the Netherlanders' struggle for freedom, nor in the Thirty Years' War, in which the leadership was finally seized by Sweden, with its relatively small physical resources.

The lack of an effective military organization naturally also governed the conduct of the civil war. Both the supporters whom King Charles I gathered about him and the Parliament's levies, even though filled with partisan zeal, were nevertheless too disorganized to fight great decisive actions. There were probably between 60,000 and 70,000 men under arms on each side, but by far the largest part of each force was used to garrison cities and fortified castles, so that the battles in the open field were fought out by no more than 10,000 to 20,000 men. On both sides there were officers and men who had been in the Netherlandish or Swedish service and had fought in battles of the Thirty Years' War. The formations that had been developed there were now carried over to England, but several years passed before they had been assimilated by the masses, so that, as in other periods of world history (in the Hussite Wars and later in the French Revolution), it was the war itself that produced the actual armies.

This transformation of the army, the replacement of loosely organized levies of citizen militia and volunteers by a qualified army, was essentially the work of Cromwell. He became an important personality in world history because he understood how to use tactically and to lead strategically this army he had created. As a member of Parliament, Cromwell had proposed a motion that the command of the militia be shifted from the king to the Parliament. When the civil war broke out as a result of this demand, Cromwell, then forty-three years old, had himself appointed a captain of cavalry and formed a squadron in his county. He had never been a soldier previously. When the parliamentary army suffered a defeat at the first rather large clash, at Edgehill on 23 October 1642, Cromwell stated to Hampden during the withdrawal:

> Your troops are mostly old, worn-out serving men, wine bibbers, and similar riffraff. On the other hand, the enemy's troops are sons of gentlemen and young men of position. Do you believe that the courage of such miserable and common fellows will ever be equal to that of men who have honor, courage, and resolution in their hearts? You must seek to raise men of a single spirit and—do not begrudge me what I am saying—of a spirit that is the equal of that of gentlemen.

He went on to say that men of honor would have to be conquered by men of religion and said he knew where such men lived. On another occasion he said that the right men were not at the top; the lawyers had more to say than the military men.

In this spirit he had at first developed his squadron and then his regiment, and in 1645, the fourth year of the war, it was decided to create a new field army based on this pattern. Previously, there had not actually existed any kind of unified parliamentary army but rather a number of military units that were maintained by the individual counties or associations of counties. The strongest of these associations, a group of eastern counties, had already joined forces with Cromwell and his county and now provided the nucleus for the "New Model." The Parliament promised this new army regular pay, no longer through the counties but from the national treasury. Although this army was no stronger than some 20,000 men, the resources at hand were still not entirely sufficient for the new organization, and the local authorities were directed to raise the necessary remaining amount by levy.

As we have heard, until then the armies on both sides had been very similar. On both sides there were officers who had served with the Netherlanders or under Gustavus Adolphus, and the officer corps on both sides consisted of noblemen. The fact that in the parliamentary army, with the passage of time, common soldiers who had distinguished themselves were occasionally appointed to officer rank still made no difference in the overall organization. Of the thirty-seven colonels and generals of the new army, nine were lords, twenty-one country gentry, and only seven of common citizen origin. It was not until the later years that more professional soldiers moved into the positions of the nobles who had taken up arms for their political and religious convictions. The difference between the two armies, therefore, is not to be sought in a possible distinction of aristocrats and democrats. The titles "Cavaliers" and "Roundheads," as if the latter had scorned the locks of the prominent man that embellished those on the other side, is misleading. Pictures of the leaders and officers of the "Roundheads," including Cromwell's, show all of them with long hair. It was only at the beginning of the civil war that the Puritans marched out with clipped hair, as if, as a lady of that day wrote, they were only marching out until their hair should have grown back in again.

In the first years of the civil war the forces of the rebels were commanded by outstanding members of Parliament, the count of Essex and the count of Manchester. While the new army was being formed, there was also established a new high command. The parliamentary generals had always conducted the war with the prospect that there would eventually be a reconciliation with the king. The count of Manchester said: "Even if we defeat the king ninety-nine times, he is still the king and his successors will also be kings. But if the king defeats us a single time, we shall all be hanged and our descendants will be slaves." Now a law was passed, the "self-renunciation acts," to the effect that the members of Parliament were no longer to hold command positions in the army. The conduct of the war was to be separated, so to speak, from politics. Parliament was to name the supreme commander and it selected for that position General Thomas Fairfax. He was given the right to appoint all the officers, colonels and captains, but still with the approval of the Parliament. If Cromwell had been a man like the others, these measures would have cut off his future. For as a member of Parliament he would have had to give up his position in the army, in which he had meanwhile moved up to lieutenant general. But the result was just the opposite. Cromwell was so highly respected among the troops that nobody dared apply the self-renunciation acts to him. Fairfax, however, was purely a soldier, an unpolitical nature. As Cromwell now remained both in the army and the Parliament, he had such an influence on General Fairfax, who was twelve years younger, that, although Cromwell was only in the second position, he actually exercised the command.

The New Model army was based on the complete elimination of the character of militia levies and the formation of a strongly disciplined, purely military organization. It was their religion, however, that formed the basis of the discipline. We must constantly remember that the army was very small in comparison with the population. It was a corporation of like-minded comrades, both a troop and a sect. It has aptly been compared with the crusaders or the knightly orders. The English revolutionary army, therefore, was completely different, for example, from what was later to be the French revolutionary army, and also completely different from a German lansquenet army. In common with the French revolutionary army it found its cohesiveness in a specific religious-political attitude, but it was the opposite, because it represented not a mass levy but a select group. The lansquenets also represented a select group, but theirs was a warriorhood of the lowest kind, animal courage without any ideal purpose, whereas in the Independent Army it was a warriorhood in the service of an idea. During the French Huguenot wars the formation of a unified army like that of Cromwell was never arrived at. The armies in those wars, which were constantly interrupted by peace treaties and armistices, continued to have the character of levies of nobles or burghers and bands of mercenaries.

In Cromwell's army, as in the armies of the latter part of the Thirty Years' War, the cavalry formed between a third and a half of the total force. Most of the men had their own horses and their own equipment. They received such generous pay that they were able to live as gentlemen, and there were among them many educated men who considered this service to be a good position.

"Our men," an old royalist officer once said to a Puritan officer, "had the sins of men, drinking and chasing women; yours had the sin of the devil, spiritual arrogance and rebellion."

Since the officers were appointed and not elected, the principle of authority was strongly maintained. "I order; every man obeys, or he is dismissed," Cromwell once wrote. "I tolerate no contradiction from anybody." "A similar uniform"—this was the issue at stake—"is a necessity, for our men have often fought with one another because of the difference in their uniforms."[2] Even in the highest position, this authority held true. Although the commanding general very often held councils of war with his colonels, he did not consider himself bound by their conclusions but issued his orders as he saw fit.

Military discipline, which, according to Cromwell's expression, "had its footing in the passion and truth of belief," was used to form firmly cohesive tactical bodies of the horsemen through drills and practice. At the beginning of the civil war the count of Essex had believed he could dispense with thorough drilling of the militiamen; it was sufficient, he thought, if they understood only the most essential aspects. Cromwell, on the other hand, required not only that efficient men be made captains but also that they be given time to drill their troops.

The horsemen in the service of the king were not lacking in courage either, and in Prince Ruprecht of the Palatinate, who was his nephew and a son of the Winter King, Charles I had a very reputable cavalry general of long experience in the Thirty Years' War. The count of Essex once despaired that they could ever form a cavalry equal to that of the king. But the superiority that Cromwell's "Ironsides" eventually developed was based not only on their courage but also on their discipline, which enabled their leaders to reassemble them immediately after an attack. Hoenig (II, 2, 435) establishes the point that in all four of Ruprecht's campaigns up to his end as a cavalry general at Naseby, the weakness that the horsemen did not reassemble after the attack was repeated time after time, and he concludes that the prince did not understand the necessity for this. Are we to believe that? A cavalry general who did not learn from one repetition of a bad experience how necessary the assembling was after the attack, how dangerous a disorderly pursuit or even plundering? I would like to believe the prince realized it. But realization did not mean execution. It was a question of military training, a very difficult work requiring continuous moral effort, which the Puritans were able to accomplish because of their religious strength of soul, while it was impossible for the Royalists. At Marstonmoor as at Naseby, it was this difference in the opposing cavalry regiments which decided the day. At Naseby, to be sure, the parliamentary army, contrary to earlier estimates, also had a large numerical superiority.[3]

I may leave aside the account of Cromwell's individual campaigns and battles. His particular talent was not so much his leadership as the formation of his army as described above.[4] But let us add a few interesting details, which also apply to the general military system of the period.

When the civil war started, pikemen and musketeers were still formed side by side. In the sources I have not found any specific manner as to how they were to be placed with respect to each other. It is often mentioned that in battles the pikemen repulsed mounted attacks and also that pike battalions clashed with one another. As on the Continent, in England too the musket gradually won the upper hand over the pike. It is often reported that in close combat the musketeers used their weapons as clubs. As an important factor favoring attainment of a dominant position by musketeers, Firth, p. 108, points out the greater marching ability of the musketeers, because they wore no armor. In the first years of the civil war the hardest marches were no longer than 10 to 12 English miles; the longest of all was 13 English miles, that is, not quite 20 kilometers. Later, when the armor was put aside, the marches became longer but still hardly longer than 3 German miles, or some 23 kilometers.

The English did not finally do away with pikes until 1705.

At the start of the civil war the forks for the muskets were still in use, but they no longer existed in the New Model army.

In the first part of the civil war, the field recognition symbol and the recognition shout were announced before each battle, so that the soldiers on the two sides could distinguish between friend and foe. At Edgehill the parliamentarians had orange scarves, at Newbury green twigs on their hats, at Marstonmoor a white cloth or a piece of white paper on the hat. Since such a symbol could easily be lost in the thick of the fight, they also had the field recognition shout, such as "God with us" (just as the Swedes had at Breitenfeld), or, on the opposite side at Marstonmoor, "God and the king."

It was during the war that Cromwell was able to establish the standard uniform, the red tunic, which has continued to be the dress of English soldiers for two and a half centuries.

The English customarily shouted aloud while attacking, whereas the Scots moved silently against the enemy. The Scot Monro made fun of the imperial soldiers, who shouted, "Sa, sa, sa" during the attack; he said they did this like the Turks, as if shouting would frighten brave soldiers. The Danes and Swedes, too, advanced in silence.[5]

If the peculiar quality of the Puritan army was its religious character and Cromwell's accomplishment was the exploitation of this religious spirit for military formations and warrior deeds, we must also finally not overlook the fact of how this character of the army reacted on politics.

The military command was exercised first by General Fairfax and then by Cromwell, who replaced him. But when the military aspects shifted over into the political field, it was the council of officers that made the decisions, and in 1647, when the army rebelled against the Parliament, the private soldiers, too, elected a soldiers' council, the "agitators," to present their complaints. The Parliament wanted to give the country the Presbyterian Church constitution, which through its church discipline would have guaranteed the power in the country to the ruling classes.[6] The army opposed this. In the army the democratic concept opposed the aristocratic character of the traditional parliamentary constitution. They did not want to subject themselves to the spiritual authority of the Presbyterians any more than to that of the bishops, and they defended the separation of church and state, the free system of sects of the Independents. Finally, the esprit de corps of the army prevailed. The Parliament wanted to dissolve the army after it had done its duty and defeated the king. But the regiments were not willing to be disbanded. The officers were inclined to seek some kind of compromise, but the private soldiers did not agree, and the officers were finally able to keep the troops under control only by going along with their inclinations. Even Cromwell yielded to this pressure. Military obedience was restored by having a few of the ringleaders shot by order of a court-martial. But the will of the army was carried out completely, the king was executed, and the Parliament was first purged and then eliminated. After this procedure was assured, the soldiers' council disappeared. Nevertheless, we later find quite a number of the "agitators" as officers. The army governed the country, and its leader, Cromwell, also became the head of state. As narrow as was the base provided by such a small army, Cromwell was still able to maintain his position as ruler of the three kingdoms of England, Scotland, and Ireland until his death, since he used his power to carry out an energetic policy in foreign affairs and successfully to attend to the interests of the country against its competitor, the Netherlands, and the ancient enemy, the Spaniards. Cromwell is reported to have said: "I can tell you

what I do not want, but I cannot say what I do want; for I shall not
know that until it becomes necessary," and that statement can be regarded
as an appropriate self-characterization.

NOTES FOR CHAPTER V

1. The outstanding book by C. H. Firth, *Cromwell's Army*, London,
1902, covers exhaustively the subject of Cromwell as a military organizer,
the role in which he is of most interest to us. The extensive work by
Fritz Hoenig, *Oliver Cromwell*, Berlin, 1887, is not up to par. See the
review in the *Historische Zeitschrift*, 63:482, and the *Historical Review*,
Vol. 15 (1889), 19, p. 599. It was only in his later writings that Hoenig
brought his considerable talent to its full development.

2. According to Hoenig, II, 2, 269, this command originated in 1643.

3. According to an estimate by W. G. Ross, reported in the *Historische
Zeitschrift*, 63(1889):484, the parliamentary army numbered 13,500 men,
including 7,000 infantry, whereas the royal army had only 8,000 men,
half infantry and half cavalry. See Firth, p. 111.

4. Hoenig attributed to Cromwell specific creations in the tactical employment of cavalry, the formation of echelons, and so on, and saw in
him the predecessor of Frederick and Seydlitz and even the guiding spirit
for our time. I cannot agree with him on this. The entire organization
of military units of the seventeenth century with the matter of effectiveness of their weapons is too different from the conditions of the eighteenth
and nineteenth centuries to justify such comparisons. Hoenig is also in
error (I, 2, 247) when he attributes to Cromwell the formation of divisions
in the Napoleonic sense.

5. Firth, p. 101.

6. See my article "Anglicanism and Presbyterianism" in the *Historisch-
Politische Aufsätze*.

Chapter VI

Individual Battles

BATTLE OF SIEVERSHAUSEN
9 JULY 1553

The horsemen on both sides used pistols; they fired when they were so close that they "could see the white of their eyes." It is not yet a question of using the caracole. Both armies were very strong; Maurice probably had 7,000 to 8,000 horsemen, while Albrecht had a somewhat smaller number. The reports contradict one another drastically. Perhaps an objective analysis of the sources will still succeed in drawing up a reasonably certain description.

BATTLE OF ST. QUENTIN[1]
10 AUGUST 1557

Philip II had assembled an army of no fewer than 53,000 men and 70 cannon, and he besieged St. Quentin, which was defended by Coligny. The main French army was in Italy. While attempting to bring reinforcements into the city, the French were defeated by the superior enemy force, as the Spaniards took the German and French infantry units under cannon fire and broke them up with cavalry. St. Quentin then fell. The remarkable aspect of this, however, is that Philip was not capable of exploiting his success, because he could not pay his army. In November he had to discharge it or divide it up among the garrisons.

BATTLE OF GRAVELINGEN
13 JULY 1558

After the loss of St. Quentin, Henry II had his army return from Italy, and he was now once again the stronger, since Philip had been obliged to disband his army. Henry thereupon captured Calais and laid waste to Flanders. The extreme effort made by the Spaniards in the previous year now took its toll and crippled them. But after six months the situation was again reversed. The French divided up their army and also invaded Luxembourg, and the Spaniards under Egmont attacked with double numerical superiority and defeated the army that was besieging Gravelingen, between Calais and Dunkirk. Again the cavalry played a decisive role.

German lansquenets fought on both sides, and on both sides they were accused of lack of zeal, perhaps because, as lansquenets, they were unwilling to cause too much damage to one another. But this was of no help to the lansquenets in the French service; like all the others, they were cut down. With the exception of a few horsemen who escaped, the army was destroyed and the great lords were taken prisoner.

THE HUGUENOT WARS

BATTLE OF DREUX
19 DECEMBER 1562

The Protestants were stronger in mounted units, while the Catholics were considerably superior in infantry strength (Swiss, lansquenets, Spaniards, and French) and in cannon. Several infantry units on both sides were broken up by the mounted men, and the "black riders" of the Huguenots also sorely pressed the square unit of the Swiss, but they were finally repulsed.[2] A French battalion also held its own against the attacks of the men-at-arms and horsemen by placing in front of its pikemen three ranks of harquebusiers, who held the attackers in respect. And so the Catholics were finally victorious.

BATTLE OF MONCONTOUR
3 OCTOBER 1569

The Catholics were considerably stronger in cavalry and infantry. Coligny sought to protect his forces with frontal obstacles, but the Catholics enveloped them. A mutiny by the lansquenets, who were demanding their back pay, delayed the withdrawal of the Huguenots. A Swiss battalion of 4,000 men that was covering its flanks with wagons in an unusual manner beat off the attacks of the Huguenot horsemen. After the Huguenot cavalry had been driven from the battlefield, the lansquenet battalion was attacked from all sides and destroyed. The Catholics claimed to have lost only 300 to 400 men, and the Swiss, according to Pfyffer's report, lost only 20 killed. According to that report, the lansquenets did not even sell their lives dearly.[3]

ENGAGEMENT AT COUTRAS
20 OCTOBER 1587

This was the first victory of Henry IV. There were no more than 6,000 to 7,000 men on the two sides, and only horsemen and harquebusiers seem to have been engaged in the fight. Henry placed his harquebusiers in small, tightly formed units between the horsemen and instructed them not to fire at the enemy horsemen until they had approached within twenty paces.

BATTLE OF IVRY
14 MARCH 1590

The reports on this battle give a somewhat legendary impression; a critical special study is yet to be done. Although large squares of pikemen were present, the battle was fought entirely by horsemen, harquebusiers, and cannon. After the cavalry of the League was defeated, Henry IV had cannon brought up against the infantry. The Swiss then surrendered while the lansquenets and French were mowed down.

BATTLE ON THE WHITE MOUNTAIN[4]
8 NOVEMBER 1620

For almost three years the Bohemian War dragged on without ever coming to a large, decisive battle. The Bohemians were the considerably stronger force; the Moravians, Silesians, and a large portion of the Austrians were also on their side, and the Hungarians came to assist them. But with their indecisive leadership, their strength was still not great enough to capture Vienna, and eventually the emperor received so much help that he was able to go over to the offensive. The pope sent money, the kings of Spain and Poland sent troops, and Duke Max of Bavaria, as head of the League, personally led up a stately army.

Nevertheless, it was doubtful up to the last moment whether a decisive battle would occur. The duke of Bavaria insisted that they should take advantage of the great numerical superiority of the combined armies of the emperor and the League and should march directly on Prague from Upper Austria. But the commander of the imperial army, Buquoi, who up to that time had conducted a successful maneuver and guerrilla strategy, had serious doubts about risking battle in the late season. He would have preferred to limit himself to maneuvering the enemy out of Lower Austria, but Duke Max stated that they must force the enemy to do battle and win back Austria and Moravia before Prague. Buquoi gave in, but we shall see that the bold undertaking could very easily have failed.

The Bohemian army under the command of Christian of Anhalt sought to delay the advance of the enemy by taking position in front of him in advantageous positions that were difficult to attack. The allied army was resolute enough to move around in a curve toward the north. In this direction ration wagons from Bavaria could also be brought up over the passes of the Bohemian Forest, and they succeeded in doing so. Only by a forced march did the Bohemians, when they noticed that the enemy's move was really directed at Prague, succeed once more in intercepting them and taking up a defensive position on the White Mountain, about 2 miles west of Prague.

The position was very favorable, with its right resting on an animal preserve surrounded by a wall, with a fortified castle, and on the left a rather steep descent. In front of their line was a stream, the Scharka, which flowed through swampy meadows and was impassable for the enemy except on a bridge.

When Tilly audaciously had the Bavarians cross the bridge and deploy on the other side facing the enemy position, the Bohemians realized that the opportunity was at hand to fall on the Bavarians and defeat them before the imperial troops could cross the Scharka and come to their aid. Two colonels, Stubenvoll and Schlieck, called Prince Christian's attention to the favorable situation of the moment, and he was inclined to follow their advice. General Count Hohenlohe argued against it, however, pointing out that the Bavarians would be able with musketeers to hold the village of Rep, which was on the near side of the bridge, long enough for the main body to cross over and that, if the Bohemians attacked, they would give up the advantages of their outstanding defensive position. Anhalt yielded to these objections and gave up the opportunity for the attack against the enemy, who was not yet deployed, an opportunity that was certainly very promising. He decided to wage a purely defensive battle, or, as he hoped up to the last minute, so to impress the enemy with the strength of his position that they would not risk an attack at all. If that actually happened, the campaign was almost surely won for the Bohemians without a battle.

Actually, Buquoi found that he could not overlook sufficiently the enemy position on its ridge, that it was not known what kind of entrenchments had been prepared, that it was possible they would encounter artillery and musket fire which his troops would not be able to withstand, and in that case, with the defile in their rear, everything would be lost. Consequently, he would have liked to maneuver the enemy out of his position by an envelopment from the south.

But Duke Max and Tilly, both of whom wanted the battle, finally won out in the council of war that took place behind the front of the already deployed army. "Whoever wants to fight the enemy in open battle," Tilly said later, "can do this in no other way than by turning his face toward him and exposing himself to the danger of his shots." After all, it was only too clear that the enveloping move was hardly feasible and a withdrawal from the position already taken was highly dangerous. Both the numerical superiority and the morale advantage were undoubtedly on the side of the Catholic army. It had some 28,000 men against 21,000 Bohemians and had continuously pushed the enemy back to the very walls of Prague.[5] Furthermore, on the night before, the Catholic forces had carried out a very successful sudden attack on the Hungarians, which had greatly depressed this part of the Bohemian king's army, numbering no fewer than 5,000 men, and had eliminated their zeal for battle.

While the leaders on the other side were still conducting their council of war, the Bohemians were working hard to strengthen their position. While they had still been on the march, the prince of Anhalt, envisaging the position on the White Mountain, had ordered that entrenchments be dug there. He had asked the king himself, who hurried to Prague ahead of the army, to take care of these works. But little had been done, since the army had worn out the tools it had been carrying and it was necessary first of all to solicit from the government of the estates the approval of 600 talers for the procurement of shovels and spades. With somewhat more energy and attention to duty in this position and a few hours of time they could have strengthened the position on the mountain so greatly that Buquoi's concerns might very well have proven to be true.

But not only had the entrenchments not been pushed along sufficiently, but they also failed to exploit the advantage of the terrain. The right flank, with the park wall and the steep slope, was naturally very strong. On that side fewer defenders would have sufficed, so that the left flank, more easily accessible over a gentle incline, could have been reinforced or a reserve held out for a counterattack. But the entire position was occupied uniformly with two echelons, each composed of alternating rather small units of infantry and cavalry with very wide intervals between them. The 5,000 Hungarian horsemen were to have taken position partly in reserve and partly on the extreme left flank, but they shied away from this position because they thought it was exposed to the enemy artillery fire, and they all remained in the rear as a third echelon. As a result of the attack to which they had been exposed the preceding night, their morale was obviously shaken.

The Jesuit Fitzsimon, who was present at the battle in the retinue of Buquoi and to whom we are indebted for a good report on the fight, has already remarked, along with scholarly references to Livy, that the Bohemians' formation was too thin. The space between the animal preserve on the right and the slope on the left flank actually amounts to about a mile and a half,[6] and the entire Bohemian army was no stronger than 21,000 men. A very sure, superior leadership, which had the troops firmly in hand, would probably have been able to compensate for that, as we have said before, by occupying the animal preserve and the right flank more weakly and in return holding back a strong reserve to intervene wherever it might become necessary. But Christian of Anhalt was not such a commander. This fact was already apparent when he hesitated as to whether he should attack the Bavarians when they were still isolated. Even if he had been a greater man, fully confident in himself, he did not have sure control over his subordinate leaders and through them over the troops.

The Catholic army did not take advantage of its numerical superiority for an envelopment, for example, which would no doubt have been possible on the left flank of the Bohemians, where the Hungarians had not taken position. Instead, it seems that the attackers formed on both flanks an even shorter front than that of their opponents. Thus the depth of their formation was all the greater. The imperial troops and those of the League each formed five large squares of their infantry, which moved forward in checkerboard form in two or three lines, with the cavalry beside or behind them. These mounted men among the imperial troops were divided into rather small squadrons, whereas those of the League were held together in larger units.[7]

The artillery on both sides fired during the deployment, but no doubt without causing much damage on either side. The Catholic artillery was in position in the valley and had to shoot upward, and the Bohemians had only six larger cannon and a few smaller ones.

Although, as we have seen, the Bavarians had deployed first, nevertheless the first attack was made by the imperial troops on the right flank. The Bavarians had to move up a steep slope, but, contrary to Krebs' belief, that cannot have been the reason for their late entry into the battle. If they had formed up simultaneously with the imperial forces, the steeper slope would hardly have caused them to enter the fight minutes later, whereas most of the regiments of the duke, who, after all, was primarily responsible for the decision to fight, did not participate in the combat at all, because the emperor's forces had already won the battle. The reason the battle developed into a kind of flank battle is rather to be sought in the fact that, considering the divergence of opinions, a kind of compromise had been made. That is, it was decided first of all to try to determine with a large-scale skirmish whether the enemy's position was as strong and well fortified as the more fearful leaders suspected. This skirmish necessarily had to be made by the right flank, where the terrain was more visible. Since the battle immediately developed from that initial move and was also very quickly decided, it happened that the portion of the Catholic army that had deployed first and was the most eager for battle had almost nothing to do.

This idea, that they were not yet completely committed to fight, may also have contributed to the very deep type of formation. They did not want to commit too many men on the first approach but wished to hold out strong reserves.

When the imperial army, marching quickly up the gentle slope, approached the left flank of the Bohemians, they were initially opposed by the various cavalry regiments. But after a bit of movement back and forth, the cavalry units were forced to give way in the face of the attackers' numerical superiority. Then Count Thurn's infantry regiment also went into action, but it only fired its muskets at a distance of 300 to 400 paces and then turned about and took flight. In his battle report, the supreme commander saw in this conduct nothing but cowardice, but historians have explained this miserable deportment by pointing out the preceding negligence, lack of payment, and resulting poor attitude of the troops. But the situation was no doubt still somewhat different. We have seen that the Bohemians formed a very thin echelon; the individual units were shallow and drawn up at large intervals. Such a formation provides the possibility for very free movement and cooperation between the various units in keeping with the circumstances. But these circumstances must be recognized and exploited; in other words, such a thin formation calls for a completely certain and superior leadership, both in the highest commander and in the individual regiments. But we find none of this. We have already seen that the formation was uniform throughout without any real adaptation to the terrain. Now we see that only that part of Thurn's regiment advanced that stood in the first echelon,[8] and that advance took place at a moment when the neighboring cavalry was already giving way. Neither the second echelon nor the Hungarians holding back in the third echelon were moved forward at the same time. Consequently, as the first echelon of Thurn's regiment moved forward, it clashed with infantry and cavalry many times stronger. It is no wonder that the men stopped there and turned around. Why were they led forward at all,

without first allowing the enemy to come within range of the musket fire
that could be directed from the position with full effectiveness and only
then, together with the nearby cavalry, making their counterattack?
Whether such a counterattack would have succeeded is questionable, in
view of the numerical superiority of the imperial troops, since the two
forward infantry units were of course followed by three additional ones
and also by cavalry squadrons. Nevertheless, the advance of an isolated
regiment without first exploiting the advantage of the defensive position
and the defensive fire meant asking too much of the troops and could
not succeed even with the highest bravery. It is surprising enough that
the troops in the second echelon, including the rest of Thurn's regiment,
did not immediately join the flight but stood fast while the first echelon
ran to the rear through the intervals.

The battle, which started at noon, lasted no longer than one and one-

A brave mounted unit commanded by the twenty-one-year-old Christian of Anhalt, son of the commander, still succeeded in winning a surprising victory by making a bold advance from the second echelon. The
foremost echelon of the imperial troops had probably fallen into some
disorder as it advanced and was engaged by the Bohemian cavalry. When
Christian now suddenly drove into them, he threw back the cavalry that
he encountered and also broke up the one infantry square and partially
cut it down with his sabers. A few other units followed him, and the
Hungarians from the third echelon also moved forward. But the enemy
mass was too strong. Tilly sent the cavalry of the army of the League in
support, and it quickly overwhelmed Anhalt's horsemen. The Hungarians
did not even start a real attack. Faced with the continuing advance of the
Catholic troops, in which the Poles also distinguished themselves, one
regiment after the other of the Bohemians took flight or pushed into the
animal preserve on the right flank, where they were attacked simultaneously from all sides and were soon cut down.

The battle, which started at noon, lasted no longer than one and one-
half or two hours. A large portion of the Bavarian troops, who were on
the left flank, had hardly needed to do any fighting.

We have information on the formation of the two armies not only from
the various accounts of participants but also from the sketches included
in the official Bavarian campaign report, the "Journal" (printed in Munich
in 1621 by Raphael Sadeler), and in the report of accounts of Prince
Christian to King Frederick (in the "Patriotic Archives," 1787).

The "Journal" has the infantry on both sides arranged in squares and
makes only one distinction between them in that with the Catholics the
squares were surrounded by marksmen on all sides, including the rear,
whereas on the Bohemian side the marksmen were used partially around
the squares and partially in long, projecting wings on the units of pikemen.

The cavalry of the Catholics was correctly formed in much larger
squadrons in the troops of the League than among the imperial forces.

In the sketch accompanying Anhalt's report, the Bohemian troops, both infantry and cavalry, are in shallow formation, but the arrangement of marksmen and pikemen with respect to one another is not indicated. The Bavarian sketch of the Bohemians is probably fantasy; they had heard something of the wings of marksmen and based their sketch on that, but they were not familiar with the principal point, the shallow formation, about which we can have no doubt as a result of the commander's own sketch.

But why did Christian come to the idea of leaving such large intervals between his individual shallow units? The sketch gives the impression that the formation was drawn up by first having all the troops (except the Hungarians) drawn up in one echelon and then having every other unit move 300 feet forward, so that the intervals of the first echelon corresponded exactly to the frontal widths of the shallow units of the second echelon. At the moment of contact with an enemy front, each unit of the first echelon would therefore have immediately been enveloped on both flanks unless the second echelon had rushed forward in advance to close the intervals. In this formation the enemy cavalry would have been particularly dangerous for the Bohemian infantry. The explanation probably lies in the fact that the enemy, too, as Christian knew, did not form a continuous front but moved forward in deep units with large intervals. Christian may therefore have counted on the fact that wherever there was the threat of envelopment, the second echelon was close enough to dash forward in support and the wide intervals assured each individual unit the greatest freedom of action.

Nevertheless, we may raise the question as to whether the wide intervals, which isolated the units, did not bear a significant responsibility for the defeat. If the Bohemian troops, instead of forming loosely in two echelons, had formed only a single closed echelon, had awaited the attack, had brought the most effective possible fire to bear,[9] and in the final moment had made the counterattack as uniformly as possible with the whole line (of course, the Hungarians still remained as a second echelon or reserve), they would probably have had better chances for victory. Is it possible that a classical reminiscence, the unfortunate and still haunting ghost, the use of intervals of the Roman legion (Lipsius's checkerboard formation as described in Livy, 8:8) played a role here? In any case, the following period went over to closed fronts.

In a memorandum concerning the defects in the Bohemian army, probably written by Christian of Anhalt himself (printed in the *Patriotic Archives*, 7[1787]:121), there are complaints that many officers were not competent enough for that organization and had scorned the Netherlandish method of fighting, which they did not understand. Now if Christian really did understand and apply the Netherlandish method in the manner we have heard and are led to believe by his own sketch, we cannot judge too strictly the old warriors who rejected this method. As a general, Christian was obviously no less at fault than all the others, and when he complains on p. 119 that he had too few colonels because the generals took the colonels' appointments for themselves, that may have been the case, but it is again a reflection of the commander's lack of decisiveness.

A remarkably large number of peoples took part in this battle. Fighting on the Bohemian side were Bohemians, Austrians, Hungarians, and Netherlanders; the Catholic side was composed of Germans, Spaniards, Italians, Walloons, and Poles.

BATTLE OF BREITENFELD[10]
17 SEPTEMBER 1631

Not until some fifteen months after the landing of Gustavus Adolphus on the Pomeranian coast did matters come to a decisive battle in Saxony between him and Tilly, commander of the combined forces of the emperor and the League. The emperor had not been able at the very start to send a sufficient force against the Swedish king. Although, together with the League, he did have at his disposal very large numbers—a member of the Swedish council of state warned that there were no fewer than 150,000 men—nevertheless, in order to retain possession of the innumerable fortified places that had been captured up to that point of the war, these men were scattered. Furthermore, the emperor was engaged in Italy in a struggle with France over the duchy of Mantua. Hasty counterpreparations, however, were prevented by the fact that the emperor had just allowed himself to be persuaded by the electors and the League to dismiss Wallenstein. In September, two months after Gustavus Adolphus had appeared on German soil, the emperor notified Wallenstein of his dismissal.

Gustavus Adolphus had time, therefore, to capture one after the other of the Pomeranian and Mecklenburg strongholds, often only after stubborn resistance, and also through political negotiations to win over allies among the Protestant princes. In February 1631, for the first time, he stood facing Tilly, near Frankfurt on the Oder, but neither commander sought battle. By rapid marches back and forth Gustavus Adolphus succeeded in first capturing Demmin on his right flank and then Frankfurt and Landsberg on his left before Tilly was able to come to the aid of those places. But then Tilly had a stunning success on 20 May when he stormed and captured Magdeburg, which had declared for the Swedes. Nevertheless, the two opponents still did not drive directly against one another. Gustavus Adolphus was awaiting the arrival of reinforcements and the linking up with the electors of Brandenburg and Saxony. Tilly believed he could not force the Swedish king to do battle in the midst of all the fortified places he already held, and he contented himself with suppressing movements in Central Germany in favor of the Swedes. Not until Tilly had moved into Saxony and Elector Johann Georg had allied himself and his troops with the Swedes did the battle develop, some 5 miles north of Leipzig.

According to the sources, Gustavus Adolphus was even now still opposed to the challenge to do battle and only acceded to the urging of the elector, who did not want to see his country become the theater for a wasting war of maneuver. If that were true, it would not enhance the Swedish king's reputation for strategic insight. He could hardly expect any more reinforcements, and we cannot see by what diversions he could still have been able to win anything important away from Tilly. Tilly, on the contrary, was still awaiting considerable reinforcements from South Germany, and they had already arrived under Aldringer in the vicinity of Jena and could therefore be present in a few days. Tilly could probably easily have taken up a position behind the Elster which would hold the enemy up long enough.[11] For this reason he himself was supposedly not without hesitation, but the confidence of his generals and troops, who were accustomed to victory, argued in favor of the battle which the enemy seemed to want to offer on the open Leipzig plain. What could now have persuaded Gustavus Adolphus to avoid battle again? With such delays he could only lose Saxony and with it everything else, but he could not win anything else. If we look carefully at the words he himself used to report back home the decisive council of war held in Düben on 15 September, we see that he does not actually say that he is opposed to the battle but only that he presented reasons that militated against it. In other words, as a wise politician, he did not want to appear to be the one who was insisting on the battle but to ascribe this role to the elector, who had the greatest interest in sparing his country in this manner from further depredation of war. In this way one could have all the more reliance on the good will of the Saxons in the battle, and if things went wrong, they bore the responsibility.

The strength of the Swedish-Saxon army is estimated as about 39,000 men and that of the emperor and the League as 36,000. Consequently, the former was slightly stronger; its cavalry was 2,000 men stronger (13,000 against 11,000), and it had 75 cannon against only 26 on the enemy side. Tilly could hope, however, that his numerical inferiority would be compensated for by the quality of his troops, to whom the 16,000 Saxons, mostly freshly levied troops, could not stand up.

Marching out from Leipzig, Tilly had his army halt on the open plain and take position on a small rise in the ground to the right of the village of Breitenfeld, about 2 kilometers behind the Lober stream, which flows across the front. Today this stream is a very insignificant brook, but at that time, according to the reports, it must have been difficult to cross.

This formation had no natural limits, nothing on which to rest the flanks, on either the right or left, but in view of the depth of the large infantry units, the *terzios*, which provided their own flank protection, such natural obstacles were not necessary.

The allied army seems to have moved up on the level plain already deployed on a broad front while still far away, and when it came in sight of the enemy position, it moved toward the right, as advance troops skirmished between the two battle lines. The king and Field Marshal Horn agree in their reports that the reason for this movement to the right was to enable them to deprive the enemy of the advantages of sun and wind. This point is not immediately clear; although the advantages of sun and wind were old drugs on the market of the theoreticians since the time of Vegetius, Frundsberg claims to have known nothing about it. The front of a battle formation is determined by completely different and more important factors, and to undertake to shift a front that is already deployed is extremely difficult. "To attempt a significant change of direction in battle," wrote John of Nassau,[12] "is very dangerous; it is a half-flight and gives the enemy the opportunity for a flank attack." Gustavus Adolphus also says expressly that the shifting movement did not succeed because it was necessary to cross a difficult obstacle, that is, the Lober stream, in view of the enemy. The result of the movement to the right, however, was that the two battle lines did not clash squarely with one another, but the allies extended beyond Tilly's left flank. They not only extended beyond him physically, but they also outdistanced him even more potentially, since Tilly had the entire mass of his infantry, with the exception of one regiment, that of Holstein, not in the center of his line but to the right of center,[13] with twelve (eleven) regiments of cavalry on the left and only six on the right. Consequently, Gustavus Adolphus with the Swedish army encountered almost nothing but cavalry, and it must have been deployed very thinly, that is with considerable intervals, since the length of the entire battle line is given as more than 2 1/4 miles, so that on the average there were no more than five men to a pace. There must also have been large intervals between the four deep, massive infantry *terzios*, which were formed in a line.

Tilly could perhaps have attacked while the allies were still crossing the Lober stream (a situation similar to that of Anhalt on the White Mountain), but he did not do so, probably in order to allow his artillery first to fire on the enemy while he was involved in his deployment. While this was happening, the outflanking of his left flank now became apparent. To counter that, Pappenheim, who was commanding on that flank, moved toward the left, thus opening a break between the left flank, the cavalry and the Holstein regiment, and the right flank. As both sides sought to outflank each other, the fight broke out there. Pappenheim extended his line so far around the enemy flank that the second Swedish echelon was able to advance directly against him.[14]

The main body of Tilly's army could not stand by passively watching this fight, all the less so in that the Swedish-Saxon artillery now went into action, and, since it was much more numerous than that of the imperial army, its effect was greater. Tilly therefore also put his right flank and especially the entire mass of his infantry into motion. He had formed four large units, which now advanced abreast and, together with the cavalry, threw back the Saxons. How could the Saxons have withstood this attack, since not only were the battle-hardened units striking against recruits but they also had a great numerical superiority? Since a wide breach had formed between Pappenheim's flank and the right flank, which was commanded by Tilly himself, the main body of the Swedish army on the line had practically no enemy opposite it. It may also be possible that as the allies had moved toward the right, an interval had developed between the Swedes and the Saxons. That is perhaps one reason why the Swedish reports, in order to counter possible reproaches, emphasize so strongly that by the shift to the right they had wanted to deprive the enemy of the advantages of sun and wind.

As a result of the move to the left of Pappenheim's horsemen and the driving off of the Saxons, the Swedish army was enveloped simultaneously on both flanks. Indeed, a cavalry regiment under Fürstenberg moved around to the rear of the Swedes. Since almost 15,000 Saxons had been driven from the battlefield, Tilly now had a numerical advantage of almost 36,000 against hardly 25,000. But the greater tactical flexibility of the Swedes and the superior, decisive leadership of the king himself and his generals made up for the difference.

Even before the defeat of the Saxons and the envelopment of the Swedes from that side was completed, Pappenheim's horsemen were repulsed. The Swedish cavalry in its close cooperation with the musketeers proved itself tactically superior to the imperial mounted troops.[15] They allowed the enemy cavalry to approach closely; then it was received by the mus-keteers with a salvo, and the Swedish cavalry charged on it and threw it back. Even the Fürstenberg horsemen, who had moved into the rear of the Swedes, were attacked, beaten, and destroyed by troops from the second Swedish echelon, who turned about.

The decisive point, however, was on the left flank of the Swedes, where the four large units of imperial infantry now held the position from which they had driven the Saxons. How were the Swedes supposed to resist if these masses, together with their cavalry, turned to the left and attacked the exposed flank? As soon as it was seen that the Saxons were abandoning the field, Gustavus Adolphus formed a defensive flank with two infantry brigades from the second echelon, also brought up a cavalry regiment from the other flank in support, and attacked the enemy cavalry, which here had only six regiments, or, if we subtract the regiment that moved to the rear of the Swedes, only five regiments. This attack was made with close cooperation of cavalry and musketeers, as on the other flank, and Tilly's cavalry was beaten and driven from the battlefield. That had happened and was completed before the imperial infantry *terzios* had reassembled and regained their formation after the pursuit of the Saxons and before they had turned in the new direction. In fact, one of the *terzios* had moved out so far that the great cloud of dust that was stirred up prevented it from seeing what was happening. While awaiting further orders it remained out of action and did not participate further in the battle. But the three other units, abandoned by their own cavalry and attacked and threatened by the Swedes on several sides, found themselves incapable of applying their real strength, the attack by storm. One would think that with their gigantic strength they could have driven off the enemy horsemen by supporting one another mutually and then could have moved into their attack. But that did not happen. The Swedish horsemen, led with complete decisiveness, must have continued to move in simultaneously from various sides, so that the *terzios* had to fight a purely defensive battle. If I said above that Tilly enveloped both flanks of the Swedes, we must now look again at that statement. The envelopment of the right flank was already repulsed before the threat to the left flank arose, and the latter, in turn, was lifted when the Swedes aggressively opposed it. The cavalry fixed the *terzios* in place, so to speak, and now the musketeers also moved up and especially the light Swedish artillery,[16] which released its hail of shots against the thick masses, in which no shot could miss. Again, this situation resembles Cannae, except that the increased effectiveness of the missile weapons greatly facilitated the Swedes' work of destruction of the surrounded units.

Gustavus Adolphus wrote later that only three of his seven infantry brigades had really fought in the battle. These were principally the two brigades that fought against Tilly's *terzios* and the infantry that participated in repelling Pappenheim's troops and destroying Fürstenberg's cavalry.

Pappenheim's horsemen, although they were much more numerous, perhaps 7,000 against 4,000, had nevertheless accomplished nothing because the Swedish horsemen worked closely with their foot soldiers and had the effective support of the musketeers. Pappenheim was not completely defeated; he reports that he reassembled his men but could not lead them forward again into the fight, and on the following day "in the brightest sunshine he withdrew them in the face of the enemy." On the contrary, on the other flank the imperial cavalry was in the minority, not quite 4,000 against at least 5,000 Swedish cavalry, which was also augmented by two Saxon regiments that had held out. The imperial infantry, with its weak contingent of musketeers and not yet ready again to attack, offered little support. And thus the different combat arms, since they did not achieve tactical cooperation, were overcome individually by the combined arms of the enemy, first the cavalry and then the infantry.

Tilly, who was wounded several times and rescued only with difficulty, had taken up the withdrawal toward Halle, probably along behind the line of the Swedes. He was perhaps with Fürstenberg's horsemen, who were cut down in the rear of the Swedes. Pappenheim and the fourth *terzio*, the one that had not fought any more in the second act of the battle, had first taken the road toward Leipzig and did not join up again with Tilly until the next day. Since Tilly still had a considerable number of troop units in Northwest Germany, this eccentric withdrawal had been envisaged from the start in the event the battle had an unfavorable outcome. In like manner, in his flight the elector of Saxony had also failed to take the route to the rear toward Düben, but had moved toward the flank in the direction of Eilenburg.

Tilly's captured infantry straightway went over into the service of the Swedes, so that their army was stronger after the battle than before.

BATTLE OF LÜTZEN[17]
16 NOVEMBER 1632

Wallenstein had driven into Saxony and captured Leipzig. Gustavus Adolphus came from South Germany to drive him out. Wallenstein had been reinforced to such an extent by Pappenheim, who marched up the long distance from Maastricht, that Gustavus Adolphus could not risk attacking him immediately, and the reinforcements on which he himself could still count, a Lüneburg-Saxon corps under Duke Georg, were on the far side of the Elbe near Torgau, so that Wallenstein was between the two enemy armies. Gustavus Adolphus took up a fortified position north of Naumburg on the Saale, which he so developed that Wallenstein, despite his numerical superiority, could not risk attacking him. For a few days the two armies stood facing one another and suffered greatly from the severe November weather. Finally, Wallenstein decided to move his troops into winter quarters in the Saxon cities, and as soon as Gustavus Adolphus became aware of that, he took up the offensive in the hope of joining up with Duke Georg or of defeating the imperial forces before they had reassembled. Wallenstein had the advance of the Swedes held up by light troops and very cleverly took up a position in which he could hope to fight a favorable defensive battle. It did not lie directly across the march route of the Swedes but turned its right flank toward that route. This flank, however, which rested on the small city of Lützen and wet meadowland that was difficult to cross, was unassailable. The Swedes, therefore, in order to make contact with the imperial troops, had to move around in a large detour and thus lose time, which not only helped the further assembling of the imperial forces but was also used to fortify even further with hard digging the position, which was already protected by strong frontal obstacles. When Gustavus Adolphus learned on the first day of his advance (15 November) that the enemy was in position close in front of him, he swung around toward him in order to attack very early the next morning. He himself had 16,300 men, including 5,100 horsemen and 60 cannon, among which were the light regimental pieces, against which Wallenstein at first could employ only 12,000 men, including 4,000 horsemen, with 21 heavy cannon and an uncertain number of light cannon.[18] But a fog that prevented any visibility delayed the Swedes' attack until ten o'clock in the morning. At noon 1,400 more horsemen joined the imperial forces; between two and three o'clock 1,500 infantrymen arrived, so that now there were all together 14,900 men fighting against 16,300.

The older accounts have the imperial troops at Lützen still fighting in about the same awkward formations as Tilly's army at Breitenfeld. But that is not correct. Wallenstein had already given up the rectangular formation and had ordered the formation with a depth of ten ranks for the infantry. He had also incorporated the light regimental cannon and had assigned marksmen to the cavalry.[19] Nevertheless, the Swedish army continued to be superior qualitatively; it had the lighter musket without the fork, had a formation only six ranks deep, and had the advantage of every veteran army against a newly formed one.

Finally, despite the strong position of the emperor's forces, the numerical and qualitative superiority of the Swedes won the upper hand. Although Wallenstein's infantry center remained unbeaten, his cavalry was so shaken up that he did not risk continuing the battle on the next day, despite the fact that the arrival of 4,000 men of Pappenheim's infantry in the evening of the day of the battle, when darkness had already fallen, had given him a not insignificant numerical superiority. If this infantry had arrived a few hours earlier, it might well have changed the fortunes of the day in favor of the imperial army. And it appears not entirely impossible that Wallenstein, from a purely tactical viewpoint, could even have resumed the battle on the following day and still have held his own, at least defensively. The Swedes, too, had moved back somewhat during the night, but they were of course still awaiting the arrival from Torgau of the Lüneburg-Saxon corps,[20] and that was the decisive point, so that Wallenstein gave up the contest and evacuated Saxony.

Scholars have claimed that it is incomprehensible why Wallenstein, considering the proximity of the Swedish army, had his troops go into winter quarters. But it was impossible to have them camp in the open any longer in the very severe November weather. The mercenaries would have deserted. He was obliged either to go into quarters or evacuate Saxony without a battle and impose the maintenance of the troops on the imperial country of Bohemia. The danger of a sudden attack was eliminated by alertness; and the enemies, too, were of course not assembled. Finally, Gustavus Adolphus himself was in no way certain of success, and the outcome of the battle wavered back and forth. Wallenstein would have been thinking very narrow-mindedly if, in order to avoid the risk of a possible battle, he had sacrificed Saxony from the start and intended to take up the withdrawal toward Bohemia.

The flanking position that he chose appears very unusual, although, as we saw, it gave him great tactical advantages. In case of a real defeat, it blocked him from Bohemia and left open only a withdrawal toward Northwest Germany. The fact that he risked this must be considered as a strong deed and testimony to his strategic boldness.

We can say of this battle almost more definitely than of other battles that it was governed very strongly by chance. Of course, Gustavus Adolphus had intended to attack the imperial forces at the very break of day. If that had been done, he would have been sure of a brilliant victory. But the fog delayed the Swedish attack, and during this time not only did the imperial forces strengthen their position by hard digging, but also reinforcements were approaching that were to establish a situation of almost numerical equality. On the other hand, the last reinforcements, the 4,000 men of Pappenheim's infantry, which would have given Wallenstein numerical superiority, were late on their march from Halle (about 19 miles), although they had already been alerted on the previous night, with the result that they did not arrive until after nightfall, when the fight was ended. And finally, even though the Swedes were victorious, their triumph was nevertheless tempered by the death of the king.

At the time of the battle the main body of the Saxons was in Silesia under Arnim; two corps were operating against him, led by Maradas and Gallas. A considerable additional force of the Catholic party was still available to the elector of Bavaria. Although it was a principal battle, Lützen was nevertheless fought with only portions of the two forces and, on an absolute basis, with very small numbers of troops.

BATTLE OF NÖRDLINGEN[21]
27 AUGUST/ 6 SEPTEMBER 1634

In 1634, after the assassination of Wallenstein, the imperial-Bavarian army, under the command of Crown Prince Ferdinand and the leadership of General Count Gallas, turned toward Bavaria and besieged Regensburg. In order to relieve the city, Bernhard, moving up from the Upper Palatinate, joined forces south of the Danube with Horn, who moved from Lake Constance. Surprisingly enough, Bernhard had left a corps behind for the siege of Forchheim, while Horn had left forces at Lake Constance and in the Breisgau, so that the combined army appeared too weak for a direct attack on the besiegers of Regensburg. While they now held up for the siege and capture of Freising, Moosburg, and Landshut, Regensburg finally fell.

After this success, the imperial army split up, and Ferdinand marched toward Bohemia, which was being threatened by a Swedish corps with the Saxons, while the Bavarian-League army intended to await at Ingolstadt the arrival of a large Spanish supporting army that was moving up via the Tyrol. Bernhard and Horn, instead of now moving directly against the Bavarians as we would expect, in order to defeat them before the arrival of the Spaniards, also split their forces and allowed their troops to rest. When the Saxons now withdrew from Bohemia, Ferdinand was able to turn about again, join forces once more with the Bavarians, capture Donauwörth, and turn his attention to the siege of Nördlingen. Were the Swedes also to allow this important Protestant city to fall into the hands of the Catholics?

Bernhard, who at Regensburg had already argued for an attempt to relieve the city, now demanded, although he did not deny the superiority of the enemy, that they should press for a battle. Horn opposed this, and in fact a decision to attack directly the army besieging Nördlingen was never taken. After having awaited reinforcements in a camp at Bopfingen, no more than 10 kilometers west of Nördlingen, they decided to press the besiegers more closely and to take up a position on the Ulm-Nördlingen road that would at the same time facilitate the movement of rations to the Swedes from Ulm and Württemberg while cutting off the supplies to the imperial army on the road from Donauwörth. The march, a distance of almost 10 miles, led in an arc from the position at Bopfingen, directly westward from Nördlingen onto a ridge southwest of the city, the Arnsberg. It appears that Bernhard, who was in command of the point, moved up somewhat closer to the city than Horn had expected, because it was only at such a close distance that the intended effect, the pressure on the supply route of the imperial army, could be accomplished. But the route that had to be taken from Bopfingen led through a difficult defile and forest, and before Horn's troops, who were following Bernhard's, had overcome these obstacles, the imperial troops had occupied a height, the Allbuch, which would have been a part of the allies' position and had to form its right flank. During the fight for this height darkness fell. The following morning Horn attempted with all his force to storm the Allbuch, while on his flank, the left one, Bernhard conducted only a holding operation.[22] But all the courage of the Swedes was to no avail against the great superiority of the enemy. For if the allies had finally brought up the largest part of the corps they had previously left behind in front of Forchheim and in South Germany, the emperor's troops had in the meantime been joined by the long-awaited Spaniards. It appears that their numerical superiority amounted to not much less than about 40,000 against 25,000.[23]

When Field Marshal Horn now realized that he was capable neither of capturing the Allbuch nor of maintaining the fight until evening, toward noon, covered by a cavalry advance, he took up the withdrawal, while Bernhard still held his hill. But now it was the turn of the imperial forces to attack. Bernhard's troops also had to give way, and they crossed through Horn's retreating troops, since the Ulm road was directly behind the left flank and Horn's troops, of course, had never arrived in their assigned position but had fought with their rear against this road, that is, forming a hook with Bernhard's units. Under all these unfavorably blended circumstances, the army of the Protestants collapsed completely, their infantry was almost wiped out, Horn was taken prisoner, and Bernhard only managed to escape with difficulty.

We are tempted to assume that Bernhard, by moving up so close to the enemy camp that he could reach it from the heights with his cannon, was aware that he would thus bring on the battle and forced his reluctant colleague in the high command into the battle against his will, because he knew that the situation in Nördlingen was already desperate and the city could fall at any moment. If we also consider that the Swedish commanders certainly did not know the huge discrepancy in the strengths of the two forces, there seems to be nothing that would make this concept impossible. In reality, however, it might have been otherwise. If Bernhard had been so eager to bring on the tactical decision, he would from the start have had to avoid splitting his forces and would have sought the battle especially during the time when Ferdinand was in Bohemia. If the Swedes had succeeded by their bold flank march in arriving without a fight on the dominating position southwest of the city or in taking the Allbuch on the first evening or early the next morning, it is still not so certain that this would have led to the battle. At least Bernhard, who no doubt knew the imperial forces were somewhat stronger but not significantly so, could assume that they would not risk an attack on the strong position held by the Swedes but would withdraw and give up Nördlingen. It was only because the march through the defile lasted too long and the Swedes did not completely reach the position intended by Bernhard and so had to fight for it that the battle was brought on. Consequently, we must consider this battle as belonging to the category of meeting engagements rather than pitched battles.[24]

The losses of the Swedes were estimated at 10,000 to 12,000 men, over half of the army. The infantry was practically destroyed. The Catholic army is supposed to have lost no more than 1,200 to 2,000 men, and that is very possible, since the attack on the Allbuch position was undoubtedly more costly for the Protestants than for their opponents, but the greatest losses, especially in men captured, did not occur until the withdrawal.

Concerning the activity of the individual arms and their cooperation—in fact, on the truly tactical situation in general—there is nothing of significance to be gleaned from the available reports. Of importance, however, and great interest, to make the point once again, was the strategic factor that neither of the two sides desired or planned the battle as such but that it developed from the fight for possession of a piece of high ground, that is, the execution of a maneuver which, if it succeeded, would have forced the Catholic army either to give up the siege of Nördlingen or to attack the Protestants in a very advantageous position.

BATTLE OF WITTSTOCK[25]
4 OCTOBER 1636

In the summer of 1636, after a long siege, the combined imperial army and Saxons captured Magdeburg, while the Swedish army commanded by Baner remained north of that city, at Werben, and felt too weak to relieve the city.

Now the armies approached one another, and on both sides plans were made to bring on reinforcements of troops from the Weser or from Pomerania, but without either side's absolute desire to seek a decisive battle. Baner considered an incursion into Saxony, while the allies planned to maneuver him back in order to capture one by one the places still remaining in the hands of the Swedes. Finally, at Wittstock in the Priegnitz the battle was brought on when Baner, who had already been maneuvered back into Mecklenburg, marched around the enemy and finally attacked him from the south.

If the battle should have taken place in the manner that is normally assumed, it would be one of the most astonishing battles in world history.

Baner supposedly had only something over 16,000 men, or perhaps at most 1,000 more than that, whereas his enemies had a strength of 22,000 to 23,000 men and occupied a position that was not only naturally strong but was also strengthened artificially. Seeing that the enemy front was impregnable, Baner divided his army and enveloped both flanks simultaneously. If we also assume that there was no longer a significant difference in the training and tactics of the troops on both sides and that the battle was fought with a completely reversed front, it would have to be placed even above Cannae with respect to the boldness of the plan and the greatness of the triumph. For if Hannibal was able to violate the rule that the weaker side could not simultaneously envelop both flanks because he was sure of the absolute superiority of his cavalry and for that reason had every justification for seeking the decisive battle, we cannot see on what reason Baner based his hopes for victory. Nor can we see why he would have felt that the battle was necessary at any price precisely at this time, since, without taking too great risks, he could have continued maneuvering.

The advantage that Baner had was that the two flanks of the enemy position did not rest on good natural points and could be enveloped without too great a detour. Furthermore, the woods in front of the enemy line hid the movements of the Swedes. And so it happened that Baner, with his right flank under Torstensson, came quite by surprise into the flank of the Saxons, who were on the left of the enemy line. But the Saxons held fast and formed a new front, and soon the imperial troops, under their commander, Field Marshal Hatzfeldt, came to their aid from the other flank, while the enveloping column of the Swedes on that side and the reserves that they had left in the center under Vitzthum were awaited in vain. If the assumed relative strengths were correct, the combined Saxon and imperial forces would now necessarily have been twice as strong as Torstensson, and we cannot see how he could have withstood their attack for three hours in the hard-fought fight that wavered back and forth.

The plan and the conduct of the battle cannot be understood until we assume that the Swedes were at least equal to the allies in strength or perhaps even somewhat stronger. In the last few weeks Baner had moved up considerable reinforcements to join him, including finally the garrison of Brandenburg, more than 1,000 men, to whom the Saxons had permitted free passage after the capitulation, whereas the allies had not yet had the 5,000 men who had taken Brandenburg under General Klitzing rejoin the main body. Therefore, even if the statement of the imperial commander that he had only 12,000 men against 22,000 Swedes,[26] in order to excuse his defeat, may have been far from the truth, it is in any case not impossible that the Swedes had a certain numerical superiority on hand.

And so it happened that the right flank of the Swedes, although it could not be victorious, was still able to hold its own, even though it gradually drew almost the entire enemy army against it. Now, as darkness descended, the other wing of the Swedes appeared in the rear of the allies, who, with their units already very confused with one another, did not risk continuing the fight but took up their withdrawal in the night, resulting in the loss of cannon and the breaking up of their units. According to a remark by Montecuccoli (*Works*, 2:58), Baner won the battle "with twelve fresh squadrons that finally appeared at sundown, when all the imperial troops were already exhausted."

Even if he did not defeat a numerically stronger force, Baner's fame as a field commander is not diminished on that account. He was far from striving primarily to bring on the decisive battle, but when the situation developed in such a way that the enemy had weakened himself by pursuing smaller objectives and Baner felt himself equal to the enemy, he took advantage of the opportunity. He did not shy away from the march around the enemy and the reversed front, and, realizing that the frontal obstacles that were supposed to protect the enemy also at the same time prevented him from counterattacking, he dared to divide the Swedish army. Since this maneuver succeeded, he definitely had the upper hand. For an attack from the front and the rear simultaneously, as it finally developed for the Swedes, is naturally the stronger type, even with equal forces. The only possibility for the defender to avoid thus being caught in the tongs is a counterattack at the appropriate moment, the destruction of one part of the attackers before the other intervenes. The imperial troops had not succeeded in doing that, and so they necessarily had to lose in the end. But their last mistake lay in the fact that, instead of contenting themselves with the smaller objective and conquering Brandenburg, they did not assemble all their forces and press for the tactical decision. It is true, of course, that bold decisions were made very difficult by the fact that the high command was shared by the elector, Johann Georg of Saxony, and the emperor's Field Marshal Hatzfeldt. Furthermore, after the capture of Magdeburg, the army had been forced to remain inactive for four weeks because of a shortage of rations, munitions, and money, and the troops refused to move into the field without their pay.

In the victory of Frederick the Great at Torgau we shall learn of a similar conduct of battle.

EXCURSUS

STRENGTH ESTIMATES

In order to estimate the strength of the allied army, Schmidt depends on an army roster that the Swedes claim to have found on an imperial quartermaster in Havelberg before the battle. But it is very questionable whether this list is reliable—that is, that it does not also include the detached troops—and in like manner the further estimates that Schmidt bases on this may easily be a few thousand men too high.

Schmidt's estimate, according to which the Swedes had 9,150 horsemen and 7,288 foot soldiers, to which perhaps the garrison of Brandenburg (a good 1,000 men) should also be added, is based on a statement by Chemnitz. Nevertheless, it is questionable whether this statement is clearly reliable. Chemnitz gives the reinforcements from Lesly as only 4,000 men, whereas Grotius in a letter to Bernhard of Weimar gives the number as 7,000 (Schmidt, p. 43). On the basis of Chemnitz's statements, Schmidt estimates the reinforcements from Pomerania as 2,000 men, but the *Relationis semestralis continuatio (Continuation of the Semiannual Report)* of Frankfurt gives 2,000 men on foot and twenty-four companies of horsemen. In view of Chemnitz's somewhat indefinite method of expressing himself, I would not consider it impossible that the latter, larger figure is the right one.

Montecuccoli, in *Writings*, 2:66, claims that at Wittstock Baner profited from the advantage that the enemy army was divided.

BATTLE OF JANKAU
6 MARCH 1645

This battle, treated thoroughly by Paul Gantzer in accordance with the sources and published in the *Mitteilungen des Vereins für Geschichte der Deutschen in Böhmen*, Vol. 43, 1905, offers nothing of importance from a tactical viewpoint for the history of the art of war. There were about 16,000 men on each side. Hatzfeldt was 1,000 men stronger in horsemen, while Torstensson was stronger in cannon, 60 against 26.

	Infantry	Cavalry
Hatzfeldt	5,000	10,000
Torstensson	6,000	9,000

The Swedes won the battle as a result of superior and more certain leadership. The imperial forces made several errors, especially in that they accepted battle on terrain that was generally unfavorable for cavalry. The imperial generals acted on their own initiative counter to the intentions of the overall commander.

In order to assemble even the 16,000 men who fought at Jankau, the Saxons and Bavarians had to send help to the emperor. The Bavarians were commanded by Johann Werth.

Torstensson stated that he lost only 600 men at Jankau, while the imperial troops lost half of their strength, including 4,000 captured. Among the prisoners were Hatzfeldt himself, five generals, eight colonels, and fourteen lieutenant colonels. One field marshal, Count Götz, two colonels, and three lieutenant colonels were killed.

The battle was fought with the greatest valor on both sides.

NOTES FOR CHAPTER VI

1. H. von Koss, "The Battles of St. Quentin and Gravelingen" ("Die Schlachten bei St. Quentin und Gravelingen"), Berlin dissertation, 1914, E. Ebering Press. I am not so sure whether the analysis of Gravelingen in this otherwise very worthwhile work is appropriate. The points raised by Elkan against this work in his review in the *Historische Zeitschrift*, 116:533, apply only to secondary items, partly simple typographical errors. The question, too, of the intervention of the English ships, which Koss, with good reasons, doubts, is not significant from the military history viewpoint, but, on the basis of testimony cited by Elkan and overlooked by Koss, this point calls for further study.

2. Swiss battle reports in Segesser, *Ludwig Pfyffer and His Times* (*Ludwig Pfyffer und seine Zeit*), 1:621.

3. Special study on the battle by Gigon, *La troisième guerre de religion*, 1912. Gigon gives the Huguenots a strength of 12,000 infantry

and 7,000 cavalry and the Catholics 15,000 infantry and 8,000 cavalry. Other writers assume considerably higher numbers for the Catholics. According to Popelinière, Coligny supposedly used the method of blending the infantry and the cavalry ("d'enlacer l'infanterie et la cavallerie") in small units. The account of the battle, however, does not show that.

4. The standard monograph is by J. Krebs, Berlin, 1879. Brendel, 1875, gives nothing useful from a military standpoint. A few details are to be found in Riezler, *Sitzungsberichte der Münchener Akademie*, Phil. Abt., Vol. 23, 1906.

5. Riezler, p. 84, of course assumes that the army of the League was only 10,000 men strong and had lost 12,000 to 15,000 men from sickness in the preceding campaign. The "Hungarian fever" was raging at that time in all camps.

6. According to Anhalt, the formation of the Bohemians was 3,750 paces wide at most, and it appears as if the animal park was not included in that figure. According to the illustration in Krebs, however, the width was not even 2,000 meters, including the position in the animal park, and, remarkably enough, this was estimated on the same scale as equal to 5,000 feet. On page 171 Krebs assumes that the front was about 3,600 meters. In any case, the front was very long for the small army.

7. Later, Tilly reproached his colleague Buquoi for having divided up his horsemen into "little squadrons" ("*squadronelli*").

8. In his report Christian speaks only of Thurn's musketeers, as if there were no pikemen there at all.

9. According to Gindely, 2:119, the units (*Fähnlein*) of the Bohemian regiments were composed of 24 privates first class, 76 pikemen, and 200 musketeers.

10. The standard special study on the battle is by Walter Opitz (Leipzig, A. Deichert, 1892). The dissertation by Wangerin, Halle, 1896, is only a study of the sources without significant conclusions.

11. Opitz, p. 76, established the fact that Tilly wanted to move from Leipzig to the Elbe, in order to gain a crossing and to draw Field Marshal Tiefenbach to him from Silesia. Once he had this latter force, Pappenheim was to be detached to Mecklenburg in the rear of the Swedish king. That was the plan in case the enemy again avoided battle. For the battle itself the plan was only significant to the extent that it may have contributed to the fact that they did not want to go back behind the Elster to await Aldringer.

12. Jähns, *History of Military Sciences (Geschichte der Kriegswissenschaften)*, 1:572.

13. Following Rüstow's sample, Opitz has Tilly's infantry arranged in the form of a Spanish brigade. It may be that they were formed this way for a moment. It is not reported, and, of course, it does not matter tactically, since in their movement forward it would have been neither

possible nor advantageous to hold the four units together in some kind of prescribed figure. It is expressly stated in a French report and in Chemnitz (Opitz, p. 92) that Tilly's entire army stood in a single echelon, and Montecuccoli, *Writings*, 2:581, says that Tilly was defeated at Leipzig mainly because he had drawn up his entire army in a single, right-angled front without reserves. The discrepancy that, according to Field Marshal Horn's report, Tilly's infantry was aligned in four battalions, whereas the French report states fourteen battalions (Opitz, p. 93), can probably be explained by the fact that in the latter figure the cavalry formations are also counted as battalions. Furthermore, as in the infantry, several regiments of cavalry may have been assembled in a single tactical unit.

14. In his sketch, Opitz obviously shows the Swedes as much too wide, the Saxons as too narrow. Since it is reported of both formations that they were a good 2 1/2 miles wide (extract from Schreiber's report of 8 September. Droysen, *Archives for Saxon History [Archiv für sächsische Geschichte]*, 7:348) and the right flank of the Swedes extended beyond the enemy flank, then the imperial right flank must no doubt have extended beyond the enemy flank, the Saxons.

15. Montecuccoli, *Works*, 2:579, states that the principal reason for the Swedish victory was that they placed the musketeers between the cavalry. The cavalry had to be so formed that the enemy first had to pass through the musket fire, and in the weakened condition into which that brought him, he was then attacked by the cavalry.

16. This action by the artillery is not mentioned in the actual battle reports, but it does appear in Chemnitz and Montecuccoli. This is consistent with the fact that Tilly, in his various reports (Droysen, *Archives for Saxon History*, 7:391–392), strongly emphasized the enemy's superiority in artillery.

17. Karl Deuticke, "The Battle of Lützen" ("Die Schlacht bei Lützen"), Giessen dissertation, 1917. It was not until the appearance of this excellent study, in which the scattered sources, especially letters, were collected and studied with the greatest care with the help of the Stockholm Library, that a correct and reliable picture of the details of this battle was achieved.

18. It is not definitely reported as to whether Wallenstein had additional light pieces along with his twenty-one heavy cannon. We only know from several letters in the *Fontes rerum austriacarum (Sources of Austrian History)*, Vol. 65, that he had procured such cannon.

19. Deuticke, p. 67.

20. Unfortunately, we do not have information on the strength of this corps; it can hardly have been more than 6,000 men. On the day of the battle it was still at Torgau and would therefore not have been able to reach the vicinity of Lützen for several days. Gustavus Adolphus had ordered it to follow the route via Riesa and Oschatz in order to avoid Eilenburg and Leipzig, which were occupied by the emperor's forces.

21. The more recent monographs on this battle, on which my account is based, are principally those of Walter Struck, Stralsund, 1893, and Erich Leo, Halle, 1900. But neither of them distinguishes sufficiently between a positive decision to seek the battle and the mere risk of bringing on the battle as the result of a maneuver. Nor has the lively description of the battle by Colonel Kaiser in the *Literarische Beilage des Staatsanzeigers für Württemberg*, 1897, come to grips with this decisive point. It was only later that I became acquainted with "From Lützen to Nördlingen" ("Von Lützen nach Nördlingen") by Karl Jacob (1904), who seeks to prove that Bernhard von Weimar was unjustly exalted and Swedish Field Marshal Horn was a much better strategist. What Jacob says in Horn's favor may well be essentially correct, but his pejorative judgment of Bernhard shows prejudice and insufficient training in military history. In the points of controversy between Leo and Struck, Jacob correctly sides strongly with Struck.

22. Jacob criticizes Bernhard for attacking at all. He believes that wing should have maintained a purely defensive stance in order to cover a possible withdrawal with its full strength still available. Such conduct would have been poor testimony for the military genius of Bernhard. Of course, since the battle was lost, the defeat was all the more frightful in that Bernhard had insufficient reserves to send in to cover the withdrawal. Nevertheless, if he had remained passive in the battle for this eventuality, a victory would have been impossible, since the enemy could then have had all the more troops to employ against Horn. From all appearances, Bernhard understood his mission absolutely correctly—to keep the enemy on his flank as occupied as possible but without bringing on the decisive battle there.

23. Leo, p. 59, estimates the strength of the Catholic army between 40,000 and 50,000 men, a small portion of which remained in position facing Nördlingen, while he considers the strength of the Swedes between 19,000 and 22,000 regulars and 5,000 to 6,000 Württemberg militia. M. Ritter, *History of the Thirty Years' War (Geschichte des Dreissigjährigen Krieges)*, p. 580, agrees with these estimates, as does Jacob, p. 109. Unfortunately, we learn nothing specific about the employment and conduct of this militia in the battle. It must have been in position on Bernhard's flank and therefore probably remained unengaged in the actual battle but was overtaken by the enemy on the withdrawal and cut down. Even in Kaiser's account, where we would most likely expect it, there is nothing further of any significance.

24. Leo, p. 66, note, cites several sources to the effect that Bernhard from the very start—that is, as early as in the council of war that decided on the march onto the Arnsberg—wished to bring on the decisive battle and so recommended. But Leo's sources are not completely reliable, and it could, for example, easily be the case that remarks by the prince on

the evening of the march or the morning of the battle, when it was a question of whether or not they should seek to take the Allbuch position by force, were transposed back to the council of war.

25. The authoritative monograph is Rudolf Schmidt's "The Battle of Wittstock" ("Die Schlacht bei Wittstock"), Halle, 1876.

26. Letter to Field Marshal Count Götz, who was in command in Hesse, dated 9 October, and therefore five days after the battle. Quoted in von dem Decken, *Duke George of Braunschweig and Lüneburg (Herzog Georg von Braunschweig und Lüneburg)*, 3:277.

BOOK III

The Period of Standing Armies

General Remarks

From the start, statesmen and theoreticians alike were not unaware of the huge disadvantages of waging war with mercenaries recruited for only a limited period. We have seen how a thinker like Machiavelli and a politician like King Francis concerned themselves with the creation of military organizations of a better type, and how they failed. Progress in this area developed in a manner that no theoretician had proposed, no philosopher had devised, and nobody had foreseen. The mercenary bands were not replaced by a warriorhood of different origin; instead, they changed their character by remaining permanently under the colors and becoming standing armies. This occurred first among the Spanish, then the Netherlanders, then, as a result of the Thirty Years' War, in all the larger German areas, and finally, not until the seventeenth century was giving way to the eighteenth, among the English.

Upon his abdication, Charles V had left behind an army of 60,000 men and garrison troops numbering 80,000, and eventually this situation became a matter of general practice. The great disadvantages of discharging the troops at the end of a campaign had been obvious since time immemorial. But now men also began to realize the advantage to be derived from a permanent organization, not only politically but also militarily, in its effect on the basic efficiency of the troops.

The military organization is always the most basic factor in the existence of a nation. The entire socio-political situation of Europe was transformed with the new military organization. The standing army was the point of contention in the struggle between the princes and their Estates of the Realm, the factor that raised kings to absolute rulers on the whole continent and in England brought first the minister Strafford and then King Charles I himself to the scaffold. The ancient vassal system reappeared in the form of the officer corps of nobles. But the troops lost the malevolent and savage character of the lansquenets, were subjected to ever stricter discipline, had their ranks filled by conscription in addition to recruitment, and, as a result of this changed basic structure, also assumed changed tactical formations.

It was extremely difficult for the occidental peoples to create orderly administrative systems for the powerful armies. The condottiere, the blend of warriorhood and business entrepreneurship, maintained his position from the Middle Ages into the Thirty Years' War, where he reached his apogee, because the nation still had no agency that could have replaced the activity and ability of these entrepreneurs.

In comparison with the military entrepreneurs, the national administrations were as good as powerless. As great and extensive as were the countries, kingdoms, duchies, and counties ruled by Emperor Ferdinand II, he was still unable to raise from them even only a military force like the one the homeless adventurer Count Ernst von Mansfeld assembled time after time under his command. The huge sums with which Wallenstein worked were only minimally inherited or acquired through marriage but were principally derived from commerce in goods and minting operations—that is, from sources that a logical and correct national administration itself could have put to use. The house of Hapsburg was unable to do that. But a man like Duke Max of Bavaria was able to go as far as commanding his own army without the service of a condottiere as intermediary. Gradually then, the other larger princely houses also succeeded in doing so.

As a prerequisite, or perhaps we should say a side effect, of the great change in the army, there developed a new administration of the state, a bureaucracy whose mission was to collect the taxes required to maintain the army and, by careful handling of the economic conditions and finally of the entire welfare and agriculture, to make the country as productive as possible.

The state now appeared as a special agency, distinct from the territorial lord who administered the territory belonging to his family and also distinct from the people, who constituted only an object for this nation. This distinction also had a reaction on the concept of war and the waging of war. Hugo Grotius enunciated the principle that war was the affair of the soldier alone and no concern of the civilian.

I have said that the first nation that maintained mercenary units on a large scale on an actual continuing basis was Spain, which had to have a military force constantly in action in the Netherlands, even when there were interruptions in her wars with France. Nevertheless, the inner character of this Spanish army remained for a long time that of the mercenary band. It was only their enemy, the Netherlandish army under Maurice of Orange, that developed, as we have seen, the new qualities of the military system that accompany the character of the standing army. In the Swedish army of Gustavus Adolphus this new situation attained a higher degree, but without fully eliminating the character of the old mercenary bands. With the close of the Thirty Years' War this development, too, was completed, and we now have more or less evenly among all the nations the phenomenon of the disciplined army which is maintained in peacetime also and paid on a regular basis.

Let us examine this situation in detail as it applies in the two most outstanding examples, France and Prussia.[1]

NOTE FOR GENERAL REMARKS

1. On the origin and development of the Austrian army see *History of the Imperial and Royal Armed Forces from 1618 to the End of the Nineteenth Century (Geschichte der kaiserlichen und königlichen Wehrmacht von 1618 bis Ende des XIX. Jahrhunderts)*, published by the Directorate of the Imperial and Royal Military Archives.

Chapter I

France

Formerly, scholars considered for a time that the *compagnies d'ordonnance* marked the beginning of standing armies in France. But these companies were nothing more than a highly developed, organized form of the Middle Ages, which already had standing troops, so to speak, in the individual forces of the princes and the castle garrisons. What we designate as standing armies in the true sense has its roots not in knighthood and its accompanying warriors, but in the new infantry appearing at the end of the fifteenth century and beginning of the sixteenth. France, however, had for a long time only an insignificant infantry of its own. Charles VIII, Louis XII, Francis I, and Henry II all fought their battles primarily with Swiss soldiers and lansquenets in conjunction with the French knights. Even the civil wars which damaged France so severely for thirty years in the second half of the sixteenth century were waged principally with Swiss and German mercenaries. It was not the French themselves but the German horsemen in French territory who accomplished the development from knighthood into cavalry. The Huguenot wars did not advance the French national military system but even threw it a step backward, as we may say. A civil war depends on the supporters that each side finds in the country, who come and go more or less as they wish. The passionate partisanship that must be present to spark a civil war and is of very special strength in religious wars produced a unique revival of knighthood in the Huguenot wars. The nobles personally and of their own volition took to the field and served without pay. They fought bravely, but the reverse side of this knightly system also became apparent: when Alexander of Parma had relieved Paris in 1590, he maneuvered and avoided battle. The army of Henry IV, which consisted for the most part of nobles serving voluntarily, then had nothing to do, and it finally broke up. Henry said that in the final analysis it was only money that made the difference between him and the prince of Parma and that with better financial resources he, too, would have been able to keep his army in the field. Ranke observed that the silver from Potosi played a role in the development of the spirit of the standing armies in Europe.[1] There is no doubt that the precious metals from America helped the Spanish very significantly. But later events showed that an orderly national administration and tax system was not only equally capable but even much more effective in providing the means for regular payment of the troops. In this connection, of course, we must again note the prerequisite that the increase in precious metals following the discovery of America greatly facilitated the transition from barter economy to money economy, because the collection of taxes can only be accomplished with great difficulty in the absence of a developed money economy. In the second volume of this work we learned how strongly the collapse of the ancient money economy and the withdrawal of Europe into barter economy contributed to the breakup of the Roman legions. Now we have the counterpart to that development: with the reappearance of a money economy there once again developed disciplined standing armies.

The Huguenot wars were constantly intertwined with foreign wars. It was not until the peace of Vervins in 1598 between France and Spain that a definite end was brought to this complicated situation, and after that peace Henry IV maintained only a very small army under arms. Most of the mounted companies were disbanded and the strength of the remaining ones was greatly reduced, reportedly to 1,500 horsemen.[2] According to one source,[3] the entire army was 6,757 men strong, most of whom were mounted. Another source states that, in addition to the Guard, there remained four strong infantry regiments.[4] And a third source stated there were 100 companies, which, of course, need not have been all together more than a few thousand men strong.

The base of the French infantry was formed by those "bands" of Picardy and Piedmont, now called "the old bands" ("les vieilles bandes"), which were not considered on a par with the Swiss and the lansquenets but which, nevertheless, continued to be maintained and were transformed into regiments at the beginning of the religious war. The momentum for this move had been provided by the fortuitous situation that the two colonels general of infantry, Andelot and Condé, were both Huguenots, and a part of the "vieilles bandes" remained loyal to them. It was considered too risky simply to announce that the two colonels general were relieved, and François Guise therefore gave a new organization to those parts of their troops that remained loyal to the king (1561; definitively in 1569).[5] That was the origin of the French infantry regiments, which were gradually increased and continued in existence up to the great revolution.

Sully gives us the following picture of the condition of the French troops at the end of the civil war: recruiting for the infantry had been carried out by force, and those troops were held together only by means of the rod, prison, and the gallows. They did not receive their pay, and they sought to desert whenever they could; the provosts had to keep them together like besieged men in camp. Another French author said, "The army is basically like a stream into which all the impurities of the social body are emptied."[6]

When Henry IV was preparing in 1610 to renew the war against Catholic Spain, the reason for which he was assassinated by Ravaillac, he is supposed to have had thirteen regiments of infantry. Sully drew up a plan for an army of 50,000 men, which, "figuring the year at ten months," was to cost 15 million francs.

After Henry's assassination, France sank again to a condition of weakness and internal confusion, from which it was only gradually raised up again by Richelieu. Richelieu saw to it that France entered the Thirty Years' War against the house of Hapsburg. But since France had not been involved in a serious war for almost forty years (1598 to 1635), her military organization was still very weak. As late as 1631 Richelieu declared that France had too few men suitable to wage war, and he therefore wished to participate in the war more through politics and with money than in a direct military way.[7] In 1636, after the Protestants in Germany had suffered the defeat at Nördlingen, it was possible for the imperial general, Gallas, to penetrate deep into France and for Johann von Werth to move from Belgium to the environs of Paris. Richelieu called on the patriotism of the French people, and finally there gradually developed a real French army. New French regiments were formed, and the drill system of the Netherlanders was adopted. Turenne, who was related to the Orange family, had been trained among them. But for a long time foreigners still remained the principal strength of the army of the king of France. It is particularly worthy of note that he took Duke Bernhard of Weimar into his service, as well as retaining Bernhard's troops after the duke's death. In 1638, along with thirty-six French regiments, there were twenty-five foreign regiments.

In 1640 Richelieu boasted that France had under arms 150,000 foot troops and more than 30,000 horsemen. More recent French research, however, shows those numbers to be greatly exaggerated; presumably there were not even 100,000 men all together.[8] The companies were said to have often numbered only fifteen to twenty men, because the captains discharged them after they were mustered, in order to pocket the pay.

Four years later, in 1644, Mazarin wrote to Turenne that he wished to recruit as many Germans as possible, since the number of deserters among the French amounted to almost two-thirds.[9] Recruits were sought in Ireland, Scotland, Sweden, and Prussia.

In 1670 the total strength of the army was figured to be 138,000 men, including 45,000 foreigners, or more than one-third of the total.

In 1789, at the outbreak of the Revolution, the French army numbered seventy-nine French and twenty-three foreign infantry regiments and a total of 173,000 men. But we are unable to determine how many of these were actually under the colors and doing service.[10]

As we know, the regiments were originally administrative units, an assemblage of a varying number of units (*Fähnlein*) of varying strengths. The tactical units were the squares or battalions, and they, too, were of varying strength and composition, according to the circumstances. In 1635 the battalions in France were made subordinate units of the regiments. The battalions were supposed to be of equal strength, but a regiment could have more or fewer battalions.

It was particularly difficult to transform the old *compagnies d'ordonnance* into cavalry regiments. The captains did not wish to be incorporated into the new organization; jokes were made concerning the light horses, which could not carry a heavily armored knight. The first test of this organization, in 1635, had to be abandoned after seven months, and the independence of the companies was once more established. As late as 1638 and 1639 regulations were issued requiring under pain of death that the horsemen were always to carry their weapons on their marches, on guard duty, and so on.

In spite of all the difficulties, the new system gradually took hold, and the French nobility also produced commanders like Turenne and Condé, who knew how to use the new military system.

The cavalry abandoned the traditions of the knightly manner of fighting so completely that in 1676 Louis XIV had to order that officers were to wear the cuirass on pain of dismissal, while the men did not wear it. In an attack the officers formed the first rank of the squadron. After 1715, the officers, too, with the exception of the generals, gave up the cuirass and wore a leather coat like the men.[11]

The real organizer of the new military system was Michel Le Tellier, who took over the position of state secretary of war in 1643 and turned it over to his son Louvois in 1668.[12] Even Richelieu had not yet been able to bring any real order into the military organization.

In the first years of the minority of Louis XIV, the Venetian ambassador Nanni reported of the French soldiers that they were clad in rags and barefooted and that the cavalry was poorly mounted but still they all fought like madmen.

The decisive point was the pay. The Venetian ambassador Angelo Correr reported that of 100 ducats which the king provided, only 40 were used for their real purpose, while 60 were wasted or embezzled. The troops were paid so poorly and irregularly that it was impossible to keep them under control.

Le Tellier created a class of civilian officials, the intendants, who were assigned to the military commands. Only the commanding general himself was superior to them; all the other officers had to obey them. They participated in every council of war the general held and in all decisions on military, diplomatic, and administrative subjects. They were to give the commanders their advice. Finances, fortifications, rations, munitions, hospitals, courts-martial—all these items depended on them.

In order to supervise the paying of the troops, Le Tellier ordered first of all that it was always to be done in the presence of the intendant or of his subordinate official, the military commissar, the military chief, and the mayor or respected inhabitants of the places where the troops were billeted. Then it was ordered that the captain was no longer to distribute the pay at all, but this was to be done by the intendant or one of the military commissars and that the pay was no longer to be given out in connection with a review but at regular intervals, usually monthly.

In 1650, in the disturbances of the Fronde, Le Tellier had once again to grant the governors themselves the responsibility for raising the taxes in their provinces needed to maintain the fortresses and garrisons. But as early as 1652 he withdrew this concession and definitively established the purely royal administration.

At the same time he saw to it that his intendants and their commissars held inspections constantly, even unexpectedly and during a march, checking the full presence of the unit. In each case they were to send an exact report to the minister. These commissars arrested refractory officers and confiscated their possessions.

Condé, Du Plessis-Praslain, and Turenne, as commanders, sometimes still gave their own money, even their silver service, in order, at the time of greatest need, to protect the soldiers from starving, even if not to pacify them. Even Le Tellier himself advanced funds, to say nothing of the greedy Mazarin.

As long as the tax system was not functioning promptly, Le Tellier introduced paper money that was given to the soldiers and then exchanged for cash when the taxes were received. It was not only Richelieu who still had very poor finances but also Mazarin, who, no doubt, gathered riches for himself but was not concerned about the national finances. Under Louis XIV regular payment in cash gradually became normal.

During the Thirty Years' War the corps of troops were still small, half-independent republics. The lieutenant generals considered themselves to be of equal authority and refused to subordinate themselves to one another. Le Tellier established the concept of the military hierarchy. In doing so, he had to treat the Weimar army with particular care, since it was organized somewhat differently from the French and had its own esprit.

The appointment of officers was gradually withdrawn from the higher leaders, and the entire existence of the officers was made completely dependent on the will of the king. The heads and sons of the leading aristocratic families, as colonels, remained the proprietors of regiments, often assuming this position as very young men. They took this position, however, only in military actions and otherwise lived principally at the court. The actual command was in the hands of the lieutenant colonel, who was named arbitrarily by the king from among the captains and was an experienced officer who had served through the grades.

Le Tellier did away with the abuse whereby higher officers held several positions and received the salaries for them. He also sought to establish the rule that even if the courtly colonels did not do so, nevertheless the other officers actually were to remain with their troops and not spend their time enjoying themselves in Paris.

He limited the luxury of the higher officers and specified for each position the maximum number of horses the incumbent might have; a captain of infantry was allowed four, a lieutenant three, and a provost two.

When the "old bands" were formed in France, few noblemen entered the service,[13] and consequently, as in Germany, men of various backgrounds who distinguished themselves rose to positions of leadership. But as early as the sixteenth century efforts were made to draw the officers to the maximum extent from the traditional, outstanding warrior class, the nobility. For example, even the Huguenot leader de la Noue had that requirement.[14] As the large standing army was now gradually formed from the time of Richelieu and under Louis XIV, there arose a noteworthy conflict. The entire spirit of the nation and the government called for an officer corps formed exclusively of nobles. The number available, however, was not sufficient. The old noble families were in many cases impoverished and unable to afford the additional expense that was necessary for a suitable standard of living in the officer corps. On the other hand, numerous young men in the upper bourgeoisie and in families of functionaries were inclined toward the military profession. The nobility, however, sought to maintain its position by excluding all others and claimed the officer positions as its natural heritage, and the government was guided by the effort to favor, maintain, and foster the nobility as much as possible. An unopposed blending in the officers' corps would in time have eliminated the special position of honor of the nobility. As the nobility provided the officers and the officer corps considered itself as nobility, there thus existed within the population a specialized class tradition with its own customs, concepts of honor, and claims, which, in its relationship to the court, those surrounding the king, exercised a firmly anchored social dominance. Furthermore, the recruiting of the officer corps from the special hereditary class created and strengthened between the officer corps and the men a cleavage that divided the army into two basically different components. This division applied in all the armies of Romanic-Germanic Europe and was then also taken over under Peter the Great of Russia. This separation was the truly characteristic feature of this period, and it gave those armies a stamp that was significantly different from that of the Roman legions and the Swiss and lansquenets of the sixteenth century.[15]

A special circumstance served to strengthen the tendency to maintain the French officer corps as nobility. Despite their appointments by the king, it happened often that officers sold their positions to others. This occurred particularly when older nobles who intended to retire sought in this way to gain an addition to their pension. Such an agreement with a successor was called a "concordat," and very great sums were paid as a result. But it was not always the most capable men who moved up in this way, and nothing can spoil the moral base of discipline more than the promotion of unsuitable elements to the higher command positions.[16] But Marshal Belle-Isle, under Louis XV, vainly took great pains to suppress this abuse, and since there was more wealth in the bourgeois families whose sons were attracted by military service than in most of the noble families, the struggle against the sale of positions led to a reaction against the commoners. If no members of the bourgeoisie were admitted, they would then not be able through their wealth to compete with the nobility for the desired positions. And thus through the entire period until the Revolution we see edict after edict which sometimes permitted access to the officer corps by bourgeois, sometimes made this more difficult, and sometimes ruled it out completely. In 1629, under Richelieu, it was proclaimed that a soldier who proved himself could advance to the grade of captain and even further if he was worthy of it. As liberal as that might appear, this edict was still based on the attitude that the officer corps was essentially noble. Just as Monluc rose to the highest position of the military hierarchy in the sixteenth century, so too did Catinat as a bourgeois in the seventeenth. In general, however, the situation was such that, although the number of bourgeois officers, the commoners, was quite high, only very seldom did they reach the higher command positions, and at times acceptance in the officer corps was so strictly controlled that it almost amounted to exclusion. A principal means of providing acceptance in the officer corps for commoners was the creation of a feigned nobility: a certificate signed by three or four nobles to the effect that the aspirant was a noble was supposed to suffice for his acceptance, and such a certificate was not very difficult to come by. Consequently, a few years before the Revolution (1781) an edict proclaimed that proof must be given of four paternal ancestors. This meant that the sons of newly ennobled men were also excluded from officer positions or that they could be admitted only as a result of special favor.[17]

The officer class, as it was formed in the course of the seventeenth century, was therefore a further development of that hereditary warrior class of the Middle Ages, knighthood, transformed not only outwardly in its combat methods, but also internally as a result of the adoption of the strict forms of discipline and of the military hierarchy, with promotion according to the judgment of the commander. In 1685 there appeared a book, *La conduite de Mars*, which aspired to teach the officer the duties associated with his status and give him rules of conduct, and which, to quote Jähns (2:1255), formed the transition from the code of honor of the noble to the military service regulations. The officer was supposed to obey but not to forget his position and was to take advantage of every opportunity to make his fortune. The book also taught that piety was an advantage.

In the French army the number of officers was surprisingly very large in comparison with the number of men. According to one statement in the general staff documents on the wars of Frederick the Great (1:114), around 1740 there was one officer for every eleven men and therefore the lieutenants, too, were also all armed with muskets. In Prussia at that time there were some twenty-nine men to each officer, at the death of Frederick about thirty-seven, and in our time about fifty men per officer. Even if the ratio of one to eleven is based on an error, nevertheless the number of officers was relatively much higher than today.[18]

If the acceptance of bourgeois elements into the officer corps had never been completely stopped, there also remained inside the army itself at least one narrow bridge that led over from the world of the men into the world of the officer class. Between the noncommissioned officers and the officers were the *"officiers de fortune,"* something like the deck officers of the navy or more recently the first sergeant-lieutenants. They were considered as only noncommissioned officers but often came from educated families. By proving his ability, the *"officier de fortune"* could be received in the officer corps in middle age. Their professional knowledge and their strong sense of duty were very important for the cohesiveness of the troop, especially in the cavalry, where many prominent gentlemen did not concern themselves particularly with their service. It was from this level of the army that Marshal Bernadotte, the later king of Sweden, came. He was the son of a respected lawyer and a personality so important and later also so imposing that he must have attracted attention to himself even as a young man. Nevertheless, at the outbreak of the Revolution he was twenty-six years old, had already been a soldier for ten years,[19] was not yet a lieutenant, and even if he eventually received the officer's epaulets, he hardly had any prospect of going higher than the rank of captain.

The regiments were brought up to strength by recruiting, for which purpose Le Tellier assigned them in 1645 specifically limited recruiting districts. In 1666 the period for which the enlistment was made was limited to four years, and captains were forbidden, on pain of reduction in rank, to hold under the colors beyond that period men who did not volunteer. From time to time there was also still a levy of knights, the *arrière-*

ban—in 1674, 1675, 1689, 1703, and even in 1758 in the Seven Years' War. But hardly had they reported when they were sent home again from the army camp as unusable, and there resulted from this a means of taxing the nobility; instead of mounting up for service, one could satisfy his obligation with the payment of a release fund. In 1639 the levied nobleman had to provide two infantrymen as substitutes for himself.

As late as 1661, when Louis XIV ascended the throne, there was still no general uniform in France. Only individual companies of some regiments were clad uniformly by their captains, even though Le Tellier in the 1640s had already had uniforms and weapons manufactured on standard patterns. In the wars of religion the opposite sides were distinguished by scarves and also by jackets (*casaque, hoqueton*) of various colors, which were often changed depending on the leaders and other circumstances.

In 1666 Le Tellier issued a regulation prescribing the same caliber for all muskets, twenty bullets to the pound.

There were but few barracks; soldiers were billeted in civilian quarters, and precise regulations governed their relationship with their landlords, both for those billeted on a standing basis and those troops on the march. Under Louis XIV more and more barracks were built.

From 1666 on, rather large troop units were often assembled in training camps and were drilled not only in tactics but also in maneuvering against one another.

For the system of rations, Le Tellier created regular depots, which became of the greatest importance for strategic operations. Le Tellier himself went into the field from time to time to direct and supervise the distribution of rations. We shall have occasion later to speak of the effectiveness of this system of ration depots.

Richelieu had already established field hospitals. Le Tellier made funds available for them, both for the purpose of caring for the soldiers and from a humanitarian viewpoint. In the eighteenth century the French were considered to be particularly well cared for in this respect. The general intendant, du Verney, wrote during the Seven Years' War to Clermont, the army commander, that the French nation was perhaps the only one that had field hospitals with its armies, for humanitarian reasons and also because they had few men and had to be economical with them. He went on to say that the field hospitals were, of course, not like those in the garrisons.[20]

A particular drawback of the old mercenary armies had been the huge train. The soldiers liked to take along their wives into the field to have their meals provided by them and to be nursed by them in case of illness or wounds. As a result of the organization of the orderly system of ration depots and the field hospitals, the help provided the soldiers by these women became so unnecessary that it was possible to forbid the women to be taken along, and Le Tellier even forbade the soldiers to marry.

Nevertheless, the great extent to which these standing armies still lived with the attitudes of the mercenary system is shown by the continuing practice of ransoming prisoners of war for money. In 1674 an agreement was made between France and Spain which established a specific tariff for ransoms: 400 francs was paid for a colonel, and 7 1/2 francs for an infantry private.[21]

Le Tellier also concerned himself with the disabled veterans. Quite a number of them were assigned to monasteries, which they had to maintain, while others were assembled in companies and fed in return for the performance of certain services. But they preferred to desert and move to Paris, where they lived by begging. Punishments were established against civilians who gave them alms, and beggars themselves were even threatened with the death penalty. In 1674 Louis XIV founded the Hôtel des Invalides.[22]

The work of Michel Le Tellier was, as we have already mentioned, continued and perfected by his son, François Michel, who bore the title of marquis de Louvois. In 1662, at the age of twenty-one, he became his father's assistant, and six years later, when he was twenty-eight, he became his father's successor as independent minister of war (1668).

When the peace treaty of Aachen ended the War of Devolution in 1668 and the army was to be reduced, Louvois did not discharge the appropriate number of troop units, as was the custom previously, but reduced the strength of each individual regiment while retaining their complete staffs, so that thenceforth the army could easily be enlarged again by assigning new recruits to the existing regiments. It was only through this method that the idea of a standing army was really brought to fulfillment. The esprit of a unit, once that unit is part of the standing army, regenerates itself. Not only was there a saving of the time that would have been necessary for the assembling of completely new troop units, in case of war, but these old regiments also had the very important qualitative advantages of old troop units in comparison with new ones.

In order to make the entire strength of the army available for the active waging of war, in 1688 Louvois created the militia regiments, which were to take over the garrison service. While the field army was based on voluntary recruitment, the men for the militia regiments were provided by the communities and were therefore levied in one way or another. Soon, however, the militia regiments were also employed here and there in action in the field, and in the War of the Spanish Succession their troops were simply incorporated into the field regiments.

With this turn of events there had therefore been recourse, if indirectly, to a form of conscription, even though mild and on a small scale, for the field army as well. But long before that, in 1677, Louvois had already written on one occasion that it was no excuse for desertion if a soldier explained that he had been levied by force; for if that was valid, nobody would be left in the units, according to Louvois, for there was hardly anybody who could not raise some objection to the manner in which he was enlisted.

Under Henry III it was once ordered that, as in Germany, any bogus soldier used as a filler for pay purposes was to have his nose cut off. They did not dare to punish those who were really guilty, the captains. Now things had changed. But it was still a very long time before this type of fraud was really eliminated. As late as 1676, under Louvois, the order concerning the cutting off of noses was repeated.

As the most important service of Louvois for the French army we may consider his administrative accomplishments, the constant, often brutal, energy and industriousness with which he carried out and perfected the system created by his father, broke down all resistance, rooted out violations, and exercised watchful control everywhere. Wherever he suspected an error or an irregularity, he appeared personally and took the necessary action. With respect to this activity he can be compared to some extent with Frederick William I.

The well-planned organization of the French army even survived the defeats of the War of the Spanish Succession and proved itself in the Seven Years' War. In 1760 Ferdinand von Braunschweig fought with a French army which was stronger and no worse organized and equipped than when it had appeared under Louis XIV on the east of the Rhine. The French numbered no fewer than 140,000 men.[23]

NOTES FOR CHAPTER I

1. *French History (Französische Geschichte)*, 1:369.
2. Susane, *Histoire de la cavallerie française*, 1:82.
3. *Campaigns of Prince Eugene (Feldzüge des Prinzen Eugen)*, 1:507.
4. Susane, *Histoire de l'infanterie*, 1:78.
5. The Spanish *terzios*, which were created in 1544, may have served as a model; their relationship to the *columellas* is not clear.
6. Mention, *L'armée de l'ancien régime*. 1900.
7. Ritter, *German History in the Period of the Counterreformation (Deutsche Geschichte im Zeitalter der Gegenreformation)*, 3:518.
8. André, *Le Tellier*, p. 26.
9. André, p. 217.
10. According to Susane, Ed. of 1876, p. 312, at the beginning of 1791 the rank and file of the infantry did not number more than 125,000 men.
11. Susane, *Histoire de la cavallerie française*, pp. 136, 154.
12. Louis André, *Michel Le Tellier et l'organisation de l'armée monarchique*, Paris, Felix Alcan, 1906. This is a large work, supported by

many documents. At times the tendency to emphasize Le Tellier's accomplishments is somewhat too strong. In 1900 the French War Ministry published a work entitled *Historiques des Corps de Troupe de l'armée française (1569–1900)*. The introduction gives a summary of the important references since the work by Daniel in 1721. The book contains a tabular presentation of all troop units since 1589 without any further source studies, as well as the names of the commanders, of the battles in which the units participated, and so forth.

13. Susane, p. 100. De la Noue concludes that the Spanish infantry was better than the French from the fact that so many noblemen were in the Spanish service (Jähns, p. 564). A remarkable account of weekly changes of the Spanish commanders, determined by lot, is reported for the year 1538 by Jovius, Book 37, Ed. 1578, pp. 364, 366.

14. *Discours* XIV, Ed. 1587, p. 338.

15. The first trace of a distinction in principle between officers and noncommissioned officers I find in a remark by de la Noue in *Discours* XIII, Ed. 1587, p. 322. In that passage he praises the Spanish for obeying the orders of even simple sergeants, and their officers all the more.

16. I. G. Hoyer, *History of the Art of War (Geschichte der Kriegskunst)*, p. 188, who was still familiar with the living tradition, considers that the principal reason for the poor discipline of the French in the eighteenth century was the selling of officer positions. But we may not observe such points in isolation and then consider them as basic causes. In the English army, too, the sale of positions was common, and it not only maintained its discipline, but this deformity even offered the advantage that an outstanding man, if he was also rich, could attain a higher command position at a very young age. Thus Wellington became a lieutenant colonel at age twenty-three.

17. The relationship of the noble and bourgeois officers in the French army is treated very thoroughly in the book by Louis Tuetey, *The Officers under the Ancien Régime, Nobles and Commoners (Les officiers sous l'ancien régime, nobles et roturiers)*, Paris, 1908.

18. Puységur, Chap. VI, p. 50, estimates sixteen to seventeen men for each officer, but on p. 103, some twenty-five men per officer. Sicard, *Histoire des institutions militaires des Français*, 2:229, estimates twelve to thirteen men per officer (79,050:6553), and on p. 244, nineteen to twenty men (686:35 in the infantry battalion). Susane, *Histoire de l'infanterie française*, 1:278, has fifteen men per officer (685:35). Berenhorst, *Observations (Betrachtungen)*, 1:61, estimates eighteen men for one officer (900:50). Susane adds to his numbers the statement that in 1718 the number was found to be much too large and consequently the number of companies was reduced, but in 1734 they were again increased. Hoyer, *Geschichte der Kriegskunst*, 2:505, states that, as a result of the reforms of the minister of war, St. Germain, the strength of the companies was

fixed at 125 souls, including seven or eight officers. Chuquet says the number of French officers in 1789 was about 9,000. In Austria, too, the number of officers at the time of Prince Eugene was very large. Montecuccoli required thirty-three officers for 1,500 men. In December 1740 Prussia had 3,116 officers for about 100,000 men, and in 1786 5,300 officers for some 200,000 men. The Thüna regiment in 1784 numbered fifty-two officers and 2,186 noncommissioned officers and men, including forty reserves, consequently one officer for forty-two men. *Militär-Wochenblatt*, 1909, col. 3768.

19. The statements in the biographies by Sarrans-Jeune and Kläber, concerning Bernadotte's entrance into service, do not agree completely.

20. Daniels, *Preussische Jahrbücher*, 77:523.

21. Hoyer, *Geschichte der Kriegskunst*, 2:199. According to Nys, *International Law (Le droit international)*, 3:512, the first treaty on ransoms was made in 1550 between Maurice of Saxony and Magdeburg. The ransom was not to exceed one month's pay. Heffter-Geffcken, *International Law (Völkerrecht)*, section 142, names as the oldest agreement concerning the exchange of prisoners and ransoms a treaty between France and Holland in 1673. Pradier-Fodéré, *Traité de droit international public*, 7:45, refers to still other treaties. At times the maximum limit for a ransom was fixed at the pay for a quarter of the year.

22. The first promise to care for the sick and wounded that I can remember having read is contained in a pay contract of Stralsund of 1510 (Beck, *Artikelsbriefe*, p. 118), where care of the wounded and of disabled veterans is promised.

23. Daniels, "Ferdinand von Braunschweig," *Preussische Jahrbücher*, 80:509. See also 79:287.

Chapter II

Brandenburg-Prussia

Basically, the German princes' need for an efficient military system was even more pressing than that of the king of France, since their resources were not sufficient to enable them, at least in wartime, to recruit large mercenary bands, as the king of France did. In the German areas there was no lack of extensive and energetic attempts to create a new military system. They were based on both the traditional feudal obligation of the nobility and the general obligation for defense of the homeland, which had never been completely forgotten. Experienced military leaders were appointed in return for fixed pay, standby money (*Wartegeld*), so that they would be ready in time of need to take command of a levy of vassals or a "delegation" of burghers and peasants. The larger territories, such as Bavaria, Württemberg, the Palatinate, Saxony, and Prussia, even established rather numerous organized militia units. In this regard special mention should be made of Count Johann of Nassau, a brother of that William Louis who so successfully assisted Maurice of Orange in the creation of his army. Count Johann, deeply impressed by the new ideas on the military system as they were put into effect by his relatives in Holland, wanted to introduce them in Germany. He saw the gathering clouds of the War of Religion and advised the Estates to arm themselves by replacing the recruited soldiers by a national levy, but he went even further.

Maurice of Orange's successes had brought him at that time such great prestige that the devotees of Mars from all of Protestant Europe had gathered in his camp in order to be initiated into the new military system.

The art of war of the Netherlands was no longer based, however, on simple experience, but on study and knowledge. Therefore in 1617 Johann established in his capital, Siegen, a military and knightly school for young nobles and the sons of patricians, where the art of engineering, fortifications, artillery, tactics, mathematics, Latin, French, and Italian were to be taught. As the director of this school he called on John Jacob von

Wallhausen, concerning whose origin and life we unfortunately do not know much more than that he was in the Netherlands, called himself "the appointed colonel of the guard and captain of the meritorious city of Danzig," and in the years from 1614 to 1621 published a long series of theoretical writings on military subjects. These writings are a mixture of real knowledge and good judgment and at the same time often uncritical fantasy.[1] He is capable of recommending that the cavalry form for defense in a circle or a square,[2] and he deploys the infantry in formations shaped like a cross and an octagon. Nevertheless, his writings were very successful and were also translated into French. The author, however, as one might suspect from his writings, was of an uncertain character and was discharged after a few months. The Siegen military school was soon abandoned, and in 1623 Count Johann died without having created anything of a lasting nature.[3]

Nor did the militia organizations have any success. These levies did not stand fast when faced with the professional warriors, the mercenaries.[4] The men of the Palatinate gave way when the Spaniards came, the Saxons took to their heels at Breitenfeld, and Prince Elector Maximilian wrote that his Bavarians, in 1632 when the Swedes were approaching, "could not be used with any effect, and the expense for them had been in vain."[5] The Württembergers still participated in the battle of Nördlingen and seem to have been destroyed there. Unfortunately, there is no more definite report as to how they fought.

Brandenburg, although it should have been looking toward a broader concept of politics as a result of its imminent union with Prussia, Pomerania, and the areas in Westphalia and on the lower Rhine, nevertheless entered the Thirty Years' War with still less preparedness than those other territories named above. While the entire number of obligated vassals was estimated at 1,073 horses, and they were divided into companies, that was only on paper, and when the Berlin burghers were supposed to hold target practice in 1610, they said that was too dangerous, since it would frighten pregnant women.[6] A war with recruited mercenaries, however, meant, as the Brandenburg chancellor wrote in 1610, that "half the enemy was inside the house and the entire enemy at the door."[7]

In Prussia the high council presented the duke a "defense plan" in 1622, but George William rejected it (19 February 1623), "because experience makes it more than clear that the national organization in the Palatinate for the protection of the country, in case of war and combat, contrary to the expectations of all persons, actually accomplishes nothing."[8]

We can say that from the Hussite Wars until the Thirty Years' War, that is, for more than 200 years, the theory and practice in the German military organization contradicted each other. In theory, the vassal service, citizen levies, and militia continued to be talked about; in practice, however, the wars were fought by mercenaries.

In 1557 the prince elector of Saxony issued an order to the town of Delitzsch: "It is our solemn command that you, along with your citizens, be in a state of good readiness, so that you and they may unhesitatingly move out on further orders." In 1583 it was ordered "that our obedient vassal counts, knightly lords, burghers, and other subjects and their relatives be at all times well equipped and ready to move out." Only in case of "obvious sickness" were substitutions by men of equal rank to be allowed.[9]

If we possessed such capitularies from the time of Charlemagne! What would legal and constitutional history have concluded from that, and what kinds of systems would they have erected on that base! But these were nothing but empty words without any content.

The small life guard that the princes had in the sixteenth century was called the "servants of the court." The prince elector of Brandenburg had 200 men in this group, or a few more.

When danger approached, the Estates approved a small troop for a short period. In 1626, when Wallenstein and Mansfeld were approaching Brandenburg, they said they were ready to observe the neutrality of the territory if the prince elector really closed off his country. But he had no soldiers for that purpose, and although the Estates had approved 3,000 men, it was too late and then only for three months. They stated that it was unnecessary to maintain warriors, since for 100 years they had paid large and heavy taxes for that purpose and had still received no protection.

And so the troops of the two opposing sides moved without hindrance through the country, and in 1628 it was estimated that Wallenstein had already taken 200 tons of gold from the country. For two tons the country could have formed a very considerable force.[10]

The alliance with Gustavus Adolphus provided the occasion for forming a few Brandenburg regiments, but it obligated the prince elector principally to the payment of money.

Six years later, when the prince elector shifted to the side of the emperor, the plan was to form a very significant Brandenburg army with imperial financial support, an army that was obligated "to the Holy Roman Emperor and in his place to His Grace, the Prince Elector of Brandenburg." Its mission was to be the expulsion of the Swedes from Pomerania, but in the following year the Brandenburg minister Schwarzenberg was already reporting to the prince elector: "Your Princely Grace was to have provided 25,000 men, whom this poor land had to maintain and who would bring the country to complete ruin. Some 5,000 reported to the general rendezvous in the presence of Your Princely Grace and of Lieutenant General Count von Gallas hardly five weeks ago. At present, as your Princely Grace's officers themselves state, there are hardly 2,000 mounted and on foot present." The origin of this situation was naturally the fact that they were not able to assemble the money. We have seen what this situation was during those years even in the largest and richest kingdom of Europe, France. An effective tax administration is not so easily created, and all the less so when the Estates opposed it in the extreme. It was not simply that they did not want to pay the taxes, but behind the financial question was the constitutional question. When the Prussian Estates rejected the prince elector with his soldiers for their protection, Schwarzenberg wrote:[11] "They would have been great fools if they had tolerated it; indeed, if the prince elector came to Prussia so strong, they would have had to fear that he could make laws for them and do whatever he wished." And so it was indeed, later, under the son and even more under the great-grandson of this prince elector, who built his sovereignty "like a rock of bronze."

The sources tell us that the Great Elector, immediately after his assumption of power, released the Brandenburg troops from their double obligation to the emperor and to the prince elector and thereby created the independent Brandenburg army. Thus we are told that the real fruit of all the pain and suffering of the Thirty Years' War was the birth of the Brandenburg-Prussian army.

This concept must be modified very significantly. Frederick William in no way took up the scepter with the decision to free the princely power from the parallel power of the Estates and to make that power independent by means of a standing army obligated only to the elector. On the contrary, the advocate of the monarchical concept was the counselor of his father, Schwarzenberg, and the reproach to George William made by his contemporaries was not that he wanted too little but rather too much. As early as 1640 the Estates requested Schwarzenberg "not to treat them as rebels and slaves." The principal reproach that this minister merited was his slovenly administration. He himself saw to it that whenever there was money in the treasury, his demands were satisfied first, while the troops were not paid and went about in rags. The new master, completely engulfed in the complaints of the Estates concerning the tyrannical regime of Schwarzenberg, did not immediately recognize the seat of the illness but initially had no other wish than to put an end to his father's overextended plans and to arrange an armistice with the Swedes as the result of "the sad and bloody condition of the country." And he also wished to reduce the army to a small strength, although not to disband it completely. In the end there remained in Brandenburg 125 horsemen and 2,150 foot soldiers, who were intended not as field troops but as fortress garrisons and therefore consisted entirely of musketeers. The main difficulty in this reduction was satisfying the overdue demands of the soldiers, for which an attempt was made to secure the necessary resources by sharply deducting from the colonels, which in turn led to conflicts with them. Margrave Ernst, a cousin of the elector, finally assembled with difficulty 1,380 talers to satisfy the horsemen. The organizational creations of Schwarzenberg, the military chancellery and the military treasury, which were of course manned by very questionable persons,[12] were disbanded, and the colonels were again given the right to appoint their subaltern officers. In a bit of advice from the elector to his sons, which was written down a generation later (1667), he said: "I constantly regret that at the beginning of my reign, to my greatest disadvantage, I allowed myself to be led astray and followed the advice of others against my will"—that is, advice to depend more on alliances than on one's own strength.[13]

What the elector finally kept in the way of troops, although it was still something more than the Estates wished, was no longer a field army, and, at the insistence of the Estates, except for the garrisons in the newly won strongholds of Kolberg, Halberstadt, and Minden, it was reduced below the strength that had been present back in 1631, when Gustavus Adolphus appeared.

It was not until fifteen years after his accession to power that Prince Elector Frederick William formed a real army, when he was forced in 1655 to take sides in the war that broke out again between Sweden and Poland, an offshoot, so to speak, of the Thirty Years' War. In continuing struggle with the Estates he had managed to obtain, instead of the one-time approvals, taxes for a longer period (in 1653 the military allocation for six years), or he had raised these taxes by force without approval.[14] An imperial law (1654), which obligated the subjects "to provide helpful contributions to the manning and maintaining of the necessary fortresses, fortified places, and garrisons," was of aid to the prince. Of no less importance was the fact that hard work brought so much order into the administration that the available resources were not squandered but were used in accordance with their purpose. Thus the elector managed in 1656 to form in Prussia a unified army of 14,000 to 18,000 men in which all the areas now united under his hegemony were represented. With this army he joined forces with the Swedes under Charles X, half-way by compulsion, to be sure, and he took part in the battle of Warsaw.

After the peace of Oliva in 1660, the field army was once again reduced to 4,000 men, aside from the garrison troops, but now the principle was adopted of maintaining a permanent military force even in peacetime. Up to that point all the measures taken by the elector can be understood only as calling for the formation of troop units only when actual or threatening warlike developments occurred. Now, however, despite all the opposition of the Estates, the *miles perpetuus* (permanent soldiery), in accordance with the Swedish model, on which the elector expressly insisted, was established,[15] and when Frederick William died, he left a well-organized army of 29,000 men.

The history of the developing Brandenburg-Prussian army is at the same time the history of the Prussian nation.

The base of the Prussian administration was the division of the country into districts (*Kreise*) with the district president (*Landrat*) at their head. The *Landrat* was a nobleman residing in the district and recommended by the large estate owners of the district and appointed by the elector. He supervised the relationships of the inhabitants with troops billeted there or marching through, assigned responsibility for the delivery of produce for their rations, allocated billets, prescribed the provision of transport, and collected the taxes to pay the troops or to compensate for the damage they caused.

Above the district presidents was the War Chamber, which stemmed from the Superior War Commissariat, which continuously prescribed and administered taxes and deliveries, supervised the construction of military facilities such as buildings, depots, and forts, paid the troops, and maintained roads and bridges. By uniting these war chambers with the chambers which administered the royal domains (1723), Frederick William I created *Bezirks-Regierungen* (district governments), which are still in existence today.

Originally, the field marshal was at the head of the entire military system, blending both command and administrative functions. Then the administration was separated and was first entrusted to an individual and then (1712) to a council, the General Commissariat. By blending this with the administration of the domains, just as he had done at the next lower level, Frederick William I created the General Directorate (1723). From this entity there stemmed not only the War Ministry but also most of the present existing ministries, especially the Finance Ministry and the Ministry of the Interior. Consequently, from the historical viewpoint, the mother of the Prussian central administration was the army intendancy.[16]

Wallenstein had required of the regions he occupied not only that they provide billets and rations for the troops but also that they provide the soldiers' pay, and that included the officers, for the highest of whom the salary was very large. What the regions did not give was forcibly collected by the troops themselves. In the cooperation of the civil authorities with the military commanders there had developed a kind of administrative system that took care of the troops and still spared the country to the extent that it was not completely ruined and economic life could continue. In peacetime the administration (except recruiting) had remained in the hands of the civilian authorities, who systematically collected taxes and improved the tax system.[17] Of particular importance and effectiveness for Brandenburg was the general excise tax, the inland revenue, which was introduced in 1667 in imitation of the Dutch pattern.

Once the standing army was created, it quickly began to grow. This was caused first by the requirements for the wars against Louis XIV, then by the complexities of the great Northern War, and, when it had ended, by the initial efforts toward becoming a great power, under Frederick William I, and finally by the policy of conquest of Frederick the Great. For this purpose, it was important to find men, as well as money.

Money came from the constantly developing and more demanding tax system, the more logically and intensively exploited domains, good control, and finally also the subsidies, which since 1688 the sea powers were willing to pay German princes for providing troops in the wars against Louis XIV. From 1688 to 1697 Brandenburg received no less than 6,545,000 talers, a third of her total military expenses.[18] Among the accusations with which the court cabal caused the fall of the excellent minister Dankelmann was also the question of why they were financially embarrassed, since, after all, the subsidies must have made the prince elector rich.

Now the procurement of manpower caused more concern than the procurement of money. Voluntary recruiting was no longer sufficient. In the Thirty Years' War we have already heard occasionally of forcible impressment for military service. Montecuccoli (*Works*, 2:469) proposed that "the orphans, bastards, beggars, and paupers" who were being cared for in the hospices should be trained as soldiers in military training institutions, after the pattern of the janissaries. That was never attempted in a practical way; such cadet corps for the common man would have cost too much and produced too little. No other method was found than to develop forcible impressment into a system.

The officers seized suitable men wherever they found them and forced them through mistreatment to have themselves enlisted. Or, on the other hand, the civil officials were allocated a certain number of recruits to be provided to the regiments from their district. The arbitrariness of these actions undermined all legal concepts and caused the most serious damage to the country. Abuses and corruption were the inevitable results. Officers as well as officials used their recruiting power for impressments and then released the levied men in return for payment. "The officers," states an order of 10 February 1710, "make bold to carry on frequently 'a regular commerce' with the private soldiers, discharging them in return for money or selling them to other regiments and companies."[19] The peasants were no longer willing to bring their produce into town because they feared they would be seized there and turned over to the recruiters. Younger men crossed over the border in droves in order to escape service. The governor of Pomerania reported in 1706 that the subjects would be "totally ruined" by the recruiting methods and other burdens. It was reported from Minden in 1707 that young farm hands were no longer to be obtained because the recruiting had driven the young men into the neighboring provinces. In 1708 a regulation prescribed that all the men fit for service who "were contributing nothing to the public good were to be quietly levied and delivered to the fortress," where the governor was to turn them over to the recruiting officers. The situation became even worse under Frederick William I. While it is true that his accession to power coincided closely with the end of the French wars and the king himself did not wage costly wars, aside from the short participation in the Northern War, nevertheless his need for manpower increased, since he doubled the size of the army. From all the provinces came the complaints of the authorities who said that the recruiting was driving men out of the country and was threatening to destroy the economy. The population opposed the recruiting with force, and the general auditor complained about the extensive bloodshed that resulted from this. Although the king issued an order concerning the others, who were supposed to be preventing the violence, since he himself recommended the levying and taking by force of disobedient burghers and peasants and such servants "who did not do good," or expressed the warning for voluntary recruitment in this way: "that is, that there be no excesses and extreme acts of force in the process, so that no complaints will be heard," so "lesser acts of force" seemed to be allowed, and in reality everything remained the same.

In theory, however, there developed, without being recognized by the period or the creator himself, a change of the greatest importance in the relationship of the army to the national commander and through him to the nation.

In addition to the army that depended on recruitment, in 1701 King Frederick I had also organized a territorial militia which carried on the old obligation to defend the country and in which burghers and peasants were "enrolled," as it was stated. Frederick William I, immediately after his accession to power, had disbanded this militia as of minimum value militarily, but he adhered to the principle of obligated service and carried it over to the standing army. Forced by necessity, a change had been made from voluntary recruiting to forcible impressment, without any possible ethical or legal basis. Now Frederick William I declared (edict of 9 May 1714) that young men were "by their natural birth and the special order and command of the highest God, responsible and obligated to serve with their property and blood;" "eternal salvation depends on God, but everything else must depend on me." This has been considered by some as the proclamation of the great principle of general military obligation. But this concept is in error. It was only the proclamation of the principle of the unlimited power of the nation as embodied in the king to dispose of its subjects as it pleased, according to its needs. The idea that the entire citizenry was called to fight for the nation was completely absent, and no one would have denied that concept more strongly than Frederick William I himself. In his eyes military service was a profession just like others, a profession that could be practiced well only if it was exercised by men with the necessary technical training. Whoever was a soldier was a soldier and, where possible, was to remain one his whole life long. If there had been a sufficient number of voluntary recruits,

Frederick William I would have been completely satisfied. The fact that he also had his subjects levied for service and proclaimed them obligated for this was only a further step in the same concept and the same practice that we have also seen in France under Louis XIV.[20] But it was precisely through this step-up that the army and the people established a relationship to one another that did not exist previously, and from a practical viewpoint the levy under Frederick William I became the precursor of the general military obligation that was proclaimed a hundred years later.

After agreements were reached quite often by which a regiment was assigned a specific district for its recruiting, the king issued a general order of this kind in 1733, which, as the "canton regulation," attained a somewhat legendary fame.[21]

This idea seems so simple and apparent that we cannot help wondering that it did not come about until so late, in the twentieth year of the rule of this king.[22] The basic concept continued to be voluntary recruitment, and the expression "recruitment" was even retained when it later became a question of completely regular levying, but the assignment of a definite district, not only for the regiment but also for each company, gave the recruiting activity of the captains a completely different character. The captains were in many cases property owners or relatives of property owners and had preferred to "recruit" the sons of peasants from these properties. This patriarchal relationship was not without value, but it was now broken, and personal zeal in recruiting was very limited. The incentive for the resulting very extensive reform was given by the experience that the captains in their open competition in recruiting mutually crossed over into the territory of others, sought to steal away the recruits, and fell into quarrels.

The principal advantage of the new system was that a limit was established on the arbitrariness with which any captain could decide whether or not a suitable man had to become a soldier. Furthermore, the higher classes and certain groups among the people who seemed to be particularly useful for the economic life of the country were protected by decrees. The nobility, the sons of officials, the sons of burghers who were worth more than 10,000 talers, those of merchants and manufacturers, officials in the economy, peasants possessing their own house and farm and their only sons, the sons of ministers who themselves were studying theology, the workers in those industries favored by the mercantile-minded king—all of these were "exempted" from the canton obligation. In time these exemptions were greatly broadened. But the limits they established were often only indefinite or broader than one would suspect. For example, the sons of ministers were only exempt if they themselves were studying theology—that is, neither all theologians nor all sons of ministers. The city of Berlin did not constitute an "enrollment district," but officers were nevertheless allowed "to enroll here and there unemployed people of low extraction, for example, the children of shoemakers, tailors, and similar common people." Consequently, enough arbitrariness remained, and this would have been completely intolerable if an external factor had not drawn very definite limits on it. That was the preference of the period and especially of Frederick William I for "long fellows." No soldier was to measure less than 5 feet 6 inches. As a result of this limit, the great majority of young men were assured from the start of not being recruited. On the other hand, men of 5 feet 10, 5 feet 11, and more, were able to avoid the recruiters only with difficulty, even if they belonged to the exempted groups. "Don't grow; otherwise the recruiters will catch you," mothers are supposed to have said to their fast growing sons.

Since there is no inherent assurance that the big person is particularly brave, tough, healthy, or even strong, this situation seems to have been simply a question of the princely mood. And the basic point for this was nothing more than the pleasure associated with things stately and impressive. We find the same phenomenon back in the Roman legions (Vol. II, p. 165). The advantage, however, was that this gave an objective standard for the levy, and the arbitrary aspect that revolted moral sensitivity was pushed back. The human being, in questions concerning his life, wants the decision made by fate and not by man. In the nineteenth century, for the same reason, selection by lot was introduced.

The captains enrolled those boys of "promising appropriate growth" who seemed suitable to them as early as at the age of ten; they were allowed to wear a special tuft (*"Puschel"*) on their hats and received a pass that was to protect them from recruitment by other captains.

After the Seven Years' War King Frederick issued new provisions governing enrollment which extended the exemptions, removed the levying from the captains, and turned it over to a commission in which the civil authorities worked together with the regiments. The provision that only tall men were to be levied remained, and this even led to the special stipulation that of several sons of a peasant the smallest was to take over the farm.[23]

The mercenary armies had taken their replacements from the countries of all the lords, wherever they happened to be available. The levy, which now made it possible to bring the armies up to strength, did not in any way exclude the recruitment of foreigners. On the contrary, the canton arrangement was really only an expedient, because recruitment in foreign countries could not suffice quantitatively or qualitatively without additional men from the levy. The more foreigners one could enlist, the better, it was believed, because the work force for the country was maintained. The subject was more useful when he earned money and paid taxes than when he did military service. Frederick the Great established as a goal in 1742 that two-thirds of the companies should consist of foreigners and one-third of natives.[24] Recruiting was carried out in those German areas that maintained no troops at all or only a small number, especially in the free cities. There was also very strong recruitment in Poland and Switzerland. The Prussian recruiting officers were not ashamed to use any stratagem and any deception where possible, even force, in order to obtain useful tall men for the army of their king. Even the life guards of the lesser German princes were not secure from having the king of Prussia "levy" from their number. Another large source was provided by the deserters, who for some reason or other, especially because they feared a punishment, abandoned their colors and did not like civilian work or could not find any. From a list of the year 1744 that has survived by chance, we can deduce that in a company of the Rettberg Regiment, of 111 foreigners, 65 "had already served other potentates," that is, had deserted. In another company the number was 92 of 119.

During his wars, Frederick the Great always had recruiting for his army carried out in neighboring countries as well and even in enemy territory, in Mecklenburg, Saxony, Anhalt, Thuringia, and Bohemia, and he even had prisoners of war impressed into his service. After the surrender at Pirna, he even attempted to attract the men of the entire Saxon army into the Prussian service after the officers had been discharged. He even left them together in their battalions and gave them only Prussian officers. Of course, that ended up badly; a number of these battalions mutinied, shot their commanders, and deserted to the Austrians.

In 1780 the king ordered that persons who were found guilty of unauthorized writing and stirring up his subjects could be sentenced to military service after completing their punishment.

With this kind of recruit material, desertion naturally occurred on a huge scale. There was hardly any military document of the king that did not concern itself with the prevention of desertion. In peacetime, desertion was facilitated by the fact that in Prussia, the "kingdom of the many borders," as Voltaire called it, few cities were more than two days' march from the border. The soldiers were forced to watch one another from moment to moment, and even the peasants were obliged, on pain of strict punishment, to block the way to deserters, arrest them, and turn them in.

In a letter of instruction of King Frederick dated 11 May 1763 the officers were also told to study the terrain. We might think this was for purposes of combat, but the entire difference not only in the training but also in the spirit of the armies of the eighteenth and nineteenth centuries appears when we compare our assumption with the actual content of that letter of instruction. It reads:

Since His Royal Majesty has also found that most officers are so lazy in their garrisons as not even to familiarize themselves with the terrain around their garrison, something which is of the greatest necessity for all officers to know when they are looking for deserters, therefore His Royal Majesty orders regimental commanders to give their officers leave for a day so that they may become familiar with the mountainous terrain, the defiles, narrow and sunken roads, and the like, and this is to be done in all garrisons whenever the regiments change their quarters.

In wartime the prevention of desertion always had to be kept in mind on marches and in camp. There were to be no night marches, no camp close to a forest, and on marches through forests hussars were to move along beside the infantry. The French ambassador Valory, who accompanied Frederick into the field in 1745, reported that, from fear of desertions, the commanders had not risked sending patrols out even to a distance of only a few hundred paces.[25] Even the strategic movements were affected by this situation; in 1735 Frederick William I, on the advice of Leopold of Dessau, refused to have his troops march through a severely ravaged area on the Moselle because it offered the most dangerous opportunity for desertion.[26]

Was it at all possible to fight battles and win with soldiers of this background and character? In the Thirty Years' War prisoners of war had already been incorporated on a large scale into the victor's forces. These mercenaries were indifferent as to which side they fought on; for them, war was their calling and their trade, and they shifted over from one service to another without any inner qualms. With the impressed soldiers of the eighteenth century it was to some extent the same situation. Now, however, a very large part, and in the growing armies a larger and larger part, took up service with so many inner reservations that they could not have produced a useful warriorhood in the forms of the old mercenary system. The creation of troop units capable of fighting from unwillingly impressed men was only possible and can only be understood from the fact that the old mercenary bands had now shifted over into the formations of the standing army with its discipline.

The recalcitrance of the lansquenets could never be completely broken, because the moment arrived when the army was disbanded and the rights of the commanders disappeared. The state of subordination was only a temporary limitation on the person and not a lifelong habit. As the regiments took on a permanent existence, discipline achieved a completely new base. Even in the Thirty Years' War, with all the lack of discipline of the mercenary bands toward the exterior vis-à-vis the population, there was still on the interior a very well-developed dominance on the part of the military hierarchy, a real discipline, produced by the imperative law of war itself, and this discipline was now not only maintained in peacetime but also strengthened more and more. We have learned how Maurice of

Orange again discovered the art of drill, or one might say that he developed it into a real technique, and the Swedes adopted it from him. This technique was now constantly improved and used to bring the men under the control of their officers and to subject them to the will of their leaders. Marching in step, the positions of the musket, the goose step, precise sentry duty, the firing of salvos, and the regulations for saluting were all means of indoctrinating the will of the man into the will of the commander. But to drill a unit to the point of effectiveness required much work and strong methods. As Dilich already drew the distinction in 1607, the individual had first to be trained and then the unit—platoon, company, battalion, and the larger units. The first drill regulations in Germany were created by Landgrave Maurice of Hesse. Wallhausen, *Kriegskunst zu Fuss*, p. 70, had already written that when a man had been told once or twice how he should form up and he still did not do it, "then a good beating is called for; for whoever will not have it without blows, must learn with blows." It must already have been quite severe at that time, for Johann of Nassau considered it necessary to point out as a bad custom the practice of punishing men at drill at the will of the leaders with beating or lashing.[27] He believed one should only punish with the "regiment" or "mace," since with them there was less abuse to be feared.

In his regulation of 1726, Title IV, Article XI, p. 222, Frederick William I prescribed:

A new man must not go on guard or do other duties for fourteen days; in this time he himself must at least learn to drill, so that he can do service, and everything must be taught to a new recruit by kind explanations, without scolding and shaming, so that he is not at the very start made to feel depressed and fearful but will develop pleasure and love for his service. And at drill the new recruit must also not suddenly be so strongly attacked, much less be mistreated with blows and the like, especially if he is a simple or non-German fellow.

Frederick the Great once expressly prescribed:[28] "At drill nobody must be struck or pushed or scolded. A man learns to drill with patience and method, not with blows." But he goes on to say: "When a recruit objects or refuses to do what he is commanded, or is malicious...then he must be put under control, but still in a reasonable way." In reality, all reports indicate that there was only too much beating at drill. But nothing is farther from the truth than the idea that drilling was a useless kind of play. The captain who had drilled his men to the point of following his command at every instant with the movement of every rank could hope to lead them forward with his word of command also against enemy fire, and the tactical evolutions that led Frederick's armies to victory were based on the precise movements of the companies.

Even men of but little good will could be incorporated into the tactical bodies that were firmly welded together by discipline and drill. They had to obey the command of the officer and go along with the others. The better the discipline became and the more one could depend on it, the less value was placed on the good will and other moral qualities of the recruit. Thus the various characteristics of the standing army mutually raised one another, so to speak: the mass brought elements that were of themselves unwarlike and unwilling, while discipline made them useful and made possible the incorporation of larger and larger masses of this type. The worse the material was, the more necessary was the firm formation, the discipline that caused the individual almost to disappear in the tactical body. On the other hand, drilling produced discipline and discipline made possible exactness and refinement of the drill, which was pushed further and further and treated the individual as an almost readily exchangeable cog in the machine. Even those who were originally enlisted completely against their will, through downright deception or brutal force, became quite accustomed to this existence and adopted more or less the spirit and the pride of their unit.

In the Prussian army it was not only the private soldier who was subjected to the strictness of discipline but also the officer. After the battle of Mollwitz, when the young king made many changes in the army, especially in the cavalry, he acted with such severity that more than 400 officers are said to have requested discharge.[29]

Frederick himself states, and the events confirm his point, that despite all the unreliable and bad elements, there still existed, even in the private soldiers of his army, a strong military concept of honor. In his *General-Prinzipien* he describes his army as follows:

> Our troops are so excellent and agile that they assume their battle formation in no time at all, and hardly ever can they be subject to a surprise enemy attack, because their movements are very rapid and nimble. If you wanted the service of musketeers, what troops are capable of such strong firing as ours? Our enemies say that they are standing before the wrath of hell when they have to stand up to our infantry. If you wished that our infantry should attack in no other way than with the bayonet, what infantry would march toward the enemy better than they, with a strong and steady pace, without wavering? Where is one to find more coolness in the most extreme danger? If it is necessary to wheel in order to fall on the enemy's flank, this movement is accomplished in a moment and completed without the slightest trouble.
>
> In a country where the military class is the most outstanding,

where the best of the nobility serve in the army, where the officers are men of birth, and where even inhabitants of the country, that is, the sons of the burghers and peasants, are soldiers, in that country one can be sure there has to be a *point d'honneur* in troops formed of such men. And this is really strong among them, for I myself have seen that officers prefer to stand their ground and die rather than yield, to say nothing of the fact that even private soldiers will not tolerate among them any who show some kind of weakness, men who in other armies would certainly not be discharged. I have seen officers and private soldiers seriously wounded who nevertheless do not abandon their posts nor wish to retire even to have their wounds bandaged.

We find it difficult today to give up the idea that the soldier is a young man. In the old Prussian army about half of the army was over thirty years of age and no small number were over fifty, with a few even more than sixty. The average age of the noncommissioned officers can be estimated at about forty-four years.[30]

In conjunction with the increase of the standing army in peacetime came the idea that expenses could be lowered by placing part of the army on leave. Under Frederick William I this practice was systematically developed and was gradually increased more and more. Not only were the natives sent home, but also the foreigners were excused from service as "men off watch." They looked for some kind of civilian occupation, so that Frederick William I in his regulations expresses concern "that they not forget their trade and that they remain soldiers and do not again become peasants or burghers." Only in the training period from April to June was the army really assembled. Those who remained under the colors were occupied principally with guard duty.[31]

Characteristic of the nature of the standing armies, as they developed in the second half of the seventeenth century, was the sharp distinction between the body of troops and the officer corps, as we have already seen in the French army. In Prussia this distinction was even sharper than in France, in that the officers from the bourgeois class were even less numerous here and the intermediate level of *"officiers de fortune"* was lacking. Further research is needed to determine how this sharp cleavage within the armed forces gradually developed.[32] Originally, the word "officer" had a broader meaning and included the noncommissioned officers and even the bandsmen. Then there came the separation based on the fact that the noncommissioned officers belonged to the same social class as the privates. Therefore the officer corps in the modern sense broke off to form a separate class that was composed exclusively or almost exclusively of nobles. A noteworthy indication of this development in the sense of a complaint is to be found in the *Simplizissimus*. It pictures the military hierarchy as a tree with the soldiers sitting on the lowest branches and above them the *"Wamsklopfer"* (backbeaters). The description continues:

> Above them the trunk of the tree has an interval which is a smooth section without twigs, covered with wonderful materials and un-usual soaps of envy, so that no fellow, unless he be of the nobility, can climb up it either by manliness, ability, or knowledge, no matter how good a climber God made him. Above the same place sat those with the companies (*Fähnlein*), some of whom were young and some considerably older. The young ones had been pushed up by their cousins, but the old ones in part had climbed up by themselves, either on a silver ladder, which is called *"Schmieralia"* (bribery) or on a step which fortune had placed for them because of a lack of other men.

To repeat the point, this development was common to all the European countries but in no nation did it reach such sharp distinctiveness as in Prussia. Immediately after his accession to the throne, Frederick William I commanded that "never is anyone other than a nobleman to be appointed as a lance-corporal (aspirant)," and after the end of the War of the Spanish Succession he discharged the officers of the bourgeois class.[33] Frederick the Great, whenever the young officer aspirants were presented to him and he discovered a commoner among them, personally pushed him out of the line with his cane. Only in the case of outstanding talent did he appreciate commoners; for example, he had great regard for General Wunsch, the son of a Württemberg pastor.

In the artillery and the hussars the situation was not quite as strict as in the infantry and cavalry. Indeed, artillerymen were still considered an intermediate step between technicians and soldiers, and the hussars, as light cavalry, were supposed to form a troop of daring adventurers, so to speak, who were basically denied permission to marry. The hussar was supposed to seek his happiness by the saber, said Frederick, and not by the sheath (vagina). To other officers, too, he gave his consent for marriage only if the bride could be shown to have a sufficient fortune and was, like her husband, of the nobility.

The young nobles (*Junker*) were often taken into the army at the age of only twelve or thirteen.

In 1806, of the 131 commoner officers of the infantry of the line, 83 were in garrison battalions and only 48 in the field regiments. As in France, however, there also occurred in Prussia cases of men assisted by bogus titles of nobility. There are accounts of affable chancellery officials who knew how to insert the decisive three letters into the personnel documents.

The original relationship between the officer and the national commander was, as with the lansquenets, a mutual contract—a capitulation, as it was called. Even Derfflinger once refused to follow the Great Elector to war because of a broken capitulation. The lower officers were appointed by the colonels, but gradually this practice shifted over to a system of appointment by the commander-in-chief himself.

The hierarchical pyramid from ensign and lieutenant up to field marshal, or let us say from the private soldier to the field marshal, was almost the same in all the European nations. Spanish, Italian, French, and German influences were all to be found in this system, which was taken over from one people to another.[34] The word "marshal" underwent the most remarkable changes. It actually meant only a stable groom, but it was transferred to quite a number of civilian functions, while in the French military it retained the meaning of blacksmith and cavalry sergeant, but at the same time it rose to be the title of the highest commander. The title "field marshal" appeared in the sixteenth century as a cavalry colonel, as counterpart of the "commander of the infantry regiment" (at Sievershausen Albrecht Alcibiades had three field marshals), but since the cavalry originally was the army, the field marshal also appeared as administrative officer or camp prefect (see p. 60 above). Montecuccoli (2:210) lists this sequence: generalissimo, lieutenant general, field marshal, general of cavalry, general of artillery, lieutenant field marshal.

Prussia was a nation that was fortuitously formed as a result of inheritances, a nation stretching from the Polish (later Russian) border to the Dutch border, the individual territories of which were not held together by any kind of internal interests but exclusively by the dynasty. The dynasty created the bureaucracy and the army, the two elements that formed the unity of this nation. In the absence of any other large factor, it could only be the knightlike vassal loyalty that bound the officer corps to the supreme commander. The formation of the officer corps therefore was a continuation of the traditions of the old warrior nobility, which of course was much more strongly represented in the marches and colonial areas, Brandenburg, Prussia, Pomerania, and Silesia, than in the old German regions west of the Elbe. Time and again in his writings Frederick returned to the point that commoners were not suitable as officers, since their attitude was oriented toward profit rather than honor. But he did not simply attribute to the nobleman the correct qualities for military service; he also required that the nobleman actually serve, and Frederick William I, to the despair of parents, had mounted agents pick up boys by force from the estates of nobles and bring them to the cadet corps for military education. In order to retain their children, a number of parents attempted in vain to show proof that they did not belong to the Prussian nobility. The king, however, stood fast by his order and had them told that he would take good care of their boys.[35] Frederick, too, had the young nobles in Silesia levied in this manner.

The education that the cadet corps provided, however, hardly surpassed that of the *Volksschule*, and there were very few men of really higher education in the Prussian officer corps. The concept of those princes of the Goths that he who learned to fear the schoolmaster's stick would not be a brave warrior (Vol. II, p. 388) had not yet died out among the nobility. Leopold von Dessau is supposed to have had nothing at all taught to his son Maurice, in order to see what pure nature could do. Frederick himself preferred the company of Frenchmen. It is no wonder that, when Berenhorst could write that in 1741 something was ordered by columns, the lords had asked one another: "What in the world are columns? It means I follow the man in front of me and wherever he marches, I do too."[36] Even into the second half of the nineteenth century there were staff officers and generals in our service who as original speakers of Low German (*Plattdeutsch*) could not distinguish between the dative and the accusative. On this point I can add a nice personal contribution. In 1879, when I intended to take my pupil, a young prince, to the cadet corps and was discussing this with the chief of the military training and education system, a general of cavalry, he assured me: "I place a special emphasis on grammar" ("auf *der* Grammatik" instead of "auf *die* Grammatik").

In the period of the lansquenets, both officers and soldiers were governed by the same articles of war. The formation of the officer corps of nobles led to special conditions. Soon after acceding to the throne, Frederick William I established new articles of war for the noncommissioned officers and privates (12 July 1713), and in 1726 he issued a special service regulation for the officers. It stated that the officer was to obey without question in the service, "unless his honor was impugned." Frederick the Great later clarified that in such a way that the insulted officer had to remain quiet as long as his service lasted; "but as soon as his service is completely over, the officer can seek appropriate satisfaction for the insult."

The aristocratic officer corps guaranteed to the king the loyalty and efficiency of the army. As a result of the discipline, the officer corps was to have the men so well under control that they followed in spite of any danger, for the soldier had to fear his officer more than the enemy. When the king was not satisfied with the performance of a few units in the battle of Zorndorf, he recommended to the officers the use of the rod. The Roman centurion, too, had of course controlled his company with the staff from the grapevine, and the Roman legion that was disciplined with the help of this instrument defeated Greeks and barbarians, Hannibal and the Gauls, and conquered the world.

I repeat the point here that the lansquenets in their time had the right to choose a "leader" or "ambassador," who represented them as their "constant mouthpiece, father, and trustee" in dealings with the officers. When he was appointed, he promised the men: "to speak for them at all times as his sons and to bring to the attention of the high command the needs of each individual, and requests, and sickness." He also represented their interests in matters of pay, and the soldiers promised him they would support him as a single man, even if he "spoke one word too many" to them and thereby came into disfavor with the high command. "Whatever happens to the leader on behalf of his soldiers is also to happen to the entire unit." Even before the Thirty Years' War Wallhausen opposed this position and demanded that it be eliminated: "In the unit the 'leader' does more harm than good. He is only its agitator and the advocate of the soldiers in mutinies."[37] How different was the situation now in the eighteenth century, from such arrangements! The more it was realized that the better disciplined troop was superior to the less disciplined one, the more subjective welfare and personal rights were forced to give way before this law of war, and the requirement for subordination to the will of the commander had not only broken the opposition of the old lansquenet but had also created the machinery for a severity that formed the strongest contrast to the concepts of humanity, concepts that were produced precisely by this same century. The power of the Prussian officers over their subordinates was unlimited and was not even tempered by the right to complain. The only consideration which caused even a tough captain to use care and reason was that he might make the man unfit for service by abuse or drive him to desertion, for in that case he would have had to provide the enlistment bonus for the man's replacement. In the Guard this factor did not exist, for here it was not the captains but the king who bore the expenses of recruiting. For this reason, however, Frederick found it appropriate in his regulation for the Guard already cited above (p. 253) to say expressly that punishment must be reasonable and it might not be said in administering discipline: "Let the devil take him, the king has to give us another one." If an officer "struck a fellow unhealthy," he was to pay him and was to be sentenced to six months in Spandau. The captains were to take better care of their men, but "they cost them nothing, and so they do not ask anything about them."

The concept that the captains had to have an interest in the well-being of their men in order to care for them is also found in the writings of the marshal of Saxony. In his *Rêveries* he rejects the idea of having recruits provided by the Estates, because the captains then let them waste away.

The running of the gauntlet, however, ended not infrequently with the man's being beaten to death.

The reader has no doubt noticed that the formation of the Brandenburg-Prussian army was based strongly on the French pattern. Indeed, this was the period in which French culture was the world culture, and German education, especially, was completely under the influence of the French. The Brandenburg army received a special reinforcement from the Huguenots who were driven out of France and found a new home in our country. In 1688, of 1,030 Brandenburg officers, at least 300 were French, that is, far more than one-fourth. In 1689, when Prince Elector Frederick III himself was commanding on the Rhine, four of his twelve generals were Huguenots. Many French expressions were also adopted in the language of the army.

If we compare the French and Prussian armies of the eighteenth century, we see that, despite the similarity of the basic elements, there were considerable differences.

With the French, drill was limited to practice of the necessary movements. With the Prussians there was daily drill, and the service made continuous demands on officers and men. The officers had to live near their men so that they could form up with them at a moment's notice.[38]

In Prussia the officer corps was unified, whereas in France there was a difference between the noble and bourgeois officers and particularly between the nobility of the court and the landed nobles. Here we see the prominent young regimental commanders and generals who attain their positions without having gone through the strict school of the real officer's training. That can be an advantage on the one hand, because it provides the possibilities of promoting those who are really capable to the top leadership positions at a young age. In the final analysis, however, this factor is not the least important when we seek the seat of the illness that ate away at the army of the lily banner. The court generals of the War of the Spanish Succession and the Seven Years' War, who corresponded with Madame de Maintenon and Madame de Pompadour concerning their war plans and were continuously intriguing against one another, were lacking in the strong warrior resoluteness which is the most decisive quality in army leadership in the long run. They were not wanting in personal courage and zeal but in the truly warrior attitude that governs the whole man. If we ask why the French army, despite its great numerical superiority, was able to accomplish nothing in the Seven Years' War against the troops of three small German countries, Hanover, Braunschweig, and Hesse, who were reinforced to only a small extent by some Prussians and English, we come back again and again to this point.[39]

Both the Prussian and the French armies filled their ranks to a very considerable degree with foreigners. In France, however, these foreigners formed their own regiments; in Prussia there were, of course, on a temporary basis, small foreign units—Huguenots, Bosnians, Hungarian hussars, Polish uhlans—but for the most part the foreigners were assigned as recruited soldiers to the same regiments as the levied men of the cantons. In 1768 the army is supposed to have had only about 70,000 natives as compared with 90,000 foreigners.[40] It would appear to be a very great advantage of the French army that it had principally a national character, but this advantage was in no way militarily important in the eighteenth century, since it was precisely the offal of the nation that was to be found in the army. Nevertheless, this difference became of great importance in world history. The national character of the French army was not great enough to give it special strength, but it was important enough to prevent the strictness of the Prussian discipline, which bordered on barbarism. The French army did not have punishment by beating, to say nothing of the unlimited right of officers and noncommissioned officers to administer beatings.[41] In Prussia, with the large number of bad elements that were foisted on the army, this was indispensable.

When the discipline in the French army had become very shaky after the repeated failures and defeats of the Seven Years' War, the minister of war, Saint Germain, attempted to raise it by adopting Prussian methods and introducing punishment by beatings. The French had sufficient self-respect not to put up with that, and the attempt had to be given up, but now there was a complete breakdown of discipline. This process continued inexorably as the nation as a whole turned away from the authority of the monarchy and adopted the concept of the sovereignty of the people. The great French Revolution, which brought on the new epoch of world history, was made possible by the fact that the army abandoned the king and joined the popular movement. The foreigners, the Swiss regiments, remained loyal to the king, while the French regiments deserted him. Even after the outbreak of general war, all attempts to bring a halt to the movement and restore order, first under Lafayette and then under Dumouriez, failed precisely because of the opposition of the army, in which national pride outweighed loyalty to the national commander-in-chief, who had taken a position opposed to the national concept. The fact that Prussia was not a national state and had no national army prevented the appearance of such an inner conflict there. The faults of the Prussian army lay in a completely different area, as was to be shown in a frightful way in 1806.

Lastly, as a final difference between the Prussian and French armies, let us not fail to realize how much larger the military levy of Prussia was in comparison with the population and its economic strength.

France seems to have reached the high point of its armed strength under the monarchy in the last year of the Seven Years' War, 1761 [sic], when it had 140,000 men under the colors in Germany and 150,000 at home and in the colonies, for a total of 290,000.[42] That would be about 1 and 1/5 percent of her population. At the outbreak of the great Revolution the army was only 173,000 men strong (seventy-nine French infantry regiments and twenty-three foreign regiments—see p. 229 above), which was about 0.7 percent of the population.

The Prussian army numbered almost 100,000 men in December 1740, which was 4.4 percent of the 2.24 million inhabitants.[43] At the death of Frederick the army was 200,000 strong, or 3 and 1/3 percent of the population, of which number, however, not even half (82,700 men) were under the colors for ten months of the year, but that still amounted to twice the ratio in France.[44]

NOTES FOR CHAPTER II

1. The Netherlander Le Hon (Hondius) wrote concerning Wallhausen (Jähns, 2:1039):

Wallhausen has made a large book of the drills of a regiment which do not occur among us and were also not used by the Prince of Orange...which are nothing more than fantasies that one puts on paper and which cannot be applied by any officer or soldier, indeed not by the author himself, who, like Icarus, wants to fly so high that he must fall down from above, who thinks that by putting figures on paper they must be heard by many people.

The Frenchman Bardin called Wallhausen's *Kriegskunst zu Fuss* "an illegible confused mixture, from which there is nothing to be learned" (Jähns, 2:1042).

2. In his defense let it be noted that even a soldier like Montecuccoli wrote something similar: "If one wishes to form a unit of lancers, not for the attack but for defense, one can give it a square formation, facing toward all four sides." Round or spherical formations were also recommended. *Writings (Schriften)*, 1:352.

3. L. Plathner, "Count John of Nassau and the First Military School" ("Graf Johann von Nassau und die erste Kriegsschule"), Berlin dissertation, 1913.

4. Around 1559 Count Reinhart Solms wrote a military encyclopedia, which Jähns, 1:510, calls "Military Government" ("*Kriegsregierung*"), in which he emphatically rejects the idea of the militia, since the men would run away when the situation became serious. Lazarus Schwendi was in favor of the militia (Jähns, p. 539). General von Klitzing drew up a report for Duke Georg of Braunschweig-Lüneburg in which he stated that, according to his experience, militiamen could not stand up to recruited troops. He recommended mixing recruited soldiers and those who were levied. Von dem Decken, *Duke George of Braunschweig-Lüneburg (Herzog Georg von Braunschweig-Lüneburg)*, 2:189.

5. The militia was only used with success once in a secondary role; when the duke moved into Bohemia in 1620, he used the militia to protect his country against the Union. Krebs, *Battle on the White Mountain* (*Schlacht am weissen Berge*), p. 32.

6. When the burgomaster of Augsburg in 1544 forced all the citizens to procure weapons and participate in daily drills, the entire city rose up against this procedure and said it was nonsense, an unnecessary waste of time and money, since, in view of the importance of Augsburg's industries, this purpose could better and more cheaply be accomplished with paid mercenaries. Schmoller, *Tübinger Zeitschrift*, 16:486.

7. Jany, *The Beginnings of the Old Army* (*Die Anfänge der alten Armee*), p. 2.

8. Jany, 1:10. Krollmann, *The Defense Work in the Kingdom of Prussia* (*Das Defensionswerk im Königreich Preussen*), 1909.

9. Meynert, *History of the Military and of Army Organizations in Europe* (*Geschichte des Kriegswesens und der Heerverfassungen in Europa*), 2:99.

10. In June 1625 the total cost of deliveries in Hesse taken by the billeted troops of the League since 1623 only in the cities and the villages subject to the princes (and not the villages of the nobility), without counting robberies and destruction, was estimated as 3,318,000 imperial talers. This was much more than ten times the amount approved by the Estates three years earlier for the landgrave, but with which the country had not been able to be defended. M. Ritter, *German History* (*Deutsche Geschichte*), 3:260. Gindely estimates the total contributions raised by Wallenstein in his first period of command as between 200 and 210 million talers. The city of Halle alone showed that from December 1625 to September 1627 it had paid 430,274 guilders.

11. Droysen, *Prussian Politics* (*Preussische Politik*), 3:1, 49.

12. von Bonin, "The War Council of the Electorate of Brandenburg, 1630–41" ("Der kurbrandenburgische Kriegsrat, 1630–1641"), *Brandenburgisch-Preussische Forschungen*, 1913, p. 51 ff.

13. Researchers are not yet completely in agreement on the content and the nature of the reduction of 1641 and of the strength until 1656. J. G. Droysen's concept that it was principally a question in 1641 of a relief from the double obligation to the emperor and the prince elector and that the young ruler simultaneously broke the opposition of the colonels and the Estates in order to create the unified army thenceforth obligated only to the prince has now been generally dropped. Meinardus, "Minutes and Accounts of the Brandenburg Privy Council" ("Protokolle und Relationen des Brandenburgischen Geheimen Rats"), introduction to the first and second volumes. Article, "Schwarzenberg" in the *Allgemeine Deutsche Biographie*. Article in the *Preussische Jahrbücher*, Vol. 86, by Schrötter, "The Brandenburg-Prussian Army Organization Under

the Great Elector" ("Die brandenburgisch-preussische Heeresverfassung unter dem Grossen Kurfürsten"), 1892. Brake, "The Reduction of the Brandenburg-Prussian Army in the Summer of 1641" ("Die Reduktion des brandenburgisch-preussischen Heeres im Sommer 1641"), Bonn dissertation, 1898. In this connection see also Meinardus, *Historische Zeitschrift*, 81:556, 82:370. Jany, "Die Anfänge der alten Armee." *Urkundliche Beiträge zur Geschichte des preussischen Heeres (Documentary Contributions to the History of the Prussian Army)*, Vol. 1, 1901.

14. Ferdinand Hirsch, "The Army of the Great Elector" ("Die Armee des Grossen Kurfürsten"), *Historische Zeitschrift*, 53(1885):231.

15. This important observation is made by B. von Bonin in the *Archives for Military Law (Archiv für Militärrecht)*, 1911, p. 262.

16. See the article "The Prussian District President" ("Der preussische Landrat") in my *Historical and Political Essays (Historische und politische Aufsätze)*, where the difference between the Prussian, English, and French administrative systems is discussed.

17. Ritter, "Wallenstein's System of Contributions" ("Das Kontributionssystem Wallensteins"), *Historische Zeitschrift*, 90:193. In Wallenstein's army administration, which attempted to assure that, despite all their contributions, the burghers and peasants could tolerate them quite well, Ranke has already recognized the "trait of the national prince" in the great condottiere.

18. von Schrötter, "The Bringing of the Prussian Army to Strength Under the First King" ("Die Ergänzung des preussischen Heeres unter dem ersten Könige"), *Brandenburgisch-preussische Forschungen*, 1910, p. 413.

19. Schrötter, *Brandenburgisch-preussische Forschungen*, 23:463.

20. As an analogy to the way the old "Land Defense" was carried over into the standing army, let us note a negotiation between the emperor and the Lower Austrian Estates in 1639. The Estates wanted to establish the principle that the land defense could only be used within the territorial borders. The emperor demanded that every twentieth man be provided and proposed for consideration "whether these men could better be used by assigning them to a special corps or whether they should be incorporated as fillers in the old regiments." According to Meynert, *Geschichte des Kriegswesens*, 3:10.

21. The standard study is Max Lehmann's "Recruitment, Service Obligation, and System of Leaves in the Army of Frederick William I" ("Werbung, Wehrpflicht und Beurlaubung im Heere Friedrich Wilhelms I."), *Historische Zeitschrift*, Vol. 67, 1891. A very clear insight of the structure of the Prussian army in the eighteenth century, based word for word on the sources, is given in the work of Erwin Dette, *Frederick the Great and His Army (Friedrich der Grosse und sein Heer)*, Göttingen,

Vanderhoeck und Ruprecht, 1915. I have taken several characteristic observations verbatim from this excellent work.

22. It is all the more remarkable when, according to Schrötter, p. 466, at the death of Frederick I there already existed a levy system along controlled lines, with exemption of those with special possessions, that was quite similar to the situation created by the "canton regulation." It appears that the purely arbitrary aspect of the levying by the officers was completely consonant with the forceful character of Frederick William I.

23. Courbière, *History of the Brandenburg-Prussian Military Organization* (*Geschichte der Brandenburgisch-Preussischen Heeresverfassung*), p. 119. When reference is made on p. 120 to men of 3 inches and under 3 inches, this seems to me to stem from a writing error. As the smallest height, which was waived only under conditions of a complete scarcity of manpower, as in the last year of the Seven Years' War, we can regard 5 feet, 5 inches (1.70 meters). See Grünhagen, *Silesia under Frederick the Great* (*Schlesien unter Friedrich dem Grossen*), 1:405. Reimann, *History of the Prussian Nation* (*Geschichte des preussischen Staates*), 1:154, claims that even in garrison regiments men could not be less than 5 feet, 3 inches tall. According to Koser, *Friedrich der Grosse*, 1:538, Frederick required in the older regiments men of 5 feet, 8 inches in the front rank and 5 feet, 6 inches in the second rank. For the newer regiments, these requirements were 5 feet, 7 inches and 5 feet, 5 inches, respectively.

24. A report of the government of the electoral march of 1811 states: "In earlier times, as filler replacements, only such a moderate number of natives was required that only those subjects who were completely dispensable were enlisted, and that was determined by the civil authorities."

25. *Studies in Brandenburg-Prussian History* (*Forschungen zur Brandenburgisch-Preussischen Geschichte*), 7:308.

26. Ranke, *Werke*, 27:230.

27. Jähns, 2:914.

28. Excerpted from *Tactical Training* (*Taktische Schulung*), p. 687.

29. von Osten-Sacken, *Prussia's Army from Its Beginnings to the Present* (*Preussens Heer von seinen Anfängen bis zur Gegenwart*), 1911, 1:173.

30. These numbers are estimated for the regiment that was named "Thüna" in 1784 and "Winnig" in 1806. Ollech, "Life of Reiher" ("Leben Reihers"), *Militär-Wochenblatt*, 1859, p. 11. Kunhardt von Schmidt, *Militär-Wochenblatt*, 1909, col. 3771. The latter correctly assumes that, in view of the uniformity throughout the army, these lists give a picture not only of the individual troop unit but of the entire infantry of the period. Similar age relationships already existed in 1704. Schrötter, p. 453.

31. M. Lehmann, p. 278.

32. Basta (Book I, Chap. 6—consequently, long before the Thirty

Years' War) was already complaining about the start of the practice of filling the captains' positions only with aristocrats, even when they were completely inexperienced, so that no private soldier any longer had the hope of moving up, except in very exceptional cases. According to Löwe, *Organization of Wallenstein's Army (Organisation des Wallensteinschen Heeres)*, p. 86, most of the colonels and generals in the Thirty Years' War were nobles, but among the lower officers there were still quite a number of former privates. G. Droysen, "Contributions to the History of the Military System During the Period of the Thirty Years' War" ("Beiträge zur Geschichte des Militärwesens während der Epoche des 30jährigen Krieges"), *Zeitschrift für Kulturgeschichte*, Vol. 4, 1875, emphasizes strongly, in opposition to Gansauge, that there was not yet any officer corps at that time.

33. Schrötter, *Brandenburgisch-Preussische Forschungen*, Vol. 27.

34. Treated very clearly by Richard M. Meyer, "The Military Titles" ("Die militärischen Titel") in the *Zeitschrift für deutsche Wortforschung*, Vol. 12, Book 3 (1910), p. 145.

The 1726 regulation of Frederick William I shows a great similarity to a Spanish regulation. Jähns, 2:1577, believes that it goes back directly to the Spanish. Erben, in the *Mitteilungen des kaiserlichen und königlichen Heeresmuseums*, 1 (1902):3, seems to refute that. I hesitate to make any definitive judgment.

35. Schmoller in the *Historische Zeitschrift*, 30:61.

36. *Observations on the Art of War (Betrachtungen über die Kriegskunst)*, section 13.

37. G. Droysen, "Beiträge," *Zeitschrift für deutsche Kulturgeschichte*, new series, 4(1875):592.

38. "Report of the Ambassador Valory of 1748." Ed. Koser, *Brandenburgisch-Preussische Forschungen*, 7(1894):299. Valory stresses the marching in step of the Prussians so strongly that we may doubt whether the French had it.

39. Daniels, "Ferdinand von Braunschweig," *Preussische Jahrbücher*, Vols. 77, 78, 79, 80, 82.

40. According to Frederick's so-called *Military Testament*, there are supposed to have been 110,000 natives and 80,000 foreigners in 1780, but the numbers are not entirely certain, since natives who were not from the regimental canton were also counted as foreigners.

41. The *Militia Gallica* by Wallhausen (*French Military Service*; translation of a book by Montgommery), p. 44, precisely states how broad was the power of punishment of each position. The colonel was allowed to strike and kill with the sword, even officers. The sergeant-major had similar authority, but he could also strike with the staff, that is, with his measuring stick. Nobody was to feel insulted by this. The captain was

allowed to strike with the flat of his sword. The lieutenants and sergeants could do likewise on the march or in the trenches, but in garrison only against their direct subordinates. The ensign was allowed to do this only when substituting for the lieutenant or captain. The sergeant (in contradiction to the foregoing!) could strike only on the march, in battle, on guard duty, and in the trenches, with the shaft of the halberd, and not with the sword, if a soldier left his post, but not in garrison or for other reasons.

42. Daniels, *Preussische Jahrbücher*, 82:270.

43. According to the estimates of the *General Staff Work*. That was, therefore, at the moment Frederick started the war. Ranke, 3:148 cites a memorandum, according to which Frederick William I, on his death, had left behind 83,484 men, including 72,000 men in the field army; other statements show up to 89,000 men. According to Schrötter, the Prussian army on 2 January 1705, when it had been strongly reinforced with the assistance of the subsidies of the sea powers, already amounted to 47,031, and with the militia 67,000 men, that is, almost 4 percent of the population.

44. *Preussische Jahrbücher*, 142:300.

Chapter III

Drills. Changes in Tactics in the Eighteenth Century

The Thirty Years' War was fought by an infantry consisting of a mixture of units of pikemen and musketeers. The firing of the musket was too slow and too uncertain to protect a musketeer unit from a cavalry attack in the open field. This protection was to be assumed by the pikemen. But even Mendoza, who thought the pike had an advantage over all other weapons, himself stated on one occasion (Chap. I, p. 98) that the pikes only seldom clashed with one another in open battles, and the firearm was the principal weapon. That was, then, at the end of the sixteenth century, and in 1630, during the Thirty Years' War, the military author Neumair von Ramsla wrote: "The long spears are more of a weakening of warfare than its nerve. The firearms arm the long spears."

It was reported as something extraordinary when foot troops fought with pikes and swords;[1] for example, at Leipzig in 1642 it was said that "the imperial foot troops ran directly onto the pikes of the Swedes." Grimmelshausen, in his *Springinsfeld* (1670), jokes: "Whoever strikes down a pikeman whom he could spare is murdering an innocent man. A pikeman harms no one who does not himself run into the spear." Nevertheless, the pikemen did hold their own. As late as 1653 the Great Elector ordered that a third of his infantry in the garrisons be equipped with pikes (that is, converted to field troops) and diligently drilled with them.[2]

In the battle of Enzheim (1674) the pikes still played a role, as Turenne had a large square of pikemen formed against a large-scale mounted attack by the Germans, with the musketeers in the middle. The horsemen did not risk moving up to it.[3]

Toward the turn of the century, however, the pikes gradually disappeared from the European armies. The boar spears or chevaux-de-frise, which were supposed to protect the infantry against cavalry in the transitional period, did not attain any practical significance.[4]

The combination of the matchlock and the pike side by side was replaced by the uniform weapon of the bayonet musket with the flintlock.

This also gave the standing army a completely different appearance from that of the preceding mercenary bands. Quite early the idea arose of inserting "an awl" into the barrel of the musket in order to convert it into a spear.[5] The decisive invention, however, came after the middle of the seventeenth century in the form of a tubular socket which was attached around the musket barrel, so that this weapon could be used simultaneously as a firearm and a close-combat weapon. But this bayonet was still very bothersome in the loading process, and the new technique did not become completely useful until the invention of the cross arm, which made possible rapid and easy loading with the bayonet fixed.

About this time the matchlock was replaced by the flint,[6] whose advantages, especially in rainy weather, were obvious. But the disadvantage of the not entirely certain spark seemed so great that in 1665 Le Tellier strictly forbade the new weapon in the French articles of war. Flintlocks that were found at inspection were immediately to be broken by the commission and to be replaced at the expense of the captains in whose units they were found. Consequently, there was built a weapon with both a matchlock and a flintlock, but soon the simple musket with the flintlock won out. A whole series of small improvements, in the powder pan, the touchhole, the pan cover, the iron ramrod instead of the wooden one, in the rings for the insertion of the ramrod,[7] in the musket stock, and especially also the paper cartridges—these improvements constantly made the weapon more effective and at the beginning of the eighteenth century already gave it a form which was then retained with but little change for more than a century. The Wars of Liberation were fought with almost the same musket as the Seven Years' War.

The continuing use and improvement of the firearm gradually caused the infantry to discard its protective armor and iron helmet as early as the latter part of the Thirty Years' War, and this was reflected in improved marching ability.

As a result of the better training of the soldiers in the standing army, the constantly improved firearm could also be used more and more effectively. In the formation with six ranks the muskets could all be used only in conjunction with the caracole, and this easily fell into confusion. Now the six-rank formation was reduced to four ranks, and finally with the Prussians to three, so that, by having the first rank kneel, all available firearms could be fired simultaneously.[8] Frederick the Great even sought to close up the formation so that for four men the width was no longer four paces but only three.[9] By constant practice the rapidity of fire in this formation was increased to the maximum degree. In view of the great inaccuracy of the individual shot, the idea of aiming was abandoned from the start, to include even any training in aiming, and the effect was sought in the most rapid possible mass fire, the salvo fired on command. If Frederick still prescribed that the firing should not be too hasty, "because a fellow must first see where he is firing," aiming was later even directly forbidden. On the other hand, the greatest importance was placed on having the salvo fired simultaneously, sounding like a single shot. It was assumed that the simultaneous impact of so many shots would strengthen the demoralizing effect.

At Fontenoy (1745) the French and the English-Hanoverian guards approached within fifty paces of one another without firing. The officers on both sides courteously offered each other the first shot. The English fired the first salvo, which was so murderous that the French guard was almost completely wiped out and the remainder took flight.

Scharnhorst taught in his *Taktik* (section 178) that individual firing was to be most carefully avoided. Only salvos were to be fired. For ten men who fell at the same time would cause a battalion to retreat sooner than the loss of fifty who fell gradually and at different places. Furthermore, the men would fire away their cartridges, and their many shots would make their muskets unusable. The flints would become blunt and the cartridges could only be placed by force into the clogged barrel. Finally, the officers would lose the control of their men.

The salvos were preferably fired by the whole battalion or by platoon. The battalion drawn up in three ranks was divided into eight platoons. The platoons fired in turn very quickly in the sequence 1,3,5,7,2,4,6,8, so that the fire had a continuous rolling effect. In this way a cavalry attack found no lull in the firing when it could have broken in. But this ideal was attainable only on the drill field. According to Lloyd,[10] Frederick himself supposedly said that firing by platoon would be the best if it could really be accomplished. Berenhorst recounts that only the first salvo might perhaps be fired as prescribed, or two or three platoons might have fired in order.[11] He writes:

There then followed a general firing away and the general rolling fire, where each man who has loaded presses the trigger, ranks and files become mixed, the men of the front rank cannot succeed in dropping to their knees, even if they wanted to, and the officers from the lowest up to the generals can no longer do anything with the mass but must wait to see whether it will finally move forward or to the rear.

This description bears the stamp of the exaggerated caricature typical of Berenhorst's writings in general; nevertheless, it is correct to the extent that in battle the precision of the drill field was more or less lost.[12]

The attack was supposed to proceed in such a way that the whole line of infantry was to move forward under continuous fire by platoons and finally close with the enemy with the bayonet. But things almost never reached the point of actual bayonet combat; at the moment when the attacking side actually approached, the defender already gave up his opposition. Frederick once wrote that it should be impressed upon the soldiers that it was to their own advantage to close with the enemy, and the king would guarantee them that the enemy would not fight again.[13] We recognize how completely these tactics correspond to the composition of the army: the common soldier has nothing to do but obey. He is led forward in step with an officer on the right, an officer on the left, and another behind. The salvos are fired on command, and finally the formation breaks into the enemy position, where an actual fight is no longer expected. With such tactics, not so much depended on the good will of the soldier, provided he was only under the control of the officer, and one could risk enlisting even very strange elements.

Legendary concepts have been formed concerning the speed with which the salvos could be fired. For example, General von Bernhardi, *On Present-day Warfare* (*Vom heutigen Kriege*), 1:22, 1912, writes that the Prussian infantry in the eighteenth century was supposed to have fired up to ten shots a minute. But that is such an obvious impossibility that the suspicion arises that this did not mean shots by the individual soldiers but the salvos of the platoons; that is, not the same unit fired ten shots per minute, but the battalion accomplished ten platoon salvos in a minute. But the report actually means that the individual man could fire, if not ten times, at least eight times in a minute. In reality, at the time of the Seven Years' War, two to three times, and later barely four times was the absolute fastest rate that could be reached with live cartridges in salvos by command. (See excursus.)

The range of the infantry musket was short; we might say up to 300 paces. Targets could hardly be hit at 400 paces.[14]

The most difficult problem was firing while moving, something that has remained a problem even in our time, with the extended line of skirmishers. The ideal was to have platoons, as they constantly moved forward, halt and fire in alternation. But that was impossible in battle, since experience taught that once the unit had halted to fire, it was difficult to bring it back into motion, and between the second and third Silesian Wars the concept was formed that it was best to have the infantry assault without shooting and to use firing only for pursuit and defense. In that case the preparatory fire was accomplished solely by the light battalion cannon, which were drawn by their crews and accompanied the infantry. Since the effective fire had a range of only 300 paces and the regular fire was to be opened only at 200 paces—indeed, with the Austrians, only 100 paces[15]—there arose the question as to whether, when the attackers were so close, it was not best to storm forward at once instead of holding up for firing, a pause that added to the effectiveness of the enemy fire. The marshal of Saxony, in his *Rêveries*, which inspired Frederick to compose his poem on the art of war, had proposed attacking without firing. Prince Maurice of Dessau expressed the wish (1748) that he might once in his life receive from His Royal Majesty the order "to move on the enemy without loading." In fact, even at the beginning of the Seven Years' War Frederick had ordered the attack without firing, and in the research of the Military History Section and even more strongly in the *Militär-Wochenblatt*, 40(1900):1004, the opinion is expressed that with this procedure the combat methods of the German infantry underwent the most radical change that they ever experienced, and that was to its disadvantage. This was said to be a fateful error on the part of the king, a point forcefully proven on the terrible days at Prague and Kollin. But another reviewer in the same source (94:2131) correctly opposed this point by stating that the king had, after all, only forbidden firing in the sense of demanding a great deal in order to get a certain amount.[16] It was claimed that he wanted to limit the firing as much as possible but assumed that the unit, if it could not advance otherwise, would still fire. At Leuthen the attack was again made with firing, and in December 1758 the king even directly rejected the idea of attacking without firing. Consequently, the prohibition of firing was not so much an earth-shaking change in tactics as it was an experiment in a task for which there was no clear rational solution.

We may add that, according to a good source,[17] despite the abundant fire of the Prussians, the losses they caused the enemy were no greater than those that they themselves suffered from the enemy fire. The principal gain, therefore, that the Prussian army derived from its firing exercises was an indirect one, comparable to the exact drills and the goose step: that is, the strengthening of discipline, the training in maintaining order, and the firmness of the tactical body.

Since the square formation of the infantry had been shifted to a shallow formation, experience had shown that a single line could be broken up or penetrated only too easily, and the infantry had therefore been formed in two lines, one behind the other, two echelons. We are familiar with the echelon formation as a product of the Second Punic War. But the origin and the development of echelon tactics in antiquity and in the modern era were different. The reason for this formation and its purpose were the same, however, despite the difference in weapons. While the second echelon as such was not capable of using its weapons, it was ready to fill breaches in the first echelon,[18] give support to weak spots, conduct flanking movements, and, in case of necessity, also to repulse attacks from the rear. The thinner the first echelon had become, with its formation in three ranks, the more it needed such support from a second echelon, which, under certain circumstances, was even followed by a third and a fourth. Unlike the first echelon, the second did not have to form a continuous line but could leave intervals between the battalions and could therefore have fewer units. The distance between the echelons varied from 150 to 500 paces.[19]

In order to support to some extent the flanks, which were very vulnerable in such a formation, a battalion was stationed between the two echelons facing toward the flank, so that the overall formation could be compared to a long rectangle.

The more shallow the formation became, the longer was the front. That situation is very advantageous for the effectiveness of the weapons, especially if the attacker succeeds in outflanking the enemy, but it is very difficult to carry out. It is not easy even to have a rather large mass form on a long front and align the men on a level drill field, but moving them forward in line and unbroken, and over uneven terrain at that, can be accomplished only by completely trained leaders and well-drilled troops. Lloyd says that in order for a cohesive battle formation to move forward a little more than 1 kilometer, it often required several hours, and Boyen (1:169), in his memoirs, recounts that his experiences taught him that a battalion deployed in line on a day of battle could be moved in orderly fashion only very seldom or hardly at all. The commander's voice could not be heard far enough in the confusion. In his *History of the Art of War* (*Geschichte der Kriegskunst*), which appeared in 1797, Hoyer wrote:

> Because it was not easy to dress such a long line properly and was almost impossible to have it deploy from a column, the most clever tacticians experimented with both formations. They took pains to show how one could move an army in different columns both forward and to the rear and then form the army for the assault in one or two lines. These maneuvers required of the troops a flexibility to which they were formerly unaccustomed.

Untiring zeal was applied in the Prussian army not only to work on the traditional training but also to strive for greater and greater perfection, speed, and flexibility and to seek new and refined formations in the employment of the troop units. The king himself, the generals with the princes of Braunschweig and Anhalt in the Prussian service, and the entire officer corps were filled with the same zeal. The most remarkable product of this creative activity was the oblique battle formation.[20]

As the original deep formation of the infantry had been transformed to a constantly more shallow formation in order to strengthen its fire power, the infantry had assumed a formation in which it was not only very difficult to move in orderly fashion but also the concepts of flank and wing attained constantly greater importance. In a square formation the front and flanks are equally strong. In a linear formation the flank becomes weaker the more shallow it is, and the distinctiveness of the wing becomes more important the longer it is. The idea arises of seeking a decision in battle not by a direct frontal attack but by an attack on a wing or on the flank.

For this reason we already find in the Thirty Years' War that an army that is forming up for a defensive battle seeks to protect its flanks with some kind of terrain obstacle (on the White Mountain in 1620). We also find attempts made to attack the enemy in his flank (Wittstock, 1636).[21]

In the War of the Spanish Succession we find the wing battle. One did not attack the entire front simultaneously but refused one of his wings by providing it with smaller forces in order with the other, stronger wing to overwhelm the opposite enemy portion of the line, enveloping it where possible. Höchstädt seems to have been planned in keeping with this method, but in any case it was not executed in this way. Ramillies and Turin were wing battles, but that was determined more by special terrain conditions than by this method itself. Malplaquet, however, was completely planned as a wing battle, although, of course, as a result of several errors, it was not fought through as such.

The theory, too, began to take into account the new problem. Formerly, it had proceeded from a study of antiquity and had continuously nourished itself on that period. Now the oblique battle formation of Epaminondas was remembered, as well as the statement by Vegetius:

> When the two armies clash, one withdraws his left wing from the enemy right wing outside the range of all missile weapons. Our right wing, which must consist of our best troops, both infantry and cavalry, then presses forward against the left wing of the enemy, closes with him in hand-to-hand combat, and breaks through or envelops him in order to be able to attack him in the rear. Or one can carry out with the left wing what we have said about the right.

The first more modern theoretician, if we leave aside a doctrinaire composition of Duke Albrecht of Prussia,[22] seems to have been Montecuccoli. In his work *On the Art of War* (*Von der Kriegskunst*), 1653 (appeared in German in 1736: *Werke*, 2:68), he gives the rule: "Assign the best troops to the wings and begin the battle from that side which is felt to be stronger, and the weaker side is to hold the enemy in place." Similar ideas are expressed in other writings (2:352).

Obviously basing his idea on this statement, Kheverhüller, in his *Short Concept of all Military Operations* (*Kurtzer Begriff aller militärischer Operationen*), published in 1738, writes: "Place the best men on the wing, start to make contact on the same side where one believes he is strongest, and attack the enemy later where one is weak, engaging him with skirmishing or the advantage of the terrain."

The Frenchman Folard, from whose extensive work on Polybius Frederick the Great had an extract drawn up on which he himself collaborated, published before his principal work a book entitled *New Discoveries on Warfare* (*Nouvelles découvertes sur la guerre*), in which he treats very thoroughly the battles of Leuctra and Mantinea (Part II, Chap. 7), points out the advantages of the oblique battle formation, and praises the genius of Epaminondas.

Frederick learned even more from another Frenchman, Feuquières, than from Folard and took over literally no small part of his writings into his own instructions. But as best I can see, Feuquières does not mention the oblique battle formation. When Frederick mounted the throne, therefore, the idea of the oblique battle formation already existed and was also already in practical use. But the theory on this was neither fully developed nor widespread, and its practice, despite a few attempts, had still not accomplished anything important. Nevertheless, we must assume that in the circles of thoughtful military men it must have been customary to speak of the oblique battle formation. It was a concept that was already circulating. Precisely at that time, old Marshal Puységur (died 1743) was making his last attempt to finish his great work, *Art de la Guerre*, which he had already started almost a half-century earlier and which was then published by his son in 1748. In this work the oblique battle formation ("ordre oblique") is clearly and exhaustively discussed (Edition of 1748, 1:161 ff; 2:45 ff. Index, 2:234). There can be no doubt that Frederick, who once wrote that he had read just about everything that had ever been written on military history, already had in mind the thought of the oblique battle order when he went into his first war. At Mollwitz we find that the king made the right wing of his army stronger than the left, especially with heavy artillery, and, according to his own expression, "refused" the left wing.[23] Nevertheless, it was not a true wing battle, since in the end it was not the advanced right wing but a forward movement of the left, which had suffered only very small losses, that brought about the decision. Consequently, it has been customary to consider the oblique attack of the Prussians at Mollwitz as being not at all an example of the oblique battle formation but rather as a simple chance occurrence. I, too, was long inclined toward this interpretation, but on the basis of the studies by Herrmann and Keibel, I have reached the conclusion that the other concept is the correct one. In any case, from Mollwitz on, the idea of the oblique battle formation was the completely dominant one in the battle formations as well as in those of Frederick's battles that were fought through to a decision.

The application of this idea was quite peculiar to the personal and creative aspects of the king's battle tactics. The practical and theoretical beginnings of this concept that already existed had still not borne any real fruit. The idea itself was easy and was very old, but its application was difficult.

It is, of course, simple to make one wing stronger than the other. But if the enemy realizes that, he either does the same thing or charges forward against the weaker wing of the attacker. The oblique battle formation does not become fully effective until it succeeds in enveloping the enemy wing with the attacking wing. The enemy, however, does not willingly offer his flank but forms up with as much of a right angle as possible to the enemy direction of approach. The attacker therefore has the task of making a large wheeling movement or change of direction in view of the enemy. That was all the more difficult in that the development of the basic tactics required that the entire battle front had to form a line as continuous as possible.[24] Puységur once said that the battalions had previously been formed with intervals as on a chess board, but many large battles had been lost as a result of this, since each battalion could be outflanked through the intervals.[25]

He went on to say that the intervals had therefore been made smaller, but that particular formation in which the battalions and squadrons were drawn up without any intervals at all was undoubtedly the strongest one. And this is what was done everywhere in Frederick's period. It was therefore a question of advancing this continuous front, with cavalry and artillery, obliquely, enveloping the enemy where possible.[26]

The oblique formation of itself does not, of course, provide any advantage. The advantage arises only from the fact that the attacking wing is also the stronger one, and the refused wing, by being held back, ties down a larger enemy force. The oblique approach march with the superior force must therefore take place not only along its whole line but also so fast that the enemy cannot take any countermeasures and the attack is effective through its surprise effect. The highest degree of the oblique battle formation is reached when it succeeds in outflanking and enveloping the enemy front.

In the documents of the Great General Staff, the concept of the oblique battle formation is limited to the infantry and its continuous unbroken front. The king supposedly did not hit upon this idea until the period between the second and third Silesian Wars. According to this theory, the oblique battle formation was a completely special subform of the wing battle and was to be sharply distinguished from it. In principle, such a specific determination of the terminology cannot be rejected. In this degree of sharpness, however, it is not indicated and not applicable, because practically and historically the limits are fluid and neither the cavalry nor the artillery may be excluded.[27] I would therefore like to define the matter in this way: the oblique battle formation is that particular form of the wing battle in which the entire battle line forms a front with the smallest possible intervals or even one that is completely continuous. An essential element of the wing battle is that one wing is advanced while the other is held back and that the attacking wing is reinforced and where possible strikes the enemy front on the flank or even in the rear. These characteristics, therefore, also apply to the subform of the flank battle, the oblique battle formation. The oblique battle formation becomes a subform of the wing battle in conformance with the basic tactics of the period, from which, with inherent logic, it grows and is developed. The reinforcing of the attacking wing can consist of strengthening the infantry by sending out an advance echelon, an "attack," as it was called, in front of the first echelon or having a reserve follow, or also by reinforcing the cavalry or artillery.

If we have already heard that the simple deployment of an army in line was in no way to be taken for granted but rather a tactical work of art, this was all the more the case in the deployment into an oblique formation. At first Frederick simply ordered the one wing to march faster than the other. But that, of course, did not work out. Breaks in the front necessarily developed, and when the battalion commanders sought to fill the intervals, the formation broke up in disorder. During the decade from 1746 to 1756 Frederick worked with tireless energy both theoretically and practically to find the most suitable form for the execution of his idea.[28] One by one he conceived and tested no fewer than eight different methods to achieve his oblique deployment. Finally, the attack in echelons seemed to him to be the best type.

Later, until 1806, this echelon attack, in which the battalions did not form up simultaneously but aligned themselves beside one another like steps, was developed and practiced with the greatest zeal, but its importance was greatly overestimated. The result, in the final analysis, was only that the successive battalions within a very short time, hardly minutes between the one battalion and the next, stood in the same line with the wing battalion that started the attack. The only battle in which the oblique battle formation with echelons was carried out more or less in accordance with the concept was Leuthen. Even there it was not the echelon attack that was decisive but the fact that the king succeeded in directing the Prussian army in its approach march with an unsuspected change of direction, unnoticed by the enemy, against the left wing of the Austrians. He changed the approach march by wings into one by echelons; that is, the four columns in which the Prussians were moving up, each consisting of a part of the first echelon and the corresponding part of the second, with a fifth column as the advance echelon, turned by platoons at an angle and marched a good 2 miles along the enemy front until they had arrived opposite the Austrians' most extreme left wing. There the platoons, which had maintained a sufficient distance from one another, wheeled into line.[29] In this way, three echelons, including the advance echelon, were formed, and the hussars took position behind them as a fourth echelon. In this formation they attacked the Austrian wing without outflanking or enveloping it, but they were numerically stronger as a result of the depth of the four echelons. The fact that the battalions now attacked not completely simultaneously but in echelons was not of special significance and was even mentioned only rather incidentally by the king in his own account.[30] The oblique formation that the Prussian front formed in the face of the Austrian front at the moment of the attack was somewhat increased, so to speak, by the sequential attacking of the battalions. The overwhelming aspect, however, was the short, compressed formation that turned exclusively against the left wing of the Austrians while leaving the right wing of the 4-mile-wide Austrian front completely out of contact. Thus the left wing of the Austrians was defeated before it could be reinforced by the right wing. Although the Prussians numbered only 40,000 against more than 60,000, they still had the numerical superiority in each individual element of the battle.

The important factor, therefore, was not the echelon attack and not even the oblique arrangement of the attack but the tactical maneuver as such, the flexibility that allowed the commander of a Prussian army to lead it in complete order along the enemy front and to approach an enemy wing, or where possible to envelop it, so quickly that the enemy did not succeed in disrupting this maneuver by an offensive move on his own part.

Similar ideas were in no way completely unknown to the enemies either. The battle of Rossbach is a precise counterpart to Leuthen. Hildburghausen and Soubise attempted to move around the Prussian army, but while they were marching, the Prussians, who had already deployed, attacked, drove into their march columns, and by the strength of their assault completely overwhelmed the enemy with hardly any losses of their own. If the Austrians at Leuthen, instead of standing fast in their defensive positions, had made such an offensive push into the marching Prussians at the right moment, they would certainly have won the battle.

Infantry combat from the Thirty Years' War to the War of the Spanish Succession quite often turned into a loose series of local fights that were carried on very stubbornly. The more exacting drills and the constantly stronger emphasis on the tactical unit also changed the character of combat. The struggle for localities was avoided where possible, since it broke up the tactical body. Frederick expressly forbade that the soldiers be placed in houses. General von Höpfner gives a very correct picture of Frederick's tactics in his *History of the War of 1806 (Geschichte des Krieges von 1806)*, p. 480:

In these tactics everything depended on achieving the decision with the first blow. The entire mass moved forward in line, fired a few battalion salvos, and then resorted to the bayonet. Whatever could not be accomplished in this way was simply not to be accomplished. The great king had no doubt realized the critical aspect of this combat method when he thus in a single move threw all his forces into the abyss of the battle. But he hardly knew any other antidotes than the attack with a withheld wing and in echelons, in which situation at least one part of the army still remained at his disposal for the moment. But that was not a drastic measure but one to be used against an enemy who was not overrun by the first blow, leading after a few moments to a parallel battle with all the forces.

It is, of course, impossible to draw a sharp distinction. Even under Frederick the first blow did not always decide everything; in some cases rather long battles developed, but it can be said in general that, remarkably enough, under Eugene and Marlborough the battles were more similar to those of Napoleon than were those of Frederick. The commanders and the troops moved more freely. It was precisely the excellent training in the mechanics of military movements and actions on the Prussian drill field that bound them to this technique and made more flexible combat difficult.

The Prussians, while strengthening linear tactics to the highest effectiveness, not only failed to diminish its natural weakness thereby, but rather increased it. These well-aligned, salvo-firing battalions were brought into disorder by every unevenness of the terrain and could fight neither in villages nor in forests. This situation was all the more critical in that the Austrians, in their Croatians, possessed a very useful light infantry composed of sons of nature who understood how to conduct combat in scattered situations. The Prussian salvo fire was not effective against these irregulars, who were firing from covered positions. At Lowositz and Kollin they also played an important role in the drawn battle, and the fact that the Prussians were victorious at Leuthen was perhaps partly due to the apparent absence of the Croatians.

At the start of the Seven Years' War, the king formed four free battalions as light infantry, and at the end he had twenty-six. But these free battalions were unable to stand up to the pandours and Croatians. In the border inhabitants, who themselves were still half-barbarian and lived in continuous warfare with the Turks, Maria Theresa had a unique source of warrior ability, one that was lacking for the king of Prussia. Again and again he complained of what great harm these undisciplined bands caused him in guerrilla warfare by their covering moves and the observation of his own movements. How much the Prussian free battalions actually accomplished can be recognized only in part and uncertainly from the sources. Although individual successful moves are recounted, the king himself did not have very high regard for these units. On 24 May 1779 he wrote General Tauentzien that the officers of these battalions were "in general, slovenly and poor material." For him, these units were only an unavoidable evil, so to speak, and they were all the less capable of accomplishing something outstanding in that Frederick himself did not correctly grasp their nature and did not give them any training compatible with that nature. In order to accomplish something in scattered combat, the men would either have had to possess a strong warlike tendency, like the Croatians, pandours, and Cossacks, or a very strong willingness, which could be systematically trained for military accomplishment. But there was no room in the Prussian officer corps for the thought of such a training. No less a person than Ferdinand of Braunschweig wrote of the Austrian pandours and Croatians that they "are always hidden behind trees like thieves and robbers and never show themselves in the open field, as is proper for brave soldiers."[31] The king himself did not think very differently. Was he systematically to develop such a reprehensible spirit in his own army? But since they were, after all, indispensable, there arose a hideous monster.

The Prussian free battalions had a composition that was not better but even worse than the line battalions. They did not have natives but were adventurers, deserters, and vagabonds who differed from the regular infantry only through the fact that they were lacking in the one element that made the other force strong, that is, discipline. Men impressed by force could be taught to carry out in the dressed alignment that which was required of them, but not in the combat of marksmen, where the individual took cover in keeping with his own perception and desire, moved forward, and fought in the same spirit. It is surprising enough that individual leaders like Mayer, Guichard, and Count Hardt were still able to fight successfully with these units that were almost robber bands.[32] In addition to the free battalions, *Jäger* (*chasseur*) companies were formed for similar purposes, but, quite to the contrary, they were composed of particularly effective, reliable men, sons of native foresters, who were themselves thus given the prospect of appointment in the forest service.

We have followed the development of the cavalry up to the time of Gustavus Adolphus, who did away with the caracole, reduced the pistol to the function of an auxiliary weapon, and ordered the closely formed shock action with the broad sword as the principal method of attack. The development continued in this direction. Everything depended on making the shock action with a completely closed formation as long and as fast as possible. But that was very difficult. Very many drills were necessary for this, and these drills were very hard on the horses. Consequently, the colonels, who wished to spare their horses, had them move at the trot in shorter attacks or only with a short gallop at the end. Although Prince Eugene ordered the attack at full gallop, he was not able to carry this off. Frederick William I did not understand the mounted arm, and as outstanding as the infantry he had trained proved itself to be in the battle of Mollwitz, just as little, on the other hand, was accomplished by the Prussian cavalry in this battle. It was completely overwhelmed and driven from the battlefield by the Austrian cavalry, which was, to be sure, numerically superior. King Frederick infused it with a new spirit; in the very next year it behaved completely differently at Chotusitz, and in the decade before the Seven Years' War, the accomplishments of the cavalry became continuously greater. Whereas in 1748 Frederick had still been content with attacks of 700 paces, in 1755 he required 1,800 paces, the last of which were covered at a full gallop. He required of his commanders that they never allow themselves to be attacked but were always themselves to attack. "When the great wall, closely formed, suddenly strikes the enemy impetuously, in this manner, he cannot possibly offer any resistance." Von Seydlitz is supposed to have expressed this idea once by saying that the cavalry won the battle not with the saber but with the riding whip. Or with the expression "In the attack, in a group of six men, he is a scoundrel who lets himself be squeezed out behind." The closed tactical body enveloped the individual horseman to such an extent that the king wished to see the hand-to-hand combat eliminated as much as possible, for "the common soldier would then decide the matter," and one could not depend on that. Consequently, the squadrons were to ride not only with the men closed together completely, stirrup to stirrup or even knee to knee, but also in the first echelon there was to be hardly any interval between squadrons. The attack was to carry through the first enemy echelon, driving it along before the attacker and breaking up the second enemy echelon as well, and only after this second success did Frederick consider hand-to-hand combat as permissible.[33]

In the Seven Years' War the Austrian cavalry supposedly still fired before using the saber.[34]

In France the development was hindered by the fact that horses and equipment belonged to the captains until a reorganization by the duke of Choiseul (between 1761 and 1770), and the captains wanted to avoid any wear and tear. The walk and the trot were the only two gaits. It was Count St. Germain who first brought about the attack at a full gallop in 1776.[35]

General von der Marwitz wrote of the attack at the gallop:[36]

This mass must always break through. It is possible that half of it may be shot up or will fall into a sunken road, causing hundreds to break their necks. But it is impossible for it to hold up or turn around, for in this confusion, raging, and uproar, when many hundreds of horses dash forward in a tight mass, even the best horseman no longer has control of his horse; all of them are running away. But even if one man or another should keep his horse under control, there can be no thought of stopping, for he would then immediately be overridden by those bolting behind him. Consequently, there can be no doubt; if such an attack is undertaken, it will create a breach or the regiment will not be seen again.

What happens now if two such attacks should clash with one another? As we have heard above that actual bayonet combat hardly ever occurred, so, too, according to a study by General Wenninger,[37] the case of two squadrons clashing with one another with their full weight and closed formation never occurred. In such a situation both sides would collapse.

General Pusyrewski, in his *Study on Combat* (*Untersuchung über den Kampf*), Warsaw, 1893, writes in the same vein:

> A real clash never exists; the moral impression of one of the opponents overthrows the other a little earlier or a little later, even if it should be not until they are the length of a nose apart. Before the first saber thrust, one side is already beaten and turns to flee. In a real clash both sides would be destroyed. In actual practice, the victor loses hardly a man.

General von der Marwitz states that the picture is completely different in an attack on infantry. In *Schriften*, 2:147, he writes:

> Whoever has ever participated in a cavalry attack, riding against the enemy, knows very well that not a single horse shows any desire to penetrate into the approaching mass, that on the contrary, they stop and try to turn around every time. If the attack is not to fail completely, every horseman must prevent his animal from doing that.

That is, he must force him ahead.

In order to accomplish this, the French rode in a tight formation but slowly.

This battle cavalry was very unsuited for the important task of reconnaissance, or even of pursuit. It has been said that the leaders of that period did not understand how to use cavalry for reconnaissance. In 1744, when Frederick had advanced into Southern Bohemia, he felt as if he were cut off, and despite the fact that he had a cavalry force of almost 20,000 men, he was unable to determine for quite a long time where the Austrian army was. The same thing happened again in 1759 to the army of Count Dohna, which had the mission of driving into Posen and fixing the Russians. The *General Staff Work*, 10:175, wrote that it was apparently believed that one should not allow this expensive and hard-to-replace arm to get out of direct control, and if on one occasion individual patrols were actually sent out at considerable distance, nothing happened to make it possible for them to report back in timely fashion. But this awkwardness might also be more basically due to the fact that the cavalry included many unreliable men, certainly not nearly as many as the infantry, but still too many to allow one to send them out through the countryside on their own in patrols. As in the case of the infantry, the entire spirit of the training was not aimed at the accomplishment of the individual warrior but of the firm tactical unit. Reconnaissance missions, however, require the training of each individual to the point of self-reliance and individual initiative. It was therefore not so much the lack of ability of the higher commanders as it was the natural result of the entire organization that determined the high but one-sided effectiveness of the cavalry.

Frederick recognized this failing at an early stage, and, as with the infantry, he also formed for the cavalry a special arm to fill this lack. These were the hussars, who were not counted as part of the cavalry. Frederick's father had left him only nine squadrons of hussars; Frederick increased their number to eighty. He saw in them men who were eager for war, adventure, and booty, who, if given a half-degree of freedom, were not ready to desert but could for that very reason be used to prevent desertions in the other troop units. But for the same reason, they were too loosely organized for that which he required of his cavalry in battle. At Leuthen they formed a fourth echelon behind the infantry. They were counted on particularly in pursuits.

Even before the Seven Years' War, however, the training of the hussars became more similar to that of the other mounted regiments.

More than a fourth of Frederick's field army in December 1755 was composed of mounted men (31,000 as compared with 84,000 infantrymen). In the first half of the sixteenth century the foot troops had been much larger proportionately; in the second half of the century, as the transformation of knights into cavalry was completed, the latter increased again, and at times in the Thirty Years' War it reached half the strength of the entire army and even more. In the standing armies, the less expensive arm, the infantry, increased again. Under the Great Elector, the cavalry was only one-seventh of the army strength. Then it was again gradually increased up to its maximum strength under Frederick.

As with the other two arms, the artillery, too, was constantly improved and increased in its effectiveness. As a special new creation, Frederick formed the horse artillery. Let us not go into the details of the cannon, which tended now in the direction of lighter weight and mobility, and then toward strengthening as a result of heavy caliber and grouping in batteries. The principal change in this arm—that is, the huge increase of heavy artillery—originated not with the Prussians but with the Austrians, who sought and found in these heavy guns their protection against the aggressive spirit of the Prussians. Frederick then reluctantly agreed with the necessity of following the Austrians along this path. At Mollwitz the Austrian army had 19 cannon, one to every thousand men, while the Prussians had 53, or 2-1/2 for every thousand men. At Torgau the Austrians had 360 cannon, or 7 for every thousand men, and the Prussians had 276, or 6 per thousand men.

EXCURSUS

RAPIDITY OF FIRE IN THE EIGHTEENTH CENTURY

The standard study on this subject is in the "Tactical Schooling" ("Taktische Schulung"), *Kriegsgeschichtliche Einzelschriften*, Book 28/30, p. 434. But since several important sources were not drawn on, there is still something to be added. The question is interesting not only from a practical viewpoint but also methodologically, since we can judge from it how easily, even among experts, false ideas are formed and traditions spring up on such technical questions that are of themselves quite simple, ideas and traditions that hardly seem assailable but that we nevertheless may not trust. In this connection, I am thinking of the unlimited trust that is usually placed in the statements of Polybius on military matters.

The conclusion of the study in the "Taktische Schulung" is that, shortly before the Seven Years' War, a competent musketeer could load without command four or five times in a minute, and the platoon could fire five salvos on command in two minutes, and this was increased to almost three per minute.

The document adds:

> Let us remember only the large number of individual moves that were necessary at that time for loading; that is: musket to the right side, half-cock, take the cartridge, break it open, shake the powder onto the pan, close the pan, throw the musket around to the left side (foot) without sprinkling powder from the open cartridge, place the cartridge in the barrel and shake out all the powder, withdraw the ramrod, grip it part way down, insert it into the barrel, push down strongly twice, replace the ramrod and raise the musket, that is, to a position in front of the middle of the body in order to take aim or to shoulder arms in accordance with the following command, in case the weapons were not to be fired immediately. It then immediately becomes clear why all of this, including firing, could not be done five times in a minute.

When the cylindrical ramrod and the conical touchhole were introduced, a report of Count Guibert on a maneuver in 1773, consequently without balls, states that a speed of thirty cartridges in 8-1/2 minutes—that is, 3-1/2 shots per minute—was attained. Although the cylindrical ramrod had the advantage of not needing to be turned around, it also had very great disadvantages, according to Guibert.

The regulation of 1779 required that practice in loading and firing with powder for the recruits "had to take place daily and be continued until the new men could fire four times in a minute."

Berenhorst wrote that "at least 15 seconds were needed to load and fire with ball cartridges," and therefore it was impossible to get off a full four shots in a minute; "with blank cartridges one could fire six times per minute."

To this, however, I add the following evidence: While he was present in Breslau in 1783, the inspector general, Lieutenant General Count Anhalt, required in an order to all the regiments stationed there (Archives in Zerbst) that "the man was to fire seven times and load six times with powder (that is, with powder cartridges but without balls), and without cartridges (that is, as a dry run) he must have fired a full eight times and loaded eight times, if he was properly drilled."

Scharnhorst, in his manual (*Taktik*, p. 268, Edition of 1790), states that experience showed that with the new musket troops could fire between five and six times per minute. But his own reckoning by seconds leads only to five times.

In his work *On the Effectiveness of the Firearm* (*Ueber die Wirkung des Feuergewehrs*), which he published in 1813, Scharnhorst said (p. 80) that in a test where ten infantrymen fired twenty aimed shots in sequence, the fastest one required 7-1/2 minutes, while the slowest needed between 13 and 14 minutes. On p. 95 it is reported of another test that 5 to 8 minutes were needed for ten aimed shots. In the best test, therefore, not quite three shots were fired per minute, and in the second test only two.

In the valuable book *Memorable Events Characteristic of the Prussian Army under the Great King Frederick II. From the Testament of a Prussian Officer* (*Denkwürdigkeiten zur Charakteristik der preussischen Armee unter dem grossen König Friedrich II. Aus dem Nachlass eines preussischen Offiziers*), by von Lossow, Glogau, 1826, p. 259, it is said that after the "discovery of the funnel-shaped breach screw" it was possible to fire six times per minute and to load the seventh time. "But since this was overdone, King Frederick William II abandoned it."

Decker, *Tactics of the Three Arms* (*Taktik der drei Waffen*), 1833, p. 138, reports that the rate of fire had been increased to between seven and eight shots per minute.

Gansauge, *The Brandenburg-Prussian Military System* (*Das brandenburg-preussische Kriegswesen*), 1839, p. 132, says that "after the Hubertusburg treaty it was required of the Prussian infantry that it fire the musket four times per minute."

In order to understand these crass contradictions, we must distinguish between the shooting of the individual man and that of the closed unit; between the achievement of individuals, especially talented ones, and the average achievement; between practice without powder, with powder, and with powder and ball; between shooting without command and the shooting of entire units on command.

Of importance in military history, of course, is only live firing, which goes considerably more slowly than firing with blanks, because the ball must be rammed down into the barrel. Furthermore, individual firing drops out of the picture. It is a question of the firing of entire platoons with balls, whether with or without command.

Following are a few cases that differ from the foregoing evidence.

Berenhorst reports expressly "six times" only in speaking of practice cartridges.

In like manner, Count Anhalt speaks only of practice cartridges.

In accordance with the above, we may assume that Decker and Lossow also had only practice cartridges in mind.

There remains the important evidence of Scharnhorst in his *Taktik*, where he undoubtedly intends to speak of live firing and states "five times" or even "five to six times."

Scharnhorst's evidence is opposed to the statement by Berenhorst, who requires "at least" 15 seconds per shot, that is, not quite a full four shots per minute, and also to Gansauge, who speaks of four shots. Berenhorst writes as a contemporary, while Gansauge, who entered the army in 1813, still had a living tradition at his disposal.

The question arises as to whether the invention of the conical touchhole, which eliminated the sprinkling of the powder on the pan, and of the cylindrical ramrod, which eliminated the double turning of the rod, really made so much difference as to allow the increase of speed from three times at the most (at the time of the Seven Years' War) to five times?

Who would dare to doubt a statement by Scharnhorst if it were the only one passed on to us? But he is opposed not only by the evidence of Berenhorst and Gansauge, but in the third edition of his *Taktik*, edited by Hoyer, the figure of the first edition is also reduced to "four to a maximum of five firings per minute."

When Scharnhorst wrote his work, he was a lieutenant of the Hanover artillery. Consequently, I cannot escape the assumption that he was deceived by a report based on the usual practice firing with blank cartridges.

When it is stated in his work of 1813 that, with a musket that was still further improved, it was still possible to fire only between two and not quite three shots per minute, even for the best marksmen, we must note that this refers to aimed firing.

The result, then, was that the Prussians entered the Seven Years' War with the technique of being able to fire two and a half to three unaimed salvos per minute, a rate that was later increased to nearly four salvos as a result of technical improvements in the musket. This rate was also still being achieved in 1806.

We are to reject not only a rate of ten or even eight times per minute, but also Koser, who assumes five to six shots per minute (*Friedrich der Grosse*, 3:377). And Bronsart von Schellendorf, the later minister of war, in the polemic treatise *A Glance Back at Tactical Retrospectives* (*Ein Rückblick auf die Taktischen Rückblicke*), 1870, went too far when he wrote, p. 5:

> If we remember that the muzzle-loading musket did not prevent the infantry of the great king from firing four to five times per minute in close formation, a rate of fire which we have not noticeably exceeded with the needle gun, it is really difficult to trace a radical change of tactics from the introduction of the breech-loading rifle.

Still graver, however, was the error in the first volume of the *General Staff Work* on the wars of Frederick the Great, where it is stated concerning a period when only two and a half shots per minute could be fired (p. 140): "Thus it was possible through continuous drilling to reach a rate as high as five times per minute for loading and firing, an achievement that was three times as fast as the normal rate elsewhere and that therefore had to assure the Prussian infantry an indisputable superiority."

General von Caemmerer once told me that with the old needle gun a good unit could fire five times in a minute and that a noncommissioned officer who came from the firing school was greatly admired because he fired seven times per minute.

With the Minié gun, with which the Prussian army was armed for a short time previously, firing was at the rate of one and a half shots per minute.

NOTES FOR CHAPTER III

1. Rüstow, *Geschichte der Infanterie*, 2:42 ff.

2. Jany, p. 108.

3. Pastenacci, *Battle of Enzheim* (*Schlacht bei Enzheim*).

4. In the battles of Klissow (1702) and Fraustadt (1706), the Saxon infantry tried unsuccessfully to protect itself against the Swedes with chevaux-de-frise.

5. According to Würdinger, *Military History of Bavaria* (*Kriegsgeschichte von Bayern*), 2:349, such an "awl spear" appears in a Passau armory register of 1488.

6. According to sources cited by Firth in *Cromwell's Army*, p. 87, a light musket with a flintlock was already in widespread use as a hunting weapon by the German peasants at the start of the seventeenth century.

In 1626 with these muskets the peasants completely wiped out imperial regiments that Christian of Braunschweig had defeated.

7. At this point I wish to assemble a number of data concerning the technical improvements of the firearm, without claiming accuracy for each individual date. From this listing, however, we gain an overall view as to how gradually such a development occurs, step by step.

Of significance in the references is the work by Thierbach in the *Zeitschrift für historische Waffenkunde*, Vol. II, "On the Development of the Bayonet" ("Ueber die Entwicklung des Bajonetts") and also Vol. III.

Second half of the sixteenth century: paper cartridges for horsemen. 1608: loading in 95 tempo. 1653: paper cartridges initially without the ball. Spak, in the *Festschrift für Thierbach*, claims to prove that muskets without forks were given to the regiments for the first time in 1655. 1670: introduction of cartridges in the Brandenburg infantry. 1684: flintlock muskets introduced in Austria. 1688: the bayonet reportedly invented by Vauban. 1690: introduction of paper cartridges in France (Jähns, 2:1236). 1698: Leopold von Dessau adopts the iron ramrod in his regiment. 1699: bayonet with cross-arm. 1703: final abandonment of the pikes by the French. 1708: abandonment of the pikes by the Netherlanders, according to Coxe, *Life of Marlborough* (*Leben Marlboroughs*), 4:303. 1718: the iron ramrod adopted in the whole Prussian army from this year on. 1721: abandonment of pikes by the Russians. 1733: loading with bayonets fixed in Prussia (Jähns, 3:2498). 1744 (or possibly 1742): the iron ramrod in Austria. 1745: the iron ramrod in France. *The Well Drilled Prussian Soldier* (*Der wohl exerzierte Preussische Soldat*), by Johann Conrad Müller, "Free Ensign and Citizen of the Town of Schaffhausen," 1759, states on p. 18 that shortly before the current campaign Frederick had had new stocks placed on all the muskets and had the foremost ring for the ramrod made in funnel form so that the rod could be brought more securely into place. The author also states that the grips described by him could not be done with the wooden ramrod. 1773: replacement of the conical ramrod in Prussia by the cylindrical rod.

Thierbach states that in tests which Napoleon had made in 1811, every seventh shot was a misfire; according to Schmidt, *Hand Firearms* (*Handfeuerwaffe*), p. 38, of every 100 shots, 20 were misfires and 10 were ignition failures. In tests that were conducted by the French government in 1829 with the same flintlock musket, there was only one misfire for every fifteen shots.

8. The standard study is the article "The Tactical Training of the Prussian Army by King Frederick the Great during the Period of Peace from 1745 to 1756" ("Die taktische Schulung der preussischen Armee durch König Friedrich den Grossen während der Friedenszeit 1745 bis 1756") in the *Kriegsgeschichtliche Einzelschriften*, published by the Great General Staff, Vol. 28/30, 1900.

9. *Taktische Schulung*, p. 663.

10. Jähns, p. 2105.

11. Berenhorst, *Observations on the Art of War, Its Progress, Its Contradictions, and Its Reliability* (*Betrachtungen über die Kriegskunst, über ihre Fortschritte, ihre Widersprüche und ihre Zuverlässigkeit*), 1797, pp. 239–240.

12. *Taktische Schulung*, p. 665.

13. The prince of Ligne reports that on a single occasion in his many campaigns, in the engagement at Mons (1757), he heard bayonets striking against one another. Berenhorst states that in military history there is not a single properly confirmed example that the rifles of opposing sides had crossed one another and there had been hand-to-hand fighting. Emperor William I also paid no attention to the use of the bayonet in the training of soldiers, since he believed it had no practical value.

14. Scharnhorst, 3:273, states that many tests had shown that the firing against a line of cavalry resulted in 403 hits of 1,000 shots at 100 paces, 149 hits at 300 paces, and 65 hits at 400 paces. In the case of a platoon well drilled in aiming, there were considerably more hits at the greater distances, up to twice as many. At 400 paces "the effect was hardly to be taken into consideration." Against infantry, of course, the effect was considerably smaller. For more on this subject, see *Taktische Schulung*, p. 431. In Firth, *Cromwell's Army*, p. 89, the range of the muskets of the sixteenth and seventeenth centuries is given as 600 paces, according to the evidence of several confirming sources, and it is not impossible that this range was greater than that of the musket of the eighteenth century.

15. Austria. *Regulations of 1759* (*Regulament von 1759*). Jähns, p. 2035.

16. In agreement with *Taktische Schulung*, p. 446.

17. General Staff, *Military History Monographs* (*Kriegsgeschichtliche Einzelschriften*), 27:380.

18. "Dispositions for the Battle of Zorndorf" ("Disposition für Schlacht bei Zorndorf"), *Militärischer Nachlass des Grafen Henckel*, 2:79. "On the wing that is supposed to attack, there will be three echelons. If a battalion in the first echelon is broken up or repulsed, the battalion of the second echelon standing directly behind it is to move immediately into the first echelon, and one from the third echelon must replace it in the second echelon so that the battalion that is broken up and repulsed must form again in good order and advance with the others."

19. Montecuccoli, *Schriften*, 2:350. The Austrian Military Field Regulations of 1759 state 500 paces (Jähns, 3:2035). The *Regulations for the Royal Prussian Infantry* (*Reglement vor die Königliche Preussische Infanterie*) of 1726 in Title XX, Article 1, " . . . that one cannot shoot that far with any musket ball."

20. The *General Staff Work* and the two monographs 27 and 28/30 added very valuable new material on this subject, but in the end they stray into a description of the oblique battle order that is much too narrow. It has been rejected by Lieutenant Colonel Schnackenburg in the *Jahrbücher für Armee und Marine*, Vol. 116, Book 2, 1900. The basis for the correct concept had already been found by Otto Herrmann in the *Brandenburg-Prussian Studies (Brandenburgisch-Preussische Forschungen)*, 5(1892):459, and the entire problem was solved once and for all in the exemplary study of Rudolf Keibel, outstanding in its source critique, completeness, and reasoning, which appeared in the *Brandenburgisch-Preussische Forschungen*, 14(1901):95. A final effort by Jany to defend the concept of the General Staff in the *Hohenzollern-Jahrbuch*, 1911, has been refuted by O. Herrmann in the *Brandenburgisch-Preussische Forschungen*, 27(1914):555.

21. Montecuccoli, 2:581, also calls Nieuport, Breitenfeld, and Alterheim wing battles. Breitenfeld did indeed become a wing battle, although it was not planned that way.

22. Jähns, 1:520, 522.

23. The details are to be found in Herrmann, p. 464.

24. Clausewitz ("Seven Years' War"), *Work*, 10:56, writes: "According to the prejudices and the arrangements of that period, 40,000 or 50,000 men could not fight in any other way than by forming in advance in a cohesive battle formation." The reproach which is felt in the word "prejudices" seems unjustified; it was a result dictated by the nature of things. Because the lines were so extremely thin, they had to be unbroken. Every interval would have offered an extremely dangerous point for a penetration.

25. According to Jähns, 2:1521.

26. Frederick himself, in his *General-Prinzipien* (Article XXII, No. 7), describes "my oblique order of battle" in this manner:

One refuses the enemy one wing and reinforces the one that is to attack; with the latter you direct all your efforts against a wing of the enemy that you take in the flank; an army of 100,000 men, if taken in the flank, can be beaten by 30,000 men, for the affair is then quickly decided.

27. Even the continuous line of the infantry was by no means maintained rigidly by the king; rather, he freed himself in keeping with the circumstances. This point is proven by O. Herrmann for the battles of Prague and Kollin, *Brandenburgisch-Preussische Forschungen*, 26:499 and note on p. 513.

28. It was their observation and follow-up of this work in all its details that led the General Staff astray in placing the beginning of the oblique

battle formation in this decade and limiting it to the cohesive infantry front. But even in the writings of the General Staff itself this limitation is not strictly adhered to, and the work thereby becomes involved in inner contradictions, in contradictions with King Frederick, and in contradictions with a document written personally by the chief of the Historical Section, von Taysen.

29. Tempelhof describes the approach march as follows:

> There was no more beautiful sight. The heads of the columns were constantly abreast of one another and separated from one another by the distance necessary for the deployment; the platoons maintained their intervals as exactly as if they were marching in a review."

30. As a reason for the echeloned attack, he states that, as a result of this formation, no special command was needed for the left wing to move into the battle. The interval of the individual battalions from one another amounted to fifty paces—that is, not even 1 minute's march. The forward point of the right wing had a distance of 1,000 paces from the tail of the left wing, or no more than 10 to 15 minutes of marching time.

That it was not the echelons that brought victory was also recognized by Dietrich von Bülow (Jähns, 3:2139). Major Jochim, "The Military Testament of the Great King" ("Das militärische Testament des Grossen Königs"), supplement to the *Militär-Wochenblatt*, Vol. 7, 1914, claims, contrary to the *General Staff Work*, p. 26, that the echelons were formed not by battalions but by brigades (five battalions). He regards the oblique battle formation not as a combat formation at all, but rather as a movement formation, and he decisively rejects the traditional exaggerated estimate of its value. For him, the oblique battle formation was only an "expedient for the open plain with no cover." According to the "Dispositions for the Battle of Zorndorf," as printed in the *Military Testament of Count Henckel Donnersmarck* (*Militärischer Nachlass des Grafen Henckel Donnersmarck*), 2:78, every two battalions together formed one echelon.

31. Letter of 8 August 1745. *Generalstabswerk*, "Wars of Frederick the Great" ("Kriege Friedrichs des Grossen"), 1:24.

32. Kurt Schmidt, "The Activity of the Prussian Free Battalions in the First Two Campaigns of the Seven Years' War" ("Die Tätigkeit der preussischen Freibataillone in den beiden ersten Feldzügen des siebenjährigen Krieges"), Berlin dissertation, 1911. Erwin Dette, op. cit., p. 78 ff. On Hardt's successes in 1759, see *Generalstabswerk*, 10:124.

33. *Militär-Wochenblatt*, 62(1895):1602; 73(1899):1832. The French ambassador Valory wrote in his report for 1748 concerning the Prussian cavalry at the time of the death of Frederick William I, *Brandenburgisch-Preussische Forschungen*, 7:308:

The horses are accustomed to the fire, and the rider dismounts from his horse, leaving the bridle on his neck, and he places himself at the head of the squadron in order to fire by rank of platoons and of battalions like the infantryman, and no horse moves from his place. I have seen entire half-squadrons double their ranks fleeing from the horses' heels.

34. von Canitz, *Information and Observations on the Fates of the Mounted Forces (Nachrichte und Betrachtungen über die Schicksale der Reiterei)*, p. 7.

35. According to Desbrière and Sautai, *Organisation et tactique des trois armes*, Paris, 1906.

36. *Writings (Schriften)*, 2:176.

37. *Kavalleristische Monatshefte*, 1908, p. 908, "On the Details and Results of Mounted Clashes" ("Ueber Verlauf and Ergebnis von Reiterzusammenstössen").

Chapter IV

Strategy

The transition from the strategy of the Middle Ages into the ideas and conduct of war of the modern period was treated by Machiavelli. We have found that the new development begins with the reappearance of the tactical body of the infantry with the close-combat weapon. It is only from this point on that there was a true strategy again in the full sense of the word.[1] The often repeated saying that war in the Middle Ages was the application of brute force but that it had become a science since the Renaissance raises ideas which must be rejected in every respect as false. Neither was war in the Middle Ages nothing but brute force, nor did it then become a science. War is always an art and can never become a science. The relationship of art to science can only exist in the fact that it is brought to an understanding of itself by means of theoretical—that is, scientific—considerations and in this way becomes all the more capable of training its masters. We have seen that tactics has indeed been influenced by scientific study in its development, without, of course, having become a "science." Whether that also applies to strategy, or to what extent it applies, we will learn as we progress in our study.

We have already seen in the chapter on Machiavelli that the nature of strategy leads to a central problem, the problem of the double form of strategy, the strategy of annihilation and the strategy of attrition, a problem that necessarily dominates all strategic thought and action.

The first natural principle of all strategy is to assemble one's forces, seek out the main force of the enemy, defeat it, and follow up the victory until the defeated side subjects itself to the will of the victor and accepts his conditions, which means in the most extreme case up to occupation of the entire enemy country. The conduct of war in this manner presupposes a sufficient superiority; it may be that the superiority suffices to win a first great victory but still is not great enough to take over the entire country or even only to besiege the enemy capital. It is also possible that the opposing forces are so equal that from the start only moderate successes can be expected. One may not so much place his hopes on completely defeating the enemy as on wearing him out and exhausting him by blows and destruction of all kinds to the extent that in the end he prefers to accept the conditions of the victor, which in this case must always show a certain moderation. That is the nature of the strategy of attrition, whose great problem is always a question of whether or not a tactical decision, a battle with its dangers and losses, is to be sought, whether or not the prospective gains from a victory outweigh the losses. If in the one case it is the principal task of the commander to devote his entire mental powers and energy to gaining for his own army the greatest possible advantages in the decisive action and to make his victory as great as possible, in the other case his analysis considers in which places and in what way he can find the enemy vulnerable while guaranteeing his own army, his country, and its people from harm. He will wonder whether he should besiege a fortress, occupy a province, cut off the enemy's supplies, attack by surprise an isolated portion of the enemy's army, alienate one of the enemy's allies, win over an ally for himself, but most importantly, whether an occasion and a good chance arises to defeat the enemy's main force. Consequently, battle plays a role both in the strategy of annihilation and that of attrition, but the difference is that in the former strategy it is the one means that outweighs all others and draws all others into itself, while in the strategy of attrition it is to be regarded as one means that can be chosen from among several. The possibility of forcing the enemy to such an extent, even without battle, that he accepts the conditions sought by our side leads in its ultimate degree to a pure maneuver strategy that allows war to be conducted without bloodshed. Such a pure maneuver strategy, however, is only a dialectical game and not any real event in world military history. Even if one side should actually propose such a method of waging war, it still does not know whether the other side is thinking in the same way and will continue with such ideas. The possibility of a decision by battle therefore always remains in the background, even with those commanders who wish to avoid bloodshed, and so the strategy of attrition is not at all to be equated with a pure strategy of maneuver; rather, it is to be regarded as a type of warfare that is hostage to an internal contradiction. Its principle is a polarized one or one with a double pole.

In antiquity we have already become acquainted with the contrast between the strategy of annihilation and the strategy of attrition, and the appearance of the new form of war immediately brought this problem again to the forefront. When the Swiss descended from their mountains into the surrounding regions, they naturally had no other principle than to seek out the enemy as fast as possible and to attack and defeat him. But this very same principle could be turned against them. It was known that they always wished to return home again soon; it was also always difficult for the national leaders to obtain the pay for them over a long period. Therefore, if one succeeded in avoiding their attack and outlasting them in unassailable positions, one could hope to win the campaign without risks and without battle. This was the thought of La Trémouille when he was besieging Novara in 1513 and received the report that a Swiss relief army was approaching. He could have moved out against this army to defeat it before it joined forces with the garrison of Novara. La Trémouille rejected this idea and marched off in order to avoid contact with the Swiss by maneuvering, but he was overtaken by them and defeated. Very soon, however, experience showed that the war was never in any way won by such a victory. Had it therefore been logical to fight the battle? We have seen how even Machiavelli's intellect paused in the face of this problem and was not capable of resolving it. His own logic led him toward the strategy of annihilation, but the ancient sources, represented by Vegetius, recommended the strategy of attrition. In practice as in theory, this latter strategy retained the upper hand. The victory of the imperial forces at Pavia had the strongest direct effect; the captured King Francis had to agree to the most difficult conditions in the peace treaty of Madrid. But within a few years not all the pieces of this gain, but certainly very important ones, were lost again, and we could raise the question as to whether the investment had paid off.

And thus the battle of Pavia in 1525 remained the last completely great decisive action in this period of warfare. Wars did not cease, but entire campaigns were conducted without any real battle, and whenever a battle did take place, as at Ceresole in 1544, it had no results.

It is not difficult for the commander who wants to avoid battle to find positions which are so difficult to approach that the enemy, even if he has a considerably stronger force, prefers to renounce the risk. Natural advantages in the terrain are strengthened by field fortifications. A strategic offensive, therefore, does not automatically reach its climax in a battle but often wears itself out in a simple gain of space, the occupation of a region that can be exploited. The most favored objective is the siege and capture of a fortress, the possession of which then allows the victor to dominate an entire region and confronts the enemy with the task of reconquering it if he wishes to have it back in the peace treaty. This is all the more applicable the more the attitude of the seriousness of relying on the fortune of battle has become fixed in the minds of the leaders and it is not expected that the enemy will make an attack in force on a position that is even only tolerably good. But possession of such areas and such positions could also be achieved by fortunate maneuvering, while the enemy was relatively soon recovered from the direct loss of the battle, provided it did not result at the same time in considerable losses of territory or fortresses. Even the very maintaining of the status quo in the war, which forces both sides into heavy expenses, can bring one closer to accomplishing the goal of the war when one side faces the bottom of the purse sooner than the other side and can be moved toward submission for this reason. "For war," wrote a Swiss author of military history in 1664, "has a great hole and a wide snout, and when the money ends, then the game also ends."[2] Every war is strongly influenced by the economic factor, for it is impossible to fight without equipment and rations. But the wars with mercenary armies are in the most outstanding sense economic wars, for the armies have no other basis at all but the economic one. From Machiavelli to Frederick, therefore, we hear repeated the saying that he who has the last taler in his pocket wins the war.[3] But Machiavelli had already turned this saying around by stating that whoever had soldiers could also obtain money. The one saying is just as right and just as wrong as the other one. If it is the question of money that holds the upper hand, the strategy tends to be one of maneuver, whereas, if it is the soldier that is more important, the tendency is to do battle. This is the same polarity which resides in the fact that the instrument through which the political goal is to be reached, the army, itself is always the stake, and under all circumstances it is more or less seriously damaged. In the strategy of annihilation one does not need to be concerned with these damages, since one hopes that victory will bring complete success and an early end of the war and one does not fear the reaction. In the strategy of attrition, however, one's own damages must be taken very carefully into account. For if victory and even a repeated victory do not bring an end to the war, then the question arises whether the expense of restoring an army damaged by its victory is not as important as the victory itself. The warring monarchs therefore very frequently warned their field commanders not to risk too much, and they set as the most important objective not positive success, but, as Prince Elector Max of Bavaria wrote to his Field Marshal Mercy, the "saving of the army." When Margrave Ludwig of Baden attacked the Turks in foolhardy fashion, the imperial ministers reproached him for sacrificing the troops carelessly and needing a new army for every campaign. Especially niggardly with the employment of its troops was the merchant government of the States-General, but even Frederick the Great wrote in his *General-Prinzipien* in the first article, after describing the wonderful capabilities and skill of his army: "with troops like these one could dominate the whole world if their victories were not just as costly for them as for their enemies."

This consideration carries the most weight in coalition wars, where the victor has made sacrifices and later perhaps has to recognize that the profit fell not to him but to his ally, perhaps precisely all the more so when the victor now no longer has the strength to protect completely his own interests.

A principal expedient in the double-poled strategy was the field fortification. At the battles of Murten and Nancy, Charles the Bold had, of course, already sought to protect himself against the Swiss with field fortifications. The first truly modern battle, Cerignola (1503), between the French and Spanish in Lower Italy, took place around a wall and a ditch that the Spaniards had erected in great haste before their front. From that time on until the end of the *ancien régime*, field fortifications played their role, often a decisive one. In the Huguenot wars, when the cavalry had again taken its important place, de la Noue tells us that ditches were dug every night in order to gain protection against sudden attacks from a distance. Gustavus Adolphus, too, fortified every camp in which he remained with his army longer than one night. Not seldom it was a question of whether one side succeeded in arriving a few hours before the other and erecting a field fortification which the enemy did not dare to storm. The battle on the White Mountain in 1620 was lost because the necessary spades from Prague were not brought up quickly enough. Daun always operated against Frederick, spade in hand. Frederick was originally opposed to field fortifications, since his troops were protected from surprise attacks by their speed, and he always wanted to conduct combat on the offensive, in which case fortifications would only have been a hindrance for him. On occasion he even spoke out against them with a certain passion[4]—one of the few points on which he differed not only practically but also theoretically from his contemporaries—and if, despite this, he states in his *General-Prinzipien*, Article VIII, "We surround our camps with a trench, just as the Romans did formerly," he says that this was to prevent night operations of the light troops with which the enemy was so well provided, and also to prevent desertion. As protection in the rear in the case of a siege (circumvallation), the king was willing to allow entrenching (*"retranchierung"*), but even there he believed it would be better to move out against the approaching relief army of the enemy. In the most extreme emergency, after a lost battle or against a foe three times as strong, one would have to have recourse to fortifications. So in 1761, when the Russian and Austrian armies had finally succeeded in joining forces against him in Silesia, he did indeed save himself with the entrenchments at Bunzelwitz. No doubt on the basis of this experience, he then was converted in his writings after the Seven Years' War even to a basic recommendation of field fortifications.[5]

The question of whether to fight, in view of this strength of the tactical defenses, sometimes was not decided on the spot but at home by the government, even though days and weeks could pass before the question, the report, and the reply had gone back and forth. In 1544 the duke of Enghien sent his master of the camp, Monluc, from Upper Italy to the king in Paris to request permission for a battle. Monluc managed to win the permission against the opposition of the ministers. Enghien was victorious at Ceresole, but his victory had no results.

The same situation obtained in the Seven Years' War between Daun and Vienna and between the Russian commanders and St. Petersburg.

We have as the type of a weak campaign of maneuver the campaign of of the Schmalkaldics in 1546, and it is certain that the allied Protestant princes, especially at the start, when the emperor still had no troops, proceeded much too timidly.[6] But Ranke has already said that one cannot always repeat the angry words of Schärtelin concerning Landgrave Philip, that he was not willing to make the final tough decision; that all the fords and all the ditches were too deep for him and all the swamps too broad. Once such strategic attitudes have developed, as we have learned them for this period, it is very difficult to lead into a great action an army composed of men with a variety of interests and with a divided high command. Even the emperor, when he had numerical superiority, still contented himself with maneuvering and eventually was victorious not as a result of combat but through politics, by persuading Duke Maurice to invade the territories of the prince elector of Saxony. Then the loose alliance of the Schmalkaldics was not sufficient to leave behind and keep assembled an army for the defense of South Germany. On this point, the historian of this war, Avila, wrote:[7]

> The emperor never had the opportunity to fight under equal, to say nothing of advantageous, conditions. Even under equal conditions, however, he could not have fought, for such a victory brings many losses, and a weakened army, even though victorious, would not have been capable of bringing Germany—especially the cities—under his control.[8]

In the Huguenot wars very bloody battles took place, but strategically they still had only the value of small combat actions, since the Catholic side, even if it was much stronger and victorious on the battlefield, was not strong enough to see the war through to the point of overcoming its enemies by capturing all their fortified places.

It was also on this very point that all the efforts of the Spanish failed to reconquer the rebellious Netherlands.

The strategy of the Thirty Years' War was determined by the very complicated and frequently shifting political conditions and by the numerous fortified cities and the armies that were always numerically weak in comparison with the large areas involved. A man like Gustavus Adolphus, who had the grandiose boldness to march against the emperor from the distant and small kingdom of Sweden, who had brought all of Germany under his domination, a hero of such authority and initiative, still found himself obliged to proceed forward only step by step, feeling his way cautiously. Clausewitz called him "a learned commander full of careful and wise estimates." In another passage he said: "Gustavus Adolphus was not at all a bold invasion and battle commander; he preferred the artful, maneuvering, systematic type of war." Not until some fifteen months after his landing in Germany did matters lead to the decisive battle at Breitenfeld. Wallenstein, to whom Clausewitz attributes an "almost fearful energy" and the "fearsome respect which his entire army had for him," nevertheless never fought an offensive battle. Torstensson, on the other hand, continuously sought battle but without having his strategy, for all that, basically exceed the framework of a strategy of attrition. Nor could it have done so. As a result of the large number of paradoxes, the Thirty Years' War is very interesting from a strategic viewpoint, and it also offers shifts that have not yet been sufficiently researched. The strength of the assembled masses of troops was at times very great; for example, in 1627 the emperor had at his disposal at least 100,000 men, and in 1630 a similar number. At the end of 1631, when Wallenstein returned, there were between 30,000 and 40,000 men on hand, and in the spring of 1633 their total was 102,000, of which the main army at Münsterberg numbered 43,000. At the end of the campaign there was still a total of 74,000.[9]

Nevertheless, the operating armies that fought the battles were small. On the White Mountain, the united army of the emperor and the League numbered some 28,000 men; at Breitenfeld Gustavus Adolphus had 39,000, including the Saxons, and at Lützen 16,300 men. In his camp at Nuremberg, Wallenstein did not have 50,000 to 60,000 men, as has often been reported, but only 22,000.[10] Torstensson's armies were no stronger than 15,000 to 16,000 men. Many of the available combat forces were used for garrisons in the numerous fortified cities. The ratio of the cavalry in the field armies grew to as much as half, indeed even to two-thirds, of the total army. At Jankau in 1645 the imperial troops numbered 10,000 horsemen and 5,000 foot troops.

The theater of operations shifted repeatedly from the Baltic and the North Sea to the Danube and Lake Constance, from Vienna—indeed from Siebenbürgen—as far as the vicinity of Paris. The most distant marches could be accomplished, since the armies, with their small numbers, could be fed by the regions they marched through, and both Protestants and Catholics found in the south and in the north adherents who offered them bases of support. Consequently, the strategic aspects were always determined to a high degree by political viewpoints, so that a history of the art of war may be allowed to overlook following up the individual details as long as they are not necessary in the analysis of the individual, particularly noteworthy, battles.

A new period for strategy was ushered in with the wars of Louis XIV, which were characterized by the increasing size of the armies and the resulting problems of provisioning the troops. The medieval armies were so small that their rations could either be carried along without too much difficulty or be taken from the regions through which they marched. Turning this point about, we may also conclude from the marches and the relatively unimportant measures for provisions that the armies were very small. With the growth of the armies, we hear more and more references to rations.[11] In the *Officials' Book (Aemterbuch)*, or the *War Regulations (Kriegsordnung)*, which was composed at the end of the 1530s and broadly disseminated and extensively used,[12] it is said: "Since provisions are the most important part in warfare," and there follows a careful computation concerning rations. A similar computation is to be found in the *Kriegsbuch* of Duke Albrecht of Prussia. It applies to an army of 90,801 combatants and estimates for that number for five days 490 bread wagons, 383 wagons with bacon, butter, salt, peas, and oats and barley, 433 wagons with 100 barrels of wine and 1,000 kegs of beer. In addition, there were the oats for 45,664 horses.[13] A Nuremberg warrior, Joachim Imhof, complained in a letter from the camp of Charles V in 1543 that everything was so expensive because the soldiers plundered on the road the burghers and peasants who were bringing up supplies; only meat was said to be cheap, because the cattle was taken off by force.[14] The French army in 1515 was already taking along its own field bakeries.[15] For his campaign in Bohemia in 1620, Duke Maximilian of Bavaria had supply depots set up. In Linz he seized 300 barrels of flour with a total content of 70,000 pecks, and the Austrians had to provide him 220 wagons with four-horse teams for its transport. In his *History of the Thirty Years' War (Geschichte des 30jährigen Krieges)*, Chemnitz is full of the concerns for rations for the operations, and Duke Albrecht points out the importance of the waterways for that purpose.[16]

Under Louis XIV the armies grew to a strength three and four times as great as that of the armies of the Thirty Years' War. We might at first think that larger armies gave the commanders the possibility of greater achievements and the domination of larger areas. If both sides increased equally, however, the opposite applied. The larger army was more cumbersome not only in its movements but also because it could not live directly from the land with no further support—unless it moved forward very quickly—but it needed an organized system of provisioning to back it up. This need was intensified by the fact that the increasing strength, as we have seen, brought to the armies many elements of very little reliability, who could be held under the colors only by discipline and close supervision. If one had these troops live from the land, most of them would desert. For this reason, too, the systematic providing of rations from depots became necessary, but depots tended to place shackles on the movement of the troops. The result then reacts again on the basic cause: the more cumbersome the movement becomes, because one is bound to the depot, the less one can live from the land and the more one depends on the depot.

The theoreticians estimated that an army could not move farther than five days' march from its depot; in the middle, at a distance of two days' march from the army and three days' march from the depot, the field bakery was to be placed. The bread baked in the field bakeries was usable for only nine days; now if the wagons moved back and forth and required one day for rest and loading, the troops could receive fresh bread every fifth day and there remained a margin for unforeseen events, something that was very necessary, since a continuous rain could make the routes impassable for transport vehicles.

Westphalen describes the conditions in a rainy period in 1758: "Within sight of the depots and bakeries the army began to suffer deprivation. For a distance of less than 5 kilometers the bread wagons needed days and nights and even then had to throw off half their load en route."[17]

In 1692, in Belgium, Luxembourg could not move forward to Enghien, as he wished to do, but he had to remain for three weeks at Soignies, because his wagon pool was not sufficient for the transport of foodstuffs from Mons, where his depot was. It is hardly 18 miles from Mons to Enghien and 9 miles to Soignies.

In 1745 Frederick the Great said that it was not he who commanded but flour and forage; another time he said to Field Marshal Keith (8 August 1757): "I agree with Homer. Bread makes the soldier."

At the same time that the armies were growing and internal changes were being made, the theaters of operations changed as most of the cities removed their fortifications, and instead a few were so strongly built up that they could only be captured by long and difficult sieges. The garrisons that were thus made available added to the strength of the field armies.[18]

Charles V had been able to undertake numerous campaigns that led him from Italy, Germany, and the Netherlands deep into France. And this also still happened in the Thirty Years' War. But after Louis XIV had had Vauban fortify again whole series of border cities, such invasions were no longer possible. In a similar manner Frederick later developed the system of Silesian fortresses, in order to assure his retention of this newly won territory.

On numerous occasions, especially when Torstensson was commanding the Swedes, there arose in the Thirty Years' War situations that bore a certain similarity to the strategic situations in Frederick's wars. But Torstensson, with his army of 15,000 men, accomplished considerably more than Frederick did later. The comparison between these two, which was proposed and carried out in Hobohm's inaugural lecture at the University of Berlin, is very instructive, and I shall come back to it during our study of Frederick's strategy.[19] As we can note right away, the difference does not lie in the fact that Gustavus Adolphus or one of his successors, whether it be Bernhard of Weimar, Baner, Torstensson, Wrangel, or Karl Gustavus, had had a different concept of the nature of strategy, and in particular of the value and importance of the open battle, than Frederick had. Rather, this difference springs solely from the differences in the conditions, political as well as military, the differences in the size, character, and combat methods of the armies.

Consequently, the development is not, for example, that from a period predominantly of maneuver there was gradually a shift to a strategy based predominantly on decision by battle, but theory and practice approached in one period closer to the one pole and in the other period the other pole.

Whereas in the Thirty Years' War, up to the end, very strong battles had been fought, the first wars of Louis XIV appear as pure campaigns of maneuver. The only real battle, at Seneffe in 1674, was not intended, and it remained indecisive because Condé was not willing to risk the army and did not continue the fight. Otherwise, in the war from 1672 to 1679 there were only sieges, marches, and a few small engagements.

The third war of Louis XIV, 1688–1697, once again showed stronger tensions and passions, but the only battle that had important results was the battle on the Boyne in Ireland in 1690. There James II was defeated by William III and the Stuarts lost their throne once and for all, while Fleurus (1690), Steenkerken (1692), and Neerwinden (1693), although accompanied by much bloodshed, had hardly any effects.

As a new and frightful means of warfare there appeared the systematic laying waste of an entire border area, the Palatinate, in 1689, in order to make it more difficult for the enemy to attack on this front and to facilitate for the French the defense of the fortified places which they intended to retain, Mainz and Philippsburg. As cruel as this measure was, it still did not attain its goal, since the Germans besieged Mainz and won it back. In 1704 the allies intended to follow the same procedure in Bavaria and even started to carry it out. Prince Eugene wrote:

> Thus I see in the final analysis that there is no other means but that entire Bavaria, together with all the surrounding districts, must be totally destroyed and laid waste in order to deny the enemies the opportunity of continuing the war any longer either from Bavaria or any of the surrounding area.

There now followed the War of the Spanish Succession, with the great battles of Höchstädt (1704), Turin (1706), Ramillies (1706), Oudenarde (1708), and Malplaquet (1709), which nevertheless accomplished no more than to push the French back to their borders. At the same time Charles XII of Sweden was attempting to defeat his enemies with repeated forceful blows.

On the other hand, in the War of the Polish Succession, 1733–1735, the efforts were small, and the war was carried out without any great decisions.

The decisive battles in the War of the Spanish Succession were on some occasions very large, but they took place only seldom and, after Malplaquet, had taken no more ground. By comparison, the many battles that took place after the appearance of Frederick the Great have given rise to the idea that Frederick had absolutely no part in the double-poled strategy but was to be considered, so to speak, as the discoverer and creator of the strategy of annihilation, which Napoleon later carried to its highest point. This concept, as we shall establish more specifically, is erroneous. The frequency of decision by battle in Frederick's conduct of war has its final basis not in a particularly new principle but in the titanic nature of the makeup of the king's character, which strove for great decisions. But the means by which he believed he could win the decision that he wanted and which he developed for this purpose was the oblique battle formation. With an army of 30,000 men, he wrote, one could defeat 100,000 men if one attacked them in the flank. The maneuverability and speed of the Prussians, which far surpassed those characteristics in the other armies of Europe, gave the king the prospect of being able to carry out such flanking movements before the enemy could protect himself against them. Here is where we must seek the improvement in the inherited art of war which pushed the king toward that pole calling for battle and distinguished the picture of the Seven Years' War so significantly, not only from earlier campaigns without battle, but also from the wars of Gustavus Adolphus, Marlborough, and Eugene. Nevertheless, Frederick's conduct of war, too, remained within the limits of the strategy of attrition and even pushed back close to the pole based on maneuver, when the enemies had found in their choice of positions, their field fortifications, and the increase in their artillery the means for countering the danger of the unsuspected flank attack based on the oblique battle formation.

The factors that limited the king of Prussia even in the period of his qualitative and partly also quantitative superiority and made it impossible for him to follow up victory to the point of forcing a peace treaty, that is, from going over to a strategy of annihilation, will appear and be worked out in the course of our discussion. Let some of these points be touched on now.

First of all, there was the very large number of unreliable men in his army, a consideration that obliged him to be constantly aware of the dangers of desertion. (See pp. 251–52, above.) He begins his greatest work, the *General Principles of War (General-Prinzipien vom Kriege)*, 1748, with fourteen rules that were to prevent desertion: one should not camp in the vicinity of a forest; whenever one is marching through a forest, one should have hussar patrols ride along beside the infantry; one should avoid night marches as much as possible; one should always have the soldiers march in platoons; whenever a defile is to be passed, one is place officers at the entrance and exit, and they are immediately to form the troops again.

He emphatically forbade night attacks.

There could be no thought whatever of breaking up the units and sending them into the countryside for requisitions. Only very exceptionally did Frederick have his troops furnished provisions by local inhabitants, while on rapid marches. And the marches were also not to be too long or strenuous; otherwise, individuals would remain behind and that would have infected others.

The strategic pursuit is impossible with such an army. Even a direct pursuit was very limited by the fact that maintaining order was seen as the primary consideration. In the dispositions for the battle of Zorndorf,[20] it was expressly prescribed that, although the first echelon was not to delay "to finish off the enemy, but rather to continue its orderly march and leave the cleaning up for the second echelon," it was still expressly forbidden to pursue at a run an enemy who was driven back, but he was to be "followed up at an orderly pace." The more distant pursuit was accomplished basically only with detachments, who had the mission of following the retreat of the enemy, staying close to his march columns, and intercepting his supplies. The victorious army, as such, however, first assembled. No doubt a commander like Frederick recognized the gigantic significance of the pursuit after a victory, and he concerned himself with pursuit especially after Hohenfriedberg and Leuthen, but with no success at all after Hohenfriedberg and only moderate success after Leuthen, even though Zieten was in command. The marshal of Saxony dared, in his *Rêveries*, to bring himself to the statement "After victory, all maneuvers are good except the prudent ones." Frederick, however, more realistically advised caution in pursuits, since counterattacks could appear only too easily.[21] "Never," he wrote, "is an army less disposed for fighting than immediately after a victory. Everybody is beside himself with joy, the great mass is charmed to have escaped the extreme dangers to which they were exposed, and no person is anxious to face them again at once."

The impossibility of an annihilating pursuit reacted, in turn, on the decision to do battle itself. The risk was very great in any case, the losses were painful, but the gain to be expected was more or less limited in the absence of a pursuit. If one now increased the concern about counterattacks to the point of advising the building of golden bridges for the fleeing enemy, then it is all the more evident that the commander would not easily find, in view of the situation, that it was advisable to fight a battle. In 1536, when Francis I, by simply waiting out the situation, had forced Charles V, who had arrived in the vicinity of Marseilles, to evacuate France and withdraw across the Alps, the French reproached the king for not having caused the emperor more harm during his retreat. Later,

Jovius questioned the king about this, and he answered that he had not entirely trusted his lansquenets, but that in addition he had also adhered to the principle of the ancients, to the effect that one must not only build bridges for the fleeing enemy but also cover them with gold.

Frederick ignored such considerations, but even under his conditions the strategic offensive was short. On only one occasion at the most did he make a demonstration from afar against Vienna, the enemy capital, but he never considered it the goal of his operations. Prague (55 miles from the passes of the Erzgebirge) and Olmütz (37 miles from the border of Upper Silesia) were his real objectives. Even to go as far as Brünn, 47 miles south of Olmütz, seemed a very great undertaking, and the fact that in 1744 he went on 70 miles beyond Prague, to Budweis, he himself later acknowledged to be a mistake.

The French, of course, moved as far as Linz and Prague in the War of the Austrian Succession. But their base was not France but Bavaria, with which land they were allied.

If the strategic offensive was short and slow, it followed that it could easily turn over to a defensive or be forced into the defense. Offensive and defensive quickly alternated with one another and merged together. The strategic attack was not capable of dominating the situation forcefully and continuously in one move.[22]

Practically the most important of all the consequences of this basic condition was the regular winter rest. The suffering a winter campaign imposed on the troops was very severe. To the losses resulting from hardships and illness were added the losses from increased desertions as the unreliable mercenaries found that too much was expected of them. If the commander believed that by continuing the military action to a conclusion, he could force a peace treaty, he was willing to accept such losses. But if there was no such prospect, he considered whether the losses were not more important than the gain to be anticipated, and since both sides were considering these same points, the military action gradually came to a standstill and the armies went into winter quarters. This was done on both sides by having the main forces pull back and secure themselves from possible surprise attacks with outposts and observation. Indeed, sometimes they even reached an agreement to renounce any attacks for a specified period. The battle of Lützen and the battle of Leuthen were both dominated by the thought of winter quarters. Wallenstein, like Charles of Lorraine, believed that the campaign for that year was finished, when it was reported that the enemy was approaching, whereupon, without any positive idea of a battle, the army was deployed in a defensive position (6 November and 5 December). Sometimes a campaign was continued not only into December but even into January in order to gain some advantage or other. Frequently, the new campaign did not begin until June, so that green forage could be found in the fields for the horses.

The winter campaigns which did occur are to be regarded as exceptions.[23] The winter rest period was used to restore the army in every respect, especially to levy, to recruit, and to impress new recruits (if they were in enemy territory, recruits were even taken there), and to drill them so that they could be incorporated in the units at the beginning of the new campaign. The regiments had no special units for the training of the replacements; their functions were, so to speak, replaced by the winter rest, and one had the advantage of being able to send all who were militarily fit together into the field.

In all conduct of war the unexpected and chance play a large role, and the mastering of this dark element of uncertainty through decisiveness is one of the most important qualities of the commander. This factor became especially strong in Frederick's period because the extended, thin lines of infantry were so completely brittle. A battle could be decided in a very short time, in a moment. They did not have the possibility, through holding action, to gain more time in which to bring up reinforcements, correct errors, or break contact without serious losses.[24] Seldom was the terrain so completely in view that the commander could take it all in from afar. There could be obstacles hidden in it—ponds, swamps, cliffs—which would break up his formation and necessarily destroy the good order of the troops and lead to loss of the battle. Should the commander let the battle develop? Such a decision is very difficult. Later, I shall present examples.

Even if the enemy made an error or otherwise offered a favorable opportunity for a battle, in Frederick's period it was still difficult to exploit the opportunity, since of course the battles with linear tactics required a complete, close-ordered deployment and therefore did not allow easy improvisation. If Soor and Rossbach were improvised battles, for that very reason they are to be considered as special evidence both for the genius of the royal commander and the tactical training of his army.

Let us survey the ideas of the theoreticians from the sixteenth to the eighteenth century.

G. du Bellay recommended in 1535 that a general should never risk a battle if he was not completely convinced of having the advantage. Otherwise, he should temporize.

Lazarus Schwendi (1522–1584) claims that in war one should base his game on security and not risk too much, even when he has good chances. "Whoever can outlast or starve out the enemy by force acts foolishly if he seeks a battle. But whoever is fighting a stronger opponent, against whom he cannot hold out long, has all the more reason for having to trust to luck and risk a battle." "He who limits himself to the defensive has much to lose and little to win."

The Spaniard Mendoza wrote in 1595 (*The Art of War [Kriegskunst,* German translation, p. 146]):

Furthermore, one should also most diligently see to it that he does not start a battle, even if he should be driven to it by the most extreme necessity, and that he should not lead all his squadrons into the fight, that even if one has already gained the victory, one still does not have much to rejoice over because it has cost him so dearly and so many men; but one should creep toward the battle slowly, thoughtfully, and with a leaden foot.

In 1607 William Louis of Orange advised his cousin Maurice: "We should conduct our affairs in such a way that they not be subjected to the hazard of a battle. . . . not to move to battle except as a matter of extreme necessity."[25] He bases this concept on Fabius Maximus before the battle of Cannae.

Dilich, *Kriegsbuch,* Part 2, Book 1 (1607) warns: "Without severe need and absolutely certain advantage, one should never accept battles, as they have an uncertain and harmful outcome, for it is much better to conquer nothing than to suffer harm and lose something." With this, however, he does not mean to say that one should not fight at all; that would be foolishness. But he says one can fight advantageously after praying, in a good season, when damp air does not make the powder wet, when the enemy is tired but we are still fresh, or some other good opportunity presents itself.

J. de Billon recommended in 1612 to a commander (*The Foremost Principles of the Art of War [Die fürnembsten Hauptstücke der Kriegskunst],* German translation, 1613, p. 160):

He is never to lead his soldiers into a field battle unless he has previously trained and instructed them, but he should preferably wear the enemy down, overpower and conquer him by various movements and detours, rather than by the uncertain luck of a battle, which is such a dangerous thing that one should not allow himself to be drawn into it unless absolutely necessary and after his soldiers have become accustomed to fighting and dangers and are hardened, for this is a kind of game in which newcomers find themselves very frightened.

"Conde de Bucquoi has this credit, that he does not like to lead his soldiers to slaughter," states a brochure of the year 1620.[26]

Neumair von Ramsla, a very prolific military author of the period of the Thirty Years' War, raised the question of when a battle should be fought. He listed fifty-five reasons, among which was "when one sees that there is no other means of helping the situation."

Montecuccoli (1609–1681) wrote:

Whoever believes he can make progress without battles and can conquer anything worthwhile contradicts himself or at least expresses such a fantastic opinion that he evokes ridicule. I know, of course, that Lazarus Schwendi, a famous general, claimed that one should never risk an engagement and that he intended to proceed only defensively and steal the advantages from the enemy to a certain degree [Schwendi did not really go to this extreme of caution!— Delbrück]. But when the troops first became aware of that, how great would be their fear and how great would the boldness of the enemy become! It is absolutely necessary that one be prepared to fight and to contest the field. Of course, one should never allow oneself to be drawn into battle unthinkingly and rashly and all the less allow oneself to be forced into it, but one should recognize the right moment for it. Fabius Cunctator in no way fled from battle, but he intended to fight only when he had reasonable hope for victory.

And in another passage Montecuccoli wrote (1:328):

Whoever wins a battle wins not only the campaign but also a large piece of territory. Consequently, whenever someone knows how to appear for battle only in good formation, the errors that he has made previously in maneuvering are to be tolerated, but if he has violated the teachings of the battles, even if he had proven himself in other respects, he would still not bring the war to an end with honor.

Turenne once advised Condé that it was better to harm the enemy in the field by many fights than to besiege and capture cities.

Daniel Defoe in his *Essay on Projects* (1697; translation by Fischer, p. 118), claims that in the English civil war one still had the maxim "Defeat the enemy wherever you find him," but that now it was a question of "Never fight without obvious advantages." Consequently, he says, wars are drawn out in length, and the result is that it is not the man with the longest sword but the one with the largest purse who best withstands the war.

The campaign diary of Margrave Ludwig von Baden for 1694 states concerning an operation: "His Serene Highness was firmly resolved, in case the enemy was so inclined, to allow himself to be drawn into a decisive engagement with him. Consequently, through this desire it was made clear to his enemies that he was resolved to fight rather than allow his otherwise weakened fatherland to plunge into complete ruin." The result was a few reconnaissances.[27]

Feuquières (1648–1711) wrote military memoirs which Frederick the Great prized so highly that he assigned them to his officers for reading and ordered that they should be read aloud to the cadets at their meals. His own military writings are often closely parallel to those of Feuquières. The latter wrote:

> Because battles are the principal action of an army and often determine the outcome of the whole war or at least almost always of the campaign, one should not wage them unless it is demanded by the seriousness of the situation and important causes exist. The reasons for seeking out the enemy and fighting with him are: when one is superior to him in the number and quality of one's troops; when the enemy generals are not in agreement or have different interests, or show little capability and alertness; when it is a question of relieving a besieged place; when there is concern that the army will break up unless one forestalls that with a success or when the enemy is about to be reinforced; when one has already derived benefits from fighting; and finally when one believes one can suddenly bring an end to the entire war by means of a battle. On the other hand, one is moved to avoid an engagement when one must fear that one will receive less benefit from a victory than one would loss from a defeat; when one is not equal to the enemy, either in numbers or ability; when one is oneself awaiting reinforcements; when one finds the enemy advantageously deployed or has hopes of finding a means of breaking up the enemy army through delay and avoidance of engagements.

The Spanish marquis of Santa Cruz (1687–1732) wrote a large military work (*Reflections*), in which he spoke "of the occasions when one must seek to fight." Neither superiority in numbers nor higher quality of the troops, he believes, is a sure means against the various chance circumstances that can cause a defeat. "Nothing is more uncertain than the outcome of a battle. . . . You may not risk any battle if the position is not very favorable or if you do not know exactly the strength of the two armies."

Prince Eugene applauded this theoretician, and Frederick regarded him as one of the "classical" authors of military literature.

Marshal Puységur (1654–1743), in his *Art de la guerre* (published by his son in 1748), which was highly esteemed because of its systematic treatment, nevertheless did not establish any basic consideration as to when a battle had to be fought. But it is characteristic of his observations that he classified Turenne with Caesar as a commander and did not notice the intrinsic difference between the strategies of the two men.

Folard (born 1669) wrote, and Frederick the Great copied this passage in the extract he made: "The greatest ancient and modern leaders have never counted the enemy but only asked where they were in order to march toward them and fight them."[28]

Count Khevenhüller (1683–1744), an Austrian field marshal, wrote a *Short Concept of All Military Operations (Kurtzer Begriff aller militär-ischen Operationen)* in which he develops the reasons "for waging or avoiding battle": I. 1. Hope of victory; 2. to relieve a besieged city; 3. to support a corps under attack; 4. to relieve a shortage of rations or the exhaustion of other necessities; 5. to allow the enemy no time for rein-forcements; 6. to profit from an advantage over the enemy, for example, when he offers a flank on the march, in a pass, or when he has split his army, and for other similar reasons. II. Reasons for avoiding battle: 1. when a loss of the battle can cause a greater loss than the profit to be gained from a victory; 2. when the enemy has superior strength; 3. when one does not have all his forces assembled; 4. when the enemy has an advantageous position. N.B. The enemy often defeats himself as a result of a lack of leadership or discord in his leadership. And in another passage:

> When the commander, through his movements, can cause the enemy to move about and back and forth from one position to another and from one camp to another and is able to realize at the right moment his advantage, to defeat him, then one realizes what the art of war really is.

The polarity of the strategy of attrition appears with special clarity in the various utterings of Frederick the Great. Throughout his life they move up and down like waves, first approaching the one pole and then the other.

Before the battle of Hohenfriedberg in 1745 he wrote that he was obliged to fight it because no alternative remained. In a letter to the marshal of Saxony (3 October 1746), he admits his responsibility for having lost the campaign of 1744 by proceeding much too rashly; he said, however, having learned from experience, he would not do that again. "A Fabius can always turn into a Hannibal; but I do not believe that a Hannibal is capable of following the conduct of a Fabius."

In the *General-Prinzipien vom Kriege* (1748), it is stated in the chapter entitled "When and How One Should Wage Battles" ("Wann und wie man Bataillen liefern soll"):

> Battles decide the fate of a nation; when one wages war, one must, of course, come to decisive moments, either to withdraw from the

embarrassment of the war, or to place his enemy in similar embarrassment, or to settle the quarrels which would otherwise never come to an end.

A reasonable man must never make a move without having a good reason for it; and even less must the general of an army *ever wage battles without seeking an important purpose through them.*

Consequently, the reasons for which one fights battles are to force the enemy to lift the siege of a place belonging to you or to drive him from a province that he has occupied; furthermore, to penetrate into his own country, or to carry out a siege, and finally to break his stubborn resistance when he is unwilling to make peace, or to punish him for an error that he has committed.

One obliges the enemy to fight when one makes a forced march which brings one into his rear and cuts him off from those of his forces that are farther back, or when one threatens a city which the enemy is extremely interested in holding. But let one be very careful in making these types of maneuvers with the army, and let one be no less careful not to bring oneself into the same disadvantageous situation nor to take position in such a way that the enemy for his part can cut you off from your depots.

To all these maxims I add the point that our wars must be short and active, inasmuch as it is not suitable for us to drag things out, because a lengthy war subtly causes our admirable discipline to decline and would depopulate the country and exhaust our resources. . . . In a word, in matters relating to battles one must follow the maxim of the Hebrew Sanhedrin to the effect that it is better that one person die than the whole people be ruined.

In the *Art de guerre* (around 1750) it is stated (10:268): "And never engage without strong reasons in these fights where death makes frightful harvests."

In the *Thoughts and General Rules for War (Pensées et règles générales pour la guerre)*, 1755, no doubt written in view of the gathering storm, there is no direct recommendation to seek a decision by battle. On the contrary, in the article on campaign plans it is said that a good plan of campaign can decide the outcome of the war as a result of the advantages "which either your fighting forces, or time, or a position that you first take possession of, guarantee you." It goes on to state: "The value of a war plan lies in the fact that you yourself risk but little but put the enemy in danger of losing everything."

In 1753 Frederick had that extract from the great work of Folard prepared for his officers and personally wrote an introduction in which he said that only a few classical works were available in which one could study the art of war. "Caesar teaches us in his *Commentaries* little more than what we see in Pandour warfare; his move to Great Britain is hardly anything different, and a general of our time could use from Caesar only the employment of his cavalry on the day of Pharsalus." This expression sounds so nonsensical that we do not know at first what to make of it. But if we seek to understand it, we recognize in it the reaction of a clear and practical mind, a mind that does not let itself be bound by traditional sources, opposing a false doctrinairism. As we have seen, the theoreticians of the period wanted to force Caesar into the scheme of the strategy of attrition. Frederick noted that that was not correct; he was aware of the error, could not, of course, discover its source, and reacted against the uneasiness that this knowledge caused him by making the comparison with the Pandour warefare.

In the *Observations on the Military Talent and the Character of Charles XII (Betrachtungen über das militärische Talent und den Charakter Karls XII.)*, which was written in the fall of 1759, it is stated that the king could have limited bloodshed on a number of occasions:

There are, of course, situations where one has to fight; but one should decide to do this only if one has less to lose than to win, if the enemy either in his camps or on his marches is negligent, or if one can force him by a decisive blow to accept peace. Furthermore, it is definitely true that most generals who let themselves be easily drawn into a battle resort to this solution only because they do not know what else to do. Far from considering this as a credit to them, we regard it rather as the sign of a lack of genius.

In the introduction to the *History of the Seven Years' War (Geschichte des Siebenjährigen Krieges)*, the king designates Daun's method as "the unquestionably good one" and goes on to say:

. . . a general would be wrong if he insisted on attacking the enemy in mountainous positions or irregular terrain. The pressure of the circumstances has sometimes obliged me to resort to this extreme; but when one wages war with equal forces, one can create for himself certain advantages through ruses and cleverness without exposing oneself to very great dangers. If many small advantages can be gained, the sum of them makes for large ones. Furthermore, an attack against a well-defended position is a difficult task; one can easily be thrown back and defeated. If one wins with a sacrifice of 15,000 or 20,000 men, that makes serious inroads into an army. The recruits, even assuming that you have enough of them, replace the number of soldiers that you have lost but do not replace their quality. The country becomes depopulated as it renews the strength of the army. The troops degenerate, and if the war lasts a long time, one finally finds oneself at the head of poorly trained and poorly disciplined peasants with whom you hardly dare to appear before the enemy. In a bad situation one may courageously free oneself from the rules; only necessity can drive us to desperate means, just as one gives to the sick an emetic when there is no other medication left. But with the exception of this case, I believe one must proceed with more concern for conserving one's forces and act only with good reasons, because in war he who leaves the least to chance is the wisest.

Five years later (1768), in his military testament, the king developed the same ideas with even stronger emphasis on the advantages of the strategy of maneuver. He stated:

It is a great error to believe that battles in the open field are not just as risky as in fixed positions. On the open plain the cannon has a frightful effect, and the bad point is that if you attack the enemy, all his batteries are already emplaced, and he can fire on you when you are just emplacing yours; that makes a huge difference.

He said that he would conduct the next war against the Austrians in the following manner:

I would first conquer enough land to enable me to procure provisions, to live at the expense of the enemy, and to select as the theater of operations terrain that is most favorable for me; I would hasten to fortify my defensive line before the enemy could appear in the vicinity. I would have the terrain reconnoitered as far in all directions as patrols can be sent out; I would as quickly as possible have maps made of all the areas that would be suitable to serve our opponents as a camp, as well as all the routes that could lead into those areas. In this way I would obtain knowledge of the country, and my maps would clarify for me those positions that can be attacked and those that are unassailable, in which the Austrians might consider forming up. I would not be concerned with starting general fights, because one can conquer a position only with considerable losses and because in mountainous country pursuits cannot be decisive; but I would secure my camp strongly; I would fortify it with great care and would direct all my plans toward defeating thoroughly the enemy's detachments, for if you destroy one of his detached corps, you cause confusion in his whole army, since it is much easier to crush 15,000 men than to defeat 80,000, and while you are risking less, you are still accomplishing almost the same thing.

He said that to attack an enemy in a good position was like wanting to lead peasants armed with sticks against well-armed men.

In the "Campaign Plans" ("Projets de campagne") of 1775 the king wrote: "*Never wage a battle only for the purpose of conquering the enemy, but in order to follow plans that would be blocked without this decision.*"

There exist no kinds of utterances by the king in which he moves out of the polarity of the strategy of attrition. The French minister Choiseul, the French plenipotentiary in the Austrian headquarters, Montazet, the Austrian minister Kaunitz, and Emperor Francis I himself all expressed in different ways the principle that it was a question of destroying Frederick's army, and one can interpret that as an indication of the strategy of annihilation. Emperor Francis wrote to his brother, Charles of Lorraine, on 31 July 1757: "We must not think of the conquest of land but only of the destruction of his army, for if we can ruin his army, the lands will automatically fall to us." We never find such a statement by Frederick. On the contrary, General Lloyd and others established at that time the proposition that one could undertake military operations with geometrical strictness and wage war continuously without ever arriving at the necessity for fighting. This concept, too, is not to be found in Frederick's writings. He approaches the battle pole of his strategy with the idea that Prussia's wars had to be short and active and that the fate of wars would be decided in battles. He again approaches the maneuver pole by describing his battles as desperate expedients and adopts the proposition that waging battles was a sign of lack of intelligence, and he recommends the cutting off of detachments instead of battles. But it would be completely false to claim to see a possible self-contradiction in this discrepancy. In Machiavelli, who simultaneously pointed out the principles of the strategy of annihilation and the strategy of attrition, there resides a definite, unresolved contradiction. Frederick represented in a completely clear and indisputable manner the attitudes of the strategy of attrition, in the nature of which lies the possibility that, according to the circumstances or perhaps even mere moods, the one method or the other receives more emphasis or is employed. Frederick himself often expressed the point that he followed the very same principles as the great French commanders Turenne, Condé, Catinat, Luxembourg, or Prince Eugene and Leopold von Dessau.[29] We may add all generals and all the theoreticians from Vegetius on, with the single exception of Machiavelli, whose ideas were self-contradictory.

If we seek a theoretical difference between Frederick and his contemporaries, it is to be found in the fact that Frederick, at the height of his military activity, from 1757 to 1759, approached the battle pole more closely than did most. We may not say more than did all, for we have seen that there are even utterances that go beyond his.

Pure theory, however, was inclined to give the advantage to maneuver. "A battle," says the regulations of the elector of Saxony in 1752, "is the most important and most dangerous operation of war. In open country without a fortress the loss of a battle can be so decisive that it is seldom to be risked and never to be recommended. The masterpiece of a great general is to achieve the final purpose of a campaign by alert and safe maneuvers without danger."

In May 1759, at the urging of the king, Prince Henry made an incursion into Franconia and destroyed the depot of the imperial army. Retzow remarks on that point that this success "must have been more valuable to the king than a victorious battle. For after a battle, an enterprising general, even though defeated, can still assemble such a force in short order as to avenge the defeat he suffered; only after the complete loss of sufficient provisions is it impossible to think of any operation of importance."

Between the Renaissance and Frederick the Great, the tactics of all arms underwent changes that gave them a completely new face from period to period. The close, deep squares of infantry became long thin lines; the heavy knights on powerful horses who sought to fight in tournament fashion became closely formed cavalry squadrons attacking at a gallop; and the artillery increased a hundredfold in numbers and effectiveness. In these three centuries, however, strategy remained the same in its basic principles. When Guicciardini describes for us how the Spanish viceroy maneuvered before the battle of Ravenna in 1512 in order to cover the cities of the Romagna against the French and to block the French from the road to Rome, what a role the providing of rations played in those maneuvers, how events finally led to the battle, and how the great victory of the French still had no lasting effect in the long run, all these things could just as easily have been recounted of a campaign of the seventeenth or eighteenth century.

In order for another strategy to be able to appear, the world political picture had to experience a change that was complete and in depth.

NOTES FOR CHAPTER IV

1. It will be worth the trouble to note that, hand in hand with the new period of strategy, there also appeared the use of an aid that became increasingly important with the passage of time, the use of maps. Jovius relates that before the battle of Marignano in 1515 there were laid out for the Swiss leaders in the castle of Milan parchment sheets on which

were drawn the roads and adjoining areas. "Membranae in medium pro-
latae, quibus mensurae itinerum et regionis situs pictura describebantur,
ut agreste ingenio homines certius deliberata cognoscerent." ("Parch-
ments were published, on which the distances of the routes and a picture
of the structure of the region were drawn, so that even men with untrained
ability might know the plans more definitely.") It is noteworthy that in
this way attempts were made to assist the peasants' lack of education.

2. Jähns, 2:1151.

3. "He who has the last piece of bread and the last crown is victorious." Gaspard (Jean) de Saulx-Tavannes, *Mémoires*, Ed. Buchon, 1836.
p. 226. Mendoza, p. 11: "Consequently, it is customarily said that the
last crown or penny holds the victory."

When Frederick planned to begin the war in 1756, he estimated that
each campaign would cost him 5 million talers and that Prussia together
with Saxony, which he planned to conquer, could afford that. The expenses increased, however, to 15 million talers annually, and he had to
request English subsidies. Maria Theresa waged war essentially with French
subsidies, but in 1761 she had used up her resources so completely that
even during the continuing war she reduced the army and discharged
troops for reasons of economy.

4. These passages are to be found in "Frederick the Great's Ideas on
War" ("Friedrichs des Grossen Anschauungen vom Kriege"), Vol. 27 of
the *Kriegsgeschichtliche Einzelschriften*, p. 268.

5. Jochim, "The Military Testament of the Great King" ("Das militärische Testament des Grossen Königs"), supplement to the *Militär-
Wochenblatt*, 1914, pp. 269, 278.

6. Lenz, *Historische Zeitschrift*, 49:458.

7. *Schmalkaldic War (Schmalkaldischer Krieg)*, German edition, 1853,
p. 90.

8. Even before the start of the Schmalkaldic War, the Venetian ambassador reported that the emperor would not fight any battle. In this
connection he noted: ". . . Protestants do not have captains . . . the
German nation alone is not suitable to do battle on its own with determination, and the emperor will avoid that but will probe and encircle the
enemy army with his light cavalry, and with the Italian infantry (which
is experienced in the business of war) he will attempt to drive them back,
wear them out, and annihilate them." Bern. Navagero, *Report from Germany of July 1546 (Relation aus Deutschland vom Juli 1546)*, Ed. Albèri,
Series 1, 1:362.

9. Viktor Löwe, *The Organization and Administration of Wallen-
stein's Armies (Die Organisation und Verwaltung der Wallensteinschen
Heere)*, 1895. Reviewed by Schrötter in *Schmollers Jahrbücher*, 1895,
Vol. 19, Book 4, p. 327. Konze, "The Strengths etc. of Wallenstein's
Army in 1633" ("Die Stärke usw der Wallensteinschen Armee im Jahre

1633"), Bonn dissertation, 1906. Hoeniger, "The Armies of the Thirty Years' War" ("Die Armeen des 30jährigen Krieges"), supplement to the *Militär-Wochenblatt*, 1914, Vol. 7, claims that at the climax of the war, when Gustavus Adolphus and Wallenstein stood facing one another, on both sides together there was a total of between 260,000 and 280,000 men under arms. That estimate is certainly somewhat high. Hoeniger gave too high a strength to the armies, especially at Nuremberg.

10. According to Deuticke, *Schlacht bei Lützen*, p. 52.

11. For the train and rations among the Swiss, see Elgger, *Military System of the Swiss (Kriegswesen der Schweizer)*, p. 117 ff.

12. Jähns, pp. 502, 505.

13. Jähns, p. 521.

14. Knaake, *Contributions to the History of Emperor Charles V (Beiträge zur Geschichte Kaiser Karls V.)*, Stendal, 1864, p. 11.

15. Spont, *Revue des questions d'histoire*, 22 (1899):63.

16. See also Rudolf Schmidt, *Schlacht bei Wittstock*, p. 49. Letter of Field Marshal Hatzfeld. Also p. 57.

17. Daniels, *Preussische Jahrbücher*, 78:487. In 1757, when Cumberland's army was marauding because of a shortage of rations, he ordered that the high provost was to have hanged without ceremony every soldier caught in the act. A priest accompanied him as he rode about, in order to comfort the poor sinners before they went to hell. Daniels, *Preussische Jahrbücher*, 77:478.

18. Montecuccoli, *Writings (Schriften)*, 2:122, states that in 1648 the Swedes held nine fortresses in Silesia. They had won them very easily, since they were not occupied, and they had then developed the insignificant older works. For this reason Montecuccoli advises that one should demolish all the old, unimportant fortresses and hold only a few really good fortresses, or have only open cities. He anticipates garrisons of only 100 to 500 men, except for Prague, which was to have 1,500. On page 135 he explains how the many fortresses were detrimental to the Spaniards in the Netherlands because they could not satisfactorily occupy and feed all of them, whereas they were useful for the Netherlanders because they were naturally strong positions and the inhabitants themselves provided the necessary defenders.

19. Printed in the *Preussische Jahrbücher*, 153(1913):423.

20. Henckel, *Military Testament (Militärischer Nachlass)*, 2:79.

21. This is excellently described in the *Kriegsgeschichtliche Einzelschriften*, 27:364. On 23 December 1757 Colonel Marainville reported of Frederick's tactics: ". . . he does not follow up his advantages. When he wins battles, he limits himself almost always to possession of the battlefield." Quoted in Stuhr, *Research and Clarifications of the History of the Seven Years' War (Forschungen und Erläuterungen zur Geschichte des 7jährigen Krieges)*, 1:387.

22. This, too, is excellently described in the *Kriegsgeschichtliche Einzelschriften*, 27:353.

23. Details on winter quarters or winter campaigns in Frederick's *General-Prinzipien*, Articles 27 and 28.

24. Here, too, as we have already seen above in the quotation from Höpfner (p. 279), is a reason for the oblique battle formation.

25. *Archives of Orange-Nassau*, 2d Series, 2:378.

26. Quoted in Krebs, *Battle on the White Mountain (Schlacht am weissen Berge)*, p. 12.

27. *The Campaigns of Prince Eugene (Die Feldzüge des Prinzen Eugen)*, 1:1:587.

28. According to the citation in *Kriegsgeschichtliche Einzelschriften*, 27:385.

29. Letter to Louis XV dated 12 July 1744. Letter to the prince of Prussia forwarding the *General-Prinzipien*.

Chapter V

Strategic Sketches and Individual Battles

BATTLE OF HÖCHSTÄDT[1]
13 AUGUST 1704

The numerical superiority of Louis XIV at the outbreak of the War of the Spanish Succession was so great that he was justified in entertaining ideas of completely subjecting the enemy similar to those of Napoleon. Allied with Elector Max Emanuel of Bavaria, he could plan assembling armies from Italy and Germany in order to drive against Vienna.

Eventually, however, the opponents gained superiority when Marlborough, against the will of his government, marched to the Danube with an English-Dutch army.

There the two sides maneuvered around each other for a considerable time. While the allies struck a heavy blow against the Bavarians by storming the Schellenberg, which enabled them to cross the Danube at Donauwörth, it was nevertheless all the more difficult to arrive at a great decisive battle, because on both sides the high command was divided. On the one side the command was shared by Marlborough and Louis of Baden, who were then joined by Prince Eugene with a third army. On the other side the two commanders, Elector Max Emanuel and the French Marshal Marsin, were joined by Tallart with a third army.

When the united French and Bavarians had taken an unassailable position before Augsburg, the allies, although much stronger, could think of nothing else to do than lay waste systematically the Bavarian countryside in order to force the elector to come to terms as a result of the misery of his people.

Since the elector stood fast, it appeared that Marlborough's army would finally have to be called home. In order to do something further, it was decided to besiege Ingolstadt with a detached corps. But when the French-Bavarian army made a countermove, Eugene and Marlborough decided to take advantage of the immediate opportunity and attack the opposing army before it had fortified its new position. "The hazardous condition of our affairs," wrote Marlborough, "requires such a powerful, if not to say desperate, solution."

In this expression the essence of the strategy of attrition is all the more apparent in that the allies only needed to pull back the corps designated for the siege of Ingolstadt, 14,000 men, in order to have a considerable numerical superiority (62,000 against 47,000). It has been thought that they had done without those 14,000 men just to get rid of their commander, Louis of Baden, with whom the other two got along very poorly. This reason, very questionable in itself, is contradicted by the fact that initially Eugene was designated to command the siege. During this period we shall find still more instances where corps of considerable importance were diverted to secondary missions and remained unavailable for a decisive battle.

The allied commanders were victorious with only a very small numerical superiority, essentially because of their superior leadership. The French and Bavarians were surprised by the attack and had not yet completed their field fortifications. Their position was not disadvantageous; Eugene was unable to advance against the enemy left, north, flank, which he was supposed to envelop, and when the first attacks were repulsed, a strong follow-up by the defenders and a shift into the attack would have offered them very good chances of success. As we have known since Marathon, there is indeed no stronger type of combat than the defense that goes over to the attack at the right moment. But this requires a great commander. The French Marshal Tallart, who was commanding at the critical spot in the center, was not only not such a general, but he also did not have at his disposal those parts of the army under his two colleagues, which would necessarily have had to take up the offensive with him. They had intended for the battle to be nothing but a defensive one; consequently, the villages of Blindheim (Blenheim) and Ober-Glauheim were so strongly occupied that no reserves were left for the offensive.[2]

Under these circumstances, Marlborough's cool vigilance succeeded, after the first attacks were beaten back, in effecting a shift of troops and pushing through between the two villages with great numerical superiority, breaking up the enemy center so that the two villages could now also be threatened and attacked from the rear. The garrison of Blindheim finally had to capitulate.

It should be noted that on the Schellenberg as at Höchstädt, the attack took place while the defensive forces were still occupied with their work on the field fortifications.

BATTLE OF TURIN[3]
7 SEPTEMBER 1706

The French besieged Turin and covered their siege with an army that was pushed out as far as the Etsch and Lake Garda. Prince Eugene assembled a somewhat stronger army, moved around the French, maneuvered them back, and with 34,000 men he marched to Turin on the south side of the Po in unusually fast marches (260 kilometers in sixteen days in frequent contact with the enemy). The duke of Modena provided him some rations. At the same time the French, who were supposed to repel him at the Etsch, arrived under the duke of Orleans, and the two armies were now of approximately equal strength, some 40,000 men. Consequently, the French felt too weak to attack the relief army and at the same time continue the siege of Turin. They sought to protect themselves against the relief force with a field fortification, a circumvallation.

The relief army, coming from the south, now moved around the besieging army until it came to a place in the northwest where the circumvallation, which was just started at the last minute, had not yet been finished. Here, between the two tributaries of the Po, the Dora and the Stura, the attack was set up with 30,000 men. The defensive forces in this sector were only 12,000 to 13,000 men strong. The allies moved up with no fewer than five or even six echelons in depth,[4] three of infantry and three of cavalry, and they finally broke through when they discovered that the right flank of the French position could be enveloped and taken from the rear through the shallow riverbed of the Stura. Now the entire line was rolled up. A sortie by the garrison of Turin also drove in and cut off the fleeing troops.

It was the troops of the duke of Orleans who were defeated, but the besieging troops under La Feuillade, as those in flight came by them, were also seized with panic and moved off toward France, unable to fight, having lost most of their cannon.

If La Feuillade had supported the duke of Orleans with even 6,000 men from his siege army, so that the duke could have formed a reserve, the Austrian attack would hardly have gained its objective. But La Feuillade did not believe that the enemy would really decide to attack the fortified line. Instead, he assumed that the enemy was only maneuvering in order to cut off supplies from the besiegers. Furthermore, he believed that the fall of the fortress, which was to be his personal accomplishment, was imminent, and he was unwilling to weaken the siege at any point. Marshal Marsin, however, who was the advisor to the young duke of Orleans, did not dare to oppose energetically La Feuillade, who was the son-in-law of Chamillart, minister of war and of finance, and who could have caused him great harm at court. Consequently, the French lost the battle because of the lack of a unified and alert leadership to an even more serious degree than they had lost the battle of Höchstädt two years earlier. On the contrary, on the other side the two commanders, Prince Eugene and his cousin, the duke of Savoy, worked together in an excellent way. Prince Eugene, who was completely lacking in egotism, even forbade that his name be mentioned in the message announcing the victory.

From this defeat of the French the theoreticians drew the conclusion that it was wrong in principle to plan to defend a siege army against a relief army by means of a circumvallation. A detailed study of the event teaches us that this conclusion is inadmissible, for the circumvallation was not attacked directly but was enveloped. Presumably, all the courage of the Prussians under Leopold of Dessau would have been in vain but for this envelopment. If the defense of the circumvallation had been well executed and led, it could have been carried out just as successfully as that of Alesia in an earlier day, and the decision of the two Savoyard cousins to risk the attack on the fortified position with a completely reversed front can be evaluated as a deed of the highest strategic boldness, an action truly demanded by fate.

1708

Marlborough's victory at Ramillies in 1706, exploited by an outstanding pursuit, had given Belgium over into the hands of the sea powers. But 1707 brought no further radical change, and in 1708, with the help of the inhabitants, who were embittered by the Dutch administration, the French won back Bruges and Ghent. Even a victory that Marlborough gained at Oudenarde on 11 July 1708 in a successful attack did not change the situation appreciably.[5] Although the English commander now proposed to push into the interior of France, a plan which has even been interpreted as an intention to attack Paris, Eugene at once opposed it, the Dutch could in no way have been won over to it, and Marlborough pointed out, in the same letter to his friend, Lord Godolphin, in which he reported all this (26 July),[6] how unpromising an advance on Paris would be: the inhabitants of the country-side would flee with their belongings into the fortified places, and the invader would enter a desert and encounter a series of fortresses positioned in a checkerboard arrangement. "If I could only lure the enemy army out for a fight!" The principal advantage of the victory of Oudenarde was, according to him, the shattering of the enemy army's morale.

Despite their defeat, therefore, the French maintained their position in Flanders and occupied Bruges and Ghent. The allies, who were unable to attack them there in their fortified places, decided to besiege Lille, and so they left the French main army behind them, so to speak. The siege of the city dragged along until deep in the winter, and after the fall of the city the siege of the citadel continued. The mighty French army moved up, marched around the besiegers in order to find a suitable place for an attack, but finally found the field fortifications with which the besiegers had covered themselves, the circumvallation line, unassailable. Even their repeated attempts to force the lifting of the siege by capturing supply transport failed, and when Lille had fallen, the allies also won back Flanders with Ghent and Bruges.

The accent of the campaign lies completely on the successfully executed siege and not on the preceding field battle, which is evaluated completely falsely if one considers the point that it was fought with a reversed front, that is, that it was based on the premise of a clear-cut result. Although he was the undoubted victor and although Prince Eugene's army was also approaching and was already nearby, and although he would also gladly have fought once more, Marlborough felt himself capable neither at once nor later of forcing a decisive battle under all circumstances and of exploiting a tactical success for the destruction of the enemy army. We are dealing here with a campaign of the strategy of attrition in the grand style, with the highest assemblage of forces on both sides. The allies won this campaign again through their leadership, the unity between Marlborough and Eugene on the one side, the lack of unity among the French commanders, the heir to the throne, the young duke of Burgundy, who was advised by Marshal Vendôme, who were also joined as a third and once again independent commander by the duke of Berwick. And so time and again the king's decision had to be sought, since he in fact expressly required that "no important decision be reached" without obtaining his orders. That presupposes a slowness in developments and in turn itself forces such a slowness, since it almost eliminates the challenge of great decisions and so enabled the allies to carry through their siege despite the proximity of the main enemy army that was lurking around them. Not battles, but positions and field fortifications brought results, without any battles being fought.

BATTLE OF MALPLAQUET[7]
11 SEPTEMBER 1709

Lille was a border city that had belonged to France for only forty years. But after its loss France felt so exhausted that Louis was willing to give up not only the real objective of his fight, the Spanish imperial monarchy for his grandson, but even Alsace. But the allies demanded from him such disgraceful concessions that he decided to fight on, and he placed in the field an army even stronger than the one of the previous year. The strategic mission of this army could be no other than to continue the war defensively, and the allies for their part also established no greater objective than to take other border fortresses, as they had taken Lille in the previous year. They first conquered Tournai and then turned against Mons, both of which, belonging to Belgium, were still in the possession of Louis. Marshal Villars, who had taken over the supreme command of the French, had been unable to prevent the fall of Tournai. When the allies now turned against Mons, he marched up as quickly as possible and would have had the possibility of attacking Marlborough while Eugene, who was in position on the other side of the fortress, was too distant to be of direct help. But Villars naturally did not know so exactly what the situation was on the other side. Marlborough was even bold enough to march toward him for a certain distance. Was France's last army to be risked? That would have been completely against the concepts and the intentions of the king. Villars therefore contented himself with occupying a position at the village of Malplaquet, which was so close to the fortress that the allies had first to drive him off in order to carry out the siege. The position, which of course was not naturally very favorable, was fortified as quickly as possible, and the allies allowed the French two complete days for this purpose so that they could first assemble all their available forces for the decisive battle. Finally, they had a superiority of some 110,000 against 95,000 French.

The battle was set up as a battle of the wings; the left wing of the French was to be attacked and enveloped with a greatly superior force, while a holding battle was to be fought opposite the center and the right wing with weaker forces. On the afternoon of the preceding day, according to some reports, several generals, including the crown prince of Prussia, Frederick William I, had started a conversation with French generals that lasted more than an hour and supposedly gave them the opportunity to survey the enemy fortifications. It can hardly be assumed that they saw something of importance, but their meeting and conversation itself in plain view of the armies that were deploying for the battle is characteristic of the soldierly spirit of the period: war and battles were for them a kind of intensified tournament.

The battle plan could not be carried through. The French position was a 3-kilometer-wide interval between two forests. While forests in front of the line or on the flanks hinder an attacker in his approach, they also conceal him. The allies had sent a large enveloping column through the forest on the northwest, but as such it was ineffective. It appears that it lost its way in the forest and was effective at the end only as a reinforcement of this wing. Thus the attack on this, the left flank of the French, against the very strong fortifications they had erected, could not penetrate. When the commander of the left flank of the allies, the crown prince of Orange, allowed himself to be drawn into making a sharp attack with his weak forces instead of the holding effort that he was supposed to conduct, he was thrown back in such a way that it would have been a simple matter for the French to overcome him completely with a counterattack. But the same fortifications which had been so advantageous for the defense hindered movement forward into the attack, and the brave Marshal Boufflers, who commanded at that point, was not able to decide on such an offensive from the purely defensive battle plan. And so the allies were still successful finally in gradually pushing the French back, so that they eventually evacuated the battlefield.

But the continuing attack against the fortifications had cost the allies no fewer than 30,000 killed and wounded, and the French, who had lost no more than some 12,000 men, moved no farther back than 5 miles from the battlefield and occupied a new position. They were no longer able to prevent the siege and the final loss of Mons. But with this loss they had continued the war for an entire year, and at its conclusion they were in a better situation than at the beginning. Tactically, Malplaquet was an unquestionable victory for the allies; strategically, however, as has been correctly said, in my opinion, the French remained the victors when one considers the campaign as a whole. This forms an inherent contradiction, but life is full of contradictions, and the strategy of attrition is especially so.

1710–1713

Malplaquet was the last large battle of the War of the Spanish Succession. The war continued for four more years as small border fortresses were besieged and captured. At first the allies held the upper hand in this activity, but then, as the English and Netherlanders left the emperor and made separate peace treaties, the French became dominant. They finally even crossed over the Rhine again, besieged and captured Freiburg, without Eugene's being able to prevent that.

1741[8]

Frederick had unexpectedly invaded and occupied Silesia and was in position with his troops on the border of Upper Silesia when the Austrians under Neipperg, with incredible boldness, appeared on an unguarded road in the midst of the Prussians and, basing their movements on the fortresses of Neisse and Brieg, which were still in their hands, they blocked the withdrawal route of the Prussian main body, which was under the command of the king himself. As Frederick himself later wrote

to Leopold of Dessau, there remained "no other possibility" than to
attack the enemy. The Prussians had almost twice as many infantry (18,000
against 9,800) and almost a threefold superiority in artillery (53 cannon
against 19), but they were much weaker in cavalry (4,600 against 6,800).[9]
As a result of the Austrian superiority in cavalry, the outcome of the
battle of Mollwitz (10 April) was very much in doubt for a while. The
Austrian horsemen had driven the Prussian cavalry from the battlefield,
and "old officers saw," as Frederick wrote in his memoirs, "the moment
arrive in which this corps, without ammunition, would be forced to
surrender." In order at least to save the king personally, Field Marshal
Schwerin persuaded him to leave the battlefield and to try to move in an
arc around the Austrians and reach the Prussian troops that were in
position farther to the north in Silesia. When the reportedly very excited
king had left, however, Schwerin succeeded in having the infantry and
artillery move forward again, and the Austrians were obliged to give way
before the superior force of the constant rolling fire. Even though the
Austrian cavalry had defeated the Prussian horsemen, their formation had
been so broken up in that process that they could not attack the enemy
infantry in its closely formed units.

The fact that the right wing of the Prussians was in advance of the left
wing (see above, p. 276) apparently did not have any influence on the
outcome of the battle. Despite his defeat, Neipperg had freed Upper
Silesia of the Prussians, and with his base on the fortress of Neisse, he
held out in Silesia for the entire summer. Frederick, although his numerical superiority rose to no less than 60,000 against 25,000, did not
dare to attack him again.[10] He was also unable to maneuver him out of
his fortified positions. Instead, the king sought to continue the war politically by bringing the French into action against Maria Theresa. And
as soon as they arrived, he made the secret verbal armistice of Klein-
Schnellendorf with Neipperg, an agreement that turned over Neisse to
him after a feigned siege of fourteen days and promised the evacuation
of Lower and Middle Silesia.

In the *General Staff Work* Neipperg is severely criticized while Frederick is praised because on one occasion he marched almost 19 miles in
a day and based his operations from the start on a tactical decision.
Neipperg is accused (p. 82) of having acted completely in the traditional
method of the old school. We can see that this criticism is very strongly
influenced by Prussian patriotism. Neipperg, with his smaller forces, truly
accomplished everything humanly possible.

It is very remarkable how Neipperg succeeded in placing his forces at
Mollwitz on the Prussians' withdrawal route. Frederick was already outside the enveloped area, when he took a day of rest at Pogarell on the
ninth, and Neipperg took advantage of this day to march to Mollwitz
and again take position in front of the Prussians. As the reason for his

stopping, the king says in his letter to Dessau and in his memoirs that he did not believe he could use his infantry—that is, their muskets—in the wet, snowy weather. On the following day fortune had it that the weather had become clear and warmer, and we have seen that the infantry fire was, in fact, the decisive factor. In the *General Staff Work* these conditions, especially the marches, are not correctly described.

1742

If the Prussians with their great numerical superiority had overcome Neipperg's army in Silesia and had then marched on Vienna, the French would no doubt have joined them, and Vienna would have been captured. With the Prussians holding back, the French were too weak for such an operation. Nevertheless, they moved forward to Prague and captured the city. Now Frederick went into motion again, breaking the agreements of Klein-Schnellendorf.

It looked as if Austria would be divided up. Bohemia was to go to Bavaria and Moravia to Saxony. The French Marshal Broglie drew up an ambitious plan, by which the Austrian army at Tabor-Budweis was to be attacked simultaneously from all sides. But Frederick did not go along with this; he simply made a movement toward Moravia, where there were no enemy troops, and he began secret negotiations with Austria, since he was not at all anxious to have that country broken up, allowing Saxony to become large and France haughty.[11] From the strategic point of view, this winter campaign is interesting in that we see how it was possible for a contemporary of Frederick to conceive and propose a plan in the spirit of the strategy of annihilation, where the conditions for it seemed appropriate, and that it was precisely Frederick who—for political reasons—rejected the plan.

The battle of Chotusitz (17 May 1742) developed as the Austrians sought to make a sudden attack on the Prussian army, which was maneuvering back and forth, and were defeated in the attempt.[12]

Maria Theresa thereupon decided to cede to Frederick Upper Silesia as well as the areas turned over to him at Klein-Schnellendorf, in order to separate him from the French.

1744

After the Prussians had again departed and the English had come to the aid of the Austrians, the French were driven back across the Rhine, and it appeared that they would also have to give up Alsace again. Then the Prussian king took up arms for the third time, conquered Prague, and pushed into Southern Bohemia. The Austrians had to move back out of Alsace, but they did not attack the Prussians directly. Instead, they appeared north of the Prussians and cut off their line of communications. For his part, Frederick was not in a position to solve the problem by means of a battle. Although he had almost 20,000 cavalry, this cavalry was not suitable for combing the land and reconnoitering the enemy. For a long time Frederick was completely without information on the enemy, and when he finally found his foes confronting him, their position seemed too favorable for him to attack. He moved back to Silesia, giving up his ration wagons, and also evacuated Prague, sacrificing his heavy cannon. The withdrawal almost broke up his army. The soldiers deserted in masses. Without a battle and almost without fairly large skirmishes, Traun had won a brilliant victory, and Frederick resolved never again to push so deeply into enemy territory.

The *General Staff Work* and especially a lecture by Major von Rössler (supplement to the *Militär-Wochenblatt*, 1891, 3d issue) hold in high esteem the king's plans for attack from 1741 to 1744, which are supposed to breathe the very spirit of the strategy of annihilation. It is correct that in those years the king theoretically came his closest to the pole based on battle, that is, if one wishes, to the strategy of annihilation, but he still fell far short. Never was the enemy army designated as the specific objective of the attack. Only in very indefinite form, without its execution ever having come closer, appears the attack on Vienna in 1744, where the joining of all the allies and a victory over the Austrian army in South Bohemia is presumed but does not call for an immediate continuation of the march toward the enemy capital, which was only a little more than 90 miles away. Instead, the plan was to go into winter quarters and take up the march on Vienna in the following year. Then they were supposed to "place their foot on the enemy's throat," but already in the more specific execution of the idea (*Korrespondenz*, 3:135) it simply says: "Advance to the Danube and even proceed to the area of Vienna, if necessary." In addition to all this, it is not improbable that Frederick did not take the great plans so seriously, since of course he had no intention of destroying Austria, and in fact he avoided great decisive actions, even when the French proposed them to him.

The false basic concept of Frederick's strategy which underlies the *General Staff Work* naturally also produces individual errors again and again. Facts must constantly be bent or covered up, but the logical consequence finally leads to the point that the intended glorification turns into reproach, because no artifice any longer suffices to force Frederick's manner of operation into the assumed scheme. This situation is very well described with respect to 1744, and the king is defended against the criticism raised in the *General Staff Work* by Max Leitzke in "New Contributions to the History of Prussian Politics and Conduct of War in 1744" ("Neue Beiträge zur Geschichte der preussischen Politik und Kriegführung im Jahre 1744"), Heidelberg dissertation, 1898.

1745

If the Austrians had followed up their success of 1744 and continued the war through the winter, we can hardly see how Prussia could have saved herself. But a winter campaign surpassed the morale capabilities and material possibilities of the Austrians, and Frederick won time to reorganize his army with tireless activity. He now left the strategic initiative to his enemies and resolved to avenge the maneuver defeat of the previous year with a victory in battle. His loyal minister Podewils urgently recommended against trusting the fate of the nation to the uncertain outcome of a battle. But the king explained to him that there was no alternative; the battle was an emetic for a sick man. He could assume that the Austrians would attempt to break into Silesia from Bohemia in the spring, and he could then exploit the advantage that the mountainous border offered him. Instead of making an attempt to block the individual mountain passes (I remind the reader what we have said in the first volume of this work concerning Thermopylae and the blocking of mountain passes), he decided to leave the passes open in order to confront the Austrians in Silesia. But he had the mountains observed very carefully and made his preparations for all the various routes that the Austrians might take. Roads and bridges were inspected, and the troops were divided in such a way that they could join forces most rapidly facing the exit from a pass from which the united Saxon-Austrian army was seen to issue. For their part, the Austrians made an attempt to attack the Prussian army by surprise at Chotusitz by means of a night march. The attempt had failed because they had underestimated the difficulties of having an army deploy in a night march. They had not started the attack until eight o'clock in the morning, and by that time the Prussians had long been aware of their presence and were in position, and the corps commanded by the king himself, that first had to be called back from a further march, was again so close that it was able to intervene in timely fashion and decide the battle in favor of the Prussians. At Hohenfriedberg on 4 June, however, Frederick had taken his preparatory measures so well that he was able to attack the left wing of the enemy army as early as four o'clock in the morning. At nine o'clock the battle was already essentially over, and the enemy was in full retreat over the mountain. The victory was brilliant and was due solely to the leadership of the royal commander. The strategic concept, the careful preparation, and the decisiveness of the execution, all were outstanding. It is only with this victory that the high regard for Frederick as a military commander began. At Mollwitz Schwerin had still had to win the victory for him; at Chotusitz the king had commanded excellently, but this was not apparent, and the Austrians even argued that they had not been beaten. The year 1744 had ended with a complete failure. But now Hohenfriedberg gave the king a reputation which never again faded. And we cannot say, for example, that the king's triumph was facilitated by special errors on the part of the enemy. Of course, in order to protect themselves against a surprise attack, they would have had to occupy certain heights on the same evening they arrived and to seize the crossings of the Strigau stream. But they did not come out of the mountains onto their camp sites until the fall of night and hardly had the possibility of orienting themselves sufficiently on all sides. Perhaps the march across the mountain could have been hastened. But, after all, it was first necessary to see whether the Prussians might not be in position directly at the opening of the pass, in which case the troop units might have run individually into their hands. But if they had planned to rest the first night while still in the mountains in order to move down into the plain the next day with a shorter march, the danger would have become all the greater that the Prussians, from whom the movement could not remain hidden, would immediately attack the troops as they debouched from the pass. The idea that the Prussians could already be in position with their entire force before sunrise the next morning and could move into the attack can hardly have occurred to the Austrian commander, Charles of Lorraine. It was precisely this completely unexpected situation that showed the genius and imagination in the deed of the Prussian king. How greatly the value of the initiative in strategy is so usually esteemed! The battle of Hohenfriedberg has taught us that all such principles nevertheless have only a relative significance. Frederick was triumphant strategically precisely because he forced the initiative on his opponent and left the strategic offensive up to him, and the execution of this action proves to us that it resulted not from a lack of offensive spirit, but from wise calculation.

Frederick followed the retreating enemy for three days. Then the military action again came to a standstill. The Austrians took up a well-secured position behind the Elbe and the Adler, and the Prussians camped facing them throughout the entire summer, almost four months, without the situation leading to any considerable military action. We see how little in the long run was the material gain from such a great tactical success as Hohenfriedberg under the conditions of that period. At that battle Frederick's strength was already no less than that of the united Austrians and Saxons (about 60,000 men), he had caused them losses of 14,000 to 16,000 men and 80 cannon while losing 4,800 men himself, and so he was now considerably stronger. If he had been governed by the principles of the strategy of annihilation, he would now have pursued without letup the enemy, whose morale was shaken, and would have attacked him again as soon as possible. Since the Austrians had lost two-thirds of their artillery and now had only 41 cannon against 192 on the Prussian side, even an attack on the Adler-Elbe position would not seem impossible from the viewpoint of a modern critic, but even if it was, the position could still have been enveloped. But such ideas were all the further from the king's mind in that he had, of course, experienced in the previous year how dangerous it was for an army like his to penetrate deeply into enemy territory and cut itself loose from its supply base. His quartermaster, von der Goltz, had already urgently warned against even crossing the mountain and advancing on Bohemian territory, since he could not move the rations forward on farm wagons.[13]

It was not long before the strategic initiative, too, again fell to the Austrians. Frederick had to weaken his forces by sending off troops to Upper Silesia and the March, which was threatened by the Saxons. The Austrians, on the other hand, reinforced their troops. Their light units successfully prevented the Prussians from foraging. In September Frederick moved back to the Sudeten passes, but before he withdrew, Prince Charles made another attempt to defeat him. The Prussians, who were now only 22,000 strong, were in a camp at Soor, between the two passes of Trautenau and Nachod; the Austrian-Saxon army, with 39,000 men, was much stronger.

Prince Charles formed a plan to attack the Prussians by surprise in the same manner as at Chotusitz and Hohenfriedberg. His forces moved up cautiously toward the Prussians and sought to deploy during the night directly in front of their camp. On the morning of 30 September at five o'clock the king received the first report. But, as always, he was already up and had assembled his generals in order to issue the orders for the day. He immediately realized that a withdrawal was no longer possible, all the less so since the Prussians had at their disposal only narrow roads between forests and cliffs, and the main road to Trautenau was already in the hands of the Austrians. The only possible salvation was in an attack. On the spot the king ordered the deployment and a march toward the right flank in order to attack in two echelons with this wing, while the left wing, composed of a single echelon, initially remained refused. The orders of the king were carried out with the great speed made possible by the Prussian discipline.

If the Austrians had opened the attack at this moment with all the strength of their superior forces, we can hardly see how the Prussian army could have held its own. Berenhorst later wrote, "The Prussians were victorious, with a disdain for military art," to which Scharnhorst replied, "They were victorious by honoring the military art." Although

Prince Charles wanted to surprize the Prussians in their camp, he had not planned to attack them directly but waited for them to withdraw hastily, expecting this withdrawal would give him the opportunity to destroy them. The light troops of the Austrians were already on the other side of the Prussian camp, and they broke in and plundered it, capturing even the entire baggage of the king himself while he was leading his troops into the battle. It was this absolute decisiveness in combat that gave the Prussians the victory, and it was the Austrian commander's caution that caused his army to lose the battle.[14] Since they themselves were still involved in their deployment and initially planned to wait until its effects were felt, the Austrians allowed the Prussian attack to come on, and even the Austrian cavalry, which was closely pressed together on a ridge, allowed itself to be attacked in position by the Prussians instead of moving against them. It was thrown back by the Prussians, and the continuing Prussian attack from this flank supported their frontal attack so that the Austrian center was defeated and their right wing took up the retreat.

Just like Hohenfriedberg, Soor was a feat of leadership, decisiveness, and discipline. Nevertheless, the strategic result of Soor was even smaller than that of Hohenfriedberg. Both victories meant salvation from the most extreme emergency and danger but nothing more. We have here the astonishing fact, completely unthinkable in a strategy of annihilation, that the victor, after remaining on the battlefield for a few more days as a matter of honor, then took up the retreat. Frederick moved off to Silesia, and the Austrians, after their failure, moved back into the camp that they had previously occupied.

They also were not deterred, after a few weeks, from once again making a large attempt to move forward. The Saxons called upon them to operate with them through the Lausitz against Brandenburg, and only three days' march beyond the Saxon border of that time lay Berlin. Frederick cut off the movement by a flanking push from Silesia into the Lausitz on 21 November and ordered the aged Dessau, who was in position at Halle with a Prussian covering army, to move forward now against the Saxons.

From these movements there developed an extremely remarkable strategic situation. Prince Charles came marching up as fast as possible with the Austrian army from the northern corner of Bohemia in order to help the Saxons. The king of Prussia was on the north bank of the Elbe a short distance in front of Dresden, but he did not join forces with Dessau, who was marching up via Leipzig. Instead, he sent Dessau only 8,500 men under General Lehwaldt via Meissen. The king himself, with the main body of his army, believed it was necessary for him to maintain contact with Silesia and cover the supply depots and the road to Berlin. When Leopold attacked the Saxons on 15 December at Kesselsdorf, a short distance in front of Dresden, the Austrians were already directly behind them. In a few hours the two armies could have joined forces, and then Dessau would be lost. Frederick reproached him most severely, and this reproach is still repeated in the latest works, because he did not march more rapidly and made a detour toward Torgau. Detailed study, however, has shown that the old field marshal acted at every moment completely appropriately for the situation and his instructions, and the difference between his concept and that of the king was caused only by the great distance between the two, the slowness of communications, and the complexity of the situation.[15] It is unavoidable that friction will arise when cooperation is attempted from various areas. Frederick could have avoided the danger if, for the sake of the victory that he surely had in prospect, he had given up his security and contacts for a few days and had led not just Lehwaldt's corps, but his entire army across the Elbe to join forces with Dessau at Meissen. If Leopold had been beaten (and he had just barely the same strength as the enemy), Frederick said later in his memoirs, he would immediately have taken up the battle again with his army, placing the defeated battalions in the second echelon. We must say that in this case the king showed himself to be not only an adherent of the strategy of attrition but also a commander completely devoted to the principles of that strategy. If it was possible to unite the two armies afterward, that indicates that the importance of the secondary reasons that prevented joining forces before the battle and for the battle was overestimated. The battle hung on the razor's edge. If it had been lost, the critics would not have spared King Frederick and indeed could not have spared him. He himself stated often enough the principle that all available forces had to be drawn in for a battle. Nevertheless, he himself acted contrary to this principle not only here, but, as we shall see, later as well, and it was not only he, but, as we have already heard, the same has been said of Eugene and Marlborough at Höchstädt. It is precisely a question of which forces a commander considers he can spare from another location in order to bring them in for the battle. Commanders of the double-pole strategy evaluated these reasons completely differently from those commanders adhering to the single-pole strategy. And in this we therefore have the explanation for Frederick's conduct at Kesselsdorf.[16] Whether he overestimated the reasons for holding his army back in this particular case is a question of less interest.

FREDERICK AND TORSTENSSON

Let us compare the campaigns of Frederick outlined above with a few campaigns of Torstensson.[17]

After Torstensson took over the command of the Swedish army in the Altmark, he suddenly moved out from there (1642), marched through

Silesia to Moravia, conquered Glogau and Olmütz, occupied these fortresses with garrisons, and then moved back again and defeated an imperial army at Leipzig on 2 November 1642. The next year he moved again to Moravia, fell back without having been able to force a battle, and followed a command from his government to defeat Denmark. The imperial army under Gallas followed him as far as Holstein. Torstensson maneuvered it back again and invaded Bohemia with the intention of "seizing a post on the Danube" and then "working back" to his base ("line of communications"). The imperial forces pulled their troops together; Saxony and Bavaria, too, the latter commanded by John of Werth, joined them, and events led to the battle of Jankau on 6 March 1645. The forces on both sides were approximately equal; the imperial forces under Hatzfeld had 5,000 infantry, 10,000 cavalry, and 26 cannon; the Swedes had 6,000 infantry, 9,000 cavalry, and 60 cannon. Both sides fought with the greatest gallantry. The Swedes won the victory as a result of their superior, sure leadership, because the imperial troops had accepted battle on terrain that was unfavorable for cavalry, the arm in which they were superior, and several generals acted on their own initiative in a manner contrary to the intentions of the commander.[18]

Torstensson moved up to the gates of Vienna, captured the bridgehead, the Wolfsschanze, and the two fortified places of Kornneuburg and Krems on the Danube. But he was too weak, with his army of hardly 15,000 men, to capture Vienna itself, and even a four-month siege of Brünn was unsuccessful. Krems remained in the hands of the Swedes for several months, Kornneuburg a year and a half, and Olmütz until the end of the war. Torstensson had, therefore, achieved his purpose of "reaching to the very heart of the emperor," but that was not sufficient to force him directly to a peace treaty. Torstensson, like Frederick, was aware of being the better fighter, and he strove for decisive battles, but he was no more capable than Frederick of exploiting the decisive battle into the winning of the war. Both men could act only in accordance with the principles of the strategy of attrition; in doing so, Torstensson gained more than Frederick, but Frederick still achieved his goal more rapidly. How can this be explained?

We have already seen that Torstensson's army was much more flexible than Frederick's, both because of its small size and also its composition, the preponderance of cavalry. But there was another special reason why Torstensson could operate and push forward more boldly than Frederick. Frederick realized that if his army were destroyed, his nation would also be lost. For that reason, in 1741 he did not force battle on the enemy, who was holding fast in a fortified position. In 1742 he fought only on the defensive, and in 1744 he risked going only as far as Budweis and then evacuated Bohemia again without a battle. And in 1745, in spite of his victory at Hohenfriedberg, he halted again after only three days' march. Torstensson risked fighting in the middle of Bohemia and pushed forward to the Danube, because in the most extreme case he was risking his army perhaps but not the nation. It had already been concluded by the Swedish senate when Gustavus Adolphus crossed the sea that an army lost in Germany would not seriously weaken Sweden in its defense, because the country held back thirty large ships and the national militia.[19] This same consideration is reported by Chemnitz from the council of war before the battle of Breitenfeld.[20] "The monarchy was so far away, and across the sea at that, that it was running no great risk for its country or had no great obstacle to overcome." Consequently, Frederick's faster success is explained not only by his military successes but also politically. After one and one-half years of war, Maria Theresa was ready to cede him a large, rich province in order to be able to defend herself against her other and stronger opponents. It is in this area, in the combining of strategy and politics, that the Frederick of the first two Silesian Wars must be sought. If it has been believed that Frederick's politics and conduct of war in that period were characterized by the following tendencies: no long war, short and powerful blows, and then an advantageous peace treaty as soon as possible—this idea reflects more a pious wish of the king than his actual moves indicated. Where are the short, powerful blows that he is supposed to have made? At Mollwitz he had to fight because he was cut off; at Chotusitz he himself was attacked; in 1744 he fought no battle at all; at Soor he was also the one attacked. The only short, powerful blows were Hohenfriedberg and Kesselsdorf. The peace treaty, which followed in 1745, however, was in no way advantageous but simply confirmed the status of possessions. It is also indispensable for Frederick's proper evaluation as a strategist to keep in mind that the decisive idea with which he started his great career was the political one, for which his bold but careful strategy served as an expedient.

TURENNE

In the Thirty Years' War, during the same period as Torstensson, the Frenchman Turenne exercised command. He must be mentioned in a history of the art of war, since he holds the position in tradition as that commander who first placed decisive emphasis on rations and preferred to forgo an advantageous undertaking rather than place his provisions in danger. He is therefore considered more or less as the creator of a maneuver strategy that is clever and active but avoids combat. It is customary to quote concerning him the expression of Clausewitz (9:193), that his art was precisely only that of his time, which would have been as exceptional in our wars as the parade sword of a courtier among knights' swords. Although this characterization and this comparison are as correct as they are impressive, they nevertheless give a false impression. Turenne, the son of a princess of Orange, was of the Dutch school, where the regular feeding of the soldier belonged to the most sacred rules of warfare. Consequently, he only took over this rule. But it may be that among the commanders of the Thirty Years' War he gave more consideration to the system of rations than did his contemporaries. In 1644, when he had forced General Mercy to withdraw from Freiburg and an energetic pursuit promised chances of a considerable success, he declined to do so and in his memoirs explained, "Since all of one's infantry was accustomed to receive baked bread and not to bake it themselves, like the old troops who had served long in Germany, it was all the less possible to follow the enemy to Württemberg in that we had no supply depots prepared there. Consequently, we did not move away from the Rhine."

Elsewhere in his memoirs we also find consideration for rations emphasized again and again, as, for example, at the relief of Arras in 1654.

Turenne's activity as a commander can be divided into two periods: the first, from the last years of the Thirty Years' War and the War of the Fronde to the peace treaty of the Pyrenees in 1659; the second, up to his death in 1675, including the first wars under the personal reign of Louis XIV. For the second period, in which the armies were two and three times as large as the armies of that first period, concern over the system of rations, as we have seen, gradually became the governing principle and also still remained as such under Frederick the Great. For all the commanders of this period, therefore, the battle sword, to remain with Clausewitz's figure of speech, became the parade sword, but it was nevertheless pointed and sharp enough to be very dangerous in the hand of a bold and able fencer, and Turenne, too, knew how to manipulate this sword with deadly effectiveness. We cannot attribute to him a battle like that of Baner at Wittstock or marches and battles of the grand scale of Torstensson's, but in 1674 Turenne maneuvered the Great Elector out of Alsace in the same way that Traun maneuvered Frederick the Great out of Bohemia in 1744. If he suffered a defeat, he immediately took up such a challenging, impregnable position that the enemy did not dare approach him again (for example, in 1652 at Orleans in the War of the Fronde), acting in this regard like Frederick the Great. On the importance of battle, he stated occasionally (concerning the year 1646) that the significant fruit of a victory was that one took control of an area and thereby strengthened himself, while the enemy was weakened. Turenne therefore occupies a very important individual position in the history of strategy and of the great commanders, but he cannot be considered as the model of a special method. Least of all can he be shown as representing a theory opposite that of Frederick, who, after all, never stated that he differed in his principles from the great French marshals.

CHARLES XII

Concerning Charles XII, I am planning a special study and intend to give here only a few indications as to the direction in which it will proceed. From the strategic viewpoint, Charles XII still belongs to the period of the Thirty Years' War, to the extent that the armies he led were very small, with a strong preponderance of cavalry. These armies therefore moved very freely over very great areas, and the motives for these movements rested more on political than military considerations. In 1707, when Charles left Saxony and stood at the height of his power, his army numbered 16,200 infantry and 20,700 cavalry, including the dragoons. At Poltawa he had a total of 16,500 combatants, of which 12,500 were led into the battle. Contrary to the situation in the Thirty Years' War, the king was opposed not by troops of equal value but of much lesser worth, but they had superior numbers. The Russian army was still being formed and was suffering from the opposition between the Russian soldiers and the officers, who were essentially drawn from foreign countries. The Polish royal army was an undisciplined medieval levy. Of the Saxons, their general, Schulenberg, himself reported to his king that they fell apart simply at the sight of the Swedes.[21] If we consider this difference in the quality of the troops, together with the broadness of the theater of war and the conditions of agriculture, roads, and climate, we see that we must here apply completely different standards from those either of the Thirty Years' War or of the wars of Louis XIV or Frederick the Great. The scion of the house of Wittelsbach on the Nordic throne was certainly not only one of the greatest heroes of world history but also a great general who led his troops correctly in battle and inspired them with his spirit and absolute confidence. But to place him as a strategist in a group with Gustavus Adolphus, Frederick, and Napoleon, there is something missing which is not settled with the words "stubbornness" or "adventurer." It is a question of seeking out and determining the mutual effects between the objective situation and the character of the actor. Both the difference in the opposing armies already cited and the political situation of the Swedish nation must be considered. This great power, which reached out all around the Baltic Sea and even had a large possession on the North Sea, still had so little definite political direction that the aged Chancellor Oxenstierna could advise his king in 1702 that he should make peace with August of Poland-Saxony and could then rent out his army to foreign potentates, something which would redound to the king's fame.

Indeed, it was with this kind of situation that the great Swiss warriorhood had also ended.

1756

In the Seven Years' War Frederick stood at the height of his power and his accomplishment. His strategic principles remained the same.

He entered the war with the awareness of his unquestioned superiority. In the ten years of peace he had increased and improved his army to a much greater extent than had his opponent. His fortresses in Silesia were strengthened. In his national treasury he had 16 million talers in cash, and he estimated that he would immediately bring the rich electorate of Saxony under his power and join its forces to those of Prussia. The two areas together had an annual surplus of income of 7 1/2 million talers, whereas Frederick estimated the expenses of a campaign at not much higher than 5 million. Politically, the king estimated that France, mindful of the old jealousy between the houses of Hapsburg and Bourbon, would give only mediocre support to Austria and would also not be capable of high financial contributions. He believed he could hold Russia back with the help of England, and even if that did not succeed, that the Russians could not accomplish much militarily; even Russia and Austria together would not be able to compete with him, since they were too weak financially. Even if Emperor Francis, in view of his title as king of Jerusalem, gave his wife an advance from his private fortune, that could not reach very far.

According to the king's estimate, conditions were so favorable that we might raise the question as to whether it would not now be appropriate for him to go over to the principles of the strategy of annihilation. The Prussian regiments could be mobilized within six days; the Saxon troops could be surprised before they were assembled; the Austrians had as yet made no preparations to speak of and first needed to fill out the vacancies in their peacetime organization. At the end of July 1756, when the situation was ripe politically, Frederick could have burst into Bohemia with overpowering superiority, and we cannot see how the Austrians, before he reached Vienna, could have offered any opposition to which he would not have been superior.

But nowhere do we find any indication that the king had even considered such ideas. At first he postponed the attack for four weeks when the French were threatening to move immediately against him. In doing so, he gave the Austrians time for their preparations and enabled the Saxons to concentrate their army in the fortified camp of Pirna. But

Frederick estimated that if he did not start the war until the end of August, the French would no longer move out in this year. He was willing to accept those disadvantages because he had no intentions of waging a campaign of destruction but planned only to occupy Saxony and a portion of Northern Bohemia. Under other circumstances that threat from the French would naturally have forced him not to put off the attack but to hasten it as much as possible in order to take care of Austria before the French had covered the long route up to the Saale. In this situation the principle "short, powerful blows and then a quick, advantageous peace" (as did happen 110 years later) would have been appropriate. But Frederick had completely different ideas. His requirement that Prussia's wars should be short and lively is not to be understood in the modern sense but in relation to the wars of the preceding period, which had lasted ten, twenty, even thirty years.

Consequently, Frederick contented himself this year with capturing the Saxon army (18,000 men) at Pirna and bringing Saxony under his control, but he not only rejected the idea of a decisive battle against the Austrians but even moved back again out of Bohemia. In this very first campaign he found out that the war would be more difficult than he had imagined. At Lobositz on 1 October the Prussians, as the result of an unsuccessful cavalry attack that was made against the orders of the king, were actually defeated, and the king had already left the battlefield when he was called back because the Prussians, after heavy fighting, had wrested from the Austrian light troops an advanced position that the Prussian generals thought to be the Austrians' main position. Now they thought the battle was won. That was not the case; the main position of the Austrians was hardly affected, and their army was fighting with the Prussians on equal terms. But the Prussians were nevertheless finally successful, because Browne did not recognize his advantage and did not continue the battle. For his plan was not to fight with the Prussians but by a surprise approach on the other bank of the Elbe, that is, by a maneuver, to give the Saxons the possibility of breaking out of their surrounded position, something which then failed.[22]

It cannot be said that it would have been absolutely too late in the year after the capitulation of the Saxons on 16 October for Frederick to conduct a campaign of destruction against the Austrians. He still had a considerable superiority, at least 100,000 against 80,000. But that is a purely doctrinaire consideration. Frederick did not give that a thought, and the internal structure of his army did not permit such a strategy.

1757

In the winter and spring of 1757 there was formed the frightful coalition of the three great military powers, Austria, Russia, and France, against brash Prussia. This alliance had been prepared for a long time but was still not foreseen in this form by Frederick and was not brought fully into being until Frederick himself moved forward.

At first Frederick had the idea of remaining on the defensive, giving up Silesia to the extent that it was not covered by the strong fortresses, and moving the main body of the army to Saxony in order, depending on the circumstances, to fall upon the Austrians or the French when and where they might approach. The initiative, therefore, was to be left to the enemies, as before Hohenfriedberg. Then Winterfeld proposed to the king that he seize the initiative himself, invade Bohemia as early as April, and defeat the Austrians before the French could appear. The king argued against this idea. The Austrians, perhaps just as strong as the Prussians, were divided like the latter into four groups on the border of Silesia and Saxony. It was very difficult for the Prussians in this season, when they would still find nothing in the fields for men and horses, to transport all their rations along with them. If one of the Austrian armies, and especially that of Browne, which was encamped on the lower Eger facing the Erzgebirge, was found in a fortified place and the king, coming from Dresden, had to turn back from this position because of a shortage of rations, then all the other columns would also be in great danger and the entire undertaking would be a failure. Consequently, Frederick improved Winterfeld's plan by having Schwerin, forcing his opponent off to the side, march out from Silesia via Jung-Bunzlau in such a way that he threatened Browne's corps from the rear, thus maneuvering it out of its fortified positions and also opening up the route for the king. In doing this, one would then also have the prospect of capturing Austrian depots, could advance deeper into the country, and would presumably find the opportunity of defeating one or another of the Austrian armies.

The plan succeeded brilliantly but not in the way in which it was intended. Schwerin reached Jung-Bunzlau and had the good fortune to arrive just in time to prevent the destruction of the Austrian depot in that city. Without this stroke of fortune, he would have been in a very desperate situation. Nevertheless, he could not now move farther in the prescribed direction toward Leitmeritz or Melnik, because the Austrians were threatening him from the other side and he could not sacrifice the depot that he captured in Jung-Bunzlau.[23] The king's plan had therefore proven to be impracticable, but also unnecessary, since Browne, completely surprised by the sudden approach of the enemy, had already given up the fortified positions on the Paschkopol and behind the Eger and had taken up his withdrawal toward Prague.

Thus it happened that the Prussian columns advancing from four different points were able to join forces at Prague without the Austrians' having been able to attack them with their own united forces while they were still separated. On the contrary, only three of the four Austrian corps were united at Prague, whereas the Prussians now had their entire army assembled there.

The Austrians now decided not to withdraw any farther but to form for battle east of Prague, where they were attacked, defeated, and surrounded in Prague (6 May). But before they could be forced to capitulate, a relief army appeared, cut off the Prussians' line of communications from Silesia, and thereby forced them into a battle under the most unfavorable conditions, in which the Prussians were defeated at Kollin on 18 June.

If we consider the definite way in which Frederick sought battle in this campaign and the final idea of completely destroying the enemy main body by encircling it, we are tempted to assume that with this campaign the king shifted to the strategy of annihilation. But as grandiose as that may seem, we find on closer inspection that with this concept we would not elevate the prestige of the king but would lower it, and we would do justice to neither his greatness as a commander nor to the truth.

If Frederick had pursued the ideas of annihilation, he would be subject to the reproach that he did not convert to that theory until it was too late. In the first year of the war he would perhaps have been able to arrive at his goal in this way, when the Austrians were still unprepared; in 1757, however, the numerical superiority of the Prussians was no longer great enough, as the results have confirmed.

Furthermore, we would have to assume that the king had not been at all aware of the nature and the extent of his own plan. Shortly before the outbreak of the war he confided his plan to his ally, the king of England, and to Field Marshal Lehwaldt (10 and 16 April), who was commanding in Prussia, but he said nothing at all of a decisive battle, speaking only of the depots he planned to capture from the Austrians. By doing so, he hoped to drive them almost completely out of Bohemia, or, as it was stated in the other letter, to push them back across the Beraun, that is, somewhat south of Prague. For him, this whole campaign would be a "coup," with which he hoped to be finished by 10 May so that he could then turn against the French or the Russians.

In the third place, if he was thinking differently and had considered completely defeating Austria in a single move, Frederick would have been guilty of a serious error in his estimate of the opposing strengths. For even if he had been victorious at Kollin and had captured the army that was bottled up in Prague, it is still extremely uncertain whether the courageous Maria Theresa would have let that force her into a peace treaty.[24]

The campaign of 1757 is therefore to be understood just like all the other campaigns of Frederick, that is, from the viewpoint of the strategy of attrition, with the condition that in this campaign Frederick came his closest to the battle pole and therefore to the strategy of annihilation. No basic change in his outlook took place, and he did not suddenly

switch from one extreme to the other. The reproach that has been directed
at him, to the effect that his original campaign plan was so "timid" that
it can hardly be understood, is just as unjustified as the opposite reproach,
with which his brother Henry taunted him after Kollin, "Phaethon has
fallen." Frederick's original plan was, as we have seen, to let the enemies
approach him so that he could then attack them, one after the other. This
plan was stepped up as the Prussians themselves drove directly against
the closest enemy, the Austrians. It was finally intensified even further
when the battle of Prague led completely unexpectedly to the enclosing
of the main body of the Austrian army in the fortress and now offered
the possibility of capturing this entire army. Even on the morning of the
battle, Frederick had hardly thought of that possibility, since the Austrians were in position facing to the north with their left flank anchored
on Prague and would therefore normally have taken the route to the south
after the defeat, bypassing Prague. With the great superiority Frederick
had at his disposal, he had left a third of his army, under Keith, on the
west side of Prague, and that force now blocked the retreat of the Austrians in that direction through the city. Frederick had also ordered Prince
Maurice to cross the Moldau above the city with three battalions and
thirty squadrons in order to continue the attack against the Austrians in
their retreat.[25] This undertaking failed since there was not a sufficient
number of pontoons, but Frederick himself was depending so little on
that move that he did not mention that order at all in his memoirs. Since
the presumed route of withdrawal was still almost 4 1/2 miles from the
Moldau, Maurice would probably not have accomplished anything of a
decisive nature with his 4,000 men. Nevertheless, Frederick's order is
proof as to how concerned he was with getting the greatest possible result
from the battle, and in this intention, too, he also approached the strategy
of annihilation. The whole combat situation, however, was changed when
it became apparent that the Austrian front was unassailable from the
north, and the Prussians marched around it in order to attack from the
east. The Austrians reacted by taking up a new front, where they now
had their backs toward the city and were finally driven back into it. It
was not until the next day that the Prussians, to their own surprise,
became aware of this and realized for the first time what a huge success
had resulted from their victory. Consequently, there now arose the idea
of capturing the entire Austrian army by starving it into submission.
Nevertheless, the king continued to act within the framework of the
strategy of attrition, for he did not contemplate, in case of success, going
on to Vienna, forcing a peace treaty, and then turning against the French
with his entire force. Instead, he assumed that he would still have to
continue the war against Austria and planned to detach only 30,000 men
against the French.

But the entire huge stroke of luck of the enclosing of the enemy army was actually, as Clausewitz has called it, a spiteful trick of fate. Frederick himself in a later document attributed the failure of his campaign plan to the fact that "the battle of Prague, which was won solely by the troops, threw the whole army of Prince Charles into Prague and thus made the siege of this city impossible." It would therefore be a complete misunderstanding of Frederick's concepts if one believed that he had intended this encirclement from the start and had left Keith's corps on the west side of Prague for that purpose. Rather, the real and original purpose of this corps, corresponding to the principles of the king, was the same one that had previously caused him to remain on the north side of the Elbe during the battle of Kesselsdorf. Just as he wished at that time to protect the roads and communications with Berlin and Silesia, now Keith was to cover the line of communications with Saxony. Since he was in position on this bank of the river, he was also given the mission of preventing the Austrians from retreating in this direction and was ordered to detach Prince Maurice across the Moldau against the assumed withdrawal route of the Austrians.[26]

Consequently, the campaign was not carried out in accordance with a previously composed plan. The basic idea, that Schwerin was to move from Silesia and by threatening Browne's flank to maneuver him out of his positions on the Eger, even turned out to be impracticable. Nevertheless, it was in the end skill and strategy that brought success, and not a simple stroke of luck. The bold advance as such, with its surprise, turned out to be so effective that the strength of morale of the enemy leadership did not stand up to it, and the Prussians were given free access to the country without opposition. Inconsistently enough, the enemy then stood fast at Prague and again gave the invaders the strongly desired opportunity to do battle.

The consistency of his logic guaranteed the royal commander against any kind of fantasy in his plans, such as the modern critics have accused him of. If he finally reached out toward something unattainable and suffered failure in doing so, posterity has not burdened him with guilt on that account, for it is said: "I love the one who strives for the impossible." How could he have been the hero who repeatedly challenged fate and bowed before no blow of misfortune if he had wished through caution to extinguish the incomparable talent that fate itself smilingly bestowed on him?

He also did not fight the battle of Kollin in order to "discourage those besieged in Prague" or because he sought the battle as a matter of principle, but because Daun had approached so closely that he could no longer cover at the same time the siege and the supply depots located on the route from Silesia (in Brandeis and Nimburg). The whole basic difference of Frederick's strategy from the other type is shown in the fact that the king, even when he moved out from Prague against Daun, had no desire or plan to attack the Austrians but intended to push them back by maneuvering. To cite a very felicitous expression by Otto Herrmann, Frederick considered it necessary to state excuses for his attack at Kollin. Another commander would have had to make excuses if he had not attacked. Because he could not get along without his depots, the king could also not allow Daun to approach still closer, as Napoleon and Clausewitz have said was necessary, so that he might then strengthen his army for the battle from the forces carrying out the siege. There was nothing else to do but attack Daun in the position he had taken or give up the siege of Prague, and in this emergency Frederick decided to risk the most extreme action and attack Daun.

But the battle of Kollin did not fail as the result of one or another individual error but because it was unwinnable from the start, as we can see the situation today. Daun had 54,000 men against 33,000 in a position so advantageous that it was not only difficult to approach but also allowed observation from afar of every movement of the attacker. At Soor Frederick defeated a largely superior force (22,000 against 39,000) and also later at Leuthen (40,000 against 60,000), but at Soor the attack of the Prussians was completely unexpected either all along the line or at the place where it succeeded, and the Austrian leadership took no timely countermeasures. Since their leadership at Kollin was capable of doing so and did not fail to do it, even if only at the last moment, the Prussians were unable to avoid defeat, and even Frederick's own idea that he could have won with only four more battalions is to be regarded as a delusion and rejected.[27]

After the Prussians had evacuated Bohemia, Frederick hit upon his first campaign idea once again, that is, not to attack the enemy in winter until they came closer to him. There can be no doubt that he would have made out better in this difficult war if he had followed this concept from the very start, for the success of his strategic offensive was lost. But the losses that Prague and Kollin had cost him could possibly be replaced in numbers but not in quality. Therefore, modern critics appear to be completely wrong in their condemnation of the first project and their enthusiasm over the execution of the plan. But the situation is not so simple. It is, of course, completely false to call the first project "timid." Even this plan already rose to the idea of a tactical offensive, and the strategic offensive was, as we have seen, only the intensification of an idea that was constantly present. Even if the material success had now been lost again, there still remained a morale gain of inestimable value, the extraordinary respect and the pious awe of the enemy leadership for the decisions that could be attributed to the Prussian king. The defeat at Kollin did not harm this prestige of Frederick, not even in the case of the victor, Field Marshal Daun. In fact, Frederick's prestige only grew as a result of the defeat. Instead of allowing himself to be depressed by this failure, he only became more convinced that maneuvers did not suffice and he had to seek to force his enemies into battles.

And so he marched toward the French and defeated them at Rossbach, not far from the Saale, and then he turned against the Austrians and defeated them in Lower Silesia at Leuthen. At Rossbach he won against a twofold superiority when, after Frederick had long sought in vain to find an opportunity to attack, Hildburghausen and Soubise decided to move into the attack themselves. They were in the process of enveloping the Prussian army for this purpose when the Prussians suddenly broke out of their camp and drove into the flanking march. Before the French and imperial troops could straighten out their formation, they were already overcome.

At Leuthen, where 40,000 Prussians faced between 60,000 and 66,000 Austrians, the Prussians succeeded in moving unnoticed, not actually into, but still up to the left flank of the fully deployed Austrians. Frederick had formed the army four echelons in depth and therefore had a very narrow front, whereas the Austrian formation, in order to have features on which to rest both their flanks, extended 5 miles. Consequently, the Prussians had numerical superiority in the area of their attack and defeated the left wing of the Austrians before their right wing could arrive in support. It was their defensive concept that brought disaster to the Austrians. While the king was occupied with the French, the Austrians had defeated the duke of Bevern before Breslau, had captured the city, and had also overcome the fortress of Schweidnitz. But now, instead of continuing the war through the winter with their numerical superiority and forcing a decision, they planned to go into winter quarters, and when the king approached, they thought it sufficient to face him in a suitable defensive position. They did not expect that he would dare to attack them in this position (5 December); they assumed that he would withdraw, and they would have been content with this result.[28] The combination of circumstances therefore had a certain similarity to that at Soor; there, too, the Austrians had believed they could attain their objective principally by deploying and did not need an actual fight at all or not until later. That gave their more resolute opponent the possibility of profiting from the tactical advantage of the flank attack and thereby compensating for the disadvantage of his smaller numbers, turning it into the opposite. Resoluteness was victorious over apathy. If the Austrians had attacked the Prussians at Leuthen while the latter were making their flanking march, as Frederick attacked the French at Rossbach, they could hardly have failed, with their largely superior numbers, to win the victory. Theoretically, they did not fail to realize this. In the spring of 1757 Emperor Francis had already given this advice to his brother Charles, the supreme commander, when Charles left to take over the army.[29] But he was lacking in the decisiveness needed to carry this out. At Prague, too, the Austrians allowed the Prussians to make their flanking march without interfering with it. And at Kollin they also failed to interfere, but there the Prussian maneuver nevertheless failed because the Austrians noticed the flanking march in time and were able to counter it with their great superiority by extending their front.

Again, at Leuthen leadership was the decisive factor, but the Prussian discipline provided it with the proper instrument, troop units whose good order, speed, and tactical flexibility guaranteed the sure execution of every command. King Frederick was able first to march forward in four parallel columns in the direction of the Austrian center and wait until he was already very near before deciding whether he would turn against the right or the left flank of the enemy. Then the change of direction and the deployment took place so quickly that the Austrians were already being attacked before they had realized the situation. No army of that period except the Prussians could have accomplished that.

It cannot be emphasized enough that it was not theory that distinguished Frederick from his opponents but only the execution. How little Frederick's opponents were lacking in theoretical insight concerning the value of a victorious battle is shown also by the Russian leadership of this year.

The "conference" in St. Petersburg gave Apraxin instructions: "We consider of no value the capture not only of Prussia but even of more distant areas if Lehwaldt succeeds in leaving this kingdom (East Prussia) and joining forces with the king." He was therefore to defeat Lehwaldt. Accordingly, the Russian guerrillas under General Sibilski were given the mission of enveloping the Prussians and holding them up until the army could move up and defeat them.[30]

1758. OLMÜTZ

Frederick went into his campaign of 1758 with a basic concept completely similar to that of the previous year. At that time he had invaded Bohemia in order to deliver the heaviest possible blow against the Austrians before the French appeared. Now he no longer needed to be directly concerned with the French. The English, encouraged by Rossbach, had now formed an army in Germany, and it could be expected that this army would hold the French in check. Instead, however, the Russians had just recently moved up dangerously close. While the Prussian troops had turned against the Swedes, the Russians had captured East Prussia in the winter without opposition, and it could be presumed that they would appear in the middle of the summer somewhere before the Oder.

Frederick's idea, therefore, was to keep the Austrians in some way or other so distant that they would not be able to join forces with the Russians, and he would then gain the freedom of movement to defeat the Russians as soon as they appeared within range in the open plain without the Austrians' being able to help them.

It was impossible to invade Bohemia again, as Frederick had done the previous year. The Prussians had their main body in Silesia in order first of all to wrest back from the enemy the last portion of his gains of the previous year, the fortress of Schweidnitz. Directly opposite the Prussian main army, close behind the passes, the Austrians were in a fortified, well-prepared position at Skalitz. If Frederick had planned to march into the Lausitz or even to Saxony, in order to launch his invasion from there, the Austrians would have observed that and would have again taken up good positions in front of him. Frederick thereupon had the idea of marching through Upper Silesia to Moravia, instead of Bohemia, and of besieging Olmütz. The king had thought on several occasions that in a war with Austria an invasion of Moravia would be more advantageous for him than a campaign into Bohemia.[31] But these considerations had nothing to do with the campaign of 1758; least of all can we attribute to Frederick the idea that he might have planned to advance on Vienna with his weak army. Instead of the 150,000 men he had had the year before, he now had a field army of only 120,000 men.[32] On the other hand, just as in the previous year, if he had succeeded in capturing Prague, he would then also have sought to bring the northern part of Moravia under his power, his idea now was that if he succeeded in taking Olmütz and thereby drawing the main army of the Austrians out of Bohemia, his brother Henry, who was in command of 22,000 men in Saxony, could perhaps succeed in taking Prague. Therefore, in the one year as in the other, the strategic concept was not an operation against the enemy capital but the occupation of the areas and fortresses closest to the Prussian borders. Bohemia was now too well defended. The Prussians therefore invaded an Austrian province whose border was as good as undefended, where they consequently met no enemy at first and left it up to the foe to decide whether he would move up and attack or take position for battle somewhere else. The decisive factor was not the geographical one, whether Bohemia or Moravia, but the factor of surprise. By invading Moravia, Frederick maneuvered the enemy out of his well-prepared position at Skalitz and now believed he had the opportunity either to bring on a battle under favorable conditions or, even without such a battle, to keep the Austrian army occupied for so long by his capture of Olmütz that he himself in the meantime could turn against the Russians and defeat them with his main army.

In 1757 he had only been able to surround Prague but not to besiege it, because the large army in the city made it impossible to open up approach trenches. Frederick now hoped to be able to overcome Olmütz with a formal siege.

As this plan seems quite similar to that of the year before, but wisely adapted to the changed conditions, in the final analysis it too, just as had the plan of the previous year, failed under the means adopted to cope with those circumstances.

Once again, as in the year before, the first act, that of surprise, was successful. As was the case with the Prussians, the Austrians, too, had much to do to repair the harm that Leuthen had caused their army. Neither army was yet ready with its preparations when Frederick, after taking Schweidnitz, suddenly moved out from there on 19 April and appeared before Olmütz on 4 May without having encountered any kind of opposition. But in order to be able to carry out the surprise, the Prussian army had not at first been able to take along its heavy siege train; in fact it could not even prepare it completely. It was not until more than fourteen days later (22 May), after Fouqué had brought up the heavy cannon and ammunition, that the siege could begin. In the meanwhile the army had not been able to do anything, since Daun, far from storming forward into battle to save Olmütz, moved from his camp at Skalitz only as far as the border of Moravia and there occupied a strong position at Leitomischl on 5 May. Although it was only some 50 miles from Olmütz, only two to three days' march from the position Frederick initially occupied, nevertheless the king had no idea of moving forward against Leitomischl to attack the Austrians there and defeat them, as would be the natural thing for a modern army, and it was indeed impossible for him to do so. It appears that Daun's position could be attacked only with great difficulty with the Prussian tactics, and if the position seemed to him not yet strong enough, he even had the option of moving farther back and drawing the Prussians away from their real objective of Olmütz, where they had to wait for their siege train.

As a result, Frederick had to attempt to carry out the siege, even though an undefeated enemy army was in position a short distance away.

This undertaking failed. It is believed that a few errors were made in laying out the siege works. This may have been the case, but we cannot place too much emphasis on that point. There exists no large military action in which similar difficulties do not occur. The decisive factor was the Austrian army. Frederick had not been capable of bringing up from the start the necessary quantities of provisions and ammunition to carry out the siege. Tempelhof estimated that for the siege train alone with the required ammunition to sustain firing for thirty days, 26,580 horses would have been necessary. In addition, others were necessary for the rations. Such huge numbers could not be assembled, and the supplies therefore had to be brought up step by step while the main Austrian army was nearby, and its detachments harassed the Prussians from all sides.

Frederick himself had the idea that the capture of a large train of munitions and rations by the Austrians at Domstadtl, 14 miles north of Olmütz, had forced him to lift the siege on 1 July. In reality, at that moment Field Marshal Daun had already successfully carried out another maneuver, of which the king was not yet aware but which would have prevented the capture of Olmütz even if the large transport train had come through successfully. For Daun, after remaining in place at Leitomischl for seventeen days, had moved up closer as soon as the actual siege had begun, and he had again occupied carefully chosen positions only a day's march from Olmütz, first to the east at Gewitsch and then on the south at Dobramilitsch and Weischowitz. The king, with his weak forces, was not able to attack these positions. But on the same day that the Prussian train was destroyed at Domstadtl, Daun had made a combined night march and forced march, more than 28 miles in twenty-four hours, and had won the left, east bank of the March, the river on which Olmütz lay, a move completely unanticipated by the king. On that bank of the river the fortress had been surrounded only weakly by the Prussians from the start. At the moment the Austrian army appeared, the Prussians were obliged to evacuate this side of the river completely, and they even destroyed the bridges behind them.[33] Daun was now in position immediately before the fortress and was able at any moment to reinforce its garrison so strongly that a storming of the place was no longer possible. Before Frederick learned that, however, he had already ordered and commenced his withdrawal as a result of the Domstadtl disaster.

In accordance with modern concepts of strategy, nothing would have prevented Frederick from now crossing the March at some point with his assembled forces and attacking Daun. After all, he would eventually find him somewhere or other in a position that would allow his battalions and squadrons to attack. But we do not find that Frederick had even considered this idea. As things now stood, the advantages a victory could have brought him were no longer comparable to the danger of a defeat and to the size of the losses to be expected. For since the loss of the large transport train, even after a victory it would not have been possible to continue the siege or the campaign in Moravia.

We must therefore give Daun credit for inflicting a defeat on Frederick almost without bloodshed, simply through the cleverness of his marches and his positions. He neither offered the Prussian king the desired occasion for a favorable battle, nor did he allow him to carry out the siege.

But it was these very characteristics, this skill of careful maneuvering that had enabled the Austrian commander to overcome the Prussian king, that now prevented him from deriving from his victory the advantage that fate now offered him with outstretched hand, so to speak.

Frederick retreated through Bohemia toward Königgrätz. He did not know how close Daun was to him already on the other side of the March, and he risked dividing his army into two parts, moving ahead himself in order to push aside any Austrian detachments that might be blocking his way and having Field Marshal Keith, who had been in command of the siege, follow with the entire huge train. As we see the overall situation today, it appears almost incomprehensible that Daun could have failed to take advantage of the opportunity to attack with all his forces this Prussian corps that moved forward only 37 miles (as the crow flies) to Zwittau in seven days and was already seriously threatened by the Austrian detachments. We cannot see how the Prussians could then have avoided a serious defeat. The king was a full day's march ahead of Keith and could not have helped him. To what extent the Prussians feared a pursuit by the Austrians is shown by the account that spread among them that the commander at Olmütz, General Marschall, when he was called upon to pursue the retreating Prussians, said: "Those men have suffered enough misfortune; let them move out in peace."[34]

War, however, is a matter of risks, and Daun intended to exercise the skill of winning without risking. This skill had just brought him a fine success. The year before he had not dared with his superior forces to attack the Prussians in order to relieve Prague but instead had approached so close to them that he cut off their provisions and had thereby lured them into attacking him and bringing on themselves the fearful defeat at Kollin. This time the events had transpired without any battle at all. Should he now again risk everything in face of the danger that the Prussians, alerted in timely fashion, might move against him with their assembled forces or that the king, who was capable of doing great things, might, as soon as he noticed that the Austrians were moving forward, turn around, and attack before they had again found one of their good defensive positions? Daun did not know very accurately with what— shall we say boldness or shall we say foolishness—the king of Prussia had separated his troops. To the disciple of modern strategy Daun's conduct seems dull, and if he had had in him something of a truly great general, he would necessarily have realized, even under the principles of the strategy of that day, that the moment had arrived when something great had to be risked, indeed when everything had to be staked in order to inflict the decisive defeat on the Prussians. It is, of course, to repeat the point again and again, the nature of the double-poled strategy that it requires, according to the circumstances of the moment, maneuver and caution or battle and boldness. But only a very great man is capable of shifting suddenly from the one principle to the other, and woe be to Daun if, not being master of both principles simultaneously, he had been only an aggressive commander! Here, on the Prussian retreat from Olmütz, that would have brought him a brilliant victory—but four or six weeks earlier, without his proven caution, he would have attacked the Prussians in order to relieve Olmütz. In other words, he would have done exactly what Frederick wanted him to do and would in all probability have suffered a defeat. In order to judge a commander correctly, we may not observe an isolated action but must see how his character is reflected in the overall situation and must give credit to those characteristics that proved unfavorable in the one situation for what they accomplished in another situation.

Since the Austrians did not pursue the Prussians, the latter arrived without losses at Königgrätz, and, surprisingly enough, the Prussians now occupied approximately the same positions in which the Austrians were encamped some three months earlier. Even now, after he sent back his entire train over the mountain to Silesia, Frederick would gladly have involved Daun in a battle, but the Austrians constantly occupied positions where Frederick was not willing to risk an attack. Maria Theresa wrote to her field marshal that he might now risk a battle, even in view of the danger of losing it, for the Prussians would turn against the Russians, and one had to seek to weaken them in advance. An astounding and, in its way, grandiose statement! Maria Theresa was willing to accept her own, perhaps greater, loss in order to cause the enemy losses as well and thereby facilitate the mission of her ally! One might think that the encounter would now necessarily have taken place, for, of course, Frederick, too, desired the battle, even at the risk of considerable losses, in order to take more troops away and be able to lead them against the Russians. But it is easier to write heroic letters from Vienna than to make heroic decisions in sight of the enemy, and it was not without good reason that the empress had celebrated Daun as the Fabius who saved the fatherland by his delaying action and that she had had impressed on the coin that was cast in his honor: "Cunctando vincere perge" ("He continues to conquer by delaying"). When Daun received the letter from the empress, he no doubt hastened out and studied the position of the Prussians, but the result was that he found the position too strong. He also did not think it advisable, for example, to move out into the open field himself and challenge the Prussians to attack. Similarly, the opportunities did not seem favorable enough to Frederick either, and after the opposing armies had maneuvered around each other almost four more weeks between Königgrätz and Nachod, Frederick marched off and left Bohemia in order to turn against the Russians.

When the supply of rations became tight at Königgrätz (the Austrians had burned the rest of their depot at Leitomischl when the Prussians approached), the king commanded that the soldiers themselves were to harvest, thresh and glean the grain, and deliver it to the bakeries. Each regiment had a specific number of bushels to deliver.[35]

This Bohemian-Moravian campaign ended for Frederick as an unquestionable strategic defeat, and in his own officer corps, Archenholtz wrote, the entire Olmütz operation was considered to be an error. Would Frederick not have acted more correctly if he had remained in place and waited with his main army in the Lausitz or in Lower Silesia until either the Austrians or the Russians came close enough to him in the open plain so that he could attack them? Just as he had originally planned in the spring of 1757?

Since the campaign finally failed, it was and is easy to explain after the fact that it would have been better not to undertake it at all. Even if the wasted expenses and the positive losses were not too great,[36] and even if the sacrifice of morale following the lifting of the siege of Olmütz was compensated for by the withdrawal that was so brilliantly executed, in a defensive situation one would have suffered no losses at all, and Frederick would have been able to be somewhat stronger at Zorndorf. It is therefore correct that Frederick would have done better to omit the Moravian operation.

So much for the objective observations. But strategy is never to be resolved in purely objective considerations. The subjectivity of the commander, too, also demands its rights. When Daun failed to exploit the Prussian withdrawal, we gave him credit precisely for being Daun; now the same thing applies to Frederick, and at the same time in the opposite way. Frederick would not have been Frederick if, after the victory of Leuthen, he had stood fast and waited until July of the following year to see whether his enemies would come. He recognized in an invasion of Moravia the chances for a positive success, and so it was impossible for him to leave these chances untested. In a testimonial of the Vienna High Council of War we read that the king of Prussia would "finally force Daun to do battle, no matter where he might take position, through his movements, in which we know that he is always superior to us."[37] Should Frederick therefore tell himself from the start that Daun would not allow himself to be drawn into a battle, and, since Olmütz was only 37 miles from the Prussian border, he would succeed in cutting off the besieger's supplies? After all, it was possible that things would go differently, and the idea that the king of Prussia was the man to take advantage of every possibility—this idea was indeed finally the factor that kept his enemies away from him, even when they were so very superior in numbers. It was just at that time that Loudon wrote to a friend that almost nothing in the world was impossible for the king of Prussia.[38] As we have said of Daun that it was the same commander who so successfully maneuvered Frederick away from Olmütz and later did not understand how to take advantage of Frederick's almost desperate situation on his withdrawal, so it is the same Frederick who undertook the Moravian campaign with small chances for success and precisely as a result of this initiative so impressed his enemy that when the campaign failed, he hardly suffered any loss.

Nor did the battle of Zorndorf on 25 August 1758 bring the decision that Frederick desired. The Russians held fast, withdrew along the Prussian front without Frederick's daring to attack them again, and while they did abandon the Neumark, they besieged Kolberg. The king could also have had this success if, instead of attacking, he had followed the advice of General Ruits and had captured the Russian train and the supplies that were separated from the army. He did indeed still make an attempt to do this after the battle, and he said, contradicting other statements, "That is better than a battle," but his attempt failed. Once again, the gain from the battle of Zorndorf was not a material one but a morale advantage: paralyzing the will of the enemies by means of their constant fear of being attacked.

But when Frederick depended completely too much on this factor, Daun succeeded in getting up his courage. He attacked Frederick in the carelessley selected camp at Hochkirch on 14 October 1758 and inflicted a serious defeat on him. Frederick again compensated for this defeat, not with a new victorious battle, but by well-planned fast marches that prevented the Austrians from exploiting and securing their advantages that could have resulted from the capture of fortresses in Silesia and Saxony.

1759

In the fourth year of the war there was a change in Frederick's strategy in that he now decided to adopt the principle of the strategic defensive, just as he had initially already considered in 1757. He now planned to remain within his borders, including Saxony, and let the enemies come to him. The two great offensives of 1757 and 1758 had, as we know, failed at Prague and Olmütz, but the defensive action following those failures had succeeded. In a memorandum written at the end of 1758, Frederick himself gave as his reason the improved defensive skill of the Austrians. They had supposedly become masters of the defensive as a result of their campcraft, their march tactics, and their artillery fire. With both their flanks well anchored, surrounded and supported by innumerable cannon, they normally formed in three lines. The first line had a gentle slope in front, so that its fire had the most extreme grazing effect. The second line was so dug in on the heights that it was at that point that the heaviest fighting would take place. There is cavalry intermixed in that line, and at the first wavering of the attacker it would drive forward and attack him. The third line had the mission of reinforcing the point against which the attacker directed his principal force. The flanks were provided with cannon like a citadel. Cavalry attacks, which a short time earlier were still normal for the start of the battle, now appeared completely impracticable in the face of such positions

and such masses of artillery. Rather, the cavalry is at first to be refused
and not to be employed until the moment of final decision and in the
pursuit.

Frederick now hoped that the Austrians, as a result of their efforts
to conquer Silesia, would eventually allow themselves to be lured into
moving down into the plain and there offer him the urgently desired
opportunity to attack. Since Daun was too cautious to do that, Frederick finally turned away from him and attempted to strike the Russians
in the Neumark. He repeated this attempt three times: at Zorndorf on
25 August 1758, at Kay on 23 July 1759, and at Kunersdorf on 12
August 1759. At Zorndorf in 1758 the result was already unsatisfactory;
in the following year at Kay and Kunersdorf the Prussians were completely defeated.

KUNERSDORF[39]
12 AUGUST 1759

The Russians with Loudon were in position before the gates of Frankfurt on the right bank of the Oder. Coming from the south, Frederick
marched by them, crossed the Oder north of their position, and since
they were covered on the north by a low swampy area, he marched around
them again so that he attacked them in an envelopment from the southeast.

Planned as a pure flanking attack, this move was initially very effective,
and it seemed that the Russian battle line would necessarily be rolled up.
Nevertheless, the attack failed in the end, since the Russian front was
also covered on the south by several ponds and streams so that the Prussians were able to attack on only a very narrow front, and the cavalry
especially, which was 13,000 horses strong, was unable to provide any
effective action. In order not to lose the cohesiveness of his battle formation, the king had not been willing to let his left wing attack around
those frontal obstacles. Consequently, the Russians were able again and
again to bring up fresh troops from the half of their battle line that was
not under attack, and the numerical superiority of these troops finally
overpowered the Prussians. Clausewitz (10:99) expresses that in this way:
"One may well say that the king fell here into the trap of his own system
of oblique order of battle," and this point is confirmed in the
Generalstabswerk.

At Kunersdorf the flanking attack was of a still more specific nature
than at Leuthen, in that the Prussians extended completely around the
Russian east wing. The relative strengths of the two sides were about the
same in both battles. The differences, which brought the Prussians victory
at Leuthen and defeat at Kunersdorf, were, first, the very greatly extended

Austrian front at Leuthen, which prevented the reinforcing of the attacked wing by the troops from the flank that was not under attack; second, the terrain the Russians occupied at Kunersdorf, which was so much more advantageous for the defense, both within their front as well as in front of their line; third, the fortifications and abatis that the Russians, who had already been occupying this position for eight days, had installed; fourth, the fact that, because of the frontal obstacles, the Russian center was not attacked, and it was therefore so easy for the Russians to move reinforcements to the wing that was being assaulted.

The king was often criticized, especially by Napoleon, for not having a stronger force at Kunersdorf for the final decision. The *Generalstabswerk* (10:84) effectively lists the reasons why he did not do so, but it clouds the principal point, namely, that these reasons are applicable and effective only under the assumption that Frederick was acting and had to act in accordance with the principles of the strategy of attrition. If Frederick had been willing to allow events to proceed to the point of temporarily giving up Saxony, he could have sent the troops of Prince Henry to the aid of Wedel at Kay, and if he had been willing to risk a part of Silesia, he could have moved Fouqué up to Schmottseifen, and he himself could have taken so many more troops with him for the decisive action at Kunersdorf. Least of all, however, is the statement on p. 85 of the *Generalstabswerk* to be accepted, to the effect that Frederick could not have let the situation come to the point of possibly having Daun "following on his heels with the largest part of his army." We may, in fact, completely reverse this statement. If Daun followed Frederick directly, he would thus have left his fortified position and would finally have offered the Prussian king the opportunity for which he had been yearning so long, the chance to attack him in the open field. The Russians could not have intervened, since they were still on the other side of the Oder. Then we would have a picture somewhat like that of Napoleon in 1815, when he hoped within two days and with the same army to defeat first the Prussians and then the English. Frederick, however, could not depend on his troops for such an accomplishment. The events before the battle of Zorndorf can be judged in exactly the same way.

PRUSSIA'S SURVIVAL AFTER THE DEFEAT OF KUNERSDORF

We normally consider the Seven Years' War almost exclusively from the viewpoint of the deeds and the strategy of King Frederick. But we may also say in precisely the opposite way: the real basic problem of the war was, how was it possible for Frederick to survive the defeat of Kunersdorf? This question is not settled with the reply that it was the lack of ability and of unity, the "divine asininity" of his opponents that saved him. Soltikoff and Daun were by no means so absolutely incapable that they did not have reasons for their actions, and it is worthwhile for us to understand these reasons.

King Frederick expected, and according to modern concepts it would probably be taken for granted, that his enemies, united, would pursue him after their victory, attack and destroy his army, capture Berlin, and thus bring the war to an end. And that is also what was demanded by the Vienna High Council of War. The Council wrote to Daun that he was not to let the defeated army out of his sight and his hands any more but was to pursue it with all possible vigor and destroy it completely. Despite the serious defeat that the Prussians had suffered, however, the accomplishment of this mission was in no way so easy and such a matter of course. Frederick's own testimony for this is not sufficiently convincing. Even if it is correct that he believed that everything was lost, wished to abdicate, and turned the high command over to General Finck, it was because he happened to be of a much more impressionable nature than was Napoleon, for example, and the subjective impressions of this man who was stunned by this fearful blow may not be treated as objective measures for judging the situation and the actions of the opponents.

The Prussian army on the battlefield of Kunersdorf had approached a strength of 50,000 men. If the king had only 10,000 men with him on the evening of the battle, nevertheless the larger half of the army was eventually saved, and the losses, severe enough, were limited to 19,000 men and the artillery. In addition to these troops, the king still had two armies under Prince Henry and Fouqué and smaller detachments in the field, some 70,000 men all together. Therefore, despite the frightful defeat and the heavy losses, very strong forces were still available, capable of maneuvering and fighting. There had been no direct pursuit after the battle, so that the men separated from their units reassembled again in the following days at Fürstenwalde, 28 miles from the battlefield. That was nothing of an unusual nature, since, as we know, pursuits in all periods have been very difficult, were only insignificant at that time, even with the Prussians, and the Russians and Austrians themselves had had very heavy losses at Kunersdorf (17,000 men).[40]

If they now resumed operations after the passage of a certain time, they had to attack the king in his position behind the Spree, and in doing so they would have the army of Prince Henry in Lausitz behind them. In view of the great numerical superiority of the combined Russian and Austrian armies, this was undoubtedly feasible, but only if the two commanders cooperated with a single idea and resolutely. Experience shows that such cooperation among allies is very difficult; not only do the generals have different viewpoints, but also behind these differing viewpoints there are greatly different interests. For the Russians, the war against the king of Prussia was simply a diplomatic war in which they were not driven forward by any inner interest to the extent of accepting unlimited dangers and losses. They were unwilling to sacrifice themselves for the Austrians. An offensive battle against King Frederick was always a risk.

Soltikoff made the remarkable statement that he was unwilling to risk anything more (*Generalstabswerk*, 11:82) or even that he wished to have nothing more to do with the enemy (*Generalstabswerk*, 10:305). The Russians were so worn out from their two victories at Kay and Kunersdorf that their moral readiness for great actions was no longer sufficient, and if they did not go along, the Austrians alone, while still enjoying numerical superiority, were still not strong enough that continued offensive operations did not seem quite dangerous to them. Daun therefore only remained true to his character and his principles when he rejected from the start the idea of bringing an end to the war with quick, heavy blows. While the idea of attacking the king or Prince Henry or of marching on Berlin was given repeated consideration, all such ventures were finally rejected. Even the capture of Berlin would mean no real gain, the Austrian commander declared, since they would not be able to occupy any winter quarters in the exhausted March. The two commanders therefore agreed to wait at first for the imperial army to occupy Saxony, which was evacuated by the Prussians, and to conquer Dresden (which also happened), and then to seek the fruit of the great victory by taking up winter quarters in Silesia.

The idea of exploiting the victory of Kunersdorf to the point of the complete subjection of Prussia must be seen as a parallel to that other idea, that King Frederick should also have brought up the army of Prince Henry for the attack on the Russians. Neither the one action nor the other fits into the framework of the conditions and the ideas of the period. If we do not demand the one action from Frederick, we may not demand the other one from Daun. Neither of them did anything incomprehensible; instead, they acted in accordance with their principles, which are already known to us. At Kunersdorf it was not the Prussian army but only half of the Prussian army that was beaten. If it now happened that this victory was exploited to the extent that Saxony and Silesia remained in the hands of the allies, they had thus attained something very great and could assume that the next campaign would force Prussia to her knees.

The plan could not be put into action, because the allies were not in agreement among themselves, and King Frederick so boldly and energetically used the forces he still had that the enemy finally moved back into the same winter quarters they had occupied the previous year, retaining only Dresden. Modern theoreticians, without understanding of the nature of the double-poled strategy, normally express little appreci-

ation of maneuvering. Let them study how Prussia was saved by maneuvering after the defeat of Hochkirch, as after that of Kunersdorf.
Three weeks after the battle, when the situation had developed to the
point that the Austrians and Russians actually planned to turn against
the remnants of the king's army and against Berlin, Prince Henry did
not attack them in the rear from the south, for example, but on the
contrary, he marched farther away from the enemy toward the south in
order to attack their communications and capture their depots. Daun
immediately turned around, gave up the plan to march on Berlin, and
the Russians and Austrians were again widely separated.

When the plan for Silesia was now to be put into action, the main
Austrian army was in Saxony. In order to be able to remain in Silesia,
the Russians would at least have had to capture Glogau, but before they
reached the fortress, the king had arrived ahead of them by forced marches
and was in such a position that they would first have had to attack and
drive him off in order to be able to take up the siege. In spite of their
great numerical superiority (Loudon was still with them), they had no
inclination toward an offensive battle, and all the less when from the very
start they had only grudgingly accepted the entire plan to conquer Silesia.
For them, Silesia was too distant from their base on the lower Vistula
and in East Prussia. The Austrians sought to draw them this far not so
much because they wished to gain this province in the peace treaty but
because it was the closest to them for their operations, was the most
convenient, and offered secure communications. But the Russians found
it to be an unduly unreasonable demand that they should make a movement that was not only very long but was also exposed to a flanking
attack from the March and from Pomerania. They could even lose East
Prussia, they thought, if they advanced so far.[41] Therefore, Soltikoff never
took seriously the Austrians' proposal to besiege Glogau, and if King
Frederick had not finally shown a careless lack of caution in sending
Finck into the rear of the Austrians, an action that resulted in his capitulation at Maxen, the defeat at Kunersdorf would have been as good as
completely eradicated.[42]

In the autumn of 1759 the king took counsel with himself in the most
earnest introspection as to whether he was on the right track with his
inclination to decisive battles. He reflected on the fate of the Swedish
king Charles XII and wrote those observations on him that we have
already cited, in which he says the king on many an occasion could have
been more sparing of bloodshed.

> There are, of course, situations in which one must fight; one should,
> however, allow himself to be drawn into battle only when the en-
> emy, either in camping or on the march, is careless or when one
> can force him to accept peace by a decisive blow. Furthermore, it

is certain that most generals who resort easily to a battle rely on this expedient only because they do not know what else to do. Far from being considered to their credit, one regards this rather as an indication of a lack of genius.

He went on to say that courage was nothing without wisdom, and in the long run a thoughtful mind was victorious over unthinking boldness.

Consequently, from then on Frederick rejected the idea of fighting with the Russians, even if a very favorable opportunity was offered him. He concentrated obstinately on looking for a weak point of the Austrians, but if we look closely, we see that in the five years of the war after Leuthen he engaged in an actual serious battle with them only once more, at Torgau. Previously, at Liegnitz, the initiative was not on his side but on that of his enemies.

1760

LIEGNITZ AND TORGAU

Urged on by the government in Vienna and the command of his empress, Daun had now decided to attack the Prussian army. The Austrians had moved into Lower Silesia from one side and the Russians from the other, and they were now separated only by the Oder.

Frederick still had only 30,000 men, while the Austrians had 90,000. The Russians, with 74,000 men, were held in check by Prince Henry with 37,000. Frederick felt himself still too weak to fight and planned only to continue maneuvering in order to protect Breslau and Schweidnitz from being besieged and to hold out in this way through the summer. Then he was saved by the attack plan of the Austrians. Spurred on by Vienna, Daun conceived the plan not only for an attack but for a battle of destruction. The Austrian corps were to move from three sides simultaneously in a night march to encircle and crush the king's army. The Prussians, by making a night march themselves, moved against the one of these corps commanded by Loudon, 24,000 men strong, threw it back in the early morning before the main Austrian force arrived, and that force now no longer dared to continue and complete the planned operation. We see, therefore, that it is absolutely false to believe that the idea of a battle of destruction was completely foreign to Daun. It was easy enough to adopt this idea, but Daun knew better than his detractors that the plan was very difficult to carry out against the king of Prussia.

The success at Liegnitz saved the king from the most extreme temporary emergency. As the year approached its end, he now attempted one more time to force fate with a heavy blow, and on 3 November 1760 he attacked

Daun in his position at Torgau. Under any circumstances he was obliged to attempt to wrest back Saxony from his enemies, and as if excusing himself, he tells us in his memoirs that he had to trust the fate of Prussia to the chance of battle because he had not succeeded by maneuvering in drawing Daun out of his position at Torgau. The victory was bought very dearly, and the results were still only moderate, since the Austrians withdrew only three days' march away and continued to control Dresden.

FURTHER DEVELOPMENT OF THE OBLIQUE ORDER OF BATTLE

The oblique order of battle can be conceived as a subtype of the wing battle, that is, the wing battle with the unified, cohesive battle front, corresponding to the elementary tactics of the period. It was successful only a single time, or, as we might better express it, it was sufficient only once, at Leuthen. After Leuthen Frederick fought only three more large, pitched battles, two against the Russians—Zorndorf in 1758, Kunersdorf in 1759—and a single battle against the Austrians, Torgau in 1760. The development after Leuthen was that the king not only marched so far along the enemy front as to outflank the one wing, but that he even marched completely around it, so that he would attack the enemy in the rear if the opponent did not make this same turn. But since he did make it, the purpose of the maneuver was not attained, and in essence the result was a frontal battle. At Zorndorf the armies even turned twice around each other in this way.

At Kunersdorf the Russian wing—we are almost in doubt as to whether we should call it the right or the left—was completely enveloped, but since the king still adhered to the principle that he had to maintain a cohesive front, a large part of the Russian army was not attacked. From these troops the part under attack could be reinforced again and again, so that the offensive power of the Prussians was finally worn down.

At Torgau Frederick applied a completely new method that we can still call a development of the wing battle. He gave up the cohesiveness of the front, divided his army into two parts, and led the enveloping part in a semicircle around the right, north, wing of the Austrians, so that he attacked them simultaneously from the front and rear. The difficulty in this procedure was that there was no way of guaranteeing simultaneous attacks by the two parts. One could neither agree on a specific time, since the duration of the enveloping march could not be estimated accurately, nor could one rely on signals, which were influenced by the wind and weather. The king's outer column had no less than 18 miles to march, and its route was through forests. Whether the king attacked too early or Zieten was too late, their attacks did not coincide.[43] Nevertheless, the battle was won, since a considerable part of the Austrians under Lascy, uncertain as to where Zieten would attack, remained in place on the left wing and left the right wing alone. Already badly shaken by the encounters with the king's corps, the Austrians could now no longer withstand Zieten's attack from the other side.

Two years earlier (23 June 1758), in a completely similar way, Ferdinand of Braunschweig had attacked the French at Crefeld with three widely separated corps, one of which moved against the enemy's rear. Despite his great superiority, the French commander, Prince Clermont, did not have the decisiveness to move out himself to attack one or the other of the isolated enemy corps. Instead, before the main body had even become engaged in real combat, he ordered the withdrawal.[44]

Napoleon sharply criticized the splitting of the attacking armies both at Crefeld and at Torgau, saying that was against all the rules of the art of war. The isolated corps could have been defeated. He also stated that Torgau was the only one of Frederick's battles in which he showed no talent.

As can be seen, we have entirely reversed this judgment, recognizing in the dividing of the attack the creative spirit that was able to achieve a final, highest development of the traditional form that was no longer productive. Napoleon's criticism ignores the difference in the tactics of the periods. Surely it was not impossible for Daun to have had Zieten attacked at Torgau while the king was still involved in his enveloping march. But the probability that Daun would make this decision and carry it out very quickly was not so great that Frederick might not risk the attempt on that account.

1761–1762

Despite his victories at Liegnitz and Torgau, Frederick was in a worse situation in 1761 than after Kunersdorf and Maxen.

He could no longer fight; he protected his army behind field fortifications (Bunzelwitz), and gradually lost his fortresses at Glatz, Schweidnitz, and Kolberg. To be sure, the Austrians, too, were so very close to the end of their strength that Maria Theresa decided (December 1761) to reduce her army, which she could no longer maintain and pay. Each regiment gave up two companies; the officers were discharged with half-pay, except for those who found openings in other companies.[45] Nevertheless, it was believed that the war could still be won, when the death of Czarina Elizabeth on 5 January 1762 completely changed the situation. The Russians not only withdrew from the Austrian alliance, but they also went over to the side of the Prussians.

As a result of this shift by the Russians, Frederick now had the numerical superiority. Nevertheless, he no longer sought a decisive battle but based his campaign from the start simply on successful maneuvering. At the end of 1761, the Austrians had succeeded in seizing the fortress of Schweidnitz, and with it as a base, they took up their winter quarters in Silesia. The Prussians were pushed back to Breslau. Instead of now risking everything in an attack on the Austrians with his assembled forces on the near side of the mountains, the king weakened his force by sending a large detachment (16,000 men) to Upper Silesia, and by an envelopment he forced Daun back behind Schweidnitz.[46]

Frederick sought to draw him out of this position, first by attacking an outpost on the left wing, but he was repelled. Then he invaded Bohemia farther to the north via Trautenau, and there lay waste the countryside. But Daun did not allow himself to be confused; he protected his depots at Braunau in timely fashion and remained at Schweidnitz. The invasion of Bohemia could easily have led to a loss such as that at Maxen.

Frederick therefore moved back out of Bohemia and now showed that it was in no way weakness and lack of decisiveness that caused him simply to maneuver.

He had the troops under Wied, who up to that point had maneuvered against the Austrian left wing, make three successive night marches, led them around Schweidnitz against the right wing of the Austrians, and there unexpectedly attacked the Austrian posts at Burkersdorf and Leutmansdorf, which were situated some 2 1/2 miles from the main body and were to cover that flank. The surprise attack succeeded, although it had to move across very rough terrain, and Daun was now obliged to withdraw so far into the mountains that the Prussians were finally able to take up the siege of Schweidnitz. Since this siege extended until 9 October, it marked the end of the campaign. In this Frederick was in no way untrue to his principles, but in accordance with the circumstances he believed he could now turn away from the dangerous and costly resort to battle. The purpose for which he had entered the war six years earlier, the winning of Saxony, could no longer be achieved in any case. It was now only a matter of the status quo ante, and that seemed possible without further battle. Of course, a victory would have hastened the final decision, but after all his experience Frederick had now approached so closely the maneuver pole of his strategy that he renounced battle under the prevailing conditions. He had abandoned the concept that Prussia's wars had to be "short and active."

1778

The Prussians invaded Bohemia over almost the same routes as they did eighty-eight years later, in 1866. Frederick came from Silesia through the pass of Nachod, while Prince Henry came from the north out of the Lausitz. In 1866 this concentric attack led to the decisive battle at Königgrätz; in 1778 the Austrians, in positions behind the upper Elbe and Isar, brought the Prussians to a standstill. These were positions that the Austrians also held for a moment in 1866. The complete difference of the times and the change that strategy had undergone in the meanwhile can be seen in the conflicting nature of these events. In 1866 the Prussians were able to force a decision that ended the war; the battles required a total of seven days. In 1778 the two sides stood observing one another with minor pushes, and after three months the Prussians withdrew over the Bohemian border mountains and called the campaign the "potato war," because it had hinged on digging out these vegetables which were only now planted on a large scale. As in 1866, the forces on both sides were of approximately equal strength.

The picture of the royal commander, as it has been imprinted on posterity, is naturally dominated by the impressions of the campaigns in which he had to struggle against a powerful superiority, held his own, and conquered. In order to understand his strategy, we must of course also consider those campaigns in which he took the field with numbers equal or superior to those of his enemies, and these campaigns form the majority. Of his twelve campaigns, four—1741, 1742, 1756, and 1762—were conducted with a definite numerical superiority. In three and a half campaigns—1744, 1745, 1778, and the first half of 1757—we may assume the opposing forces as approximately equal. In the remaining four and one-half campaigns—second half of 1757, 1758, 1759, 1760, 1761—the superiority was on the enemy side.

NOTES FOR CHAPTER V

1. All the previous descriptions of this campaign and of the battle have been significantly corrected by the careful study with its critical analysis of the sources by Rudolf Israel, "The Campaign of 1704 in South Germany" ("Der Feldzug von 1704 in Süddeutschland"), Berlin dissertation, 1913.

2. Of course, Tallart intended to attack the allies as soon as they had crossed through the mist moving across his front, and he also made a few movements toward attacking in the battle. But in view of the formation of his troops, especially the unusually strong occupation of Blindheim and the lack of a reserve, we can still say that the battle was planned as a purely defensive action.

3. The battle was first completely explained in its strategic as well as tactical sequence by Georg Schmoller, "The Campaign of 1706 in Italy" ("Der Feldzug von 1706 in Italien"), Berlin dissertation, 1909.

4. Schmoller, pp. 35–36, "The Hussars in front of the two Echelons of Cavalry."

5. Franz Mühlhoff, "The Genesis of the Battle of Oudenarde" ("Die Genesis der Schlacht bei Oudenaarde"), Berlin dissertation, 1914.

6. In Coxe, *Life and Correspondence of Marlborough (Leben und Briefwechsel Marlboroughs)*.

7. The battle is treated excellently in the 1912 Berlin dissertation by Walter Schwerdtfeger. It is to be noted particularly that the account by Rüstow in the *Geschichte der Infanterie* is corrected and expanded in very important points by this study. Sautai, too, *Bataille de Malplaquet* (1906), had already rejected Rüstow's account.

8. The wars of Frederick the Great have recently been treated comprehensively by both the Prussian and the Austrian general staffs. The Prussian work suffers from a false basic concept of the strategy of the period, which has also presented many details in a false light. The two general staff works have been compared in an excellent article by Otto Herrmann in the *Jahrbücher für die Armee und Marine*, January, 1906.

9. The *Generalstabswerk*, p. 392, states that the opposing strengths in the battle were "not significantly different from one another," but it estimates the Prussian infantry 1,200 men too low and the Austrian cavalry 1,800 horses too high. Furthermore, it does not at all take into consideration the fact that the Prussians also had 1,400 cavalry in position in the rear of the Austrians at Ohlau, who could be counted on to intervene in the battle, and also a corps of seven battalions and six squadrons, as well as five squadrons from the homeland.

10. In the introduction to the second volume of the *Generalstabswerk*, the unsatisfactory exploitation of the Prussian victory is retroactively explained by the "heavy losses of troops, which influenced most deeply the commander's easily excited spirit" and similar reasons, but the great numerical superiority of the Prussians remains unmentioned.

11. How important this viewpoint was for Frederick is explained by Senftner, "Saxony and Prussia in 1741" ("Sachsen und Preussen im Jahre 1741"), Berlin dissertation, 1904.

12. Monograph by Paul Müller. Berlin dissertation, 1905. According to the Austrian *Generalstabswerk*, 3:670, Frederick did not push his success to a complete victory because for political reasons he wished to spare Austria. That would be the direct opposite of the strategy that is normally attributed to Frederick, but it seems to me to go too far when it draws the political motive into the tactical action. It was sufficient that the victory was not further pursued strategically. The *Generalstabswerk* is to be compared with the very different account in Koser, *Friedrich der Grosse*, and Bleich, "The Moravian Campaign, 1741–42" ("Der mährische Feldzug 1741–42"), Rostock dissertation, 1901. I agree with Koser with respect to the facts, but I evaluate them very differently from the strategic viewpoint. Bleich, too, has not yet hit upon the correct points of view.

13. The account of the battle in the *Generalstabswerk* has been corrected in many respects, including the army strengths, in the comprehensive monograph by Rudolf Keibel (1899). The reproach concerning the unsatisfactory pursuit that is directed against the king in the *Generalstabswerk* is rejected by Oskar Schulz in "Frederick's Campaign after the Battle of Hohenfriedberg up to the Eve of the Battle of Soor" ("Der Feldzug Friedrichs nach der Schlacht bei Hohenfriedberg bis zum Vorabend der Schlacht bei Soor"), Heidelberg dissertation, 1901.

14. In this saying lies the key to understanding the battle of Soor, which, although it was already correctly recognized by Clausewitz (10:30), is missing in the *Generalstabswerk*. Hans Stabenow, "Die Schlacht bei Soor," Berlin dissertation, 1901.

15. This point has been strongly confirmed in detail by Hans Kania, "The Conduct of Prince Leopold before the Battle of Kesselsdorf" ("Das Verhalten des Fürsten Leopold vor der Schlacht bei Kesselsdorf"), Berlin dissertation, 1901.

16. Iwan Jowanowitsch, "Why Did Frederick the Great not Participate in the Battle of Kesselsdorf?" ("Warum hat Friedrich der Grosse an der Schlacht bei Kesselsdorf nicht teilgenommen?"), Berlin dissertation, 1901.

17. Hobohm, "Torstensson as Predecessor of Frederick the Great in the Struggle Against Austria" ("Torstensson als Vorgänger Friedrichs des Grossen im Kampf gegen Oesterreich"), *Preussische Jahrbücher*, 153:423 ff.

18. Monograph by Paul Gantzer in the *Mitteilungen des Vereins der Geschichte der Deutschen in Böhmen*, Vol. 43(1905).

19. Clausewitz, *Werke*, 9:6.

20. Hobohm, p. 436.

21. Sarauw, *The Campaigns of Charles XII (Die Feldzüge Karls XII.)*, 1881, p. 192.

22. Franz Quandt, "Die Schlacht bei Lobositz," Berlin dissertation, 1909. The *Generalstabswerk* still does not present things correctly.

23. Karl Grawe, "The Development of the Prussian Campaign Plan in the Spring of 1757" ("Die Entwicklung des preussischen Feldzugsplanes im Frühjahr 1757"), Berlin dissertation, 1903. This work, which in other respects develops the sequence correctly, makes the mistake of simply naming Leitmeritz as a march objective in the king's order to Schwerin of 3 April, whereas both Melnik and, on 17 April, Reudnitz are named.

24. That has already been proved in an outstanding way by Caemmerer, *Frederick the Great's Campaign Plan for the Year 1757 (Friedrichs des Grossen Feldzugsplan für das Jahr 1757)*, 1883, which, in other respects, challenges my concept.

25. Jany, *Documentary Contributions and Studies on the History of the Prussian Army (Urkundliche Beiträge und Forschungen zur Geschichte des preussischen Heeres)*, published by the Great General Staff, 3 (1901):35.

26. The opposite concept was represented principally by Albert Naudé, whose arguments have been thoroughly refuted by me in the *Preussische Jahrbücher*, 73:151; 74:570 (1893). See in this connection the article by Gustav Roloff in the *Deutsche Heereszeitung*, Nos. 42 and 43, 1894.

27. Credit for having clarified these conditions goes to Dietrich Goslich, "Die Schlacht bei Kollin," Berlin dissertation, 1911. See also the review in the *Deutsche Literaturzeitung* of 1 May 1915, No. 18. See also *Jahrbücher für Armee und Marine*, March 1912, p. 336. If in this article the author, Jany, jokingly refers to Frederick's concern for his depot as the loss of "flour sacks," which could not be compared with the gains from a battle, he misunderstands a basic principle of the Prussian military system and Frederick's strategy. For Napoleon, the proposal not to fight at Kollin but to allow Daun to approach still closer was simple and natural. Nothing is more characteristic of Frederick than that from the start he rejected this idea because of his concern for his rations. This point is developed very well by Goslich and misunderstood by Jany.

More recently, there has appeared an Austrian account of the battle by von Hoen, Vienna (1911), which confirms Goslich's conclusions from the Austrian sources and adds some very interesting new points. A critical review of this work that presents an excellent picture has been given by Otto Herrmann in the *Brandenburgisch-Preussische Forschungen*, 16(1913):145.

28. Gerber, *Die Schlacht bei Leuthen*, Berlin, 1901, has the right concept. The *Generalstabswerk* is off base in many respects.

29. Arneth, 5:172.

30. Masslowski, *The Seven Years' War from the Russian Viewpoint (Der siebenjährige Krieg nach russischer Darstellung)*, pp. 175, 180.

31. The considerations that Frederick mentions in his *General-Prinzipien* (1748) to the effect that it was generally more advantageous for him to attack Moravia rather than Bohemia, are based on the assumption that Saxony was not in his possession. This point is explained excellently in the study by Otto Herrmann in the *Jahrbücher für Armee und Marine*, Vol. 121. The *Generalstabswerk*, in the volume devoted to the year 1758, also abandons the concept that is still represented in the first volumes. Its discussions are filled out in a very valuable way in an article by Otto Herrmann in the *Historische Vierteljahres-Schrift*, 1912, Vol. 1. Later, the king stated that the invasion of Moravia was particularly advantageous, also under the assumption that he had possession of Saxony. Such considerations naturally have no theoretical significance. They are geographical and topographical studies that are made by every strategy in all periods, and necessarily so. In particular, the fact that Vienna was threatened more strongly from Moravia than from Bohemia is not a consideration of the strategy of annihilation, for example, but of the strategy

of attrition, for the former does not plan to threaten the enemy capital but to conquer it.

32. When Frederick was in Moravia, he had 55,000 men there, some 17,000 in Silesia, 22,000 in Saxony, and 22,000 under Dohna, as well as several thousand sick. The normal statement that he was almost as strong as in 1757 is therefore not correct.

33. The *Generalstabswerk* reports this withdrawal twice. On page 92 the Prussians moved back before Daun's approach march. On page 106 they were called back because the king planned to lift the siege.

34. Retzow, 1:293.

35. *Unpublished Reports (Ungedruckte Nachrichten)*, 2:367. Bernhardi, 1:243, has the credit for calling attention to this unique report from the diary of a junior officer. But when he adds, "No one knew how to go about requisitions," he is unfair to the resourcefulness and intelligence of Frederick and his officers.

36. Retzow, p. 294, does say expressly, "The losses in men, cannon, munitions, and rations were considerable," but we must nevertheless take into account on the other hand that Frederick had taken much of the provisions for his army from enemy territory. In Bohemia contributions were even forced. *Ungedruckte Nachrichten*, 2:367.

37. *Generalstabswerk*, 7:232.

38. Arneth, 5:388.

39. The newest study, based on the *Generalstabswerk*, is the article by Laubert in the *Brandenburgisch-Preussische Forschungen*, 25(1913):91.

40. The *Generalstabswerk* estimates the strength of the combined Russians and Austrians in the battle as 79,000, while Koser estimates only between 68,000 and 69,000 men, 16,000 of whom were irregulars. The *Generalstabswerk* gives Frederick 49,900 men, of whom the troops who covered the bridges and garrisoned Frankfurt were estimated as some 7,000 men. Koser's statement (2:25), to the effect that 53,121 men were counted at the crossing of the Oder, contradicts p. 37, where only 49,000 men are given. The origin of this error has already been discovered by Laubert, *Die Schlacht bei Kunersdorf*, p. 52.

41. This argumentation appears again and again in Masslowski, *Der Siebenjährige Krieg nach russischer Darstellung* (translated by Drygalski).

42. Clausewitz claimed to find this lack of caution so extreme that it was "hardly possible to explain it, to say nothing of excusing it." The explanation is found in the study by Ludwig Mollwo, Marburg dissertation, 1893. It is to be found in the concept of the "unassailable position," so characteristic of that period. The king assumed as certain that the Austrians were about to evacuate Saxony and that they would not attack. But Daun recognized his advantage, summoned up his courage, attacked Finck, and overpowered him with his large superiority, and that all the

more easily since the Prussian troops consisted partially of captured Russians who had come over to their service and impressed Saxons.

43. In the *Brandenburgisch-Preussische Forschungen*, 2(1889):263, Herrmann published a letter from Gaudy to Prince Henry, dated 11 December 1760, in which he says that "unfortunate cannon shots" were the cause of the premature attack. He says that the cavalry and artillery were also not yet in place.

44. Daniels, *Preussische Jahrbücher*, 78:137.

45. Arneth, 6:259.

46. On 30 June Tschernyscheff's Russian corps joined forces with the Prussians, and on 1 July the advance of the combined armies began. On 18 July came the news of the abdication of Czar Peter. During this time Frederick could have fought a battle with considerable superiority, if he had planned for it. But he planned to do so only in case the Austrians would have been obliged to detach a part of their army against the Turks.

Chapter VI

Frederick as a Strategist

As penetrating, and indeed as earth-shaking, as were the changes in tactics from the Renaissance to Frederick the Great, the principles of strategy remained the same. The closely formed deep squares of infantry became threadlike lines; the spearmen and halberdiers became musketeers; the knights who fought individually became closely formed squadrons; the few, cumbersome cannon became countless batteries. But the art of the commander presents the same countenance through all the centuries. Again and again we find the same situations and decisions initiated in the same manner and similarly motivated. Seldom did the two sides move directly against one another in order to bring on the decision. Quite often both sides or the one that felt itself weaker sought out unassailable positions. Battles were brought on as one side believed it could profit from a good opportunity; for example, it could attack before the other side had fortified its position (on the White Mountain in 1620; Höchstädt in 1704) or on the occasion of the siege of a fortress. The battles of Ravenna in 1512, Nördlingen in 1634, and Malplaquet in 1709 all originated in the same way, as the stronger side planned to besiege a fortress and the opponent sought to prevent that by taking up an advantageous position nearby and was then attacked. Kollin differed from those listed above only through the fact that the besieger moved out a bit farther to meet the relief army. Or in the opposite way, a relief army attacked an army that was essentially stronger but was involved in a siege: Pavia in 1525, Turin in 1706. A good part of the Seven Years' War revolved around the siege or defense of fortresses—Prague, Olmütz, Dresden, Schweidnitz, Breslau, Küstrin, Neisse, Glatz, Kosel, Kolberg, and Glogau, as in the struggles between Charles V and Francis I, as in the Thirty Years' War, and as in the wars of Louis XIV. The decisions by Gustavus Adolphus to fight at Breitenfeld and Lützen were made in a manner completely similar to the decisions of Frederick before the battles of Leuthen and Torgau. Every period, every campaign, and every commander showed individual traits in these decisions, and they are to be carefully considered. Gustavus Adolphus attacked Wallenstein at Lützen because he did not want to let him remain in Saxony for the winter, and Frederick attacked the Austrians at Leuthen and Torgau because he did not want to allow them to spend the winter in Silesia and Saxony, respectively. To that extent the situations were similar, but there was a considerable difference in that, for Frederick, the risk on both occasions was vastly greater than it was for the Swedish king. On the other hand, the far-reaching campaigns and the mobility of Torstensson gave his strategy a completely unique flavor, but the basic principles were nevertheless no different from those of Gustavus Adolphus. Even in the history of individual commanders we find remarkable parallels: both Eugene and Frederick fought a last great battle with large bloody losses and moderate strategic success, the former at Malplaquet and the latter at Torgau, and thereafter only conducted campaigns in which they no longer sought a decision by battle. Malplaquet was what has been termed with the age-old expression a "Pyrrhic victory," and Torgau was only a little more. From the viewpoint of world military history, therefore, the question to be asked is not so much why Frederick approached so closely to the maneuver pole after 1760 but how, after the experiences of the great commanders before him, he could allow himself to be seized by such a passion for the battle pole. We have seen that it was the improved quality of the Prussian troops, their tactical flexibility, that finally led to the idea of the oblique order of battle and made it seem feasible and that also offered new prospects strategically for bringing on a decisive battle by a bold leader with genius.

If the effects of even the largest tactical results of battle were always only limited and could not be expected as such to lead to a peace treaty, nevertheless the secondary benefits became so important that the commander could not neglect them, and to assure them he was even allowed to hold out forces from the main tactical battle. In the Thirty Years' War by far the largest part of the available troops was used for the occupation of countless fortified cities, and the battles were fought by only small armies. With Eugene and Marlborough, just as with Frederick, we have found one situation after another where in a decisive battle troops were missing who, from an ideal viewpoint, could have been on hand. In his *General-Prinzipien* of 1748, Frederick enunciated the principle that if one was simultaneously attacked by several enemies, "One must then sacrifice a province to one enemy but at the same time vigorously attack the others with his entire force, force them into battle, and use every bit of his strength to overcome them and must then detach forces against the other foes." When the anticipated situation actually arose in 1756, Frederick was nevertheless not willing to decide to sacrifice a province, and therefore he did not assemble his entire "force." Furthermore, he added in his

General-Prinzipien: "These kinds of wars ruin the armies by fatigue and the marches that one must have his men make, and such wars last so long that they finally have an unhappy ending." Consequently, he always applied to only a relative degree the principle of "operating on interior lines," as a later theory has named it. For as highly as he prized the decision by battle, he knew that he could not carry that to the point of actual destruction of the enemy and that for this reason the protection of his provinces and, in the individual case, of depots was of no smaller importance for the extended conduct of the war. When he therefore returned for the second time in a theoretical observation to the assembling of his entire forces at one point, it was for him only the last resort of despair, in order to die with honor. When his critical situation had reached its highest degree in the winter of 1761–1762 and there seemed to be no further help available anywhere, on 9 January 1762, a few days before he learned of the death of the Czarina, he indicated this solution to his brother, Prince Henry. Henry replied that by assembling all the forces at one point they would be sacrificing to the enemy depots and provinces everywhere else. The king himself had the same idea, when, despite his basic principle of being as strong as possible in a battle, time after time he fought his battles with only a part of his army because he used troops for covering purposes. At Kesselsdorf, Prague, Zorndorf, and Kunersdorf he could have been stronger on the battlefield if he had not been concerned with the consideration for protection. When he was besieging Olmütz, the Russians advanced to the Oder and threatened Berlin. Prince Henry wanted to join his army in Saxony with the troops of Count Dohna and fight the Russians in order to free the March. But the protection of Saxony seemed too important to the king, and the plan was not carried out. The fact that we have this same occurrence again and again shows us that it was not a question of fortuitous errors but of principles. It was all the easier to refrain from assembling systematically all one's forces in that the larger the force, the more difficult was the control. It was immeasurably difficult to deploy twenty or thirty battalions in line abreast and move them forward uniformly.[1] Instead of attempting to have the greatest possible strength, the idea was considered as to whether an upper limit should be drawn, whether the larger force could not become a burden and an obstacle that one was better off without. One pondered what strength was the most advantageous, that is, what strength composed a normal army. Machiavelli had already considered an army of 25,000 to 30,000 men as the best. He said that with an army of that size one could occupy such positions that he could avoid being forced into battle and could thus outlast a larger army, which, after all, could not be kept assembled a long time.[2] Turenne wanted to command only relatively small armies, 20,000 to 30,000 men at the most, but with half of them cavalry.[3] Similarly, Montecuccoli wanted no more than 30,000 men. "Battle is fought more with the mind than with the body," he wrote, "and therefore a large number is not always useful." Armies that were too large were useless.[4] Later the number was raised somewhat. The marshal of Saxony established a maximum of 40,000, and Fleming, in his work, *The Complete German Soldier (Der vollkommene Deutsche Soldat),* 1726, p. 260, wrote: "An army of 40,000 to 50,000 men of resolute and disciplined soldiers is capable of undertaking everything; indeed, it can promise itself without illusion to conquer the whole world. Any amount above this number is only superfluous and causes nothing but awkwardness and confusion." Half a century later Guibert moved the figure up to 70,000.[5] Even in Napoleon's time, Moreau is supposed to have spoken of 40,000 as the normal strength, and Marshal St. Cyr declared that it seemed to exceed human capabilities to lead more than 100,000 men.[6]

The idea of a normal army is the direct contrary of the principle of the greatest possible assembling of all forces for the battle.

How then are battles won, if not by the larger force? Assuming that ability and courage can be estimated about equally high on both sides?

Clausewitz later emphasized the theme: The best strategy is to be as strong as possible, first overall, and second, at the decisive point. This truth was so far from being taken for granted by the thinkers of the ancient school that Dietrich von Bülow considered it necessary to justify specifically the advantage of numerical superiority: it follows automatically from the necessity for not letting oneself be outflanked. "If one has more men than the enemy and understands how to make appropriate use of this superiority, the greater skill and courage of the enemy soldiers will be of no avail."[7]

Just as each individual link of the Prussian military nation was superior to the corresponding Austrian link as a result of better training and more energetic efforts, in the final analysis the strategy of Frederick was also superior to that of Daun in the same way. The Prussian troops maneuvered more skillfully, the infantry fired faster, the cavalry made a more powerful assault, the artillery was more flexible, and the administration was more reliable and made it possible to extend the five-march system to a seven- and nine-march system. All of this was brought together by a king commander who was responsible to no higher authority and had no responsibility toward a supreme war council above him to arrive at his constantly superior strategy based on boldness and flexibility.

We have learned what wonders leadership can work. But we are reminded again and again that chance, that completely blind, incalculable factor, plays a very important role. This importance of the factor of chance gradually increased in the period we have considered, to reach its highest degree in Frederick's time. Theodor von Bernhardi, in his work *Frederick the Great as a Commander (Friedrich der Grosse als Feldherr),* makes fun of Frederick's contemporaries, who claimed to see in a decision by battle a product of chance. In this concept he sees a characteristic difference between the king and not only his opponents but also his subordinate commanders, Prince Henry and Prince Ferdinand of Braunschweig. He overlooked, however, the fact that Frederick himself on many occasions, when he moved into a battle, called that a challenge of chance, just as did all the other generals of his time.[8] The author also particularly overlooked the fact that under the circumstances of the eighteenth century chance had a broader latitude to influence the decision than in any other military period, either before or afterward.

In order to exploit the effect of firearms, commanders had made their infantry lines very thin and long. But these long thin lines were now very fragile; they could easily be broken up and brought into disorder by any kind of rough terrain—slopes, swamps, ditches, ponds, and woods. Furthermore, they were very sensitive on their flanks. The deeper a formation is, the more easily the troops can move and defend themselves on their flanks as well. The more shallow the formation is, the stronger is its fire power, but the more difficult it is to move either forward or sideways.

The decision in battle therefore depended principally on whether the attacker succeeded in outflanking the defender and bringing his line up to the opponent in reasonably good order. Furthermore, the attack had to have as much surprise effect as possible, since the enemy could otherwise form a new front.

Whether all of this is successful depends to a high degree on the terrain, which the commander does not know very precisely in advance and cannot normally reconnoiter completely, and if one seeks assistance from darkness, the troops have difficulty orienting themselves correctly in the dark.

The qualitative superiority of the Prussians over their enemies was based not least of all on the fact that they overcame these difficulties more easily as a result of their more intensive drills and their better discipline. Consequently, Frederick dared to make the statement that if a flank maneuver succeeded, one could defeat 100,000 men with 30,000. In fact he did succeed at Soor and Leuthen in overcoming a very great superiority in this manner.

It was impossible to foresee, however, to what extent the favorable or unfavorable preconditions existed.

The Austrians lost Chotusitz only because they had delayed too long on their night march. The Prussians were successful on the night march that led them to Hohenfriedberg.

At Kesselsdorf we must recognize as a pure stroke of luck for the Prussians the fact that they attacked the Saxons before the arrival of the Austrians.

At Lobositz the Austrians had actually won the battle, and the Prussians carried the day only because Browne did not realize his advantage, did not pursue, and withdrew in the night.

At Prague Daun was in the process of leading his army to join the main army. The advance troops of Puebla's corps approached the battlefield as close as 7 miles in the Prussians' rear during the battle. That corps was 9,000 men strong, and, considering the wavering aspect of the battle, it could have given the decisive blow against the Prussians.

At Leuthen a chain of hills made it possible for the Prussians to keep their circling movement against the Austrian left flank hidden, something that had not been possible at Kollin.

At Zorndorf a Russian corps of 13,000 men was two days' march north of the battlefield and could very easily have joined forces with the Russian main army.

Kay could perhaps have been won for the Prussians if the column under General von Kanitz, which was supposed to circle around the Russians in a wide arc from the south, had been able to cross a stream, the Eichemühlen-Fliess.

At Kunersdorf the king succeeded in bringing his army completely into the flank of the Russians, but this advantage was given up because the terrain made it difficult to attack, problems that the king had not recognized in advance and in part could not possibly have recognized.

At Torgau everything depended on cooperation between the two halves of the army under the king and Zieten, which were advancing completely separated from each other; it was not until the very last moment that this occurred.

It is at this point that we must set about understanding the specific greatness of the Prussian king. When General Leopold von Gerlach had read Ranke's *Preussische Geschichte*, he wrote in his journal in 1852 (1:791) that Frederick's "conduct of war was often incomprehensibly weak, but it had its most brilliant moments." What appeared to Gerlach as incomprehensible weakness is the nature of the strategy of attrition, which soldiers of the nineteenth century could no longer understand. Anyone who cannot see the king against this background cannot actually avoid the condemnatory judgment. One is completely on the wrong track when he conceives of Frederick basically as an adherent of the strategy of annihilation; under those conditions, Frederick necessarily appears step by step, with very few exceptions, as a weakling who did not dare to think his own principles through to their conclusion and to apply them. Frederick's greatness is fully recognizable only for those who see him as an adherent of the strategy of attrition. In their appraisal of the role of the decisive battle, there is, as we have seen, no difference between him and his predecessors and contemporaries. He lived completely within the attitudes of the strategy of attrition, but at the apogee of his military

career he came so close to the pole of the decisive battle that the idea
could arise that he was a representative of the strategy of annihilation and
as such a precursor of Napoleon. In doing so, one would think he was
giving Frederick a special nimbus, but in reality one would thereby be
placing him in a very unfavorable light. In order for one to act in keeping
with the principles of the strategy of annihilation, certain preconditions
are necessary that were missing in Frederick's national and military organization. At every step Frederick necessarily held back behind the
demands of the strategy of annihilation. If we see him as an adherent of
this strategy, we measure him by a standard that is not appropriate for
him and would cause him to appear small and limited even in his greatest
days. The later years, however, would on their own present a definite
decline. But correctly placed in the framework and on the basis of the
strategy of attrition, there appears a picture of vitality and of spectral
greatness. In the nature of the strategy of attrition there is, as we have
seen, an irremovable element of subjectivity; I believe I am justified in
saying that Frederick's conduct of war was more subjective than that of
any other commander in world history. Again and again he forbade his
generals to hold councils of war, even to the extent of threatening the
death punishment when he turned over to Count Dohna the supreme
command against the Russians (letter of 2 August 1758). He believed that
in a council of war the more timid faction always had the upper hand.
But he demanded that risks be taken even under conditions that were
uncertain. Such a decision must always have a personal color; it is necessarily subjective. A council of war is too timid because it is too objective.
If a comparison with the creative arts is permissible, we may recall that
the seventeenth and eighteenth centuries were the period of the baroque
and the rococo, in which fantasy was allowed to work in its unbridled
subjectivity, whereas classical art restricts itself to objective forms. We
may not on this account name Frederick as a rococo hero, for example,
for with this expression we would also introduce the impression of a
certain grace and popular art, which is entirely inappropriate. This designation could more appropriately be applied to the French commanders
in the Seven Years' War. For Frederick, the comparison applies only in
the opposition his leadership shows to everything of a schematic nature.
There was, so to speak, never a natural necessity that dictated his decisions
but only his free personal will. Instead of the large-scale invasion of
Bohemia in 1757, he could have stayed on the defensive and left the
initiative to the enemy. He could often have attacked in situations where
he did not do so,[9] and he could also have refrained from attacking at
Lobositz, Zorndorf, Kay, and Kunersdorf. Theoretically, the same thing
can naturally also be said of Napoleon's decisions; from a practical viewpoint, however, the latter were determined by an internal law that leads
to the goal with logical necessity. The stronger the subjective element is

in an estimate, the greater is the burden of responsibility and the more difficult the decision. The hero himself does not see his decision as the result of a rational estimate, but, as we have seen, as a challenge of fate, of chance. Often enough this decision works against him. But if he has been true to the greatness of his character in the risk of his decision, he has to prove it even more in the steadfastness with which he faces failure. If we compare Frederick with his immediate predecessor, Prince Eugene, we see that the Prussian king's career as a commander had many more ups and downs. With Prince Eugene there was a certain viscosity of development that often peaked in his very great moments only in the course of years; with Frederick, there were in a certain year four great battles—Prague, Kollin, Rossbach, and Leuthen—and alternating victories and defeats, the overcoming of which created an even higher prestige than the victories. There is no doubt that an excessive effort was involved in the attempt to capture the entire Austrian army in Prague and that the attack against the Austrian army at Kollin, twice as strong as his own and in a completely favorable position, was extremely rash. But victories like defeats of this kind had a spiritual significance that extended beyond the military result and was almost independent of that result. That was the tremendous respect which the king gained in the eyes of the opposing commanders. Why did they so seldom take advantage of the favorable opportunities that he offered them frequently enough? They did not dare. They believed him capable of everything. If it is definitely inherent in the double-poled strategy that one proceeds to great decisive moments only with great caution, this caution rose to the level of timidity especially in the case of Frederick's principal opponent, Daun, whenever he knew he was facing Frederick personally. War is no chess game; it is a struggle of physical, intellectual, and spiritual forces. Even when we follow the campaigns of Ferdinand of Braunschweig against the French, we notice how this disciple of Frederick's schooling remained superior to his enemies simply as a result of his higher strategic courage, which accepts the danger that the enemy avoids. In 1759 Ferdinand had 67,000 men against 100,000; in 1760 he held his own with 82,000 men against 140,000. The decisive battles were smaller and less bloody, but otherwise the differences between the opponents were just the same as in the main theater of the war, the struggle of Frederick against the Austrians and Russians.

His contemporaries, headed by his brother, Prince Henry, reproached the king, often to an extreme degree, for having shed unnecessary blood; they said his art of war consisted always of fighting. The French Colonel Guibert believed (1772) that he was victorious as a result of his marches and not his battles.[10] The more modern writers, on the other hand, have claimed to see his genius precisely in the fact that he and he alone among all his contemporaries correctly recognized the nature of battle and used it to his advantage. The king himself finally actually conceded that his contemporary critics were right. He declared that his brother Henry was the only commander who made no mistakes; he abandoned the principle of battle in his last campaigns; and in his history of the Seven Years' War he declared Daun's method to be the correct one. We have also seen that the outcome of the Seven Years' War was not determined by the result of battles. If Frederick had not fought the battle of Prague and then also the battle of Kollin, followed by the battles of Zorndorf and Kunersdorf, he would have better and more easily been able to withstand the war. But that is a very superficial observation. It is correct that these battles could have been avoided, that they had their origin not in an inherent objective necessity but in the personal judgment, the subjectivity of the commander. Rossbach and Leuthen, however, were absolutely necessary, and for the commander who made those two decisions, Prague, Kollin, Zorndorf, and Kunersdorf were also a matter of necessity—a subjective necessity to be sure, but still an inherent necessity. "Phaethon has fallen," Prince Henry said mockingly after the defeat at Kollin. The comparison would have been correct if Prussia had really gone down in this fall and if the king had not found in himself the strength to rise again. But because he had this strength in himself, he was not only allowed to dare to follow the orbit of the sun, but he had to do so. He would not have been himself if he had not attempted to force fate. It would have been more advantageous objectively but was for him an inherent impossibility to enter the Seven Years' War with that more modest strategic defensive program that he followed after 1759. Indeed, he initially had it in mind in 1757, but when Winterfeld showed him the brilliant possibility of offensive success, he could not abstain from the heavenly power of such a prospect—indeed, was not permitted to abstain from it. It is from this viewpoint that not only he himself must be understood but also that the contradictory judgments of him are to be interpreted. The naive outlook of his contemporaries, who saw only his heroic side, deified him; professional criticism of his contemporaries damned him; and later authors of military history no doubt felt that the condemnation was absurd but carried their own recognition into a false category and thereby ran into insoluble inner contradictions.

Frederick wrote in the introduction to his history of the Seven Years' War that necessity sometimes forced him to seek a decision by battle. Theodor von Bernhardi taught the contrary, that necessity had forced the king to avoid fighting battles. Can there be anything more astonishing than the fact that, one hundred years after Frederick, his strategy was no longer understood in the Prussian General Staff, which published a comprehensive, well-documented work on his wars, only to find, when the work was already far along and many volumes had been published, that they had proceeded from a false basic concept? As astonishing as it is, it is not only a fact but is also not even so unnatural. Such a difference occurs easily between historical observation and the exercise of an art. Historical probing, as valuable as it is for the practitioner, is also dangerous, because it makes appear as only relatively justified so many of the things that the practitioner considers an absolute law, and must so consider them, in order to require complete certainty and firmness of the concept for the action. Only very strong spirits are capable of joining both of these, and so I want to finish this chapter with the statement that Field Marshal Blumenthal, who certainly belonged to the most determined representatives of the strategy of annihilation (in 1870 he demanded from the start a large offensive into the interior of France at the same time as the siege of Paris), one time expressed to me his agreement with my concept of Frederick's strategy, with the remark that it could once again happen.

EXCURSUS

ON THE HISTORY OF THE STRATEGY CONTROVERSY

Clausewitz is to be considered the true discoverer of the truth that there are two different basic forms of strategy. This discovery is to be found in his *Report (Nachricht)*, which was written in 1827, and therefore not very long before his death, and preceded the publication of his work *On War (Vom Kriege)*, and also in a few statements in the seventh book of that work, the refining of which he himself did not yet see as completed. Since Clausewitz never again reached the point, as he intended, of reworking his book from the viewpoint that there was a "double kind of war," and he had, neither in the army nor among scholars, a direct successor who might have continued his line of thought, his discovery of the double type of war was lost in the next generation, and there arose the idea that there was only a single true type of the conduct of war. The deviations to be found in military history were to be regarded, not as something historically determined and confirmed in the circumstances but as something arising from insufficient insight, as a distortion, a doctrinaire prejudice. When the preliminary studies for my biography of Gneisenau led me to these problems, I soon recognized the falseness of this concept, and in my capacity as historian I easily developed the statements of Clausewitz, the military philosopher, with the historical facts at hand in the direction that Clausewitz himself undoubtedly had in mind.[11] Not as a new discovery and not with the opinion of expressing something new in this area but with the idea that it was a question of a completely obvious historical truth, I published that in 1878 in a book review while I criticized the author in question for his lack of knowledge. But my concept was rejected. Colmar von der Goltz, the later general field marshal, was the first to enter the lists against me, and it became apparent that my ideas were so contradictory of the accepted opinion that I was not even understood. There arose a whole series of publications on the problem, but the main struggle I had to conduct was not so much the defense of my concept but the repulsing of unshakable misunderstanding. In the middle of this controversy stood, quite naturally, the strategy of Frederick the Great, of whom there had developed the idea that he was to be considered Napoleon's predecessor in the discovery of the true principles of strategy, whereas I presented him as a representative of the strategy of attrition, who was great, not as the result of discovering new principles, but because of the strength of his character and the greatness of his personality. The lack of understanding of my claim was so extensive that a very respected military author, General von Boguslawski, apparently completely innocently, cited *"without* a battle,"* where I had written, "by means of a battle." In particular, writers were not willing to believe that my concept represented, and was supposed to represent, a justification of Frederick, but they saw in it a malicious attempt "to pluck away at the laurel crown of the great king." Angered by this lack of understanding, I resorted to the weapon of parody and proved in the *Strategy of Pericles (Strategie des Perikles)* that under the prerequisites of the principles of the strategy of annihilation the presumably great commander, Frederick, would have been a strategic bungler, only to experience that the Prussian minister of culture in the Prussian Upper House was strongly attacked because he had appointed as professor a person who had called Frederick the Great a strategic bungler.

The root of all the misunderstanding was the expression "strategy of attrition" (*"Ermattungs-Strategie"*). I coined this phrase as the opposite of Clausewitz's expression "strategy of annihilation" (*"Niederwerfungs-Strategie"*), and I must confess that the expression has the weakness of coming close to the misconception of a pure maneuver strategy. To date I have not found a better expression, since the expression "double-poled strategy," which I then used in order to eliminate that misunderstanding, is also disputable and has not taken hold.

For a long time I stood essentially alone with my concept. The leading historians of the time, Droysen, Sybel, and Treitschke, were in agreement with Field Marshal Moltke and with the historical section of the Great General Staff, which since 1890 has been publishing the broadly documented work *The Wars of Frederick the Great (Die Kriege Friedrichs des Grossen)*, in rejecting my idea. The scholar to whom was attributed the greatest understanding of military matters, Theodor von Bernhardi, wrote a two-volume work, *Frederick the Great as Commander (Friedrich der Grosse als Feldherr)*, 1881, in order to refute my concept, which was regarded as a kind of heresy and indeed as a dangerous and harmful heresy, as the *Kreuzzeitung*, especially, repeatedly claimed. In the *Preussische Jahrbücher* Alfred Dove expressly agreed with Bernhardi's concept.

Jähns, in the third volume of his *History of the Military Sciences (Geschichte der Kriegswissenschaften)*, 1891, presented the same concept concerning Frederick's strategy as I did. He expressly rejects Theodor von Bernhardi's idea that Frederick had a different and deeper concept of the nature of strategy and in particular of battle. Jähns confirms the fact (p. 2029) that the king became great, not *because of* but *in spite of* his strategic theory. Jähns believed Frederick had been unable to break completely away from the traditional viewpoints and had arrived at a compromise between those doctrines and his own temperament. Jähns pictures the relationship between the socio-political conditions of the old monarchy, the army organization, and strategy in precisely the same way as I. There is one difference, but only to the extent that Jähns occasionally chooses somewhat too unfavorable expressions for the king, draws from the unimplemented plans of the Second Silesian War conclusions that I do not consider justified, and therefore regards Frederick's ideas at his entry into the Seven Years' War not as the apogee but rather as a decline in Frederick's greatness (p. 2027). Consequently, Jähns goes further than I do, so to speak, but he was so little conscious of this that he believed (p. 2020), judging my concept erroneously, that he was taking a mediating position between me and my opponents. When Gustav Roloff then pointed out in an article in the supplement to the *Augsburger Allgemeine Zeitung* (1893, No. 16) that our ideas were in agreement in all important aspects and that Jähns also used the same terms as I, Jähns once explained to me in a conversation the relationship between our ideas in such a way as to show that he, like everybody else, had been caught up in the misunderstanding—namely, that I wished to make of Frederick simply a so-called methodizer. Jähns had therefore felt his ideas were opposed to mine, even though he had unknowingly partially taken over my terms. But since in the *Geschichte der Kriegswissenschaften* he had come out against my concept, the doubt continued to exist in the scholarly world.

Even more unfavorable for the correct understanding was the effect of the position taken by the expert for that period, Reinhold Koser.

From the objective viewpoint, Koser, too, indeed proclaimed the same thing as I, in particular, that Frederick had not been able to apply the strategy of annihilation. In a manner completely similar to mine he also explained the objective and subjective reasons that led Frederick to the decision by battle. He claims, however, to make a distinction between Frederick's strategy and that of his opponents by considering only the latter as the strategy of attrition, since it basically wished to avoid resorting to the test by battle, whereas Frederick was anxious not to destroy his enemies by frequent resort to battle, but nevertheless to discourage and intimidate them in that way. That viewpoint can be considered if we apply it to the practice on both sides. But Koser constructs three (or even four) different theoretical basic forms of strategy: the strategy of annihilation, the Frederican strategy, and the strategy of attrition. That has an immediate confusing effect in that the expression "strategy of attrition" ("*Ermattungs-Strategie*") is taken from my terminology but is used in a completely different sense (as "a weak strategy") without the reader's being made fully aware of this difference. Objectively, however, it is easy to recognize that the historical facts do not justify Koser's division into three. What he defines in a linguistically admissible way as "strategy of attrition," namely, a pure strategy of maneuver, is a method that does not occur in the reality of military history, and if it could be proven to exist anywhere, it would surely not be among the opponents whom Frederick had to fight. None of them avoided battle as a matter of principle, as Koser would have it. Rather, they considered it and sought it whenever they believed it appropriate. At Mollwitz the Austrians forced the battle by taking position on the Prussians' line of retreat, and at Chotusitz, Breslau, and Hochkirch they attacked. At Soor they were about to do so; at Liegnitz they had indeed staked everything on a battle of destruction. And the same kind of battle was planned at Rossbach. Empress Maria Theresa and Emperor Francis, as well as the Russian council of ministers, again and again urged battle and indicated the Prussian army and not some kind or other of territorial gain as the true objective of the conduct of the war. Consequently, no difference in principle can be discovered between Frederick and his opponents. Otherwise, how could Frederick have pointed out Daun's method as the correct one? If Frederick's method, in contrast with that of his enemies, had called unconditionally for the decision by battle, he would have been untrue to himself and would have wavered uncertainly back and forth in 1762 and 1778 and when he attacked the Austrians on a grand scale only a single time in the five years following Leuthen. We can arrive at a correct appreciation of Frederick only if we find the difference between him and his opponents not in a different theory or in different principles, but in the strength of his personality, his decisiveness, the speed of his estimate, the fruitfulness of his mind, and the firmness of his will. Everything depends on this distinction, and since Koser did not arrive at a clear and definite concept on these points, the problem remained in a certain fog even after his descriptions, although they were correctly oriented from an objective viewpoint.

Otto Hintze, in his book *The Hohenzollerns and Their Work (Die Hohenzollern und ihr Werk)*, which appeared in 1915, expresses himself as follows (p. 357): "Frederick, who always preferably sought the decision by battle, in contrast with the cautious methodizers of the old school, who preferred maneuvering." In a very general way we could let that stand. But from a scholarly viewpoint it is inexact or directly false. Neither are Frederick's opponents appropriately and completely characterized as "methodizers of the old school," nor did Frederick himself "always" preferably seek the decision by battle, not even in 1756, to say nothing of 1742, 1761, 1762, or 1778. When he did seek battle, his efforts were often still not strong enough to force the enemy into it, as in 1744. Or, on the other hand, when he did fight, he himself regarded it as a kind of desperate resort, an "emetic," because there was nothing else he could do, as in 1741, 1745, and 1760.

While the historians were still wavering a great deal and were uncertain and the work concerning the wars of Frederick the Great continued in the direction that had already been taken, even if with a certain tempering, there arose in the historical section of the Great General Staff itself a new direction, and it prevailed. In 1899 there appeared in the *Kriegs-geschichtliche Einzelschriften* as Book 27 "The Concepts of War of Frederick the Great in their Development from 1745 to 1756" ("Friedrichs des Grossen Anschauungen vom Kriege in ihrer Entwicklung von 1745 bis 1756"), and this work is rooted, almost without reservation, in the soil of my concepts. It is expressly established that Frederick knowingly and definitely declined to follow a route similar to that which Napoleon was to take fifty years later (p. 375). What I called the polarity in Frederick's strategic concepts is reflected with the statement that the king's ideas had been in conflict with one another (p. 374). The idea to which Jähns still adhered, to the effect that Frederick at his first appearance broke through the traditional ideas with youthful energy, is also expressly rejected. The *Kriegsgeschichtliche Einzelschriften*, Book 27, states that even after 1746 the king still retained the viewpoint of the traditional theory, which regarded battle with mistrust (p. 267). But while the correct concept was represented in this work, the overall work on Frederick's wars was continued in the old sense, and again and again there appeared individual writings by members of the Great General Staff, who sought to claim for Frederick the basic principles of Napoleon. From the controversial references, I wish to point out the following:

Von Taysen, "The Military Testament of Frederick the Great" ("Das militärische Testament Friedrichs des Grossen"), in the *Miscellanies on the History of Frederick the Great (Miszellaneen zur Geschichte Friedrichs des Grossen)*, 1878.

Delbrück, review of the above work in the *Zeitschrift für Preussische Geschichte*, 15:217.

Colmar von der Goltz, *Zeitschrift für Preussische Geschichte*, Vol. 16, 1879, with my reply.

Theodor von Bernhardi, *Frederick the Great as a Commander (Friedrich der Grosse als Feldherr)*, 2 volumes, 1881.

Delbrück, review of the above work in the *Zeitschrft für Preussische Geschichte*, 18:541.

Von Taysen, *On Judging the Seven Years' War (Zur Beurteilung des 7jährigen Krieges)*, 1882.

Von Caemmerer, *Frederick the Great's Campaign Plan for the Year 1757 (Friedrichs des Grossen Feldzugsplan für das Jahr 1757)*, 1883.

The two preceding works were reviewed by me in the *Historische Zeitschrift*, 52:155.

Von Malachowski (Major), "The Methodical Conduct of War by Frederick the Great" ("Die methodische Kriegführung Friedrichs des Grossen"), *Grenzboten*, No. 31, 1884. Answered by me in the *Preussische Jahrbücher*, 54:195.

Delbrück, "On the Difference of the Strategies of Frederick and Napoleon" ("Ueber die Verschiedenheit der Strategie Friedrichs und Napoleons"), *Historische und Politische Aufsätze*, 1887.

Delbrück, *The Strategy of Pericles Clarified by the Strategy of Frederick the Great (Die Strategie des Perikles, erläutert durch die Strategie Friedrichs des Grossen)*, 1890.

Max Jähns, *History of the Military Sciences (Geschichte der Kriegswissenschaften)*, third section, 1891.

Von Rössler (Major), "Frederick's Plans for Attack and Defense in the First Two Silesian Wars" ("Die Angriffspläne und die Verteidigungspläne Friedrichs in den beiden ersten Schlesischen Kriegen"), *Militär-Wochenblatt*, 1891.

Fr. von Bernhardi, *Delbrück, Friedrich der Grosse und Clausewitz*, 1892.

Delbrück, *Friedrich, Napoleon, Moltke*, 1892.

Dalhoff-Nielsen (Danish captain), *Jahrbücher für die deutsche Armee und Marine*, February issue, 1892.

Fritz Hönig (Captain), *Deutsche Heereszeitung*, Nos. 18, 19, 22, 1892.

Von Boguslawski (Lieutenant General), "Strategy as Seen in Various Lights" ("Die Strategie in verschiedener Beleuchtung"), *National-Zeitung*, Nos. 169 and 175, 1892.

Gustav Roloff, *Augsburger Allgemeine Zeitung*, 1892, Supplement No. 16.

Fr. von Bernhardi, *Augsburger Allgemeine Zeitung*, 1892, Supplement No. 65.

Richard Schmitt, *Göttinger Gelehrte-Anzeiger*, 1892, No. 23.

R. Koser, *König Friedrich der Grosse*, Vol. 1, 1893; Vol. 2, 1903.

Great General Staff, Military History Section, "The Concepts of War of Frederick the Great in their Development from 1745 to 1756" ("Friedrichs des Grossen Anschauungen vom Kriege in ihrer Entwicklung von 1745 bis 1756"), *Kriegsgeschichtliche Einzelschriften*, Book 27, 1899.

E. Daniels, *National-Zeitung* of 28 December 1898 and 8 January 1899. (Polemics with Boguslawski and Jähns.)

Koser, "The Prussian Conduct of War in the Seven Years' War" ("Die preussische Kriegführung im Siebenjährigen Kriege"), *Historische Zeitschrift*, 92(1904):239. See also 93:71. Replies by me in 93:66 and 93:449.

Von Caemmerer, *The Development of the Science of Strategy in the Nineteenth Century (Die Entwicklung der strategischen Wissenschaft im 19. Jahrhundert)*, 1904. Reviewed by me in the *Preussische Jahrbücher*, 115:347.

NOTES FOR CHAPTER VI

1. This is very clearly described by General von Caemmerer in *Defense and Weapons (Wehr und Waffen)*, 2:101.

2. When the *True Advice* (Frundsberg) requires "10,000 foot soldiers, 1,500 saddle horses, and appropriate field pieces" against a powerful enemy, that, too, has the flavor of a "normal army."

3. Susane, *Histoire de l'infanterie française*, 1:106.

4. *Collected Writings (Gesammelte Schriften)*, 1:327, 364.

5. *Essai général de Tactique*, 2:41, Ed. of 1772.

6. Jähns, 3:2861.

7. Bülow, *Spirit of the Newer Military System (Geist des neueren Kriegssystems)*, p. 209.

8. In the *General-Prinzipien* (1748) in the article on the campaign plans. In the "Réflexions sur la tactique" (1758), *Oeuvres*, 28:155. To Prince Henry, dated 8 March 1760, 15 November 1760, 21 April 1761, 24 May 1761, 15 June 1761. In the introduction to the *History of the Seven Years' War (Geschichte des Siebenjährigen Krieges)*. Marlborough wrote in a similar way to his friend Godolphin after his victory at Oudenarde, saying that if it had not been absolutely necessary, he would have avoided exposing himself to the dangerous chances of a battle. Coxe, *Marlborough, Life and Letters*.

9. For example, on 15 and 16 August 1761, where, with considerable superiority, he could have attacked a Russian corps. Bernhardi, *Friedrich der Grosse als Feldherr*, 2:358 ff., describes the situation very clearly and finds the explanation only in a kind of mood, that is, that the king had determined to fight the Austrians, and not the Russians in an open battle.

10. Guibert, *Essai général de tactique*, 1:33: "Everywhere that the king of Prussia could maneuver, he had successes. Almost everywhere that he was forced to do battle, he was beaten—events that prove to what extent his troops were superior in tactics, even if they were not in courage."

11. As a predecessor we might perhaps consider a remark by Boyen in his *Contributions to Our Knowledge of General von Scharnhorst (Beiträge zur Kenntnis des Generals von Scharnhorst)*, where he states on p. 20: "In the wars of maneuver, in which skillful movements are supposed to avoid battles to some extent or bring them on only under completely favorable circumstances (the system of the Great Frederick). . . . "

BOOK IV

The Period of National Armies

Chapter I

Revolution and Invasion

After the conclusion of the Seven Years' War the political forms of Europe fell into a kind of stiff mold. The huge struggle of the seven years had ended without any territorial change in Europe and without change in the relationships of the great powers. These powers had realized that they were unable to overcome one another. Efforts were made to come to agreement without resorting to arms. The first division of Poland, which took away from Poland West Prussia, Galicia, and large eastern border areas, was carried out through diplomatic negotiations. What holds true for politics also holds true for strategy and warfare in general. We have seen how Frederick the Great was already approaching the pole of maneuver more and more during the Seven Years' War. During the last two campaigns, in 1761 and 1762, and likewise in the War of the Bavarian Succession in 1778, he fought no more battles—in 1762 even though he had numerical superiority and in 1778 even though his strength was about equal to that of the enemy. Theory followed this same route. It was believed that one could turn completely away from the decision by battle, and the method of pure maneuver was developed, as it had indeed already been done here and there at an earlier time.

Fäsch, *Rules and Principles of the Art of War* (*Regeln und Grundsätze der Kriegskunst*), 1:213 (1771) quotes the following from Turpin de Crissé: "A general must never allow himself to be forced into a battle and should not do battle except in case of necessity. But if he decides to do so, he must have the intention of sparing human blood rather than pouring it out."

The Saxon Captain Tielcke taught in 1776 that not only were customs refined by the sciences, but "that the more tactics reaches its true summit and perfection and the officers attain more insight and strength, the more seldom will battles, and indeed wars themselves, become."[1]

General Lloyd, an Englishman who served in the French, Prussian,

Austrian, and Russian armies and composed the first comprehensive and analytical work on the Seven Years' War, wrote in 1780:

> Wise generals will always prefer to base their measures on these things (knowledge of the terrain, of the science of fortification, of campcraft, and of marches) rather than allow matters to depend on the uncertain outcome of a battle. He who has an understanding of these things can initiate military operations with geometric strictness and can constantly wage war without ever finding it necessary to be forced to fight.[2]

Lloyd was in no way a common, insignificant man. For example, he stated very well (1:320) the fact that the only reasonable purpose of all maneuvering is to assemble at a single point more fire power than the enemy does.

The intelligent French military author, Count Guibert, who wrote widely read works on tactics and was received very cordially by King Frederick and permitted to observe the Prussian maneuvers in 1773, is also supposed to have written in 1789 that the great wars were ended and there would be no further battles. (I have not, however, been able to find the passage.)

Since war was supposed to be conducted by maneuvering, principles, rules, and recipes were sought for this art. Geographical studies were made in order to determine where positions could be found that were difficult for the enemy to attack and at the same time readily accessible for bringing up the necessities for one's own army. Particularly advantageous positions of this kind or fortresses were called keys to the country. It was determined that streams or mountains divided countries into separate "sectors" and that a field army had first to assemble close to these terrain features before crossing them. Forms and rules of tactics and of the warfare of fortifications were carried over into strategy. Regions were considered as curtains and bastions of a fortress. The idea that a body of troops had to guard against being attacked in the rear in combat was also applied to strategy, where under certain circumstances the exact opposite holds true—namely, on those occasions when the possibility exists of defeating the enemy on the one side before he is close from the other side and able to intervene, whereas tactically an attack from the rear is always directly effective as far as cannon and rifle can fire. Since it is advantageous in battle to be in a higher position than the enemy,[3] the strategic principle was deduced that possession of water divides was of decisive importance. The region from which an operating army drew its supplies was called its base, and efforts were made to determine what the relationship should be between the operation and its base. The simple truth that the nearer an army is to its base, the more easily it can be supplied was clothed in scholarly mathematical formulas. The line leading from the base through one's own army to the opposing army was called the line of operations; if one joined the point of the operating army with the ends of the line that represented its base, that produced a triangle. It was arbitrary but sounded very important when one taught that the distance of an army from its base could not be greater than one that formed an angle of 60 degrees and no less at the apex of the triangle.

The *History of the Art of War (Geschichte der Kriegskunst)*, by Johann Gottfried Hoyer (1797), which, incidentally, is very valuable as a historical work, indicates the attitude of the period through the fact that, in a collection on the *History of the Arts and Sciences (Geschichte der Künste und Wissenschaften)*, this work was classified as a subdivision of "mathematics." The art of war was conceived of as being the practical application of certain mathematical laws determined by theory.

The last offshoot in this direction was Dietrich Heinrich von Bülow, a brother of the later General Bülow von Dennewitz. He drew the ultimate conclusion from the nature of the strategy of maneuver by determining that the objective of operations was not the enemy army but his depots. "For the depots are the heart, through the wounding of which one destroys the assembled humans, the army." He believed that by strategic maneuvering on the flanks and in the rear of the enemy one could neutralize any victory the enemy might win with weapons. Since the infantry did nothing but fire and the firing line determined everything, the moral and physical qualities no longer came into consideration, "for a child can shoot a giant dead."

As absurd as were the foregoing ideas, we must still always consider that the basic concept, that of a pure strategy of maneuver, had been the actual result of the preceding military period. These authors, with their tendency to systematize everything, did nevertheless also create a few concepts, such as "line of operations" and "base," which proved to be very practical and have been retained by military theoreticians.[4] The military system, which had now become soulless and whose advocates those authors were, also produced those generals, like Saldern, who gave thought to such considerations as whether the infantry should take seventy-five or seventy-six steps per minute, or Tauentzien, who in the middle of the War of the Revolution, in 1793, ordered: "The pigtail must fall behind to the coattail and the sword must be high above the hip; two locks are to be in the hair with a toupee."

According to Hoyer,[5] the Prussian army made a step forward in the War of the Revolution when it shifted from the triple-rank formation of the infantry to the still thinner double rank, but in the three years of this war—even though there was a good deal of fighting—the Prussians did not fight a real battle. How little the approaching wave of the new period was suspected is clear from the fact that a number of the cited works appeared when the new period was really already at hand: Hoyer's *Geschichte der Kriegskunst* in 1797, and Bülow's *Spirit of the Newer System of Warfare* (*Geist des neueren Kriegssystems*) in 1799.

It had been only three years since the great Prussian king had died when the great internal movement broke out in France, the movement that was gradually to draw all of Europe into its maelstrom. The decisive factor for the victory of the revolution was the defection of the army, its shift from the royal side to the republican side. This victory of the revolution, in turn, radically changed not only the character of the army, but also tactics, and finally strategy, and it brought on a new period in the history of the art of war.

The repeated defeats of the French army in the War of the Spanish Succession did not significantly shake up its structure, and under Louis XV France was still able to accomplish the great external success of annexing Lorraine. The country then made two more mighty attempts to rise to a position of hegemony on the Continent and at the same time to dispute the colonial dominance of the English in America and India. The first of these was in league with Prussia, and the second, in the Seven Years' War, allied with Austria. Both efforts were in vain. The army was large and well equipped, and there was no lack of personal courage and skill on the part of the leaders. But the court generals who commanded the French army in the Seven Years' War were not capable of making the great decisions that strategy requires. I believe we may say that the study of the campaigns of the Seven Years' War in the western theater of operations is a very good preparation for the study of the causes of the French Revolution.[6] Not in the sense that great abuses or violations of duty in the ruling class and among the leading personalities would come to light. As exclusively aristocratic as were their ideas, nevertheless the court and the generals were unprejudiced enough to entrust the important position of general intendant of the army to a bourgeois official, du Verney, the son of a tavern keeper, who, even though there were complaints about him, apparently still accomplished a great deal. But everywhere there were only small intellects at the top, and the army command was restricted by personal intrigues.

The repeated failures and defeats that the French commanders experienced consumed the moral structure of the army, its discipline. Indeed, the French army had never been disciplined in the same sense and manner as the Prussian army. In France, nothing was known of the strictness and exactness of the Prussian drills, of the constant care that was applied there to this skill, day after day. The French discipline had always just sufficed to maintain external order and to lead the troops into combat. When the troops now returned home from the Seven Years' War with little fame but much bitter joking and self-criticism, there was in general not much left in the way of military authority. The minister of war, St. Germain, made a great effort to reestablish discipline in the army by introducing, in the Prussian manner, beating with the bare blade rather than the punishment of arrest. But both the officer corps and the men opposed this. Despite the bad elements from which the army was principally recruited, the soldiers were still not willing to accept beatings, and the officers refrained from the use of a procedure that they did not approve. For the spirit of humanity that emanated from the French literature of the period had also influenced the French nobility, and discipline had become lax not only in the treatment of the men but also in the officer corps itself. The strictness which one wished to reestablish would have had to permeate from the top to the bottom, would have had, as in Prussia, to apply just as strictly to the officer corps as to the private soldier. That could not be accomplished through orders from the minister of war and references to the example of the glorious Prussian army.

In 1758 St. Germain wrote to the general intendant, du Verney: "Subordination is the tie that binds the men together and creates the harmony of society; where there is no more subordination, everything falls into confusion, and chaos and disaster soon follow." But as surely as discipline produces power, so is power also a factor in creating discipline. The Bourbon monarchy no longer had this power, and as St. Germain's effort to introduce a stricter discipline failed, the harm became all the greater and the spirit of opposition was strengthened and stimulated. While it is true that the absolutism of Louis XIV had restricted the old, defiant spirit of opposition of the feudal nobility, it had nevertheless not completely eliminated that spirit. As the royal authority receded and was disputed, this opposition also sprang to life again, as such went hand in hand with democracy, and drew even the officer corps into the movement of opposition. And so it happened that in 1789 the monarchy had no army at its disposal to subdue the popular movement, and the public power went over to the National Assembly, which gave the nation a new constitution.

According to this constitution, the army was to remain a mercenary army, as previously. The introduction of compulsory service was almost unanimously rejected as being despotic. Since the constitution was based on the principle of the division of powers, the control of the army should have remained, as previously, under the monarchy, the power of the executive. This was called for by the doctrine, but, as is so often the case, the doctrine did not conform to reality. It was said that the king as head of the army would be very dangerous for the new freedom, and therefore his executive authority was restricted in the most varied ways. He was to appoint only a part of the officer corps; the other part was to be determined by a complicated system of seniority and election. Within a radius of 37 miles from the seat of the National Assembly the king was permitted to have no troops except his guard, which could not be stronger than 1,800 men. The foreign regiments were to be disbanded. In addition to the standing army, there was to be a second armed force, a citizen militia called the National Guard, which was to be not at the disposal of the king but under the control of the burgomasters elected by the people. This National Guard represented a huge force, for all the primary voters were supposed to belong to it.

Nevertheless, as the result of a reaction in public opinion, the king would no doubt have received the reins in his hand again if the internal movement had not now been complicated by a foreign war.

With all its political and national divisions, Europe is still too much of a unit for a movement like the French Revolution not to have necessarily released strong reactions even beyond the borders. It is, of course, not correct that the kings had joined together to smother the young freedom in France, but nevertheless they sought through threats to exercise pressure, protected the émigrés, who assembled in great masses on the borders and refused a friendly understanding over the feudal rights of German princes that were still in existence in Alsace. All of this was taken by the French democrats as a reason for declaring war on Emperor Francis, from which they hoped that it would not only strengthen their esprit but would also bring to France the old objective of national ambition, the annexation of Belgium. But Austria received help from Prussia, which abandoned the Frederican policy and now, joined with Austria and in opposition to the social upheaval in France, believed it could follow new paths that would lead to power and conquest.

As a result of the revolution, the French army was so disintegrated that it was as good as incapable of action. The officer corps, which had itself still been rebellious at the beginning of the movement, had completely lost the ground under its feet as the revolution progressed. The majority of officers, who could not accommodate themselves to the new ideas and conditions, left the army and the country as well.

An invasion was made into Belgium, which was hardly defended, but at the first sight of an enemy the French broke up, thought they were betrayed, and killed their officers. Before the Austrian army and the Prussians arrived, more than three months passed without any military action. In the meanwhile the French army was reinforced to some extent by levies of volunteers from the National Guard, but most of these battalions proved to be useless. Nevertheless, the French held their own. The Prussian army under the duke of Braunschweig, with its auxiliary corps, had a strength of 82,000 men; the Austrians, who had just finished a war with the Turks, were still very weak in Belgium, some 40,000 men strong. Nevertheless, the invasion was undertaken with the expectation that the great mass of the French population was loyal to the royal house and the German troops would be welcomed as liberators. This proved to be a complete delusion. When the Prussians had taken Longwy and Verdun, the French commander, Dumouriez, took up a defensive position behind the Argonne region and stood fast there, even after the Prussians had completely surrounded the position. He had 60,000 men, while the Prussians had 30,000 on the first day and 46,000 on the second day. The remainder of the army was used for security against the French fortresses in the rear that had not yet been captured (Sedan, Diedenhofen, and Metz). It was a question of whether the Prussians should risk a battle under these circumstances with a reversed front. If they were beaten, they would be exposed to destruction. And even if they had been victorious, they would hardly have been able to push forward to Paris, in view of the hostility of the population. Of course, the French troops were not capable of attacking, but they had superior numbers and were well equipped with artillery. With correct insight and with a decisiveness deserving the highest recognition, Dumouriez had limited himself to the defensive and maintained his position. After an artillery exchange which cost the two sides losses of hardly 200 men (20 September 1792), the Prussians decided to give up the idea of an attack and finally to withdraw.

Would Frederick have undertaken the attack at Valmy? If we consider the extreme boldness of his attacks at Kollin, Leuthen, Zorndorf, Kunersdorf, and Torgau, we might well give a positive answer to this question. But if we consider how strongly Frederick always warned against penetrating too deeply into foreign territory—what he called the "point"—and how an advance into Bohemia up to Budweis was already such a "point" for him, and that he never considered seriously threatening Vienna, we might well have doubts on this question and refrain from attributing this decision to the subjective aspect of his generalship, for which we cannot even establish any likelihood after the fact.

We may also pose this question in the opposite way: was it the distortion of the theory, the idea of waging war without bloodshed, that formed the basis for this decision, or, better stated, this undecision? These concepts may have had a psychological influence, but they cannot be considered as decisive. The decisive point was the realization that a considerably stronger opposition had been encountered than that which had been expected; that the support from the French population on which one had counted did not materialize, and that the invaders were therefore too weak for such a huge operation, as which even Frederick would have regarded the march on Paris.

The invasion had failed. It was repulsed not with the resources of the revolution, not with an armed levy of the population, but principally with the remains of the old royal military nation, especially the material resources—the fortresses and the artillery. Even if this old military nation had been brought into disorder and reduced by the revolution and this loss was not nearly replaced by a small number of volunteers and auxiliary battalions, so too was the Prussian-Austrian offensive very much weaker than the united forces of Eugene and Marlborough had once been. Thus the strategic conclusion of the campaign of 1792 was the natural result of the opposing forces, a result that gives us no basis for critical reproaches or personal complaints.

NOTES FOR CHAPTER I

1. *Contributions to the Art of War* (*Beyträge zur Kriegskunst*), Vol. II, foreword.

2. *General Lloyd's Treatise on the General Principles of the Art of War* (*Des H. General von Lloyds Abhandlung über die allgemeinen Grundsätze der Kriegskunst*), German edition, p. 18.

3. Frederick wrote to Fouqué in 1758: "Cannon fire and musket fire upward from a lower position have no effect, and to attack the enemy with firing from below means fighting against weapons with sticks; it is impossible."

4. The decisive statements by Bülow are collected in Caemmerer, *The Development of the Science of Strategy in the Nineteenth Century* (*Die Entwicklung der strategischen Wissenschaft im 19. Jahrhundert*), 1904, but not enough attention is given to the fact that a number of Bülow's disputed statements are very similar to some that appear in the writings of Frederick the Great.

5. *Geschichte der Kriegskunst*, 2:949.

6. E. Daniels, "Ferdinand von Braunschweig," *Preussische Jahrbücher*, Vols. 77–80, 82.

Chapter II

The Revolutionary Armies

It was not until the invasion had been repulsed that there was gradually formed in France the new military system based on the new political ideas and conditions.

First of all, the traditional mercenary army had been reinforced by battalions of volunteers. They had not yet been very effective in repelling the invasion. But when Dumouriez turned against the Austrians in Belgium after the withdrawal of the Prussians, he had such a considerable reinforcement by these volunteers that he was able to attack an Austrian corps of barely 14,000 men at Jemappes near Mons with a threefold numerical superiority and strong artillery (6 November 1792). Nevertheless, the French advanced only very irregularly under fire and were initially thrown back by the Austrians, but their superiority was nevertheless too great for the Austrians to have been able to exploit their success. They evacuated the battlefield and finally had to give up all of Belgium to the French.[1]

The reaction occurred four months later. The French were beaten by the Austrians at Neerwinden on 18 March 1793 and were driven back across the border. At that very moment, however, the Convention had already decided (24 February) to change over from voluntary recruitment to mandatory levying and had initially called up 300,000 men. They were to be determined by the communities or chosen by lot. Consequently, this law already came quite close to a universal service obligation, but it was received with the strongest opposition by the majority of the French people and was rejected. When the king was executed, the Vendée had remained calm, but when the peasant sons now were supposed to fight for the anti-religious republic, the entire countryside rose up, and soon the large provincial cities of Lyons, Marseilles, and Bordeaux and more than sixty of the eighty-three departments followed suit. Only the Seine basin with Paris and the areas of the theater of operations remained obedient to the Convention. While France was threatened on its borders by Austrian, English, Prussian, Piedmont, and Spanish armies, the interior of the country was racked with a civil war waged with frightful cruelty. Nevertheless, the republic held its own against its foreign enemies because the opponents bickered among themselves, and inside the country the republic was victorious because the democratized army with its volunteer battalions formed in 1791 and 1792 remained loyal. The widespread recruitment in the spring was successfully followed in summer by the theoretically universal military obligation, the *levée en masse* (23 August 1793). All unmarried men fit for service between ages eighteen and twenty-five were drafted without any substitutions. The army was thereby raised by 1 January 1794 to a strength, not of 1 million combatants, to be sure, as legend would have it, but still to 770,000 men, by the estimate of the duke of Aumale, and of this number about a half-million men under arms stood facing the external enemy.[2]

This gave a mighty superiority over the mercenary armies of the old powers, and at Handschoten on 8 September 1793 and Wattignies on 16 October 1793, the French, with a reported 50,000 against 15,000, and 45,000 against 18,000, respectively, were able to win advantages. But they did not yet win a true superiority, since the government of the Terror was unable to bring the great mass into shape. Of the 9,000 officers of the old army, two-thirds—some 6,000—had left the colors; of the old generals, only three—Custine, Beauharnais, and Biron—remained, and all three of them were guillotined. It was therefore necessary to form a new officer corps from the bottom up. This was made particularly difficult by the fact that the Convention remained for a long time full of suspicion of the former royal army and therefore was not willing to do away with the independent volunteer battalions. When General Custine, the conqueror of Mainz, in an order of the day, threatened to shoot deserters, mutineers, and agitators, he was reproached by the minister of war, Bouchotte, since the free man made his orders effective not through fear but through trust among his brothers. Custine replied that he was too good a republican to consider a fool as a god, even if he was a minister. Thereupon Custine was guillotined. The deputy Carnot, however, a former captain who was called by the Committee of Public Safety as minister of war in August 1793, effected the melding of the old line regiments with the volunteer battalions, built up again a useful officer corps, and succeeded to the extent of restricting to a certain degree the disorderliness, the waste, and embezzlement. The completely useless elements were again dispersed, and the war itself, so to speak, formed a new military organization for the French in 1794, the third year of the war. During the period of transition we find side by side opposing characteristics and phenomena. General Elie once reported of the new battalions that they went into battle shouting "Vive la République," "Vive la montagne,"

"Ça ira," but when the first bullets flew, the watchword was "We are lost" ("Nous sommes perdus"), and when the enemy attacked, "Every man for himself" ("Sauve qui peut"). After taking over the ministry, Carnot had to discharge 23,000 officers, since most of those who had remained under the colors had wanted to be not privates but officers. On the other hand, however, in smaller situations, where able men happened to be in charge, the revolutionary troops also fought well, even in 1793, as, for example, at the siege of Toulon, where the excellent commander of the besieging troops, General Dugommier, had as his commissar from the Convention the cynical but brave and energetic Barras and as his chief of artillery Lieutenant Bonaparte.[3] Very similar situations occurred in the civil war in the Vendée on both sides, among the rebellious peasants as well as in the republican national guards. In the excellent book on this war by General von Boguslawski (Berlin, 1894), one can learn comprehensively and reliably what these popular levies accomplished and what they were not able to accomplish.

The longer the war lasted, the more the weaknesses were overcome, and firmer military formations again took form, units that nevertheless reflected the spirit of the revolution.

The Saxon lieutenant, later general, Thielmann, was already able to write home from the revolutionary war in 1796: "We are close to the point where the great nation that we are fighting will prescribe laws for us and will command peace. We can do no other than to admire this nation. Yesterday I captured a hussar officer whose demeanor was so noble that one might well doubt finding anyone like him among us."[4] And in 1808 he testified in a memorandum: "The German soldier is more religious than the French, but the Frenchman is more ethical in that the principle of honor without compare has more effect on him than on the German."

The democratization of the army in the new military organization also brought a special advantage by lowering the demands of the officer corps. It was possible to decrease very significantly the size of the train, because the officers were now permitted only the most necessary items of baggage. No doubt, the sources exaggerate to some extent the accounts of the conveniences that the officers of the old army, right down to the lieutenants, had carried along into the field, but it is still only natural that when the officer corps and the men were brought closer together, the officers were obliged not to be too much above the men in their obvious luxury. In Prussia each lieutenant had his saddle horse and his pack horse,[5] captains had three to five pack horses, and it was normal for whole lines of wagons and carts above the prescribed number to move out behind the troops. It was said in Prussia that the French officers, of course, did not need so much equipment, since socially they were indeed nothing more than noncommissioned officers, but the Prussian officers were no-blemen and, if they were considered the same as the common man, they would feel insulted and humbled and degraded below their class.[6]

Not only the French officers but also the men had to put up with deprivation in the service of the defense of their fatherland, hardships that the mercenaries of the old days would not have tolerated. Tents were eliminated and the men bivouacked in the open air, whereas each Prussian infantry regiment was followed by no fewer than sixty pack horses carrying tents.[7]

The new military organization also gave birth to new tactics.

The armies of the eighteenth century consisted quite similarly, even if with certain variations, of professional soldiers—the officer corps, which lived under the concept of traditional knightly honor and loyalty, and the men, who were considered as more or less indifferent. Discipline forged them into firm tactical bodies, and the firmer these formations were, the more highly they were esteemed. The most perfected type was the line moving forward in three ranks firing salvos. The newer republican armies were no longer mercenary armies in the service of a lord, but they were filled with a unique idea, with a new world outlook of freedom and equality and defense of the fatherland. These ideas lost none of their strength as a result of the fact that the original volunteer service was replaced by a legal military obligation and produced a soldier material which, basically different from the old mercenaries, lent itself to being trained to the point of outstanding military qualities. In this process, however, we should remember that in the French national regiments even before the revolution there already lived a certain national spirit. This spirit, of course, was not yet militarily effective and in fact even contributed in the revolution to the dissolution of discipline and of the old army along with it but then led over into the new spirit and facilitated the transition. And so it was also with the new tactics.[8]

At first the new republican armies naturally sought to move in the traditional formations. But they were unable to accomplish what was required. They were lacking in the discipline and the drill necessary for the advance in line and the firing of salvos. Since it was impossible to hold the men together and move them in the thin lines, they were grouped in deep columns, and these columns were given fire power by having selected men or entire units move as marksmen or sharpshooters ahead and beside them.

This combat method was not completely new. Not only the Croats and the Pandours had already customarily used combat by marksmen with great success in the Frederican wars, but the Prussians, too, had formed independent battalions for the same purpose. And the French had already added individual companies of light infantry to the line infantry regiments in the War of the Austrian Succession. But all these formations were not so much intended for support of the line infantry in combat as they were for the secondary purposes of the war—reconnaissance, patrolling, raids—for which the battle infantry was less well suited. The experiences of the American War of Independence, where the people's levies had overcome the regular troops in the English pay, led a bit further. Special battalions of light infantry, fusiliers (in addition to the musketeers), were formed, and each company was given a number of marksmen with rifled muskets. The grooved-bore musket, the *Büchse*, which was invented in the fifteenth century, has the advantage of more accurate fire, while the smooth bore allows faster loading; this difference is similar to that between bow and crossbow (Vol. III, p. 386). But many theoreticians considered the advantage of faster loading as the more important one, because in the excitement of battle it was not normal to aim carefully anyway, and several musket shots, even only casually aimed, especially in the mass formation, had a stronger effect than the individual shots from the rifle, even if they were fairly well aimed.

The sharpshooters of the French revolutionary armies were followed as a reserve and for the final decisive shock by the columns. Just as the combat of marksmen had its precursors, so too did the columnar tactics of the revolutionary wars. But whereas the former was born from practice, the latter had its origin in theory. The development of infantry tactics had led to a constantly more shallow formation, for the sake of increased fire effect. But the thin line was not supposed simply to shoot but also eventually to assault. Because of the difficulty of firing while moving, the Prussians had even at times planned to make the assault without firing. That had soon been given up. But theoreticians had appeared, especially the Frenchman Folard, who had pointed out that the deeper column has a completely different shock effect than the thin line. The column necessarily broke through the line and tore it apart. It was even claimed that the column should again be given the pike instead of the musket with bayonet. Count Lippe, Scharnhorst's commander and instructor, represented this viewpoint, and the young Scharnhorst agreed with him (1784).[9] This was also reported of a French maneuver in 1778 under the duke of Broglie, one of the most competent French generals of this period, in which the combining of the preparatory fire-fight with a final attack in columns presaged the new combat method.[10] Indeed, in the battle of Bergen (13 April 1759), in the Seven Years' War, Broglie had already had his infantry fight in this way. In the entire generation between the Seven Years' War and the wars of the revolution there had been theoretical debates on the advantages of the line and the column. And even if the defenders of the line had generally held the upper hand, nevertheless, the French drill regulations of 1791—that is, already in the revolution but still untouched by its spirit—had provided, in addition to the line, for several column formations as well, including a battalion column behind the middle. The regulation itself did not draw any further conclusions from this; it was drawn up completely in the spirit of the linear tactics. The columns appear to have been formed only superficially but were not organically integrated with the combat method of the infantry.[11] In actual practice, however, the revolutionary armies now dropped what they did not approve of, the long extended lines. They used the column formation, which, while without strict order, was still useful, by combining it with the combat of marksmen, which was, of course, already known earlier but was now very much strengthened. The columns not only had the advantage of stronger shock action, but they could also move with much greater agility over the terrain than could the long lines, and they easily found cover that removed them from the observation of the enemy and the effect of his cannon.

We might characterize the new combat method by saying that the tactics of the old line infantry and light infantry were blended and the column was added from theory. But that would raise the accompanying idea that it was a question of a conscious new creation, and that would be false. I have never noticed in the sources that there was any conscious idea here, as in the national order, of creating and intending to create something new and better, but instead there was taken from the traditional forms whatever could be used, and what could not be used was dropped. Thus there arose a completely new combat method, each individual element of which, however, was related to something traditional and at hand.[12]

Even when discipline was restored and the army was again brought into firmer formations, a systematic new organization did not emerge. Napoleon did not issue a new drill regulation; instead, until 1831, the French army was trained in accordance with the regulations of 1791. Consequently, in the area of tactics, the revolution was not only tied directly to the traditional, but in its progression it even took on factors from tradition that had already been lost. That applies particularly to the discipline. Almost all of the generals who rose to the top in the wars of the revolution (Moreau was the principal exception) had already been soldiers before the revolution, most of them young lieutenants like Bonaparte. The perception that the fruit of drill was discipline and that capability in war depended on discipline had been retained, even in all the confusion and woes of the revolution. As soon as the new generals again had the army under control, they worked with energy and strictness along these lines. Immediately after the treaty of peace in 1797, Bonaparte ordered that the regulations be studied and that individual drills be held in the morning, battalion drills in the evening, and regimental drills twice a week. He personally was as zealous in his inspections "as a meticulous barracks master."[13] Once he had become army commander, he did not allow the recruits to be incorporated into the regiments until they were not only physically trained but also spiritually oriented in the military system.[14]

A strange bit of evidence as to how the old and the new, militarism and national spirit, were blended in the new French army is provided by an order of Napoleon concerning the incorporation of Negroes. When he was in Egypt, cut off from the homeland, and saw his army melting away, he wrote to General Desaix (22 June 1799): "Citizen General, I would like to buy 2,000 or 3,000 Negroes over sixteen years old and place about 100 of them in each battalion."

As long as skirmishing was a simple auxiliary activity, there had always been the danger that it would be carried too far and there would not remain enough troops under direct control of the leadership for the actual assault. Consequently, as good order was again restored, efforts were made to limit the skirmishing. The combat of marksmen, the linear formation, and columns were used simultaneously and in alternation, according to the need. The fundamental difference between the new tactics and the old was therefore not as obvious to the outside observer as one might think, and the contemporaries, especially the French themselves, were hardly conscious of the change that took place before their eyes. From quite a number of sources we can recognize how little thought was given to a systematic development of the new formations. The combat by marksmen naturally called for training the man in firing, but there was so little of such training that Bonaparte's chief of staff, Berthier, was still obliged to order in 1800, a few days before the start of the march over the Great St. Bernhard Pass: "From tomorrow, all enlisted soldiers are to fire a few musket shots; they are to be taught how to hold the musket with the correct position of the eye in order to aim, and finally how to load the musket." In this same year (1800) there appeared in Germany the excellent *History of the Art of War* (*Geschichte der Kriegskunst*) by Hoyer, which I have already mentioned. The author asks (2:891): "Has the art of war perhaps gained in its development as a result of this war (since 1792)?" "It is impossible," he says, "to answer this question with either yes or no without qualification." Then the author enumerates: increase of the use of artillery; the favorable employment of skirmishers in mountain warfare; the use of balloons for reconnaissance. "For this reason it can indeed be stated that the art of war has been expanded as a result of this war, as in any war, but that tactics has in no way undergone a complete reversal." In one passage (2:958) he speaks of the combat of marksmen in the Vendée. For him, the columns were simple groups without order, a point that is indeed correct superficially. He believes (p. 1017): "In no war has the art of field fortifications been so frequently applied as in the present one." And in another passage (Vol. I, foreword) he speaks of the improvement of the muskets, the stronger powder, the signal telegraphs that had been invented. Finally (p. 886), he believes that those generals of the revolution were victorious who had determined the positions that the old French generals had found in the border areas and that were listed in the war ministry, who understood how to read maps, and who had used them to advantage.

We who survey the progress of this development see the military history significance of the revolutionary wars not in the improvement of the powder and the muskets; those points seem so unimportant to us that we even say the wars of Frederick and Napoleon were fought with the same musket. Furthermore, what was accomplished at that time by balloon observation seems to us hardly more than a curiosity. Nobody sees an important characteristic of the revolutionary wars in the use of field fortifications or attributes the victories of the revolutionary generals to the fact that they knew how to discover from the maps the good positions determined by earlier generals. For us, the single decisive point is the new army organization, which first produced a new set of tactics, from which there would then also blossom a new strategy. Hoyer, that wise, professionally educated observer, sees the new tactics only in mountain warfare and in the Vendée, and he has no idea of the new strategy.

As general war approached, the French offered the overall command of their army to Duke Ferdinand of Braunschweig, the same man who then led the army of the coalition against them and was defeated at Auerstädt in 1806. Frederick the Great had thought so highly of the courageous prince and had praised him so much that he was considered to be the greatest living general. The Goths had once offered their crown to Belisarius, the opposing general,[15] and just as this naive plan of the Goths serves us as proof that any kind of political idea was foreign to their warriorhood, so may the French idea be evaluated as evidence that the French were without any idea that their revolution was also about to usher in a completely new military epoch.

With the new combat method the losses were considerably smaller than with the linear tactics, where the closely formed units came under grapeshot fire or overwhelmed each other mutually with their salvos. This point was already noticed by contemporaries. In 1802, on the occasion of the review of a French book,[16] Scharnhorst stated that in the revolutionary wars few of the higher generals were killed. The situation was completely different in the Prussian army in the Seven Years' War. In the very first years this very small army lost both of its field marshals— Schwerin and Keith—as well as Winterfeld and others of the most famous and oldest generals. But also in a single battle of this war (for example, Prague, Zorndorf, Kunersdorf, Torgau) more men were killed than in an entire campaign of the wars of revolution (that is, in more than four to ten battles), even including Bonaparte's campaign in Italy.

To the best of my recollection, even in 1813 Scharnhorst himself was the only Prussian general who was killed. In general, however, the losses in the course of the Napoleonic wars rose again very markedly.[17]

Among the old powers the new French combat method was considered as nothing more than a deterioration, and it was consciously rejected. The Austrian lieutenant field marshal and general quartermaster, Mack, in October 1796—that is, when Bonaparte had been victorious in Italy but Jourdan and Moreau had had to withdraw from Germany—composed a memorandum in which he listed the advantages of the old combat method. He said that the Austrian army, too, had become accustomed to the "attack as skirmishers" in Flanders, where the irregular terrain made it impossible to attack in a closed front. Furthermore, without being ordered, the infantry attack took on the same form as soon as the heat of battle caused the initial formation to disappear during its advance. The author believed one should oppose this faulty procedure because it weakened the pressure of the attack, could eliminate the first advantages in case of unexpected opposition by the enemy, and made the defeat of the dispersed troops, drunk with victory, inevitable if enemy cavalry appeared. Mack went on to say:

A regular, trained, and solid infantry, if it advanced bravely with a closed front in measured steps under the protection of its artillery fire, would not be held up in its advance by scattered skirmishers, must therefore not allow itself to be held up either by skirmishing or firing by sections but must go directly to the assault of the enemy with the greatest possible speed and constantly maintaining the greatest orderliness. This method is the true way to avoid bloodshed; all firing and skirmishing cause losses of men and decide nothing.

In Prussia the ideas were naturally of the same kind. These thoughts are very clearly explained in a memorandum, probably from the year 1800, that General von Fransecky published in a work on Gneisenau in 1856 (Supplement to the *Militär-Wochenblatt*, p. 63). It reads:

Skirmishing is the most natural of all combat methods; that is, it corresponds most closely to the instinct for survival in us; from this it follows in no way that it is the most purposeful method, as some have tried to prove. War itself, of course, is foreign to human nature; to make it more in consonance with that nature means to make it unwarlike, and that can in any case be no object of the art of war. Someone once said very accurately: "Skirmishing nourishes the natural scoundrel that still lurks in all of us, if we wish to be candid, and one must seek to suppress it." Here we are hearing many voices confusedly raised against us. The great deeds of the French army!

one shouts out to us; the boldness of their skirmishers; their attacks in closed columns in the battles in Italy! Do not all of these prove the opposite? We answer very calmly: not for us. No matter how much respect we have for experience, nevertheless we still think only too little of similar general citations to allow them to overcome our healthy judgment. But this teaches us that a person who is accustomed to enjoying always a protection against danger will be fearful when he is supposed to face it deprived of this protection. We shall nevertheless try to clarify the confusion of these voices in order to see what we can answer to them. Those who call out to us the great deeds of the French we would like to remind that the French in the campaign of '93 skirmished their way in just as well as they skirmished out in '94, in the campaign of '99 just as well in as out in 1800, and they skirmished their way out of Swabia just as well as they had skirmished their way in. We must say trivialities of this kind when we see that people no longer think these facts or no longer are willing to think them. We have the following to remark about the boldness of the French skirmishers, if it is a real boldness. Every kind of danger has its own kind of courage. The Dutchman cannot understand how one can entrust his bones to the untamed spirit of a wild horse, while on the other hand he travels the stormy waves of the ocean with the greatest calm. A man who is accustomed to stand in ranks will certainly not creep up under the cannon of a fortress as boldly as a French skirmisher; he will particularly fear the danger of being taken prisoner or of being cut down and overridden by cavalry. On the other hand, a skirmisher, deprived of the usual protection of his hedges, ditches, holes, etc., will think there is nothing else to do but run off and look for such protection.

This lack of courage, which springs from mutual lack of familiarity with danger, would of itself still not prove what we have declared above, that skirmishing weakens courage in general, or rather the scorn of danger. In order to make this point convincing, we offer the following for consideration. If the skirmisher becomes more and more courageous, this is due to the fact that he learns to realize the danger is not as great as he had thought and also that he daily becomes more clever with ruses and richer in expedients. Therefore, his scorn of danger does not grow, but he only learns how to fight danger skillfully. In cases where he cannot do this, where he cannot face danger with anything but the scorn of it, it will be seen how greatly the natural scoundrel in him has in the meantime been nurtured and grown.

Finally, as far as the battles in Italy are concerned, in which the French so completely belie the conclusions we have just drawn, opposing death with extraordinary scorn of danger, unprotected, in closely formed attacks, my reply is as follows: First, we have only too little knowledge of these dangers to be able to know what degree of courage and valor the French showed there and what kind of opposition they had to overcome. All the descriptions of these battles are rich in pompous tirades and poor in details. Generally speaking, one must judge the courage which troops have shown in combat by the number of dead and wounded, and according to very well-known figures, the war of the French Revolution cannot in this respect be compared in any way with the Seven Years' War. Second, it is not a question here of that violent courage which inspires men in the assault like a kind of passion and which is a natural dowry of the French, because they are more animated than other nations; it is a question, rather, of the cold scorn of fatal danger, which maintains order and steadfastness in continuous fighting and which we find to such an outstanding degree in the old Spanish units in the battle of Rocroi and in the Prussian army at Mollwitz, formed as it was by Leopold's spirit. Our conclusion therefore stands fast.

As a result of becoming accustomed to his combat method, the skirmisher loses the courage which is necessary for close combat. *It follows from this that line infantry must never skirmish, if it is not to lose its usefulness as line infantry.*

Those who wish to introduce skirmishing claim that there is no other way one can fight in broken terrain but by skirmishing. This is based on a major error.

When a commander with a battalion that has never skirmished but slavishly maintains its ranks goes through a wooded area, even though it be as thick as possible, in order to attack the enemy by this approach, one cannot march in rank and column, as is perfectly clear, but both ranks and files must open up somewhat, and the men must pass through individually. Now does that mean as skirmishers? Not at all! Does one intend at that moment to skirmish? Even much less! Is the nature of the closed attack lost in this case? The reply is also negative! It is the leader's intention to approach the enemy and overrun him, just as is really the case in all attacks. A battalion that attacks a battery on the most beautiful plain will not actually remain in ranks until the last moment, but this action still retains the spirit of the closed attack.

If one must avoid skirmishing with line infantry, one does not need to instruct the unit in skirmishing in peacetime; indeed, one must not instruct the unit in skirmishing, precisely for the reason that one must not allow it in war in cases where, considered as an expedient measure, it might appear harmless.

It is really no wonder that the French skirmishers, as they poured out from the interior of the kingdom by hundreds of thousands, swept away our old principles. One may perhaps be frightened by such an occurrence and lose his head a little, but one must nevertheless come back to his senses if he wants to call himself a man.

After their defeats, the old powers, too, acquired a better insight and accepted the new French combat method. Even among them there had, of course, already been a start in this direction with the light troops and the rifle marksmen assigned to the companies. This development proceeded naturally in the way of new, reformed regulations, first among the Austrians in 1806 and then in Prussia in 1809 and 1812. If, by chance, only the French and Prussian drill regulations had been retained, one would believe he had at hand documentary proof that skirmisher tactics were invented in 1812 by the Prussians. We would be all the more ready to believe that when someone discovered that as early as 1770 Frederick the Great, in his document entitled *Elements of Campcraft and of Tactics* (*Eléments de castramétrie et de tactique*), prescribed that in the attack an echelon of skirmishers of independent battalions was to precede the first unit of the line, and that the great king ordered the formation of battalions of light infantry shortly before his death. In reality, these independent battalions were not intended to have a positive effect but only to draw enemy fire on themselves. And we have learned to recognize light infantry not as a revised infantry but as an auxiliary arm. In order to create the new tactics, the new nation was essential. The individual reports that have by chance survived can always be considered as confirmed and as giving a correct picture only when it can be established that they are objectively in agreement with the overall direction of the development. In the realm of the history of the art of war, this method of analysis is of special importance. How greatly scholarship has been led astray in this area by the statement in Livy (8:8) that the Romans had already understood in very ancient times how to move and to fight in very small tactical units, or by those capitularies that happen to be preserved from the last years of Charlemagne, from which we would believe ourselves forced to conclude that the feudal system was introduced at that time! Also, in the opposite vein, we can call up these analogies in a negative way. The most far-reaching change experienced by ancient tactics was the shift from the mass pressure of the phalanx to the echelon formation in the course of the Second Punic War. But Polybius, the contemporary of the Scipios, tells us as little about this as does Hoyer, the contemporary of Bonaparte, about the shift from linear tactics to skirmisher tactics, even though we are forced to recognize the one man as well as the other as professionally educated observers of high rank. Even concerning the origin of the feudal system we are without an account based on original sources. On the decline of the Roman legions in the third century of the imperial period the situation is no different. As earth-shaking as such changes are, they still take place in certain transitions that hide them from the eyes of contemporaries. The chance occurrences in the fragmentary survival of traditional accounts or misunderstandings of an unprofessional author (like Livy) produce distortions that scholarship can eliminate only through the work of generations.

As we have explained at the beginning of this work, all military art moves between the two poles or basic forces, the courage and skill of the individual man and the cohesiveness, the steadfastness of the tactical body. The two extremes are represented on the one side by the knight, who is completely oriented toward individual accomplishment, and on the other side by the salvo-firing infantry battalion of Frederick the Great, where the individual is pressed into the machine in the role of a cog to such a degree that even fractious elements can be incorporated and made useful. The controlled combat of skirmishers, directed from above, is supposed to combine the advantages of the tactical body with the advantages of the good will of the individual man. Consequently, a prerequisite for this change is the availability of soldier material of which it can be assumed that it possesses a good will. Such a good will had been a quality of the ancient mercenaries who were voluntarily recruited. But those armies could always be only small ones. The increasing size of the armies had brought the poorer material. The new idea of defense of the fatherland brought with it not only a further enlargement but also in this mass a will that was so much better that the new tactics could be developed from it.

In the artillery, the construction of cannon had been significantly improved by Gribeauval even in the last years of the old monarchy. More and more had been learned as to where metal and weight could be reduced without weakening the solidity of the cannon. Up to that time, the heavy cannon had been moved up before the beginning of the battle to the positions designated for them, and they had normally made no change of position. It had therefore been possible to get along by having those cannon moved by peasants. But the advancing troops were accompanied by the very light battalion cannon, which were drawn by crews. Gribeauval now lightened the field cannon so extensively that on the battlefield they could be drawn by the soldiers themselves, who were provided with leather belts for this purpose. The revolution introduced horse artillery after the model of the Prussians. At the very beginning of his command, Napoleon improved this situation by militarizing the personnel transporting the cannon. The peasant boys had been only too strongly inclined to take off with the horses when they came within range of the enemy fire. Now, with the systematically trained personnel and horses, the artillery could follow the infantry also on the battlefield, as needed, and the light cannon drawn by crews were abandoned for this purpose.

If the artillery gained greatly in importance in this way because of its greater mobility, its importance, like that of the cavalry, still diminished, because the numerical growth of the armies was exclusively to the advantage of the infantry. Whereas Frederick the Great finally had seven cannon for every 1,000 infantrymen, in the wars of the revolution the ratio sank to two, indeed as low as one, cannon per 1,000 men, but then it rose again gradually under the empire. At Wagram Napoleon had somewhat more than two cannon per 1,000 men (395 to 180,000), and in 1812 about three cannon per 1,000 men.[18] The greater mobility of this artillery, however, made possible the establishment of a new tactical principle for its deployment. The fire was concentrated on a specific point, which was thus prepared for the infantry breakthrough. That could be accomplished all the more easily when it succeeded in taking the enemy by surprise. This concept, too, had appeared and been taught in the French army even before the revolution.[19]

The old armies had as their highest permanent unit the regiment, and for every battle special battle orders were issued, assigning the generals the command of echelons or parts of echelons. Combat by skirmishers, which was estimated to be of longer duration and often had to depend on mutual support of the various armed branches, made it desirable to have permanently fixed units. Consequently, the French created divisions and, later, army corps. That appears to be a purely external arrangement, but it was the exponent of a completely different spirit in battle leadership. The Frederican battle was based on a unified, powerful blow, ordered by the highest commander himself, and this shock action not only was supposed to lead very quickly to a decision but also necessarily did so. Now a battle was divided up into separate, perhaps even many separate actions, in which the division commander or even the corps commander controlled his various arms—his skirmishers, his closed infantry, his mobile artillery—in accordance with his own judgment. It was only in the development of the battle and in keeping with the circumstances that the overall commander made his decision as to the blow that was supposed to bring on the final outcome.

Although the formation by echelons was not given up, it declined in importance. Instead, of ever greater importance for the course of the battle was the withholding and employment of a reserve. Combat was no longer based on a decision caused by the first impact, but it was first of all started and then from a position of depth intensified, held back, or increased. Marshal St. Cyr wrote: "Battles are only won by reinforcing the line at the critical moment."

If we do not place too specific a meaning on the individual expressions, we may present schematically the difference between a Frederican and a Napoleonic battle in the following manner:[20]

Frederican	Napoleonic
The army forms a single, unified body.	The army is divided into corps and divisions.
The leaders of the echelons or partial echelons have no other function than to pass on the orders of the overall commander and to ride ahead of the troops, giving them an example of their disdain of death.	The intermediate leaders have independent missions and the opportunity to apply their military experience and their professional judgment.
The commander has his troops deploy and attack in conformance with a specific idea.	The commander has the battle start along the entire front and decides from moment to moment where and how he is to continue it and seek the decision ("On s'engage partout et après on voit.").
No reserves, or very small ones. First blow is the strongest one. Chance plays a large role.	Very strong reserves. Last blow is the strongest one. Chance has its importance, but it cannot overshadow superiority in numbers and leadership.

Just as the commander divides the battle into individual actions, the control of which he assigns to his subordinate generals, he also frees himself from arranging the details of the marches. Jomini reports of Napoleon that he specified the marches of the army corps on the map with a compass opened to a radius of seven to eight hours of march as the crow flies. On the march from Boulogne to the Danube in 1805 the army covered 465 miles, that is, an average of about 12 miles daily, as the crow flies.

As was the case with skirmishing, so too did the new type of warfare give the French army a second, very important characteristic. The old armies depended on the controlled provision of rations by depots. The army was always supposed to carry eighteen days of rations with it; the soldier himself carried bread for three days, the bread wagon that followed each company contained bread for six days, and the flour wagons of the quartermaster transport system carried flour for nine days.[21] Without such arrangements the strict discipline could not be maintained. The more refinements these armies had developed in their individual nature in the course of the eighteenth century, the more it had been emphasized that the soldier be cared for well and reliably by the army administration. The direct need for discipline and the general organization of the nation were in agreement on this point. War was a matter for the authorities and not the subjects; the latter, if there was no fighting in their immediate area, were not supposed to notice that there was a war. It was impressed on the soldier in the strictest way that he was to be sparing of the countryside and the populace on his marches and in camps. The French did not attach importance to such a sparing attitude. As war for them was a matter for the entire population, which was sacrificing its blood, so was the war permitted to take from the countryside whatever it needed. Whenever the depots failed, the soldiers took by force whatever they needed from the local inhabitants wherever they were at the time. This process of requisitioning very easily shifted to plundering, broke up troop units, and favored marauding, with its infectious force. If Frederick the Great had allowed that, he would have been concerned to see his army melt away as a result of desertions. Only in a few very unusual emergencies did he allow his soldiers to be fed by their hosts in billets. The French revolutionary armies also suffered greatly at the start from desertions, but these desertions had nothing to do with their rations, and there existed absolutely no disciplinary supervision to prevent this. After the unreliable elements had faded away, a very considerable portion of the army remained under the colors, and these men continued to serve as a result of their individual motivation, while of course, in their lack of discipline, they were reminiscent of the bands of the Thirty Years' War.

In 1796 General Laharpe reported to his superior commander, Bonaparte, that his troops were worse than the Vandals had ever been; two brigade commanders resigned on a single day; and Bonaparte himself wrote to the Directory that he was ashamed to command such a thieving rabble. The French, who were of course supposed to be bringing freedom to the peoples, had marched into Milan amidst the jubilation of the population, but eight days later the inhabitants rose up against them, having been brought to the point of despair by the abuses of the French; the insurgents, however, were brought under control by fusillades. No different from Bonaparte's reports from Italy was the report by Moreau from Germany on 17 July 1796: "I am doing my best to control the plundering, but the troops have not been paid for two months, and the ration columns cannot keep up with our rapid marches; the peasants flee, and the soldiers lay waste the empty houses." And a similar report came from Jourdan on 23 July: "The soldiers mistreat the country to the most extreme degree; I blush to lead an army that behaves in such an unworthy manner. If the officers take steps against the men, they are threatened; indeed, they are shot at." Nevertheless, in time the generals succeeded in taking the reins of discipline once more in hand. This was required not only for humanitarian reasons but also in the interests of the military action. In the cited report, Jourdan already pointed out that the inhabitants in their dire need were taking up arms and that it would soon be impossible to travel on the line of communications without security forces. It happened that troops who spread out requisitioning and plundering after a victorious battle were now attacked and beaten. With the restoration of good order, the old forms were again taken up appropriately both in the tactics and the supply system of the French army, and only in emergencies was the soldier forced to resort to uncontrolled individual foraging. Nevertheless, despite the very much enlarged armies, the French ration trains remained considerably smaller than in the old period. If we take into account the decrease in the baggage of the officers and the elimination of tents, it may be correct when Rüstow estimated that the entire train of the French infantry troops amounted to only one-eighth or one-tenth of the Prussian train in 1806.[22]

Frederick once wrote to Field Marshal Keith (11 August 1757) concerning a ration convoy he was awaiting: "On it I base the last hope of the nation." In Napoleon's mouth such an expression would have been an impossibility.

As far as I have seen, no contemporary author mentions how greatly the direct feeding of large military forces was made easier for the countryside as a result of the extension and increase in the production of potatoes in the second half of the eighteenth century. In the Seven Years' War this did not yet play any role. Twenty years later, the War of the Bavarian Succession was jokingly named "the potato war." In the autumn campaign of 1813, potatoes were undoubtedly of great importance.[23]

No matter how outstanding a degree of good order Napoleon had brought into his army, in the supply system the old wounds were still opened up again from time to time, and as soon as there was any kind of failure in that area, the evil of dispersed units and lack of discipline again immediately came into play.[24]

Napoleon at the same time perfected the revolution and brought it to a close. He exercised the highest power not as a result of his inherent right, but as the chosen man of the people. In a general election the French people had named him with an almost unanimous vote, first as consul and then as emperor. Despite the reestablishment of the monarchy, the army therefore retained significant qualities of the character it had newly developed under the republic. The distinction between the officer corps and the men no longer had the nature of a class division but rather of one between higher and lower education and qualification. This distinction was further bridged by the fact that even completely uneducated men who showed proven ability could advance to the grade of captain and in case of special distinction even to the highest positions. Every soldier, as the saying went, carried a marshal's baton in his knapsack. Of course, that is not to be understood as meaning that Napoleon's great marshals had been promoted from the depth of the common people; by far the majority of them, like Bonaparte himself, had been professional soldiers before the revolution. Their outstanding accomplishments were based in no small degree on the fact that the revolution, liberated from all tradition, had brought them into positions of leadership at an age when youthful strength blended with youthful ambition and boldness to accomplish the most unheard-of feats. Napoleon himself was twenty-seven years old when he took over the command of the army in Italy, and most of his marshals were only slightly older or no older at all.

The universal military obligation for the five age groups from the twentieth to the twenty-fifth year of age was again announced as a principle in 1798, but in 1800 it was limited by the provision for substitution. Even before that date it had not actually been in effect from a practical viewpoint in that young men in large numbers avoided service or, even when they were already in the army, they returned home. The administration was not strong enough and sufficiently developed to prevent that, and the offering of substitutes had also already been allowed at one time, but then it was eliminated. The conscription with provision for substitution created by the laws of 1798 and 1800 was by its nature a very flexible system and was in fact administered very mildly. Whereas each year group included at least 190,000 young men fit for service, Napoleon levied annually for the years 1801 to 1804 only 30,000 men for the active army and 30,000 for a reserve that was supposed to drill only fifteen days a year and once a month, on Sunday. On completing his twenty-fifth year, the man was to be discharged.

From 1806 on, the demands became greater and greater, and the provision for discharge at the end of the twenty-fifth year was undoubtedly no longer observed, since the war situation was now continuous. There is no positive source document and no certain number indicating how strong the actual (not the prescribed) levies were from 1812 to 1814. The only point that is certain is that, even in the period before 1805, the very moderate conscription encountered strong opposition and could be carried out only by force. The men who were levied and avoided reporting were called "refractories"; they were tracked down in the countryside by special gendarmerie units, and were led, tied up, to their regiments, or their parents and relatives were harassed with billeting, or the community was held responsible.[25]

Consequently, the reality of the situation was very different from the ideal principle of universal military service that was adopted by the revolution. We might say that this conscription was nothing else than the resumption of the system of the ancien régime: the substitutes, who continued to serve as reenlistees, formed a professional mercenary body and in addition to this group, of course, the successive kings Louis had also imposed levies. Our comparison would agree even more closely with the Prussian military organization, where the levy by cantons played an important role and provided half of the army. Nevertheless, even if it was fragmentary, much of the spirit of the republican army was carried over into the Napoleonic army, not only in the different spirit of the officer corps, the different relationship between officers and men, but also in the nature and the spirit of the body of troops themselves. Based on their origin, they were not mercenaries but were sons and defenders of the French fatherland, even when they played this role unwillingly. These were only relative and not absolute contradictions; even in the old French army, a national spirit had already existed. But the increase was so significant that we may and even must designate the contrast of the two types as a basic difference.

In comparison with Prussia, we might well say that there, on the basis of the canton regulations, the levy was just as strict and even stricter than it was in France under conscription, but in France the conscription procedure provided completely different masses of men, because France had five times as many inhabitants as Prussia, and the Prussian natives of the cantons, even if they had to a great extent a strong devotion to the king and the nation, still were necessarily without the unique power of the fatherland concept, because Prussia was only a chance dynastic nation and not a national political body. Finally, it should be noted that even if natives formed half and even more than half of the army, they were still the ones who were under the colors only a short time, whereas the men recruited in foreign countries provided continuous service and therefore stamped the whole body with their spirit, that is, the spirit of a more or less honorable military class, but not that of the defense of the fatherland.

One cannot portray this difference any better than by comparing the regulations already cited that were prescribed by Frederick in his most important instructions on the prevention of desertion with the army orders that Napoleon issued to his troops before the battle of Austerlitz. Frederick taught:

It is an essential duty of every general to prevent desertion. This can be done only through the following measures: by avoiding camping near a forest; by having the men visited often in their tents; by having hussar patrols ride around the camp; by having light infantrymen posted at night in the grain storage area and toward evening having the outposts doubled by cavalry; by not allowing soldiers to fall out of ranks but obliging the officers to lead their men in formation when straw and water are being fetched; by punishing marauding very sternly; on march days by not relieving the sentinels in the villages until the army is already formed under arms; by not marching at night; by rigorously forbidding that any soldier be permitted to leave his platoon on march days; by having hussar patrols move along on the side when the infantry is passing through a wooded area; by being alert at all times to assure that none of the necessities are lacking for the troops, whether it be bread, meat, brandy, straw, and so forth.

On the other hand, Napoleon's order of the day for 24 November 1805 reads as follows:

For the time being there shall be quiet. The corps commanders will take pains to make a list of the marauders who have remained behind without legitimate reason. The commanders will urge the soldiers to feel that those men are shameful, for the greatest punishment in a French army for not having participated in the dangers and the victories is the reproach that is directed to them by their comrades. If there should be any men who find themselves in this situation, the emperor has no doubt that they will be ready to assemble and rejoin their colors.

The releasing of prisoners of war for money, "ransoming," which was peculiar to the old mercenary armies, had already been forbidden by the French National Assembly by decrees of 19 September 1792 and 25 May 1793.

In his later years, 1812 and 1813, when Napoleon was obliged to enforce conscription ever more strictly, he too had to suffer greatly from desertion. Indeed, we can say that he lost the campaigns of 1812 and 1813 precisely because of desertion. For, as a result of the streaming of men back to the rear on the march out, he arrived in Moscow so weak that he could not continue the war, and if he started the autumn campaign of 1813 with an army that was only a little less numerous than the allies, only to be a little stronger than half the number of his opponents two months later at Leipzig, this situation was, of course, due to many reasons, but very particularly to the unheard-of numbers of desertions on the French side.

Frederick's army, too, became worse and worse in the course of the Seven Years' War, and we have seen how the king sought to compensate for the inadequate infantry by increasing his artillery. In Napoleon's case, we have seen above that exactly the same thing can be determined, even if not to the same degree. With Frederick, this internal change in the army also led to a change in strategy, whereas in Napoleon's case, as we shall see, that did not happen.

Expressed in the simplest way, the new military system that was created in and by the revolution differed from that of the ancien régime in three ways: the army was much larger, it fought as skirmishers, and it requisitioned. Of these three military characteristics, in which the new military system rose above that of the preceding period, we should finally also notice that all three did not come into effect simultaneously and from the start. The great numbers, particularly, appeared at the beginning with the levée en masse, then fell back again for a while, so that Napoleon in his first campaigns was only just equal in strength to his opponents.

NOTES FOR CHAPTER II

1. De la Jonquière, *La Bataille de Jemappes*, Paris, 1902, gives the Austrians 16,000 men on page 124, but a bare 14,000 men on page 143; on page 146 Dumouriez is said to have had between 40,000 and 42,000 men, including Harville's corps, which provided important cooperation.

2. The results of the February recruiting were estimated at 180,000 men, while the *levée en masse* of August produced between 425,000 and 450,000. Kuhl, *Bonaparte's First Campaign (Bonapartes erster Feldzug)*, pp. 32–33.

3. According to the apparently generally reliable description by Duruy in the memoirs of Barras.

4. Of course, other judgments concerning the newly formed French officer corps read in quite the opposite way; for example, von der Marwitz, *Autobiography (Lebensbeschreibung)*, edited by Meusel, 1:459.

5. According to the *Wars of Frederick the Great (Kriege Friedrichs des Grossen)* by the Great General Staff, Vol. 1, Supplement No. 2, p. 38, that had already been the case in 1740.

6. Lehmann, *Scharnhorst*, 2:147.

7. Supplements to the *Militär-Wochenblatt*, 1901, p. 436.

8. That is correctly given strong emphasis by Caemmerer, *The Development of the Strategic Science in the Nineteenth Century (Die Entwicklung der strategischen Wissenschaft im 19. Jahrhundert)*, 1904, Chap. 2.

9. Klippel, *Life of Scharnhorst (Leben Scharnhorsts)*, 1:44, note. The agreement in principle expressed here was nevertheless very limited from a practical viewpoint, according to Lehmann, *Scharnhorst*, 1:51.

10. Jähns, 3:2588.

11. Certainly with accuracy. Kuhl, p. 43.

12. A particularly valuable witness is Duhesme, who participated in the wars of the revolution from the start and in 1814, as a lieutenant general, published a book, *Essay on the Light Infantry (Essai sur l'infanterie légère)*, which he had begun to write in 1805. He shows that skirmishing was accepted only as an expedient, and on p. 114 he says that in 1793 the entire French infantry had adopted the combat method of the light infantry. This point is not expressed entirely appropriately, since, of course, the new combat method consisted not only of skirmishing but also of the following assault columns, which did not belong to the nature of the light infantry.

13. The quotations are from Kuhl, p. 44.

14. Hermann Giehrl reports very clearly and accurately from the sources concerning other branches of Napoleon's military activity in his work

General Napoleon as an Organizer (Der Feldherr Napoleon als Orga-nisator), Observations on His Means of Transport and Communications, His Methods of Working and Command, Berlin, E. S. Mittler and Son, 1911.

15. 2:360.

16. Reprinted in Klippel, 3:40.

17. In a thorough study, "The Expenditure of Manpower in the Principal Battles of the Last Centuries" ("Der Menschenverbrauch in den Hauptschlachten der letzten Jahrhunderte"), *Preussische Jahrbücher,* 72 (1893): 105, Gustav Roloff established a wavelike falling and rising of the casualty figures since the seventeenth century, in which various factors (weapons, tactics, strategy) work together and in opposition to one another.

18. Freytag-Loringhoven, *Napoleon's Military Leadership (Die Heer-führung Napoleons),* p. 43, estimated for 1809 "hardly more than one and a half cannon for 1,000 men," and for 1812 he estimates three and a half.

19. Caemmerer, *History of Strategic Science (Geschichte der strate-gischen Wissenschaft),* p. 14 f., from Colin, *L'Education militaire de Napoléon.*

20. Caemmerer gives a masterful survey of the difference in battle leadership between Frederick and Napoleon in *Defense and Weapons (Wehr und Waffen),* 2:100 ff., especially p. 108.

21. According to Lehmann, *Scharnhorst,* 2:149.

22. *History of the Infantry (Geschichte der Infanterie),* 2:296.

23. Compare Gneisenau's statement to York on the evening of the battle on the Katzbach. Delbrück, *Life of Gneisenau (Leben Gneisenaus),* 1:342. On 24 October 1805 Napoleon wrote in Augsburg to the general intendant of the army, Petit, that he had necessarily operated without depots but despite the favorable season and the repeated victories, the soldiers had suffered a great deal. "In a season when there were no potatoes in the fields, or if the army experienced some reverses, the lack of depots would lead to the greatest misfortunes."

24. Lauriston to the major general, 25 May 1813:

I must call the attention of Your Highness to the march of the troops. The lack of supplies since several days causes the soldier to dare everything in order to procure rations. There are definitely fewer stragglers than there are men who move out ahead at the moment they sight some town or village. The generals make every effort to stop this disorder; the small number of officers paralyzes these measures, especially because the officers themselves are looking for foodstuffs (Rousset, *La grande armée de 1813*).

The connection between discipline and regular rations is indicated very well in a corps order by Blücher (drawn up by Gneisenau) of 8 May

1813: "In order to maintain our discipline we must be sure to impress on the soldier on the one hand that we are using every measure at our disposal to satisfy his needs, but on the other hand we must also observe a strict economy." And it goes on to say: ". . . so that the soldier is completely convinced of the concern of his superiors . . ." Reported in the "Life of Reiher" ("Leben Reihers"), Supplements to the *Militär-Wochenblatt*, 1861, p. 84.

25. von Lettow-Vorbeck, "The French Conscription under Napoleon I") ("Die französische Konskription unter Napoleon I."), Supplements to the *Militär-Wochenblatt*, 1892, Book 3.

Generals of the Republic and Napoleon's Marshals

Dumouriez: born in 1739; already an officer in the Seven Years' War.

Kellermann: born in 1735; already an officer in the Seven Years' War.

Servan: born in 1741; a staff officer at the outbreak of the Revolution.

Carnot: born in 1753; captain of engineers at the outbreak of the Revolution.

Houchard: born in 1740; captain of dragoons at the outbreak of the Revolution.

Hoche: born in 1768; soldier in the Guard in 1784, lieutenant in 1792.

Marceau: born in 1769; soldier in 1785, sergeant in 1789, commander of a volunteer battalion in 1792.

Pichegru: born in 1761; instructor of mathematics; soldier in 1783, *officier de fortune* (see p. 234) at the outbreak of the Revolution.

Moreau: born in 1763; lawyer; commander of a volunteer battalion in 1791.

Jourdan: born in 1762; soldier in 1778 and serving with his regiment in America in 1784; for a time, house-to-house peddler; commander of a volunteer battalion in 1791.

Scherer: born in 1747; officer in the Austrian and Dutch armies; French captain in 1791.

Kléber: born in 1753; architect; for a while Austrian lieutenant; officer in a volunteer battalion in 1792.

Sérurier: born in 1742; *officier de fortune*, captain at the outbreak of the Revolution.

Berthier: born in 1753; general staff officer at the outbreak of the Revolution.

Moncey: born in 1754; second lieutenant in 1779, lieutenant in 1782.

Perignon: born in 1754; second lieutenant in 1784.

Lefebvre: born in 1755; soldier in 1770, sergeant in 1782, lieutenant in the National Guard in 1789.

Masséna: born in 1756; soldier in 1775, *officier de fortune* at the outbreak of the Revolution.

Augereau: born in 1757; soldier in 1774, deserted in 1776, became a fencing master in Prussia; returned to France at the outbreak of the Revolution and became adjutant-major (*officier de fortune*) in the Germanic legion.

Bernadotte: born in 1763; soldier in 1779, *officier de fortune* at the outbreak of the Revolution.

Brune: born in 1763; lawyer; volunteer in 1791.

Gouvion St. Cyr: born in 1764; artist painter; volunteer in 1792.

Victor: born in 1764; soldier from 1781 on.

Macdonald: born in 1765; lieutenant in 1784.

Grouchy: born in 1766; lieutenant in 1781.

Oudinot: born in 1767; soldier in 1784.

Murat: born in 1767; soldier in 1787.

Bessières: born in 1768; from a family of lawyers; soldier in 1792, second lieutenant in 1793.

Mortier: born in 1768; son of a deputy of the National Assembly; volunteer in 1791 and immediately elected captain.

Desaix: born in 1768; second lieutenant in 1783.

Ney: born in 1769; soldier in 1788.

Soult: born in 1769; soldier in 1785, noncommissioned officer at the outbreak of the Revolution.

Lannes: born in 1769; son of a stable groom; dyer; volunteer in 1792.

Bonaparte: born in 1769; lieutenant in 1785.

Suchet: born in 1770; soldier in 1792.

Davout: born in 1770; attended the Ecole Militaire in Paris, lieutenant in 1788.

Marmont: born in 1774; son of a knight of the Order of Saint Louis; second lieutenant in 1790.

THOSE LISTED ABOVE WHO WERE ALREADY OFFICERS IN THE OLD ARMY
(in addition to Lafayette, Custine, Biron, Beauharnais)

Dumouriez, Kellermann, Servan, Carnot, Houchard, Berthier, Moncey, Grouchy, Desaix, Macdonald, Bonaparte, Perignon, Davout, Marmont.

OFFICIERS DE FORTUNE

Pichegru, Bernadotte, Masséna, Sérurier.
Those who would have had the opportunity for this career: Augereau, Soult, Ney, Murat, Victor, Oudinot.

OFFICERS IN THE SERVICE OF FOREIGN COUNTRIES

Scherer, Kléber.
Those who in the Old Army would have remained privates or have become noncommissioned officers at most: Jourdan, Hoche, Marceau, Lefebvre, Lannes.
Civilians with a higher education who entered the army after the start of the Revolution: Moreau, Brune, Bessières, Mortier, Suchet, St. Cyr.

Chapter III

Napoleonic Strategy[1]

The natural principle of strategy is, as we should repeat, assembling one's forces, seeking out the enemy's main force, defeating it, and following up the victory until the loser subjects himself to the will of the victor and accepts his conditions, in the most extreme case even to the point of occupying the entire enemy country. "The destruction of the enemy armed forces is, among all the purposes that can be pursued in war, always the one that dominates all others" (Clausewitz). This, then, and not a geographical point, an area, a city, a position, or a depot, is the objective of the attack. If one side has succeeded, as the result of a great tactical victory, in destroying the enemy armed forces physically and spiritually to such an extent that they can fight no longer, the victor extends his victory as broadly as he considers appropriate for his political purpose.

The armies of the ancien régime were too small, too awkward in their tactics, and too unreliable in their composition to be able to carry out these basic principles in their conduct of war. They stood fast in front of positions that were impregnable for their tactics; they could not bypass them because they had to carry their rations along with them. They could risk going only a moderate distance into enemy country because they were not able to protect large areas and they had to guard a secured line of communications with their base under all circumstances.

Napoleon found himself freed from these fetters. From the start he wagered everything on the tactical victory that was to put the enemy army out of action, and he then followed up his victory until the enemy subjected himself to his conditions. From this supreme principle there stemmed consequences that influenced everything from the campaign plans down to each individual combat action. Since everything was based from the start on an overwhelming tactical victory, all other purposes and considerations were subordinated to this single supreme purpose, and the campaign plan was of a certain natural simplicity. The strategy of attrition is based on individual undertakings that can be formed in one way or another. At the beginning of the Seven Years' War Frederick wavered between the most varied, indeed opposite, plans. The more resourceful and the more energetic the commander is, the more possibilities loom up in his fantasy and the more subjective are his decisions. Napoleon's campaign plans had an inherent objective necessity. When we first recognize those plans and understand them, we have the feeling that they could not be different in any way, that the creative act of the strategic genius consisted simply of determining what was dictated by the very nature of things. The Empire style, which is spoken of in the history of art, with its classicism and its straight-line simplicity, permits a certain comparison with the art of war of that period as well.

Let us seek to achieve a comprehensive view of the positive results that stem directly from this contrast of the basic principles. We do not need to develop them dialectically but can read them from the deeds of the great masters, Napoleon and Frederick.

In his campaign concepts, Napoleon concentrated on the enemy army and based everything from the start on not only attacking that army but, where possible, also destroying it. Frederick, too, stated the principle: "He who wishes to save everything saves nothing. The most essential element, therefore, to which one must hold, is the enemy army." We have seen, however, that for Frederick this principle still had only a relative significance, that he deviated from it time and again and very strongly. For Napoleon, its importance was absolute. When Napoleon was involved with several enemies, he was able to overcome all of them, one after the other. In 1805 he had defeated the Austrians at Ulm before the Russians arrived; then he defeated the Russians with the remnants of the Austrians at Austerlitz before the Prussians intervened. In 1806 he again defeated the Prussians before the Russians were on hand (at Jena), and in 1807 he defeated the Russians before the Austrians had pulled themselves together again.

At the outbreak of the Seven Years' War, Frederick acted in a completely different manner. In July 1756 the situation was already completely ripe, the Austrians were not yet mobilized, and the Russians and French were far away. But instead of striking as quickly as possible, Frederick artfully delayed the start of the war until the end of August. If he had been a strategist of the school of annihilation—that is, if his resources had allowed him to follow the strategy of annihilation—we would have to decide that this conduct would have been the most serious strategic error of his entire military career. But since the plan for a total subjection of Austria was out of the question for him, even under the most favorable circumstances, he acted correctly by limiting himself for this year to the occupation of Saxony and by doing this so late that the French no longer considered it suitable to interfere with him.

We see how contradictory is the attitude of those persons who attempt to show, for the higher fame of Frederick, that in the following year, 1757, he actually had a plan for the subjection of Austria (battle of Prague, siege of Prague). If this plan had really been feasible in 1757, how much easier it would necessarily have been in 1756! Frederick's conduct is clear and consistent only on the basis of the strategy of attrition. But if this is correct, we may, on the other hand, evaluate this start of the Seven Years' War in its fundamental contrast to Napoleon's conduct in 1805 and 1806 as the finest and most fruitful proof for the natural opposition between the nature and the principles of the two types of strategy that we find in history.

Let us pursue this point further.

In the strategy of attrition we find sieges of fortresses, their prevention, and their relief in the foreground of the events. These occurred less frequently with Frederick than with his predecessors, but they were still very important. Napoleon, in all his campaigns (aside from secondary undertakings), besieged only two fortresses, Mantua in 1796 and Danzig in 1807.

Even in the case of these two sieges, he reached his decision only because at the moment he was unable to continue to pursue the war in the open field against the enemy forces with the forces he himself had available. In the strategy of annihilation, one besieges only what one absolutely cannot avoid besieging, unless it be the enemy capital itself, like Paris in 1870, or when an entire enemy army is surrounded in the stronghold, as at Metz in 1870, or when it is a question of smaller secondary actions. For Frederick, the capture of a fortress, like Neisse in 1741 and Prague, Olmütz, and Schweidnitz in 1762, was often the real objective of a campaign.

Frederick expressly proclaimed: "If you find a country where there are many fortified places, do not leave any of them behind you, but capture them all. Then you will be proceeding systematically and you will have nothing to fear in your rear."[2]

If the allies had intended to follow this Frederican principle when they invaded France in 1814, they would never have overcome Napoleon.

Frederick built canals; he used the waterways not only for commerce, but also for the provisioning of his troops. Napoleon built roads; he waged war primarily by marching.

For Frederick, battle was, according to an expression he often used, an "emetic" that one gives to a sick person. He wrote quite often, when he wished to justify his decision to do battle, that there was no other possibility left to him.[3] For him, battle was a question directed to fate, a challenging of chance, which could determine the outcome in an unforeseeable manner. Napoleon stated as his principle that he would not accept battle if he did not have a 70 percent chance of winning.[4] If

Frederick had been willing to adhere to this principle, he could hardly have fought a single battle. This does not indicate a difference in the boldness of the two commanders, for example, of which there can be no question, but it lies in the differences of the systems. If the practitioner of the strategy of annihilation were willing to consider battle as a chance decision, then the entire war would be based on chance, for it is battle that decides the outcome of the war. In the strategy of attrition, battle is only one factor among several, and the outcome of battle can be counterbalanced. Frederick once wrote, when he was considering a battle, that even if it should be lost, his situation would not thereby be any worse than was already the case.[5] Coming from Napoleon, such a statement would be incomprehensible and impossible. Under all circumstances, a lost battle or a victorious one changed for him and in his eyes the entire situation. For Prussia, Kunersdorf was something to recover from, while Jena was not. We have seen in Frederick's case how very much the statement he often made, to the effect that all available forces had to be assembled for a battle, was actually limited in practice. Napoleon really followed this through, although even that is naturally not to be taken on an absolute basis.[6] On 15 November 1805 he wrote to Marmont: "People attribute to me somewhat more talent than to others, and yet, in order to do battle with an enemy whom I am already accustomed to defeat, I never believe I have enough troops; I assemble all the forces that I can."

Frederick had the principle of drawing up as extensive a campaign plan as possible, of which he himself said from the start that it would be reduced in the execution. Again and again he confirmed his adherence to this principle. "Far-reaching campaign plans," he says in the *Political Testament* of 1768, "are undoubtedly the best ones, because in carrying them out one immediately notices what would be impracticable, and by limiting oneself to that which is feasible, one achieves more than with a small project, something that can never lead to anything great." "Such great plans are not always successful; if they succeed, they decide the outcome of the war." "Draw up four projects of this kind, and if one of them succeeds, you are rewarded for all your trouble."[7] Consequently, if we compare his initial plans with their later execution, we cannot avoid the impression that his energy was not equal to his strategic ideas. Nothing would be falser. With complete awareness he first drew up plans that exceeded the possible so that under no circumstances would he remain below that which was possible. The hard facts established their limits; he knew that they would do so and wanted it that way. His strategic ideas, therefore, may always be evaluated and estimated only with this condition. The opposite applied to Napoleon. His plans did not shrink in the execution but rather grew still larger. He said of himself:

> When I am making a campaign plan, there is nobody more timid than I; I imagine all the dangers in an exaggerated way and see all

the circumstances as black as possible; I am in a painful state of agitation. Of course, that does not prevent me from appearing completely cheerful to my staff. But once my decision is made, I forget everything and think only of those things that can make it succeed.

In the Frederican battle, everything is based on a unified, cohesive effect; the first shock is also supposed to bring on the decision. Napoleon often moved into a battle without a definite plan, without even a rather accurate idea of the enemy's position. One makes contact, he said, and then sees what is to be done. Consequently, a very significant part of the army had to remain in reserve so that the victory could be fought out with it at the point to be designated by the commander. Primarily, this difference between the Frederican battle and the Napoleonic goes back to the difference in tactics, the linear formation and the combat by marksmen. Nevertheless, a connection with strategy is also involved. The Napoleonic battle develops organically from the preceding operations, often unforeseen. The Frederican battle stems from a more or less prepared subjective decision, and it therefore rejects a long initial development and seeks the decision the faster the better.

His whole life long Frederick could not do enough weighing of strategic principles, expedients, and plans. Napoleon said: "I know only three things in war; they are to cover ten leagues per day, to fight, and to rest."

What held true for the individual battle—namely, that Napoleon allowed it to develop without any preconceived idea—also held true for his strategy. He himself said that he never had a campaign plan. And that does not stand in contradiction to the statement that we heard above, to the effect that he was very anxious as he worked out his plans. A statement by Moltke that is often quoted reads as follows:

No plan of operations extends with any degree of certainty beyond the first encounter with the main enemy force. Only the layman believes he can discern in the course of a campaign the consistent execution of an initial idea formulated in advance, thought out in all its details, and adhered to right up to the end.

It is in this sense that Napoleon, too, meant that he never had a campaign plan. Nevertheless, he naturally had a very definite idea for and during the deployment of his troops, and he carefully weighed the possibilities that could result therefrom, but without deciding in advance for any particular one. In the strategy of attrition we again and again find campaign plans determined far in advance—with Frederick no doubt not to the same extent as with his contemporaries, but nevertheless with him also, in keeping with the nature of things.

Even Napoleon was not strong enough to carry the subjection of his enemies up to the same point as, for example, Alexander the Great, who took possession of all of Persia. Even the Prussians would have fought on in 1807 if the Russians had been ready to do so. It was not only through victory but eventually also through politics that Napoleon brought his wars to an end. We could therefore say that the difference between him and his predecessor was, after all, only a relative one. But we have seen that the practical differences were fundamental in that Napoleon in fact acted in accordance with the principles logically stemming from the nature of the strategy of annihilation, no differently than Alexander the Great. He was able to do that because he was certain, or believed he was certain, that if in the end there was still something missing from the complete subjection of the enemy, if he ran out of breath, so to speak, he would still be capable of making up that deficiency through politics. Indeed, we may say that it is precisely in this point that his historical greatness lies. In accordance with his deepest inclination, Napoleon was even much more a statesman than a soldier. Neither as a young person nor later did he pursue military history or theoretical studies. All reflective military men concerned themselves with the question of whether one should not turn back from the thin lines to the deep column; there is no indication that Lieutenant Bonaparte did this. Frederick read everything there was in the way of old and more modern literature on the nature of war and military history. Of course, Napoleon, too, quite often pointed out that a soldier had to study the deeds of the great commanders in order to learn from them. He named Alexander, Hannibal, Caesar, Gustavus Adolphus, Turenne, Eugene, and Frederick. But he himself was familiar essentially, in addition to Caesar, with only the quite unmilitary biographies of Plutarch, and he preferred to read writings on politics and moral philosophy. Nothing was more characteristic of him than his behavior at the outbreak of the war of the revolution. He was a French lieutenant; if the military inclination in him had been the strongest, it would necessarily have driven him to move to the front into the fight with his regiment—all the more strongly since he adhered enthusiastically to the new political ideas. But for the whole first year the young officer avoided the war and occupied himself with somewhat adventurous plans for Corsican politics. Not until these had failed did he go to the army. But his very first large-scale campaign plan, after he had been assigned the high command in Italy in 1796, was politically based, aiming for the separation of Sardinia from Austria, and it was politically that he finally also brought the struggle against Austria to a close in 1797, when, already in position close to Vienna, he not only proposed to his defeated enemy the cession of territories (Belgium and Milan), but also offered them the possibility of a great gain (Venice). The situation was similar in his later wars; despite all his extravagant fantasy, he nevertheless also had a feel for the limits of his power. Whether this moderation had abandoned him after 1812 and no longer held him in limits, or whether an inexhaustible inherent necessity led him beyond those limits, we may at first pass over. We limit ourselves to the point that his circumstances enabled him to base his campaign plans, not on simple attrition, but on the complete overthrow of his enemy, so that he could then complete his work politically—something that was not possible for Gustavus Adolphus, the commanders of Louis XIV, Prince Eugene, and Frederick the Great.

If one were perhaps inclined to believe that the new strategy had grown of itself as a natural product on the soil of the new conditions, that would be an error. It required the creative genius of a great personality to form the new phenomenon from the material at hand. Precisely in such situations do we recognize with special clarity that world history is in no way a natural process, as the materialists believe. We realize this when we compare the first campaigns in which the new strategy was applied, the campaigns of General Bonaparte, with those of the most important of his colleagues, General Moreau.

After 1795 had passed without any decisive actions but Prussia had withdrawn as a result of the Basel peace treaty, in the spring of 1796 the French established three armies—one under Jourdan along the Middle Rhine as far as Düsseldorf, one under Moreau on the Upper Rhine, and one under Bonaparte in Italy. With the help of English subsidies, the Austrians, together with their smaller allies, had managed to establish, in opposition to the French, armies that were not only equal to them in strength but even somewhat stronger. On both sides the troops were spread over a long front in keeping with the principle of the protection of territory. Bonaparte, whose troops were stationed partly in the Alps, and partly along the Riviera almost as far as Genoa, now assembled his main force on his most extreme right flank on the Riviera, leaving his line of communications with France only weakly covered. From both sides the forces moved toward each other via the Apennine passes, but the French, although a few thousand men weaker in overall strength, as a result of their troop dispositions were stronger than their enemies in each individual battle. They defeated the central enemy column and then pushed between the Austrian and the Sardinian armies and completely won the upper hand as the general granted an advantageous armistice to the king of Sardinia.[8] Thus Bonaparte drove the Austrians back to Mantua, surrounded the remnants of their army there, and besieged them. Four times the Austrians came down out of the Alps to relieve Mantua. Each time they were defeated by the French—once when Bonaparte gave up the siege of the fortress and sacrificed his heavy cannon in order to gain numerical superiority for the decisive action in the open field.

When he had been victorious and was negotiating for the armistice at Leoben, he said to the Austrian generals: "There are many good generals in Europe; but they see too much at the same time. As for me, I see only one thing, and that is the masses of men. I seek to destroy them, because I am certain that with that everything else falls at the same time."

Somewhat later he said in Milan: "The nature of strategy consists of always having, even with a weaker army, more forces at the point of attack or at the point where one is being attacked than the enemy has." Finally, on St. Helena, he said:

> In the wars of the revolution one had the false system of dividing up one's forces, sending columns to the right and columns to the left, which is completely wrong. What truly brought me so many victories was the opposite system. For on the day before a battle, instead of having my divisions stay apart, I drew them all together at the point I wanted to overwhelm. My army was massed at that point and easily threw back whatever forces confronted it, forces that were necessarily always weaker.[9]

From an objective viewpoint, it would have been completely possible for Moreau and Jourdan to operate in Germany in the same manner as Bonaparte in Italy. The Austrians under the command of Archduke Charles were extended along a front reaching from Basel to Sieg. After a corps under Wurmser had been sent off to Italy because of Bonaparte's successes, the opposing forces were quite equal. The French, by concentrating their troops, could have attacked and defeated the various Austrian corps individually. And powerful blows were indeed intended; but the real objective was considered to be, not the destruction of the enemy armed forces, but the winning of territory. With actions of little importance the two French generals maneuvered the archduke back toward Bavaria. Moreau moved up to the Isar. In the meantime, however, the archduke had turned with his main forces against Jourdan; he now inflicted a loss on him at Würzburg and pushed him back to the Rhine. Along the Isar Moreau had more than twice the strength of his opponents; nevertheless, he too took up the withdrawal, did not know how to make any further use of his superior forces, and after four months the two opponents were again in approximately the same positions as at the start of hostilities. Public opinion, however, credited Moreau with a great strategic accomplishment for his successful withdrawal without losses through the Höllental.

The French campaign plan, with its establishment of the three armies commanded by Bonaparte, Moreau, and Jourdan, was drawn up by the minister of war, Carnot. Scholars have claimed to see in it a strategic concept of the highest style, believing that Carnot intended to have the three armies close in on Vienna. It is correct that Carnot had in mind a cooperation between the theaters of operation in Italy and Germany, but nevertheless not in the sense that the three armies, each moving forward from its separate base, were finally to join forces on the battlefield for the destruction of the enemy army. Instead, his objective was that of mutual support in order, by threatening his flanks, to maneuver the opponent back farther and farther and win territory. To a certain extent this plan can be compared with Frederick's march into Bohemia in 1757. Just as Frederick considered the nature of this plan to consist of "chasing the enemy almost out of Bohemia,"[10] but also wanted to strike the most possible blows in the process, so Carnot also wrote to the generals, pointing out to them how they would outflank the enemy and capture his depots while at the same time they were always to attack strongly and not let up with their pursuit until they had completely defeated and broken up the enemy. These instructions can serve as a perfect example for the double-poled strategy. But the difference between 1757 and 1796 is that, when the opportunity presented itself, Frederick increased his inclination for battle up to the point of waging the large battle of Prague and finally to the idea of taking the entire enemy army prisoner in Prague, whereas Moreau, with very moderate actions, remained mired in the concept of maneuver and did not go beyond that, even when the defection of the German princes from Austria had left the nation's forces significantly weakened and had given the French the unquestionable important superiority.

A comparison of the double campaign in 1800 shows quite the same picture. In 1799 the Austrians, with the help of the Russians, had driven the French out of Italy while Napoleon was in Egypt. Bonaparte, having been named first consul, initially planned to conduct the campaign in Germany. He intended to join the reserve army that he formed at Dijon with Moreau's troops, attack the Austrians in an enveloping move from Switzerland, do the greatest possible destruction to their army, and then move on Vienna. The plan turned out to be impracticable, because Moreau was not willing to be subordinated to the first consul and Napoleon had to be considerate of this older general, who, after him, was the most highly respected. It would have been too ticklish for him politically if Moreau, disgruntled, had demanded his discharge.

And so Bonaparte decided to lead the reserve army, not to Germany, but through Switzerland to Italy. He moved down from the Alps on the east side of Lake Geneva, had an auxiliary corps from Moreau move over the St. Gotthard Pass to join him, and appeared with it in the rear of the Austrians, to their great surprise. With the greatest boldness he disposed his divisions in such a way that he could confront the Austrians on any route on which they could attempt to withdraw, and yet he carefully held his units so close together that they were able to support one another mutually. When the opposing forces met one another by surprise at the village of Marengo on 14 June 1800, the Austrians, who had an assembled strength of about 30,000 men, had the advantage against the 20,000-man

French force. The battle nearly ended in a complete defeat of the French.
But the arrival of Desaix's division (6,000 men), which was ordered up
by Bonaparte, and a spontaneous cavalry attack by General Kellermann
reversed the balance. The Austrian commander, Melas, who was already
rather elderly, had already left the battlefield, and his troops were advancing with little order when the counterattack occurred with complete
surprise. Consequently, the French were victorious despite their smaller
numbers, principally as a result of the ability of their troops and of their
youthful, energetic generals. Since the battle was fought with reversed
fronts, the Austrians believed they had no further line of retreat, and
Bonaparte won Upper Italy as far as the Mincio as he granted Melas a
free withdrawal in return for evacuation of this area.

In Germany Moreau had a similar success as he drove the Austrians
back, very slowly to be sure, behind the Inn River. The difference is that
Germany was the main theater of operations, while Italy was the secondary theater, and that Bonaparte achieved the same success in the latter
area with small forces as a result of the unprecedented boldness of his
leadership as Moreau did with his methodical advance without special
risk. The comparison is not even changed by the fact that Moreau eventually won the victory of Hohenlinden on 3 December 1800, after the
expiration of an armistice. For this victory was not the fruit of a planned
strategy but, as Napoleon quite correctly called it, a "lucky encounter,"
although, of course, in very high style.[11] Again, the victory went to the
French as a result of the qualitative superiority of their troops and the
dash of the youthful General Richepanse.

Again in 1813, when Moreau, who was called by the allies to serve
with them with his strategic advice, discussed the situation of the Army
of the North with Bernadotte, he urgently advised Bernadotte not to
seize the offensive, as called for by the Trachenberg plan, since his line
of operations was too weakly secured.[12]

If we compare Moreau with Frederick and Daun, we see how men
with the same basic concepts can differ greatly from each other. Victories
such as Frederick won in his great battles were never won by Moreau.
But Moreau also never moved as far from the battle pole as the king did
in his later years. But we also cannot place Moreau in the same category
with Daun, for the Frenchman was decidedly superior to Daun in energy
and flexibility. The very youthfulness of his army gave him a flame and
a force that were not available in the traditional Austrian system.

Nothing would be more inaccurate than to hold Moreau in low esteem
because he followed the strategy of attrition. In order not to be a strategist
of that school, he would in fact have had to be a Napoleon. He would
have had to have not only the unerring certainty of understanding but
also that incomparable blend of daring and caution, of glowing fantasy
and the coolest power of analysis, of heroism and political skill that mark

Napoleon's strategy. It is still no reproach not to be a Napoleon. We have made this comparison, not to measure the two men against each other, but to clarify for ourselves that world history is based not only on conditions but that the personalities form at least one of the many elements that make up that history. The French Revolution did not yet create the modern strategy of annihilation and replace the strategy of attrition with it, but it was General Bonaparte who created this strategy with the resources of the French Revolution.[13] And he was also aware of this. He said that only a vulgar ambition could use those resources which served Louis XIV and Frederick II. This is reported by Marshal St. Cyr in his memoirs, who reproaches Napoleon for scorning rules that were universally recognized as good and for believing that they were intended only for mediocre minds.

Their contemporaries made no important distinction between the accomplishments of Generals Moreau and Bonaparte. To be sure, there was talk of an Italian school and a German school of strategy, the former referring to Bonaparte and the latter to Moreau, but neither the true nature of the contrast nor the absolute superiority of the one "school," that is, of the personality, over the other was recognized.[14] Bonaparte took it upon himself to make the coup d'état and thereby became the ruler of France, but whether he was really the man called for this by fate and the only one so called—that point was still in no way obvious to the contemporary world. This doubt led to an aftermath of the Marengo campaign which from the military history viewpoint gives us the occasion for supplementary remarks on that situation.

When Napoleon had himself elected and crowned emperor in 1804, he was still, of course, in the vestibule of his greatness, his deeds, and his fame. His fantastic move to Egypt had ended in failure and one could justifiably raise the question as to whether it was proper for him to leave his troops in the lurch there. His successes of 1796 and 1800 were brilliant, but Moreau was on the same level with him, and malicious tongues whispered that the victory of Marengo was due essentially not to Napoleon but to Desaix, who fell on the battlefield. In order to counter this idea, the emperor had an official report worked up on the campaign, which he himself corrected and which had to be reworked in keeping with his corrections. These changes distorted the truth in the grossest fashion by indicating that the commander was aware of and had figured on everything in advance and by suppressing the temporary withdrawal of the French and the critical moments of the battle. For the critical historian, these—let us say obvious—falsifications did not raise but lessened the fame of the commander. For there is no great strategic action that does not include a great risk and therefore also a critical moment, and the merit of the complete and unconditionally correct advance estimate of the situation is either fictitious or fortuitous, for such an advance estimate is possible only to a moderate extent. Was Napoleon then so little aware of his own actions, or did his vanity dupe him to such a great extent that he made a goblin of himself? He knew better. He knew that true greatness cannot be understood by the common people. Just as the people always prefer to imagine bravery in the victory of a smaller force over a more numerous one, so do they see the clearest proof of the art of command when they are shown that the great man estimated and knew everything very precisely in advance. That strategy means movement in an opaque element and that the most important quality of a commander is boldness—that is a realization that was first discovered and introduced into military science by Clausewitz. If Napoleon had let it be admitted how close he had come to losing the battle—indeed, that his main body was in fact already beaten when Desaix arrived late in the evening—the French people would not have admired his boldness but would have reproached his foolishness in dividing up his troops, from which he was rescued only through luck. Even the Athenians, of course, were not able to portray to their children the greatness of Themistocles in any other way than by the account of the clever secret message by means of which he misled the Persian king into attacking at Salamis.

Simultaneously with General Bonaparte there appeared as a commander on the world scene Archduke Charles, who was two years younger than Napoleon (born in 1771). The archduke was a reflective spirit and at an early age had already wielded the pen as well as the sword, composing numerous writings. Strategically, he was an absolute advocate of the strategy of attrition. Like Frederick the Great, he stated that one had to make every effort to make wars as short as possible and that the objective could be reached only by decisive blows, but at the same time he limited this proposition by teaching: "In each country there are strategic points that are decisive for the country's fate; because by holding them one gains the key to the country and becomes master of its resources." And he goes on to say: "The decisive importance of strategic lines makes it a law that one not allow himself to be misled into any movement, even by the greatest tactical advantages, as a result of which one becomes so distant from those lines or in such a direction from them that they are sacrificed to the enemy." Or: "The most important tactical measures seldom have a continuing usefulness as soon as they occur in places or in a direction that are not strategic."[15]

These propositions are justified and appropriate for the strategy of attrition. Indeed, a great deal depended not only on the fact that a victory was won but also on where it was won, for a victory that cannot be followed up has only a passing value, and often the follow-up is narrowly limited. We have seen how Frederick even withdrew after one of his most brilliant victories, at Soor. In the strategy of annihilation, victory does not depend on the "point" where it is won or the "strategic line" along which one moves, but the commander assumes that with victory the strategic points also fall into his hands, and he determines the strategic lines. It was precisely by sacrificing his strategic line that Napoleon, as we shall immediately see, attacked the Prussians at Jena and Auerstädt in the rear and not only conquered them but also destroyed them.[16]

Napoleonic strategy is free of any schematics. Nevertheless, a basic form reappears so frequently with Napoleon that it deserves to be discussed. In deploying, he pushes his whole force onto one wing or into one flank of the enemy, seeks to envelop him, to drive him away from his base, and in this way to destroy him as completely as possible. That was already his plan in the spring of 1800, when he planned to attack the Austrians in South Germany in conjunction with Moreau, moving out from Switzerland. That is what he did in 1805, when he attacked the Austrians along the Danube from the north, enveloping them, and for this purpose had Bernadotte march from Hanover through the Principality of Ansbach. He did the same thing the following year, when he attacked the Prussians in Thuringia, moving not from the Rhine but from the upper Main. He enveloped them so completely that the battles of Jena and Auerstädt were fought with reversed fronts, the Prussians facing toward Berlin and the French with their back toward that city. If the French had been defeated in this formation, they would have had an even more difficult withdrawal than the Prussians; pressed against the Erzgebirge and the Austrian border, they might have been destroyed. But sure of his victory, Napoleon did not hesitate to take the risk, and he was then able to wear down completely the Prussian army on its retreat, separated as it was from its base.

The Prussian General von Grawert is supposed to have correctly predicted Napoleon's operation in 1806 and to have interpreted it to the effect "that the enemy will envelop our left flank and will cut us off from the Elbe, from all our resources, that is, from the Oder and from Silesia."[17] We cannot better characterize the difference between the older and the newer strategy than by a comparison of this interpretation with Napoleon's true intention. Grawert saw everything correctly in the sense of Frederican strategy. But Napoleon was not at all concerned with "cutting off" from the "resources," which would have maneuvered the Prussian army to the rear and have opened up a piece of territory for him, but he placed himself on the Prussians' line of retreat in order to catch their army itself.

Napoleon's plan for the autumn campaign of 1813 also fits into this picture. He planned at first to take a defensive stance with his main force toward the Bohemian and Silesian armies until the Army of the North under Bernadotte was beaten and the countryside as far as Danzig was in his hands. Then the great offensive was to start in the direction from north to south, which was to cut off the Russians from their communications with their country. The plan failed because the Army of the North, commanded by Bernadotte, cautiously but logically beat back the French armies at Gross-Beeren and Dennewitz.

It was not until the renewed outbreak of the general war in 1805 that Napoleon rose to the full height not only of his fame and his greatness, but also of his strategy. The disruptions of the revolution had been overcome; the great masses, the patriotic spirit, and the new tactics were now governed by discipline; Emperor Napoleon was in a position to carry out whatever he considered right, unhindered by other powers.

The secret of the great commander is the blending of boldness and caution. We find this in Alexander when, before he undertook his campaign into the interior of Persia, he first covered his rear by conquering Tyre and Egypt and significantly strengthened his army. We find the same combination of qualities in Hannibal, when he established as his objective the separation of the Italian allies from the capital rather than the siege of Rome. We find these qualities in Scipio when, although he allowed the decisive battle to develop without a line of withdrawal, he provided in advance for his reinforcement by Masinissa. We find those qualities in Caesar, who planned to turn first against the army without a commander and then against the commander without an army. We have found the same qualities in Gustavus Adolphus and Frederick. And we find them also in Napoleon. As boldly as he challenges fate time and again, in no way does he rush into the limitless, but he knows where he must stop, shifts from the offensive into the defensive, leaves it up to the enemy to decide whether or not to attack him, and at the same time seeks to complete his victory through politics.

The best example of this conduct is the campaign of Austerlitz. Napoleon destroyed an Austrian army at Ulm, captured Vienna, and moved forward as far as the vicinity of Olmütz in Moravia, where the Russians faced him with their main force. To fight an offensive battle at such a "point" seemed too risky to Napoleon, since the enemy was numerically somewhat stronger. He initiated negotiations, and when the enemy approached, he took up position for a defensive battle. He won it (2 December 1805) by making a counterattack from his defensive position at the right moment. In order to envelop him, the enemy extended his forces very far and thus formed a thin center without any real reserves. That was the point that called for a penetrating blow. "How much time will you need to capture that height (at Pratzen)?" the emperor asked Marshal Soult, who was at his side. "Twenty minutes." "Then let us wait a quarter of an hour." It was then a question of spending this quarter-hour correctly.

Of all types of battle, the defensive-offensive battle is the most effective. Both defense and offense have their advantages and their weaknesses. The principal advantage of the defensive is the choice of the battlefield and full exploitation of the terrain and the firearms. The principal advantage of the offensive is the morale lift of the attack, the choice of the point of attack, and the positive outcome. The defensive initially always brings only a negative outcome. Consequently, purely defensive battles are only very seldom won (Crécy, 1346; Omdurman, 1898). The greatest result, however, is achieved when the commander goes over to the counterattack from a good defensive at the right moment and in the right place. We have become familiar with Marathon as the classical example of the defensive-offensive battle. Austerlitz is the modern counterpart of that battle. This battle is important for us in both its plan and execution because it shows us the commander in complete self-control, because we see here how this man with all his daring still never lost his presence of mind. His caution even extended so far that, when the approach of the enemies was reported, he gave the order to Talleyrand, who was negotiating in Vienna, to agree to an equitable peace. Although he was confident of victory, he therefore also wanted to cover his rear diplomatically in case of a defeat.

Among the most daring events in Napoleon's career was the crossing of the Danube that led to the battle of Aspern on 21-22 May 1809. Archduke Charles, with the entire Austrian army, more than 100,000 men, was on the north bank quite close to the crossing point. The French were to cross the mighty stream on a single improvised bridge. The bridge broke the first time when they had only 22,500 men across, and the second time on the following day at eight o'clock in the morning, when some 60,000 men were on the other side. But despite their fourfold superiority on the first day and their strength of still half again as many men on the second day, the Austrians did not succeed in throwing the French into the river. Archduke Charles still had reserves but he did not move them up. The entire difference between him and Napoleon comes to light in this point. For Frederick the Great, the question of the employment of the reserve did not yet really exist, since, of course, he planned to accomplish everything with the first blow, therefore made it as strong as possible, and held out no significant reserves. With the new tactics, the Austrians, too, had been obliged to accept the principle of reserves, but as the intellectual power of the archduke had not been broad enough to move him to accept the strategy of annihilation, so too was he lacking in any correct concept of the nature and use of the reserve. He established the principle: "The reserve may be brought into the battle only when its support decides the outcome beyond any doubt." "It may possibly be brought into the fight here and there if only a final push is needed for the completion of the victory; otherwise its main purpose is always to secure and cover a withdrawal."[18] Even in pursuance of this principle, as dull as it is, at Aspern every resource would have had to be thrown into the battle in order to win the most complete possible victory. There could not have been any better opportunity. But the archduke did not have the daring to accomplish that. Of course, he was still caught up in the concepts of the strategy of attrition, which attribute no particular importance to victory as such. Only a hero like Frederick the Great was still able, even with such concepts, to rise to the great challenges of fate to which his battles bear witness. Archduke Charles was too little to seize the gift that the goddess of fate smilingly held out to him at Aspern. He always looked behind him, just as his equestrian statue in Vienna shows him today with unconscious, cruel irony.

The French were defending with their infantry the two villages of Aspern and Esslingen and were holding the intervals with a weak cavalry force that made one bold attack after another. Napoleon exposed himself in the most extreme manner as he rode along the ranks of his troops amidst the firing in order to strengthen their courage. The Austrians finally forced their opponents to withdraw to the island in the Danube near the north bank, but Archduke Charles did not dare to attack them there or to exploit his success in any other way.[19] Six weeks later Napoleon had strengthened his forces to such an extent that he could renew the attempt, and this time he succeeded, in the battle of Wagram, 6 July 1809. Napoleon won the battle as a result of his great numerical superiority, by enveloping the Austrians' left wing. The large masses of artillery and infantry that he concentrated in the center did not, as is often assumed, bring on the decision. Archduke Charles has been unjustifiably praised because he had the left wing of the French attacked from the flank by an independent army corps; this appears to be a premonition of the Moltke method of waging battles. Nevertheless, the similarity is only superficial. The attack was too weak to be effective, and the archduke, although he had had enough time to prepare himself for a new crossing of the Danube by the French, had no well-thought-out battle plan at all but constantly wavered back and forth between defensive and offensive ideas.[20]

The real problem of Napoleonic strategy is the campaign of 1812. Napoleon defeated the Russians at Borodino and captured Moscow. But he had to turn back again, and in doing so he lost practically his whole army. The same thing would have happened to Frederick if he had wanted to risk taking Vienna. Even with the forces Napoleon had at his command, the strategy of annihilation had its limits. Would Napoleon have done better if he had adopted the strategy of attrition in 1812 and waged the war in Frederick's manner? Clausewitz answered this question in the negative, with good reasons, and he explained that the French emperor still had the greatest chance of winning this war if he fought by the method that had always guaranteed him victory up to that point. But as the proportion of forces on the two sides then stood, he could win neither with the strategy of attrition nor with that of annihilation. All together, according to the latest research, he had 685,000 men under arms against

Russia, including the garrisons. Six hundred and twelve thousand men crossed the border, of whom more than half, at least 350,000 men, belonged to the main army, in the center. But when he reached Moscow, he had only 100,000 men with him. In just fourteen days after the crossing of the Niemen he had lost 135,000 men, almost without combat, through desertion, poor rations, and sickness. The French half of the army consisted for the most part of very young men who had just been levied in 1811, and among them were many "refractories," who had received their military training on the Dutch islands, where they could not desert. But this training did not hold up on the advance through the barren Russian countryside. The depot system for rations did not function satisfactorily; in keeping with his custom, Napoleon had paid little attention to it and had not sufficiently considered that the Russian territory would not provide him what had been available to him in Italy and Germany.[21] Thus, he actually lost the war through desertions and the failure of the ration system, and not, for example, as a result of the Russian winter, which only wore down the remnants of his army and which, moreover, was later and milder in 1812 than in other years. If Napoleon had arrived in Moscow with 200,000 men instead of 100,000, he would probably have been able to control the conquered area, and the czar would eventually have accepted his conditions.

We can compare Napoleon's campaign of 1812 with Frederick's invasion of Bohemia in 1744, when finally, without having lost a battle, he was driven out of the country simply as a result of enemy action against his line of communications, and he sacrificed a very large part of his army. Frederick himself considered this "point" in enemy territory as an error, but he was able to build his army up again in the winter and, as a result of Hohenfriedberg, to reestablish the balance. Nevertheless, Frederick had wanted to conduct with his "point" only a campaign of the strategy of attrition, and the defeat was therefore not irreparable. Napoleon had aimed at something much larger, a complete and decisive victory, and since he had failed in that, the reaction was much more difficult. It consisted, of course, not only of the loss of the army but also very importantly of the fact that his two forced allies, Prussia and Austria, now found the courage to break with him.

The error that led to Napoleon's downfall, therefore, is not so much that he operated on a false strategic basis as that he overestimated the inner moral cohesiveness of the French people in his empire. No doubt a large portion of the French people adhered to him with respect and gratitude or was blinded by his fame and swept along. But in a very large part of the population these feelings were only weak or were even negative. Men were not willing to fight for him, and those who were levied by force deserted. While it is true that he succeeded even in 1813 in again raising a mighty army, nevertheless, in the harassing autumn campaign, even this army was destroyed to a very considerable extent, not by the enemy, but by desertion. Remarkably enough, we have no report as to what really became of the deserters of 1812. We must nevertheless assume that a very large part of them arrived back in Germany and France and were again enlisted in 1813. But since any indication on this point is missing, we cannot estimate how large the mass of recruits actually was that France provided to the emperor in these years.

The campaign of 1814, as we have learned from more intensive research, was governed completely by political motives but is interesting for a "History of the Art of War" because these political motives could be clothed in the garb of the rules of the old strategy. The one faction, under the leadership of Metternich, sought a balance with Napoleon and, in case it did not occur, favored the restoration of the Bourbons. The other faction favored the fall of Napoleon, and Czar Alexander wished to replace him with Bernadotte. In order not to fight for opposing objectives, the Austrians refused to move out and either intentionally or unintentionally clothed this reluctance with strategic considerations. They based their stand on the fact that neither Eugene nor Marlborough, both of whom were also great commanders, had ever directed their operations against Paris. The king of Prussia did not wish to continue the pursuit across the Rhine, because the Rhine formed a definite cutoff, and one had first to assemble beside such an obstacle. His adjutant general, Knesebeck, wanted to halt on the plateau of Langres because the water divide of France was there and one could therefore dominate France from this point.

In the campaign of 1815, too, the opposing natures of the two methods of strategy were again at play. Wellington, who was certainly a very important general, nevertheless still adhered to the concepts of the strategy of attrition. All together, the allied armies in Belgium were not much less than twice as strong as Napoleon (220,000 troops, a number of which, to be sure, were of very little value, against 128,000 excellent soldiers). Yet the emperor came very close to victory, because Wellington, who was always thinking of protecting himself, did not assemble his troops soon enough for the battle, consequently arrived too late at the battle of Ligny, and again on the 18th, during the battle of Belle-Alliance, he left a whole corps, 18,000 men, in position 9 miles away from the battlefield. This splitting of forces has been correctly compared with Frederick's conduct when he left Keith's corps on the other side of the city during the battle of Prague. But what nevertheless appeared as logical, even if not required, in the period of Frederican strategy was a serious error in Napoleon's time. It was counterbalanced by the fact that Gneisenau, on the other hand, guided only by the idea of the decisive battle, gave up the direct communications of the army that was beaten at Ligny with the homeland and directed his withdrawal on Wavre, close to the English, so that the Prussians could move to join them the next day.[22] As a result of the final victory, Wellington's mistakes were so overshadowed that they received but little notice. From the military history viewpoint, however, they should be strongly emphasized, not because they were mistakes, but as proof of the power and the harmfulness of false theories. The four-day campaign of 1815 can be regarded as the most complete expression of the clash between the two opposite methods of strategy. When Archduke Charles failed as he opposed Napoleon, an empty head and a weak character succumbed to a genius. But when Wellington so thoroughly misunderstood Napoleon's intentions and assumed that he planned to maneuver the English back in order to capture Brussels, and therefore failed to assemble his troops in timely fashion, that can only be explained in the case of such an important man and outstanding soldier as Wellington when we realize that he was caught up in the attitudes of the older strategy.

If Wellington had fought only in Spain and had ended his career in 1814, we would have nothing at all to reproach him for except that he had not been put to the extreme test. We would then have been able to draw from his character conclusions as to how he probably would have proved himself in such a situation. But now in 1815 he was put to the test and responded brilliantly as a tactician but failed as a strategist. He solved only the defensive part of the problem and applied his Spanish methods where they were no longer suitable. The final complete success was achieved through the fact that the army leadership of Blücher and Gneisenau so brilliantly complemented his own precisely in its weak points.

SUPPLEMENT

ON THE CONTRAST BETWEEN THE STRATEGIES OF ATTRITION AND ANNIHILATION

As I was reading the proof of the foregoing, there came into my hands the essay "Frederick the Great after the Seven Years' War and the Political Testament of 1768" ("Friedrich der Grosse nach dem Siebenjährigen Kriege und das Politische Testament von 1768"), by Otto Hintze, (*Forschungen zur Brandenburgisch-Preussischen Geschichte*, Vol. 32), which shows me that, despite Book 27 of the *Einzelschriften des Generalstabes*, the period of misunderstanding of the question of Frederican strategy is still not yet over. I wish to repeat here word for word the passage of Hintze's essay in order to show once again with the greatest possible clarity and completeness where the aberration starts or comes to light. The *Politisches Testament* itself will be published in a short time as a complementary document to the *Politische Korrespondenz* of the king; Professor Hintze was kind enough to place the proofs at my disposal, so that I am able to insert here the text of the passage in question. Hintze's own account reads as follows:

The king has in mind only a defensive war against Austria and her potential allies; but he believes that one must not start this war in a strategic defensive but must immediately start out with an effective offensive having as its objective the enemy capital. This is his old normal strategic idea, which A. Naudé had already correctly explained in the discussions on the campaign plan of 1757: one must invade Moravia with the main army and at the same time send out combat patrols along the March as far as the vicinity of Vienna. That is the most sensitive point for the Austrians; they can be forced to a peace treaty most quickly by a threat against Vienna. Of course, the advance must continue at the same time into Bohemia as well; everything else must be made to depend on the circumstances. Of course, the king had already had this idea in 1757; but then, influenced by advice from Schwerin and Winterfeld, he had replaced this idea with the concentric march into Bohemia, aiming toward a decisive battle at Prague. In 1758 he had again come back to this plan; but the stubborn resistance at Olmütz and the capture of a large train by the Austrians had ruined the plan at that time. Nevertheless, the idea remained firm in the king's head, and now it came to the fore again as the normal strategic plan that is recommended to his successor. In the War of the Bavarian Succession in 1778, Frederick himself attempted to act in accordance with it, but the difficulties that were caused by Prince Henry, who was in command in Bohemia and who wanted to have the main army nearby for the protection of his flank, also prevented the execution of the plan at that time. With respect to Russia, too, Frederick planned under some circumstances not to remain on the defensive strategically but this concept no doubt presupposed support not only by Austria, but also by England. He was thinking of a march on St. Petersburg, along the coast of the Baltic Sea; the provisioning of the advancing army was to be accomplished with certainty by a fleet that was to accompany the advance along the coast. It is not indicated where this fleet was supposed to come from; presumably this was to be done as support by an allied sea power; for in the *Politisches Testament* of 1768 Frederick expressed himself even more decisively than in 1752 against the founding of a Prussian navy.

We see that the boldness and broadness of vision of the strategic plans did not decrease after the war, but instead, they increased even more. In his chapter on the fundamental principles of warfare, the king constantly prefers the broad plans of the strategy of annihilation to the small plans of the strategy of attrition. The way in which he here explains the general concept of the campaign of 1757 shows a large, almost modern-sounding trait, and it is not always given sufficient consideration in the quarrel over the king's strategic principles. In this case, we cannot apply the usual critical method, according to which later retrospective writings in the nature of memoirs have less weight than the contemporary evidence, that which accompanies the action itself and which is available in the individual reports, often in the form of only partially preserved discussions and similar documents. These individual reports and orders retain their correct cohesiveness and background only as a result of those general ideas that are reported later. The execution usually falls short of the plan. In this respect, it depends on whether the time and the man were capable of a concept in the style of the strategy of annihilation, and in Frederick's case we must clearly answer that in the affirmative. Of course, his military resources and the general conditions that govern the conduct of war, such as, for example, the cultivation of the land, the condition of the roads, and the possibilities for providing rations, were at that time so limited that they presented greater difficulties for the execution of such plans than at the time of Napoleon or of Moltke. Frederick learned that sufficiently from experience, and therefore his conduct of war retained its fluctuating aspect, which, on the opposite side, caused it to approach once again the old methodical strategy of maneuver. Reliance on ration depots remained for him the principal base of all his operations, and he also foresaw that in the future, when opposing the Austrians, one would have to be prepared for a simple war of positions ("guerre de postes"). The campaign of 1778 confirmed this prediction.

We may agree that the boldness and broad scale of the king's strategic plans after the Seven Years' War seem not to have been lessened. That they, rather, rose even higher is no doubt supposed to be based on the idea of a march on St. Petersburg, and that does in fact certainly seem to exceed everything that the king had planned earlier. Of course, Frederick never seriously threatened even Vienna, but St. Petersburg was still a completely different matter. The explanation lies in the fleet that was supposed to accompany the army, and the commentary on this is to be found in the *Observations on the Military Talent of Charles XII (Betrachtungen über das militärische Talent Karls XII.)*. Here Frederick explains thoroughly how the Swedish king failed through the fact that, instead of advancing on St. Petersburg, he moved on Smolensk, in the direction of Moscow. In doing so he gave up his lines of communication and the possibility of feeding and supplying his army, or, as we say today, he gave up his base. As Frederick presupposed for himself a war against Russia in alliance with Austria and a sea power, he was thinking along older lines when he had the idea of a march on St. Petersburg. By having the fleet accompany him on this march, he took his base along with him, so to speak. There was no other way to defeat the Russians or bring them to terms. When fantasy once undertook to picture the war of a great coalition against Russia, Frederick, for the reason of his strategic concepts, was obliged to reject the march into the interior of Russia. Consequently, there remained only the objective of St. Petersburg, and even that only under the assumption of the accompanying fleet.

The error in Hintze's study lies in the statement: "The king constantly prefers the broad plans of the strategy of annihilation to the small plans of the strategy of attrition." This sequence shows that the author does not correctly understand the two concepts, "strategy of annihilation" and "strategy of attrition." It is well known that Frederick preferred large-scale plans to small ones, and he followed this principle all his life. In his execution he said to himself, even if the plans should shrink, if a really large plan should once succeed, one has won. But are large-scale plans therefore of themselves the strategy of annihilation? Are there not also large-scale plans in the strategy of attrition? If large-scale plans indicate the practitioner of the strategy of annihilation, then Gustavus Adolphus, Marlborough, and Eugene were also strategists of this type. Gustavus Adolphus's advance to Munich, Marlborough's march from the Netherlands to the Danube in 1704 (battle of Höchstädt), and Eugene's march from the Etsch south of the Po to Turin in 1706 were as broadly planned as anything that Frederick ever undertook. If the decisive point, therefore, is the broad scope, then the difference between the one type of strategy and the other is nothing more than a difference between significant and insignificant commanders. But this difference has been correctly understood only by that scholar who has recognized that the mission of the strategist of attrition is no less important and, as a result of its two-sidedness, is often even more difficult from a subjective viewpoint than that of the strategist of annihilation. Consequently, the difference does not lie in the larger or smaller scope of operations.

We must test the objective content of Frederick's "large-scale plans" referred to by Hintze in order to see if they belong in the category of the strategy of annihilation. He tells us that the king, in his *Testament*, recommended "putting into operation an offensive whose objective is the enemy capital." That sounds like annihilation. But in the very next sentence he speaks only of "combat patrols up to the vicinity of Vienna." It is clear that this can no longer be a question of "annihilation." Completely aside from the fact that Vienna lies south of the Danube, that not even the army but only combat patrols were supposed to advance into the Vienna area, and that there was, consequently, no question at all of a real threat to the capital, we must also take into consideration the fact that in this very same *Political Testament* those observations are recorded that have been repeated in detail above (p. 312 f.), in which the king urgently recommends against battles, not only in mountainous terrain, but also on the plain. Consequently, the king intended to try to advance into the vicinity of Vienna, but not to fight.[23] If a campaign of annihilation looks like this, then we obviously understand as "annihilation" something completely different. If the concept of "annihilation" that I have is used, then Frederick would have had to write: "We shall not be content with threatening Vienna, but we shall cross the Danube and conquer it; the Austrian army that attempts to defend the capital will be attacked and defeated."

The fact that the Frederican plan to overcome Austria by an operation through Moravia against Vienna belongs in the correctly understood strategy of attrition is also indirectly shown by the fact that Hintze, after the example of Naudé and Koser, refers to this plan as Frederick's "normal strategic concept." This expression is disputable. But if one accepts it, it is clear that the "normal strategic concept" can only have grown on the soil of the strategy of attrition. The objective that the strategy of annihilation envisages is always the enemy army; it must be sought out and defeated. He who establishes the plan for a strategy of annihilation therefore asks: Where is the enemy army presumably to be found? With Frederick, however, the question is a geographical one: Which of the two provinces under consideration offers better and more advantageous opportunities for invasion and the conduct of war? Frederick's "normal concept" consists of the fact that he has understood that an invasion of Moravia has certain advantages over an invasion of Bohemia. To impress on such a simple consideration the important name of "normal concept" makes it sound more significant than it really is. Indeed, according to the circumstances, Frederick also invaded Bohemia much more frequently than Moravia.[24]

Let us now examine the complete text of that passage in the *Political Testament* on which Hintze bases his observation. It reads as follows (p. 244):

> As often as we shall have reasons for drawing the sword against one another, we must always start by invading Saxony and from there pushing a corps along the Elbe into Bohemia. We must have a larger army in Silesia, which, placing detachments at Landshut and in the county of Glatz, penetrates into Moravia in the region of Hultschin. If we have allies who act in concert with us, we can push them beyond the Danube in our second campaign. The Turks would have to act at the same time in Hungary or a detachment of 30,000 Russians would penetrate to the Danube between Pressburg and Buda. This would be the means of seizing Bohemia in order to exchange it then for an electorate closer to our borders.

We see then that the king, even though he presupposes an alliance both with the Russians and the Turks, has in mind moving up to the Danube—but only in a second campaign. And this is supposed to be the strategy of annihilation? In July 1866 Moltke taught us something different in this area. He did not lead one part of the army to Bohemia and the other to Moravia but sought to join all forces as soon as possible for a main battle. He did not lead the Prussians up to the Danube in the first year in order to take up winter quarters then and continue the war in the following year, but he staked everything on continuing the war in a single campaign as long as it took for the enemy to accept our conditions for peace. That is what the strategy of annihilation looks like.

It seems to me that Jähns has judged more correctly than Hintze when he says of this plan, which the king developed almost identically in 1775 and 1778, that it actually amounted only to demonstrations (*History of the Military Sciences*, 3:2015).

It is surprising enough that Frederick believed that with such conduct of war he could force Bohemia away from the House of Hapsburg so that he could then trade it for Saxony. But it is no less astonishing that Hintze adheres to the idea that, from the political viewpoint, Frederick considered as defensive a war in which Prussia had the Turks and the Russians on her side and which was supposed to bring him eventual possession of Saxony.

It is, of course, no direct contradiction, but it nevertheless pulls the physiognomy of the king in opposite directions when he is supposed to be at the same time the innocuous politician who conducts only defensive wars and the fantastic strategist who with his limited means dares to defeat the most powerful enemies.

I believe I must indicate the following details in Hintze's account as erroneous.

In 1757 Frederick did not originally have the idea of an invasion of Moravia but allowed himself to be persuaded by Winterfeld and Schwerin to change his opinion. He planned to take position initially in Saxony on the defensive, and not until he had defeated the Austrians in this defense by a tactical counteroffensive did he intend, in agreement with the two generals, to move into Moravia.

Furthermore, in no way did Frederick march into Bohemia in 1757 "with the objective of a decisive battle at Prague." In his *Testament* of 1768, Frederick himself did, to be sure, express it in that manner, and I gladly admit that one may not neglect such retrospective expressions in the form of memoirs in comparison with the contemporary evidence that accompanied the action itself. In the case in question, however, this account in the form of memoirs is not a filling in of the original evidence but, on the contrary, stands in complete contradiction to the documentary evidence and does not even agree completely with the personal memoirs written five years earlier and devoted to this period, the *History of the Seven Years' War*. Consequently, the document of 1768 is certainly not a completely dependable witness.

I must also question the charge that the loss of the large train in 1758 ruined the king's plan. At the same time the train was lost, Daun had already succeeded in relieving Olmütz on the east side, and that caused the failure of the king's plan, even if the train had come through safely.

Finally, with respect to the campaign of 1778, it was, after all, not simply the personal opposition of Prince Henry but also the nature of things that prevented the king's army from marching off to Moravia while the other half was in Bohemia.

Hintze goes on to say: "It depends on whether the time and the man were capable of a concept in the style of the strategy of annihilation, and in Frederick's case we must clearly answer in the affirmative." Of course, we must do so in the sense in which Hintze understands it. But we must do the same thing in the case of Emperor Francis, the Russian Council of Ministers, Field Marshal Daun, and General Soubise, as we have seen sufficiently above. The "concept" by which Soubise planned to envelop the Prussians at Rossbach, and that by which Daun planned to encircle them completely at Liegnitz and destroy them, were as excellent as anything Frederick ever accomplished. But if Hintze refuses for that reason to designate Daun and Soubise as strategists of the annihilation school, he is thereby acknowledging that he has also applied that designation erroneously to Frederick.

He acknowledges that even more when he goes on to say:

Of course, his military resources and the general conditions that determine the conduct of war, such as, for example, the cultivation of the land, the condition of the roads, and the possibilities for providing rations, were at that time so limited that they presented greater difficulties for the execution of such plans than at the time of Napoleon and Moltke. Frederick learned this sufficiently from experience and therefore his conduct of war retained its fluctuating aspect, which, on the opposite side, caused it to approach once again the old methodical strategy of maneuver.

If we overlook the suggestion of reproach that lies in the expression "the fluctuating aspect," we could say that with this statement Hintze, completely correctly and in complete agreement with me, places Frederick in the category of the double-poled strategy or the strategy of attrition. But why then does he previously call him a strategist of annihilation? We may not assume of a scholar like Hintze that he contradicts himself in such a direct manner. The explanation lies simply in the fact that he uses the expressions "strategy of attrition" and "strategy of annihilation" in a completely different sense than that in which I formulated this terminology and in which I use it. In that case, of course, there must result one misunderstanding after another. It is exactly as with Koser, who also used my terminology without making it clear to himself and his readers that with these words he was indicating a different meaning from mine. Anyone who understands by "strategy of attrition" a conduct of war lacking in energy and force and by "strategy of annihilation" a conduct of war that is ingenious and bold will not easily escape from his surprise that I count Frederick as one of the strategists of attrition.

In particular, there is still to be said concerning Hintze's last statements that the reasons why Frederick could not be a strategist of annihilation are presented only very incompletely, and it is precisely the main points that are missing. The progress in the "cultivation of the land, the condition of the roads, and the possibilities for providing rations" in the eighteen years between Frederick's last campaign and Napoleon's first campaign had not been so great as to make possible a completely different strategy. Of course, Hintze also says simply "greater difficulties [for Frederick] than at the time of Napoleon." If it were only a question of "greater difficulties," we would have to say: "Difficulties are there to be overcome," and from Hintze's expression we could again interpret a reproach for Frederick. But in reality it is in no way a question of "difficulties," but of impossibilities. Everything depends on our understanding these impossibilities in order to judge Frederick correctly. Since Hintze has not done that, we have once again the result that by wishing to glorify Frederick particularly by characterizing him as a strategist of annihilation, he makes him so small as a result of the limitations that he is forced to add that we are confused. Once again I am reminded of the parody in which I proved that Frederick would be a "strategic bungler" if we intended to consider him as a strategist of annihilation. Frederick already protected himself against this procedure by jokingly saying about Voltaire that he took his military course only under Homer and Virgil. Voltaire, however, praised Charles XII, who (in keeping with the principles of the strategy of annihilation) unremittingly pursued the fleeing Russians and hastened from battle to battle.

NOTES FOR CHAPTER III

1. *Napoleon as Commander* (*Napoleon als Feldherr*), by Count York, is a popular and frequently read book, and I have taken points here and there from it; nevertheless, its most important points must be rejected. The author depends, to his detriment, more on Jomini than on Clausewitz. It is as if the old Gneisenau-York antagonism once more was expressed here, as if the grandson of General York was unwilling to recognize the friend and disciple of Gneisenau, Clausewitz. His study of the sources is often insufficient, and we must particularly reject the idea that Napoleon's power was declining from 1809 on and that he fell because of his own doings. A principal passage that he cites as proof (2:95, letter to Clarke of 21 August 1809) is based on an erroneous translation. Napoleon does not say that one may be allowed to fight a battle only "when one has no new turn of fortune to hope for," but that one should not fight as long as one can hope that the chances of success will still increase. See note 4, below.

2. *Thoughts and General Rules for War* (*Pensées et règles générales pour la guerre*), 1755. Article: "Projets de campagne."

3. See p. 313 above; further, to Winterfeld, 5 August 1757: "I intended to march between Reichenbach and Bernstädtel in order to cause him (the enemy) jealousy over Görlitz; if this works, that will be good,

but if he is unwilling to move from Zittau, I will be forced to attack him where I find him. I do not know anything else to do."

4. To the minister of war, Clarke, 21 August 1809: " . . . that battles should not take place if one cannot estimate in his favor 70 chances for success out of 100, even that one may fight a battle only when one has no new chances to expect, since by its nature the outcome of a battle is always doubtful; but once the decision is made, one must conquer or perish."

5. To Prince Henry, 8 March 1760.

6. The passages in which Napoleon expresses himself in favor of keeping all his troops assembled before the battle are collected in an excellent study by Balck, "Napoleonic Preparation for Battle and Battle Leadership" ("Napoleonische Schlachtenanlage und Schlachtenleitung"), supplements to the *Militär-Wochenblatt*, Book 2, 1901.

7. Similarly in *Oeuvres* XXIX, pp. 70, 78, 91, 143. "Réflexions sur les projets de campagne," 1775. "Exposé sur le gouvernement prussien," 1776. "Réflexions sur les mesures à prendre au cas d'une guerre nouvelle avec les Autrichiens," ("Reflections on the Measures to Be Taken in Case of a New War with the Austrians"), 1779.

8. For the details, the reader is referred to "Studies on the First Phase of the Campaign of 1796 in Italy" ("Studien zur ersten Phase des Feldzuges von 1796 in Italien"), by Erich Eckstorff, Berlin dissertation, 1901, where the completely false accounts by Jomini and Count York are refuted and an error by Clausewitz is also corrected.

9. The three quotations are from Kuhl, *Bonaparte's First Campaign, 1796 (Bonapartes erster Feldzug, 1796)*, Berlin, 1902, p. 319.

10. Letter to Field Marshal Lehwaldt of 16 April 1757.

11. The French historians, for example, Martin and Thiers, find Napoleon's judgment to be inspired by his own self-love, which was not willing to recognize anybody on a par with him. It may be that such a feeling had something to do with this somewhat disparaging expression. But that Moreau, in contrast to Bonaparte, was "methodical" is conceded even by his admirers, or if one wishes, it is pointed out by them; for example, in a study in the Parisian war archives (Dépôt de la guerre) of 1829. Quoted by Lort de Sérignan, p. 212.

12. Wiehr, *Napoleon and Bernadotte in the Autumn Campaign of 1813 (Napoleon und Bernadotte im Herbstfeldzug 1813)*, p. 61.

13. The comparison between the strategy of Moreau and that of Napoleon was correctly presented for the first time in the two dissertations— Theodor Eggerking, "Moreau as Commander in the Campaigns of 1796 and 1799" ("Moreau als Feldherr in den Feldzügen 1796 und 1799"), Berlin, 1914; and Siegfried Mette, "Napoleon and Moreau in Their Plans for the Campaign of 1800" ("Napoleon und Moreau in ihren Plänen für den Feldzug von 1800"), Berlin, R. Trenkel, 1915. Alfred Herrmann's

work, *Marengo*, Münster, 1903, is interesting but at times overcritical, and it often sees errors in Napoleon's conduct of war precisely in those places where his greatness actually lies. See in this connection the review by E. Daniels, *Preussische Jahrbücher*, 116:347. The correct concept of the campaign, based most appropriately on the sources, is to be found in the work by Major De Cugnac, *La campagne de Marengo*, Paris, 1904. Review by von Caemmerer, *Militärische Literaturzeitschrift* 2 (1905): 86.

We learn about Moreau in 1813 from his conversation with Bernadotte in the *Collection of the Orders of Charles John, Royal Prince of Sweden* (*Recueil des ordres de Charles Jean, Prince royal de Suède*), Stockholm, 1838, p. 11. He did not exercise a noticeable influence.

14. Even in the book *Napoléon et les grands généraux de la révolution et de l'empire*, by Lort de Sérignan, Paris, 1914, despite the generally correct orientation, the really important aspect of the problem is still not yet grasped. The author considers only Davout as a complete disciple of Napoleon. He considers Lecourbe, Desaix, and St. Cyr as disciples of Moreau. The frequently expressed statement, which is also accepted by Sérignan, that Napoleon formed no disciples but only tools, I would like to reject expressly.

15. These passages are from the *Basic Principles of Strategy* (*Grundsätze der Strategie*), 1813.

16. The theories and writings of the archduke are treated excellently by Heinrich Ommen in *The Conduct of War of Archduke Charles* (*Die Kriegführung des Erzherzogs Karl*), Berlin, E. Ebering, 1900. The army organization, tactics, rations system, and so on, are also treated very clearly in this work. In his discussion of strategy, however, Ommen makes a mistake. He understands the old strategy too much as a simple strategy of maneuver, which it became only in those cases where it stiffened, and he therefore brings the archduke into an opposition to that strategy, an opposition which did not actually exist (p. 13). See W. Kraus, "Die Strategie des Erzherzogs Karl 1796," Berlin dissertation, 1913.

17. Rühle von Lilienstern, *Report of an Eyewitness of the Campaign of Prince Hohenlohe* (*Bericht eines Augenzeugen vom Feldzug des Fürsten Hohenlohe*), 1807, 1:63.

18. See my article "Erzherzog Carl" in the *Recollections* (*Erinnerungen*), p. 590. See also in this connection *Kriegsgeschichtliche Einzelschriften*, 27:380, where older theoreticians are cited, whose teachings were adopted by the archduke.

19. August Menge, *The Battle of Aspern* (*Die Schlacht bei Aspern*), Berlin, Georg Stilke, 1900. Holtzheimer, "Schlacht bei Wagram," Berlin dissertation, 1904. In his book *Napoleon as Commander*, 2:247, Count York compared Napoleon with Frederick and Archduke Charles in the following manner:

If the Napoleonic strategy possessed a grandeur in its plans and a boldness in its execution that I, at least, cannot recognize to the same degree in Frederick or Archduke Charles, on the other hand the behavior of the latter two does not show the decline from the earlier summit; they remained true to their own conduct, even if this never reached the full military greatness of the Napoleonic.

This kind of comparison must be rejected in every respect. Neither did Napoleon decline from his summit, nor may the archduke be compared with Frederick in this way, nor may the difference in their epochs be ignored in the comparison between Napoleon and Frederick, nor may the change in Frederick himself be left out of consideration. If one claimed to measure strategists only by the "grandeur of their plans and the boldness in their execution," then of course it would be precisely Frederick who "declined from his summit."

20. In conjunction with this battle, Napoleon once developed for an Austrian officer the difference between his conduct of battle and that of the Austrians (quoted, for example, in Knesebeck's *Trilogie*, and in Ranke, in "Hardenberg," *Werke*, 48:125). Ranke finds that it is a generalized description of the second day of Wagram. The passage here reads as follows:

> You normally move forward in small corps that are brought together as a whole by your battle plan; you make your dispositions on the day before the battle, when you do not yet know the enemy's maneuver. In doing so, you can only take into account the terrain. I do not deploy before the battle; during the night before the battle I keep my troops carefully assembled. At the first rays of the sun, I reconnoiter the enemy. As soon as I am informed about his movements, I make my dispositions, but they are based more on the enemy than on the terrain.

I cannot find that in this point Napoleon hit precisely on the difference between the French and the Austrians. It is rather the difference between the offensive battle and the defensive that he portrays. For that reason it is applicable to the battle of Wagram. At Austerlitz, however, Napoleon, too, made his battle plan on the preceding day and deployed his troops in conformance with the terrain. If there was on the other side no commander who waited until the morning of the battle to order the approach march and the attack, but instead the general staff provided for a detailed disposition, that still does not mean that the important and decisive difference of the opposing arrangements is to be found precisely in this point.

21. On 11 October 1805 Napoleon had Berthier write to Marmont as follows:

In all the letters that General Marmont writes me, he speaks to me about rations. I repeat to him that in the wars of movement and invasion that the emperor is waging there are no depots; it is the business of the commanding generals of the corps to provide for themselves the means of feeding the troops in the areas through which they march.

On 8 July 1812 word was sent to Poniatowski that His Majesty was very dissatisfied to see that he spoke of pay and bread when it was a question of pursuing the enemy.

22. The account in my *Gneisenau* is supplemented by an article "General Wolseley on Napoleon, Wellington and Gneisenau" in my *Recollections, Articles, and Speeches (Erinnerungen, Aufsätze, und Reden)*.

23. See "On the Difference, etc." ("Ueber die Verschiedenheit, usw") in my *Historical and Political Essays (Historische und Politische Aufsätze)*, p. 273; 2d Ed., p. 269 f., and "Frederick, Napoleon, Moltke," p. 45, where it is explained that even when a battle was in prospect, as was actually the case in 1778, that did not change anything in the strategic basic character of the war plan. After all, there are also battles in the strategy of attrition.

24. Koser, *Friedrich der Grosse*, 2:400 (4th Ed.), understands it in this way: "In keeping with Frederick's theory, the final decision in a war between Prussia and Austria would necessarily take place in Moravia." A similar comment is on p. 457. In another passage (p. 585) it was quoted, on the other hand, that "the main blow was to be struck at the enemy by the capture of Prague," from which he would not be able to recover. The error lies in the fact that a decisive significance is attributed to the question "Bohemia or Moravia?" as such. The significance, however, varies according to the circumstances. As practice has indeed shown, on one occasion it is the one country, and on the other occasion the other country where it appears more advantageous to seek the decision. In theory, a campaign into Moravia offered many advantages, but they were not so great as to prevent Frederick very frequently from preferring to move into Bohemia.

Chapter IV

Scharnhorst, Gneisenau, Clausewitz

The Frederican system of warfare had collided with the new French system for the first time at Valmy, had then continued the struggle for two more years, 1793 and 1794, and in this time had still shown itself to be qualitatively superior. For political reasons, but militarily undefeated, Prussia withdrew from the war in the spring of 1795 as a result of the Treaty of Basel. When she again crossed swords with the French eleven years later, the French had in the meantime developed into the soldiers of Napoleon, and now Prussia collapsed at the first blow. We do not realize the full nature of this event if we say with Queen Louise that Prussia had gone to sleep on the laurels of Frederick the Great. As proud as they were of the inherited fame, criticism and reform movements were also quite active and the old and the new were already locked in combat before the crisis. Even before the French themselves were fully aware of their own creation in tactics, the then Hanoverian Major Scharnhorst entered in his diary on 10 July 1794: "The present French war will strongly shake up the accepted tactical system in a few points," and toward the end of the century (1797) he wrote several essays in which he elaborated on the sentence "It is an established fact that the French skirmishers have decided the greatest part of the affairs in this war," and he added his proposals for the development of the tactics that still pre-vailed in the German armies.[1] He wished to link the old and the new together organically. It seemed to him out of place to give up the linear formation or to loosen up all the infantry into marksmen, but he proposed that the third rank be used for the skirmishing battle.[2] In any case, the third rank had not been very useful for the salvo, and in the revolutionary war the transition had already been made to the formation in two ranks. Carried out as a general rule, however, that resulted in uncontrollably wide and dangerously thin lines. Now, by having a third of the infantry move out as skirmishers and taking for that purpose not the first rank, but the third, the old, well-ordered, and firmly cohesive front remained and was able to profit from its advantages. But the marksmen, who moved forward around the flanks of the battalions, strengthened the fire power of the whole much more intensively than when they remained in the third rank of the linear front, where they, furthermore, still took their place again to reinforce the front in an emergency. The retention of the close-ordered front for salvo fire and finally for the attack seemed so important to Scharnhorst that he did not even want the men of the first two ranks to be taught to fight as marksmen.

Even when Scharnhorst was taken over into the Prussian service in 1801, his ideas were still in no way accepted. Of course, General Prince Hohenlohe did introduce, for the same Silesian regiments that he later commanded at Jena, skirmishing by the third rank (1803). But in the same year Field Marshal von Möllendorff issued an order in Berlin in which he directly forbade aiming while firing; the soldiers were supposed "to hold the rifle horizontally while keeping the head erect."[3]

It is clear then that the old and the new were already struggling with one another in Prussia before 1806, but in every important respect the old was unshaken, and the army, in its composition, was still completely of the old Frederican type. As such, however, it was not poorer, as might be expected, but better than in Frederick's time. Its discipline was un-shaken, and the officer corps was brave, but the spirit had disappeared, the leadership was miserable, the enemy was a giant, and so the army necessarily had to go down to defeat. In other works I have expressed myself in detail concerning this period and these events, the catastrophe, the reconstruction, and the final victory of Prussia, and I do not intend to repeat those points here.[4] The result was that Prussia now accepted for itself the ideas of the French Revolution to which it had succumbed, was rejuvenated with the help of those ideas, extended itself again in the area of the military even more so than formerly, and worked out the ultimate possibilities both practically and theoretically.

It should be added here that Austria, too, after the defeat of 1805, revised the old tactics under the direction of Archduke Charles and blended the tactics of skirmishers and columns in a clever manner with the linear formation to the extent that this was possible with an army lacking a national basis.[5] I have already cited above (p. 403) the argumentation of General Mack as to why the tactics of skirmishers should be rejected. A critical witness as to how different the spirit of the old military pedagogy was and how difficult it necessarily was to effect the transition into the new spirit is a report of Lieutenant Field Marshal Bukassowicz to the Imperial War Council in 1803:

> In the Turkish war a troop unit at Besania-Damm was ordered to lower its bayonets to half the height of a man, and since the men had not learned to do anything else, the unit remained as motionless

as a statue. The Turks took advantage of this and moved in under the muskets with bared knives and immediately cut off the feet of the soldiers, as a result of which the troops had to learn from experience that they were to jab with the bayonet at the command "Jab!"[6]

The Russians were still governed by Suvorov's words: "The bullet is a foolish woman, but the bayonet is a whole man." As late as 1813 only the light regiments used skirmisher tactics in the Russian army; the rest of the infantry was not at all familiar with combat by individuals.[7]

In Prussia, Scharnhorst, as minister of war, transformed the old mercenary army into a national people's army by eliminating foreign recruitment and establishing the universal military obligation, which the French had again dropped. This idea encountered so much opposition that it could not be put into effect during the preparatory period but only at the moment of the revolt (9 February 1813). And at first it was also announced only for the duration of the war, but in 1814 it was again put into effect and accepted definitively through the efforts of Boyen, the disciple and successor of Scharnhorst.[8]

Although combat as skirmishers had become of the greatest importance for the French, as we have seen, it remained an uncultivated plant. In Prussia, as already previously in Austria, these tactics were now systematically introduced by regulations based on the proposals that Scharnhorst had already made in writing in 1797. The three-ranked linear formation, with its salvo fire that swept everything away in front of it, remained the basic formation. But the third rank was supposed to move out as skirmishers for the battle of marksmen, and in case of necessity even the whole battalion might be spread out as skirmishers. (In this respect, Scharnhorst now moved out beyond his proposal of 1797.)[9]

The battalion deployed in line was not supposed simply to deliver salvo fire but was also supposed to be able to apply the striking force of its depth in the attack. In order to make this possible, Scharnhorst established, also in keeping with the French model, the "column toward the middle," two platoons wide and four platoons deep. The battalion was able to deploy into line from this column with the greatest imaginable speed or from the line to form the column, since the outer platoons from the right and the left simultaneously placed themselves behind those in the center.

The "column toward the middle" was twelve men deep, or when the marksmen were deployed, eight men deep (since the battalion numbered four companies or eight platoons). That was the normal depth of the Greek phalanx, and it was therefore, according to the older concepts, still a linear formation, but with respect to the formation in three ranks that had been established in the eighteenth century, it was already a column.

Just as Scharnhorst carried over the French organizational ideas to Prussia and at the same time renewed them, so was Gneisenau, who had already supported Scharnhorst in the reform of the army, the one among Napoleon's opponents who had completely adopted the latter's strategy, so that he was able to strike the mighty one with his own sword. The great mission of the allies in the autumn campaign of 1813 was to unite their armies, which were in position in Brandenburg, Silesia, and Bohemia, forming a semicircle around Napoleon, on a single battlefield without giving the opponent the opportunity to strike them individually and defeat them from his central position. This task was accomplished when the Silesian army, as Napoleon intended to close with it after its crossing of the Elbe at Wartenburg on 3 October, did not withdraw across the Elbe but, sacrificing its communications, marched around Napoleon and joined the Schwarzenberg army on the Saale in Napoleon's rear. This maneuver cut Napoleon off from France and could have resulted in the encirclement and destruction of his entire army by the superior forces of the allies. Schwarzenberg's chief of staff, Radetzky, had also already drawn up a plan along these lines, that even up to our time has been misunderstood and distorted in the grossest manner, as if its purpose were not so much to destroy the French army as to force it by maneuver to withdraw without a battle in the sense of the old strategy. Radetzky's ingenious plan was broken up by the intervention of Czar Alexander at the behest of his military advisor, General von Toll. The allied armies separated once again and gave the French free passage on their withdrawal route toward the west.[10]

A move of similar type and boldness as the march from the Elbe to the Saale in 1813 was the march in 1815 from Ligny via Wavre to La Belle-Alliance.[11] Both maneuvers were all the more effective in that Napoleon had not reckoned with them and consequently made false moves himself in 1813 by attacking into thin air and in 1815 by failing to order Grouchy's corps to the battlefield at the right time. "These animals have learned something," he shouted.

To complete a great phenomenon in the real world, it must also have its theory. It is remarkable enough that even the theoretical thinker who was able to clarify Napoleon's strategic actions belonged to the Prussian army—Clausewitz, a disciple of Scharnhorst and a friend of Gneisenau. How these three men are to be interrelated is strongly expressed in the sentence that Gneisenau wrote to Clausewitz when Scharnhorst's remains were transferred to the Veterans' Cemetery in Berlin from Prague, where he had died: "You were his John, and I only his Peter, although I was never disloyal to him as the other Peter was to his master."

Before Clausewitz did so, the French Swiss Jomini had already undertaken to analyze Napoleon's art of war. He was a talented, widely read, and very prolific author, and he also understood well and described as early as 1805 the decisive point in the Napoleonic strategy, his drive toward the decisive battle, but he still did not penetrate the real nature of Napoleonic action and his strategy in general. That would have required the special drive toward deep philosophic exploration that had filled life in Germany since Kant and Hegel and awakened in the Prussian officer the interpreter of the god of war whose acts had overturned the old world and had forced mankind to build a new one. Jomini sought the nature of strategy in the lines of operation and tested the advantages of the inner and outer lines of operation. Clausewitz recognized that bases and lines of operation and other aspects pertaining to them were, to be sure, very useful concepts to be understood and to clarify situations but that rules for plans and decisions could not be derived from them, because in war all the elements of action are uncertain and relative. Consequently, strategic action cannot be of a doctrinaire nature but must spring rather from the depth of character. War, however, is an action of politics, and strategy can therefore in no way be isolated but must always be considered only in its relationship to politics. Whoever complains that politics had interfered in the conduct of war is saying something that is logically nonsensical, and he really means that the political interference as such seems false to him. Correct politics can also direct strategy in only a correct way—that is, provided the statesman does not think incorrectly in military matters. In the most critical decisive moments, politics and strategy are not to be distinguished from one another, and the universal historical effect of the great strategist emanates from his personality as a whole. Frederick's moderate war plan at the outbreak of the Seven Years' War and the intensification of his plans in the following year were completely determined by political factors, consideration of the allies of the empress, and not because he believed he could surely defeat the Austrians with his oblique battle formation. Rather, because he had become imbued with the idea of honorable defeat, he risked the attack against superior forces at Leuthen.

The superiority that lifted General Bonaparte above all the other brave and brilliant soldiers of the revolutionary armies was rooted not only in his eminent military qualities but just as much in his sense of politics. For it was only his political superiority that allowed him to carry out his far-reaching strategic ideas, because he envisioned capping his military success politically before a reaction destroyed what had been won. The fact that Napoleon did not reckon with the reappearance of the Prussians on the day of La Belle-Alliance can logically be considered an error on his part that is hard to understand. But it is precisely here that his heroism lies. If he had expected the arrival of the Prussians, he would not at all have been able to accept battle against the oppressive superiority and would have ended as did Bazaine in 1870, who from the start despaired of success and finally had to capitulate without having fought out a battle. Even Napoleon was in no way able to win the campaign against the overwhelming enemy numbers under two commanders like Wellington and Gneisenau. But the fact that he came very close to victory and finally went down to defeat not in shame but with fame created for him personally an unforgettable brilliance and for his people a source of spiritual strength from which it has again and again drunk new life.

The period from the Renaissance to the end of the ancien régime shows an unending series of great soldiers and army commanders. But in the first half of the period we cannot yet claim that they merited the expression "great strategist." Despite the mighty battles that we have encountered, the dimensions of the military events are not great enough, or, better expressed, the military aspect in the overall relationship of things takes place still more in the sphere of individual military deeds against the political background than in that unity of politics and military action that forms the nature of strategy.

The great strategists in the full sense of the word begin only with Gustavus Adolphus. In Wallenstein, the statesman and organizer play a greater role than the strategist as such. The great commanders of the school of Gustavus Adolphus, Cromwell, the series of great French marshals under Louis XIV, are surpassed in the memory of later generations by Eugene of Savoy and Marlborough. This period finds its summit and its conclusion in Frederick the Great. For a long time he was attributed a special position by being considered the precursor of Napoleon. We have now recognized this concept as false and rejected it. Frederick was not a precursor but one who brought a period to its end and highest point. It was only through Clausewitz's deeper philosophical understanding of the concept of strategy in combination with politics and his associated psychological analysis of the nature of army leadership that full understanding of the similarity as of the difference of the two masters of warfare has been defined. Clausewitz himself recognized this result of his reflections, but he did not carry it to completion. In a "report" that he wrote on 10 July 1827 and that is placed at the head of the work he left behind, *Vom Kriege*, he considers redoing this work once more from the viewpoint that there is a *double art of war*, that is, the one "in which the purpose is the overthrow of the enemy," and the one "in which one only intends to make a few conquests on the borders of the country." The "completely different nature" of these two efforts must always be separated from one another. Clausewitz died in 1831, before he could carry out this work. To fill out the lacuna that he left has been one of the purposes of the present work.

With the appearance of Clausewitz's works after his death in 1831, the Napoleonic period of the history of the art of war comes to a close, so to speak. It leads into the new period to the extent that Moltke's ideas were built on the works of Clausewitz. This new period is defined in its content by the new technology, not only of weapons but also of transportation and all the resources of life, from the railroads and telegraph to the foodstuffs, which increased in such unlimited proportions in the course of the nineteenth century.

This is the point to which I wished to bring this work. What followed, included in the phenomenal rise of Prussia and its final collapse, will have to be undertaken later by others.

NOTES FOR CHAPTER IV

1. Lehmann, *Scharnhorst*, 1:254.

2. According to the supplement in Lehmann's *Scharnhorst*, 1:543, Prince Ferdinand of Braunschweig was perhaps the very first to express this idea of using the third rank for the skirmisher fight, when in January 1761 he commanded a general in the Hanoverian light troops to equip the third rank with grooved-bore muskets.

3. *Documentary Contributions to the History of the Prussian Army* (*Urkundliche Beiträge zur Geschichte des preussischen Heeres*), Vol. 5, "The Combat Training of the Prussian Infantry of 1806" ("Die Gefechtsausbildung der preussichen Infanterie von 1806"), by Jany, 1903. Möllendorff's order reads as follows: "The position of the musket must be shown to the men better, so that they no longer lean their head against the stock and aim, as formerly, but press the butt against the shoulder, holding the head upright, and thus hold the musket horizontally as His Majesty the King primarily reminded them and commanded at this year's review." In 1807 the Reorganization Commission recommended the "introduction of stocks more definitely curved, which make aiming possible." Scherbening, *The Reorganization of the Prussian Army* (*Die Reorganisation der preussischen Armee*).

4. *Life of Gneisenau* (*Leben Gneisenaus*), 3d Ed., 1907. Supplemented by the article "New Information on 1813" ("Neues über 1813"), *Preussische Jahrbücher*, Vol. 157, July, 1914. "General von Clausewitz"; "The Prussian Officer Class" ("Der preussische Offizierstand")—both articles in the *Historical and Political Essays* (*Historische und politische Aufsätze*), 2d Ed., 1907. "On Max Lehmann's *Stein*" ("Ueber Max Lehmanns *Stein*"), *Preussische Jahrbücher*, Vol. 134, 1908. "From Arminius to Scharnhorst" ("Von Armin bis Scharnhorst"), in the collection *In Defense and Weapons* (*In Wehr und Waffen*), edited by von Caemmerer and von Ardenne.

5. Very well explained by Ommen, *The Conduct of War of Archduke Charles* (*Die Kriegführung des Erzherzogs Karl*).

6. The same thing is reported by Valory of the Prussian cavalry in 1742, *Brandenburgisch-Preussische Forschungen*, 7:310. Valory wrote that an outstanding Prussian officer had told him that in the battle of Chotusitz, when the closely formed Prussian squadrons had reached the enemy, it was first necessary to shout to the men that they were to strike with their sabers. Frederick himself told the same thing to Count Gisors. Rousset, *Le comte de Gisors*, p. 105.

7. According to A. Müffling, *My Life* (*Mein Leben*), p. 31.

8. Fr. Meinecke, *Life of Boyen* (*Leben Boyens*).

9. These instructions are from the year 1809, and they were then assembled as training regulations in 1812. As a continuation of the distinction between line infantry and light infantry, there still also remained the difference between the musketeer (or grenadier) battalions and the fusilier battalions, but this difference can be passed over, since it had no practical significance.

10. The history of the wars of liberation has in no work been at the same time more extensively developed and more confused than by the *Memorable Recollections from the Life of the Imperial Russian General of Infantry Carl Frederick Count von Toll* (*Denkwürdigkeiten aus dem Leben des kaiserlichen russischen Generals der Infanterie Carl Friedrich Grafen von Toll*) by Theodor von Bernhardi. The book is excellently written, the author is a competent military analyst, and the papers left by Toll provided him the most valuable material—it is no wonder that for a long time his judgment enjoyed an almost saintly respect. I, too, long deferred to his authority and only by laborious research learned to overcome his prejudice, point by point.

11. Critical extremists have also puttered around with this great deed. In addition to my *Gneisenau*, these have also been very well rejected by Caemmerer in *The Wars of Liberation. A Strategic Survey* (*Die Befreiungskriege. Ein strategischer Ueberblick*), 1907.

Index

Aachen, treaty of, 236
Administrations, national: gradual development by, of tax system, 224, 228; of Prussia, 246-47; weakness of, 224
Aelian, 156-57, 159
Age: of *Junker* at entry in Prussian army, 256; of soldiers in Prussian army, 255
Agitators, 191
Aiming, 271; prohibited by von Möllendorf, 450
Alba (duke of): army of, trailed by camp followers, 65; on space occupied by horseman, 121, 138 n.12; withdrawal of, from Alkmar, 155
Albanians, as light horsemen (*stradioti*), 117
Albertus Magnus, 24-25
Albrecht (duke of Prussia), 120
Albrecht Achilles, on firing of harquebuses, 148
Albrecht Alcibiades of Brandenburg, 257; in battle of Sievershausen, 123, 193; in battle of Saint Vincent, 126; in command of "Black Horsemen," 121; training of horsemen with pistol, 123
Albrecht von Stein, at Bicocca, 90
Alençon (duke of): in battle of Marignano, 85; in battle of Pavia, 93
Alexander I (czar of Russia), 438, 452

Alexander the Great, 426
Alfons (duke of Este), in command of artillery at Ravenna, 75-78
Alkmar, 155
Allbuch, 210-11
Alrammah, Hassan, 24-25
Alsace, 328
Alviano (Venetian general), 81, 110
American War of Independence, 399
Ancien régime, army of, compared with French revolutionary armies, 414, 421
Andelot (colonel general of infantry), 228
Anghiari, battle of, 16
Anhalt (prince of). *See* Christian, prince of Anhalt
Annihilation, strategy of, 109; aspects of, 432-33; contrast of, with strategy of attrition, 439-44; impossible with armies of *ancien régime*, 421; in modern sense, created by Napoleon, 431. *See also* Strategy
Antwerp, "fury" of, 160
Apraxin, 346
Arabs, role of, in development of gun powder, 24
Ariosto, condemnation of firearms, 30
Armagnacs, 68
Armor: of infantry discarded, 270; necessity for lightening of, 135; de la Noue on, 130-31

Army strengths: in battle of Breitenfeld, 203; in battle of Hohenfriedberg, 330; in battle of Kunersdorf,
367 n.40; in battle of Lützen, 208; in
battle of Mollwitz, 326; in campaigns
of Frederick the Great, 363; competitive tendency to increase, 63; in
English civil war, 186-87, 192 n.3; of
"normal" army, 371-72; of Sweden,
181 n.2; in Thirty Years' War, 299
Arnim, 209
Arnsberg, 210
Arras, 336
Arrière-ban, 234-35
Articles of War, 60
Artillerists: as soldiers, 407; as technicians, 34, 256
Artillery: in battle of Breitenfeld, 204,
206; in battle of Ceresole, 95; in battle of Ravenna, 75-76; in battle on
White Mountain, 198; effectiveness
in battle, 36, 75-76; fire of, concentrated, 408; French, in Italy in 1495,
47 n.27; of French revolutionary
army, 393; improved by Gribeauval,
407; heavy, increased by Austrians,
284; horse, creation of Frederick the
Great, 284; horse, in French revolutionary armies, 407; increase of, in
army of Gustavus Adolphus, 177;
increased and improved, 284; Napoleon III on, 49 n.36; opinion of Jovius on, 36
Aspern, battle of, 435-36
Attack, firing in, 271-72
Attrition, strategy of, 108; alternation
of offense and defense in, 305; analysis of, 293-315; army at stake in,
296; contrast of, with strategy of annihilation, 439-44; economic aspects
of, 296; importance of field fortifications in, 296-97; misunderstanding
of, in strategy controversy, 378-80;
strategy of Frederick the Great, 374-
78; typical of Machiavelli's period,
109; variation between poles of, 302.
See also Strategy
Auerstädt, battle of, 433

Augereau, Pierre (marshal of France),
418-19
Aumale, in battle of Saint Vincent, 126
Austerlitz, battle of, 422, 434-35, 447
n.20
Austrians: in battle of Chotusitz, 329;
in battle of Hohenfriedberg, 329-30;
in battle of Kollin, 341, 343-44; in
battle of Leuthen, 345; in battle of
Prague, 340-43; in battles of French
Revolution, 392; cavalry of, in Seven
Years' War, 282; in coalition of
1757, 339-40; defensive skill of, 353;
increase of heavy artillery by, 284;
losses of, at Kunersdorf, 356; new
drill regulations of, 406; renewal of
army after 1805, 450
Avila, Gil Gonzalo de (Spanish historian): on formation of imperial
mounted troups, 119-20; on pistol in
Schmalkaldic War, 42; on strategy in
Schmalkaldic War, 298; on use of
cannon in Schmalkaldic War, 36

Bacon, Roger, 24-25
Bakeries, field, of French army, 300-
301
Balloon observation, 401-2
Baner, Johann Gustafsson (Swedish
general), 178; in battle of Wittstock,
212-14; double envelopment by, 212-
13; strategy of, 301
Barbarossa, 59
Barletta, 41
Barracks, 235
Barras, Paul, 397
Barrel: forged on spindle, 38; rifled, 38
Barwick, 40
Basel, treaty of, 449
Bashkirs, 40
Basic poles of military art, 407
Basta, Georg: on appointment of inex-
perienced nobles, 266 n.32; on com-
parison of cuirassiers and lancers,
132; contradictions in writings of,
132; criticized by Wallhausen, 132-
34; on dragoons, 142 n.35; on im-
portance of discipline in cavalry,

132, 160; on light cavalry, 132; military experience of, 132; on pay, rations, booty, 160; writings, 132

Battalion, equivalent to infantry square, 59

Battle: defensive—offensive, most effective, 434-35; efforts to avoid, 387-88; risks in, 306-15; role of, in strategy, 294; tactical results of, limited, 370

Battle leadership; Frederican compared with French revolutionary armies, 408; Frederican compared with Napoleonic, 408-9; youthfulness of, under Napoleon, 411-12

Bavaria: militia in, 241-42; plan of Eugene to lay waste, 302

Bavarians, as lansquenets, 10

Bayard, Pierre du Terrail, 12, 13, 36

Bayonet, 269-70, 283, 289 n.13, 450-51

Beauharnais, Alexandre de (French general), 396, 418

Bellay, Guillaume du (French general), 306

Bellay, Martin du: on musket fork, 38; on siege of Parma, 42; on types of mounted troops, 118

La Belle-Alliance, 438, 452-53

Bergen, battle of, 399

Bernadotte, Jean (marshal of France, king of Sweden), 418-19; in command of Army of the North, 430, 433; considered to replace Napoleon, 438; officier de fortune, 234; victories of, at Gross-Beeren and Dennewitz, 434

Bernhard von Weimar (duke of Saxony-Weimar): in battle of Nördlingen, 210-12, 218 nn.21, 22; in service of France, 229; strategy of, 301

Bernhardi, Friedrich von (German general), 272, 381-82

Bernhardi, Theodor von, 372-73, 456 n.10; in strategy controversy, 379, 381

Berthier, Louis-Alexandre (marshal of France), 401, 417-18

Berwick, Jacques Stuart, duke of (marshal of France), 323

Besania-Damm, 450

Bessières, Jean-Baptiste (marshal of France), 418-19

Bevern, duke of, 345

Bezirks-Regierungen, 246

Bicocca, battle of: army strengths in, 87; impatience of Swiss before, 87-88; lack of pursuit, 90; preliminary situation, 86-87; press from rear in, 55; Swiss attack at, 88-89

Billon, J. de, 139 n.15, 165, 307

Bi-polar strategy, 108

Biron, Armand-Louis, duke de Lauzun (French general), 396, 418

Black Band, 10; destroyed at Pavia, 92-93

Black Horsemen, 121-22

Blenheim (Blindheim), in battle of Höchstädt, 320, 363 n.2

Blide, 34-35

Blücher, Gebhardt Leberech von (Prussian field marshal), 439

Blumenthal (Prussian field marshal), 378

Boar-spears, 179, 269

Boguslawski, von (Prussian lieutenant general): in strategy controversy, 379, 381; on French revolutionary war, 397

Bohemians, in battle on White Mountain, 195-202

Bombards: of large size, in sieges, 31; at Saluerno, 25; of Vienna, 32. See also Cannon

Bonaparte. See Napoleon Bonaparte

Bonnivet, Guillaume Gouffier de (French admiral), 14

Booty, in mercenary armies, 62

Borodino, battle of, 436

Bouchotte, 396

Boufflers, Louis-Francois de (French marshal), in battle of Malplaquet, 325

Bourbon, Charles III, constable of, 110

Bow: accuracy of Mongolians with, 51 n.55; in battle of Leipzig, 40; com-

pared with harquebus, 38, 40; penetrating power of, 51 n.55; retention
of, 40; use of by Kalmucks, 40; used
in conjunction with harquebus, 39
Boyen, Hermann von (Prussian general), 451
Boyne, battle on the, 302
Brandenburg: alliance of, with Gustavus Adolphus, 243; economy of,
threatened, 248; excise tax in, 246;
failure of, to raise large army, 243;
life guard of elector of, 243; loss of
gold to Wallenstein, 243; unprepared
for Thirty Years' War, 242
Brandenburg—Prussian army: birth of,
244; formed basis for Prussian nation, 245-46; Huguenots as officers
in, 260; manpower for, 247; money
for, 247; reduction of, by Frederick
William, 244
Braunschweig, Charles William von,
duke of (Prussian field marshal), 392
Braunschweig, Ferdinand von, duke of
(Prussian field marshal), 373; in battle of Crefeld, 361; offer to, to become commander of French army,
402; criticism by, of pandours and
Croatians, 281; as disciple of Frederick the Great, 376; against French
army in 1760, 237; zealous efforts
of, to refine formations, 274
Breitenfeld, battle of, 202-7, 369; approach and deployment in, 204;
army strengths in, 203; effect of artillery in, 205; formation of Tilly's
army in, 216 n.13; importance of, to
Gustavus Adolphus, 178; participation of Scots in, 174-76; preliminary
actions, 202-3; similarity of, to Cannae, 178, 206; as wing battle, 290
n.21
Breslau, 369, 380
Brieg, fortress of, 325
Broglie, Victor-François, duke of (marshal of France): in battle of Bergen,
399; plan to attack Austrians at Tabor-Budweis, 327
Browne, Maximilian (Austrian general):

in battle of Lobositz, 339, 374; in
campaign of 1757, 340
Bruges, 322-23
Brune, Guillaume (marshal of France),
418-19
Bukassowicz (lieutenant field marshal),
450
Bülow, Dietrich Heinrich von, on im-
portance of depots, 372, 389
Bülow, Friedrich Wilhelm von Denne-
witz (Prussian general), 372, 389
Bunzelwitz, battle of, 297, 361
Buquoi, count of (commander of impe-
rial army), 307; in battle on White
Mountain, 196-97
Burgundians, 4-6, 14
Burgundy, duke of, 323
Burkersdorf, 362
Byzantium: instrument of, projecting
fire, 26; role of, in development of
gunpowder, 23-24

Cadet corps, 257-58
Caemmerer, von (Prussian general),
382 n.1; on Frederick the Great's
campaign plan for 1757, 381; on the
development of the science of strat-
egy in the nineteenth century, 382
Caesar Borgia, 17, 107
Caesar, Julius, 312
Campaign costs: of Frederick the
Great, 316 n.3, 338; of Maria Ther-
esa, 316 n.3
Campaign of maneuver, 297-98
Campaign plans: of Frederick the
Great against Austria, 313-14; Fred-
erick the Great on, 311; of Napo-
leon, 424-25
Campaign of 1758: preliminary situa-
tion, 346-47; siege of Olmütz, 348-
49; strategic concept of, 347-48
Campaign of 1759, 353-59; Frederick's
change of strategy for, 353
Campaign of 1778, 362-63; "potato
war," 363
Campaign of 1812, 436-37
Canals, built by Frederick the Great,
423

Cannon: at Bioule in 1347, 28; components of, 31; early fabrication of, 25, 32; effectiveness of, against infantry square, 50 n.41; of Frankfurt, 32; ignition of, 37; improved by Gribeauval, 407; "Lazy Greta," 34; light (leather), in army of Gustavus Adolphus, 179, 182 n.8; light, in preparatory fire, 272; loss of, by Frederick, 328; Machiavelli's opinion of, 36; mounts for, 33; names of, 36; of Nuremberg, "Chriemhilde," 32; protection for, 32; rapid growth of, 31; ratio of, to infantrymen, 408; sacrificed by Napoleon at Mantua, 427; in Schmalkaldic War, 36; in sieges, 34; transportation and loading of, 32, 36; use of, by English at Orleans, 33; use of, by Turks at Constantinople, 34; varied projectiles, 33

Cannonballs: of cast iron, 33, 48 n.28; early, of stone, 31; effectiveness of, 35; use of, by English at Orleans, 34; use of, by Turks at Constantinople, 35

Cannon-masters, 33-34

Canton regulation, 249

Caracole, 125; abandoned by Gustavus Adolphus and Wallenstein, 177; in battle of Moncontour, 123; development of, 124; first mention of, in battle of Dreux, 123; Hermann Hugo on, 137; influence of, on discipline, 124; no mention of, by Basta or Wallhausen, 134; de la Noue on, 129; use of, after introduction of linear formation, 176; use of, by Spanish militia, 148

Cardona (Spanish general): in battle of Ravenna, 73-78; at siege of Prato, 105

Care for sick and wounded, 65-66, 235, 239 n.22

Carignano, 94

Carnot, Lazare, 417-18; campaign plan of, 428-29; as minister of war, 396-97

Catinat, Nicolas de (marshal of France), 233, 314

"Cavaliers," 187

Cavalry: in armies of condottieri, 17; in attack compared with awaiting an attack in place, 144 n.43, 145 n.47; Austrian, in Seven Years' War, 282; in battle of Breitenfeld, 206; in battle on White Mountain, 197-201; development of, among "German Horsemen," 121-22; development of, from knights, 127-36; development of shock action of, 281-83; difference between, and knights, 117; against foot troops, 151; in France, 282-83; fully developed, 136; Hermann Hugo on, 136-37; ineffectiveness of Prussian, at Mollwitz, 281; importance of, in Cromwell's army, 189; against knights in Huguenot Wars, 135-36; against Mamelukes in Egypt, 136; necessity for drill and discipline in, 121, 135; new spirit of, under Frederick the Great, 282; patrols of, unreliable, 284; reorganization of, by Gustavus Adolphus, 177, 179; recruiting of, 125; start of, in modern sense, 121, 135; unsuitable for reconnaissance, 283-84, 328

Ceresole, battle of, 43-44, 55, 94-97, 295

Cerignola, battle of, 41, 73

Chance aspects of battle, 306-11, 372-73, 376, 423

Charles, archduke (Austrian commander), 428, 432, 439; in battle of Aspern, 435-36; failure of, to use reserves, 435-36; revision of Austrian tactics by, 450; theories of, 432

Charles the Bold, 101

Charles of Lorraine: at Hohenfriedberg, 330; lacking in decisiveness, 345-46; at Soor, 331-32; surrounded in Prague, 343

Charles I (king of England), 189; executed, 191, 223; at start of civil war, 186

Charles V (Holy Roman emperor),

223, 301; on effectiveness of pistols at Châlons, 42; invasion of France by, 97; leveling movement among mounted troops of, 119; muster held by, at Vienna, 93-94; resumption by, of fight for Upper Italy, 86-87; against Schmalkaldic army, 56; study by, of Caesar, 101; on Tunisian campaign, 41

Charles VIII (king of France), 14, 47 n.27, 49 n.36, 54, 227

Charles X (king of Sweden), 245

Charles XII (king of Sweden), 302, 312, 337-38, 358

Charles XIV (king of Sweden). See Barnadotte

Chemnitz, Philip Bogislav: concern for rations, 300; description by, of Gustavus Adolphus, 178-79. Work: History of the Thirty Years' War, 300

Chevaux-de-frise, 269

China, role of in development of gunpowder, 23-24

Choiseul, Etienne-François, duke of, 314; reorganization of French cavalry by, 282

Chotusitz, battle of, 327, 329, 373, 380; Prussian cavalry in, 282

"Chriemhilde," 32

Christian, prince of Anhalt: in battle on White Mountain, 196-202; son of, in cavalry counterattack on White Mountain, 200

Circumvallation, discredited by French theoreticians, 322

Cividale, battle of, 25

Clausewitz, Karl von (Prussian general), 441 n.1; on battle formations, 290 n.24; on battle of Prague, 343; on boldness in battle, 432; clarification by, of Napoleon's strategic actions, 452; compared with Jomini, 453; on double art of war, 454; on Frederick the Great at Kunersdorf, 354; on Frederick's lack of caution before Maxen, 367 n.42; on Gustavus Adolphus, 298; on Napoleon's campaign of 1812, 436; on overall

strength and concentration of forces, 372; relationship of, with Scharnhorst and Gneisenau, 452; on relationship of war and politics, 453; on strategy, 378-79; on Turenne, 335-36; on Wallenstein, 299. Works: Seven Years' War, 290 n.24; On War, 378, 421, 432

Clermont, prince of, 361

Coalition of 1757 against Frederick the Great, 339-40

Coligny, Gaspard de (French admiral): in battle of Moncontour, 194-95, 215 n.3; in battle of St. Quentin, 193; concern of, for rations, 61; on conduct, 71 n.10

Colleoni, 47 n.25

Colonna, Fabricio (Spanish general), 73, 74-77

Colonna, Prosper (Spanish general), 87-90, 109-10

Column: against linear formation, 274, 399-400; in tactics of French revolutionary armies, 398-99; "toward the middle," 451

Commands, emphasis on, by Maurice and William Louis, 159

Commissars, military, in French army, 231

Committee of Public Safety, 396

Commoners: Catinat, 233; Monluc, 233; as officers in French army, 232

Campagnies d'ordonnance, 227; basis of French army, 13; marksmen of, at Guinegate, 4-6; transformation of, into cavalry regiments, 230

Concentration of forces for battle, 370-71

Condé, Louis II, prince of (French marshal), 314; in battle of Lens, 181 n.4; in battle of Seneffe, 302; contribution by, of own money for soldiers' pay, 231; as Huguenot, 228; understanding by, of new military system, 230

Condottieri, 224; armies of, principally cavalry, 17; interest of, in ransom for prisoners, 16; opinion of, by historians, 16; role of, in Italy, 16

Conscription: civil war resulting from, in France, 395-96; in French army under Convention, 395; in French army under François Le Tellier, 236-37; *levée en masse*, 396; in Napoleonic armies, 412-13; in Prussia, 413, 451

Convention, 395

Cordes, des (French general), 4-6

Cornput, 159

Corps, army, created in French revolutionary army, 408

Cossacks, 40, 281

Council of war, forbidden by Frederick the Great, 375

Courage, lack of, among skirmishers, 404-5

Courts, military, 60-61

Coutras, battle of, 136, 195

Creazzo, battle of, 81

Crécy, battle of, 29, 435

Crefeld, battle of, 361

Croatians, 280-81, 398

Cromwell, Oliver, 454; creation of "New Model" army by, 187; discipline of, 188-89; as head of state, 191-92; importance of cavalry in army of, 189; insistence of, on drills, 189; on members of opposing armies, 187; as organizer, 190; place of, in history, 185; position of, in "New Model" army, 188, 191; transformation of army by, 186

Crossbow: compared with harquebus, 38; French recommendation for readoption of, 40; used in conjunction with harquebus, 39; use of, by mounted men under Charles V, 41

Cruelty of warfare, 68

Cuirass, 230

Cuirassier: compared with lancer by Basta, 132; compared with lancer by Wallhausen, 133; incident of French, at Bicocca, 128-29; as light horseman armed with pistol, 125

Cumberland, Guillaume-Auguste, duke of (English general), 317 n.17

Custine, Adam-Philippe, count of (French general), 396, 418

Cyzicus, siege of, 23

Dadizeele, Jean, 4, 6

Dalhoff-Nielsen (captain), 381

Daniel (colonel): shift of, to service of Swedes, 67

Daniels, E., 382, 394 n.6

Dankelmann, 247

Danzig, 423

Daun, Leopold Joseph (Austrian field marshal), 374, 376, 443; analysis of actions of, 356-57; in battle of Liegnitz, 359; in battle of Torgau, 359-61; compared to Fabius, 351; compared with Frederick the Great, 372; double-poled strategy of, 350; forced back in 1762, 362; Frederick the Great on, 312; at Kollin, 343-44; movement of, away from Russians, 358; at Olmütz, 348-53; reliance of, on field fortifications, 297; victory of, at Hochkirch, 353

Davila, 151. Work: *History of the Huguenot Wars*, 151

Davout, Louis Nicolas (marshal of France), 418, 446 n.14

Deception in musters, 65, 229, 237

Defense: alternation of, with offense in strategy of attrition, 305; development of Austrian skill in, 353; favored by new methods of warfare, 108, 147

Defoe, Daniel, 308

Delbrück, Hans, on strategy of Frederick the Great: attacks on, 378-80; at issue with concept of Hintze, 441-44; misunderstanding of concepts of, 378-79

Delfzyl, 162

Dennewitz, battle of, 434

Depots: of Duke Max of Bavaria, 300; importance of, 315, 389; importance of, to Frederick the Great, 440; need for, in wars of Louix XIV, 300-301; protection of, 371

Desaix de Veygoux, Louis (French general), 401, 418, 446 n.14; in battle of Marengo, 430-32

Desertion: in campaign of 1812, 437; measures against, by Frederick the Great, 251-52, 303-4, 413, 414; in Napoleonic armies, 413-14; from Prussian army in 1744, 328

Dessau. *See* Leopold of Dessau

Dietrich von Bülow. *See* Bülow, Dietrich Heinrich von

Dijon, 82

Diplomacy, 387

Discipline: in army of Florentine republic, 104; in army of Gustavus Adolphus, 177; in army of Maurice of Orange, 161, 163; basic to modern cavalry, 121, 135; Basta on importance of, in cavalry, 132; in Cromwell's "New Model" army, 188-89; development of, through drill, 253-54, 373; furthered by firing drills, 273; influence of *caracole* on, 124; in lansquenet armies, 68-69, 106, 252; Machiavelli's lack of appreciation of, 106; of officers, 254; in standing armies, 252-54

Division (army unit), created in French revolutionary army, 408

Dohna, count, 283, 371

Dove, Albert, 379

Dragoons, 125, 142, 142 n.35

Dresden, 369

Dreux, battle of, 123-24, 194

Drill: as basis for discipline, 253-54; *caracole* as, 124; in Cromwell's army, 189; emphasis on commands, 159; emphasis on, by Maurice, 157-59; in firing, 273; on forming quickly, 158; limiting effects of, 280; necessary for lancers, 132; necessity for, in development of modern cavalry, 121; opposition to, by veterans, 159; in Prussian army, 253, 373; regulations for, 253

Drill regulations, 400, 406

Droysen, G., 181 n.2, 379

Dugommier, Jacques-François Coquille (French general), 397

Dumouriez, Charles-François (French general), 261, 392-93, 417, 418; at Jemappes, 395

Dutch, imitation by, of Swiss military system, 4

East Prussia, 346

Eberstein, Georg von (Wolkenstein), 12

Echelons: in attack, 291 n.30; in battle of Leuthen, 278; in formation of Maurice of Orange, 157-58, 169 n.14; as Frederick's solution for oblique formation deployment, 278; necessity of, with thin lines, 273

Economic aspects of strategy of attrition, 296

Economy, money: transition to, from barter economy, 228

Edgehill, battle of, 176, 187

Egmont, Lamoral, count of (imperial general), 194

Eguiluz, 57 n.2

Egypt, 136, 401, 431

Elie (French general), 396-97

Elizabeth (czarina of Russia), 361

Emanuel Philibert of Savoy, 121

"Emetic," Frederick the Great's view of battle as, 329, 380, 423

Emigrés, 392

Engelbert, count of Nassau, 5

Enghien, duke of (French general), 94, 297

England: army of, in Germany in 1758, 346; failure of, to intervene on Continent, 185; military organization of, 185-86

Entrenching, by mercenaries, 62

Envelopment, 373

Enzheim, battle of, 269

Ernst von Mansfeld, count, 224

Ernst, Margrave, 244

Essex, Robert Devereux, count of, 188-89

Esslingen, 436

Estates: in Brandenburg, 243; complaint of, against Schwarzenberg, 244; against Frederick William, 245; in Prussia, 244

Eugene, prince of Savoy (imperial general), 280-81, 303, 314, 325, 393, 427, 454; in battle of Höchstädt, 319-20; in battle of Turin, 321-22; compared with Frederick the Great, 376; failure of, to concentrate forces for battle, 370; plan of, to lay waste Bavaria, 302; in siege of Lille, 323

Europe, political forms of, after Seven Years' War, 387

Events of 1708, 322-23

Events of 1741, 325-27

Events of 1744, 327-29

Events of 1745, 329-33

Events of 1756, 338-39

Events of 1757, 339-46

Events of 1758, 346-53

Events of 1761-62, 361-62

Fairfax, Thomas (general), 188, 191

"Fanterie," 14

Fate, battle as a challenge of, 377

Feldwebel, 71 n.2

Ferdinand von Braunschweig. See Braunschweig, Ferdinand von

Ferdinand II (Holy Roman emperor), 224

Ferdinand III (Holy Roman emperor), 209

Fermor (general), 40

Ferraruoli, 122, 132

La Feuillade, Louis (marshal of France), 321

Feuquières: on reasons for accepting and avoiding battle, 309; writings of, borrowed by Frederick, 276, 309

Field marshal, 60, 257

Field regulations, 59

Finance Ministry of Prussia, 246

Finck (Prussian general), 356, 358

Firearms: addition of sights, 38; advantages of, over bow, cross-bow, 38; aiming, 38; of assistance to knights, 41; in battle of Ceresole, 96; date of invention of, 30; development of, 27-28; distrust of, by Machiavelli, 39; early illustrations of, 26; first significant use of hand, at Barletta, 41; first use of, in Europe, 25; hand, 36-41; importance of, at Cerignola, 41; initial use of, as complements to other weapons, 41; numbers of, increased by Gustavus Adolphus, 177; opposition to, 30-31; pistols, 41-42; recoil of, 37; rifled barrel, 38; role of, in development of mankind, 31; spread of, throughout Europe, 28; in strong defensive positions, 147; superiority of, over spears, 175, 269; technical improvements to, 288 n.7; use of, as club, 38; use of, long after gunpowder, 27; various types, 38

Firing: accuracy of, 289 n.14; advantage of drills in, 273; without aiming, 271; in attack, 271; avoidance of, in attack, 272-73; competitive, 51 n.49; complications of, 285; dependent on loading process, 27; at Fontenoy, 271; invention of, 23-27; lack of training in, in French army, 401; positions for, 37; rapidity of, 270, 272, 285-87; of salvos at Breitenfeld, 176

Firth, C. H. Work: Cromwell's Army, 192

Fitzsimon (Jesuit), 198

Flank protection, 274-75

Fleming, 372

Flemish, 6-7

Flintlock, 270

Fleurus, battle of, 302

Florence: compared with Rome, 106; end of republic of, 105; horsemen of, at Ceresole, 96; organization of republic of, 103; position of Machiavelli in government of, 102; republic of, threatened by Medici, 103

Florence, militia of: creation of Machiavelli, 102; danger to republic, 102-3; lack of discipline in, 104, 106; lack of overall commander, 104; limited authority of captains, 103-4; organization of, 103-5; in siege of Prato, 105; subjection of Pisa by, 105

Folard, 310-11; on effectiveness of column, 399; on oblique battle formation, 276

Fontenoy, battle of, 271

Foreigners: in French army, 227, 229, 391; in Prussian army, 250-51, 413

Fork (musket), 38, 175

Formations: combination of skirmishers and column, 401; in French revolutionary armies, 398-401; infantry, shift to double rank, 389; line versus column, 274, 399-400; mobility and control of, by Maurice, 158; new, created by Maurice, 157-58; oblique, 274-79; refined, 274; Rüstow on simplification of, 170 n.16; Swedish, 174-75, 180; tested with lead soldiers and on drill field, 159

Fortifications, city, 49 n.36, 301

Fortifications, field, 323; at battle of Höchstädt, 320; digging of, required by Maurice, 161-62; failure to complete, on White Mountain, 197; of Frederick, at Bunzelwitz, 361; importance of, at Cerignola, 73; importance of, in strategy of attrition, 296-97; initial opposition of Frederick the Great to, 297; of Russians at Kunersdorf, 355

Fortresses, 301, 388, 393, 423

Fouqué, 348

Francesco Maria, duke of Urbino, 110

Francis I (Holy Roman emperor), 314, 338, 345, 380, 392

Francis I (king of France): in battle of Marignano, 84-86; in battle of Pavia, 91-93; campaign maneuver of, Avignon to Italy, 110-11; captured, 93; claim of, to Milan, 82; creation of "legions," 14; dependence of, on Swiss and lansquenets, 227; on "golden bridges" for enemy withdrawal, 304-5; move of, on Milan, 83; obligation of, for mercenaries' pay, 62; recapture of Milan, 91; in

siege of Pavia, 91; in treaty of Madrid, 295

Francs-archers, 4, 13

Fransecky, von (Prussian general), on skirmishing, 403-6

Frederick I (king of Prussia), 248

Frederick II, the Great (king of Prussia): analysis of strategy of, 314-15, 374-78, 422-25; on attack without firing, 273; in battle of Kollin, 341, 343, 344; in battle of Kunersdorf, 354-55; battle leadership of, compared with Napoleon, 408-9, 425; in battle of Leuthen, 345; in battle of Liegnitz, 359; in battle of Lobositz, 339; in battle of Mollwitz, 325-26; in battle of Prague, 340-43; in battle of Rossbach, 345; in battle of Soor, 331-32; in battle of Torgau, 359-60; in battle of Zorndorf, 352-53; on Caesar, 312; campaign of 1758, 346-53; campaign plans of, 311, 424; capture of Saxon army by, 339; change of strategy by, in 1759, 353; changing plans of, 340, 422; on Charles XII, 312; closing of formation by, 270; combination of strategy and politics, 335; compared with Daun, 372; compared with Eugene, 376; compared with Torstensson, 301-2, 333-35, 370; controversy over strategy of, 378-82; on Daun's method of warfare, 312, 377; on decision to do battle, 312-13; on defense, in 1745, 329; dependence of, on rations, 301; description of Prussian army by, 254-55; desertion in army of, 251-52, 303-4, 328, 413; exemptions from military service by, 250; failure of, to unite forces for battle of Kesselsdorf, 332-33, 370; on firing of salvos, 270-71; on Folard, 311-12; "free battalions" of, 280-81, 406; impressionable character of, 326, 364 n.10; increase of cavalry by, 284; infused cavalry with new spirit, 281; initial opposition of, to field fortifications, 297; intention of, to abdicate, 356; invasion of Bohemia by, 362-63; lack of vigorous pursuit after Hohenfriedberg, 330-31; limitations on advance, 305; loss of fortresses, 361; loss of ration wagons and heavy cannon, 328; marches of, 376; measures of, against desertion, 251-52, 303-4; misconception of strategy of, 303; not a precursor of Napoleon, 375; opposed by coalition of Austria, Russia, France, 339-40; Otto Hintze on strategy of, 439-40; plan of, to attack Vienna, 328; plans of, compared with Napoleon, 422, 424; postponement by, of start of campaign, 338, 422; preference of, for company of Frenchmen, 258; prestige of, as military commander, 330, 344, 352, 376; on Prince Henry, 377; prohibition by, of council of war, 375; on punishment at drill, 253; recruiting by, 251; rejection by, of ambitious French plan, 327; relative strengths in campaigns of, 363; reluctance of, to fight Russians, 358-59; siege of Olmütz by, 348-57; situation of, at start of Seven Years' War, 338; situation of, in 1761, 361; statements by, on strategy, 310-14; as strategist of attrition, 375; strategy of, 1741 to 1744, 328; strategy of, compared with Gustavus Adolphus, 369-70; strategy of, misunderstood by Great General Staff, 377; strength of personality of, 380, 422; subjective aspects of strategy of, 352, 375-76, 377; tactics of, 279-80; unreliable men in army of, 303-4; use by, of oblique battle formation, 276; use of waterways by, 423; victory of, at Prague, 328; view of battle as challenge of fate, 376-77, 423; weakness of reconnaissance of, 328. Works: *Art of War*, 311; *Elements of Campcraft and Tactics*, 406; *General Principles of War (General-Prinzipien)*, 254, 370, 371; *History of the Seven*

Years' War, 377; *Military Testament*, 313; *Observations on the Military Talent and Character of Charles XII*, 312; *Political Testament*, 424; *Thoughts and General Rules for War*, 311

Frederick William (elector of Brandenburg), 244-46, 269, 284, 336

Frederick William I (king of Prussia), 246-50, 253, 255, 257-58, 267 n.43, 281, 324

Free battalions, 280-81

French: allied with Frederick, 326; in battle of Rossbach, 345; cavalry of, 14; character of, unsuited for early infantry service, 14, 18; driven back across Rhine, 327; efforts of, to improve army, 13-15, 18; infantry of, 14; lansquenets in service of, 18-19; "old units" of Picardy, Piedmont, 13; origin of infantry of, 13; recapture of Bruges and Ghent by, 322; successes of, in War of Spanish Succession, 325; Swiss in service of, 18

French army: abandonment of king in French Revolution, 261, 390; arrangements for disabled veterans of, 236; cavalry of, in eighteenth century, 282-83; compared with Prussian army, 259-62; condition of, in early years of Louis XIV, 230; condition of, at end of civil war, 228-29; desertions in, 229, 410; court generals of, 390; discipline of, 410; drill regulations of, 400, 406; field bakeries of, 300; before French Revolution, 390; further reform of, by Le Tellier's son, 236-37; foreign regiments in, 229-30, 260; foreign regiments disbanded, 391; Huguenot wars, detrimental to, 227; humaneness in, 261, 391; intrigue among generals in, 260; lack of training in firing, 401; levy of, compared with Prussia, 261-62; national character of, 261; national infantry of, insignificant, 227; new tactics of, in French

Revolution, 398-401; officer appointments in, 231-34; officers of, in French Revolution, 396-97, 411; "old bands" as base of infantry of, 228; organization of, in seventeenth century, 230; origin of infantry regiments of, 228; privations of, in French Revolution, 397-98; ration system of, 409-10; recruiting for, 229, 234-35; reorganized by Le Tellier, 230-36; in Seven Years' War, 390; "a stream carrying all the impurities of the social body," 229; soldiers of, compared with Germans, 397; strength of, 261; strength of, after Vervins treaty, 228; strength of, in 1670 and 1789, 229-30; strength of, in 1794, 396; in Thirty Years' War, 229; Swiss and lansquenets in, 13, 227; in War of Spanish Succession, 390; in wars of French Revolution, 391-414; weakness of, after Henry IV, 229

French Revolution: armies of, 391-414; conduct of volunteer battalions of, 396-97; creation of divisions, corps, 408; defection of army in, 390; discipline in armies of, 410; importance of new army organization of, 402; influence of, on other countries, 392; introduced new period in warfare, 390; new tactics of, 398, 402, 449; officers of, compared with Prussians, 397-98; soldiers of, compared with Germans, 397

Fröhlich (Swiss captain), 95

Froissart, 29

Fronde, 231, 336

Frundsberg, Georg: in battle of Bicocca, 87, 89, 128-29; in battle of La Motta, 55, 81; in battle of Pavia, 91-93, 111; Lutherans in service of, 67; marksmen in rear guard of, 40; marksmen in unit of, 148. Work: *True Advice and Reflections of an Old Well-tested and Experienced Warrior (Trewer Rath . . .)*, 55-56, 120

Fueter, E., 112 n.2

Fürstenberg, 205-7

Fusiliers, 399

Galicia, 387

Gallas, Matthias von (Austrian general), 209, 243, 334

Gallerate (treaty of), 83

Garrisons: of fortified cities, 299; made available for field army, 301

Gäschuff, Konrad, 8

Gascons, 14, 55; at Ceresole, 95-96; at Ravenna, 77

Gaston de Foix, duke of Nemours (French general), in battle of Ravenna, 74-78

Gauntlet, running of: in army of Gustavus Adolphus, 177, 182 n.10; in Prussian army, 259

General-Prinzipien of Frederick the Great, 254, 296-97, 370, 371

Genoese, as marksmen, 17

George William, elector of Brandenburg: regulations of, for support of wandering mercenaries, 69-70; rejection of defense plan by, 242

Gerlach, Leopold von (Prussian general), 374

"German horsemen," 121; effectiveness of pistols of, in battle of St. Vincent, 126; fathers of European cavalry, 121-22

German military organization: practice in contradiction to theory from Hussite wars to Thirty Years' War, 242

Germans, imitation by, of Swiss military system, 3

Gertruidenborg, siege of, 162

Ghent, 322-23

Giovacchino da Coniano, 57 n.3

Glatz, 361, 369

Glogau, 358, 369

Gneisenau, Neidhardt von, count (Prussian field marshal), 444 n.1, 454; adoption by, of Napoleonic strategy, 452; in four-day campaign of 1815, 438-39

"Golden bridges" for enemy withdrawal, 304-5
Goltz, Colmar von der (German field
marshal), 331; in strategy controversy, 378, 381
Gonzalo of Ayora, 16, 17
Gonzalo of Cordova: in battle of Barletta, 41; composition of army of,
15; first victory of, at Cerignola, 15,
73; inability of, to curb mercenary
disorders, 64; Life of, by Jovius, 15
Gravelingen, battle of, 194
Grawert, von (Prussian general), on
Napoleon's campaign plan of 1806,
433
Great Elector. See Frederick William
Great General Staff: on battle of Mollwitz, 326; concept by, of oblique
battle formation, 277; contradictions
in publications of, 381; on Freder-
ick's strategy from 1741 to 1744,
328; misunderstanding by, of Fred-
erick's strategy, 377-78, 381; new di-
rection of studies of, 381; on oblique
battle, 277, 290 n.28; on rapidity of
fire, 285; on sparing cavalry, 283.
Works: General Staff Works, 283,
290 n.20; Taktische Schulung, 285,
289 nn.9, 12, 16
Great Strategists, 454
Greek fire, 23
Gribeauval, Jean-Baptiste Vaquette de
(French general), 407
Groningen, 67
Gross-Beeren, battle of, 434
Grouchy, Emmanuel de (marshal of
France), 418, 452
Guasto, del (Spanish general), 44, 94-
97
Gui, Johann, 35
Guibert, count (French colonel), 372,
376, 383 n.10, 388
Guicciardini: opinion of condottieri,
16; praise by, of Prosper Colonna's
caution, 109-10; on Swiss losses at
Bicocca, 90. Work: Historia d'Italia,
49 n.36, 50 nn.38, 41
Guichard, 281

Guinegate, battle of, 4-7
Guise, François de Lorraine, duke
(French general), 228
Gunpowder: formula for, via Byzantium, 24; granulation of, 29; ingredients, 23-24, 29; invention of, 23-26;
list of references on, 44 n.1; "lump
powder," 46 n.17; use of, for military purposes in China, 24
Günther of Schwarzburg, as leader of
"Black horsemen," 121
Gustavus Adolphus (king of Sweden),
303, 427, 454; in battle of Breitenfeld, 203-6; in battle of Lützen, 207-
9; capture of strongholds by, 202;
characteristics of, 178-80; characterization of, by Clausewitz, 298; death
of, 209; discipline in army of, 177;
formation of, at Lützen, 208; increase by, of small arms and artillery, 177; perfected Maurice's art of
war, 173; religious influence in army
of, 178; reluctance of, to bring on
battle of Breitenfeld, 203; reorganization of cavalry by, 177, 281; strategy of, compared with Frederick the
Great, 369-70

Hadank, Karl, 15, 98 nn.12, 18
Hand grenades, use of, in China, 24
Handschoten, 396
Hardt (count), 281
Harquebus: in battle of Ceresole, 96;
in battle of Pavia, 42-43; compared
with bow, 40; compared with musket, 42; gradual introduction of, 38-
39; manipulation of, 39; opinion of
Machiavelli on, 39; too weak against
armor, 38; use of, by mounted
troops, 118-19
Harquebusiers: distinguished from
musketeers in army of Maurice, 158;
Hermann Hugo on, 137; mounted,
formed in squadrons executing caracole, 125
Hatzfeldt (imperial field marshal): in
battle of Jankau, 215, 334; in battle
of Wittstock, 213-14

"Hedge" formation, 126; abandoned
by Tavannes, 127; de la Noue on,
130-31; struggle between, and squadron formation, 134-35, 143 n.41
Hegel, 453
Height, requirements for, in Prussian
army, 250, 265 n.23
Henry, prince of Prussia (brother of
Frederick the Great), 315, 347, 359,
371, 373, 376; Frederick the Great
on, 377; in invasion of Bohemia,
1778, 363; reproach by, of Frederick, after Kollin, 342
Henry, duke of Guise, 124-25
Henry II (king of France), 118, 194;
dependence of, on Swiss and lansquenets, 227
Henry IV (king of France), 155, 227;
in battle of Coutras, 195; first to understand and exploit new cavalry,
136; on use of cavalry at Ivry, 151,
182 n.9, 195; small army of, after
Vervins treaty, 228; strength of army
of, in 1610, 229
Herreruelos, 122
Hesse, landgrave of, 123
Hildburghausen (Austrian general),
279, 345
Hintze, Otto: concepts of, challenged
by Delbrück, 441-44; on the strategy
of Frederick the Great, 439-40.
Work: Frederick the Great after the
Seven Years' War and the Political
Testament of 1768, 439
Historical accounts: misleading aspects
of, 406-7
Hobohm, Martin: authority on Machiavelli, 101; defended by Delbrück
against Fueter's criticism, 112 n.2;
opinion of, on Florentine com-
mander, 104; on spear length, 54.
Work: Machiavelli's Renaissance of
the Art of War, 19nn.6, 7
Hoche, Lazare (French general), 417,
419
Hochkirch, 380
Höchstädt, battle of, 302, 319-20, 369;
high command in, divided on both

sides, 302; preliminary situation,
319; as wing battle, 275
Hohenfriedberg, battle of, 304, 373,
437; army strengths in, 330; brilliant
leadership of Frederick in, 329-30;
losses in, 330-31
Hohenlinden, battle of, 430
Hohenlohe (count), 159
Hohenlohe, prince (Prussian general),
450
Holstein, in battle of Breitenfeld, 204
Hönig, Fritz (captain), 381
Höpfner, von (German general): description of Frederick's tactics by,
279-80
Horn (Swedish field marshal): in battle
of Breitenfeld, 204; in battle of Nördlingen, 210-12, 218 nn.21, 22; captured after battle of Nördlingen, 211
Horse artillery: created by Frederick
the Great, 284; in French revolution-
ary armies, 407
Hospitals, field, in French army, 235
Hôtel des Invalides, 236
Houchard, Jean-Nicolas (French general), 417, 418
Hoyer, Johann Gottfried: on development of art of war after 1792, 401-2;
on line and column, 274; on sale of
officer positions, 238 n.16; on treaties governing ransoms, 239 n.21.
Work: History of the Art of War,
238 n.16, 390
Hugo, Hermann, 136-37
Huguenots: attacks by horsemen of, at
Dreux, 123; conduct of, 71 n.10; as
officers in Brandenburg army, 260
Huguenot Wars, 194-95; detrimental to
French military system, 227; "German horsemen" in, 121-22; influence
of religion in, 67; knights against
cavalry in, 135-36; opposing sides in,
too weak for conclusive victories,
298; start of modern European cavalry in, 121-22
Hugues de Candilhac, 28
Hungarian cavalry, in battle on White
Mountain, 197-201

Hungarian fever, 216 n.5
"Hungarian order," 94
Hussars, 118, 256
Hussites, use by of cannon in siege, 34

Impressment: for Brandenburg-Prussian army, 247; of enemy prisoners, 251
Independent Army. See "New Model" army
Infantry: armor of, discarded, 270; combat of, at Breitenfeld, 175-76; combat of, at Edgehill, 176; combat of, under Gustavus Adolphus, 179; decline of, to secondary role at Coutras and Ivry, 136; formation of, reduced to four ranks, 270; increase of, in standing armies, 284; light, 400; of line, never to skirmish, 405; origin of name, 14-15; regiments of French army, origin of, 228
Infantry battalion of Frederick the Great, as a basic pole of the military art, 407
Infantry square: against cavalry, 151; against infantry square, 53; new formation of, 53; numbers of, 56-57; pressure from rear in, 54-55; relative positions of, 150-51; shock action of, 55; in Spanish army, 150; in "Spanish brigade," 151; Swiss contribution to world history, 86; width and depth of, 56
Ingolstadt, siege of, 321
Intendants in French army, 230-31
Intervals, in unit of pikemen, 163-68
"Ironsides," 189
Italy: danger of dependence on military leaders in, 19; decline of infantry of, 18; role of condottieri in, 16; strategies of Sforzas, Braccios in, 16; warlike country in fourteenth and fifteenth centuries, 16
Ivry, battle of, 136, 151, 195

Jacob von Ems, in command of German lansquenets at Ravenna, 75
Jäger companies, 281

Jähns, Max, 442; on "hook firearm," 51 n.48; on low forts, 49 n.36; in strategy controversy, 379, 381. Work: *History of the Military Sciences,* 49 n.36, 379, 381
James I (king of England), 185
James II (king of England, Scotland, Ireland), 302
Janissaries, 44, 153 n.15, 247; adoption of musket by, 149
Jankau, battle of, 215, 299, 334
Jemappes, battle of, 395
Jena, battle of, 422, 424, 433
Johann Friedrich of Saxony, 61
Johann Georg (elector of Saxony): allied with Gustavus Adolphus, 203; in command with Hatzfeldt at Wittstock, 214
Johann of Nassau, 158, 241-42, 253
John of Werth, 334
Jomini, Antoine-Henri, 409, 444 n.1, 446 n.19; analysis by, of Napoleon's art of war, 453; compared with Clausewitz, 453
Jourdan, Jean-Baptiste (marshal of France), 403, 417, 419; in command of army on Middle Rhine, 427-28; on poor discipline, 410
Jovius: on artillery, 36; on attack at Düren, 119; on battle of Ceresole, 95; on Duke Francesco Maria of Urbino, 110; on Italian infantry, 17; on lack of pursuit by Francis I, 305; on mounted crossbowmen of Charles V, 41; opinion of condottieri, 16; on Pavia, 42-43; on "snail" at Marignano, 148; on spear length, 53-54; on Vienna muster, 93-94; on wheel lock pistols in imperial cavalry, 41. Works: *Life of Gonzalo of Cordova,* 15, 41; *Life of Pescara,* 42
Julius II (pope), allied with Venice and Spain, 73
Jung-Bunzlau, capture of depot at, 340
Junker, in Prussian army at young age, 256
Jussuf, 24

Kalmucks, use of bow by, 40
Kanitz, von (Prussian general), 374
Kant, 453
Kappeler, Friedrich, 9
Karl Gustavus, 301
Karlstein, 34
Kay, battle of, 354, 374
Keith (Prussian field marshal): in battle of Prague, 342-43; in siege of Olmütz, 350; killed in action, 402
Kellermann, François-Christophe (marshal of France), 417, 418; in battle of Marengo, 430
Kesselsdorf, battle of, 332-33, 371, 373
Kheverhüller, count (field marshal): on reasons for waging and avoiding battle, 310; on wing battle, 275. Work: Short Concept of all Military Operations, 275
Kléber, Jean-Baptiste (French general), 417, 419
Klein-Schnellendorf, 326-27
Klitzing (general), 213
Knesebeck (Prussian adjutant general), 438. Work: Trilogie, 447 n.20
Knights: aided by firearms, 41; Burgundian, at Guinegate, 5; against cavalry in Huguenot wars, 135-36; decline of French men-at-arms, 126; difference between, and cavalry, 117; French, ineffective at Novara, 80; holding back of, in attack, 129; horsemen accompanying, 142 n.33; Mamelukes, 136; as one basic pole of the military art, 407; as one type of mounted troops, 118; transition of, to cavalry, 127-36, 230
Kolberg, 353, 361, 369
Kollin, battle of, 280, 341, 343, 344, 369, 376
Königgrätz, 351
Kornneuburg, 334
Kosel, 369
Koser, Reinhold: on "Bohemia or Moravia?", 448 n.24; in strategy controversy, 380, 382. Work: King Frederick the Great, 382
Krems, 334

Kreuzberg, 25, 28
Kunersdorf, battle of, 371, 374, 424; army strengths in, 367 n.40; attack by Prussians, 354-55; losses in, 402; preliminary moves, 354; Prussia's survival after, 355-59; Russian field fortifications at, 355; terrain at, 355; wing battle in, 360
Küstrin, 369
Kuttler, Hans, 8

Lafayette, Marie-Joseph, marquis of (French general), 261, 418
Laharpe (French general), 410
La Motta, battle of, 17, 55, 81
Lance: compared with pistol, 122, 126, 130, 132-33; discarded by Maurice of Orange, 134; effectiveness of, 137; generally discarded by end of sixteenth century, 134; wounds caused by, 137-38. See also Spears
"Lance of the raging fire," 24, 25
Landrat, 246
Landrecy, last use of mixed combat, 136
Lannes, Jean (marshal of France), 418, 419
Lanspessades, 14
Lansquenets: after discharge, 68-69; armament of, at Bruges, 10-11; in battle of Calliano, 9; in battle of Ceresole, 95; in battle of Marignano, 84-85; in battle of Moncontour, 195; in battle of Novara, 79-81; in battle of St. Quentin, 194; composition of, 10; expansion of, 18; decline of, 126; difference between, and Swiss, 9; failure of, at Pont-à-Mousson, 9; first clash with Swiss, 12; first victory over Swiss, 86-90; meaning of word, 7-8; "Order of," 8; origin of, 7-9; parade of, in 1495, 11-12; personal rights of, 259; in service of France, 14, 18-19, 227; systematic training of, 10; with Swiss, 9
"Lanze spezzate," 14
Lascy (Austrian general), 361

Lautrec, Odet de Foix (marshal of France), in battle of Bicocca, 88
"Law of the long spears," 61
Lazarus Schwendi: on deception in muster, 65; on risk of battle, 306
"Lazy Greta," 34
Leave system, under Frederick William I, 255
Lechuga, 57 n.2
Lecourbe, Claude (French general), 446
Lefebvre, François-Joseph (marshal of France), 418, 419
Lehwaldt (Prussian field marshal), 332, 341
Leipzig, battle of (1642): effectiveness of light cannon in, 179; shift of prisoners to victor at, 67
Leipzig, battle of (1813), Russian archers in, 40
Leitomischl, 348, 349, 351
Leo (emperor), influence of *Tactics* of, on Maurice and William Louis, 156-57, 159
Leopold I of Dessau (Prussian field marshal), 252, 314; in battle of Kesselsdorf, 332-33; in battle of Turin, 322; lack of education of son of, 258; efforts of, to refine formations, 274
Letter of articles, 60
Leuthen, battle of, 369-70, 374, 376; army strengths in, 345; attack in, with firing, 273; hussars in, 284; leadership of Frederick in, decisive factor, 346; pursuit following, 304; tactical maneuver of major importance in, 279; use of oblique battle formation with echelons in, 278-79
Leutmansdorf, 362
Levée en masse, 396, 414
Liegnitz, battle of, 359, 380
Ligny, 438, 452
Lille, siege of, 322-23
Limaçon. See "Snail"
Linear formation: compared with column, 399-400; disadvantages of, 274
Lippe, count, 399
Lipsius, Justus: on discipline, 156; on

field fortifications, 161; on Roman infantry under attack by cavalry, 151. Work: *de militia Romana*, 156
Lloyd (general), 314, 387-88
Loading: development of procedures for, 37; process of, basic to firing, 27
Lober stream, at Breitenfeld, 204
Lobositz. See Lowositz
Lombards, as marksmen, 17
"Long fellows," in Prussian army, 250
Long spears: in battle of Guinegate, 5; carried by lansquenets at Bruges, 10; disadvantages of, 11. See also Spears
Longwy, 392
Lorraine, annexed by France, 390
Losses in battle: in Napoleon's campaign of 1812, 436-37; reduced in French revolutionary wars, 402; in Seven Years' War, 402
Lotbüchsen, 36
Loudon (Austrian general), 354, 358-59
Louis of Baden, in battle of Höchstädt, 319-20
Louis XI (king of France), 13
Louis XII (king of France), 18-19, 73; dependence of, on Swiss and lansquenets, 227
Louis XIV (king of France), 232, 246-47; absolutism of, 391; action of, after loss of Lille, 323-24; condition of army in early years of, 230; construction of barracks by, 235; *Hôtel des Invalides* established by, 236; improvement under, of military pay system, 231; numerical superiority of, at outbreak of War of Spanish Succession, 319; wars of, fought by ever larger armies, 299-300
Louis XV (king of France), 390
Louvois, marquis de. See Le Tellier, François-Michel
Lowositz, battle of, 280, 374
Ludovico Moro, duke of Milan, 11
Ludwig von Baden, margrave, 308-9
Luther, Martin, condemnation of firearms by, 30-31
Lützen, battle of, 174, 177, 369-70; army strengths in, 208; opposing

formations in, 208; preliminary
movements, 207; Wallenstein in,
207-9
Luxembourg, François-Henri de Mont-
morency-Bouteville, duke (marshal
of France), 314

Macdonald, Alexandre (marshal of
France), 418
Machiavelli, Niccolo, 371; construction
by, of theoretical system based on
Romans, 101; contradictions in theory of, 109; distortions by, of con-
temporary conditions, 111; distrust
of firearms, 39; hostility of, to mer-
cenary system, 112; opinion of can-
non, 36; opinion of condottieri, 16;
position of, in Republic of Florence,
101-2; statements of, on strategy,
109; theory of strategy of, 107, 111.
Work: *Renaissance of the Art of
War*, 39, 101
Mack, Karl (Austrian lieutenant field
marshal), rejection by, of new
French combat method, 403, 450
Madfaa, 24, 26, 27, 28, 47 n.20
Madrid, treaty of, 295
Magdeburg, 202, 212
Mainz, 302
Malachowski, von (major), 381
Malplaquet, battle of, 302, 369-70; action of, 324-25; army strengths in,
324; losses in, 325; preliminary
movements, 323-24; strategic victory
for French, 325; tactical victory for
allies, 325; as wing battle, 275, 324
Mamelukes, 136
Manchester, count of, in English civil
war, 188
Maneuver, campaigns of: as exercised
by Turenne, 335-36; in first wars of
Louis VIV, 302; Frederick the Great
on, 313; furthered by limit on payment of troops, 108; by Gustavus
Adolphus, 298; by imperial army in
Southern France in 1524, 111; increasingly frequent, 1761-1789, 387;
by Moreau and Jourdan, 428; Prus-

sia saved by, 358; by Schmalkaldics,
297-98; spear squares ineffective in,
147
Manpower, for Brandenburg-Prussian
army, 247
Mansfeld, Ernst von (Protestant gen-
eral), 162, 243
Mantua, 423, 427
Maps, 315 n.1, 402
Maradas (general), 209
Marbot, Antoine-Marcellion, baron of
(French general), 40
Marceau, Francois-Séverin (French
general), 417, 419
Marching: Dilich on, 169 n.6; from
Elbe to Saale in 1813, 452; of lans-
quenets, 11; from Ligny via Wavre
to La Belle-Alliance, 452; by troops
of Frederick the Great, 376; by
troops of Napoleon, 423
Marck, de la, count, 79
Marcus Graecus, 24
Marengo, battle of, 429-30; distortions
by Napoleon in report on, 431-32
Maria Theresa, 280, 380; cession by, of
Upper Silesia, 327; permission of,
for battle, 351; reduction of army
by, 361
Marignano, battle of, 81-86
Marksmen: at Ceresole, 55, 95; of
compagnies d'ordonnance at Guinegate, 4-5; in French revolutionary
armies, 398-401; increase in numbers
of, 147-48; of Italians, 17; mounted,
of Camillo Vitelli, 41; protection for,
148-50, 152 n.14, 158; in rear guard,
40; as skirmishers, 148
Marlborough, John Churchill, duke of
(English general), 280, 303, 393, 454;
in battle of Höchstädt, 319-20; failure of, to concentrate forces for battle, 370; in siege of Lille, 323;
victory of, at Oudenarde, 322; victory of, at Ramillies, 322
Marmont, Auguste de (marshal of
France), 418; on rations, 448 n.21
Marriage: forbidden to French soldiers

by Le Tellier, 235; restrictions on, in Prussian army, 256
Marschall (Austrian general), at Olmütz, 350
Marseilles, siege of, 110
Marshal, meaning of title, 257
Marsin (marshal of France), in battle of Höchstädt, 319-20
Marston Moor, battle of, 190
Marwitz, von der (general), description of cavalry attack, 282-83
Masséna, André (marshal of France), 418, 419
Masses: financial strain caused by, 108; increase of, 108; use of, in infantry square, 63
Matchlock, 37
Mathematical formulas for warfare, 388-89
Maurice, prince of Dessau: on attack without firing, 273; in battle of Prague, 342
Maurice, landgrave of Hesse, creator of first drill regulations in Germany, 253
Maurice of Nassau, prince of Orange: abandonment of lance by, 134; creation of new formations by, 157-58; creator of officer status, in modern sense, 161; discipline of, 161-63; emphasis of, on drill, 157, 159; free withdrawal granted by, at Groningen, 67; increase by, of marksmen/spearmen ratio, 158; initial development of standing army by, 224; insistence of, on prompt payment of troops, 160, 163; military reforms of, based on Machiavelli, 155, 156; position of, 156; relationship of, with William Louis of Nassau, 156, 159; sieges by, 162; studies of ancient authors by, 156-57
Maurice, elector of Saxony: in battle of Sievershausen, 123, 193; training by, of horsemen with pistol, 123
Max, duke of Bavaria: as army commander, 224; in battle on White

Mountain, 196-97; supply depots of, 300
Max Emanuel, elector of Bavaria, in War of Spanish Succession, 319
Maxen, 358
Maximilian (Holy Roman emperor): artillery of, 36; in battle of Guinegate, 4-7; demands of, at end of Swabian War, 12; fear of, by Flemish, 6-7; mutiny of lansquenets of, 64; as spearman in ranks, 8
Maximilian Sforza, 78-79, 82
Mayer, 281
Mazarin, Giulio, cardinal, 229, 231
Medical care, in mercenary armies, 65-66
Melas, Michael, baron (Austrian general), 430
Mendoza, Bernardino de (Spanish general): on cavalry awaiting attack in place, 145 n.47; on formations, 57 n.2; history of war in the Netherlands, 131; on lance against pistol, 132; on mounted troops at Mooker Heide, 122, 132; on pike compared with firearm, 269; on slowness to bring on battle, 307; on squadron depth, 132. Works: Theory and Practice of War, 131; History of the Netherlands War, 140 n.20
Mercenaries: development of, into standing armies, 223; revulsion of Machiavelli to, 112
Mercenary armies: discipline of, 63-64, 66; disorders in, 62; entrenching duties, 62; field regulations for, 59-60; influence of religious affiliation in, 67; mistreatment of population by, 64; mutinies in, 64; not interested in "cause," 67; officers in, 59; pay of, 61-63; rations of, 61; units of, 59; women camp followers, 65. See also Lansquenets; Swiss
Mercy, Franz (imperial general), 336
Metternich-Winneburg, Klemens Lothar Wenzel, prince of, 438
Metz, 423
Milan: captured by French, 78; French

claim to, 82; in hands of French, 86; move on, by Francis I, 83; recaptured by French, 91; taken by Swiss, 82
Military organization, basic factor in existence of nation, 223
Military profession, 248
Military school, at Siegen, 241-42
Military service, compulsory: civil war resulting from, in France, 395-96; initially rejected by National Assembly, 391; introduced by Convention, 395; *levée en masse*, 396; in Napoleonic armies, 412-13; in Prussia, 413, 451. See also Conscription
Military terms, adopted in German from other languages, 70
Militia: created by King Frederick I, 248; criticism of, 262 n.4, 263 nn.5, 6; of English counties, 185-86; failure of, 242; in France in seventeenth century, 236; in larger German territories, 241-42; of Republic of Florence, 102-6
Mines, ground, use of in China, 24
Minié gun, 287
Mistreatment of population by mercenaries, 64
Mixed combat: Hermann Hugo on, 137; last example of, at Landrecy, 136
Modena, duke of, 321
Möllendorf, von (Prussian field marshal), prohibition by, of aiming, 450
Mollwitz, battle of, 325-27, 380; army strengths in, 326; artillery in, 285; ineffectiveness of Prussian cavalry in, 281; oblique battle formation in, 276
Moltke, Helmuth von, count (Prussian field marshal), 443; in campaign of 1866, 442; on campaign plans, 425; new period in art of war, 455
Moncey, Bon-Adrien Jeannot de (marshal of France), 418
Moncontour, battle of, 194-95; use of *caracole* in, 123
Mongolia, 23
Monluc, Blaise (marshal of France),

233; on efficiency of *reîtres*, 131; on marksmen, 148; on shock action at Ceresole, 55
Mons, 324, 325
Monro (Scottish officer), 174, 191
Montecuccoli, 371; on demolition of fortresses, 317 n.18; on military hierarchy, 257; proposal for obtaining manpower, 247; on ratio of musketeers to pikemen, 181 n.4; on reasons for accepting battle, 308; on wing battle, 275. Work: *On the Art of War*, 275
Mooker Heide, battle on the, 122, 132, 145 n.47
Moreau, Jean-Victor (French general), 372, 400, 403, 417, 419; campaign of, compared with Napoleon, 427-28; in campaign of 1800, 429-30; compared with Frederick the Great, 429; compared with Frederick and Daun, 430; compared with Napoleon, 430-31; on poor discipline, 410; strategic advice to allies in 1813, 430; withdrawal of, 428
Mortier, Adolphe (marshal of France), 418, 419
Moscow, 436
Mounted troops: accompanying knights, 142 n.33; armament of, 122; "Black horsemen," 121; changes in, 117; depth and breadth of formation of, 120-21; difference between, and infantry, 117; at Düren, 119; formation of, recommended in *True Advice...*, 120; gradually equipped with firearms, 118-19; of Huguenots at Dreux, 123; increased need among, for light horsemen, 119; leveling movement among, 119; light, *stradioti*, 117; against marksmen and pikemen, 149; at Mooker Heide, 122; in parade at Metz, 118; at Ravenna, 117; in Schmalkaldic War, 119-21; slow, steady approach ride by German, 119; transition of, from knights to cavalry, 127-36; various

types of, 118-19. *See also* Knights; Cavalry

Murat, Joachim (marshal of France), 418, 419

Muschamp (Scottish lieutenant colonel), on attack of musketeer battalion at Breitenfeld, 175-76

Musket: accuracy of, 289 n.14; compared with harquebus, 42; compared with rifle, 399; with flintlock and bayonet, 269-70; with fork, 38; improvements to, 270, 401-2; increased power of, 38; range of, 272; rapidity of fire of, 272, 285-87; use of, by janissaries, 44; use of, in wet weather, 327

Musketeers: in army of Maurice of Orange, 158; in battle of Breitenfeld, 206; in Cromwell's army, 190; execution of *caracole* by, 176; ratio of, to pikemen, 181 n.4; in Swedish formation, 175, 179

Muster, deception in, 65, 229, 237

Napoleon Bonaparte: actions of, at outbreak of French Revolution, 426; at apogee of fame and strategy in 1805, 434; battle leadership of, compared with Frederick the Great, 408-9, 425; in battle of Marengo, 429-30; in battle of Wagram, 436; blend of boldness and caution in operations of, 434; campaign plans of, simple, 421-22, 424-25; campaign plans of 1806 and 1813, 433-34; in campaign of 1800, 429-30; in campaign of 1814, 438; in campaign of 1815, 438; compared with Frederick the Great, 422-23; compared with Moreau, 430-31; concentration of forces for battle, 424, 428; concentration on one enemy flank, 433; conscription under, 412-13; creative genius and personality of, 427; creator of modern strategy of annihilation, 431; criticism by, of Frederick at Kunersdorf, 355; criticism by, of Frederick at Crefeld and Torgau, 361; crossing of Danube by, and battle of Aspern, 435-36; decisions of, based on chances of success, 423; dependence of, on marches, 423; dependence of, on politics, 426-27; desertions in armies of, 413-14, 437-38; distortions by, in report on Marengo, 431-32; in Egypt, 431; emphasis of, on drill, 400; freed from fetters of older armies, 421; as head of state, 411; Italian campaign of, compared with Moreau, 427-28; lack of support for, in France, 437-38; as lieutenant at Toulon, 397; losses of, in 1812, 436-37; on Mamelukes in Egypt, 136; marches of, 409, 423; marshals of, 411, 417-19; plan of, to buy Negroes, 401; primarily a statesman, 426; reports of, on poor discipline, 410; republican spirit in armies of, 412-13; in Russian campaign of 1812, 436-37; training of recruits by, 400-401; unforgettable fame of, even in defeat, 454

Napoleon III, Charles-Louis (emperor of France), on width and depth of squadron, 138 n.12, 139 n.15. Work: *History of the Artillery*, 49 n.36

Naseby, battle of, 189

National Assembly, 391

National Guard, 392

Naumburg, 207

Navarro, Pedro de (Spanish general), in battle of Ravenna, 74-77

Needle gun, 287

Neerwinden, battle of, 302, 395

Negroes, 401

Neipperg (Austrian general), in battle of Mollwitz, 325-26

Neisse, fortress of, 325, 326, 369, 423

Nemours, duke of, 41

Netherlands army: based on orderly economy, 160; organization of, 160-61

"Netherlands brigade," 158

Neumair von Ramssla: reasons of, for accepting battle, 308; on superiority of firearms over spears, 175. Work:

Recollections and Rules of the Military System, 175
"New Model" army: composition of, 187-88; created by Cromwell, 187; discipline in, 188-89; drills in, 189; field recognition symbols of, 190; importance of cavalry in, 189; influence of religion in, 188, 190-91; musketeers and pikemen in, 190; rebellion of, against parliament, 191; uniform of, 190-91; will of, dominant, 191
Ney, Michel (marshal of France), 418-19
Nieuport, battle of, 163, 290 n.21
Nijmegen, 162
Nobles: in battle of Béthune, 12; feigned, in France, 233; feigned, in Prussia, 256-57; in front rank at Guinegate, 5; as officers in French army, 231-34; at Padua, 12; in Prussian officer corps, 255-58; sons of, inducted in cadet corps, 257-58; in training of lansquenets, 12
Nördlingen, battle of, 369; analysis of, 211; army strengths in, 211; development of, 210; losses of Swedish army in, 211; opposing views of Protestant leaders before, 210; preliminary movements, 209-10; Württemberg militia in, 242
"Normal army," 371-72
Northern War, 246
Noue, de la (French captain and author): on attacks by knights, 129; on *caracole*, 124; on cohesiveness of *reîtres*, 129; on Coligny's concern for rations, 61; on depth of squadron, 121, 131; on French armor, 130; on "hedge" formation versus depth, 131; on ineffectiveness of *caracole*, 129; on infantry against horsemen, 151; on lance and pistol, 130; military experience of, 129; on numbers of marksmen, 148; on orderliness during marches, 130; on pistol range, 123; requirements of, for nobles as officers, 232

Novara, battle of, 295; army strengths in, 79; French wooden fortress, 79; ineffectiveness of French knights in, 80; preliminary moves, 78
Nuremberg, giant cannon of, "Chriemhilde," 32

Oath of obedience, 60
Ober-Glauheim, 320
Obligation, military: under King Frederick William I of Prussia, 248-49; under Louis XIV, 249. *See also* Conscription; Military service, compulsory
Oblique battle formation, 274, 276-79, 360-61
Offense: alternation of, with defense in strategy of attrition, 305; favored by new methods of warfare, 108
Officers: appointments of, in Prussian army, 257; "commerce" of, in recruiting, 247; development of, from knighthood, 233-34; discipline of, 253; distinction between, and men, 255; duties of, 234; in French army of seventeenth century, 231-34; of French Revolution, 396, 397, 411; hierarchy and titles of, 257; Huguenot, in Prussian army, 260; lack of higher education among, in Prussia, 258; in mercenary armies, 59, 64-65; *officier de fortune*, 234; ratio of, to men, 234, 238 n.18; sale of positions as, 233, 238 n.16; severity of, in Prussian army, 259
Officier de fortune, 234, 255, 419
"Old bands," as base of French infantry, 228
Oliva, treaty of, 245
Olmütz, siege of, 334, 347-49, 369, 371, 423
Omdurman, battle of, 435
Orange, crown prince of, at Malplaquet, 324-25
Orleans, duke of, in battle of Turin, 321-22
Oudenarde, battle of, 302, 322

Oudinot, Nicolas-Charles (marshal of France), 418, 419
Oxenstierna, 337

Paetel, Georg, 139 n.16
Palatinate: laid waste by French, 302; militia in, 241-42
Pandours, 280, 281, 312, 398
Pappenheim (imperial general), in battle of Breitenfeld, 204-9
Paris, 423
Parliament, English: purged, then eliminated, 191; rebellion of Cromwell's army against, 191; "self-renunciation acts," 188; at start of civil war, 186
Parma, prince of, 162, 227
Patrols, cavalry, 284
Pavesen, 99 n.12
Pavia, battle of, 91-93, 295
Pay: difficulties with, in Spanish army, 160; emphasis on regularity of, by Maurice, 160, 163; irregularity of, in French army in early seventeenth century, 230; irregularity of, in mercenary armies, 61, 63; system of, reformed by Le Tellier, 231
Pérignon, Dominique-Catherine de (marshal of France), 418
Personal rights: forfeited in Prussian army, 259; of lansquenets, 259; retained in French army, 261
Pescara, Fernando Francisco de Avalos, marquis of (Spanish general), 36; in battle of Bicocca, 87-90; in battle of La Motta, 81; in battle of Pavia, 42-43, 91-93, 111; in battle of Ravenna, 74-77; in France with Bourbon and imperial army, 110; inability of, to control mercenary disorders, 64; wish of, to avoid battle, 108
Peter III, czar of Russia, abdication of, 368 n.46
Petrarch, on firearms, 29-30
Philip of Hesse: on demands of mercenaries, 62; as entrepreneur, 61; limitations of, on requisitioning, 61; marksmen in units of, 148; necessity of, for nobles among knights, 121

Philip, landgrave, 36, 298
Philip I, the Handsome (king of Spain), 16
Philip II, (king of Spain), 194; in battle of St. Quentin, 193
Philosophic exploration, in Germany, inspired by Kant, Hegel, 453
Picards: in "old bands," 228; at Ravenna, 77
Pichegru, Charles (French general), 417, 419
Piedmont, "old bands" of, 228
Pien-King, 24
Pikemen: in battle of Enzheim, 269; in Cromwell's army, 190; decline of, 177; against firearms, 269; against horsemen, 148; intervals in units of, 163-68; as protection for marksmen, 150, 181 n.4; in Swedish formation, 174-75, 179
Pinkin Cleugh, battle of, 40
Pirna, 338-39
Pisa, 105
Pistols, 41-42; as arm of mounted men, 122, 125, 140 n.21; aversion to, 126; in battle of Sievershausen, 123; at Ceresole, 42, 96; at Châlons, 42; compared with lance, 122, 126, 130; first large-scale victory of, 126; against lance, 126; origin of name, 52 n.64; practice firing of, from horseback, 140 n.22; range of, 123; use of, by mounted marksmen in France, 42; wheel lock, 42
Du Plessis-Praslain, 231
Podewils, 329
Poland, division of, 387
Poles, opposite, of strategy of attrition, 302
Political forms, in Europe, after Seven Years' War, 387
Political Testament of Frederick the Great, 439-40
Politics: dependence of Frederick the Great on, 335, 453; dependence of Napoleon on, 426-27, 453
Poniatowski, 448 n.21
Popelinière, Lancelot Voisin, sire de la:

on *caracole* at Moncontour, 123-24; in command of Huguenot company, 141 n.27

Potatoes, 411

"Potato war," 363, 411

Potosi, 228

Prague, 369, 371, 374, 376, 423; battle of, 340-43; captured by French in 1742, 327; conquered by Frederick in 1744, 328; losses in battle of, 402

Precious metals from America: aid of, in development of Spanish standing army, 228

Presbyterian Church, 191

Profoss, 60

Provinces, protection of, 370, 371

Prussia: administration of, 246-47; allied with Austria against French Revolution, 392; army intendancy, 246; composition of nation of, 257; defense plan for, rejected, 242; development of, tied to development of Brandenburg-Prussian army, 245-46; forces of, still available after Kunersdorf, 356; initial efforts toward becoming great power, 247; militia in, 241-42; new drill regulations for, 406; survival of, after Kunersdorf, 355-59; withdrawal of, from war in 1795, 449

Prussian army: ages of soldiers in, 255; compared with French army, 259-62; description of, by Frederick the Great, 254-55; desertion in, 251-52; distinction between officers and men in, 255-56; drill in, 253; essentially unchanged before 1806, 450; foreigners in, 250-51; establishment of, by Frederick William, 245; formed basis for Prussian nation, 245-46; growth of, 246-47; levy of, compared with French, 261-62; integration of foreigners in, 260; maneuverability and speed of, 303; recruiting for, 248-51; rejuvenation of, 450; restrictions on marriage in, 256; severity of officers in, 259; stiffness of linear formation

of, 280; superior quality of, 371. *See also* Brandenburg-Prussian army

Prussian navy, 440

Puebla (Austrian general), 374

Punishment: at drill, 253, 258; in French army, 266 n.41

Puritans, in parliamentary army, 188

Pursuit: after Hohenfriedberg and Leuthen, 304, 330-31; lack of, after Soor, 332; not possible for Frederick, 304; risks in, 304

Pusyrewski (general), on cavalry combat, 283

Puységur, Jacques-François de Chastenet, marquis of (marshal of France), 309-10; on intervals in battle formation, 277; on oblique battle formation, 276. Work: *Art de la Guerre*, 276

Quitzow, Dietrich von, 34

Quitzow, Hans von, 34

Rabutin: description by, of Metz parade, 118-19; description by, of parade execution of "snail," 148. Work: *Commentaires*, 143 n.37

Radetzky, 452

Raitri. See Reîtres

Ramillies, battle of, 302; Marlborough in, 322; as wing battle, 275

Ranke: on imperial army after siege of Marseilles, 111; on Swiss at Bicocca, 90. Work: "Hardenberg," *Werke*, Vol. 48, 447 n.20

Ransom: agreement on, between France and Spain in 1674, 236; interest of condottieri in, 16; limitations on, 68; treaties on, 239 n.21

Rapidity of fire, 272, 285-87

Rations: Chemnitz on, 300; depots for, established by Le Tellier, 235; difficulties of transport of, 301, 331; emphasis on, by Turenne, 335-36; in French revolutionary armies, 409-11; in mercenary armies, 61; old system of, in French army, 409; shortage of, in campaign of 1812, 437; in Thirty

Years' War, 299-301; use of waterways for transport of, 300
Ravaillac, 229
Ravenna, battle of, 55, 73-78, 369
Recoil, of hand firearm, 37
Recoil hook, 37, 51 n.48
Reconnaissance, unsuitability of line cavalry for, 283-84, 328
Recruiting: of cavalry, 125; in mercenary armies, 61; in Prussia under "canton regulation," 249-50
Recruits, 306, 400-401
"Refractories," 412; in campaign of 1812, 437
Regiment, composition of, 59
Reisner: on incident of cavalry charge at Bicocca, 128-29. Work: *Life of Frundsberg*, 128
Reîtres: cohesiveness of, 129; description of, by Tavannes, 127-28; as fathers of European cavalry, 121; versus "hedge," 143 n.41, 144 n.42; in Huguenot wars, 121; praised by Monluc, 131; troops needed to defeat, 124
Religion, influence of: in army of Gustavus Adolphus, 178; on conduct, 71 n.10; in Cromwell's army, 188, 190, 191; in determining choice of warring sides, 67
Renaissance of the Art of War (Machiavelli), 101
René, count of Lorraine, 9
Renzo da Ceri, 110
Reserve: in battle of Aspern, 435; importance of, in French revolutionary armies, 408
Reyd (secretary of William Louis of Nassau), 159
Ribaudequin, 29, 46 n.16
Richelieu, Armand-Jean du Plessis de, cardinal, 232; boast by, of French strength, 229; participation of, in Thirty Years' War, 229; unable to bring order into military organization, 230
Richepanse (French general), 430
Rifle, 38, 399

Roads, built by Napoleon, 423
Rockets, use of, in China, 24
Roloff, Gustav, 416 n.17; in strategy controversy, 379, 382
Romagna, 17
Roman candle, 24
Romont, count of, 4-6
Ronco River, 74-77
Rossbach, battle of, 279, 306, 345, 376, 380
Rössler, von (major), 328, 381
"Roundheads," 187-88
Ruits (Prussian general), 353
Ruprecht, prince of the Palatinate, as cavalry commander, 189
Russia, campaign in, 1812, 435-36
Russians: in battle of Kunersdorf, 354-55; in battle of Zorndorf, 352-53; capture by, of East Prussia, 346; in coalition of 1757, 339-40; instructions from, to Apraxin, 346; lack of agreement with Austrians, 357; losses of, at Kunersdorf, 356; shift of, to Prussian side, 361; slow to adopt skirmisher tactics, 451; war of, against Frederick, a diplomatic one, 357; widely separated from Austrians, 358
Rüstow: on "Hungarian order," 94; on "Netherlands brigade," 158; on simplification of tactical formations, 170 n.16; on "Spanish brigade," 151, 216 n.13; on "Swedish formation," 174-75, 180

Saint Anthony, original patron saint of artillerists' guild, 34
Saint Barbara, patron saint of artillerists, 34
Saint-Cyr, Gouvion, Laurent (marshal of France), 372, 408, 418, 419, 431, 446
Saint-Germain, Claude Louis, count (French war minister): efforts of, to improve discipline, 390-91; introduction of cavalry attack at gallop, 282; reforms of, 238 n.18, 261

Saint-Luc. Work: *Observations militaires*, 138 n.12
Saint Petersburg, 346, 440, 441
Saint-Quentin, battle of, 193
Saint-Vincent, battle of, 126
Saldern (general), 389
Saltpeter, in gunpowder, 23
Saluerno, siege of, 25
Salvos, 176, 270-71
Santa Cruz, marquis of, on risks of battle, 309. Work: *Reflections*, 309
Sarissa, length of, 54
Savelli, Jacopo, 104
Savoy, duke of, in battle of Turin, 322
Saxons: in battle of Breitenfeld, 205; in battle of Kesselsdorf, 332, 373; in battle of Wittstock, 213; concentration of, at Pirna, 338; with imperial forces in 1645, 334; planned move by, against Brandenburg, 332; threat by, to March, 331
Saxony, militia in, 241-43
Saxony, marshal of, 372; on attack without firing, 272-73; on pursuit, 304. Work: *Rêveries*, 272
Scharnhorst, Gerhard von (Prussian general), 399; establishment of national army by, 451; on firing of salvos, 271; on French revolutionary wars, 449; ideas of, not accepted in Prussian army, 450; introduction of "column toward the middle," 451; introduction of universal military obligation, 451; mortally wounded in action, 402-3; on rapidity of fire, 286-87. Work: *Taktik*, 271
Schellenberg, 320-21
Schemaeddin-Mohammed, 24
Scherer (French general), 417, 419
Schinner (cardinal), role of, in battle of Marignano, 83-85
Schmalkaldic army: campaign of maneuver by, 297-98; composition of mounted troops of, 121; formation of, on Danube facing Charles V, 56
Schmalkaldic war: formation of imperial horsemen in, 119-20; use of cannon in, 36; use of pistol in, 42

Schultheiss, 60
Schwarz, Martin, 8
Schwarzenberg, 243, 244, 452
Schweidnitz, 345, 347, 361, 362, 369, 423
Schwerin (Prussian field marshal), 326; capture of depot at Jung-Bunzlau, 340; killed in action, 402
Sclopus, 25
Scots: at Breitenfeld, 176-77; in Swedish army, 174, 175-76
Sea powers, subsidies of, to Brandenburg, 247
Seneffe, battle of, 302
Sérurier, Philibert (marshal of France), 417, 419
Servan de Gerbey, Joseph (French general), 417, 418
Seven Years' War, 338-63; political forms in Europe after, 387
Seydlitz, Friedrich Wilhelm von (Prussian general), 282
Sforza, Franz, duke, 88
Shock action of cavalry, 281-83
Sibilski (Russian general), 346
Siegen, 241
Sieges, 369
Sievershausen, battle of, 193; army strengths in, 193; use of pistols in, 123
Sights for firearms, 38
Sigismund, duke of Tyrol, 9
Signal telegraphs, 401
Silesia, 325-27
Sittich, Marx, of Embs, at Pavia, 91-93
Skalitz, 347
Skirmishing, 401, 415 n.12; gradually accepted in Austria and Prussia, 406; rejected by General von Fransecky, 403-6; Scharnhorst on, 449
Small arms, increased by Gustavus Adolphus, 177. *See also* Firearms; Pistols
Smythe, Sir John, 40
"Snail" (*limaçon*): among horsemen as *caracole*, 123; used by lansquenets at Bruges, 11; used by marksmen at Marignano, 148

"Snow from China," 24
Soderini, 103
Soldier, importance of good will of, 407
Soltikoff (Russian general), 356-58
Soor, battle of, 306, 331-32, 380
Soubise, Charles de Rohan, prince of (marshal of France), 279, 345, 443
Soult, Nicolas (marshal of France), 418, 419; in battle of Austerlitz, 434
Spangenberg, 25, 28
Spanish: in battle of Ceresole, 95; in battle of Ravenna, 55; creation by, of national mounted force, 122; development of, into outstanding infantry, 15, 19; difficulties of, with army pay, 160; first standing mercenary army, 224; imitation of Swiss military system, 3, 15; infantry formation of—"Spanish brigade," 151; initially inferior to Swiss, 15; invasion by, of Florentine republic, 105-6; length of spears of, 54; in the Netherlands, 155; opposition of, to new formations and drills, 16; too weak to win out in Netherlands, 298
"Spanish brigade," 151, 216 n.13
Spears: gradually abandoned toward 1700, 269; inferiority of, to firearm, 175; length of, 53-54; square of, ineffective in war of maneuver, 147. See also Lance; Long spears; Pikemen
Squadron: in depth, start of development of cavalry, 135; Napoleon III on width and depth of, 138 n.12; struggle between, and "hedge" formation, 134-35, 143 n.41
Square, battle formation of Germans, 50 n.41
Standing armies: better training of, 270; development of, from mercenaries, 223; discipline in, 252; further development of, by Gustavus Adolphus, 224; increase of infantry in, 284; new qualities characteristic of, developed by Maurice of Orange, 224; in Spain, 224

States-General, 160, 161, 163
Steenkerken, battle of, 302
Steenwyk, 162
Stradioti, 117, 122
Strategy: of annihilation, 293, 421, 423; of attrition, 108, 293, 294, 295-315, 374, 423; basic principle of, 293, 421; "bi-polar," 108, 294, 302; campaign of 1815, direct contrast of two forms of, 439; changed by French Revolution, 390, 402; Clausewitz on, 378, 421; contrast between, of attrition and annihilation, 439-44; controversy over, of Frederick the Great, 378-82; decisions on, by home governments, 297; of Frederick the Great, analysis of, 374-78, 439-44; of Frederick the Great, double-poled, 303, 314; of Frederick the Great in 1744, 328; of Frederick the Great in Seven Years' War, 338-53; of Frederick the Great, misunderstood by Great General Staff, 377-78; of maneuver, 294; modern, of annihilation, created by Napoleon, 431; of Napoleon, compared with Frederick the Great, 423; problem of, unsolved by Machiavelli, 107, 111, 295; role of battle in, 294; statements on, by Frederick the Great, 310-14; subjective aspects of, 352; of Swiss, 294-95; of Thirty Years' War, 298-99; of Torstensson, 333-35; of Turenne, 335-37; unchanged from Renaissance to French Revolution, 315, 369
Strategy controversy, 378-82
Stuhlweissenburg, 9, 42, 64
Subjective aspect of Frederick's strategy, 352
Subsidies, to Brandenburg from sea powers, 247
Suchet, Louis (marshal of France), 418, 419
Suleiman, sultan, 42, 94
Sully, Maximilien, duke of, 228-29
Surprise, 373
Susane: on origin of dragoons, 142

n.35; on origin of French infantry, 13. Works. *Histoire de la cavallerie française*, 142 n.35; *Histoire d l'infanterie française*, 382 n.3

Swabians: at Bicocca, 90; as lansquenets, 10

Sweden: development of, as military nation, 173; lack of definite political direction in, 337-38; organization of government of, 173-74; parliament of, 173-74; willing to risk army in Germany, 335

Swedish army: in battle of Breitenfeld, 203-7; in battle of Jankau, 215, 334; in battle of Lützen, 207-9; in battle of Nördlingen, 209-12; in battle of Wittstock, 213; concept of drill in, 174; discipline of, 174; first national army, 174; formation of, 180-81; other nationalities in, 174; size of, 174; strength of, 181 n.2

"Swedish formation," 174-75, 181

Swiss: in battle of Ceresole, 95; in battle of Marignano, 81-86; in battle of Novara, 78-81; contribution to world history of, creation of infantry, 86; defeated by lansquenets at Bicocca, 86-90; destroyed at Pavia, 93; difference between, and lansquenets, 9; first clash with lansquenets, 12; in French army, 227; imitation of, 3; as instructors, models for French, 13; with lansquenets, 9; length of spears of, 54; in Milan, 82; military system of, 3; opportunity of, to form large nation, 82, 86; opposition of, to treaty of Gallerate, 84; political limitations of, 82-83; in service of France, 14, 18; strategy of, 294-95

Swords: carried by lansquenets, 11; in front rank, 55

Sybel, Heinrich von, in strategy controversy, 379

Tactics: changes caused by French Revolution, 390, 398, 402; changes in, from Renaissance to Frederick

the Great, 369; new nation a prerequisite for new, 406; revised, in Austria and Prussia, 450; Scharnhorst on, 449

Tallart, Camille d'Hostun, duke of (marshal of France), in battle of Höchstädt, 319-20, 363 n.2

Talleyrand-Périgord, Charles Maurice de, 435

Tauentzien (general), 389

Tavannes, Gaspard de Saulx de (marshal of France): on armor, lance, and pistol, 127-28; on *caracole* in battle of Dreux, 123; on *caracole* in battle of Moncontour, 123; change of cavalry formation by, 127; on combat against *reîtres*, 127; on depth of mounted formation, 121; as marshal in Huguenot wars, 127; opposed to *caracole*, 128; on pace of cavalry attack, 128; as page at Pavia, 127; on shorter training time, 135. Work: *Teachings of a True Military Leader*, 127

Tax system: in Brandenburg, 246-47; gradual development of, 224; needed for regular payment of army, 69, 228

Taysen, von, in strategy controversy, 381

Le Tellier, François Michel, marquis de Louvois: compared with Frederick William I, 237; conscription under, 236-37; continuation by, of father's reforms, 236-37; retention by, of complete regimental staffs when army reduced, 236

Le Tellier, Michel: creation of intendants, 230-31; introduction by, of uniforms, standard musket, ration depots, field hospitals, 235; prohibition by, of flintlocks, 270; recruiting system of, 234-35; regularization of pay system by, 231; reorganization and reform of French army by, 230-36

Terni, siege of, 25

Terrain, 373, 388

"Terror," in French Revolution, 396

Terzio, 150; in battle of Breitenfeld, 204, 206
Theories on warfare, late eighteenth century, 388-89
Thérouanne, 4-6
Thielmann (Saxon lieutenant), 397
Thirty Years' War: armies of, lived from land, 299; army strengths in, 299; majority of troops in, garrisons of cities, 370; strategy in, 298-99; wide-ranging theater of operations of, 299; strategy of, determined by political viewpoints, 299
Thurn, count: infantry of, on White Mountain, 199-200
Tielcke (Saxon captain), 387
Tilly, Johann Tserclaes, count of: in battle on White Mountain, 196-97; capture of Magdeburg by, 202; defense position of, at Breitenfeld, 203; infantry of, defected to Swedes, 207; losses of, at Leipzig, 179; withdrawal of, from Breitenfeld, 207
Toll, Carl Friedrich, count of (Russian general), 452, 456 n.10
Torgau, battle of, 360, 369-70, 374; artillery in, 285; losses in, 402; new method of wing battle in, 360
Torpedo, 25
Torsion engine, revived by Johann Gui, 35
Torstensson, Lennart, count of Ortala (Swedish general): army of, 334; in battle of Jankau, 215, 334; in battle of Wittstock, 213; capable of risking army, 335; compared with Frederick the Great, 301-2, 333-35; 370; move of, to gates of Vienna, 334; movements of, in 1642, 333-34; strategy of, 299, 334-35; superior leadership of, 334
Touchhole, 37
Toulon, 397
Tournai, 324
Trabanten, 10, 64
Trachenberg plan, 430
Train: loss of, by Frederick, at Olmütz, 349; reduced in French revo-lutionary armies, 397-98, 411; reduced by Le Tellier, 235
Traun (Austrian general), victory of, without battle, in 1744, 328, 336
Traupitz, Laurentium, on Swedish formation, 180-81. Work: Art of War According to the Royal Swedish Manner..., 174
Trecate, 79, 81
Treitschke, Heinrich von, in strategy controversy, 379
La Trémouille (marshal of France), 79, 82, 295
Trewer Rath. See True Advice
True Advice and Reflections of an Old Well-tested and Experienced Warrior: on administration of oath, 60; on broad front, 56; on mounted formations, 120
Trivulzio (marshal of France), 36, 79, 85
Trunnion, for cannon, 33
Tschernyscheff (Russian general), 368 n.46
Tungus, 40
Turenne, Henri de la Tour d'Auvergne, viscount of (marshal of France), 314, 371; in battle of Enzheim, 269; Clausewitz on, 335-36; contribution by, of own money for soldier's pay, 231; emphasis of, on rations, 335-36; introduction by, of Netherlands drill, 229; maneuver ability of, 335-36; at Orleans, 336; preference of, for battles rather than sieges, 308; strategy of, 335-37; understanding of new military system, 230
Turin, battle of, 302, 321-22; as wing battle, 275
Turks, 149, 153 n.15, 280
Turpin de Crissé, 387

Uhlans, 126-27
Ulm, battle of, 422
Uniforms: in Cromwell's army, 190-91; in French army under Le Tellier, 235

Vaila, battle of, 17
Valdes, 57 n.2
Vasa dynasty, 173; Gustavus Vasa, 173
Valmy, battle of, 393, 449
Vastadores, at Pavia, 91-92
Vauban, Sébastien Le Prestre, seigneur de: fortification of border cities by, 301
Vegetius, 295
Vendée, 395, 397, 401-2
Vendôme, Louis-Joseph (marshal of France), 323
Venetians, in reserve at Bicocca, 88
Venice, Republic of, 17
Verdun, 392
du Verney, general intendant of French army, 235, 390, 391
Vervins, peace treaty of, 228
Veterans, disabled, arrangements for in France, 236
Victor, (Victor) Perrin (marshal of France), 418-19
Vieilleville, François de (marshal of France), 14. Work: *Mémoires*, 14
Vienna: High Council of War in, 356; muster at, 93-94
Villars, Claude, duke of (marshal of France), in battle of Malplaquet, 324
Vitelli brothers, 17, 41, 107, 118
Vitzthum (Swedish general), in battle of Wittstock, 213
Voisin, Lancelot. *See* Popelinière

Wagram, battle of, 436, 447 n.20
Wallenstein, Albrecht von (imperial general), 454; assassination of, 209; in battle of Lützen, 207-9; Clausewitz on, 299; defensive position of, at Lützen, 207; dismissal of, 202; as entrepreneur, 59, 224; formation of, at Lützen, 208; on lance and pistol, 122; requisitioning by, 263 n.10, 264 n.17; taking by, of gold from Brandenburg, 243, 246; taking of prisoners limited by, 68
Wallhausen, Johann Jacobi von: criticism by, of Basta, 133-34; criticism of, by Hondius, 262 n.1; director of

military school at Siegen, 241-42; distinction by, between light and heavy cavalry, 126; on French punishments, 266 n.41; on lancer versus cuirassier, 133-34; on organization of Prince Maurice, 160-61; on punishment at drill, 253; writings of, 242. Works: *Art of Dismounted Warfare*, 160; *Art of Mounted Warfare*, 133; *Militia Gallica*, 266 n.41
War as an art, 293; scientific aspects of, 293; to become less frequent, 387
War of Bavarian Succession, 411
War of Devolution, 236
War Ministry of Prussia, 246
War of Polish Succession, 302
War, "Potato," 363
War of the Spanish Succession, 236-37, 303; Höchstädt, 275, 302, 319-20; last four years of, 325; Malplaquet, 275, 302, 323-25; Oudenarde, 302; Ramillies, 275, 302; Turin, 275, 302; wing battle in, 275, 302
Wartegeld, 241
Water power, importance of, in manufacture of cannonballs, 33
Waterways: for transport, 300; use of by Frederick the Great, 423
Wattignies, 396
Wavre, 438, 452
Weakness of commanders in preventing mercenary disorders, 64
Weimar army in French service, 231
Wellington, Arthur Wellesley, duke of (English general), 454; in campaign of 1815, 438-39; compared with Frederick the Great, 438; lieutenant colonel at age 23, 238 n.16; strategy of, 438-39
Werth, John of, 334
West Prussia, 387
White Mountain, battle on the, 195-202, 369; army strengths in, 197; Bohemian defensive position in, 197-98, 200-201; counterattacks, 199-200; development of, 199; formation of Catholic army in, 198, 200; incompleteness of field fortifications, 197;

nations allied with Bohemians in, 195; preliminary actions, 195-96
Wied (Prussian general), 362
William III (king of England, Scotland, Ireland), 302
William Louis, prince of Nassau: cooperation of, with Maurice of Orange, 156, 159; on digging of field fortifications, 161-62; interest of, in military reform, 156, 159; sieges by, 162; on slowness to accept battle, 307
William of Orange, 155-56
Willoughby, lord, 176
Wing battle, 275-79, 290 n.21, 360
Winkelried, Arnold: in battle of Bicocca, 89; in battle of Marignano, 84; transposed in legend to battle of Sempach, 90
Winterfeld (Prussian general), 340, 402
Winter rest, 305-6
Wittstock, battle of, 178, 212-14
Wolkenstein (Georg von Eberstein), 12

Women, as camp followers, 65-66
Wounds, by lance, 137-38
Wrangel, Karl Gustav (Swedish general), 301
Wunsch (Prussian general), 256
Wurmser (Austrian general), 428
Württemberg, militia in, 241-42

Ximenez (cardinal), 148

York, count: comparison by, of Napoleon, Frederick the Great, Archduke Charles, 446, n.19; false accounts by, 445 n.8; failure to recognize Clausewitz, 444 n.1. Work: Napoleon as Commander, 444 n.1

Zieten, Hans Joachim von (Prussian general), 304, 360-61, 374
Zorndorf, battle of, 289 n.18, 304, 352-53, 354, 371, 374; losses in, 402; as wing battle, 360